PRAISE FOR *PUTIN'S PEOPLE*

"A fearless, fascinating account of the emergence of the Putin regime . . . [Belton] has an unrivalled command of the labyrinthine history of share schemes, refinancing packages, mergers, shell companies, and offshore accounts that lay bare the stealthy capture of the post-Soviet economy and state institutions by a coterie of former KGB officers . . . The result reads at times like a John le Carré novel."
—Daniel Beer, *The Guardian*

"In her deeply researched new book, Catherine Belton tells a dark tale of Vladimir Putin's rise to power and his twenty years as leader of Russia . . . Belton, a former Moscow correspondent for the *Financial Times*, digs deeper. Hers is a story about Putin, his KGB colleagues, businessmen and mobsters pieced together through interviews with many relevant players."
—Anders Åslund, *The Washington Post*

"The plot sounds like a geopolitical thriller. Amid an empire's collapse, the secret police funnel money out of the country, creating a slush fund to rebuild their old networks. They regain power, become spectacularly rich and turn on their enemies, first at home—and then abroad."
—Edward Lucas, *The Times* (London)

"A staggering achievement of reporting . . . The level of depth [Belton] reaches, and the analysis of the details which are, by design, entirely opaque transactions and financial arrangements, is simply incredible. Belton follows the money."
—Joshua Huminski, *Diplomatic Courier*

"Through meticulous research into financial networks, Belton investigates Vladimir Putin's political ascent via the KGB ties at the center of her story. She captures the texture of Putin's government: its approach to power, its ambition, its cynicism, its desire to reverse the defeats of 1989 and 1991 and then to translate KGB formulas into a new international affairs paradigm."
—Michael Kimmage and Matthew Rojansky, *The New Republic*

"Relentless and magnificently detailed . . . *Putin's People* is a serious, absolutely timely warning. No book has documented the Russian president's leadership so indefatigably and compellingly. If you want to grasp in full how Russia has become the nation it has in the last twenty years, this is the book you've been waiting for."
—Julian Evans, *The Telegraph* (London)

"As Catherine Belton's powerful and meticulously reported new book shows, the apparent anarchy of the post-Soviet world has instead given way to a massive concentration of wealth and power, which is used by the new Russian elite to quash dissent at home and project force abroad . . . A narrative tour de force."
—*The Economist*

"[Catherine Belton's] book is fast-paced, thoroughly researched and packed with new—or at least not widely known—facts . . . This is the best kind of journalist's book, written with an eye for a well-turned story and compelling characters, and steering mercifully clear of academic theorising. And what tales Belton has to tell."
—Owen Matthews, *The Spectator*

"A book that western experts on modern Russia acknowledge as vital to our understanding of the Putin phenomenon . . . Belton draws on published sources and deep-throat contacts to plot a course through the maze of crooked financial manoeuvres—the sleights of hand, the back-room deals, the 'loans' from state banks, the kick-backs on contracts—that Putin and his courtiers got up to as they systematically drew the wealth to themselves as inexorably as iron filings to a magnet."
—Tony Rennell, *Daily Mail* (London)

"Catherine Belton is quite simply the most detailed and best-informed journalist covering Russia. One hears so much grand punditry about the country, but if you want to know the terrifying facts, from the nexus of KGB, business, and crime that was Putin's petri dish to the complex reality of the relationship with Trump—and if you want to see how all this combines into a whole new system—then this is the book for you."
—Peter Pomerantsev, author of *This Is Not Propaganda* and *Nothing Is True and Everything Is Possible*

PUTIN'S PEOPLE

HOW THE KGB
TOOK BACK RUSSIA
AND THEN TOOK ON
THE WEST

CATHERINE BELTON

PICADOR

FARRAR, STRAUS AND GIROUX
New York

To my parents, Marjorie and Derek,
as well as to Richard and to Catherine Birkett

Picador
120 Broadway, New York 10271

Copyright © 2020 by Catherine Belton
All rights reserved
Printed in the United States of America
Originally published in 2020 by William Collins, Great Britain
Published in the United States in 2020 by Farrar, Straus and Giroux
First Picador paperback edition, 2021

Library of Congress Control Number: 2020933664
Picador Paperback ISBN: 978-1-250-78732-3

Our books may be purchased in bulk for promotional, educational, or business use. Please
contact your local bookseller or the Macmillan Corporate and Premium Sales Department at
1-800-221-7945, extension 5442, or by email at MacmillanSpecialMarkets@macmillan.com.

Picador® is a U.S. registered trademark and is used by Macmillan Publishing Group, LLC,
under license from Pan Books Limited.

For book club information, please visit facebook.com/picadorbookclub or
email marketing@picadorusa.com.

picadorusa.com • instagram.com/picador
twitter.com/picadorusa • facebook.com/picadorusa

1   3   5   7   9   10   8   6   4   2

'Russian organised-crime leaders, their members, their associates, are moving into Western Europe, they are purchasing property, they are establishing bank accounts, they're establishing companies, they're weaving themselves into the fabric of society, and by the time that Europe develops an awareness it's going to be too late.'

Former FBI special agent Bob Levinson

'I want to warn Americans. As a people, you are very naïve about Russia and its intentions. You believe because the Soviet Union no longer exists, Russia now is your friend. It isn't, and I can show you how the SVR is trying to destroy the US even today and even more than the KGB did during the Cold War.'

Sergei Tretyakov, former colonel in Russian Foreign Intelligence, the SVR, stationed in New York

Contents

PART THREE

Illustrations

Dramatis Personae

Putin's inner circle, the *siloviki*

Igor Sechin – Putin's trusted gatekeeper, a former KGB operative from St Petersburg who rose in power as deputy head of Putin's Kremlin to lead the state takeover of the Russian oil sector. Later became known as 'Russia's Darth Vader' for his ruthless propensity for plots.

Nikolai Patrushev – Powerful former head of the Federal Security Service (FSB), the successor agency to the KGB, and current Security Council chief.

Viktor Ivanov – Former KGB officer who served with Putin in the Leningrad KGB and oversaw personnel as deputy head of Putin's Kremlin during his first term, leading the Kremlin's initial expansion into the economy.

Viktor Cherkesov – Former senior KGB officer who ran the St Petersburg FSB and was a mentor to Putin, moving with him to Moscow, where he remained a close adviser, first as first deputy head of the FSB and then running the Federal Drugs Service.

Sergei Ivanov – Former Leningrad KGB officer who became one of the youngest ever generals in Russia's foreign-intelligence service in the nineties and then rose in power under Putin's presidency, first as defence minister and then as Kremlin chief of staff.

Dmitry Medvedev – Former lawyer who started out working as a deputy to Putin in the St Petersburg administration when he was in his early twenties, and followed closely in Putin's footsteps thereafter: first as a deputy head of the Kremlin administration, then as its chief of staff, then as Putin's interim replacement as president.

The custodians, the KGB-connected businessmen

Gennady Timchenko – Alleged former KGB operative who rose through the ranks of Soviet trade to become co-founder of one of the first independent traders of oil products before the Soviet fall. Worked closely with Putin from the early nineties, and according to some associates, before the Soviet collapse.

Yury Kovalchuk – Former physicist who joined with other KGB-connected businessmen to take over Bank Rossiya, a St Petersburg bank that, according to the US Treasury, became the 'personal bank' for Putin and other senior Russian officials.

Arkady Rotenberg – Former Putin judo partner who became a billionaire under Putin's presidency after the state awarded his companies multi-billion-dollar construction contracts.

Vladimir Yakunin – Former senior KGB officer who served a stint undercover at the United Nations in New York, then joined with Kovalchuk in taking over Bank Rossiya. Putin anointed him chief of the state railways monopoly.

'The Family', the coterie of relatives, officials and businessmen closely surrounding the first Russian president, Boris Yeltsin

Valentin Yumashev – Former journalist who gained Yeltsin's trust while writing his memoirs, and was anointed Kremlin chief of staff in 1997. Married Yeltsin's daughter Tatyana in 2002.

Tatyana Dyachenko – Yeltsin's daughter who officially served as his image adviser, but was essentially gatekeeper to the president.

Boris Berezovsky – Former mathematician who made his fortune running trading schemes for carmaker AvtoVAZ, the producer of the boxy Zhiguli car that epitomised the Soviet era, and inveigled his way into the good graces of Yeltsin and his Family. When he acquired the Sibneft oil major, he became the epitome of the intensely politically-wired oligarchs of the Yeltsin era.

Alexander Voloshin – Former economist who started out working with Berezovsky on privatisations and other schemes, and was transferred to the Kremlin in 1997 to work as Yumashev's deputy chief of staff. Promoted to chief of staff in 1999.

Roman Abramovich – Oil trader who became Berezovsky's protégé and associate. Once described by Alexander Korzhakov, Yeltsin's security chief, as 'cashier' to the Yeltsin Family (a claim denied by Abramovich). Later said to have a 'good relationship' with Putin.

Sergei Pugachev – Russian Orthodox banker who was a master of the Byzantine financing schemes of Yeltsin's Kremlin, and then became known as Putin's banker too. Co-founder of Mezhprombank, he straddled the worlds of the Family and the *siloviki*.

The Yeltsin-era oligarch who crossed Putin's men

Mikhail Khodorkovsky – Former member of the Communist Youth League who became one of Russia's first and most successful businessmen of the *perestroika* era and the 1990s.

The mobsters, footsoldiers for the KGB
St Petersburg

Ilya Traber – Former Soviet submariner who became a black-market antiques trader in the *perestroika* years, and then an intermediary between Putin's security services and the Tambov organised-crime group, controlling St Petersburg's most strategic assets, the sea port and the oil terminal.

Vladimir Kumarin – Tambov organised-crime boss who lost an arm in an assassination attempt and became known as St Petersburg's 'night governor', joining in business with Putin's men, most notably with Ilya Traber.

Moscow

Semyon Mogilevich – Former wrestler, known as 'the Brainy Don', who at the end of the eighties became banker to the leaders of Russia's most powerful organised-crime groups, including the Solntsevskaya, funnelling cash into the West and setting up a criminal empire of drugs and arms trafficking of his own. Recruited in the seventies by the KGB, he was 'the criminal arm of the Russian state'.

Sergei Mikhailov – Alleged head of the Solntsevskaya organised-crime group, Moscow's most powerful, with close ties to many of the KGB-connected businessmen who later cultivated connections with New York property mogul Donald Trump.

Vyacheslav Ivankov ('Yaponchik') – Mobster dispatched by Mogilevich to Brighton Beach, New York, to oversee the Solntsevskaya's criminal empire there.

Yevgeny Dvoskin – Brighton Beach mobster who became one of Russia's most notorious 'shadow bankers' after moving back to Moscow with his uncle, Ivankov, joining forces with the Russian security services to funnel tens of billions of dollars in 'black cash' into the West.

Felix Sater – Dvoskin's best friend since childhood. Became a key business partner of the Trump Organization, developing a string of properties for Trump, all the while retaining high-level contacts in Russian intelligence.

Prologue

Moscow Rules

It was late in the evening in May 2015, and Sergei Pugachev was flicking through an old family photo album he'd found from thirteen years ago or more. In one photo from a birthday party at his Moscow dacha, his son Viktor keeps his eyes downcast as Vladimir Putin's daughter Maria smiles and whispers in his ear. In another, Viktor and his other son, Alexander, are posing on a wooden spiral staircase in the Kremlin presidential library with Putin's two daughters. At the edge of the photo, Lyudmilla Putina, then still the Russian president's wife, smiles.

We were sitting in the kitchen of Pugachev's latest residence, a three-storey townhouse in the well-heeled London area of Chelsea. The late-evening light glanced in through the cathedral-sized windows, and birds chirped in the trees outside, the traffic from the nearby King's Road a faint hum. The high-powered life Pugachev had once enjoyed in Moscow – the dealmaking, the endless behind-the-scenes agreements, the 'understandings' between friends in the Kremlin corridors of power – seemed a world away. But Moscow's influence was in fact still lurking like a shadow outside his door.

The day before, Pugachev had been forced to seek the protection of the UK counter-terrorism squad. His bodyguards had found suspicious-looking boxes with protruding wires taped to the under-carriage of his Rolls-Royce, as well as on the car used to transport his three youngest children, aged seven, five and three, to school. Now, on the wall of the Pugachevs' sitting room, behind the rocking horse and across from the family portraits, the SO15 counter-terrorism squad had installed a grey box containing an alarm that could be activated in the event of attack.

Fifteen years before, Pugachev had been a Kremlin insider who'd manoeuvred endlessly behind the scenes to help bring Vladimir Putin to power. Once known as the Kremlin's banker, he'd been a master of the backroom deals, the sleights of hand that governed the country then. For years he'd seemed untouchable, a member of an inner circle at the pinnacle of power that had made and bent the rules to suit themselves, with law enforcement, the courts, and even elections subverted for their needs. But now the Kremlin machine he'd once been part of had turned against him. The tall, Russian Orthodox believer with a dark beard and a gregarious grin had become the latest victim of Putin's relentlessly expanding reach. First, the Kremlin had moved in on his business empire, taking it for itself. Pugachev had left Russia, first for France and then for England as the Kremlin launched its attack. Putin's men had taken the hotel project the president had granted him on Red Square, a stone's throw from the Kremlin, without any compensation at all. Then his ship-yards, two of the biggest in Russia, valued at $3.5 billion, were acquired by one of Putin's closest allies, Igor Sechin, for a fraction of that sum. Then his coal project, the world's biggest coking-coal deposit in the Siberian region of Tuva, valued at $4 billion, was taken by a close associate of Ramzan Kadyrov, the strongman Chechen president, for $150 million.[1]

In the process, Putin's men had blamed him for the collapse of Mezhprombank, the bank he co-founded long ago in the nineties that had once been the key to his power. The Kremlin authorities had opened a criminal case claiming Pugachev had caused the bank's bankruptcy by transferring $700 million from it to a Swiss bank account at the height of the 2008 financial crisis. The Kremlin paid no regard to Pugachev's claims that the money was his own. It seemed to matter little that the takeover of the shipyards by Sechin at a fraction of their value was the biggest reason for the shortfall in the bank's funds to creditors.[2]

The hand of the Kremlin seemed clear. 'People within the state manipulated the rules against him in order to bring the bank down, unsurprisingly benefiting themselves,' said Richard Hainsworth, a long-standing Russian banking expert.[3]

It was a typical story for a Kremlin machine that had become relentless in its reach. First, it had gone after political enemies. But now it was starting to turn on Putin's onetime allies. Pugachev was the first of the inner circle to fall. And now the Kremlin had expanded its campaign against him from the brutal closed-door courts of Moscow to the veneer of respectability of London's High Court. There, it obtained a freezing order against his assets with ease, tying the tycoon up in knots in the courtroom along the way.

Ever since Pugachev had left Russia, the Kremlin had pursued him. At his home in France, he'd been threatened by stooges sent by Mezhprombank's liquidator. Three members of a Moscow mafia group had taken him out to a yacht off the coast of Nice and demanded he pay $350 million to guarantee his family's 'safety'. It was 'the price of peace', they told him, the price for making the Russian criminal case against him for the Mezhprom bankruptcy go away, documentary evidence shows.[4] In the UK courts, Pugachev had been a fish totally out of water, incapable of operating according to their unfamiliar rules and procedures. He was too accustomed to the backroom deals of his Kremlin past, too accustomed to slipping through the net of rules and regulations because of his position and power. He hadn't done himself any favours. Convinced of the righteousness of his position, that he was the victim of the latest Kremlin asset grab, he believed himself above the regulations of the British courts. He'd failed to stick to court orders related to the asset freeze, and had burned through millions of pounds from an account he'd kept hidden from the UK court. He believed the disclosure rules were beneath him, petty compared to the calamity that had befallen his business empire, and no more than part of a Kremlin campaign to hound and frustrate him at every turn. The Kremlin, however, had become adept at pursuing its enemies through the UK court system, while a PR machine was honed to fill the pages of the UK tabloids with allegations of the Russian oligarch's stolen wealth.

The Kremlin had first observed how the UK court system operated during Roman Abramovich's victory against Boris Berezovsky, the exiled oligarch who'd become Putin's fiercest critic, in a case that seemed to some to turn Russian history on its head. Berezovsky was the fast-talking onetime Kremlin insider who had tried – and failed – to sue his erstwhile business associate Roman Abramovich, a former federal governor, for $6.5 billion in London's High Court. The judge over-seeing the case, Dame Elizabeth Gloster, had taken a dim view of Berezovsky's claim that he'd partly owned one of Russia's biggest oil majors, Sibneft, and a stake in Rusal, Russia's biggest aluminium giant, with Abramovich, and that Abramovich had forced him to sell his stakes at a knockdown price. Mrs Justice Gloster said she found Berezovsky to be 'an inherently unreliable witness',[5] and sided with Abramovich, who'd claimed that Berezovsky had never owned these assets; he'd merely been paid for providing political patronage and protection. The judgment was greeted with some surprise in Russia, where Berezovsky had been widely viewed as an owner of Sibneft. Berezovsky cried foul. Mrs Justice Gloster had declared at the outset of the trial that her stepson had represented Abramovich in the early stages of the case. Though Berezovsky's lawyers claimed his involve-ment was more extensive than had been disclosed, they did not appeal.[6]

The Kremlin had further honed its operations in the UK court system through its pursuit of Mukhtar Ablyazov, a Kazakh billionaire who happened to be the biggest political foe of the Kazakh president, a key Kremlin ally, Nursultan Nazarbayev. Ablyazov was pursued by Russia's state deposit insurance agency, which charged him with siphoning more than $4 billion from the Kazakh BTA Bank, of which he had been chairman, and which had branches across Russia. The Russian agency hired a team of lawyers from the top London law firm Hogan Lovells, who launched eleven civil fraud lawsuits against Ablyazov in the UK, as well as a freezing order on his assets. Private detectives had traced the siphoned $4 billion to a network of offshore companies controlled by the Kazakh tycoon.[7]

But in Pugachev's case, no stolen or hidden assets appeared to have been found. No fraud claims had ever been launched in the UK, or anywhere else outside Russia. Instead, on the basis of a Russian court ruling alone, the same team from Hogan Lovells had won the freezing order against Pugachev's assets, and ably ran rings around him while he chafed at the multitude of court orders that came his way. He'd been interrogated over asset disclosures, and found to have given false evidence over whether the sale of his coal business had been conducted by himself or by his son. It didn't seem to matter to the judge that the sale had been forced through at a price that was less than one twentieth of the business's real value. What mattered was whether he'd followed procedure and declared all the assets that remained under his control. Pugachev had been forced to hand over his passports to the court, and was banned from leaving the UK during a prolonged period of questioning over his asset disclosures as the Kremlin's lawyers tightened the legal net. He'd run through a series of lawyers who in turn seemed baffled by a case that had never been heard on its merits in the UK, while others viewed him mendaciously as easy prey. Spoilt by the flood of Russian cases that Moscow's tycoons were willing to pay top prices for airing in London's High Court, legal firms padded their bills to astronomical sums for work that was never done, as documents show. PR firms offered to defend Pugachev's image for £100,000 a month. 'He's on our territory now,' said one partner at a global law firm representing him.

At first Pugachev had believed the case against him was being driven by unruly Kremlin underlings anxious to draw a line over their expropriation of his business empire. But as the campaign expanded, and Pugachev began to fear for his physical safety, he became convinced that it was being guided by Putin himself. 'How could he do this to me? I even made him president,' he said that evening as he sat in his Chelsea kitchen, still shell-shocked by the visit from SO15 and the suspicious devices found underneath his cars.[8] A former friend sent by the Kremlin to London had told him that Putin was personally managing every step of the campaign against him, warning: 'We have control of everything here, we've got everything all stitched up.'

Pugachev had long detected the growing influence of Kremlin cash in London. Long before the legal attack started, he said, he'd met a string of English lords who'd guffawed and shaken his hand, and told him how great they thought Putin was. In those days they believed Pugachev was 'Putin's banker', as the press had called him then, yet they'd still asked him to donate to the Conservative Party without any question or thought. All his former friends from the Kremlin kept relatives and mistresses in town, who they visited at weekends, flooding the city with cash. There was Sechin's ex-wife, Marina, who kept a house with her daughter here. There was Igor Shuvalov, the deputy prime minister, who owned the most prestigious flat in the city, a penthouse overlooking Trafalgar Square. There were the sons of Arkady Rotenberg, Putin's billionaire former judo partner, who attended one of the country's most vaunted private schools, while his ex-wife Natalya shopped and sued her husband for divorce in London's High Court. There was the deputy speaker of the State Duma, one of Russia's most vocal patriots, Sergei Zheleznyak, who'd long raged against the influence of the West, yet his daughter Anastasia had lived in London for years. The list of officials resident in London was endless, said Pugachev. 'They have sorted themselves out very well on this small island with terrible weather,' he sniffed. 'In the UK, the main thing was always money. Putin sent his agents to corrupt the British elite.'

The city had grown used to the flood of Russian cash. Property prices had surged as first tycoons and then Russian officials had bought up high-end mansions in Knightsbridge, Kensington and Belgravia. A string of Russian share offerings, led by the state's Rosneft, Sberbank and VTB, had helped pay the rents and wages for the offices of London's well-heeled PR and legal firms. Lords and former politicians were paid lavish salaries to serve on Russian companies' boards, although they were granted little oversight of corporate conduct. Russia's influence was everywhere. Alexander Lebedev, the former KGB officer and banker who'd positioned himself as a champion of the free press in Russia, had acquired London's most-read and influential daily, the *Evening Standard*, becoming a fixture at the capital's soirées and on the lists for the most sought-after dinner invitations. Another was Dmitry Firtash, a Ukrainian tycoon who'd become the Kremlin's gas trader of choice, and who despite his links to a major Russian mobster wanted by the FBI, Semyon Mogilevich, had become a billionaire donor to Cambridge University. His chief London minion, Robert Shetler-Jones, had donated millions of pounds to the Tories, while influential party grandees served on the board of Firtash's British Ukrainian Society. There were other less noticeable players. At least one of them had slipped through the cracks to become close friends with Boris Johnson, then London's mayor, at the top of the Tory elite. 'Everyone has gotten used to spies wearing dark glasses and looking suspicious in films,' said Pugachev. 'But here they are everywhere. They look normal. You can't tell.'

Pugachev had no idea whether the envoy sent by the Kremlin to warn him that it had everything stitched up in the UK was telling the truth, or whether he'd been sent merely to frighten him. But at some point – after he found the suspicious-looking devices on his cars, and after he first got wind that Russia was going to seek his extradition from the UK – he decided he didn't want to risk waiting to find out. Despite his previous closeness to Putin, and his extensive contacts with the Kremlin's clan of former KGB men known as the *siloviki*, a meeting set up for him with a top-level official from the British Foreign Office had been cancelled at the last minute. Instead he'd been told by a visiting Kremlin agent that he should meet a man Russian intelligence had cultivated in MI6. Everything was being turned on its head. He feared that the UK government was preparing a deal with the Russians to extradite him. He wondered too about the fate of his friend Boris Berezovsky, the arch Kremlin critic who in March 2013 had been found dead on the floor of his bathroom in his country mansion in Berkshire, his favourite black cashmere scarf round his neck, an unidentified fingerprint left at the scene. For some unknown reason, Scotland Yard didn't investigate, leaving it to the local Thames Valley Police, which called it a suicide and closed the case.[9] 'It looks like there is an agreement with Russia not to make a fuss,' Pugachev worried.[10]

And so one day in June 2015, a few weeks after we'd met in his Chelsea home, Pugachev was suddenly no longer in the UK. His phones had all been switched off, ditched by the wayside as he ran. He'd ignored the court orders forbidding him to leave the country. He hadn't even told his partner, the mother of his three young children, the London socialite Alexandra Tolstoy, who was left waiting late into the night for him to appear at her father's eightieth birthday party. He'd last been seen in a meeting with his lawyers, at which they'd warned him he'd need £10 million to secure bail on an imminent Russian extradition request – cash to which Pugachev didn't have access. A few weeks later he surfaced in France, where he'd gained citizenship in 2009, and where French law protected its citizens from extradition to Russia. He'd fled to the relative safety of his villa high in the hills above the bay of Nice, a fortress surrounded by an impenetrable high iron fence, a team of bodyguards and a battery of security cameras at every turn.

The ease with which the Kremlin had been able to pursue its case against him in London seemed to Pugachev, as the Russians would say, like the first *lastochka* – the first swallow of spring. It was the arrival of Moscow rules in London, where the Kremlin could twist and distort the legal process to suit its agenda, where the larger issue of its expropriation of Pugachev's multi-billion-dollar business empire could be artfully buried in the minutiae of rules related to the freezing order and whether Pugachev had correctly followed them. Pugachev was no angel, of course. It was not at all clear what had happened to the $700 million he'd been accused of siphoning from Mezhprombank. But a series of asset disclosures, unquestioned by the UK High Court, had revealed that $250 million of that money had been returned to the bank, while the trail of the remainder had been lost in companies liquidated by a former Pugachev ally who was now working closely with the Kremlin. Later, Swiss prosecutors, asked by Russia to block Pugachev's Swiss bank accounts, said they'd found no evidence that any crime was committed when the $700 million was transferred from Pugachev's company accounts in Mezhprombank to the Swiss bank account at the height of the 2008 crisis.[11]

But even though the Kremlin lawyers had not opened a fraud case against him in the UK, even though there appeared to be no trail of stolen funds, the legal pursuit of Pugachev was relentless. Lawyers working for the Russian State Deposit Agency insisted they had him 'bang to rights' over Mezhprombank's bankruptcy. 'If you get cash from a regulator, you should take it to help the bank survive, not fund a payment to yourself,' one person close to the legal team said.[12] Despite the Kremlin having expropriated his business empire, and his having begun to fear for his life, Pugachev was found in contempt of court for fleeing the UK, and sentenced in absentia to two years in jail. During the contempt hearings he was frequently branded a liar. He'd flouted the rules of the freezing order. He'd not only fled the country, but transferred funds from the sale of two cars to France. One of the judges presiding over the case, Justice Vivienne Rose, found she could not 'safely rely on any evidence he gave'. A New Zealand trust he'd set up to hold tens of millions of dollars in properties, including his Chelsea home, was later found to be a sham.

For all his flaws, Pugachev insisted he had been caught in a Russian state vendetta pursued through the UK courts. The Kremlin seemed intent on quashing any notion that he'd ever been well-connected in the Kremlin, or that he could have any knowledge that could be damaging to it. It had been able to suppress any political connotation to the case by leveraging the diminishing knowledge of Russia in the UK intelligence services, which had been distracted by monitoring the Islamic terrorist threat, and Pugachev's own low profile. Before things had got tough in London, Pugachev had never given an interview in his life. Few knew who he was. Most people believed it was the recently deceased oligarch Boris Berezovsky who had helped bring Putin to power. Lawyers at Hogan Lovells had been told that Pugachev was a nobody, and the case against him had nothing to do with politics. 'I've not seen any evidence of what he was doing in the Kremlin,' said one person close to the legal team. 'We have to be extremely careful. Pugachev seems to say whatever he wants. The people I have spoken to just say he was a blatant crook.'[13]

But in fact Pugachev had worked at the heart of the Kremlin, and had been privy to some of its deepest secrets, including how it was exactly that Putin came to power. This seemed to be one of the main reasons the Kremlin was so intent on pursuing him, and making sure he was tied up in legal knots. Even before the Kremlin took over his business empire, he'd been seeking to leave Russia, to escape the endless intrigue of business there. Already, he'd been sidelined by Putin's KGB allies from St Petersburg, and he'd begun seeking French citizenship in 2007. For those on the inside, Pugachev was being punished precisely for seeking to exit the tight-knit system that ruled Russia, the mafia clan which no one was ever meant to leave. 'Pugachev was like a kidney. He was essential for the functioning of the system. But he lost his mind and thought he could leave and work on his own business. Of course the order was given to destroy him,' said a senior Russian banker involved in financial operations for the Kremlin.[14]

In the rush of his flight from the UK to France, Pugachev left behind a number of telltale signs. Detectives working for the Kremlin's lawyers had swooped in to raid his Knightsbridge office on a court order issued in the days after his disappearance. Among the reams of documents, there were a number of disc drives. On one of the disc drives were recordings: the Russian security services had been secretly taping every meeting he held in his downtown Moscow office since the end of the nineties.

One of the recordings vividly documents Pugachev's candid and rueful feelings about Putin and his own role in bringing him to power. The tape records Pugachev sitting in his office with Valentin Yumashev, former president Boris Yeltsin's son-in-law and chief of staff, discussing over dinner and fine wine the tense state of affairs as Moscow hurtled through yet another political crisis. It was November 2007, and just a few months remained before Putin would come to the end of his second consecutive term as president, at which point Russia's constitution dictated that he must step down. But although Putin had made vague statements about becoming prime minister after standing down as president, there was not yet even a whisper of his real intentions. In the warren-like corridors of the Kremlin, the former KGB and security men who had risen to power with Putin had been jostling for position, bickering and backstabbing in hopes that they, or their candidate, would be selected as his successor.

Pugachev and Yumashev quietly clinked glasses as they discussed the standoff. The uncertainty over the succession was bringing back strong memories of 1999, when they'd assisted Putin's rise. It seemed to them an age ago. By now they had been eclipsed by Putin's KGB allies from St Petersburg. By now they were almost relics from a totally different era. The system of power had changed irrevocably, and they were still struggling to understand what they'd done.

'You remember how it was when he came into power?' says Pugachev on the tape. 'He would say, "I am the manager. I have been hired."' In those days, Putin had appeared reluctant to take the leading role, and seemed malleable and compliant to those who'd helped bring him to power. 'Between us, at the beginning I think he had the idea to become rich, to live a happy life, to decide his own personal issues,' Pugachev goes on. 'And in principle, he decided these issues very quickly . . . But as the four years of his first term passed he understood things had happened that would never allow him to step down.'

Putin's first term had been drenched in blood and controversy. It led to a sweeping transformation of the way the country was run. He faced a series of deadly terrorist attacks, including the siege of the Dubrovka theatre in Moscow by Chechen terrorists in October 2002. The hostage-taking ended with more than a hundred dead when the Russian security services botched the storming of the theatre and gassed the very theatregoers they'd been trying to free.

Putin's battles with rebels from the restive northern Caucasus republic of Chechnya had caused thousands of deaths, including the 294 who died in a string of apartment bombings. Many in Moscow whispered Putin's security services were behind these bloody attacks, not least because the end result was a security clampdown that strengthened his power.

The freewheeling oligarchs of the 1990s were soon brought to heel. It had taken just one big case against the country's richest man for Putin and his men to rein in the market freedoms of the Yeltsin era, and to launch a takeover by the state.

'He would have gone gladly after four years, I think,' Pugachev continues. 'But then all these controversies happened. With the West now, there is such a serious standoff that it's almost the Cuban missile crisis. And now he's gone even deeper . . . He understands that if it goes further, he will never get out.'

For both these men, the power construct built by Putin, by which the president had accumulated so much power that everything now depended on him, looked the very opposite of stable. 'It's a pyramid. All you have to do is knock it once and it will all collapse . . . He understands all this, but he can't change himself.'

'I don't have the feeling he understands any of this,' says Yumashev.

'It would be strange if he said everything I did is backward,' Pugachev interjects. 'Many of the decisions he makes are based on his convictions of how the world is run. The subject of patriotism – he believes this sincerely. When he says the collapse of the Soviet Union was a tragedy, he believes this sincerely . . . He just has such values. What he does he does sincerely. He sincerely makes mistakes.'

Putin had often justified his consolidation of all levers of power – which included ending elections for governors, and bringing the court system under Kremlin *diktat* – by saying such measures were necessary to usher in a new era of stability, ending the chaos and collapse of the 1990s. But behind the patriotic chest-beating that, on the face of it, appeared to drive most of the decision-making was another, more disturbing factor. Putin and the KGB men who ran the economy through a network of loyal allies now monopolised power, and had introduced a new system in which state positions were used as vehicles for self-enrichment. It was a far cry from the anti-capitalist, anti-bourgeois principles of the Soviet state they had once served.

'These people, they are mutants,' says Pugachev. 'They are a mixture of homo-soveticus with the wild capitalists of the last twenty years. They have stolen so much to fill their pockets. All their families live somewhere in London. But when they say they need to crush someone in the name of patriotism, they say this sincerely. It's just that if it's London they're targeting, they will get their families out first.'

'I think it is a terrible thing,' says Yumashev. 'Some of my friends who work in the Kremlin now say – with absolute sincerity – how great it is they can get so rich there. In the nineties, this was unacceptable. You either had to go into business or work for the country. Now they go and work for the state to earn money. Ministers hand out licences to make money. And of course all this comes from the boss . . . The first conversation [Putin] has with a new state employee is, "Here is your business. Share it only with me. If someone attacks you, I will defend you . . . and if you don't [use your position as a business] you are an idiot."'

'Putin said this himself,' says Pugachev. 'Openly. I remember, I was speaking with him. He said, "What is that guy waiting for? Why isn't he earning? What is he waiting for? He has the position. Let him make money for himself." These are now like people who have drunk blood. They can't stop. Now it is state officials who are the businessmen.'

'There are very few real businessmen left,' Yumashev agrees, shaking his head sadly. 'The atmosphere . . . The atmosphere has changed so much in the country. The air has changed. It's suffocating now. Suffocating.'

The two men sigh. Everything has changed – apart from their ability to idealise their own roles. 'What was great about the nineties was that there were no lies,' Yumashev continues.

'Absolutely,' says Pugachev. 'For me, my whole life, the truth was equivalent to freedom. I earned money not for riches, but for freedom. How much can you spend? As long as you have enough to buy two pairs of jeans, that's fine. But a certain independence gave me one thing: I don't need to lie.'

It seemed to the two men that the president had become surrounded by yes-men, all of whom proffered lengthy toasts to Putin, telling him he had been sent by God to save the country, while they served at his pleasure. Yet it seemed to Pugachev that these yes-men understood the deep hypocrisy of the system, the sham democracy represented by the Kremlin's ruling party, United Russia, and how deeply corrupt it had become.

'Look at the people around VV [Putin], who say Vladimir

Vladimirovich, you're a genius!' Pugachev continues. 'I look at them
– and they don't believe in anything. They understand it's all crap.
That United Russia is crap, the elections are crap, the president is
crap. But they understand all this, and then they go on stage and
say how great everything is. And all the toasts they make, which are
total lies. They can sit and tell . . . rubbish about how they have
always been together, ever since they were sitting on the school
bench. But at the same time the guys sitting in the office next door
are saying, "As soon as he comes out, let's finish him off." There is
such cynicism. I don't think they feel comfortable. The ones who
have power . . . I am sorry for them. They're stealing from all sides,
and then they come out and speak about how Putin is fighting
against corruption. I look at them and think, this is the end. I'm
sorry for them . . . VV was always asking, "What is that word beginning with s? *Sovest* – conscience." They don't have receptors for this.
They don't understand it. They forgot the word and what it means.
They've gotten totally messed up.'

All the achievements of the Putin era so far – the economic
growth, the increase in incomes, the riches of the billionaires that
had turned Moscow into a gleaming metropolis where sleek foreign
cars filled the streets and cosy cafés opened on street corners – boiled
down to the sharp increase in the oil price during the Putin years,
they agree. 'In 2000 the oil price was $17 and we were happy,' says
Yumashev. 'When you and I were in power it was $10, $6. The best
time for me was when it hit $16 for two to three weeks. Now it's
$150, and the only thing they're doing is building awful houses for
themselves.'

'The state is doing nothing with the money. They could have
transformed the country's infrastructure. But he thinks everything
will be stolen if we build roads . . . Time is passing so quickly,' says
Pugachev.

'Eight years have gone. In 2000 we gave the boss such a smoothly
oiled machine. Everything worked. And what did we get?' asks
Yumashev.

'We didn't understand that he wasn't going to drive things forward.
I thought he was liberal, young,' Pugachev replies.

'For me it was principally important that he was young,' says Yumashev.

'You understand it turned out he was from a different species.'

'Yes. They are different people,' Yumashev agrees.

'They are different, special people. This was something we didn't understand. The person who understood this very well was Ustinov [the prosecutor general],' says Pugachev. 'He told me, "You understand, the guys from the security services, they are different. Even if you were to suck all their blood out and then put on a different head, they would still be different. They live in their own system. You will never be one of them. It is an absolutely different system."'

The recording offers a unique window into the unguarded views of two men who had brought Putin to power, and their horror at the system they'd help create. This book is the story of that system – the rise to power of Putin's KGB cohort, and how they mutated to enrich themselves in the new capitalism. It is the story of the hurried handover of power between Yeltsin and Putin, and of how it enabled the rise of a 'deep state' of KGB security men that had always lurked in the background during the Yeltsin years, but now emerged to monopolise power for at least twenty years – and eventually to endanger the West.

This book began as an effort to trace the takeover of the Russian economy by Putin's former KGB associates. But it became an investigation into something more pernicious than that. First research – and then events – showed that the kleptocracy of the Putin era was aimed at something more than just filling the pockets of the president's friends. What emerged as a result of the KGB takeover of the economy – and the country's political and legal system – was a regime in which the billions of dollars at Putin's cronies' disposal were to be actively used to undermine and corrupt the institutions and democracies of the West. The KGB playbook of the Cold War era, when the Soviet Union deployed 'active measures' to sow division and discord in the West, to fund allied political parties and undermine its 'imperial' foe, has now been fully reactivated. What's different now is that these tactics are funded by a much deeper well of cash, by a Kremlin that has become adept in the ways of the markets and has sunk its tentacles deep into the institutions of the West. Parts of the KGB, Putin among them, have embraced capitalism as a tool for getting even with the West. It was a process that began long before, in the years before the Soviet collapse.

Putin's takeover of strategic cash flows was always about more than taking control of the country's economy. For the Putin regime, wealth was less about the well-being of Russia's citizens than about the projection of power, about reasserting the country's position on the world stage. The system Putin's men created was a hybrid KGB capitalism that sought to accumulate cash to buy off and corrupt officials in the West, whose politicians, complacent after the end of the Cold War, had long forgotten about the Soviet tactics of the not too distant past. Western markets embraced the new wealth coming from Russia, and paid little heed to the criminal and KGB forces behind it. The KGB had forged an alliance with Russian organised crime long ago, on the eve of the Soviet collapse, when billions of dollars' worth of precious metals, oil and other commodities was transferred from the state to firms linked to the KGB. From the start, foreign-intelligence operatives of the KGB sought to accumulate black cash to maintain and preserve influence networks long thought demolished by the Soviet collapse. For a time under Yeltsin the forces of the KGB stayed hidden in the background. But when Putin rose to power, the alliance between the KGB and organised crime emerged and bared its teeth. To understand this process, we must go back to the beginning of it all, to the time of the Soviet collapse.

For the men who helped bring Putin to power, the revanche has also brought a reckoning. Pugachev and Yumashev had begun the transfer of power in desperate hurry, as Yeltsin's health failed, in an attempt to secure the future of the country – and their own safety – against what they believed to be a Communist threat. But they too had forgotten the not too distant Soviet past.

The security men they brought to power were to stop at nothing to prolong their rule beyond the bounds of anything they'd thought possible.

'We should have spoken to him more,' sighed Yumashev.

'Of course,' said Pugachev. 'But there wasn't any time.'

PART ONE

1

'Operation Luch'

ST PETERSBURG – It's early February 1992, and an official car from the city administration is slowly driving down the main street of the city. A grey slush has been partially swept from the pavements, and people are trudging through the cold in thick anonymous coats, laden with bags and hunched against the wind. Behind the fading façades of the once grand houses on Nevsky Prospekt, shops stand almost empty, their shelves practically bare in the aftershocks of the Soviet Union's sudden implosion. It's barely six weeks since the Soviet Union ceased to exist, since the fateful day when Russia's president Boris Yeltsin and the leaders of the other Soviet republics signed their union out of existence with the stroke of a pen. The city's food distributors are struggling to react to rapid change as the strict Soviet regulations that for decades controlled supply chains and fixed prices had suddenly ceased to exist.

In the bus queues and at the impromptu markets that have sprung up across the city as inhabitants seek to earn cash selling shoes and other items from their homes, the talk all winter has been of food shortages, ration cards and gloom. Making matters worse, hyperinflation is ravaging savings. Some have even warned of famine, sounding alarm bells across a city still gripped by memories of the Second World War blockade, when up to a thousand people starved to death every day.

But the city official behind the wheel of the black Volga sedan looks calm. The slight, resolute figure gazing intently ahead is Vladimir Putin. He is thirty-nine, deputy mayor of St Petersburg and the recently appointed head of the city's foreign relations committee. The scene is being filmed for a series of documentaries on the city's new administration, and this one centres on the youthful-looking deputy mayor whose responsibilities include ensuring adequate imports of food.[1] As the footage flickers back to his office in City Hall at Smolny, Putin reels off a string of figures on the tonnes of grain in humanitarian aid being shipped in from Germany, England and France. There is no need for worry, he says. Nearly ten minutes is spent on careful explanations of the measures his committee has taken to secure emergency supplies of food, including a groundbreaking deal for £20 million-worth of livestock grain secured during a meeting between the city's mayor, Anatoly Sobchak, and British prime minister John Major. Without this act of generosity from the UK, the region's young livestock would not have survived, he says.

His command of detail is impressive. So too is his grasp of the vast problems facing the city's economy. He speaks with fluency of the need to develop a class of small and medium business owners as the backbone of the new market economy. Indeed, he says, 'The entrepreneurial class should become the basis for the flourishing of our society as a whole.'

He speaks with precision on the problems of converting the region's vast Soviet-era defence enterprises to civilian production in order to keep them alive. Sprawling plants like the Kirovsky Zavod, a vast artillery and tank producer in the south of the city, had been the region's main employer since tsarist times. Now they were at a standstill, as the endless orders for military hardware that fuelled and eventually bankrupted the Soviet economy had suddenly dried up. We have to bring in Western partners and integrate the plants into the global economy, says the young city official.

With sudden intensity, he speaks of the harm Communism wrought in artificially cutting off the Soviet Union from the free-market relations linking the rest of the developed world. The credos of Marx and Lenin 'brought colossal losses to our country', he says. 'There was a period of my life when I studied the theories of Marxism and Leninism, and I found them interesting and, like many of us, logical. But as I grew up the truth became ever more clear to me –

these theories are no more than harmful fairy tales.' Indeed, the
Bolshevik revolutionaries of 1917 were responsible for the 'tragedy
we are experiencing today – the tragedy of the collapse of our state',
he boldly tells the interviewer. 'They cut the country up into republics that did not exist before, and then destroyed what unites the
people of civilised countries: they destroyed market relations.'

It is just a few months since his appointment as deputy mayor of
St Petersburg, but already it is a powerful, carefully crafted performance. He sits casually straddling a chair backwards, but everything
else points to precision and preparation. The fifty-minute film shows
him on the judo mat flipping opponents over his shoulder, speaking
fluent German with a visiting businessman, and taking calls from
Sobchak about the latest foreign aid deals. His meticulous preparation
extends to the man he specifically requested to conduct the interview
and direct the film: a documentary film-maker known and loved
across the Soviet Union for a series he made intimately charting the
lives of a group of children, a Soviet version of the popular UK television series *Seven Up*. Igor Shadkhan is a Jew, who recently returned
to St Petersburg from making a series of films on the horrors of the
Soviet Gulag in the far north; a man who still flinches at the memory
of anti-Semitic slurs from Soviet times, and who, by his own admit-
tance, still ducks his head in fear whenever he passes the former
headquarters of the KGB on the city's Liteyny Prospekt.

Yet this is the man Putin chose to help him with a very special
revelation, the man who will convey to the world the fact that Putin
had served as an officer in the feared and hated KGB. It is still the
first wave of the democracy movement, a time when admitting this
could compromise his boss, Sobchak, a rousing orator who rose to
mayor on a tide of condemnation of the secrets of the old regime,
of the abuses perpetrated by the KGB. To this day, Shadkhan still
questions whether Putin's choice was part of a careful rehabilitation
plan. 'I always ask why he chose me. He understood that I was
needed, and he was ready to tell me he was from the KGB. He
wanted to show that people of the KGB were also progressive.' Putin
chose well. 'A critic once told me that I always humanised my subject
matter, no matter who they were,' Shadkhan recalls. 'I humanised

him. I wanted to know who he was and what did he see. I was a person who had always criticised the Soviet authorities. I endured a lot from them. But I was sympathetic to him. We became friends. He seemed to me one who would drive the country forward, who would really do something. He really recruited me.'[2]

Throughout the film, Putin artfully takes opportunities to stress the good qualities of the KGB. Where he served, he insists in response to a delicate question on whether he abused his position to take bribes, such actions were considered 'a betrayal of the motherland', and would be punished with the full force of the law. As for being an 'official', a *chinovnik*, the word need not have any negative connotation, he claims. He'd served his country as a military *chinovnik*; now he was a civilian official, serving – as he had before – his country 'outside the realm of political competition'.

By the end of the documentary, Shadkhan appears to have fully bought in. The film concludes with a nod and a wink to a glorified KGB past: Putin is shown surveying the icy river Neva, wrapped against the cold in a fur hat, a man of the people behind the wheel of a white Zhiguli, the boxy car ubiquitous in those days. As he watches over the city with a steely and protective gaze, the film closes to the strains of the theme tune from a popular Soviet TV series – *17 Moments of Spring* – that made a hero out of an undercover KGB spy who had infiltrated deep into Nazi Germany's ruling regime. It was Shadkhan's choice. 'He was a person exactly of his profession. I wanted to show how it turned out that he was still in the same profession.'

Putin, however, had taken care in the interview to give the impression that he'd resigned from the KGB as soon as he'd returned to Leningrad, as St Petersburg was then called, in February 1990. He told Shadkhan that he'd left for 'all kinds of reasons', not for political ones, indicating that he'd done so before he started working in May of that year with Sobchak, then a law professor at Leningrad's State University and the fast-rising star of the city's new democratic movement. Putin had returned to the tsarist-era capital from five years of service in Dresden in East Germany (the German Democratic Republic, or GDR), where he'd served as liaison officer between the KGB and the Stasi, the East German secret police. Later legend had it that he'd confided to a colleague that he feared he might have no better future than working as a taxi driver on his return.[3] Apparently he was keen to create the impression that he'd cut all ties to his old masters, that Russia's rapidly changing order had cast him adrift.

What Putin told Shadkhan was just the start of a string of falsehoods and obfuscation surrounding his KGB career. In the imploding empire that he had returned to from Dresden, nothing was quite as it seemed. From the KGB villa perched high on the banks of the river Elbe overlooking Dresden's still elegant sprawl, Putin had already witnessed at first hand the end of the Soviet empire's control of the GDR, the collapse of the so-called socialist dream. The Soviet Union's Warsaw Pact power bloc had shattered around him as its citizens rebelled against the Communist leadership. He'd watched, first from afar, as the aftershocks began to reverberate across the Soviet Union and, inspired by the Berlin Wall's collapse, nationalist movements spread ever more rapidly across the country, forcing the Communist leader Mikhail Gorbachev into ever more compromise with a new generation of democratic leaders. By the time of Putin's interview with Shadkhan, one of those leaders, Boris Yeltsin, had emerged victorious from an attempted hard-line coup in August 1991. The abortive putsch had sought to turn the clock back on political and economic freedoms, but ended in resounding failure. Yeltsin banned the Communist Party of the Soviet Union. The old regime, suddenly, seemed to have been swept away.

But what replaced it was only a partial changing of the guard, and what happened to the KGB was a case in point. Yeltsin had decapitated the top echelon of the KGB, and then signed a decree breaking it up into four different domestic services. But what emerged in its place was a hydra-headed monster in which many officers, like Putin, retreated to the shadows and continued to serve underground, while the powerful foreign-intelligence service remained intact. It was a system where the rules of normal life seemed to have long been suspended. It was a shadowland of half-truths and appearances, while underneath it all factions of the old elite continued to cling to what remained of the reins.

Putin was to give several different versions of the timing and circumstances of his resignation from the KGB. But according to one former senior KGB officer close to him, none of them are true. He would tell interviewers writing his official biography that he resigned a few months after he began working for Sobchak at the university, but his resignation letter had somehow got lost in the post. Instead, he claimed, Sobchak had personally telephoned Vladimir Kryuchkov, the then KGB chief, to ensure his resignation at the height of the hard-line August 1991 coup. This was the story that became the official version. But it sounds like fiction. The chances of Sobchak reaching Kryuchkov in the middle of a coup in order to secure the resignation of one employee seem slim at best. Instead, according to the close Putin ally, Putin continued receiving his paycheque from the security services for at least a year after the August coup attempt. By the time he resigned, his position at the top of Russia's second city's new leadership was secure. He'd penetrated deep into the country's new democratic leadership, and was the point man for the administration's ties with law enforcement, including the KGB's successor agency, the Federal Security Service, or FSB. His performance as deputy mayor, as clearly presented in the Shadkhan interview, was already slick and self-assured.

The story of how and when Putin actually resigned, and how he came to work for Sobchak, is the story of how a KGB cadre began to morph in the country's democratic transformation and attach themselves to the new leadership. It's the story of how a faction of the KGB, in particular part of its foreign-intelligence arm, had long been secretly preparing for change in the tumult of the Soviet Union's *perestroika* reforms. Putin appears to have been part of this process while he was in Dresden. Later, after Germany reunified, the country's security services suspected he was part of a group working on a special operation, 'Operation Luch', or Sunbeam, that had been preparing since at least 1988 in case the East German regime collapsed.[4] This operation was to recruit a network of agents that could continue to operate for the Russians long after the fall.

*

DRESDEN – When Putin arrived in Dresden in 1985, East Germany was already living on borrowed time. On the verge of bankruptcy, the country was surviving with the help of a billion-DM loan from West Germany,[5] while voices of dissent were on the rise. Putin arrived there at the age of thirty-two, apparently fresh from a stint training at the KGB's elite Red Banner academy for foreign-intelligence officers, and began work in an elegant art deco villa with a sweeping staircase and a balcony that overlooked a quiet, brightly-painted neighbourhood street. The villa, surrounded by leafy trees and rows of neat family homes for the Stasi elite, was just around the corner from the grey sprawl of the Stasi headquarters, where dozens of political prisoners were held in tiny windowless cells. Hans Modrow, the local leader of the ruling Communist Party, the SED, was known as a reformer. But he was also heavy-handed in his efforts to clamp down on dissent. All around the eastern bloc, the mood of protest was increasing amidst the misery and shortages of the planned economy and the brutality of state law-enforcement agencies. Sensing an opportunity, US intelligence agencies, with the help of the Vatican, had quietly started operations to funnel printing and communications equipment and cash to the Solidarność protest movement in Poland, where dissent against the Soviets had always been the strongest.

*

Vladimir Putin had long dreamed of a career in foreign intelligence. During the Second World War his father had served in the NKVD, the Soviet secret police. He'd operated deep behind enemy lines trying to sabotage German positions, narrowly escaping being taken prisoner, and then suffering near fatal wounds. After his father's heroics, Putin had been obsessed from an early age with learning German, and in his teenage years he'd been so keen to join the KGB that he called into its local Leningrad office to offer his services even before he'd finished school, only to be told he had to graduate from university or serve in the army first. When, in his early thirties, he finally made it to the elite Red Banner school for foreign-intelligence officers, it was an achievement that looked to have secured his escape from the drab struggle of his early life. He'd endured a childhood chasing rats around the stairwell of his communal apartment building and scuffling with the other kids on the street. He'd learned to channel his appetite for street fights into mastering the discipline of judo, the martial art based on the subtle principles of sending opponents off balance by adjusting to their attack. He'd closely followed the local KGB office's recommendation on what courses he should take to secure recruitment into the security services and studied at the Leningrad University's law faculty. Then, when he graduated in 1975, he'd worked for a while in the Leningrad KGB's counter-intelligence division, at first in an undercover role. But when he finally attained what was officially said to be his first foreign posting, the Dresden station Putin arrived at appeared small and low-key, a far cry from the glamour of the station in East Berlin, where about a thousand KGB operatives scurried to undermine the enemy 'imperial' power.[6]

When Putin came to Dresden, there were just six KGB officers posted there. He shared an office with an older colleague, Vladimir Usoltsev, who called him Volodya, or 'little Vladimir', and every day he took his two young daughters to German kindergarten from the nondescript apartment building he lived in with his wife, Lyudmilla, and the other KGB officers. It seemed a humdrum and provincial life, far away from the cloak-and-dagger drama of East Berlin on the border with the West. He apparently played sports and exchanged pleasantries with his Stasi colleagues, who called their Soviet visitors 'the friends'. He engaged in small talk on German culture and language with Horst Jehmlich, the affable special assistant to the Dresden Stasi chief, who was the fixer in chief, the lieutenant-colonel who knew everyone in town and was in charge of organising safe houses and secret apartments for agents and informants, and for procuring goods for the Soviet 'friends'. 'He was very interested in certain German idioms. He was really keen on learning such things,' Jehmlich recalled. He'd seemed a modest and thoughtful comrade: 'He never pushed himself forward. He was never in the front line,' he said. He'd been a dutiful husband and father: 'He was always very kind.'[7]

But relations between the Soviet spies and their Stasi colleagues were sometimes fraught, and Dresden was far more than the East German backwater it may have appeared to be. For one thing, it was on the front line of the smuggling empire that for a long time served as life support for the GDR's economy. As the home of Robotron, the biggest electronics manufacturer in East Germany, producing mainframe and personal computers and other devices, it was central to the Soviet and GDR battle to illicitly obtain the blueprints and components of Western high-tech goods, making it a key cog in the eastern bloc's bitter – and failing – struggle to compete militarily with the rapidly developing technology of the West. In the seventies, Robotron had successfully cloned the West's IBM, and it had developed close ties with West Germany's Siemens.[8] 'Most of the East German high-tech smuggling came through Dresden,' said Franz Sedelmayer, a West German security consultant who later worked with Putin in St Petersburg and started out in the eighties in the family business in Munich selling defence products to NATO and the Middle East.[9] 'Dresden was a centre for this black trade.' It was also a centre for the Kommerzielle Koordinierung, a department within the East German foreign trade ministry that specialised in smuggling operations for high-tech goods under embargo from the West. 'They were exporting antiques and importing high-tech. They were exporting arms and importing high-tech,' said Sedelmayer. 'Dresden was always important for the microelectronics industry,' said Horst Jehmlich.[10] The espionage unit headed by East Germany's legendary spymaster Markus Wolf 'did a lot' for this, added Jehmlich. He remained tight-lipped, however, on what exactly they did.

The Dresden Stasi foreign-intelligence chief, Herbert Kohler, served at the same time as head of its information and technology intelligence unit,[11] a sign of how important smuggling embargoed goods was for the city. Ever since Germany was carved up between East and West in the aftermath of World War II, much of the eastern bloc had relied on the black market and smuggling to survive. The Soviet Union's coffers were empty after the ravages of the war, and in East Berlin, Zürich and Vienna organised-crime groups worked hand in hand with the Soviet security services to smuggle cigarettes, alcohol, diamonds and rare metals through the black market to replenish the cash stores of the security services of the eastern bloc. Initially the black-market trade had been seen as a temporary necessity, the Communist leaders justifying it to themselves as a blow against the foundations of capitalism. But when, in 1950, the West united against the Soviet-controlled bloc to place an embargo on all high-tech goods that could be used for military means, smuggling became a way of life. The free choices of capitalism and the drive for profit in the West were fuelling a boom in technological development there. By comparison, the planned socialist economy of the eastern bloc was frozen far behind. Its enterprises were bound only to meet annual production plans, its workers and scientists left to procure even the most basic goods through informal connections on the grey market. Isolated by the Iron Curtain, smuggling became the only way for the eastern bloc to keep up with the rapidly developing achievements of the capitalist West.[12]

The East German foreign trade ministry set up the Kommerzielle Koordinierung, appointing the garrulous Alexander Schalck-Golodkowski as its chief. Its mission was to earn illicit hard currency through smuggling, to bankroll the Stasi acquisition of embargoed technology. The KoKo, as it was known, answered first to Markus Wolf's Stasi espionage department, but then became a force unto itself.[13] A string of front companies was set up across Germany, Austria, Switzerland and Liechtenstein, headed by trusted agents, some with multiple identities, who brought in vitally needed hard currency through smuggling deals and the sale of illicit arms to the Middle East and Africa.[14] All the while, the Soviet masters sought to keep a close eye on these activities. The KGB could access all the embargoed high-tech blueprints and goods collected by the Stasi.[15] Often, the Stasi complained that the intelligence-gathering was a one-way street.

At the time Putin arrived in Dresden, West Germany was becoming ever more important as a source of high-tech goods. The KGB was still recovering from a major blow in the early eighties, when Vladimir Vetrov, an officer in its 'Directorate T', which specialised in procuring Western scientific and technological secrets, offered his services to the West. Vetrov handed over the names of all the KGB's 250 officers working on 'Line X', the smuggling of technology, in embassies across the world, as well as thousands of documents which provided a breakdown of the Soviets' industrial espionage efforts. As a result, forty-seven agents were expelled from France, while the US began to develop an extensive programme to sabotage the Soviets' illicit procurement networks.

The KGB was doubling down on its efforts in Germany, recruiting agents in companies including Siemens, Bayer, Messerschmidt and Thyssen.[16] Putin was clearly involved in this process, enlisting scientists and businessmen who could assist in the smuggling of Western technology into the eastern bloc. Robotron's status as the biggest electronics manufacturer in East Germany made it a magnet for visiting businessmen from the West. 'I know that Putin and his team worked with the West, that they had contacts in the West. But mostly they recruited their agents here,' said Putin's Stasi colleague Jehmlich. 'They went after students before they left for the West. They tried to select them and figure out how they could be interesting for them.'[17]

But Jehmlich was far from aware of all the operations of his KGB 'friends', who frequently went behind the backs of their Stasi comrades when recruiting agents, including in the Stasi itself. Jehmlich, for instance, claimed he'd never heard that Putin used a cover name for sensitive operations. But many years later, Putin told students he'd adopted 'several technical pseudonyms' for foreign-intelligence operations at that time.[18] One associate from those days said Putin had called himself 'Platov', the cover name he'd first been given in the KGB training academy.[19] Another name he reportedly used was 'Adamov', which he'd taken in his post as head of the House of Soviet–German Friendship in the neighbouring city of Leipzig.[20]

One of the Stasi operatives Putin worked closely with was a short, round-faced German, Matthias Warnig, who was later to become an integral part of the Putin regime. Warnig was part of a KGB cell organised by Putin in Dresden 'under the guise of a business consultancy', one former Stasi officer recruited by Putin later said.[21] In those days, Warnig was a hotshot, said to have recruited at least twenty agents in the 1980s to steal Western military rocket and aircraft technology.[22] He'd risen fast through the ranks since his recruitment in 1974, becoming deputy head of the Stasi's information and technology unit by 1989.[23]

Putin mostly liked to hang out in a small, lowlit bar in the historic centre of Dresden called Am Tor, a few tram stops into the valley from his KGB base, where he'd meet some of his agents, according to one person who worked with him then.[24] One of the main hunting grounds for operations was the Bellevue Hotel on the banks of the Elbe. As the only hotel in the city open to foreigners, it was an important hive for recruiting visiting Western scientists and businessmen. The hotel was owned by the Stasi's department of tourism, and its palatial restaurants, cosy bars and elegant bedrooms were fitted out with hidden cameras and bugs. Visiting businessmen were honey-trapped with prostitutes, filmed in their rooms and then blackmailed into working for the East.[25] 'Of course, it was clear to me we used female agents for these purposes. Every security service does this. Sometimes women can achieve far more than men,' said Jehmlich with a laugh.[26]

We may never know if Putin took his hunt further afield into the West. We cannot trust the authorised accounts of his KGB contemporaries. He himself has insisted he'd never done so, while his colleagues liked to tell instead of the long, lazy 'tourist' trips they took to neighbouring East German towns. But one of Putin's chief tasks was gathering information on NATO, the 'main opponent',[27] and Dresden was an important outpost for recruiting in Munich and in Baden-Württemberg five hundred kilometres away, both home to US military personnel and NATO troops.[28] Many years later a Western banker told me the story of his aunt, a Russian princess, Tatiana von Metternich, who'd married into the German aristocracy and lived in a castle, near Wiesbaden, West Germany, where the US Army had its main base. She'd told her nephew how impressed she'd been by a young KGB officer, Vladimir Putin, who had visited her in her home and taken confession religiously, despite his background in the KGB.[29]

While Putin operated under the radar, in the background, the ground was beginning to shift beneath his feet. Parts of the KGB leadership were becoming ever more cognisant of the Soviet Union's flagging capacity in the struggle against the West, and had quietly begun preparing for a different phase. Soviet coffers were running on empty, and in the battle to procure Western technology, despite the extensive efforts of the KGB and the Stasi, the eastern bloc was always on the back foot, always playing catch-up and lagging ever further behind the technology of the West. In an era when US president Ronald Reagan had announced a new initiative to build the so-called 'Star Wars' system that would defend the United States from nuclear-missile attack, the Soviet bloc ploughed ever greater efforts into securing Western technology, only to become ever more aware of how behind they were.

Since the early eighties, a few progressive members of the KGB had been working on a transformation of sorts. Ensconced in the Institute for World Economy in Moscow, they began working on reforms that could introduce some elements of the market to the Soviet economy in order to create competition, yet retain overall control. When Mikhail Gorbachev took office as General Secretary of the Communist Party in 1985, these ideas were given impetus. Gorbachev launched the political and economic reforms of *glasnost* and *perestroika*, which aimed for a gradual loosening of control over the country's political and economic system. Throughout the eastern bloc, the mood of protest was rising against the repression of Communist rulers, and Gorbachev pressed his colleagues across the Warsaw Pact to pursue similar reforms as the only way to survive and stay ahead of the tide of resentment and dissent. Aware that a collapse could nevertheless be on its way, a small handful of KGB progressives began preparing for a fall.

As if seeing the writing on the wall, in 1986 Markus Wolf, the Stasi's venerated Spymaster, resigned, ending his reign over East Germany's feared foreign-intelligence unit, the Hauptverwaltung Aufklärung, where for more than thirty years he'd ruthlessly run operations for the Stasi, known for his ability to relentlessly exploit human weaknesses to blackmail and extort agents into working for him. Under his watch the HVA had penetrated deep into the West German government, and had turned numerous agents thought to be working for the CIA. But now he'd somehow suddenly dropped all that.

Officially, he was helping his brother Konrad write his memoirs of their childhood in Moscow. But behind the scenes he too was preparing for change. He began working closely with the progressive *perestroika* faction in the KGB, holding secret meetings in his palatial Berlin flat to discuss a gradual liberalisation of the political system.[30] The plans they spoke of were similar to the *glasnost* reforms Gorbachev had launched in Moscow, where informal political movements were gradually being allowed to emerge and media constraints were being relaxed. But though the talk was of democracy and reform, the plan was always for the security services to remain in control behind the scenes. Later it turned out that Wolf had secretly remained on the Stasi payroll throughout.[31]

Ever more aware of the risks of Communist collapse, in the mid-eighties the KGB quietly launched Operation Luch, to prepare for a potential regime change ahead. Wolf was kept fully aware of it, but his successor as head of the Stasi foreign-intelligence arm was not.[32] In August 1988 the KGB sent a top official, Boris Laptev, to the imposing Soviet embassy in East Berlin to oversee it.[33] Officially, Laptev's mission was to create a group of operatives who would work secretly in parallel with the official KGB residency to penetrate East German opposition groups. 'We had to collect information on the opposition movement and put the brakes on any developments, and prevent any moves towards German reunification,' he later said.[34] But in fact, as the anti-Communist protests grew and the futility of such efforts became ever clearer, his mission became almost the opposite of that. The group instead began to focus on creating a new agent network that would reach deep into the second and third tier of political circles in the GDR. They were looking for agents who could continue to work undercover for the Soviets even in a reunified Germany, untainted by any leadership role before the collapse.[35]

The signs are that Putin was enlisted to play a part in this process. In those days he served as Party secretary,[36] a position that would have put him in frequent contact with Dresden's SED chief Hans

Modrow. The KGB appear to have hoped that they could cultivate Modrow as a potential successor to the long-serving East German leader Erich Honecker, apparently even believing he could lead the country through modest *perestroika*-like reforms.[37] Vladimir Kryuchkov, the KGB foreign-intelligence chief, paid a special visit to Modrow in Dresden in 1986.[38]

But Honecker had refused to step down until the bitter end, forcing the KGB to dig deeper to recruit agents who would continue to act for them after the fall of the eastern bloc. Kryuchkov would always insist that he never met Putin then, and to deny that Putin played any part in Operation Luch, as did Markus Wolf.[39] But the West German equivalent of MI5, the Bundesamt für Verfassungsschutz, believed the reverse. They later questioned Horst Jehmlich for hours on what Putin had been up to then. Jehmlich suspected that Putin had betrayed him: 'They tried to recruit people from the second and third tier of our organisation. They went into all organs of power, but they didn't contact any of the leaders or the generals. They did it all behind our backs.'[40]

Other parts of the Stasi also began secretly preparing. In 1986, Stasi chief Erich Mielke signed off on plans for a squad of elite officers, the Offiziere im besonderen Einsatz, to remain in power in case the rule of the SED suddenly came to an end.[41] The most important phase of securing the Stasi's future began when they started moving cash via their smuggling networks through a web of firms into the West, in order to create secret cash stores to enable them to maintain operations after the fall. A senior German official estimated that billions of West German marks were siphoned out of East Germany into a string of front companies from 1986.[42]

Putin's Dresden was a central hub for these preparations. Herbert Kohler, the head of the Dresden HVA, was closely involved in the creation of some of these front companies – so-called 'operative firms' – that were to hide their connections with the Stasi and store 'black cash' to allow Stasi networks to survive following a collapse.[43] Kohler worked closely with an Austrian businessman named Martin Schlaff, who'd been recruited in the early eighties by the Stasi. Schlaff was tasked with smuggling embargoed components for the construction

of a hard-disc factory in Thüringen, near Dresden. Between the end
of 1986 and the end of 1988 his firms received more than 130 million
marks from the East German government for the top-secret project,
which was one of the most expensive ever run by the Stasi. But the
plant was never finished. Many of the components never arrived,[44]
while hundreds of millions of marks intended for the plant, and from
other illicit deals, disappeared into Schlaff front companies in
Liechtenstein, Switzerland and Singapore.[45]

These financial transfers took place at the time Putin was serving
as the main liaison officer between the KGB and the Stasi in Dresden,
in particular with Kohler's HVA.[46] It's not clear whether he played
any role in them. But many years later, Schlaff's connections with
Putin became clear when the Austrian businessman re-emerged in
a network of companies in Europe that were central cogs in the
influence operations of the Putin regime.[47] Back in the 1980s Schlaff
had travelled at least once to Moscow for talks with Soviet foreign-
trade officials.[48]

Most of what Putin did during the Dresden years remains
shrouded in mystery, in part because the KGB proved much more
effective than the Stasi at destroying and transferring documents
before the collapse. 'With the Russians, we have problems,' said Sven
Scharl, a researcher at the Stasi archives in Dresden.[49] 'They destroyed
almost everything.' Only fragments remain in the files retrieved from
the Stasi of Putin's activities there. His file is thin, and well-thumbed.
There is the order of Stasi chief Erich Mielke of February 8 1988,
listing Major Vladimir Vladimirovich Putin as receiving a Bronze
Medal of Merit of the National People's Army. There are the letters
from the Dresden Stasi chief Horst Böhm wishing Comrade Putin
a happy birthday. There is the seating plan for a dinner celebrating
the seventy-first anniversary of the Cheka, the original name for the
Soviet secret police, on January 24 1989. There's the photograph
marking the visit of more than forty Stasi, KGB and military officers
to the First Guards Tank Army Museum. (Putin peeps out, almost
indistinguishable among the grey mass of men.) Then there are the
photographs, uncovered only recently, of a loutish and bored-looking
Putin in light-grey jacket and bright suede shoes holding flowers

and drinking at an award ceremony for the Stasi intelligence unit's top brass.

The only trace of any operative activity connected to Putin is a letter from him to Böhm, asking for the Dresden Stasi chief's assistance in restoring the phone connection for an informant in the German police who 'supports us'. The letter is short on any detail, but the fact of Putin's direct appeal to Böhm appears to indicate the prominence of his role.[50] Jehmlich indeed later confirmed that Putin became the main KGB liaison officer with the Stasi on behalf of the KGB station chief Vladimir Shirokov. Among the recent finds was one other telltale document: Putin's Stasi identity card, which would have given him direct access to Stasi buildings and made it easier for him to recruit agents, because he would not have had to mention his affiliation with the KGB.

Many years later, when Putin became president, Markus Wolf and Putin's former KGB colleagues took care to stress that he had been a nobody when he served in Dresden. Putin was 'pretty marginal', Wolf once told a German magazine, and even 'cleaning ladies' had received the Bronze Medal awarded to him.[51] The KGB colleague Putin shared an office with on his arrival in Dresden, Vladimir Usoltsev, who was somehow permitted to write a book on those times, took care to emphasise the mundanity of their work, while revealing zero detail about their operations. Though he admitted that he and Putin had worked with 'illegals', as the sleeper agents planted undercover were called, he said they'd spent 70 per cent of their time writing 'senseless reports'.[52] Putin, he claimed, had only managed to recruit two agents during his entire five years in Dresden, and at some point had stopped looking for more, because he realised it was a waste of time. The city was such a provincial backwater that 'the very fact of our service in Dresden spoke of how we had no future career', Usoltsev wrote.[53] Putin himself claimed he'd spent so much time drinking beer there that he put on twelve kilos.[54] But the photographs of him in those days do not suggest any such weight gain. Russian state television later proclaimed that Putin was never involved in anything illegal.

But one first-hand account suggests the downplaying of Putin's activities in Dresden was cover for another mission – one beyond the edge of the law. It suggests that Putin was stationed there precisely because it was a backwater, far from the spying eyes in East Berlin, where the French, the Americans and the West Germans all kept close watch. According to a former member of the far-left Red Army Faction who claimed to have met him in Dresden, Putin had worked in support of members of the group, which sowed terror across West Germany in the seventies and eighties: 'There was nothing in Dresden, nothing at all, except the radical left. Nobody was watching Dresden, not the Americans, not the West Germans. There was nothing there. Except the one thing: these meetings with those comrades.'[55]

*

In the battle for empire between East and West, the Soviet security services had long been deploying what they called their own 'active measures' to disrupt and destabilise their opponent. Locked in the Cold War but realising it was too far behind technologically to win any military war, ever since the sixties the Soviet Union had found its strength lay in disinformation, in planting fake rumours in the media to discredit Western leaders, in assassinating political opponents, and in supporting front organisations that would foment wars in the Third World and undermine and sow discord in the West. Among these measures was support for terrorist organisations. Across the Middle East, the KGB had forged ties with numerous Marxist-leaning terror groups, most notably with the PFLP, the Popular Front for the Liberation of Palestine, a splinter group of the Palestine Liberation Organisation that carried out a string of plane hijackings and bomb attacks in the late sixties and seventies. Top-secret documents retrieved from the archives of the Soviet Politburo illustrate the depth of some of these connections. They show the then KGB chief Yury Andropov signing off three requests for Soviet weapons from PFLP leader Wadi Haddad, and describing him as a 'trusted agent' of the KGB.[56]

In East Germany, the KGB actively encouraged the Stasi to assist in its 'political activities' in the Third World.[57] In fact, support for international terrorism became one of the most important services the Stasi rendered to the KGB.[58] By 1969 the Stasi had opened a clandestine training camp outside East Berlin for members of Yassar Arafat's PLO.[59] Markus Wolf's Stasi foreign-intelligence unit became deeply involved in working with terrorist groups across the Arab world, including with the PFLP's notorious Carlos Ramirez Sanchez, otherwise known as Carlos the Jackal.[60] Stasi military instructors set up a network of terrorist training camps across the Middle East.[61] And when, in 1986, one Stasi counter-intelligence officer, horrified at the mayhem that was starting to reach German soil, tried to disrupt the bombing plots of a group of Libyans that had become active in West Berlin, he was told to back off by Stasi chief Erich Mielke. 'America is the arch-enemy,' Mielke had told him. 'We should concern ourselves with catching American spies and not bother our Libyan friends.'[62] Weeks later a bomb went off at the La Belle discothèque in West Berlin, popular with American soldiers, killing three US servicemen and one civilian, and injuring hundreds more. It later emerged that the KGB had been aware of the activities of the bombers, and knew exactly how they'd smuggled their weapons into Berlin.[63] Apparently all methods were to be permitted in the fight against the US 'imperialists'.

One former KGB general who defected to the US, Oleg Kalugin, later called these activities 'the heart and soul of Soviet intelligence'.[64] The former head of Romania's foreign-intelligence service, Ion Mihai Pacepa, who became the highest-ranking eastern-bloc intelligence officer to defect to the US, had been the first to speak openly about the KGB's operations with terrorist groups. Pacepa wrote of how the former head of the KGB's foreign intelligence, General Alexander Sakharovsky, had frequently told him: 'In today's world, when nuclear arms have made military force obsolete, terrorism should become our main weapon.'[65] Pacepa also stated that KGB chief Yury Andropov had launched an operation to stoke anti-Israeli and anti-US sentiment in the Arab world. At the same time, he said, domestic terrorism was to be unleashed in the West.[66]

West Germany had been on edge ever since the far-left militant

Red Army Faction – also known as the Baader-Meinhof Group after its early leaders Andreas Baader and Ulrike Meinhof – launched a string of bombings, assassinations, kidnappings and bank robberies in the late 1960s. In the name of toppling the country's 'imperialism and monopoly capitalism', they'd killed prominent West German industrialists and bankers, including the head of Dresdner Bank in 1977, and had bombed US military bases, killing and injuring dozens of servicemen. But by the end of the seventies, when the West German police stepped up a campaign of arrests, the Stasi began providing safe haven in the East to members of the group.[67] 'They harboured not just one but ten of them. They lived in cookie-cutter buildings around Dresden, Leipzig and East Berlin,' said the German security consultant Franz Sedelmayer.[68] The Stasi had provided them with false identities, and also ran training camps.[69] For four years, from 1983 to 1987, one of their number, Inge Viett, had lived under a false name in a Dresden suburb, until one of her neighbours travelled to West Berlin and saw her face on a wanted poster there. She was one of West Germany's most wanted terrorists, known as the 'grandma of terrorism', accused of participating in the attempted assassinations of a NATO commander-in-chief and the commander-in-chief of US forces in Europe, General Frederick Kroesen.[70]

Initially, after the fall of the Wall, the West German authorities believed the Stasi had provided only refuge and false identities to the Red Army Faction members. But as prosecutors continued to investigate the Stasi's role, they found evidence of a much deeper collaboration. Their investigation led to the arrest and indictment of five former Stasi counter-terrorism officers for conspiring with the group to bomb the US's Ramstein army base in 1981, and attempting to kill General Kroesen.[71] Stasi chief Erich Mielke was indicted on the same charges. One former Red Army Faction member emerged to tell how the group would frequently be used by the Stasi to transport weapons to terrorists in the Arab world.[72] Another former member spoke of working in the eighties as a handler for the notorious Carlos the Jackal,[73] who had lived for a time under Stasi protection in East Berlin, where he lived it up in the city's most luxurious hotels and casinos.[74] Inge Viett later confessed that she'd attended a training camp in East Germany to prepare for the 1981 attack on General Kroesen.[75]

But amid the tumult of German reunification, there was no political will to root out the evils of the GDR's past and bring the Stasi men to trial. The five-year statute of limitations on those charged with collaboration with the Red Army Faction was deemed to have passed, and the charges dropped away.[76] The memory of their crimes faded, while the KGB's involvement with the Red Army Faction was never investigated at all. But all the while the Soviets had overseen the operations of the Stasi, with liaison officers at every command level. At the highest level KGB control was so tight that, according to one former Red Army Faction member, 'Mielke wouldn't even fart without asking permission in Moscow first.'[77] 'The GDR could do nothing without coordination with the Soviets,' said a defector from the senior ranks of the Stasi.[78]

This was the environment Putin was working in – and the story that the former Red Army Faction member had to tell about Dresden fitted closely with that. According to him, in the years that Putin served in East Germany, Dresden became a meeting place for the Red Army Faction.

Dresden was chosen as a meeting place precisely because 'there was no one else there', this former Red Army Faction member said.[79] 'In Berlin, there were the Americans, the French and the British, everyone. For what we needed to do we needed the provinces, not the capital.' Another reason the meetings were held there was because Markus Wolf and Erich Mielke wanted to distance themselves from such activities: 'Wolf was very careful not to be involved. The very last thing a guy like Wolf or Mielke wanted was to be caught red-handed supporting a terrorist organisation . . . We met there [in Dresden] about half a dozen times.' He and other members of the terrorist group would travel into East Germany by train, and would be met by Stasi agents waiting in a large Soviet-made Zil car, then driven to Dresden, where they were joined in a safe house by Putin and another of his KGB colleagues. 'They would never give us instructions directly. They would just say, "We heard you were planning this, how do you want to do it?" and make suggestions. They would suggest other targets and ask us what we needed. We always needed weapons and cash.' It was difficult for the Red Army Faction to purchase weapons in Western Germany, so they would hand Putin and his colleagues a list. Somehow, this list would later end up with an agent in the West, and the requested weapons would be dropped in a secret location for the Red Army Faction members to pick up.

Far from taking the backseat role often ascribed to him during his Dresden years, Putin would be among the leaders in these meetings, the former Red Army member claimed, with one of the Stasi generals taking orders from him.

As the Red Army Faction sowed chaos across West Germany in a series of vicious bomb attacks, their activities became a key part of KGB attempts to disrupt and destabilise the West, the former member of the terror group claimed. And, as the end loomed for Soviet power and the GDR, it's possible that they became a weapon to protect the interests of the KGB.

One possible such attack came just weeks after the Berlin Wall's fall. It was 8.30 in the morning on November 30 1989, and Alfred Herrhausen, chairman of Deutsche Bank, was setting off from his home in Bad Homburg, Frankfurt, for his daily drive to work. The first car in his three-car convoy was already heading down the road that was his usual route. But as Herrhausen's car sped to follow, a grenade containing 150 pounds of explosives tore through his armoured limousine, killing him instantly. The detonator that set off the grenade had been triggered when the limousine drove through a ray of infrared light beamed across the road.[80] The attack had been carried out with military precision, and the technology deployed was of the highest sophistication. 'This had to be a state-sponsored attack,' said one Western intelligence expert.[81] Later, it emerged that Stasi officers had been involved in training camps at which Red Army Faction members had been instructed in the use of explosives, anti-tank rockets and the detonation of bomb devices through photo-electric beams just like the one used in the Herrhausen attack.[82]

Herrhausen had been a titan of the West German business scene, and a close adviser to West German chancellor Helmut Kohl. The attack came just as reunification had suddenly become a real possibility.

This was a process in which Deutsche Bank could stand to gain massively from the privatisation of East German state enterprises – and in which Dresdner Bank, where Putin's friend the Stasi officer Matthias Warnig would soon be employed, was to battle with Deutsche for the spoils. According to the former Red Army Faction member, the attack on Herrhausen was organised for the benefit of Soviet interests: 'I know this target came from Dresden, and not from the RAF.'[83]

For the former Red Army Faction member those days now seem long ago and far away. But he can't help but remember with regret that he was no more than a puppet in Soviet influence games. 'We were no more than useful idiots for the Soviet Union,' he said with a wry grin. 'This is where it all began. They were using us to disrupt, destabilise and sow chaos in the West.'

When asked about the Stasi and the KGB's support for the Red Army Faction, a shadow falls across the still spry face of Horst Jehmlich, the former Dresden Stasi fixer-in-chief. We are sitting around the dining table of the sunlit Stasi apartment he's lived in ever since the GDR years, just around the corner from the Stasi headquarters and the villa of the KGB. The fine china is out for coffee, the table is covered with lace. The Red Army Faction members were only brought to the GDR 'to turn them away from terrorism', he insists. 'The Stasi wanted to prevent terrorism and stop them from returning to terrorist measures. They wanted to give them a chance to re-educate themselves.'

But when asked whether it was the KGB who were in fact calling the tune, whether it was Putin who the Red Army Faction members were meeting with in Dresden, and whether the order for the Herrhausen attack could have emanated from there, the shadow across his face becomes darker still. 'I don't know anything about this. When it was top-secret, I didn't know. I don't know whether this involved the Russian secret service. If it is so, then the KGB tried to prevent that anyone knows about this material. They will have said that this is a German problem. They managed to destroy many more documents than us.'[84]

The former Red Army Faction member's story is near-impossible to verify. Most of his former comrades are either in prison or dead.

Others allegedly involved in the meetings back then have disappeared off the grid. But a close Putin ally from the KGB indicated that any such allegations were extremely sensitive, and insisted that no connection between the KGB and the Red Army Faction, or any other European terrorist group, had ever been proved: 'And you should not try to do so!' he added sharply.[85] At the same time, however, the story he told about Putin's resignation from the security services raised a troubling question. According to this former KGB ally, Putin was just six months from qualifying for his KGB pension when he resigned – at thirty-nine, he was far younger than the official pension age of fifty for his rank of lieutenant-colonel. But the KGB doled out early pensions to those who'd given special service in terms of risk or honour to the motherland. For those who were stationed in the United States, one year of service was considered as one and a half years. For those who served time in prison, one year's service was considered three. Was Putin close to gaining an early pension because one year's service counted as two, as a result of the high risk involved in working with the Red Army Faction?

Many years later, Klaus Zuchold, one of Putin's recruits in the Stasi, offered some partial details of Putin's involvement in other active measures then. Zuchold, who'd defected to the West, told a German publication, *Correctiv*, that Putin had once sought to obtain a study on deadly poisons that leave few traces, and planned to compromise the author of this study by planting pornographic material on him.[86] It's not clear whether the operation ever got off the ground. Zuchold also claimed that Putin's activities included a role as the handler of a notorious neo-Nazi, Rainer Sonntag, who was deported to West Germany in 1987, and who returned to Dresden after the Wall's fall and stoked the rise of the far right.[87] By the time I sought out Zuchold to ask him about Putin's alleged work with the Red Army Faction, he had long gone to ground, and didn't respond to interview requests. According to one person close to Western intelligence, he was under the special protection of the Bundesamt für Verfassungsschutz.

*

While working with the Red Army terrorists may have been Putin's training ground in active measures against the imperialist West, what happened when the Berlin Wall came down was the experience he would carry with him for decades to come. Though it had become ever clearer that the eastern bloc might not hold, that social unrest could tear it apart and that the reverberations could reach into the Soviet Union itself, still Putin and the other KGB officers in Dresden scrambled to salvage networks amid the sudden speed of the collapse.

In a moment, it was over. There was suddenly no one in command. The decades of struggle and covert spy games seemed done. The border was gone, overwhelmed by the outpouring of protest built up over so many years. Though it took another month for the protests to reach Dresden, when they came, Putin and his colleagues were only partially prepared. While the crowds massed in the bitter cold for two days outside the Stasi headquarters, Putin and the other KGB men barricaded themselves inside the villa. 'We burned papers night and day,' Putin said later. 'We destroyed everything – all our communications, our lists of contacts and our agents' networks. I personally burned a huge amount of material. We burned so much stuff that the furnace burst.'[88]

Towards evening, a few dozen protesters broke off and headed towards the KGB villa. Putin and his team found themselves almost abandoned by the nearby Soviet military base. When Putin called for reinforcements to protect the building, the troops took hours to arrive. He telephoned the Soviet military command in Dresden, but the duty officer merely shrugged, 'We cannot do anything without orders from Moscow. And Moscow is silent.'[89] It seemed to Putin a betrayal of all they had worked for: the phrase 'Moscow is silent' rang through his head for a long time. One by one, the outposts of empire were being given up; the geopolitical might of the Soviet Union was collapsing like a house of cards. 'That business of "Moscow is silent" – I got the feeling then that the country no longer existed. That it had disappeared. It was clear the Union was ailing. And it had a terminal disease without a cure – a paralysis of power,' Putin said later.[90] 'The Soviet Union had lost its position in Europe. Although intellectually I understood that a position built on walls cannot last, I wanted something different to rise in its place. But nothing different was proposed. That's what hurt. They just dropped everything and went away.'[91]

But not all was lost. Though the fierceness of the protests and the timing of the ensuing collapse appeared to have taken the KGB by surprise, parts of it, together with the Stasi, had been preparing for that day. Parts of the KGB had been planning for a more gradual transition in which they would retain an element of influence and control behind the scenes.

Somehow, the KGB officers in Dresden managed to get one of their Stasi counterparts to hand over the vast majority of the Stasi's files on their work with the Soviets before the protesters burst into the Stasi headquarters. Putin's colleague from the earlier Dresden days, Vladimir Usoltsev, recounted that a Stasi officer handed over the files in their entirety to Putin. 'Within a few hours, nothing remained of them apart from ashes,' he said.[92] Reams of documents were taken to the nearby Soviet army base and thrown into a pit, where it was planned that they would be destroyed with napalm, but they were burned with petrol instead.[93] A further twelve truckloads were spirited away to Moscow. 'All the most valuable items were hauled away to Moscow,' Putin later said.

Over the next few months, as they prepared their exit from Dresden, they were provided with special cover from the powerful head of the KGB's illegals department, Yury Drozdov, the legendary officer in charge of overseeing the KGB's entire global network of undercover sleeper agents. The Dresden station chief, Vladimir Shirokov, told of how Drozdov made sure he was watched over from six in the morning to midnight. Finally, in the dead of night Shirokov and his family were driven to safety across the border to Poland by Drozdov's men.[94] Later, one of Putin's former colleagues told journalist Masha Gessen that Putin met with Drozdov in Berlin before he travelled home.[95]

The Dresden KGB 'friends' disappeared into the night, leaving little trace, abandoning their Stasi colleagues to face the people's wrath. It was a pressure Horst Böhm, the local Stasi chief, seemed unable to bear. In February the following year he apparently took his own life while under house arrest. 'He didn't see any other way out,' said Jehmlich. 'To protect his house, he removed all the fuses and then he poisoned himself with gas.'[96]

Two other Stasi commanders in neighbouring regions were also reported to have killed themselves. What precisely they feared most, we may never know, as they died before they'd been questioned on their roles. But for the KGB, although they'd been forced to abandon their posts, some of their legacy at least had been left intact. Part of their networks, their illegals, remained hidden far away from scrutiny and sight.[97] Much later, Putin would speak with pride of how his work in Dresden had mostly revolved around handling the illegal 'sleeper agents'. 'These are unique people,' he said. 'Not everyone is able to give up their life, their loved ones and relatives and leave the country for many, many years to devote themselves to serving the Fatherland. Only an elect can do this.'[98]

After Hans Modrow, backed by the Soviets,[99] took over as East Germany's interim leader that December, he quietly allowed the Stasi's foreign-intelligence arm, the HVA, to liquidate itself.[100] Untold assets disappeared in the process, while hundreds of millions of marks were siphoned off through the Liechtenstein and Swiss front companies of Martin Schlaff. Amid the jubilance of reunification, the voices of defectors from the Stasi to the West were rarely heard. But a few of them spoke out. 'Under certain conditions, parts of the network could be reactivated,' one such defector said. 'Nobody in the West has any guarantee as to whether some of these agents will be reactivated by the KGB.'[101]

*

When Putin returned home to Russia from Dresden in February 1990, the impact of the Berlin Wall's collapse was still reverberating across the Soviet Union. Nationalist movements were on the rise, and threatening to tear the country apart. Mikhail Gorbachev had been thrust onto the back foot, forced to cede ever more ground to emerging democratic leaders. The Soviet Communist Party was gradually starting to lose its monopoly on power, its legitimacy coming ever more under question. In March 1989, almost a year before Putin's return to Russia, Gorbachev had agreed to hold the first ever competitive elections in Soviet history to choose representatives for a new parliament, the Congress of People's Deputies. A ragtag group of democrats led by Andrei Sakharov, the nuclear physicist who'd become a dissident voice of moral authority, and Boris Yeltsin, then a rambunctious and rapidly rising political star who'd been thrown out of the Politburo for his relentless criticism of the Communist authorities, won seats and debated against the Communist Party for the first time. The end was rapidly nearing for the seven decades of Communist rule.

Amidst the tumult, Putin sought to adapt. But instead of earning a living as a taxi driver, or following the traditional path after a return home from foreign service, a post back at the Centre, as the Moscow headquarters of the KGB's foreign-intelligence service was known, he embarked on a different kind of mission. He'd been ordered by his former mentor and boss in Dresden, Colonel Lazar Matveyev, not to hang around in Moscow, but to head home to Leningrad.[102] There, he was flung straight into a city in turmoil, where city council elections, also competitive for the first time under Gorbachev's reforms, were pitting a rising tide of democrats against the Communist Party. For the first time, the democrats were threatening to break the Communists' majority control. Instead of defending the old guard against the democrats' rise, Putin sought to attach himself to Leningrad's democratic movement.

Almost immediately, he approached one of its most uncompromising leaders, a doughty and fearless newly elected member of the Congress of People's Deputies, Galina Starovoitova. She was a leading human rights activist, known for her uncompromising honesty as she railed against the failings of Soviet power. After she had given a resounding speech ahead of the city council elections, Putin, then a pale-eyed and unremarkable figure, walked up to her and told her how impressed he'd been by her words. He asked whether he could assist her with anything – including perhaps by working as her driver. But, suspicious of such an unsolicited approach, Starovoitova apparently resoundingly turned him away.[103]

His first post instead was as an assistant to the rector of the Leningrad State University, where in his youth he'd studied law and first entered the ranks of the KGB. He was to watch over the university's foreign relations and keep an eye on its foreign students and visiting dignitaries. It seemed at first a sharp demotion from his Dresden post, a return to the most humdrum work reporting on foreigners' movements to the KGB. But it was no more than a matter of weeks before it landed him a position at the top of the country's democratic movement.

Anatoly Sobchak was the university's charismatic professor of law. Tall, erudite and handsome, he'd long won students over with his mildly anti-government line, and had risen to become one of the new democratic movement's most rousing orators, appearing to challenge the Party and the KGB at every turn. He was part of the group of independents and reformers that took control of the city council after the March 1990 poll, and by May he'd been anointed the council's chairman. Almost immediately, Putin was appointed his right-hand man.

Putin was to be Sobchak's fixer, his liaison with the security services, the shadow who watched over him behind the scenes. From the start, the posting had been arranged by the KGB. 'Putin was placed there. He had a function to fill,' said Franz Sedelmayer, the German security consultant who later worked with him. 'The KGB told Sobchak, "Here's our guy. He'll take care of you."' The position in the law faculty had merely been a cover, said Sedelmayer, who believed that Sobchak himself had long been working unofficially with the KGB: 'The best cover for these guys was law degrees.'[104]

Despite his democratic credentials and his blistering speeches against abuses of power by the KGB, Sobchak understood all too well that he would not be able to shore up political power without the backing of parts of the establishment. He was vain and foppish, and most of all he wanted to climb. Along with hiring Putin, he'd also reached out to a senior member of the city's old guard, appointing a Communist rear admiral of the North Sea Fleet, Vyacheslav Shcherbakov, as his first deputy in the Leningrad city council. Sobchak's fellow members of the city's democratic movement who'd made him their leader were horrified at the choice. But, compromise by compromise, Sobchak was climbing his way to the top. By the time the city held elections for mayor in June 1991 he was the front-runner and won with relative ease.

When, that August, a group of hard-liners launched a coup against the Soviet leader, Sobchak relied on part of the old guard – in particular Putin and his KGB connections – to see himself, and the city, through a defiant stance against the attempted putsch without any bloodshed at all. Threatened by the increasing compromises Gorbachev was making to democrats driving for change, the coup plotters had declared a state of emergency, and announced that they were taking over control of the Soviet Union. Seeking to prevent Gorbachev drawing up a new union treaty that would grant the leaders of the restive Soviet republics control and ownership of their economic resources, they'd essentially taken Gorbachev hostage at his summer residence at Foros, on the shores of the Black Sea.

But in St Petersburg – as Leningrad was now named once again – as in Moscow, the city's democratic leaders rebelled against the coup. While members of the city council manned the defences of the democrats' headquarters in the tattered halls of the Marinsky Palace, Putin and Sobchak garnered the support of the local police chief and sixty men from the special militia. Together, they persuaded the head of the local television company to allow Sobchak on air on the first evening after the coup.[105] The speech Sobchak gave that night denouncing the coup leaders as criminals electrified the city's residents, and brought them out in the hundreds of thousands the next day, when they gathered in the shadow of the Romanovs' Winter Palace to demonstrate against the coup. Sobchak rallied the crowd with powerful calls for unity and defiance, but in the main he left the most vital and difficult mission to his deputies, Putin and Shcherbakov. That first tense night of the putsch, after making his televised address, he buried himself deep in his office in the Marinsky Palace, while Putin and Shcherbakov were left to negotiate with the city's KGB chief and the Leningrad region's military commander to make sure the hard-line troops approaching in tanks did not enter the city.[106] While Sobchak addressed the crowds gathered on the

Palace Square the following day, Putin and Shcherbakov's negotiations had stretched on. And when the tanks came to a rumbling halt that day at the city limits, Putin disappeared with Sobchak and a phalanx of special forces to a bunker deep beneath the city's main defence factory, the Kirovsky Zavod, where they could continue talks with the KGB and military chiefs in safety through an encrypted communication system.[107]

By the time Putin and Sobchak emerged from their bunker the next morning, the coup was over. The hard-liners' bid to take power had been defeated. In Moscow, elite special units of the KGB had refused orders to fire on the Russian White House, where Boris Yeltsin, by then the elected leader of the Russian republic, had amassed tens of thousands of supporters against the coup's bid to roll back the freedoms of Gorbachev's reforms. What remained of the legitimacy of the Communist Party was in tatters. The leaders of Russia's new democracy were ready to step up. Whatever his motives, Putin had helped them be in a position to do so.

All the while, true to his KGB training, Putin had reflected everyone's views back to them like a mirror: first those of his new so-called democratic master, and then those of the old-guard establishment he worked with too. 'He would change his colours so fast you could never tell who he really was,' said Sedelmayer.[108]

2

Inside Job

*

'What we've discussed is how the darkest forces never give up. The French Revolution, the Soviet one, all the others, appear first as a liberating struggle. But they soon morph into military dictatorship. The early heroes look like idiots, the thugs show their true faces, and the cycle (which isn't what revolution means) is complete.'

Christian Michel

*

MOSCOW, August 25 1991 – It was late in the evening when Nikolai Kruchina trudged wearily through the door to his flat in the closely-guarded compound for the Party elite. Just four days before, on August 21, the attempted coup by Communist hard-liners seeking to preserve Soviet power had collapsed in failure. And now, the institutions Kruchina had served for most of his life were being dismantled in front of his eyes. The evening before, he'd held a series of high-level meetings with the powerful boss of the Central Committee's International Department, Valentin Falin, and he seemed exhausted.[1] The KGB watchman outside his home noticed his downcast gaze, his clear reluctance to talk.[2]

The changes in those four short days had come thick and fast. First, the pro-democratic Russian leader Boris Yeltsin had signed a decree, broadcast live, suspending the Soviet Communist Party and ending its decades of rule. Yeltsin's defiant stance against the hard-line leaders of the attempted coup had put him firmly in the ascendant. He now by far eclipsed Gorbachev, who stood timidly to the side of the podium as Yeltsin addressed the Russian parliament. Arguing that the Communist Party was to blame for the illegal coup, Yeltsin ordered that the sprawling, warren-like headquarters of the Party's Central Committee on Moscow's Old Square be immediately sealed. Filed in hundreds of its rooms were the secrets of the Soviet Union's vast financial empire, a network that spanned thousands of administrative buildings, hotels, dachas and sanatoriums, as well as the Party's hard-currency bank accounts and untold hundreds, perhaps thousands, of foreign firms set up as joint ventures in the dying days of the regime. Through these bank accounts and other connected firms, the strategic operations of the Communist Party abroad – and those of allied political parties – had been funded. It was the engine room of the Soviet struggle for supremacy against the West. This was the empire Kruchina had administered as the chief of the Communist Party's property department since 1983. Its sudden sealing felt like a symbol of all that was lost.

Kruchina's wife turned in early that night, leaving her husband alone, she believed, to spend the night sleeping on the couch. But early the next morning she was awoken by a knock on her door. It was the KGB watchman. Her husband, she was told, had fallen to his death from the window of their seventh-floor flat.[3]

There were no apparent signs of disturbance, and the watchman said he'd discovered a crumpled note lying on the pavement next to Kruchina's body. 'I'm not a conspirator,' it said. 'But I'm a coward. Please tell the Soviet people this.'[4] The KGB immediately declared his death a suicide. But to this day, no one knows what exactly happened – or if they do, they are not willing to tell. Those who were at the centre of events in those days, like Viktor Gerashchenko, then the head of the Soviet state bank, prefer to limit their explanations to a Delphic 'He fell.'[5] Others like Nikolai Leonov, then the powerful head of the KGB's analytical department, insist that Kruchina was a victim of a 'deep depression' that set in at the empire's collapse.[6]

A little over a month later, the same thing happened to Kruchina's predecessor as property department chief. On the evening of October 6, Georgy Pavlov fell to his death from the window of his flat. His death, at the age of eighty-one, was also recorded as a suicide. Eleven days after Pavlov's death, another high-ranking member of the Party's financial machine fell to his death from his balcony. This time it was the American Section chief of the Communist Party's international department, Dmitry Lissovolik. Again, it was recorded as a suicide.

What linked the three men was an intimate knowledge of the secret financing systems of the Communist Party at the time the KGB was preparing for the transition to a market economy under Gorbachev's *perestroika* reforms. The property department Kruchina and Pavlov oversaw had been understood to have a value of $9 billion.[7] Western experts estimated its foreign holdings at many times more.[8] But in the first few days after the Communist Party's collapse, Russia's new rulers were bewildered to discover that the Party's coffers were nearly empty. Rumours abounded that officials, overseen by Kruchina, had siphoned billions of roubles and other currencies through foreign joint ventures hastily set up in the final years of the regime.[9] Russian prosecutors, originally ordered by Yeltsin to investigate the Communist Party for its role in the August coup attempt, were soon redirected to investigate what had happened to the Party funds.

Although Yeltsin ordered the offices of the Central Committee on Old Square to be sealed, Valentin Falin, the head of the committee's International Department, which oversaw the funding of foreign operations, immediately ordered his subordinates to start destroying documents.[10] What lay in the archives could provide a roadmap to the crimes of the Communist regime and, most importantly of all, to the cash that had been stashed away.

The most top-secret operations had been run out of Room 516, which had housed the International Department's special section for 'Party technology'. It was headed by Vladimir Osintsev, a specialist in black operations, who ran Communist Party influence campaigns to sow discord in countries where the existence of the Party was illegal, such as El Salvador, Turkey, South Africa and Chile. When the Russian prosecutors finally entered this room months later, in October 1991, reams of shredded files were found in ribbons across the floor. But signs of the lengths Party operatives had gone to run sleeper agents under deep cover remained. The prosecutors found piles of foreign passports and stamps from many different countries, heaps of other blank travel documents, and official stamps and visas waiting to be forged. There was a huge photo album filled with pictures of people of all types and races, a selection of wigs and beards, and even rubber moulds for faking fingerprints.[11]

One of the International Department's employees, Anatoly Smirnov, had rebelled, and smuggled out what he could.[12] The top-secret documents he managed to extract included details of hundreds of millions of dollars in payments to Communist-linked parties abroad. One such document, dated December 5 1989, showed an order for the Soviet state bank to transfer $22 million directly to Falin for the Party's International Fund for left-wing organisations.[13] Another, dated June 20 1987, ordered Gosbank, the central bank of the USSR, to transfer $1 million to the Party's curator for international affairs to provide the French Communist Party with additional funds.[14] The physical transfer of the money to France was to be organised by the KGB.

To Smirnov, the fact that the Party was regularly dipping into state coffers to fund its political and influence operations abroad meant that 'a crime was being committed against our people'.[15] For him, this was a red line. It was against Soviet law. The Party's operations should have been funded from the donations it collected from members, not from state coffers.[16]

The Russian prosecutors calculated that more than $200 million had been transferred out of the Soviet Union to fund Communist-linked parties in the USSR's final decade of existence; Smirnov put the total at many times more.[17] The sums transferred by more surreptitious means, for more clandestine activities, remained unknown.

But as the team of prosecutors trawled through what remained of the Central Committee's archive, they began to find documents that cast light on the myriad of unofficial, secret schemes via which billions of dollars more in funds seemed to have been siphoned out.

One such scheme involved what the Soviets called 'friendly' firms. These were the crony companies at the heart of the vast system of black-market operations that kept the eastern bloc afloat. Many of them were involved in the smuggling of embargoed technology. They included the string of front companies the East German trade official Alexander Schalck-Golodkowski deployed across East Germany, Austria, Switzerland and Liechtenstein. Others were involved in selling much-needed equipment to the Soviet oil, nuclear power and manufacturing industries at prices that were inflated many times over, while the profits were used to fund the activities of the Communist Party and other leftist movements in Italy, France, Spain, the UK and elsewhere.[18]

The money the CPSU would send directly to fund Communist Parties' activities was nothing compared to the amounts sent via the friendly firms, said Antonio Fallico, a senior Italian banker with close ties to the top of the Soviet elite, and later to the Putin regime too. The official donations the Italian Communist Party received annually from the Soviet Union were 'only about $15–20 million. This is not even money.' The real funding, he said, came from the intermediaries. 'All Italian firms who wanted to do business in the Soviet Union had to pay money to these firms . . . This was a colossal flow of money.'[19] A list of forty-five such 'friendly firms' was disclosed by prosecutors rooting through the archives. Among the mostly obscure import-export firms was at least one well-known name: Robert Maxwell's Pergamon Press, a vast publishing house that had long been a channel for the sale of Soviet science books to the West.[20] Just days before the list was published, the body of the controversial former Labour MP and media tycoon had been found floating in the Atlantic Ocean not far from his yacht.

Other companies working with the Soviet regime that stayed off the radar included titans of European industry such as Fiat, Merloni, Olivetti, Siemens and Thyssen, according to a former KGB operative who worked closely with Putin in the nineties, and another businessman who worked in these 'friendly firms' during Soviet times. This businessman, who would speak only on condition of anonymity, said his firm had supplied military goods under the guise of medical equipment: 'The medical equipment – it was a façade. Behind it, the firm produced very serious military equipment. It was the same with Siemens and with ThyssenKrupp. All of them were providing dual-use equipment to the Soviets. These friendly firms were not just fronts, the way things operate now. It was major European companies.' [21]

The network of friendly firms was not only involved in imports. According to one former aide to Gorbachev, some of them were engaged in barter operations that had been under way since the 1970s under Brezhnev. [22] The state oil-export monopoly Soyuznefteexport had, for instance, engaged in an elaborate scheme to barter oil for embargoed goods. It had first delivered oil via traders to vast storage reservoirs in Finland, where the oil's origins were disguised before a web of intermediaries sold it on in exchange for embargoed technology and other goods, according to a former Soyuznefteexport associate. Fertiliser exports, too, had long been part of these schemes.

For the Russian prosecutors trying to investigate the Party's finances, the traces of these schemes presented the biggest red flag. Untold fortunes in oil, metals, cotton, chemicals and arms had been transported out of the Soviet Union, either through barter schemes or export deals, and sold at knockdown prices to the intermediary friendly firms in the West. Under the export deals, the friendly firms would buy the raw materials at the Soviet internal price, which was fixed low under the rules of the planned economy, enabling them to reap vast profits when they sold them on at world market prices: the global oil price, for example, was almost ten times higher than the internal Soviet price in those days. [23] They could then stash the funds away into a web of accounts in friendly banks in Europe, such as Switzerland's Banco del Gottardo, and tax havens in Cyprus, Liechtenstein, Panama, Hong Kong and the British Channel Islands. The fortunes they made could be deployed for the activities of the Communist Party abroad, for active measures to destabilise the West. Most importantly of all, the entire process was overseen by the KGB, whose associates manned the friendly firms and controlled much of the Soviet trade ministry. 'The friendly firms sold what they had acquired for global prices. The profit was never returned to the Soviet Union,' wrote the prosecutor general tasked with overseeing the investigation, Valentin Stepankov. 'All contact with the friendly firms was carried out by the KGB.'[24]

The siphoning of commodities had rapidly accelerated in the final years of the Soviet regime. Later, the onetime head of economic analysis for Soviet military intelligence, Vitaly Shlykov, claimed that a large part of the Soviet Union's huge military stockpiles of raw materials – literal mountains of aluminium, copper, steel, titanium and other metals – that had been intended to keep the Soviet military machine running for decades to come, were fast dwindling by the time of the Soviet collapse.[25] Prosecutors, however, found only scraps of information. The raw-materials deals had left barely any trace.

But as they searched the debris and destruction, the reams of shredded paper on the floor, the prosecutors found one vital document, which looked as if it might provide a partial key to what happened in the twilight years of the Communist regime. It was a memo, dated August 23 1990, signed by Gorbachev's deputy general secretary Vladimir Ivashko, and it ordered the creation of an 'invisible economy' for the Communist Party.[26] The top Party leadership had evidently recognised that it urgently needed to create a network of firms and joint ventures that would protect and hide the Party's financial interests as Gorbachev's reforms sent the country hurtling into chaos. The Party was to invest its hard-currency resources into the capital of international firms operated by 'friends'. The funds and business associations would have 'minimum visible links'.

An even more telltale document was found in Nikolai Kruchina's apartment. When investigators arrived after he had plunged to his death, they found a file lying on his desk. Inside were documents that pointed to a potentially vast network of proxies managing funds for the regime.[27] One of the documents they reportedly found had spaces left blank for the name, Party number and signature of the Party member signing up to become a trusted proxy, a *doverennoye litso*, or custodian of the Party's funds and property.

'I _____ CPSU member since _____, Party number _____, with the following confirm my conscious and voluntary decision to become a trusted custodian of the Party and to carry out the tasks set for me by the Party at any post in any situation, without disclosing my membership of the institute of trusted custodians.

I pledge to preserve and carefully deploy in the interests of the Party the financial and material resources entrusted to me, and I guarantee the return of these resources at the first demand. Everything I earn as a result of economic activities with the Party's funds I recognise as the Party's property, and guarantee its transfer at any time and any place.

I pledge to observe the strict confidentiality of this information, and to carry out the orders of the Party, given to me by the individuals authorised to do so.

Signature of CPSU member _____

Signature of the person taking on the duty _____'[28]

The prosecutors scrambled to unravel what this document might mean. Few of the Party leadership and other members of the Party elite they questioned would reveal anything. Most claimed that they had been unaware of any such schemes. But the prosecutors' team struck lucky when they came across Leonid Veselovsky, a former colonel in the foreign-intelligence directorate of the KGB. Fearing a wave of repressions, Veselovsky spoke openly of how he'd been one of a number of top KGB foreign-intelligence operatives drafted in to help manage and hide the Party's property and wealth.[29] The foreign-intelligence officers were brought in for their knowledge of how Western financial systems worked. They reported to Kruchina, the property department chief, as well as to Vladimir Kryuchkov, the KGB chief, and Filip Bobkov, then the first deputy head of the KGB, and Vladimir Ivashko, the treasurer of the Central Committee.

Veselovsky, a specialist in international economics, had been transferred from his post in Portugal in November 1990 to work on the plan to create an 'invisible economy' for the Party's wealth. It was he who proposed the system of 'trusted custodians', or *dover-enniye litsa*, who would hold and manage funds on the Party's behalf. He'd prepared a series of notes for Kruchina with proposals for disguising the Party funds to protect them from confiscation. These included investing them in charitable or social funds, or anonymously in stocks and shares. The process was to be led by the KGB.

'On the one hand this will ensure a stable income independent of the future position of the Party. And on the other, these shares can be sold at any moment through stock exchanges and then trans-ferred to other spheres to disguise the Party's participation while retaining control,' he wrote. 'In order to conduct such measures there needs to be an urgent selection of trusted custodians who can carry out separate points of the programme. It could be possible to create a system of secret Party members who will ensure the Party's exist-ence under any conditions of these extreme times.'[30]

In another note, he suggested the creation of a network of compa-nies and joint ventures, including brokerages and trading firms, in tax havens such as Switzerland, where the shareholders would be the 'trusted custodians'.[31]

Just as the Stasi had begun preparing, transferring funds into a network of front companies before the fall, the KGB was readying the Party for regime change, fully aware that its monopoly on power was becoming ever more precarious. To some operatives of the foreign-intelligence network drafted in to work on the scheme, when they received the orders from Kryuchkov to start creating private companies it was a clear signal that the game was up for the Communist regime. 'As soon as this happened, I understood it was the end,' said Yury Shvets, a senior officer in the KGB's Washington station until 1987.[32]

But when, after the botched coup attempt of August 1991, the Soviet Communist Party was suddenly no more, it was not at all clear what had happened to the structures created to preserve its wealth, or who was in charge of them. For the Russian prosecutors investigating, the documents left behind in the archives and in

Kruchina's flat provided only the faint outlines of the network. The figures and cogs in the schemes, the trusted proxies, the *doverenniye litsa* managing the funds, the network of companies, joint ventures and brokerages were hidden.[33] When later questioned about the documents, former members of the Politburo insisted that the collapse had come so swiftly and unexpectedly that no one had had time to implement Ivashko's plans for the 'invisible economy'.[34] But the prosecutors found plenty of signs that the project had been at least partially activated, and was long under way – and that it appeared to be led by the foreign-intelligence arm of the KGB.

Veselovsky's career was just one indication. Two weeks before the August coup attempt he had resigned his position and headed for Switzerland, where he took up a post at a trading firm named Seabeco that was the epitome of a KGB-backed 'friendly firm',[35] and that had sold vast amounts of raw materials from the Soviet Union. It was headed by a Soviet émigré named Boris Birshtein, who in the seventies had gone first to Israel and then to Canada, where he set up a string of joint ventures, including one with a leading light of Soviet foreign intelligence.[36] The KGB appeared to have its fingerprints all over Seabeco's rise. 'None of this could have happened without the patronage of the KGB,' said Shvets.

When questioned, former KGB chief Vladimir Kryuchkov admitted that the trading firm had been created as a channel for the Communist Party's funds. But he insisted again that the plans had never been implemented – there'd been no time before the collapse of the regime.[37] But telltale signs emerged of Seabeco's continued association with the KGB. A taped telephone conversation between a Seabeco associate and a Russian foreign-intelligence chief was leaked, in which the two men openly discussed the trading network they'd set up.[38] This Seabeco associate, Dmitry Yakubovsky, went public with claims that Seabeco had received tens of millions of dollars to finance KGB operations in Europe.[39]

Any remaining chance the prosecutors might have of following the money trail, however, seemed to evaporate completely when Veselovsky disappeared from his post in Switzerland without a trace. Without adequate funding and only a scanty paper trail, the prosecutors soon ran into a brick wall. Inside Russia, they'd been able to trace the transfer of billions of roubles from Kruchina's property department to more than a hundred Party firms and commercial banks.[40] But their attempts to recover any of it were simply stonewalled.[41]

The new Yeltsin government seemed to have little interest in finding any of the funds amid the chaos of the Soviet collapse. For one brief moment that seemed to change, when Yegor Gaidar, Yeltsin's round-faced new reformist prime minister, announced with great fanfare that the government had hired Kroll, a top international investigations firm, to hunt down the Party cash. But, a \$1.5 million contract and a year scouring the globe for the missing Party funds later, Kroll appeared to have made even less progress than the prosecutors had. Apparently, there was nothing to report. 'They didn't find anything,' said Pyotr Aven, the government minister whose initiative it was to bring in Kroll in the first place. 'They found nothing more than the accounts of a handful of top-level bureaucrats. They had no more than half a million dollars on the accounts.'[42]

The problem was, it seemed, that the government did not want the funds to be found. The reason Kroll came back largely empty-handed was that it received no assistance from the Russian government at all. The firm had been blocked from working with the Russian prosecutors. 'The Russian government was not interested in us finding anything, so we did not,' said Tommy Helsby, a former Kroll chairman who worked on the probe.[43] 'All the government wanted to do was use our name in a press conference.' It only wanted to give the impression that a real search was under way.

The task was made more difficult by the fact that, rather than through straightforward bank transfers, much of the wealth of the Soviet Union appeared to have been transferred, via friendly firms like Seabeco through the raw materials trade. Another big operator in these trades, said Helsby, was the controversial Geneva-based Glencore founder, commodities trader Marc Rich.[44]

The KGB foreign-intelligence operatives who had been behind the creation of the scheme now held the keys to the hidden wealth.

'At the end, when the Soviet Union collapsed, when the music stopped, these KGB men were the men who knew where the money was,' said Helsby. 'But by then they were the employees of a non-existent Soviet state.'

Some of them, however, stayed on; fragments of the KGB's foreign-intelligence networks were being preserved. Behind the scenes, amid the chaos, 'some of them continued to manage money for the KGB', Helsby said.

The night Nikolai Kruchina plunged to his death was the night the Communist Party's wealth was transferred to a new elite – and part of it had gone to the foreign-intelligence operatives of the KGB. Some of the cash had already undoubtedly been stolen, squirrelled away by top Party bosses and organised crime. But the foreign-intelligence operatives were the men who controlled the accounts when Yeltsin signed the Soviet Communist Party into history. Kruchina may have been grappling with the despairing realisation that the men who handled the funds were no longer under his control. Equally, he may have been sent to his death by those same men, to make sure he could never tell.

'Kruchina was most probably frightened that he could be asked where all the property had gone,' said Pavel Voshchanov, a former spokesperson for Yeltsin and a journalist who spent many years investigating the Party's stolen wealth. 'Kruchina gave the orders, but now he didn't know where it all was. The state was being destroyed. The KGB was being destroyed. And already no one knew where these KGB guys were – and who they were.'[45]

*

The story of the prosecutors' search for the missing Party wealth was fast forgotten in the tumult of the collapse. But what the prosecutors found then was a blueprint for everything that was to come later. The smuggling schemes, the friendly firms and the trusted custodians became the model on which the Putin regime and its influence operations would be run. The fact was that parts of the KGB foreign-intelligence elite had begun preparing for a market transition ever since former KGB chief Yury Andropov became Soviet leader in 1982. In the early eighties a handful of Soviet economists had begun to quietly discuss the need for a move to the market, whispering in the privacy of their kitchens about the chronic inefficiencies of the Soviet economy and publishing underground treatises on the need for reform. At the same time, there was a growing realisation among a tight-knit group within the intelligence elite that the Soviet economy was in a death spiral, that it was impossible to maintain the empire of the eastern bloc, let alone run broader influence and disruption campaigns in South America, the Middle East and Africa, and in the West. 'If you want to have a policy of being a great empire you should be able to spend a huge amount of money,' said one person who worked closely with reform-minded foreign-intelligence chiefs in those days.[46] 'It was not within our means to compete with the US. It was very costly and very difficult, impossible perhaps.' Even before progressive elements within the KGB began tentatively preparing for a possible transition in East Germany, they'd been pushing for sweeping reform in the Soviet Union itself.

The Soviet economy was being drained of resources by the push to build up military production and compete with the West at the expense of everything else. The Communist state was, in theory, succeeding in delivering its socialist vow of providing all workers with free education and healthcare. But in practice the planned economy simply didn't work. Instead there was a corrupted system under which the ordinary people the Communist state was supposed to protect lived largely in poverty. The Communist state could access plenty of natural resources for corrupt trading schemes, but it was failing to develop light industry to produce competitive consumer goods. There was no private ownership, or even any understanding of what profit was. Instead, the government handed down production quotas to each and every enterprise, controlled all earnings and fixed prices for everything. There was no motivation for anyone, and the system just didn't work. Consumer goods prices were fixed at incredibly low levels, but because of this there were acute shortages of everything – from bread, sausages and other foodstuffs, to cars, televisions, refrigerators and even apartments. The shortages meant queues and rationing, sometimes for months on end. Informal connections and payoffs to officials were often the only way to jump weeks-long queues for the most basic necessities – for shoe repairs, for a hospital bed, for coffins and funeral rites. The overweening power of the Soviet bureaucracy had built corruption deep into the system, while under these conditions the black market flourished.[47]

In the late sixties black marketeers, known as *tsekhoviki*, began to set up underground factories in which spare parts and materials siphoned from the state-owned plants were used to produce goods outside the regulated economy. Such activities could result in jail sentences of ten years or more, but increasingly these factories' output was becoming the only way to make up for at least some of the shortages of the Soviet planned system. Hard-currency speculators would trawl the halls of the Soviet Intourist hotels, risking prison to buy dollars from visiting foreign tourists at an exchange rate far more advantageous to the tourist than the fixed Soviet one. It was a good deal for the speculators, too. In the system of Soviet shortages, anyone with access to hard currency was king. Dollars would gain you access to the well-stocked Bereyozki shops reserved for the Soviet elite, where the shelves were crammed with the quality foodstuffs and other luxuries of the West. It would enable you to buy Western clothing, Western pop music, anything produced outside the stagnating and dreary Soviet economy – all of which could then be sold on for vast profits. The shortages in the Soviet economy ran so deep that, according to the former KGB foreign-intelligence operative Yury Shvets, everyone was for sale. Factory directors fiddled the books to give materials to the black marketeers in return for a cut of the profits. Law-enforcement officials turned a blind eye to the currency speculators marauding through Soviet hotels in return for bribes and access to the hotel buffet.[48] And at the top of the pyramid, ever since the seventies, the Party elite had been taking a cut of the smuggling and trading schemes. All of it undermined any efforts to improve production. 'The Soviet Union could not even make a pair of tights or shoes,' said Shvets. 'Prostitutes would give themselves for one night for one stocking, and then the next night for the other. It was a nightmare.'[49]

It was the members of the security service's foreign intelligence who saw most clearly that the system had to change. They were the ones who could travel and could see how the market economy operated in the West, how the socialist system was failing to keep up with the technological progress of the Western world. Among them was a legendary Soviet military-intelligence chief, Mikhail Milshtein, a strapping, Kojak-bald man with thick bushy eyebrows who'd served for decades in the US and then returned to Moscow to head the intelligence department at the Soviet military academy. In the seventies he moved to the Institute for the USA and Canada, a think tank that worked closely with Falin's influential International Department, where he was among those working on ways to engineer a rapprochement with the West. In the halls of the institute, an elegant pre-Revolutionary building tucked away down a narrow, leafy street behind Moscow's main thoroughfares, Milshtein worked with other associates of the Soviet foreign-intelligence elite on disarmament proposals. He forged close ties with the former US secretary of state Henry Kissinger as he sought ways out of what he called 'a vicious circle' of standoff with the West.[50]

Across town, deep in the southern suburbs of the city, in a dark and sprawling seventies-era tower block, a group of economists at the Institute for World Economy and International Relations, known as IMEMO, began working on reforms that would start to relax the Soviet state's monopoly on the economy. Among them was Rair Simonyan, a bright young economist in his early thirties who was the son of a high-ranking Soviet military-intelligence general. He worked closely with his deputy Andrei Akimov, a foreign-intelligence operative who would later be sent to head the Soviet Union's bank in Vienna, and subsequently became one of the most important financiers behind Vladimir Putin's regime. Simonyan made research trips to East Germany, where he saw clearly how far behind the Soviet economy lagged. 'It was a different world,' he said.[51]

As early as 1979, Simonyan had worked on a reform that would bring foreign capital into the Soviet economy through the creation of joint ventures between foreign and Soviet businesses. It was a bold measure that would erode the Soviet monopoly on all foreign trade, and it was immediately vetoed by the institute's director. But when a new director was appointed under Andropov in 1983, 'an absolutely different life' began, recalled Simonyan. The new director was Alexander Yakovlev, a former ambassador to Canada who would become a mentor to Gorbachev and the godfather of his *perestroika* reforms. Simonyan worked closely too with Yevgeny Primakov, a mandarin-like foreign-intelligence operative who'd worked many years in the Middle East under cover as a correspondent for the Soviet newspaper *Pravda*, forging close ties with Saddam Hussein in Iraq and other leaders in the Soviet patronage system there. Throughout the seventies, Primakov worked at IMEMO, cooperating closely with Milshtein at the US Institute for the USA and Canada, and took over as director of IMEMO when Yakovlev was promoted to the Politburo. He was now heading one of the main nests for the progressives in foreign intelligence. IMEMO became an engine room for the *perestroika* reforms.

Under Andropov, a new generation of economists was being educated. The twentysomething Yegor Gaidar discussed far-reaching market reforms that he believed were crucial to the survival of the Soviet bloc with the equally youthful Pyotr Aven. Both of them worked at another key research institute in the early eighties, the All Soviet Institute for Systems Research, and both of them were from the heart of the Soviet elite. Aven's father had been one of the country's most respected academics, while Gaidar's had worked under cover of being a correspondent for *Pravda* in Cuba, where he rose to the rank of admiral. Fidel Castro and Che Guevara visited him in his home, and his son grew up surrounded by high-ranking Soviet generals. Both Gaidar and Aven were to play leading roles in the market reforms of the new Russia. 'All the market reformers who later came to prominence – from Gorbachev to the young reformers – were brought up in institutions created by Andropov,' said Vladimir Yakunin, a close Putin ally from the KGB and later a senior Russian official. 'The first market reforms were mapped out at these institutions.'[52]

Once Andropov had taken over as leader, progressive factions in the KGB, led by the foreign-intelligence directorate and the economic-crime directorate, began to experiment with the creation of a new class of entrepreneurs who would operate outside the confines of the Soviet planned economy. They began with the black marketeers, the *tsekhoviki*. 'The real *perestroika* started under Andropov,' said Christian Michel, a financial manager who for more than a decade handled funds for the Soviet and then the Russian regimes. 'The message was given out to turn a blind eye to the black market. He knew the country was otherwise headed for mass starvation.'[53] 'There was a conscious creation of a black market,' agreed Anton Surikov, a former senior Russian military-intelligence operative. 'It was impossible to work in the black market without KGB connections and without protection from the KGB. Without them, no shadow business was possible.'[54]

What had begun as corruption within the system became a KGB-cultivated petri dish for the future market economy, and a stopgap measure to fill the shortages of the command economy. The black marketeers were mostly from the Soviet Union's ethnic minorities. Often they had very little choice, their careers having been blocked due to the prejudices of the Party elite. 'The only people who went into it were the people who had no prospects in the normal Soviet system, the ones who had hit a glass ceiling and could go no further,' said Michel. 'These were the ethnic minorities: the Georgians, the Chechens, the Jews.'

The black-market experiments also marked the beginning of a sudden acceleration in the transfer of the Soviet Union's vast wealth through KGB-associated friendly firms. This was the beginning of the looting of the Soviet state. It was also the beginning of what became a mutually beneficial alliance between the KGB and organised crime that stretched through Boris Birshtein's Seabeco in Switzerland, an outfit named Nordex in Vienna, and to New York through a metals trader named Mikhail Cherney and his Brooklyn-based associate Sam Kislin. Birshtein and the owner of Nordex, Grigory Luchansky, were Soviet émigrés recruited by the KGB to transfer state and Party wealth on the eve of the Soviet collapse, the Swiss intelligence service later said.[55] Later, Birshtein and Kislin were to become part of a network funnelling money from the former

Soviet Union into America, including – indirectly - into the business empire of Donald Trump.

*

While Putin was in Dresden, the KGB progressives in Moscow were beginning the second stage of their market experiment. They began to cultivate and create their own entrepreneurs from the ranks of the Communist youth league, the Komsomol.

Their eyes soon fell on Mikhail Khodorkovsky, an intensely driven young Muscovite in his early twenties who'd risen to become a deputy chief of his local Komsomol. Khodorkovsky was escaping from a childhood spent in a communal apartment in the north of Moscow where he learned from an early age the dangers of falling through the cracks of Soviet society. The other family who shared his parents' two-room apartment were a clear demonstration to him of many of the things that could go wrong in life: the father was a half-crazed Bolshevik who would wander through the flat without his trousers, scaring Khodorkovsky's mother; the son was a drunk,[56] and the daughter a member of 'the world's oldest profession', according to one of Khodorkovsky's former partners. 'The whole atmosphere there firmly propelled him to follow Lenin's principle of "Learn, learn and learn again". He understood that if you did not try hard and work hard in life you weren't going to get anywhere.'[57] By the time Khodorkovsky was a teenager his family had moved out of the shared flat, but its atmosphere left a lasting imprint. His parents were engineers, and Khodorkovsky began work at the age of fourteen, earning extra cash by sweeping the yard after school.[58] When we met many years later, after he had experienced a meteoric rise and an equally dizzying fall, he told me his ambition in life back then was to become the director of a Soviet factory, but that he feared his father's Jewish ethnicity would hold him back.[59]

In those days Khodorkovsky looked like a thick-necked street hustler, dressed in jeans and a denim jacket, with thick glasses and a dark moustache. But his intense focus helped propel him to the top of the local Komsomol, where he started out organising discos for the students at the Mendeleyev Institute for Chemical Science. He demonstrated such entrepreneurial flair that he was soon invited by the top of the Moscow city Komsomol to run an ambitious new initiative called 'scientific youth centres', known as NTTMs, which were to act as intermediaries for Moscow's top scientific research institutes, finding ways to turn research into cash and providing computer programming. They were also to be given access to a potentially vast source of funds, known as *beznalichiye*. In the Soviet Union's skewed Alice-in-Wonderland planned economy, profits meant nothing, and everything – from the cost of materials to the price of the finished product – was determined by state planners. All the state enterprises had to do was rigorously follow the annual plan for production handed down by the state. As a result, the plants weren't meant to hold any more cash in their accounts than what they needed to pay wages. What they held instead were accounting units called *beznalichiye*, or non-cash. Real cash was in such short supply as a result that one real rouble could be worth ten times as much as a *beznalichiye* rouble.[60]

Soviet law forbade any enterprise from exchanging the non-cash units for real cash. But under Gorbachev's reforms, the NTTMs were to be given permission to swap the *beznalichiye* for real cash simply by moving the funds from one account to another. This unlocked huge amounts of capital, and generated enormous profits. By then Khodorkovsky had teamed up with a cybernetics graduate, Leonid Nevzlin, a smooth-talking political animal with intense green eyes and a debonair air, and Vladimir Dubov, an employee of Moscow's Institute of High Temperatures. They were given a helping hand from the top. Dubov's place of employment was one of the Soviet Union's most secretive research institutes, a gigantic scientific complex deeply involved in research for laser weapons and the Star Wars race. Its head, Alexander Sheindlin, granted the team access to 170,000 roubles, a vast sum in those days. He didn't even ask what they would do with the money.[61]

Khodorkovsky and his partners moved into the vanguard of a new movement created by Gorbachev's *perestroika* reforms, forming one of the country's first 'cooperatives', essentially the Soviet Union's first privately-owned businesses. Groundbreaking laws passed in 1987 allowed private businesses to be set up in the parts of the economy where shortages were most acutely felt – consumer goods, shoe repairs and laundry services. A year later the laws were extended to allow entrepreneurs into the Soviet Union's most lucrative business, the trade of raw materials. Khodorkovsky and his team put the *beznalichiye* from the Institute of High Temperatures to extremely profitable use, exchanging it for hard currency earned by state timber exporters, and then using the money to import computers. Their actions, however, were still partly directed from on high. The Soviet economy was in dire need of Western technology, its computer systems were lagging far behind. But the Western embargo on high-tech goods made the import of computers a difficult process. Khodorkovsky and his partners needed to use the secret trading channels set up by the KGB.[62]

'The new generation of businessmen did not appear from nowhere,' said Thomas Graham, a former senior director for Russia on the US National Security Council. 'They had people who were helping them. There were certain elements in the Soviet government and in the first directorate of the KGB who had a sense of how the Western world worked and understood the need to change.'[63]

'Gorbachev was pushing it. It was official policy,' said Christian Michel, who by 1989 had become a money manager for Khodorkovsky's new wealth. 'There were two directorates of the KGB that were specifically interested in this. One was the directorate for the black market and economic crimes. And the second was the foreign-intelligence department, because they understood better than the rest of the Politburo what was happening, and because they had access to a lot of money. They wanted a better return on what they had, so they gave it to people like Khodorkovsky and said, "Go and play."'[64]

When we met, Khodorkovsky insisted that he was unaware he was part of any KGB experiment. He claimed that he was too young, too obsessed by his bid to succeed to notice that he may have been part of a broader plan. But for years, he said, his activities seemed to him only a job, and it was only in 1993 that he realised the business he ran could be considered his own. All the while, he'd received instructions: 'They asked, "Could you supply computers here, could you supply computers there? Could you do this, could you do that?" They had the right to issue orders. But always they asked.'[65] (He would not, however, say who these masters were.)

Hundreds of young businessmen began to set up cooperatives. Most of them sought to import computers or trade in consumer goods. But the most successful of them, the ones who entered the raw-materials trade or went into banking, were the ones with the most powerful connections. One such black marketeer from the Komsomol was Mikhail Fridman, an exceptionally bright and ambitious twenty-something with a round face and a pugnacious air who'd essentially been barred from attending Moscow's best universities due to unofficial anti-Semitic quotas. He'd studied instead at the Moscow Steel and Alloy Institute. In addition to focusing on his studies he hawked theatre tickets to barter goods.[66] With friends he created another of the first cooperatives, Alfa Foto, which first washed windows, then imported computers, and then became one of the very few operators allowed to expand into the commodities trade. The outfit was renamed Alfa-Eko, and sank roots deep into Switzerland as one of the very first Soviet–Swiss joint ventures. 'It was all under Soviet control,' said a former government official who knew Fridman's operations well.[67]

*

The KGB sought to keep tight control over commodity exports, but after the 1988 law was passed allowing cooperatives to participate in trade, its task became ever more difficult. The directors of state enterprises joined the goldrush, creating their own cooperatives to export the huge stores of raw materials – aluminium, steel, copper and fertilisers – held by the plants they ran. They were taking over industrial cash flows, privatising their companies from the inside out before anyone had ever mentioned the word privatisation. Though the KGB attempted to maintain its grip over the most strategic commodities – oil in particular – parts of the raw-materials trade were rapidly becoming a free-for-all. Gorbachev's reforms had let the genie out of the bottle. The Soviet state was being looted, and most importantly, the power the Communist Party held over the economy – and the country itself – was being eroded fast.

A little-noticed line in the law on cooperatives allowed for the creation of financial or credit businesses – in other words, the creation of banks. Khodorkovsky was among the first to pay attention. He'd gone to a local branch of the Soviet state housing bank, Zhilsotsbank, to ask for a loan for his cooperative, and was told he could be granted one, but only if he created a bank first. Once again, he received a friendly helping hand from on high. Zhilsotsbank agreed to become one of the founders of his bank, eventually registered as Menatep Bank, and the head of the Institute of High Temperatures joined its board. Khodorkovsky contributed capital from the NTTM profits, and soon began making himself loans to fund his computer-import business. Then he found a loophole that allowed him into an even more lucrative trade: the exchange of hard currency. It was now that his business really took off. He could change roubles for dollars at the official fixed state price of sixty-five kopecks to the dollar, and then sell computers at a price worth forty roubles to the dollar.[68] The profits were enormous. The Soviet central bank granted Menatep one of the first licences to trade hard currency, and soon the bank was transferring huge amounts of money abroad.

The floodgates had opened for the transfer of hundreds of millions of dollars into accounts abroad through hard-currency trading. Most of it had happened just as Gorbachev's deputy general secretary Vladimir Ivashko was signing off on the plan for the 'invisible economy' for the Party wealth, and the KGB's Leonid Veselovsky was proposing creating the system of trusted custodians, or *doverenniye litsa*. For years, Moscow legend held that Khodorkovsky's Menatep Bank was one of the main conduits for the transfer of Communist Party wealth abroad. Khodorkovsky has always denied this, but at least one senior Moscow financier and two former senior Russian foreign-intelligence operatives say that Menatep was a key front for the transfer of the Party's cash. 'A lot of money was lost from the Central Committee. I know for sure Khodorkovsky was one of the actors in this,' said the financier.

*

Gorbachev first indicated that he was terrified at the process his economic reforms had unleashed in early 1989. He and his government were proposing to limit how much the owners of the new cooperatives could earn. The plan was that they – and their workers – could pay themselves only a hundred roubles a day, while the rest of the money they made would have to be kept in a special account at a state bank. Gorbachev was clearly trying to stem the looting of the Soviet state: already it was becoming clear that the coffers were running dry. But the proposal met with an immediate backlash. One of the cooperative owners, Artyom Tarasov, the Soviet Union's first publicly declared rouble millionaire, publicly campaigned against it and won the support of half the Politburo, including Alexander Yakovlev and the former KGB chief Viktor Chebrikov.[69] Gorbachev had always only wanted gradual reform, that would keep the economy within the confines of the socialist state. But now, in the rush for riches, the unity of the Party leadership itself was cracking, with a deepening rift between progressives and old-guard conservatives. One by one, the progressives were giving their support to Boris Yeltsin, the upstart former member of the Politburo who was increasingly challenging Gorbachev's rule – and members of the KGB secretly joined them. Yeltsin had gained a platform as a leader in his own right under Gorbachev's own political reforms, first when he was elected chairman of Russia's Supreme Soviet in 1990, and then when he was elected president of the Russian Federation, in the first such elections in June 1991.

The handpicked new young wolves of Russia's economic transition were rallying behind Yeltsin, while reform-minded political giants such as Alexander Yakovlev moved to his side too. Khodorkovsky and his team financed part of Yeltsin's presidential election bid, helping to run part of his media campaign and forging ties deep within his administration.[70]

*

By the time the five black Volga sedans drove up to the wrought-iron gates of Gorbachev's summer residence in Foros on the Black Sea coast that fateful evening of August 18 1991, the Communist Party of the Soviet Union was already essentially finished.

Parts of the KGB never seemed to support the hard-line coup. The plotters had declared that the KGB chief Vladimir Kryuchkov was with them, but Kryuchkov stepped back from taking decisive action to quash protests against the coup. The KGB didn't arrest Yeltsin when he landed back in Moscow from Kazakhstan the morning after the plotters took control; nor did the elite KGB special unit, the Alfa troops, detain him as they lurked in the bushes outside his Moscow dacha while he mulled over his next steps. Instead, Yeltsin was able to make his way unhindered to the White House, the seat of the Russian parliament's power, where he led a defiant protest against the coup as tens of thousands flocked to support him. When the plotters finally gave the order to storm Yeltsin's stronghold on the afternoon of the third day of the coup, the Alfa troops declined to fire on the White House. Kryuchkov withdrew the order when three men were killed in the early hours of the morning, after a group of protesters had barricaded a nearby street from incoming tanks. No one wanted to spill any more blood.

Progressives in the Party and the KGB had clearly begun to back the democratic leaders, because they didn't want the flood of cash to stop.[71] 'Part of the KGB supported Yeltsin,' said Andrei Illarionov, an economic adviser to Putin in the first years of his presidency. 'They saw Yeltsin as an alternative who would carry out market reform.'[72]

'The businesses and the people who stood at the roots of *perestroika* decided they needed more,' said Rair Simonyan, the young economist with ties to military intelligence who'd led reform efforts at the Institute for World Economy. 'It became a political process because it became clear to them that otherwise all their efforts would go into a dead end. Gorbachev was just too indecisive.'[73]

For a long time, hard-liners in the KGB barked about how the collapse of the Soviet system was engineered by agents of the United States. Many were convinced the US had acted to leverage weaknesses within the system and help stoke protests for independence across the Warsaw Pact – and there was some truth to that. It was whispered darkly that Alexander Yakovlev, the godfather of Gorbachev's *perestroika* reforms, was planted as an agent of the CIA at the top of the Politburo to demolish the Soviet empire, and that Boris Yeltsin was a US stooge. But the truth is that the revolution that ended seven decades of Communist rule was largely bloodless because many within the system did not want the Party or socialism to survive. 'The very upper echelon of the Soviet *nomenklatura* was wiped away, and part of the second and third tier took over the country,' said the US National Security Council's Thomas Graham. 'These people had realised that if you stripped away ideology they could live even better. The country fell apart because these people from the second and third echelon had no interest in it surviving. They had figured out a way of surviving better in the new system.'[74]

Ultimately, when it came, the collapse had been an inside job. The men at the top of the KGB's foreign intelligence had decided 'to blow up their own home', according to one former senior operative.[75]

And when the Russian prosecutors came calling in the search for the Communist Party's missing wealth, it was the sentinels of the foreign-intelligence directorate who did everything they could to block them. Leading the cover-up was Yevgeny Primakov, the former head of the Institute for World Economy, which had quietly been a leading force behind the reform drive, who soon after the coup would be anointed by Yeltsin as Russia's new foreign-intelligence chief.[76] 'Primakov decisively sabotaged the only serious attempt to undo the massive theft that depleted Russia's treasury,' said Richard Palmer, a CIA station chief for the former Soviet Union in the early nineties.[77]

All the while, Primakov and his close associate, the onetime military-intelligence chief at the Institute for the USA and Canada, Mikhail Milshtein, had been working on plans to end their country's standoff with the West. But under the cover of Soviet emigration they'd also been sending a new group of agents into the West to guard and generate part of the hidden cash networks of Russia's foreign intelligence.[78] Money was being funnelled out and reserved for a later, more covert game. A senior Russian foreign-intelligence operative, Sergei Tretyakov, later claimed that tens of billions of dollars had been transferred to maintain the foreign-intelligence networks of the KGB.[79] Hundreds of foreign shell companies and Soviet joint ventures had been created in the year leading up to the coup, some founded by the Soviet émigrés, others by the handpicked emissaries from the Komsomol.[80]

The Soviet empire might have been lost, but the foreign-intelligence progressives knew that the battle against the West was unsustainable under the command economy anyway. For them, the end of the Communist empire did not mean an end to hostilities, but an opportunity to eventually continue them under new auspices.

New Day

When Boris Yeltsin, blinking in the sunlight, strode out of the Russian White House in the middle of the hard-line coup on the afternoon of August 19 1991, the world believed it had gained an icon for a new age. Defying the military hardware surrounding the White House, Yeltsin clambered stiffly on top of one of the tanks, shaking the hands of the soldiers manning its guns as he went.

In the euphoric days that followed, the symbol of the KGB's overpowering might, a statue of the founding father of the Soviet secret police, Felix Dzerzhinsky, was winched away from its plinth in front of the KGB headquarters on Moscow's Lubyanka Square. Western bankers and government officials were soon hurrying to Russia to advise Yeltsin's new government on the creation of a market economy. The new cabinet was partly staffed with bright young economists, including Yegor Gaidar and Pyotr Aven. Russia was to integrate into Western markets, and a new era of cooperation was hailed.

Although in October 1991 Yeltsin signed an order abolishing the KGB and breaking it up into four different domestic services, his appointment of Vadim Bakatin to head the organisation in the final months before its break-up was an early sign that change was going to be cosmetic. Bakatin was an inexperienced outsider who'd served briefly as interior minister in the final years of the Soviet regime, and his new KGB comrades ran rings around him. He himself admitted to the Moscow journalist Yevgenia Albats that he had little control over his employees, and that he knew they were manipulating him and withholding information from him: 'I am absolutely convinced that whatever the *komitetchiki* don't want me to know, I won't know,' he told her.[81] And once the KGB had officially been broken up, under Primakov's stewardship the powerful foreign-intelligence service, now renamed as the SVR, remained intact. Even though tens of thousands of apparently demoralised officers resigned from the service to join the rush into business, part of the system merely went underground. Like Putin with Sobchak, 'they stayed in the shadows', said one former intermediary for the KGB, speaking on condition of anonymity.[82] 'They didn't really get rid of anything. They changed the façade and they changed the name. But nothing else really changed.' While officially the SVR's budget was shredded, unofficial sources of funding were soon found.

Even though the Russian government was struggling in the chaos of the Soviet collapse to pay pensions and the wages of teachers, doctors and other state workers, the new prime minister, Yegor Gaidar, made sure to find funds to maintain strategic outposts for foreign intelligence. One such payment was $200 million in 1992 to Fidel Castro's regime in Cuba for Russia's foreign-intelligence service to continue to use its Lourdes listening station for eavesdropping on the US. The payment was made through a convoluted barter scheme, swapping oil products for sugar imports – exactly like the smuggling schemes deployed by the KGB through friendly firms.[83] The $200 million transfer was made at the same time as Russia's official state budget for 1992 was $148 million. Later that year, Gaidar diverted an entire $1 billion loan from the International Monetary Fund, aimed at stabilising the Russian economy, to bail out one of the most important financial outposts of Russia's foreign-intelligence network, Eurobank, the Soviet state bank in Paris.[84]

For the first half of the nineties, the KGB remained a potent force behind the scenes. Its operatives were still everywhere, employed as advisers for trade or government relations or as security chiefs. Until 1995, most of the oil sector remained in state hands, its exports watched over by the foreign operatives of the KGB. 'You found this virtually everywhere, in all the companies, in all the government agencies,' said Christian Michel. 'Through their networks, they were a lot more than individuals. These men from the KGB controlled networks, and without them nothing would move.'[85]

At first, many of the senior KGB operatives involved in forging Russia's market transition went to work for the young tycoons they'd helped create through Gorbachev's *perestroika* reforms.[86] They were mostly there simply to take their cut, but in some cases they had control. 'They said, "You'll make money and kick it back to us,"' said Yury Shvets, the former foreign-intelligence operative.[87]

But as the young tycoons gained wealth and power under the market reforms launched by Yeltsin's government, gradually they began to eclipse their former sponsors in the KGB. A new Russia seemed to be emerging, in which the former Komsomol members became brash symbols of the new capitalist age. Khodorkovsky and his team from Menatep even issued a manifesto, issuing 50,000 copies of a screed handed out on the streets that proclaimed the virtues of getting rich: 'Our compass is profit. Our idol is his financial majesty capital.'[88] Their goal was 'to become billionaires', and they wanted to demonstrate that there was nothing wrong with getting wealthy after decades in which making a profit was considered a crime. But they benefited from an inside track to riches from the start.

The market reforms of Gaidar's new government aimed to bring the market to Russia as fast as possible – regardless of the consequences. They were encouraged by a team of American economists from Harvard led by Jeffrey Sachs, who hoped to emulate the success of so-called 'shock therapy' reforms in Poland, where two years before a rapid transition to the market seemed to have been successfully launched.[89] But in Russia, the legacy of the Soviet state weighed far more heavily. Gaidar's market reformers were in a minority, and the corrupted system in which they launched the reforms only further warped the economy. Only those, like Khodorkovsky, who'd set up banks in the final years of the Soviet Union were in a position to benefit. For a while, however, the American economists seemed to go along with that. They believed they were helping create a new class of entrepreneurs, and seemed ready to do anything that would help break the hold of the Soviet old guard.[90]

When the Yeltsin government freed prices overnight on January 1 1992, lifting decades of Soviet controls, the young tycoons made money, while the population and the government struggled to survive. The price-freeing unleashed a devastating bout of hyper-inflation, as suppliers and producers struggled to overcome the shortages long built into the Soviet economy. Unlike in Poland, where inflation had soon settled after an initial surge, Gaidar was contending with a wily old-guard central bank chief, Viktor Gerashchenko, who'd once worked at the pinnacle of the Soviet foreign-bank network funding the operations of the KGB, and who now continued to print money no matter what. Prices of consumer goods soared by 400 per cent, sometimes many times more. While the hyperinflation ravaged the government's spending power, and wiped out what little savings the population had, Khodorkovsky and other young tycoons were able to hedge against devaluation. They could access hard currency through their banks, and were able to swiftly transfer any rouble income into dollars.

The tycoons also benefited from the next planned market reform of the Gaidar government, the privatisation of state enterprises. The only people with funds to participate in the so-called mass privatisations were the narrow elite who had already taken over much of the enterprises' cash flows under Gorbachev's *perestroika* reforms: the young businessmen from the Komsomol, the black marketeers, the organised-crime groups, the KGB and the state directors.

Privatisation at a time of hyperinflation could only further concentrate the country's wealth in the hands of this small group, said Grigory Yavlinsky, one of Russia's most principled economists, who'd argued strongly for more gradual reforms. 'How is it possible to have privatisation when money has been wiped out as an insti-tution? There can only be a criminal privatisation. The next step was criminal privatisation.'[91]

'When Gaidar tried to conduct the first privatisations, everything had already been seized,' said Gleb Pavlovsky, a former Kremlin adviser.[92] 'Gaidar's biggest mistake was that when he began his reforms he considered that what was before him was still the Soviet economy of 1987. But already the Soviet economy did not exist.' The Gaidar government had sought to keep the privatisation process open to all, by giving plant workers vouchers to take part in the sell-offs. But the workers were often forced to exchange their vouchers for cash, or even for bread, just to survive the hyperinflation.

The new tycoons from the Komsomol benefited most of all when the Yeltsin government granted their banks access to deep stores of cash, without their having to lift a finger. Instead of having its own treasury, the government authorised the tycoons' banks to hold strategic funds from the Russian budget on deposit. It was a get-rich-quick scheme for the chosen favourites of the Yeltsin regime. They could direct hundreds of millions of dollars in government funds into high-yielding investments, sometimes even into the privatisation auctions, while the government was left waiting for the disbursal of its funds. Vital programmes such as defence spending or aid for citizens half-abandoned in the crumbling industrial wastelands of Russia's far north were delayed or simply unpaid, while the government was fobbed off with promissory notes. The government was being bled dry, while the new wolves of the Russian economy concocted elaborate schemes to avoid paying taxes or customs duties.

Faster and more adept in the ways of the market than their one-time masters in the KGB, the young tycoons from the Komsomol were becoming a sort of Frankenstein's monster, fast outrunning the men who had made them. The real turning point, when control of the economy appeared to transfer irrevocably into the hands of the new tycoons, came towards the middle of 1995. Russia was entering the final year before the first post-Soviet presidential elections, and the government's coffers were empty. Wages and pensions were months in arrears, and Yeltsin's approval ratings were terrifyingly low, at 6 per cent. The tycoons feared a return to Communism, that would strip them of their fortunes and could even land them in jail. Even more importantly, they'd long been eyeing the crown jewels of Soviet industry, the state's biggest industrial giants. What they'd acquired so far was small-scale compared to the vast resources still under the control of the state.

Vladimir Potanin, the smooth-talking son of a senior Soviet diplomat, who'd become one of the country's major new bankers, concocted what seemed an ingenious scheme. He proposed that the young bankers offer to help out the cash-strapped Yeltsin government with a series of loans. As collateral, the tycoons would take stakes in a select handful of the nation's biggest enterprises. The tycoons would manage the enterprises, and could sell off their stakes if the government was unable to pay the loans back. When the idea was first floated, outside observers scoffed that it would never gain any traction. The potential for corruption, they said, was too great.[93] It would be too easy for the bankers simply to sell the stakes to themselves.

But the young tycoons had powerful friends in the Yeltsin government. Prime among them was Anatoly Chubais, the red-haired deputy prime minister and close Gaidar ally who'd been the architect of the privatisation programme so far. With strong support from the team of US economists, Chubais had been intent on breaking the hold of the state over the economy at any cost. Too much of industry was still in the hands of the state, of 'red' Soviet-era directors and the KGB, while the threat of a return to Communism seemed all too real. If the government signed off on the bankers' proposal, it would create a major new class of property owners overnight, as well as filling empty government coffers with a proposed $1.8 billion in loans. The tycoons would then back Yeltsin to the hilt against the Communists to preserve their new wealth. Chubais believed it would signal a final victory for liberal reformers over the forces of the old guard.

But the scheme would become one of the original sins of Russia's market transition. It tainted everything, and opened the way for constant threats over the legality of the property the young tycoons acquired at that time. It became known as the loans-for-shares privatisations, an insider deal that transferred the nation's resource wealth into the young bankers' hands at a knockdown price. Far more financially nimble, and able to access much bigger pools of ready cash through the rapid growth of their banks and the government deposits they held, the young tycoons outmanoeuvred their former KGB masters. The combined forces of the KGB and the former Soviet directors managed to win only two of the auctions for stakes in oil companies: 5 per cent of an oil firm named Lukoil, and 40 per cent of Surgutneftegaz, whose managers went to great lengths to keep the young bankers away. The nearest airport to the Siberian oil town of Surgut, where the sale was being held, was shut down, and armed guards manned roadblocks across the main routes in.[94]

Most of the rest of Soviet industry passed into the hands of the young bankers, in auctions that were widely seen as rigged. Potanin won the prize he'd long coveted – a controlling stake in the world's biggest producer of nickel and platinum, Norilsk Nickel, a sprawling plant high above the Arctic Circle whose profits in 1995 stood at $1.2 billion. He'd done so by extending a loan of just $170 million to the government – and when, as expected, the still cash-strapped government defaulted on the loan after Yeltsin secured his election victory, the way was clear for Potanin to win the stake in an auction for little more than the loan price. Khodorkovsky had long been targeting Yukos, an oil producer in west Siberia which controlled some of Russia's largest reserves. He took control of it after lending the government $159 million for a 45 per cent stake, and then paying a further $150 million in investment for an additional 33 per cent. Another oil giant, Sibneft, was won for $100 million through the efforts of Boris Berezovsky, who already controlled sales at Russia's biggest carmaker and chaired a bank of his own. Most of these bankers were still barely in their thirties, but with the help of sympathetic government officials running the auction process, they were able to secure the foundations of fortunes that within a few years would be worth billions, and then tens of billions, of dollars. Berezovsky was soon crowing that a group of seven bankers controlled 50 per cent of the nation's economy.[95]

The loans-for-shares auctions marked a huge shift in the control of the economy. It was the moment the tycoons were transformed from mere bankers to owners of the biggest assets in the country, with access to some of the most lucrative cash flows. 'This is when they started to reinvent themselves,' said Christian Michel. 'They acquired real assets. They became much more than banks.'[96]

By the end of the nineties, the young tycoons were starting to turn around the Soviet legacy of falling production, deep debts and neglect. But for the members of the security services that had helped create these new billionaires, the loans-for-shares auctions was a moment they would never forgive or forget, and would be the kernel for the KGB's later revanche. Before then, in the shadows, the KGB men had still been able to control much of the cash flow from the nation's oil wealth. But now they'd been outwitted and outpaced, and the financial reins had largely been taken out of their hands. 'This was the turning point when [the young tycoons] took control,' said Rair Simonyan, the ally of Yevgeny Primakov who'd worked on the early *perestroika* reforms. 'It changed the entire paradigm.'[97]

But in those days, the tycoons of Russia's new order were giddy at their new wealth. They were fast becoming oligarchs who held considerable sway over the weakened Yeltsin government. The remaining members of the old-guard security services who had served in government had been ousted amid scandal in the run-up to the presidential elections, and Western-leaning reformers like Chubais had been left to take the lead. Fresh from his successful engineering of the loans-for-shares sell-offs, Potanin took a post as Yeltsin's deputy prime minister, while Berezovsky was appointed secretary of the Security Council. Chubais became Yeltsin's chief of staff. It was the apotheosis of their era. The country, it seemed, was theirs. The forces of the KGB appeared to be receding into the background.

But, said the former senior foreign-intelligence operative Yury Shvets, the oligarchs 'all forgot to whom they owed a debt'.[98] In the rush to shore up their positions, in the battle to accumulate more wealth, Khodorkovsky and the others didn't notice that nearby, in

St Petersburg, there was a chill in the air. Things were being run differently there. Isolated from the goldrush of Moscow's economic boom, the forces of the KGB were exerting far greater control, in a city where the economy was tougher and darker, in the violent scrabble for cash.

3

'The Tip of an Iceberg'

ST PETERSBURG – On the south-western edge of St Petersburg, where the Gulf of Finland starts to join the Baltic Sea, a tangle of cranes and containers juts out across the elegant façades of the pre-Revolutionary palaces across the bay. On one small island, twisted heaps of scrap metal and piles of timber lie in wait for tankers, while across a channel the red-brick buildings that were once the customs house and the warehouses for the city's finest pre-Revolutionary merchants somehow still stand, half-abandoned among the heavy machinery. Far out on the western edge, a concrete jetty leads to the place sometimes called the 'Golden Gates', a concrete sprawl of oil-storage facilities that mark St Petersburg's most strategic outpost, the oil terminal that was the battleground for some of the 1990s' most vicious bandit wars.

The archipelago of islands is home to St Petersburg's sea port, and through its channels Russia's tumultuous history has always run deep. When Peter the Great founded St Petersburg in the early eighteenth century, he did so in the hope that it would become Russia's greatest sea port, a vital link between the vast country's Eurasian land mass and the markets of the West. Thousands of serfs toiled and died to realise his vision of stately Baroque mansions and elegant canals rising out of the freezing and muddy marshes. St Petersburg was always intended as Russia's 'window on the West', a port city that would drag the country kicking and screaming out of its medieval and Asiatic past, no matter what the cost.

Ships carrying cargoes of cloth, tea, silk and spices began to arrive in ever greater numbers from the colonial empires of the West, while

Russia's imperial riches of timber, furs, hemp and potash steamed out. St Petersburg's merchants and noblemen thrived, but as the city's population exploded, its workers were among the world's most downtrodden. Dockers hauled cargoes on and off the ships on their backs, unprotected from the ice and bitter winds that gripped the port for half of the year. When Vladimir Lenin gathered the city's workers to overthrow the rule of the provisional government in 1917, the dockers were foremost among them. When the city, by then named Leningrad, came under blockade by the Nazis during the Second World War, the sea port was on the front line of the heart-rending struggles to survive starvation and bombs.

And when Russia juddered out of its third revolution of the twentieth century, the St Petersburg sea port again had a defining role to play. It became the ground zero for an alliance between the KGB and organised crime that was to expand its influence across Russia, and later into Western markets and institutions too. It was the starting point for the business alliances of the city's deputy mayor, Vladimir Putin, who worked closely with the organised-crime leader who ran it, and the oil trader who gained a monopoly on exports through its oil terminal. The relationships forged then, through an elaborate web of barter and export deals, became a model for how Putin's Russia would be run.

In the early nineties, the port was one of the darkest places in a city riven by gangland shootings and violent battles for cash. 'The story of the sea port is a very criminal and dirty story,' said one former senior official in the St Petersburg city council.[1] 'The port was totally criminalised. There was a lot of shooting,' according to a former member of the biggest local crime gang, the Tambov group.[2]

The group who eventually took it over were part of a nexus of organised-crime and KGB men that came to rule the roost in St Petersburg in the nineties, and Vladimir Putin was at the centre of it. If in Moscow the forces of the KGB had stayed largely in the shadows, in St Petersburg they were much more visible. St Petersburg's economy was far smaller than Moscow's, the battle for cash much more vicious, and the mayor's office had tentacles extending into most businesses. The main reason for the potency of the KGB's reach in St Petersburg was that mayor Anatoly Sobchak had little interest in the day-to-day running of the city. He left it to Putin, who ran the foreign-relations committee, which oversaw all trade and much of the rest of the city's business, and to his other deputy, Vladimir Yakovlev, who was in charge of the city's economic affairs.

Sobchak and his deputies moved the mayor's office from the Marinsky Palace, where St Petersburg's democrat-run city council had its seat, to the warren-like offices of the Smolny Institute, from which the Communist Party had run the city since the days of Lenin's takeover. The legacy they inherited was desperate. The city's coffers were empty. There was no cash to pay for imports, and the shop shelves were fast emptying. Domestic food production was in a parlous state. Grain was left to rot at the roadside by inefficient state collective farms, while a series of bad harvests made things even worse. They not only had to deal with the food crisis, but also with an explosion of crime. In the chaos of the Soviet collapse, the institutions of power appeared to be melting away. Organised-crime groups moved in to fill the vacuum, running protection rackets extorting local businesses and taking over trade.

From his office behind the stately columns and fading façade of the Smolny Institute, Sobchak seemed incapable of dealing with the deteriorating situation. He was a convincing and powerful orator who prided himself on his appearance, but his relations with what remained of the city's law enforcement were fraught. 'Sobchak was a moron,' said one former senior KGB officer who worked for a time with Putin in St Petersburg. 'He wanted to wear the sharpest suits, and he could give speeches for hours on end. He loved all the attributes of power, and his wife wanted to live like an aristocrat. He liked to travel in limousines, but someone needed to work. Who was going to clean the shit from the streets and deal with the bandits?'

Few in law enforcement would even take Sobchak's calls. 'The former chairman of the St Petersburg KGB would not even go into a room with him,' the former KGB officer said. 'If you tried to explain to him how security worked, it would be the same as explaining nuclear physics. But with Putin, you could explain. You could say, "Volodya, there is this situation and there is this one." And when he had to phone up the police to sort out situations, for him they would not put down the phone.'

So Sobchak came to rely on Putin, who had maintained a network of connections with the top of the city's KGB: his former mentor in the Leningrad KGB's feared dissident-fighting Fifth Directorate, Viktor Cherkesov, was the new head of St Petersburg's FSB, the KGB's successor agency. Putin became the point man for dealing with law enforcement. He 'was someone who could phone someone and say, "We have to do something, otherwise there's going to be a nightmare,"' the former KGB officer said. 'He could agree with a general who before had handled special forces, who could tell him how to handle something and maybe provide back-up. They were people with connections. The system had collapsed, but part of it had remained.'[3]

What emerged out of the chaos and collapse – and Sobchak's ineffectiveness – was an alliance between Putin, his KGB allies and organised crime that sought to run much of the city's economy for their own benefit. Instead of seeking to impose order for the good of the city's population, the only order they imposed was mostly for themselves. Above all, the collapse meant opportunity for their own enrichment – and, in particular for Putin and his allies in the KGB, for the creation of a strategic slush fund that was to preserve their networks and secure their position for years to come. The slush fund had its roots in the barter schemes of KGB-run friendly firms. Later they extended to the sea port, and then to the oil terminal itself. Running through it all was St Petersburg's Tambov organised-crime group. It was a business, according to one former local FSB officer, that consisted of 'murder and raiding': 'The arms of the Tambov group were covered in blood.'[4]

*

It was near the end of 1991 when Marina Salye first noticed something was wrong. The firebrand democrat, who at one point had rivalled Sobchak as St Petersburg's democratic leader, had been tasked by the head of the city council to find ways out of the food crisis. A doughty geologist in her mid-fifties with soft greying hair and shadows sunk deep under determined eyes, Salye was relentless. That autumn, she'd successfully pushed for the city to introduce a system of ration cards. It was the first time food had been rationed since the terrible days of starvation of the Leningrad blockade.[5] She'd now decided to push for a barter scheme that would allow the city to exchange raw materials for imports of food. It seemed the only way out of the impasse. A system had already been set up on a federal level to deal with the crisis that was facing the entire country. The Moscow government had begun issuing quotas that allowed the export of set quantities of natural resources held by state-owned enterprises, such as oil products, metals and timber, in exchange for food. But as Salye began to push the mayor's office to apply for the export quotas for St Petersburg, she got wind of rumours that Putin's foreign-relations committee had already been granted them. 'What quotas? Where are the quotas? Officially no one knew anything,' she later told an interviewer.[6] When she tried to extract more information from the mayor's office, no one answered her letters. The scheme, she found out, had been under way since at least the beginning of December, and no one had been informed.[7] The biggest problem of all was that the expected food imports were nowhere to be found. As the city entered the new year, it had only one month's worth of food reserves left.[8]

Salye launched a parliamentary inquiry demanding information on the deals.[9] When Putin eventually bowed to demands and addressed the city council, pale-eyed and defiant, he turned up with just two pages of notes, and told the MPs that everything else was a commercial secret.[10] What he told parliament differed greatly from the documents Salye was eventually able to retrieve from the State Customs Committee and other officials as she ramped up her investigation.[11]

By the time she'd pieced everything together, it had become clear that Putin's committee had handed out more than $95 million in export licences to an obscure web of front companies, while virtually none of the food imports expected in return had arrived.[12] A further $900 million worth of export quotas had been granted by the federal government, including one for $717 million worth of aluminium.[13] It was impossible to tell whether Putin had gone ahead and handed out the additional $900 million in quotas to other firms which also disappeared with the proceeds, as Salye had been unable to access any further documentation. But she suspected that he had.[14]

As Salye and her deputies dug through the paperwork, the scandal seemed to grow. State customs officials and St Petersburg's representative from the foreign trade ministry had written to Putin complaining that he'd issued the export licences in violation of laws governing such barter deals.[15] An expert opinion commissioned by Salye's committee warned that the companies involved were so obscure they could disappear with the proceeds from the sales overnight.[16] Most of them were to receive mind-blowing commissions for their services: 25 to 50 per cent of the value of the deals, instead of the usual 3 or 4 per cent.[17] A handful of the contracts appeared to allow the companies to purchase raw materials for far less than the market price. One quota awarded by Putin allowed for an outfit created just two months before the scheme took off to acquire 13,997 kilograms of rare-earth metals for two thousand times less than the global market price, enabling it to reap vast profits when it sold it all on world markets.[18]

The scheme Salye had uncovered was almost identical to the practices deployed by KGB joint ventures in the dying days of the Soviet Union, which had led to a flood of raw materials being siphoned out of the country from state-owned enterprises at the low internal Soviet price, while the profits from the subsequent sales at much higher world prices remained in bank accounts abroad. In those days, any outfit that wanted to export raw materials had to receive a special licence to do so from the ministry of foreign trade, whose ranks were mostly manned by associates of the KGB. When the Russian government launched a series of barter schemes intended to staunch the looming humanitarian crisis following the Soviet collapse, the deals followed a similar route. But Putin had special permission to award his own quotas, licences and contracts for the city's so-called oil-for-food deals, bypassing the need to agree each one with the ministry.[19] He'd been granted this by Gaidar and the minister for foreign trade himself, Pyotr Aven, the same bespectacled economist who'd worked closely on reforms with Gaidar in the early eighties, and who stood aside from criticism of Putin when the deals came under scrutiny.

One of the contracts Putin handed out was to a Soviet-Finnish joint venture called Sfinks, which at the end of December 1991 was awarded a quota to trade diesel fuel, cement and fertiliser in exchange for 200,000 tonnes of livestock grain.[20] Another was a Soviet-German entity named Tamigo, given a licence to trade five hundred tonnes of copper in return for supplies of sugar and cooking oil.[21] Dzhikop, the outfit that was awarded the contract to acquire 13,997 kilograms of rare-earth metals for two thousand times below the market price,[22] was co-run by the brother of one of Putin's university classmates who shared Putin's love for martial arts.[23] Another recipient of diesel oil quotas was a firm called Interkommerts, run by Gennady Miroshnik, a convicted criminal who'd participated in a scheme that siphoned 20 million Deutschmarks from funds earmarked for the relocation of the Soviet Union's armed forces from East Germany.[24] Later, Putin's wife Lyudmilla told a friend that Interkommerts was linked to East Germans her husband met in Dresden.[25]

The barter deals 'were handed out to his friends,' said Alexander Belyayev, the then head of the St Petersburg city council who oversaw Salye's investigation.[26] 'They had to be given to people Putin trusted. There was no legal tender process then, so it was clear they would be given to people he knew personally, to people he could control. For the oil-product sales, this was mostly connected to Kirishi. They were near monopolists. This was Timchenko, Katkov, Malov.'[27]

The men Putin was apparently handing the deals to appeared to represent far more than a network of friends. One of them, Gennady Timchenko, was a spry man with a charming smile who was fluent in German and English, with a smattering of French. He and his partners, Andrei Katkov and Yevgeny Malov, had set up the Kirishineftekhimexport oil trader when Gorbachev first loosened trade in 1987, granting seventy organisations, including the Kirishi oil refinery near Leningrad, the right to trade outside the Soviet monopoly.[28] All Katkov and Malov had done at their previous posts in the Soviet foreign trade ministry was stamp and file papers for export deals, and they leapt at the chance to enter into their own business. Timchenko appeared to be a different matter. His official biography said he'd worked as a senior engineer at the foreign trade ministry. But according to three people familiar with the matter, he'd taken a very different route. He'd studied German together with Putin at the KGB's Red Banner Academy before Putin was sent to Dresden and Timchenko to Vienna and Zürich,[29] where, two former senior officers for the Russian foreign-intelligence service said, he had worked as an undercover agent in Soviet trade organisations.[30] It's possible, according to a third former officer speaking to Russian newspaper *Vedomosti*, that he was sent there to handle bank accounts funding the KGB's networks of illegals.[31] 'I don't rule out that Timchenko knew Putin then,' one of the former officers archly told me.[32] Timchenko has repeatedly denied any connection to the KGB, saying any such connection is untrue. A senior Russian banker with ties to the security services also indicated he had links to Putin during his Dresden days.[33]

While Timchenko has also previously denied that his Kirish-ineftekhimexport had ever been involved in the scandal-racked oil-for-food deals, adding later that all his firm's activities were 'transparent and legitimate', one of Timchenko's former partners told me his firm had participated, as did two other associates. They insisted that all the food they'd been tasked with importing had been delivered to St Petersburg.[34] But overall, the scheme ended disastrously: only a tiny fraction of the food due to be imported had ever turned up. Instead, Salye suspected, KGB networks were being preserved. Salye told a friend she felt her inquiry had uncovered 'the tip of an iceberg'.[35] What lay beneath, she believed, was a huge structure that had its origins in the foreign slush funds of the KGB, the networks of which the scheme was designed to maintain.

Salye, it turns out, was probably right.

*

'Salye was a fool! This all happened. But this is absolutely normal trading operations. How can you explain this to a menopausal woman like that!'[36] It was May 2013, more than twenty years since the scheme was set up, and Felipe Turover, a former senior officer for the foreign-intelligence directorate of the KGB, was telling for the first time the story of how he helped Putin set up the St Petersburg oil-for-food scheme.

We were sitting in the sun on the terrace of a café in Boadillo del Monte, a sleepy market town in the hills near Madrid. The scheme that had been publicly presented in the early nineties as a mechanism to bring in vitally needed imports of food, Turover claimed, actually had a different purpose. It was never really intended that the food would arrive. There were much bigger problems to deal with: 'All this bullshit about the report of Marina Salye. This was absolutely beside the point. The situation was one of total collapse. There was an absolute lack of federal finance for projects, and Moscow only drank and stole. In order for everything not to collapse, we had to do something. It was like a ship without a captain, and when you try to turn the wheel it falls off. This was what it was like. If we had not started work, then St Petersburg would have drowned in shit.'

Built like a bodybuilder, with a shaved head and dark glasses, Turover had a demonic laugh and a treasure trove of stories about the Soviet collapse. He was from the elite of the Soviet foreign-intelligence service. His father had taught languages at the KGB Red Banner Academy, and served as a translator to Leonid Brezhnev; Giulio Andreotti, the long-serving Italian prime minister, was among his friends. In Soviet times Turover had worked closely with Vladimir Osintsev, the legendary *komitetchik* who headed the so-called 'Party Technology' division of the Central Committee's International Department, running black operations and illegals deep into countries where the Communist Party was banned. In the chaos that followed the Soviet collapse, Turover had been charged with finding ways to pay debts owed to the 'friendly firms' at the heart of the clandestine financing schemes of the KGB and Party influence operations abroad – many of which also supplied crucial equipment, including for energy infrastructure, to the Soviet Union at a marked-up price.

The problem was that when the USSR collapsed, Russia had agreed to take on all the foreign debts of the former Soviet republics in exchange for their foreign property, and had then promptly pronounced itself bankrupt. An international moratorium had been announced on all Russia's foreign debts. Turover, who needed to bypass this in order to pay the friendly firms without anyone finding out, claimed that the barter schemes were in fact set up as a way to do so. Eventually he'd set up a channel for payments through a small Swiss bank in Lugano, documents show. 'We could not say we paid someone and did not pay Philip Morris,' he said. 'This was not a small matter. For some things we needed to pay right away. If we did not pay for equipment for nuclear power plants, then we would have a catastrophe. When the country stopped existing, everyone had stopped supplies.'

Turover had been sent to St Petersburg, he said, to help Putin set up his own scheme to pay off debts to some of the friendly firms. One of them, he claimed, was an Italian outfit called Casa Grande del Favore, which he said was one of a handful of engineering firms capable of the delicate operations required for repairs of the sewerage system that criss-crossed St Petersburg's myriad of canals: 'We had to pay, because without completion of the work St Petersburg would be covered to the tops of its cupolas in crap.' He'd advised Putin to set up the oil-for-food scheme, he said, because 'We needed to have operative instruments to be able to pay someone off fast.'[37]

Turover was essentially admitting that from the start the scheme had been intended not to bring in imports of food, but to create a hard-currency slush fund for the city. But without any oversight, there was no way of telling whether any of the funds were actually used to pay off the debts to the friendly firms, or whether they were in fact funnelled to networks of KGB agents still operating abroad. Turover claimed that there was no other way to operate, because the Russian state bank in charge of foreign operations, Vneshekonombank, was in a state of collapse. All of its accounts had been frozen January 1 1992, when the Russian government announced it had run out of funds. 'It was a pure necessity,' said Turover. 'It was not possible to pay the expenditures of the city any other way.'[38] Any hard-currency accounts officially connected to City Hall would be frozen, along with the other accounts impounded under the Soviet bankruptcy: 'If they'd kept it on the accounts of the city, it would mean the same thing as keeping the cash in VEB.

But if you had funds somewhere in foreign accounts, in Liechtenstein, then you could pay immediately.'[39]

Russia's central bank had used the same reasoning when it tried to explain away a scandal that emerged later in the nineties, when it emerged that it had transferred tens of billions of the country's hard-currency reserves through a small offshore firm in Jersey named Fimaco, which had been established in November 1990, shortly after Ivashko ordered the creation of the 'invisible Party economy'. The secret transfers through Fimaco, the Russian central bank chief later argued, had been necessary to protect the funds from being seized after the Soviet Union pronounced itself bankrupt, and to pay off the foreign debts of the Soviet international banking network.[40]

But there was zero oversight over any of the transactions, and rather than paying down debts, many suspected most of the money was used to fund the foreign networks of the KGB. In many ways, the central bank's Fimaco operations and Putin's oil-for-food scheme were cut from the same cloth. They looked to be part of the black cash of the Russian regime, and were so lacking in transparency that they could just as easily be used as the personal slush funds of the officials running Russia. Turover insisted that Putin never stole from the slush funds he helped create through the oil-for-food scheme. 'But he spent money, of course. Of course he spent some of the money, and somehow managed this money, because he needed to travel, to pay for hotels, and he probably needed to eat as well.'[41]

In essence, what had been created was what in Russian criminal parlance is called an '*obschak*', a common cash pot or slush fund for a criminal gang. It was a model based on handing out riches to a tightly controlled network of close allies, where the lines between what was to be used for strategic operations and what was for personal use were always conveniently blurred. This model became the basis for the kleptocracy of the Putin regime, and later its influence operations too – and it was based on the clandestine networks and payments systems of the KGB.

As for Salye, she was sidelined as a political figure. Sobchak blocked any further investigation of his young protégé's oil-for-food deals. In the mid-nineties she moved to Moscow, where her voice was drowned out in the capital's political din. On the eve of Putin's election as president, however, she resurfaced to publish the first in-depth investigative article on the deals, titling it 'V. Putin – The President of a Corrupt Oligarchy!' Although her findings created a furore among liberals, they had little impact nationwide. Soon after the election she withdrew to the depths of the countryside near the border with Finland, miles down a boneshaking road from the nearest town. Only a handful of journalists made the journey to interview her there. But the scheme, and her investigation of it, remained her abiding obsession till the day she died, just weeks after Putin began his third term in 2012. She knew she'd glimpsed the true nature of his regime in those deals.[42]

Submariner, Soldier, Trader, Spy

The KGB men who took over St Petersburg with Putin were far more commercially minded than the generation that had gone before. Though they mourned the collapse of the Soviet empire, many in the younger, middle echelon of the security services like Putin had fast embraced the tenets of capitalism and rejected the dogma of the Communist Party. For this new generation, it had been Communism that failed the empire, leaving them high and dry in Afghanistan and abandoning them in East Germany. 'They saw Communism as having betrayed them,' said Andrei Illarionov, the former presidential economic adviser to Putin.[43] They were the product of the operations the KGB launched in the final years of Soviet rule to create networks of foreign firms. The secrecy surrounding these activities meant that from the beginning, the methods of the KGB men of the eighties resembled money-laundering operations.

Once the oil-for-food scheme was done, Putin's allies began to move in on the sea port, which initially together with the oil terminal and a fleet of ships was part of a vast state holding company known as the Leningrad Baltic Sea Fleet, or BMP. For the St Petersburg KGB men, the BMP had long been a strategic asset and the story of how Putin's people took it over is inextricably bound up with the forging of an alliance between Putin's City Hall and the city's most notorious organised-crime group, the Tambov group. In Soviet times, the KGB had manned the fleet's ships as trade aides to the captains.[44] They knew intimately its trade routes, its cargoes, the contraband and the money to be made. In its heyday, hundreds of ships had set out from Leningrad carrying oil products, metals and grain, while others arrived from as far away as South America carrying fruit, sugar and smuggled goods, vital for underground operations and cash. In those days, the BMP represented the city's most strategic cash flow. Even in 1991, the year of the Soviet collapse, its net profits were in the hundreds of millions of dollars.[45] It was not only the owner of nearly two hundred passenger and cargo ships, it also controlled the entire Leningrad sea port, including its oil terminal, as well as the neighbouring ports in Vyborg and Kaliningrad. It was the key to the city's wealth.

The man who ran the Baltic Sea Fleet at the time of Yeltsin's revolution, Viktor Kharchenko, was an avowed liberal who under Gorbachev's *perestroika* reforms had won the government's permission to carve out the company as his own fiefdom. Square-jawed and built like a tank, Kharchenko had become increasingly independent. He'd risen from a childhood spent in an orphanage to become one of the city's most revered businessmen. In 1990, under his watch, the BMP became an enterprise he rented from the state, which kept 50 per cent of its profits for reinvestment.[46] He'd grown close to Yeltsin, and when the Communist regime collapsed in the wake of the failed August putsch, he unceremoniously kicked all the KGB men out of the fleet.[47]

Kharchenko was carving out a separate power base just at the time the St Petersburg KGB men most urgently wanted to keep control of the cash flow. In the chaos of the Soviet collapse, and with organised-crime groups also trying to get a piece of the port and the oil terminal, it took over a year for them to exact their revenge.

One of the first moves was made quietly. Late one evening in February 1993, Viktor Kharchenko was returning home from a meeting with Yeltsin in Moscow when police stopped the Red Arrow train he was travelling on just outside St Petersburg. He was hauled off the train, charged with siphoning $37,000 out of the Baltic Sea Fleet, and jailed.[48]

Kharchenko was released on bail four months later, but he was removed from his post in charge of the BMP. The St Petersburg KGB men installed their own director, sold off the fleet of ships one by one and transferred them to a myriad of offshore companies. In the process, one of the BMP's directors was shot dead.[49] 'It was a real raider attack,' said one of Kharchenko's associates. 'They sold off the ships for nothing. Everything disappeared. They siphoned everything out of the country.'[50]

Kharchenko's former associates still fear to speak of what happened back then, or about who was behind the attack. But the footprints of the local KGB men were everywhere. 'They needed to clean their boots and eat,' said one. 'They didn't pay attention to anyone. They just took BMP and looted it.'[51]

The raid was a foretaste of operations that were to come later. The KGB men had bent St Petersburg's law enforcement to their will to take over the city's most important trading link. Kharchenko had been removed as BMP chief at a crucial moment. At the same time, the port and the oil terminal were being carved out from the Baltic Sea Fleet into separate entities, and privatised by Putin's City Hall. 'They pulled out the harbour walls from BMP,' said a former Kharchenko associate.[52]

Submariner

As City Hall began to privatise part of its stake in the sea port, Ilya Traber, an alleged St Petersburg mobster later named by Spanish prosecutors as an associate of the Tambov organised-crime group, was quick off the mark.[53] His men bought up shares from the port's workers, who'd received them as vouchers, as soon as the sell-off began. The process was violent. 'There were huge violations in the privatisation of the port. But all this was covered up,' said a former Traber associate.[54] From the beginning, Traber seemed to have an inside track. On paper, the state retained a 49 per cent stake in the port: 20 per cent through the federal property ministry, and 29 per cent through St Petersburg's City Hall. But a clerk at the City Hall

Property Department somehow lost the City Hall voting rights to the 29 per cent stake through a 'mistaken' stroke of a pen, leaving Traber and his associates free to do as they wished.[55]

'The raider takeover would not have happened without help from the mayor's office,' said a former city FSB officer.[56] After a series of violent struggles, Traber, who'd become the quintessential intermediary between the St Petersburg KGB men and the Tambov group, established control over the oil terminal too.[57] He'd first arrived in Leningrad in the early eighties, as an ex-officer from the Soviet nuclear submarine fleet. A squat and burly man with a thick neck and close-set eyes, he'd washed up at a city-centre bar named Zhiguli,[58] a favourite haunt of Leningrad's street thugs and budding black marketeers. Traber worked there as a barman and administrator, and in the bar's dark reaches he began to trade in hard currency, and then in the city's rich collection of tsarist-era antiques. He soon cornered the market, earning himself the nickname 'Antikvar'. By the end of the eighties he was moving his business out of the black market and into the light, setting up the city's finest antiques store on Nevsky Prospekt. There he established ties with St Petersburg's newly-elected mayor Anatoly Sobchak and his wife Lyudmilla Narusova, who became frequent customers, forging a close friendship with Traber that was to last long after Sobchak's time in office.[59]

Traber had always worked closely with the city's KGB, without whose assistance it wouldn't have been possible for him to smuggle antiques. 'It was clear he had deep ties with the city's law enforcement,' said a former senior official from the city parliament.[60] He was also 'in business with the Tambov group', said a former FSB officer who worked in the St Petersburg contraband division.[61]

Soldier

At that time, the Tambov was becoming the city's most powerful organised-crime group. Its leader, Vladimir Kumarin, had served time in jail in 1991 following a violent battle with another of the city's mafia groups. After he emerged from prison, with the help of Putin, Traber and his men, the Tambov began taking control of St

Petersburg's entire fuel and energy business. The battles with rival gangs continued: in 1994, Kumarin lost one of his arms in a bomb attack. By that time, however, he was creating the St Petersburg Fuel Company, or PTK, which became the city's monopoly domestic oil distributor, while Ilya Traber was taking over control of the sea port and the oil terminal on the Tambov's behalf.[62] (Later, Spanish prosecutors described Traber as a co-owner with Kumarin of PTK.[63]) Kumarin became so powerful that he was known as St Petersburg's 'night governor'. In essence, he was the dark side of City Hall.

Putin seemed to be central to these manoeuvrings, the point man providing logistical support from the mayor's office. Together with his trusted deputy Igor Sechin, who towered over a lectern in an anteroom outside Putin's office vetting all who entered, he was the one who issued the licences that allowed Traber to control the port and the oil terminal. He was the one who granted Kumarin's PTK an exclusive contract to supply fuel for the city's ambulances, buses, taxis and police cars.[64] The first sign of his cooperation with the Tambov group came late in the summer of 1992, when his Foreign Relations Committee registered a Russo–German joint venture, the St Petersburg Immobilien Aktiengesellschaft, or SPAG, for investing in the city's real-estate business. Much later, German prosecutors would allege that SPAG was a vehicle for laundering illicit funds for the Tambov group, as well as for a Colombian drugs cartel.[65] During his stint as St Petersburg's deputy mayor, Putin served on SPAG's advisory board. The Kremlin said this was no more than one of many such 'honorary' positions he held as deputy mayor. But one of SPAG's co-founders said he met Putin five or six times to discuss SPAG's St Petersburg business.

Trader

For Gennady Timchenko, the alleged former KGB operative who'd apparently known Putin since their days studying spycraft together at the Red Banner Academy, gaining access to the oil terminal had also always been key. He prided himself on his powers of persuasion and, in later interviews, he'd often explain his success with a nod and a wink about his ability to sell anything to anyone.[66] Since childhood he'd been part of the Soviet elite. His father held a senior rank in the armed forces, and he spent some of his early years in East Germany. His knowledge of German helped secure him a job in Soviet foreign trade and, according to former associates, propelled him into the ranks of the KGB, where he allegedly worked undercover as a trade representative in Vienna and Switzerland. Through his connections he forged a partnership with a former senior KGB officer, Andrei Pannikov, a thick-set man with a broad grin and hands as big as dinner plates. Pannikov had studied offshore finance at the Soviet Trade Institute, and then, with the blessing of the KGB's foreign-intelligence chief Leonid Shebarshin, set up the first joint venture to be licensed to export oil products outside the Soviet monopoly.[67] Timchenko's Kirishineftekhimexport oil trader formed a partnership with Pannikov's Urals Trading – and for a time, from 1990, Timchenko headed Urals' branch in Finland. According to a report by French intelligence, the company had initially been set up by the KGB in the eighties as part of a network of firms to transfer assets for the Communist Party[68] – a claim Timchenko denied.

Even with all their connections, for at least two years Timchenko and Pannikov were unable to gain access to the St Petersburg oil terminal.[69] Not only was it part of Kharchenko's fiefdom, but as the power of the Soviet Union fractured, it became a vicious battleground for the city's warring criminal groups. The oil trader Timchenko co-founded had ready access to supplies as the in-house trading arm of the nearby Kirishi refinery, part of the Surgutneftegaz oil company. But without access to the St Petersburg terminal, it was forced to export its oil by rail to neighbouring ports in Estonia or Finland, a much costlier route.[70]

Gaining control of exports through the St Petersburg terminal became so important that Timchenko turned to Putin for assistance. In January 1992, together with Pannikov's Urals Trading, Timchenko set up a joint venture with Putin's Foreign Relations Committee called 'Golden Gates'.[71] They aimed to bypass the existing terminal, beset by rival gangs and under Kharchenko's ultimate control, and raise Western financing to build a new, upgraded terminal.[72]

This was the first time the ties between Putin and Timchenko had emerged into the open. For almost a year, Putin led discussions with France's BNP Paribas on a credit facility for the new oil terminal, backed by exports through Urals Trading.[73] But the talks fell apart when one of the key negotiators, a former KGB officer operating in Paris named Mikhail Gandorin, died just before the loan was to be approved.[74] 'It looked like he'd been given something,' one former Timchenko partner involved in the process said. 'He called me two days before he died, and he couldn't speak.'[75] That summer another member of the Golden Gates group, Sergei Shutov, was threatened and told to stay away from the project.

The project was under severe attack, with St Petersburg's mafia groups, including the Tambov, battling each other to gain control of revenues from the existing terminal. The pressure mounted to such a degree that, according to two senior Western bankers, Putin sent his two young daughters away to Germany for their safety.[76] There is no indication Timchenko had any involvement in the violent struggles that accompanied Traber's takeover of the port and oil terminal. But eventually, instead of building a new terminal, the way was opened for him to win a monopoly on exports through the existing terminal.[77]

One former Traber associate, a former Timchenko partner and a former KGB associate claimed Timchenko would only have been able to gain such a monopoly through forging some kind of working relationship with Traber. 'Traber always had good relations with Timchenko,' said one of Traber's former associates. 'The monopoly Timchenko won on exports would only have been possible through such ties.'[78] 'If you need to ship oil and the port is full of bandits, then you need to agree,' said a former senior KGB officer who worked with Putin in the nineties. 'There was no way to go through without their agreement.'[79]

Lawyers for Timchenko said the relationship was no more than a 'commercial, arm's-length' one, while any suggestion Timchenko had any involvement with organised crime, corruption or any other improper or illegal activity in St Petersburg, whether 'via Mr Traber or in any other way', was false and libellous. In 2011, a Timchenko representative told Russia's *Novaya Gazeta* Timchenko was acquainted with the co-owner of Traber in the sea port and oil terminal, Dmitry Skigin, but the two men had not engaged in any joint business projects.[80]

At the same time, Timchenko was drawing on a network of KGB-linked foreign bankers to finance his trading operations. First, there was Dresdner Bank, headed in St Petersburg by one of Putin's former Stasi comrades, Matthias Warnig, who'd worked with him in Dresden as part of a KGB cell.[81] Then there was Andrei Akimov, who'd worked with Yevgeny Primakov at the Institute of World Economy before becoming the youngest head of the Soviet foreign bank in Vienna, where, in the year before the Soviet fall, he set up his own private venture, IMAG, which provided financing to Timchenko.[82]

All the while, Putin assisted, issuing the licences allowing Timchenko to use the oil-storage facilities at Traber's sea port, and helping facilitate supply arrangements between Timchenko's Kirishineftekhimexport and Kumarin's PTK.[83] Kumarin, meanwhile, joined the board of both outfits' supplier, the Kirishi oil refinery.[84]

'It was all very well organised,' said Maxim Freidzon, co-owner of another oil trader in the city. 'Putin and his guys ensured support from City Hall. Because of his KGB past, he could help with the logistical organisation. It was all one team.'[85]

The alliance that was forged then took KGB traditions from before the Soviet collapse and put them to a still more commercial use. 'As far as I remember, the symbiosis between the bandits and the KGB had always existed,' said Freidzon. 'The KGB had worked with the bandits in the currency markets and in prostitution rings. They were sources of information. It was a natural symbiosis: neither of them had any moral limits. The bandits were like the infantry for them. They would take all the risks.'[86]

Putin's interest in St Petersburg's sea port and oil terminal often seemed more direct than that of a state official responsible for the city's share. The alliance he built with Ilya Traber and his men troubled even visiting businessmen. When one was brought in to help arrange financing for the port, he was whisked from the city's Pulkovo airport straight to Traber's lair in an armoured car, accompanied by police and Traber's guards. On arrival at the high-gated compound in a back street, he was escorted past armed guards and snarling German shepherds. After passing through several rooms adorned with icons, he arrived at an inner chamber where Traber was waiting, wearing a tracksuit bottom and slippers, a thick chain with a huge gold cross around his neck – the uniform of the city's bandits. The businessman was left in no doubt about whom he was meeting. 'It was like in the movies,' he said. 'My heart stopped when I saw him.'[87]

The scene was far from what he had expected when he was invited by an official from City Hall to assist with financing the port. But after a tense discussion with Traber, he received the nod of approval. The next day he was taken to more salubrious surroundings: the downtown law offices of one of Traber's business partners, Boris Sharikov, on one of St Petersburg's most picturesque canals. Also at the meeting was a former KGB officer who'd become another of Traber's partners, as well as Putin and the City Hall property chief Mikhail Manevich, and a smooth-talking thirtysomething named Dmitry Skigin, who the businessman was to learn owned the port jointly with Traber. Skigin was the acceptable face of the port, a mild-mannered geek, fluent in the language of international finance, a disciplined businessman who went mountain climbing in his spare time and spoke English and French. His father Eduard was close to Putin, according to Monaco intelligence.[88] But according to two of Skigin's former business partners, he was also a front for another St Petersburg crime boss, a pugnacious former boxer named Sergei Vasilyev, with whom Traber had agreed a fragile peace for joint control of the port, and later for its oil terminal.[89]

The alliance St Petersburg's administration forged with the Tambov group became embedded deep in the city's infrastructure. With the help of Putin's men in City Hall, the sea port become a major hub for smuggling drugs from Colombia into Western Europe, former senior KGB officer Yury Shvets later testified to a London court. One of Putin's closest allies in the St Petersburg security services, Viktor Ivanov, had assisted the Tambov group in taking over the sea port, while Putin provided protection from the mayor's office, he said.[90] (Ivanov strenuously denied the claim, but other signs emerged that the St Petersburg port was a vital channel for drug trafficking.[91])

Control of the port became so strategic that when, in 1997, the Property Department chief Mikhail Manevich sought to return the voting rights City Hall had lost to its 29 per cent stake during its privatisation, he was shot dead by a sniper as he drove to work.[92]

'Manevich was pushing for it all to be returned to the state,' said a former Traber associate. 'The leverage that he had was that he could refuse to extend the licence for the long-term rent of the port including the oil terminal. And for this he paid with his life.'[93] Vyacheslav Shevchenko, a former member of the St Petersburg parliament and a close Manevich ally, reportedly testified to the police murder inquiry that in the final days of his life Manevich had been deeply troubled by the situation at the port: 'On his request, I went twice to the port and spoke with the head of the port. I made a proposal that the English insurance company Lloyds should come to analyse the port's financial situation. A week later, two of Traber's bandits visited me and told me if I went to the port again my head would be cut off with an axe.'[94]

Traber refused to comment for this book, saying the allegations were 'fantasy and slander'.[95] Just three months after Manevich's murder, the port's shareholders agreed to extend a new long-term management contract for the port to a new Traber company, OBIP, owned by a Liechtenstein foundation called Nasdor Incorporated.[96] Later, the only person who ever dared to speak out publicly about the looting of the Baltic Sea Fleet was the city's mayor at the time it occurred, Anatoly Sobchak. Long after he had stepped down he wrote a newspaper article in which, for the first and only time, he publicly criticised the actions of the city's post-Soviet KGB. 'The prosecutors, the FSB and the policemen who took part in this should be charged with abusing their position and for causing the country enormous loss,' he wrote.[97] Four months later he was dead. 'I fear this was what cost Sobchak his life,' said an associate of Kharchenko.[98]

In the eyes of Putin's KGB allies, the alliances they forged then were necessary as the only way to restore some degree of control in the chaos of the Soviet collapse. The organised-crime groups were the infantrymen they needed to help control the masses, the men on the street – as well as in the prisons, according to one of Putin's associates then. This was a typical KGB practice, forged in the Soviet past, when Putin for instance had run illegals through East Germany. 'They worked with people. This is what they did,' said a former KGB officer who worked with them. 'Imagine you need to calm down a bunch of alpha males. If you can't shoot them, this is terribly difficult work.'[99] But the argument that they needed to do this if they were to bring order was only a self-justification behind the power grab. The oil-for-food scheme had also been set up ostensibly to save the city – whether to bring in food or to pay down debts. But all it had achieved was to create a network of black cash to preserve the power and the networks of the KGB.

In the skein of these relationships, another thread led to one of the structures set up for the Communist Party's 'invisible economy' in the final days of its rule. This was Bank Rossiya, a small St Petersburg bank which was one more key intermediary in some of the oil-for-food barter deals. Like many of the institutions and firms set up by the Party in the dying days of the regime, when the August 1991 putsch failed and the Soviet Communist Party was banned, control of Bank Rossiya passed noiselessly into the hands of representatives of the KGB. Its new shareholders included a senior KGB officer and two KGB-connected physicists who specialised in rare-earth metals, materials so rare, and so strategic, that trade in them could only be handled by members of the KGB.

Spy

When the senior KGB officer Vladimir Yakunin returned to Leningrad in February 1991, a year after Putin, from a posting under-cover at the United Nations in New York, he was shocked by the conditions that greeted him. He had come from a comfortable residence in New York to the grime of a working-class area of Leningrad, where the street lamps rarely shone and his wife would return home from the shops in tears because the only thing on the shelves was pickled cucumbers. 'In essence, the country that had sent me to work abroad, and in which I grew up and where my children were born, had ceased to exist,' he said. 'So too had the values – the social and moral values – which were the fundamental basis for any society. The entire country had descended into a certain darkness.'

It seemed to him that everything he'd once believed in had collapsed: 'We were brought up in the spirit of loyalty to the Party and to the people. We really did believe we were doing something useful for our country and for our people.' But like many in the foreign-intelligence services, he'd long been able to see that the Party leadership was failing: 'There was no one who knew how to deal with the growing problems . . . The gap between reality and ideological dogma led to deep distrust in the country's leaders.'[100]

Although the loss of empire and the loss of the decades-long Cold War hit men like Yakunin hard, he was among those who moved fast to embrace Russia's new capitalism. And while he said he hankered for the days of certainty, for the morality and values that he believed lay at the foundation of Communism, that did not stop him from leaping into business before the Soviet Union had even collapsed, to pocket vast amounts of cash both for himself and, more importantly, to help preserve the networks of the KGB.

For four years after the Soviet collapse, Yakunin remained an officer in the security services, never resigning his post. Although he insisted that he hadn't been taking orders, he admitted that the aim of his and his partners' business activities was partly to preserve what they could: 'We needed to redirect ourselves. We needed to create commercial enterprises that would earn money . . . We were all part of this process. The traditions of communication and cooperation remained.'

Yakunin joined forces with associates from St Petersburg's prestigious Ioffe Institute for Technology and Physics, where he'd worked overseeing the institute's international connections before being sent to New York. Among them was Yury Kovalchuk, then thirty-nine and a leading physicist of his day. Kovalchuk had a high forehead and a hawk-like gaze, and he worked closely with Andrei Fursenko; both of them were deputies in the Ioffe Institute's work on sensitive semiconductor technologies deployed in laser and satellite systems. This was an area at the heart of the KGB's special interest, in which all manner of smuggling schemes had been deployed to bypass embargoes and steal technology from the West (Yakunin was believed to have worked on technology smuggling when he served undercover in New York). Their expertise landed Yakunin, Kovalchuk and Fursenko a lucrative assignment: a deal to sell a batch of rare-earth metals, including rare and strategic isotopes used in the aerospace and military industries, and in semiconductor technology.[101] They were given the deal by a senior general in the KGB, said Yakunin. Once they'd pulled it off, one of the joint ventures they'd created, Temp, landed 24 million roubles in profits.[102] It was a huge sum in those days, and it helped them take over Bank Rossiya.

The three men had set up a string of such joint ventures in the final months before the Soviet collapse, as the KGB stepped up preparations for the transition to a market economy, and they'd already been working closely with Bank Rossiya. In the aftermath of the failed August coup, said Yakunin, they had briefly feared that they might go out of business when their accounts in Bank Rossiya were frozen, along with the rest of the property of the Communist Party. But their connections, and the cash they made in the rare-earth metals deal, saved them. High-ups in the local Party and the KGB gave them the nod to take over Bank Rossiya and bring it back to life. 'We were people who were well-known in the party structures of the city of Leningrad,' said Yakunin. 'We had many contacts, and people trusted us. We were allowed to take a controlling stake in Bank Rossiya precisely because these people trusted and respected us.'[103]

From the beginning, Bank Rossiya had been strategically connected to the foreign-relations committee run by Putin. Its offices were in the Smolny Institute, which had become the city's mayor's headquarters, and it began to play a key role in the creation of the *obschak*, the common cash pot for Putin's men. The city's KGB-connected businessmen, including Yakunin, Kovalchuk and Fursenko, almost religiously continued to follow the prescriptions of the KGB laid out in the twilight years of the Communist regime, when trade was to be ordered through joint ventures with foreign entities. All joint ventures were set up on the approval of Putin's committee, and most were directed to open accounts with Bank Rossiya. In one instance, millions of dollars were siphoned from the city budget through Bank Rossiya's accounts into a network of such companies linked to Putin's men. The cash had been funnelled through a fund known as Twentieth Trust. At one point the scheme had threatened to embroil Putin in a criminal case. Like many of the slush funds created by Putin's men, the money had gone towards strategic needs such as funding election campaigns, and also for personal acquisitions such as luxury properties in Finland and Spain for city officials.[104]

As Putin and his KGB men became more secure in their control of the city's economy, they began to dream their own bourgeois dreams. One transfer in particular paid for a five-star hotel trip for Putin and the head of Twentieth Trust to Finland, where they met an architect from the St Petersburg government and most likely discussed plans for the building of a group of dachas, according to a senior police officer who investigated the case.[105] 'Soviet people always have a dream to have a dacha,' said a Putin associate from then.[106] 'The understanding was that it was not just important to have a good piece of land, but also to have the right neighbours.'

The patch Putin chose to while away his weekends in peace and tranquillity was far down a highway snaking north from St Petersburg through the forests and lakes of Karelia. Near the border with Finland, an unsignposted road led to a snug group of wooden houses on the shores of the Komsomolskoye lake, renowned for its excellent fishing. Before Putin moved in, the road had been no more than a dirt track. But soon after the new inhabitants arrived it was asphalted over, and lights were installed.

The villagers who'd lived peacefully for generations on the coveted stretch of land on the lakeshore saw new, more powerful electrical lines installed, though none of the power reached their homes. Instead they were asked, one by one, to move away, and were either given money to leave or provided with new ready-built houses further inland. Their powerful new neighbours built imposing Finnish-style chalets on vast tracts of land. They formed a group that became known as the Ozero dacha cooperative, and took over the lakeshore, from which their former neighbours were cut off by a high new fence. When the newcomers had parties, the old inhabitants could only watch the festivities and fireworks from afar. They knew not to object. 'My mother told me a simple thing: don't fight the strong and don't sue the rich,' said one of them.[107] The only inhabitant who tried to fight lost every stage of her trial.

The men who moved to Lake Komsomolskoye with Putin were the blue blood of his KGB acquaintances. Mostly shareholders of Bank Rossiya, they included Yakunin, Fursenko and Kovalchuk. All of them had been connected to Putin since even before the St Petersburg days. 'These were people who were close to Putin from before,' said one former Putin associate.[108] 'They hadn't got there because of their work or their knowledge – but just because they were old friends.'

This was a principle that was later expanded across the entire country. After Putin became president, he and his allies from the Ozero dacha group began to capture strategic sectors of the economy, creating a tight-knit network of loyal lieutenants – trusted custodians – who took control of the country's biggest cash flows and excluded everyone else. Bank Rossiya was to form the core of the financial empire behind this group, and it was to spread its tentacles throughout Russia, and deep into the West too.

Those who'd worked with Putin at the sea port and the oil terminal also followed him when he vaulted to power. Timchenko was prime among them, first in the shadows working, according to two former associates, as an unofficial adviser, and then becoming the nation's biggest oil trader. The men who ran the St Petersburg sea port under Traber's watch were to take the first senior positions in Gazprom, the state gas giant, as Putin began to take over the country's biggest and most strategic assets. Then, when Putin made his first moves to take back the nation's oil industry from Western-leaning oligarchs like Mikhail Khodorkovsky, Timchenko and Akimov were part of the core group who benefited.

But in those days in the nineties, when they were just starting

out, it was difficult to imagine that they would ever make it so far.
The members of the Ozero dacha cooperative kept themselves to
themselves, rarely speaking to the former neighbours who they'd
moved away from the shores of the lake. But after Putin moved to
Moscow, the weekend visits became rare. The houses they'd built
were left empty, like ghosts on the edge of the lake. 'It became too
small for them here. They had absolutely different opportunities in
Moscow,' said one of the neighbours.[109]

*

When Putin was suddenly appointed to a senior position in the
Kremlin in Moscow in the summer of 1996, one of the senior KGB
generals who'd watched closely over his St Petersburg career
pronounced himself satisfied with him. 'He began his career as an
official from zero,' the general, Gennady Belik, later told a reporter.
'Of course he made mistakes. The issues for him were absolutely
new . . . The only people who don't make mistakes are the ones that
don't do anything. But by the end of his activities in St Petersburg,
Vladimir Vladimirovich had grown a great deal.'[110]

Belik was a veteran of the KGB's foreign-intelligence service, and
in St Petersburg he'd overseen a network of firms trading in rare-
earth metals. He'd been a mentor of sorts to Putin as he managed
the city's economy, while according to one close ally Putin also stayed
in touch with former KGB chairman Vladimir Kryuchkov.[111] But
although Putin's men had dominated much of the city's economy,
the amounts of cash they were dealing with in St Petersburg were
minuscule compared to what the young Western-leaning tycoons
like Khodorkovsky were taking over in Moscow. They were far away
from the action as the new oligarchs of the Yeltsin era began to carve
up the country's industrial wealth. For many of the St Petersburg
KGB men, what was going on in Moscow represented the collapse
of the Russian state. Vladimir Yakunin, for one, saw the country as
being seized by a cabal of corrupt members of the Party elite and
by men like Khodorkovsky who he called 'criminals'.[112] The KGB
men saw Yeltsin as a drunken buffoon, a mid-ranking Communist

Party official who danced to the tune of the West and who was now handing over the country's strategic enterprises for a song to a corrupt gang of rapacious businessmen. 'People had given their lives. They'd served honestly and put their lives at risk. But all they got was a finger up their ass from a drunk bastard who by the way was no better than a local Communist Party leader,' said a former KGB officer who worked with Putin in St Petersburg.[113]

Though it seemed far from likely then, Putin's move to Moscow was the first step towards changing that equation. His promotion had happened at a moment when he should in fact have been down and out. In the summer of 1996, Anatoly Sobchak had just lost his campaign for re-election as St Petersburg's mayor. Putin, as his campaign manager, had been partly responsible. Sobchak lost by a whisker: by 1.2 per cent – the equivalent, his widow Lyudmilla Narusova later said, of the occupants of one large apartment building. Whispers circulated that Sobchak's defeat had been organised by Yeltsin, who wanted him out, as the flamboyant and charismatic Sobchak could have posed a challenge to Yeltsin's own battle for re-election as president a few months later. Narusova was convinced of that: 'He'd become too independent. Yeltsin saw him as his competitor, and therefore the order was given that the elections were to be a farce.'[114] Before the campaign had even begun, Sobchak was targeted by a criminal investigation over bribery allegations. Many believed it was part of a dirty tricks campaign by the old-guard security men surrounding Yeltsin.[115]

The allegations undoubtedly impacted the outcome of the election, and Putin resigned from the St Petersburg administration immediately after the loss. Kremlin spin doctors telling the official story of Putin's career have always stressed his loyalty to Sobchak in stepping down, and the risk he took in facing unemployment because of his principles. But in fact he was out of work for less than a month before he was invited to Moscow, initially to take up a prestigious position as a deputy head of the Kremlin administration. He had been helped along the way by Alexei Bolshakov, a dinosaur from the Leningrad defence establishment and most likely from the KGB, who'd somehow become Yeltsin's deputy prime minister.

Although Putin's appointment was unexpectedly blocked by Anatoly Chubais, the Western-leaning privatisation tsar who'd become Yeltsin's new chief of staff, he was not abandoned. Instead, he was asked to head the Kremlin's fabled foreign property department, which had inherited all the Soviet Union's vast overseas holdings after the collapse – the stately trade and diplomatic missions, the network of arms bases and other military installations, clandestine or otherwise. Though it was an empire in which much had already gone unaccounted for, it represented a strategic core of the nation's imperial wealth, and for Putin this was a prestigious promotion indeed.

It was the beginning of a dizzying rise. Within seven months of his move to Moscow, Putin was promoted further still. First, he was made head of the Control Department, a core institute of Kremlin power, where he was charged with making sure the president's orders were carried out across the nation's unruly regions. 'They didn't just take Putin from the street,' said one close ally. 'He was known in Moscow as an adviser to Sobchak, as an influential person in St Petersburg . . . I think this transfer was planned.'[116] Then, a year later, he was promoted to become the Kremlin's first deputy chief of staff in charge of the regions, the third most powerful role in the Kremlin after the president. After just three months in that role he was appointed to head the FSB, the successor agency to the KGB, for the whole of Russia. He was only a lieutenant colonel at the time, and it was unheard of for anyone other than a general to head the FSB. The FSB generals were said to be aghast, but Putin's allies insisted that his status as first deputy chief of staff gave him a rank equivalent to a general. It was just that it was in civilian terms, they said.[117]

Yeltsin's son-in-law Valentin Yumashev, a good-natured former journalist who'd risen to become Yeltsin's chief of staff, insisted that Putin's miraculous rise was down to his outstanding qualities. 'Among my deputies, he was one of the strongest,' he told me. 'He always worked brilliantly. He formulated his views exactly. He would analyse the situation exactly. I was always happy I had such a deputy.'[118] But for others who had known him in St Petersburg, Putin's elevation was taking on a surreal quality. Some of his former associates questioned whether he was being propelled by the KGB generals who'd mentored his career from the beginning. 'You could make the case that he'd first been given the task to infiltrate the democratic community through his work with Sobchak,' said one. When Sobchak had become surplus to requirements, had Putin played a role in helping make sure he lost? 'It's totally possible that Putin was following the orders of the Kremlin, and that when he completed this task he entered the Kremlin and became so important,' said the former associate. 'If you suppose this was a special operation to liquidate Sobchak as a contender, then everything becomes clear.'[119] But others argued that Sobchak had become increasingly controversial in St Petersburg in any case, mainly due to what many saw as his arrogance. It hadn't taken much to make his bid for re-election touch and go.

However he got there, once Putin assumed his role as director of the FSB, he soon began to clean up the stains from his St Petersburg past. One of his greatest enemies from those days was Yury Shutov, a former Sobchak deputy who'd clashed with Putin and had been collecting compromising material on him – on the oil-for-food deals, on the privatisations of the city's assets and on his ties to the Tambov group. Soon after Putin's appointment, Shutov was arrested at gunpoint. He'd long been a deeply controversial figure and rumours of his ties to the St Petersburg underworld ran deep. But once Putin became FSB chief, the suspicions turned into legal charges. He was charged with ordering four contract killings and attempting two others. Though he was briefly freed by a local court which ruled that there was no legal basis for a criminal case, Shutov was swiftly arrested again, and dispatched to Russia's toughest penal colony, known as the Beliy Lebed, or White Swan, in Perm, in the depths of Siberia. He never emerged from it. The material he'd gathered on Putin's ties to Tambov simply disappeared, said Andrei Korchagin, a former city official who had known Shutov well: 'He was Russia's first and only real political prisoner.'[120]

An even more disturbing omen came just four months after Putin's appointment as FSB chief. Galina Starovoitova, the same stout and tweedy human rights activist with soft brown hair who Putin had approached for work after his return from Dresden to Leningrad, was shot dead at the entrance to her apartment building late one evening in November 1998. She was by then St Petersburg's leading democrat, its most vocal crusader against corruption. The whole city was in mourning after her death, the nation in shock. Many commentators linked her killing to tension surrounding elections to the local parliament that were to be held the following month. But one of Starovoitova's former aides, Ruslan Linkov, who was with her at the time of the shooting but somehow escaped with his life, believed she was killed because of her corruption investigations.[121] One of her closest friends, Valeria Novodvorskaya, another leading democrat, was convinced the St Petersburg security men had ordered her murder: 'They were clearly behind the scenes. They held the hand of the killers.'[122] A former partner of Ilya Traber said the biggest threat to Starovoitova could have come from the St Petersburg *siloviki* who controlled the sea port, the fleet and the oil terminal: 'She had a dossier on the group of people who controlled the oil business in St Petersburg. Traber told me about this. He said, "Why the hell did she start looking into the oil business?" This is why she was killed.'[123] Later, a former FSB officer who'd investigated her death told me he suspected it was indeed Tambov that organised it: 'We understood that we would not be able to get anywhere with the case.'[124]

The events that accompanied Putin's rise were ominous. But the country was hurtling towards another financial crisis, and the warning signs, it appeared, were not noticed by anyone. Yeltsin's health was failing, and if at least one account is to be believed, the generals of the KGB were preparing to return. One evening in Moscow, soon after a financial crash that obliterated the Russian economy in August 1998, a small group of KGB officers and one American gathered for a private dinner. Among them were the former KGB chief Vladimir Kryuchkov; Robert Eringer, a former security chief for Monaco who'd dabbled as an informant for the FBI; and Igor Prelin, an aide to Kryuchkov and one of Putin's senior lecturers at the Red Banner spy institute. According to Eringer, Prelin told the other guests that soon the KGB would return to power: 'He said, "We know someone. You've never heard of him. We're not going to tell you who it is, but he's one of us, and when he's president we're back."'[125]

4

Operation Successor:
'It Was Already After Midnight'

*

'Everyone forgot. Everyone thought that democracy would just
be there. Everyone was thinking only about their own personal
interests.'

Andrei Vavilov, former first deputy finance
minister in Yeltsin government[1]

*

Plan A

MOSCOW – It was summer 1999, and a deathly quiet had
descended on the Kremlin. In the warren-like corridors of
the main administration building, the only sound was the steady
whirr of electric motors as cleaners polished the parquet floors. In
the distance, the clopping heels of a lone presidential guard on patrol
echoed down the halls. Offices once overflowing with petitioners
queuing for favours now stood largely empty, their former occupants
huddled far from Moscow in their dachas, nervously drinking tea.
'It was like being in a cemetery,' said Sergei Pugachev, the Kremlin
banker who'd also happened to serve as an adviser to a succession
of Kremlin chiefs of staff. 'It was like a company that had gone
bankrupt. All of a sudden there was nothing there.'[2]
For Pugachev and the other members of Yeltsin's inner circle,

widely known as the 'Family', who were the Kremlin's few remaining occupants, a tense new reality had begun. Yeltsin had been in and out of hospital ever since October, and outside the walls of the Kremlin, it seemed, a coup was being prepared. Piece by piece, the foundations of Yeltsin's rule were being dismantled, a consequence of the past summer's disastrous rouble devaluation and default on $40 billion in government debt. The easy money, the free-for-all for the well-connected few that had defined the boom years of the market transformation had ended in a spectacular bust. The government had spent four years funding the country's budget through issuing short-term debt, creating a pyramid scheme in which the only winners had been a handful of oligarchs, the young wolves of the Yeltsin era. For a time, the tycoons had used surging interest rates on government bonds and a fixed exchange rate to pocket the proceeds of a surefire bet, while the central bank burned through its hard-currency reserves keeping the rouble stable. It had all come crashing down in August 1998, and once again the Russian population had borne the brunt of the blow. Many of the oligarchs' banks had collapsed in the crisis, but while they themselves had managed to funnel most of their fortunes away offshore, the general population's savings were wiped out. The parliament, then still dominated by the Communists, was in uproar. Forced onto the defensive, Yeltsin had been backed into appointing a prime minister from the top echelons of the KGB, Yevgeny Primakov, the former spymaster who'd run the foreign-intelligence service and had long been a sentinel of the networks of the KGB. Racked by ill health, his regime in tatters, Yeltsin had retreated to the Black Sea resort of Sochi, while Primakov brought a string of Communist deputies, led by the former head of the Soviet economic planning agency Gosplan, into his government. Yeltsin was repeatedly hospitalised, and a Kremlin aide gently hinted that he was to take a back seat from then on.[3]

One by one, members of the Communist old guard had been settling on perches at the top of the government, and now that they were taking control of the cabinet, financial scandal after financial scandal targeting the excesses of their opponents in the Yeltsin ruling elite was beginning to emerge. Leading the corruption charges was Yury Skuratov, Russia's rotund and seemingly mild-mannered prosecutor general. Until early that year, he had attracted more attention for his ability to quietly close down criminal cases than for opening them. Now, however, amid the widespread outrage that accompanied the country's financial collapse, he'd begun to target top-level corruption. First, he'd launched a broadside against the central bank. In a letter to the Communist speaker of the State Duma, he zeroed in on how the bank had secretly funnelled $50 billion of the country's hard-currency reserves through Fimaco, the obscure offshore company registered in Jersey[4] – a revelation that opened a Pandora's box of insider trading and siphoned funds through the government debt market.

Behind the scenes, several more threatening probes were under way. One was a case that could lead directly to the financial accounts of the Yeltsin Family. It focused on Mabetex, a little-known company based in the Alpine Swiss town of Lugano, near the Italian border, which throughout the nineties had won billions of dollars in contracts to renovate the Kremlin, the Russian White House and other prestigious projects. Initially the probe, launched by Skuratov in tandem with Swiss prosecutors, appeared to focus on kickbacks apparently paid to middlemen close to Pavel Borodin, the jovial and earthy Siberian party boss who'd ruled over the Kremlin's vast property department since 1993. But behind that lay a potentially bigger affair. And those in the Kremlin who were ruling in Yeltsin's stead knew this only too well. 'Everyone was scared about what was going to happen,' said Pugachev. 'No one dared to come to work. Everyone was shaking like rabbits.'[5]

The groundwork for the case had been laid quietly. Part of the old guard, particularly those waiting in the shadows in the security services, had been looking for ways to oust Yeltsin since the beginning of his rule. They had long viewed his overtures to democracy with disgust, and when he appealed to Russia's regions to take as much freedom as they could swallow, they saw it as part of a Western plot to weaken, and ultimately destroy, the Russian Federation. Still set in the zero-sum thinking of the Cold War, they regarded Yeltsin as being in thrall to the US government, which they liked to believe had helped to install him and destroy the Soviet Union in the first place. They despised his apparent friendship with US president Bill Clinton, and believed the market reforms they themselves had developed, and which had helped bring Yeltsin to power, had been perverted to create the oligarchic rule of the *semi bankirschina* – the seven bankers who'd outrun their former KGB masters to take over much of the economy. They cared nothing for Yeltsin's democratic achievements: in their view he was an addled alcoholic incapable of leading the country, while the Yeltsin Family, which included his daughter Tatyana, his chief of staff (and future son-in-law) Valentin Yumashev and various acolytes of the oligarch Boris Berezovsky, was an unholy alliance that had illegally taken power behind the scenes, and was leading the country towards certain collapse.

'A certain group of people understood that things could not continue this way,' said one of the participants in this plot, Felipe Turover, the former KGB operative who'd worked with Putin on the St Petersburg oil-for-food scheme. 'The whole operation was started out of necessity. There was no other choice. It had to be done. Yeltsin was a drunk and a heavy drug addict. It is a matter of fact that the country was ruled by his daughter, by a bunch of idiots who were only looking after their own interests . . . The governors were disobeying the Kremlin. The regions were starting to almost become independent countries. We needed to get rid of that scum.'

Turover refused to disclose the names of the security officials in the group plotting to remove Yeltsin from power. But it was clear that they were angling to replace him with Primakov, who as a former spymaster was one of their number. From the start, the group was looking for evidence directly linking Yeltsin to financial corruption; for something that would taint the president irredeemably, overcoming the widespread and age-old Russian view that the country's problems were due to the poor decisions and corruption of the courtiers, the boyars surrounding the tsar, and not the president himself. 'Because he'd been praised as the great democrat, no one knew how to get rid of him,' said Turover. 'The only clear path was a legal path. It had to be clear to the people that it wasn't the case that the tsar was good and without fault, while the boyars were the bad guys. When the president is a thief himself, then everything is clear. We needed to have something concrete.'[6]

Turover was the informant who found and then disclosed the material that formed the basis of the case. From his perch overseeing clandestine payments of Soviet-era strategic debt, he had been gathering and sifting *kompromat* – compromising material – on the inner financing of the Yeltsin regime for years, in the hope that the right moment would come. As a close friend of the former head of the KGB's black-ops department for financing illicit operations abroad, he'd been a member of the KGB security establishment since the eighties. Turover was the same wisecracking, tough-talking foreign-intelligence officer who had helped Vladimir Putin set up the oil-for-food scheme in St Petersburg in the early nineties – the scheme that created a strategic slush fund for Putin and his allies from the KGB. He'd helped set up other clandestine schemes that he said were to ensure the payment of the strategic debts of the Soviet Union to the so-called 'friendly firms', but which were almost certainly also slush funds for the KGB.

Documents show that many of these schemes had run through Banco del Gottardo, a small bank hidden away on the outskirts of Lugano, at which Turover was appointed as an adviser.[7] Banco del Gottardo was chosen, Turover said, because 'We needed a very small bank with a very dirty reputation.'[8] It had been the overseas arm of Banco Ambrosiano, the Vatican-linked bank that had collapsed in scandal in the eighties, with its chairman Roberto Calvi found dead, hanging from London's Blackfriars Bridge. Now numerous Russian black-cash financing schemes were run through its accounts, including a web of barter and commodities-export schemes through which billions of dollars had been siphoned.

It was another sign that for all Yeltsin's attempts at market reform, for all his efforts to build a new Russia out of the rubble of the Soviet collapse, the old ways of the *komitetchiki*, the KGB men, still prevailed behind the scenes. Although Yeltsin had tried to man the ranks of his government with so-called 'young reformers' who sought to liberalise the Russian economy from the control of the state and run the country along the transparent lines dictated by the institutions of the West, the rules of business were still skewed in favour of insiders close to the state, and to the foreign-intelligence community. It was through these schemes that the Yeltsin Family had been compromised, and it was all the more telling that the blow to the freedoms Yeltsin had sought to bring to Russia came from a member of the KGB foreign-intelligence establishment. Yeltsin had been unable to pull either his country or his own family out of the practices of the past.

Banco del Gottardo hosted the accounts of Mabetex, the obscure Swiss company which handled the Kremlin renovation contracts, and this was where the links to Yeltsin and his family appeared. When he'd first uncovered these ties, Turover said he'd initially objected to handling any cash flow related to Yeltsin or his family. 'But then I stopped, because I decided that all this could come in handy for the future.'[9]

Among the Banco del Gottardo accounts he oversaw, Turover had discovered credit cards for Yeltsin and his family. They'd been issued by the founder of Mabetex, a pugnacious Kosovar Albanian named Behdjet Pacolli, who'd worked in the netherworld of financing and construction for the Soviet regime since the seventies.[10] Pacolli, once an aide to the Yugoslav Communist Party boss, had long been involved in black-cash financing schemes through the sale to the Soviet regime of embargoed dual-use military goods, said Turover.[11] On the face of it, the credit cards looked like an out and out bribe by Pacolli, paid directly into the pockets of Yeltsin and his family, while the fact that they were paid out of a foreign bank account was a direct breach of a law banning Russian officials from holding such accounts. Yeltsin's daughter Tatyana had spent the most, running up bills worth $200,000 to $300,000 every year.[12] A further $1 million had apparently been spent by Yeltsin during an official visit to Budapest.[13]

By the standards of today's multi-billion-dollar corruption scandals, the sums are almost laughable. But in those days the equation was absolutely different. The balance of power had already fast been shifting away from the Kremlin to Primakov's White House. The old guard and the Communists were on the rise. In the aftermath of the financial crash, Yeltsin's popularity ratings were at an all-time low of 4 per cent. The Communist Party, which still dominated the Duma, scheduled impeachment hearings to put Yeltsin on trial for everything they deemed as sins of his rollercoaster rule: the disastrous war in Chechnya that had taken the lives of so many Russian soldiers, the dissolution of the Soviet Union, and what they claimed was the 'genocide' of the Russian population – the market reforms that had led to plummeting living standards and, they believed, to early deaths for millions of Russians. Revelations about the credit cards were intended to be the final straw. 'Primakov was meant to stand up in the Federation Council and tell the senators the president was a thief,' said Turover.[14]

The investigation also threatened to draw uncomfortably close to the much bigger sums that had washed through an oil exporter called International Economic Cooperation, or MES, that held accounts in Banco del Gottardo and was inextricably linked with the Kremlin reconstruction contract. MES had been granted contracts from the Russian government to sell more than 8 per cent of the country's total oil and oil-product exports, its annual turnover nearing $2 billion in 1995.[15] It had been active since 1993, when old-guard members of the Yeltsin government had sought to take back control of the oil trade, reinstating a system of special exporters, known as *spetsexportery*, through which all oil companies had to sell their oil.[16] It was an insider game that lined the pockets of a small and murky group of traders mostly close to the security services in the Yeltsin administration. MES had initially been created as a means of financing the restoration of the Russian Orthodox Church after decades of destruction and oppression under Soviet rule. But the billions of dollars in crude it was granted by the Russian government, export tariff-free, far surpassed any amount ever spent on the restoration of the Church.

MES was like a souped-up version of the slush funds created through Putin's oil-for-food scheme. None of its operations were transparent, and the lines between what was strategic and what could be spent on personal needs and bribes had become conveniently blurred. Mostly, it generated black cash used to make sure politics went the way of a faction of security men in the Kremlin supporting Yeltsin. 'The authorities always needed money. It would seem there is the state budget. But if you need finances to ensure a vote in parliament goes a certain way, you're not going to get the cash from the state budget,' Skuratov later told me.[17] MES's activities were closely tied to Mabetex and the Kremlin reconstruction project. When Pavel Borodin, the Kremlin property department chief, initially asked the government for funding for the Kremlin reconstruction project, he was told the budget had no cash.[18] So he asked for oil contracts to be sold through MES to finance it instead. But the decrees issuing the oil quotas for MES – first for two million tonnes, and then for another 4.5 million tonnes – were all classified.[19] No accounting of how the proceeds were spent was ever published. And then, as if the oil sales through MES had never been granted, the government made an official announcement that it was going to finance the Kremlin reconstruction by raising $312 million in international loans.[20] MES looked to have got away with as much as $1.3 billion in proceeds from the oil sales, and no one could explain where the money had gone.[21]

In the middle of it all was Sergei Pugachev, the Kremlin banker who would later flee to London and then Paris. A tall, gregarious expert in the art of backroom deals, he'd teamed up with Borodin while the bank he co-founded, Mezhprombank, was the main creditor of the Kremlin property department.[22] In those days the property department was a sprawling fiefdom, controlling billions of dollars' worth of property retained by the state following the Soviet collapse.[23] With Pugachev's help it doled out apartments and dachas, medical services and even holidays to members of the Yeltsin government. It was a Soviet-style patronage network that to all appearances extended to the Yeltsin Family too: Pugachev said he'd bought an apartment through Mezhprombank for Yeltsin's daughter Tatyana.[24]

Officials' wages were still paltry compared to what could be earned in business in the boom of Russia's market transition, and Pugachev insisted that what the property department did was the only way to keep state officials honest, and stop them from taking bribes. But essentially the department was the ultimate Kremlin slush fund, and it gave Borodin a position of great power, including the ability to make or break careers. 'People were queueing to see him,' said Pugachev. 'If you were a minister, you didn't get anything if Borodin didn't give you it. If you needed an apartment, a car, any resources you had to go to Borodin to get it all. It was a very influential position.'[25]

Pugachev would not explain the extent of his involvement with MES. But his Mezhprombank had helped bankroll the operation,[26] and he'd developed a deep friendship with the head of the Russian Orthodox Church, Patriarch Alexei II, working closely with him ever since his appointment.[27] Pugachev had nursed the Kremlin reconstruction project, and guided its every step. He was an adept of the Byzantine financing schemes of Yeltsin's Kremlin, and reaped a fortune for himself along the way. He'd somehow managed to set up a financial arm of Mezhprombank in San Francisco in the early nineties,[28] and spent large parts of the year in the United States. His direct access to the Western financial system further ingratiated him with the senior officials of Yeltsin's government. 'I could explain to them how the Western financial system worked,' he said. He rented the most expensive house in San Francisco, and later bought a fresco-covered villa in the south of France, high on the hills over-looking the Bay of Nice. He'd become close to the Yeltsin Family, in particular to Yeltsin's daughter Tatyana, when he'd worked as part of a team helping to secure Yeltsin's re-election in 1996, bringing in a team of American spin doctors who ran a US-style campaign that helped boost Yeltsin's flagging ratings and focused on the threat of a Communist return.[29]

All the while, Pugachev worked closely with Behdjet Pacolli, the owner of Mabetex. He personally oversaw the entire Kremlin recon-struction project, from the signing of the contract to the renovations themselves, he said. From the beginning, it was a lavish operation. Though he insisted that he tried to make sure the Kremlin got the best price possible, it seems that no expense was spared. Wood from twenty-three different types of tree was used to recreate the ornate patterns of the Kremlin Palace floor. More than fifty kilograms of pure gold was purchased to decorate the halls, and 662 square metres of the finest silk to cover the walls.[30] The Kremlin was to be transformed to its tsarist-era glory after decades of Communist rule in which all the treasures of pre-Revolutionary times – the mosaic floors, the precious ornamentation, the golden mirrors and chandeliers – had been ripped out and replaced with the plainest of decorations. Two thousand five hundred workers toiled day and night to create a palace fit for Russia's new tsar.[31] Every last detail had to pass under Pugachev's gaze. When Yeltsin asked why an urn had been placed outside his office, snapping 'We don't smoke here,' Pugachev had it swiftly removed. And when Yeltsin asked why the new floors creaked and squeaked, he gently explained that there were now caverns of cables beneath them to carry the Kremlin's top-secret communications.[32]

When it was all completed, visiting foreign leaders were awed by the grandeur they saw. US president Bill Clinton and German chancellor Helmut Kohl could not help but gasp when they were shown the vaulted gold-leafed ceilings of the Ekaterinsky Hall, dripping with golden chandeliers. 'And these people are asking for money from us?' Kohl remarked.[33]

The reconstruction had cost around $700 million,[34] at a time when Russia was receiving billions of dollars in foreign aid, supposedly to help it survive. But the financing that had been disbursed by the state for it was many times higher. The oil quotas MES had received alone were worth as much as $1.5 billion, while Yeltsin had signed off on an official decree for $300 million in foreign loans. Pugachev had also leaned on the first deputy finance minister, Andrei Vavilov, to approve an additional $492 million in guarantees for a treasury bill programme for the Kremlin property department – apparently another scheme to fund the reconstruction programme.[35] None of it was accounted for.

Pugachev had been aware of the credit cards for the Yeltsin Family soon after Pacolli issued them. 'I said to him, "Why did you do it?" He thought if he gave them the cards he would have them on a leash. He understood it was criminal, that this would mean the president was essentially taking bribes.'[36] He said he was also aware of bigger sums that had apparently gone to the Yeltsin Family. Later it emerged that $2.7 million had been transferred to two accounts in the Bank of New York in the Cayman Islands held in the name of Yeltsin's daughter Tatyana's then husband, Leonid Dyachenko.[37] A lawyer for the oil firm Dyachenko ran later said the funds were for work he'd done.

So when, on a cold grey morning in late January 1999, Swiss prosecutors sent in helicopters and several dozen armed vans to raid Pacolli's Mabetex offices in Lugano and left with a truckload of documents, it was, to put it mildly, a bit of a shock.[38] Pugachev and Borodin were immediately informed by Pacolli, and the news travelled like a poisoned dart to Yeltsin's daughter Tatyana, who in her father's absence was acting as unofficial head of state, and to the man who was later to become her husband, Valentin Yumashev, or 'Valya', as he was affectionately known, who until recently had been the Kremlin chief of staff.[39] For Pugachev it was a threat because of all the sums that had washed through MES. For Tatyana and Yumashev, it could potentially lead to the credit cards and other, larger, sums that appeared to have been transferred to private offshore accounts.

Quietly, without anyone being informed, the prosecutor general Skuratov had opened a criminal investigation into the possible siphoning of funds for the Kremlin reconstruction through Mabetex.[40] For the past few months he'd been working in the shadows with the Swiss prosecutors' office, but until the raid, no one had been aware that he'd launched an investigation. He'd received he first batch of documents on the case in the weeks immediately following the August 1998 default. To avoid interception, the Swiss prosecutor general Carla del Ponte had sent them to him via diplomatic pouch to the Swiss embassy in Moscow.[41] A few weeks later, towards the end of September, Skuratov held a secret meeting with del Ponte, skipping town from an official visit to Paris to meet her in Geneva. It was there that he first met Felipe Turover, the KGB informant who started it all, who soon made a clandestine visit to Moscow to give official witness testimony.[42] Only Skuratov's closest deputy was in the know.[43] He'd also consulted, on the quiet, with the old-guard KGB prime minister Yevgeny Primakov.[44] But once Skuratov sent the order for the raid in Lugano in January, the secret was out. 'All our efforts to ensure the confidentiality of the case collapsed,' he said. 'Under Swiss law, del Ponte had to show Pacolli the international order that was the basis for the raid. Of course he contacted Borodin immediately.'[45] Turover too was upset by the sudden end to the secrecy: 'She [del Ponte] didn't need to make so much noise. She didn't need to send all those helicopters. It was a signal to Moscow they had taken the books.'[46]

The raid marked the moment when Pugachev began a tense game of cat and mouse to bring about the removal of Yury Skuratov as prosecutor and end the case. It was then too that Pugachev – and the Yeltsin Family – began the chess game for their own survival that helped propel Vladimir Putin to power. It was the tipping point when they realised they were totally under siege.

'It took them just four days to get organised,' said Skuratov.[47]

*

When Pugachev looks back now and remembers it all, he says, parts of it seem like a blur: the constant telephone calls, the meetings stretching far into the night. Some of the dates are mixed up, remembered only by the time of year, how the weather was outside the window. But the meetings themselves, the important ones, are remembered distinctly, inscribed forever into his brain. Others are recorded in diary entries from those times.[48] Those were the days when Russia's future was decided, when Pugachev was trying to act so fast, in the belief that he was countering the threat of takeover by Primakov's alliance with the Communists – as well as saving his own and the Yeltsin Family's skin – that he didn't notice he was ultimately helping to usher in the KGB's return. Pugachev's story was the untold, inside account of how Putin came to power. It was the one the Yeltsin Family never wanted aired. At the time of the raid on Mabetex, Primakov's political star was rising, and an alliance he'd forged with the powerful Moscow mayor Yury Luzhkov and other regional governors was already threatening to bring down the curtain on the Yeltsin regime.

Skuratov's criminal case could bring them a still more powerful weapon.

For years, Pugachev had developed his own network within the Russian prosecutor's office. Like any powerful Russian institution, it was a den of vipers, where deputies jostled for position and collected *kompromat* on each other. Pugachev's particular ally was Nazir Khapsirokov, the wily head of the prosecutor's own property department, a sort of miniature version of the Kremlin department overseen by Borodin. With the power to issue apartments and other benefits to prosecutors, Khapsirokov, who was a master of intrigue, wielded the same ability to help make or break careers within the prosecutor's office as Borodin and Pugachev did in the Kremlin. 'In essence he was my guy in the prosecutor's office,' said Pugachev. 'He brought me all the information. He told me an uprising was being organised against Yeltsin. Then he brought me a tape. He told me, "Skuratov is on it with girls."'[49] Pugachev said that at first he didn't believe Khapsirokov: such a tape would be the ultimate *kompromat*, powerful enough to cost Skuratov his job and close down the Mabetex case.

Pugachev took the tape back to his office, but, unused to handling technology himself, he was unable to get it to play on his video recorder – he fumbled and fumbled with the settings, trying to find the right channel. Eventually he had to enlist his secretaries' help. As soon as they managed to switch it on, he regretted that they'd become involved. The grainy footage of the rotund prosecutor general cavorting naked on a bed with what appeared to be two prostitutes made for grim viewing. Pugachev cleared his throat, red-faced. But his secretaries made a copy of the tape nevertheless. Pugachev believes it was a decisive moment. 'If we hadn't made a copy, then none of this would have happened,' he said. 'History would have been different. Putin would not have been in power.'

He said he gave the original tape to Valentin Yumashev, Yeltsin's son-in-law and former chief of staff, who essentially still occupied the same position behind the scenes.[50] Yumashev was to take it to Nikolai Bordyuzha, a former general from the Russian border guards who'd recently been appointed official Kremlin chief of staff in

Yumashev's place. Bordyuzha was then to call in Skuratov and tell him about the tape, and that his behaviour did not befit the office of prosecutor general.

Always prone to overstating his role, Pugachev said that no one else knew how to act: 'They were all still shaking.' Bordyuzha awkwardly held the meeting with Skuratov, who agreed on the spot to resign. Bordyuzha then handed the tape to him, as if to indicate that it should all be forgotten among friends.

Instead of securing Skuratov's removal, that Kremlin meeting on the evening of February 1 led to an endless standoff. The position of prosecutor general had been protected under special laws seeking to enshrine its independence. For Skuratov's resignation to come into force, it had to be accepted by the Federation Council, the upper chamber of parliament. But many of the senators in the Council at that time were already aligning themselves with Primakov and Moscow's mayor Yury Luzhkov against the Kremlin. They were intent on protecting Skuratov. While he disappeared from sight for weeks, apparently to receive treatment at the Central Clinical Hospital, the Council stalled on putting his resignation up for a vote.

By that time the Yeltsin Family was dealing with the beginnings of a potential coup. Just a few days after the January raid on Mabetex, Primakov had laid down the gauntlet with a public challenge to Yeltsin's hold on power. With the backing of parliament he announced a political non-aggression pact, ostensibly to end the mounting tension between the Communist-led Russian Duma and the Kremlin.[51] The Duma was to agree to drop its impeachment hearings and set aside its constitutional right to topple the government with a no-confidence vote, at least until the parliamentary elections at the end of the year. In return, Yeltsin would give up his right to dismiss both the Duma and the Primakov government. Yeltsin was scandalised by the proposal, which had been agreed and announced without his being informed at all. 'Because this all happened behind his back he was absolutely flabbergasted,' said Yumashev, who was still Yeltsin's most trusted envoy in those days.[52] 'The main thing was that Primakov was already not hiding from the people who worked with Yeltsin that he intended to be the next president.' Making matters worse, Primakov had also proposed that Yeltsin should be granted immunity from future prosecution for any illegal deeds he might have committed during his eight-year rule. It was as if he believed Yeltsin had already agreed to step down.

The friction between Primakov and the Yeltsin Family was immediate. Primakov had sent shivers down their spines when, hours before Skuratov was summoned to the Kremlin and told to consider resigning over the *kompromat* tape, Primakov had called for space to be freed in Russia's prisons for businessmen and corrupt officials.[53] 'We understood that if he really did come to power that he had in his head a totally different construct for the country,' said Yumashev.[54] And when the next day, in a final show of defiance just hours before his resignation was announced, Skuratov had sent prosecutors to raid the oil major Sibneft, it was a move clearly directed at them.[55] Suspicions had long circulated that relations between Sibneft and the Yeltsin Family were too close, that the company had been the basis for Boris Berezovsky to become the consummate insider oligarch. Sibneft had sold oil through two trading companies: one of them, Runicom, was owned by Berezovsky's associate Roman Abramovich; the other, a more obscure outfit known as Belka Trading, was owned and run by Tatyana's then husband, Leonid Dyachenko.[56] 'The raid on Sibneft was deadly dangerous for the Yeltsin Family,' said one close Berezovsky associate.[57] Clearly trying to contain the damage, they began trying to distance themselves from Berezovsky, who had become politically toxic for them.

Yumashev had already stepped down from his post as chief of staff in December.[58] He said he'd done so when he first realised that Primakov was aiming for the presidency, which went far beyond the bounds of their agreement when Yeltsin first forwarded him as prime minister. They'd intended for Primakov to be a caretaker prime minister while Yumashev and Yeltsin searched for a suitable successor to take over the presidency. 'It was my personal responsibility that Primakov was brought in,' said Yumashev. 'Now he was behaving in violation of all our agreements.'[59] There was also a suggestion that Yumashev's replacement as chief of staff with a security man, Nikolai

Bordyuzha, an officer from the border guards, was part of an effort to remove the taint of the Family from Yeltsin's rule.

Sergei Pugachev claimed that he took it upon himself to try to reach a deal behind the scenes with the Federation Council, to make sure Skuratov was eliminated from view.[60] But the politically powerful regional governors on the Council were consolidating around Primakov and Luzhkov against the Kremlin. In the meantime, the ever-rising tension over Skuratov's investigation was starting to reach the top layers of Yeltsin's Kremlin. Horrified at where it might lead, they began to drop away one by one. First, Yeltsin was hospitalised again, for a bleeding ulcer. Then Nikolai Bordyuzha wound up in the Central Clinical Hospital after apparently suffering a heart attack shortly to be joined there by Pavel Borodin, the earthy head of the Kremlin property department and the focus of the Mabetex probe.[61] The Kremlin was rapidly emptying, and in the apparent vacuum Skuratov slipped back to work.[62]

On March 9, more than a month after Skuratov was supposed to have departed, the Federation Council finally scheduled the vote on his resignation.[63] Yet still Pugachev's efforts to secure the governors' votes for his removal failed. On the day of the vote, March 17, Skuratov arrived unexpectedly to address the Council, and gave a blistering speech claiming he was under attack from powerful enemies close to the Russian president, and calling on the senators to reject his resignation.[64] They voted down his resignation almost unanimously.

Rumours of a tape compromising Skuratov had already wafted through the media. But, stung by the collapse of the vote, Yumashev and the still little-known Vladimir Putin, who the summer before had been appointed head of the FSB, took matters into their own hands, claimed Pugachev. They handed the copy of the tape to a federal TV channel, which then aired it to millions of viewers across the country, with little regard for the modesty of Skuratov or the feelings of his family. They just wanted him out. 'Skuratov is an idiot,' said Pugachev. 'We wanted to deal with it decently, but he dug in his heels.'[65]

It was then, Pugachev said, that he first began to really notice Putin. The day after the video was aired, Putin gave a press conference together with Sergei Stepashin, the country's interior minister, at which he vowed that the tape was authentic. In comparison to Putin's clear, insistent manner, Stepashin kept his eyes glued to the floor, as if embarrassed to be part of the show. Pugachev said it was then that he began to see Putin as someone he could rely on:[66] 'He spoke very coolly. He looked like a hero on TV. This was the first time I noticed. No one else was thinking of him then. But I thought, he looks good on TV. We'll make him president.'[67]

Despite everything, Skuratov was still in position, and was increasing the pressure over the Mabetex affair. On March 23, while Swiss prosecutor Carla del Ponte was visiting Moscow again, matters reached boiling point. Skuratov sent a team of prosecutors to seize documents from Borodin's property department, as well as to the Moscow offices of Mabetex.[68] The raid by a prosecutor on a Kremlin office was unprecedented. The Family – and Borodin and Pugachev – were in shock. The theatrics were already ominous, but the old guard had a further point to make. That same day, a leading Communist lawmaker, Viktor Ilyukhin, stepped up the pressure another notch, holding a press conference at which he claimed he'd received evidence that part of the $4.8 billion bailout loan granted to Russia by the International Monetary Fund at the height of the 1998 financial crisis had been siphoned off to companies linked to the Yeltsin Family, including $235 million through what looked to be an Australian bank, Bank of Sydney, to a company 25 per cent owned by Leonid Dyachenko.[69] The media furore reached fever pitch, with political analysts saying they were no longer sure whether Yeltsin could secure the support of the army.

Pugachev said he returned to the Federation Council to press for another vote on Skuratov's resignation.[70] But the former Communist senator who led it once again indicated that he had more powerful backers elsewhere. Pugachev then went to see Luzhkov, the Moscow mayor, whose voice was carrying ever greater weight with the senators of the upper chamber. But Luzhkov had been trying to stack the parliamentary vote against the Kremlin ever since the August financial crisis hit. He'd developed his own ambitions for power, said Yumashev: 'Luzhkov was working actively in the Federation Council.

He was telling the heads of the regions, "I will be president and I will give you this and do this for you. We are fighting the president, and the prosecutor general for us is a powerful resource." In essence, there was a fight for the future of the presidency.'[71] 'Luzhkov was boasting he had 40,000 guys from the Moscow interior ministry behind him, as well as the local FSB,' said Pugachev.[72] 'Primakov and Luzhkov had been working to get the support of tens of thousands across the mid-level of the army. This was starting to look like a real state coup.' One Russian tycoon close to Luzhkov said the Moscow mayor's political weight had indeed risen rapidly: 'Against the background of the flailing Yeltsin, it was clear he was the new centre of power. Marshals and generals began coming to him. They came to bow to the new tsar. They were asking for orders from him.'[73]

What happened next, Pugachev insists, was motivated by the best intentions. He said that he could not allow Primakov and his crew to come to power and endanger the freedoms of the Yeltsin years, and that he'd felt the stench of Soviet stagnation and corruption as soon as Primakov and his team had entered the White House: 'The first thing they did was ask for bribes. I'd spent so much effort making sure the democrats remained in power and the Communists were kept out,' he said, referring to his efforts in Yeltsin's 1996 re-election campaign. 'You need to understand that the Yeltsin Family were normal people. This was nothing compared to the corruption you see today. My idea was not to let it all collapse.'[74] But fears over the money trail Skuratov was pursuing and where it could lead undoubtedly weighed heavier still.

Skuratov had spent the morning of April 1 handing over a report to Yeltsin on what he said were the illegal Swiss bank accounts of twenty-four Russians.[75] By the evening, Yeltsin's Kremlin had launched another attempt to oust Skuratov from his post. Skuratov's deputy, Yury Chaika, and the chief military prosecutor Yury Demin were called in to the office of the Kremlin chief of staff, by then a Berezovsky associate named Alexander Voloshin, a slight, bearded economist.[76] There, Voloshin, together with Putin, Nikolai Patrushev, who'd risen with Putin through the St Petersburg KGB and had served for the past four years in senior positions in the FSB, and

Pugachev leaned on them to launch a criminal case against Skuratov, claimed Pugachev. They wanted him suspended for cavorting with the prostitutes.

Chaika and Demin were scared. 'They didn't understand why they were there. It was like a meeting of deaf and blind,' said Pugachev. 'They were both frightened. "How can we open a criminal case against the prosecutor general?" they said. They were looking at who was there at the meeting. Putin was no one then, Patrushev was no one. They looked at us and thought, "We'll end up outsiders, and then we'll be accused of organising a state coup." I could see this going through their heads. I understood this in five minutes. So I called them away individually.'

Pugachev said he went to a meeting room opposite Voloshin's office. First, he called in Chaika. 'I asked him, "What do you want to open a criminal case?" But I saw there was no chance. Then I called in Demin, and asked him, "Are you ready to be prosecutor general?"' Seeing that his offers of rich rewards and promotions in return for cooperation were having little effect, Pugachev asked them to at least explain in detail what would be needed to open a criminal case. 'We talked for six hours, going over it all. They said only a prosecutor general could launch a case against a prosecutor general. I said, "Look," to Chaika, "you are the first deputy and you will become the acting prosecutor general. You can open a case against the former prosecutor general." But he said, "No, the Federation Council has to sign off on it." I said that if there was no criminal case, the Federation Council wasn't going to sign off on it. And we went round and round in circles for hours. I understood that it was not possible to deal with them, that nothing was going to work out.'

It was already after midnight, and Pugachev was rapidly running out of options. He had one avenue left. In the small hours of the morning, he called the head of the Moscow city prosecutor's office at home. 'I said, "I need you." He said, "Yes, Sergei Viktorovich, what do you need?" I told him I couldn't tell him by phone. But he asked me again what the problem was. He said, "You have to tell me." So I sent one of my guys round to his house with a note.'[77] But the Moscow prosecutor appeared to have little desire to respond in person. Pugachev believes Chaika called him and warned him off. When Pugachev phoned him again a little while later, he advised Pugachev to call the prosecutor on duty for the night instead.

This man was Vyacheslav Rosinsky, a grey man in glasses who that night was in a terrible state. He had been drinking – his daughter had recently committed suicide, hanging herself in her flat, and he was still mourning the loss. But Pugachev sent a car to bring him into the Kremlin nevertheless. As Rosinsky was driven through the Kremlin gates, said Pugachev, 'he was flabbergasted. He had no idea where he was being taken. When he got to my office, he sat there in a drunken funk. He was very down. But I told him, "Look, it's all very simple. You can open a criminal case against the prosecutor general." I showed him the charge sheet' – which of course had been prepared in advance. 'He told me what I needed to change. And then he signed.'[78]

Pugachev began to think about what he could offer in return. 'I told him I couldn't make him deputy prosecutor general immediately. But he said, "That's all right. I don't want that. If possible, I'd like to be the prosecutor general of Moscow."' Pugachev told him he'd make it happen. Although in the end he couldn't pull it off, that didn't matter. The criminal case accused Skuratov of abusing his position, and led to his immediate suspension by Yeltsin. His position was undermined when the prostitutes on the tape testified that they were paid for by a relative of a businessman and banker who'd been under investigation by Skuratov.

For a while, Skuratov still fought tooth and nail against his suspension. He slammed the tape as a fake, and said the criminal case was a political stitch-up aimed at preventing him from investigating corruption at the top of the Kremlin. He said it had been launched illegally – and the Moscow military prosecutors' office, called in to investigate, agreed. The Federation Council rejected his resignation again in a second vote, even after the criminal case had been launched. Voloshin, the recently-appointed chief of staff, gave a disastrous speech, stumbling and stammering over his lines as he was heckled by senators. The Kremlin's loss for a second time was heralded in all the newspapers the next day as signalling the end of

Yeltsin's power. 'Today, April 21 1999, presidential power in Russia collapsed,' said one leading governor.[79]

Primakov and his coalition of the Communist-led Duma and regional governors in the Federation Council – as well as the KGB men propelling the Mabetex case – looked to have the Family on the rails. But at some point, it seems they went too far. Pugachev said he tried to frighten Luzhkov and Primakov into backing down with threats that they'd be charged with sponsoring a state coup, while agreeing with Yumashev that he could offer Luzhkov the prime ministership just in case.[80] But Pugachev's manoeuvrings would never have amounted to anything had not Yeltsin returned to the political scene and roared.

For months Yeltsin had been in and out of hospital, further weakening his position in relation to Primakov, who in his absence was seen to have taken over the reins of power. But by April he'd gathered his strength for a final showdown. Just three days before the Duma was scheduled to begin impeachment hearings, Yeltsin, with an animal-like instinct for survival and a penchant for dramatic political gambits, decided it was time to act. He called Primakov to the Kremlin and told him he was fired. He was to be replaced by Sergei Stepashin, the interior minister, who'd been a close Yeltsin ally since the early days of the democratic movement and had served as one of the earliest heads of the FSB. Though the media had long speculated that Yeltsin might make such a move, it still came as a shock. Yeltsin had waited till the final moment. 'He understood that if he waited three more days it could be too late,' said Pugachev.[81] 'The Duma was absolutely unprepared,' said Yumashev. 'Many of our colleagues in the Kremlin considered it was suicide, that we would turn the Duma even more against us. But in fact the opposite happened. We showed all the strength of Yeltsin. He was absolutely calmly firing such a powerful force as Primakov, and the Duma was cowed by this show of strength.'[82] There was nothing Primakov could do, and his dismissal took the wind out of the Duma's sails.[83] Amid fears that Yeltsin could dissolve parliament, the impeachment vote collapsed just days later.

The KGB's Plan A had failed. 'Primakov should have been president in this scheme,' sighed Turover. 'During the second Federation Council vote on Skuratov, he was meant to stand up and say, "The president is a thief." He was meant to present the evidence. It would have been enough. The impeachment hearings had already been scheduled. It would have been enough for him to stand up and say, "I have the legitimate power to end all this." He had all the proof. But he didn't have the balls. At the last moment, he lost his nerve.'[84]

Though Skuratov insisted that he had never been playing a political game, that he was just seeking to bring an end to corrupt dealings in the Kremlin, he also understood all too well that Primakov could have finished Yeltsin's rule: 'There were two centres of power then. On the one hand there was the legislative power – the Federation Council and the government of Russia, led by Primakov and the Moscow mayor's office. And then there was Yeltsin at the top of power, and the Family on the other side. And of course, if the Federation Council and Primakov had agreed and put on the pressure, the Family would have crawled away. Everyone would have supported Primakov. The secret services would have supported him. The Family would have scuttled away like cockroaches. And Yeltsin, due to health reasons, would have transferred the presidential powers to Primakov, and the country would have been different. But Primakov . . . he is a very careful person. Perhaps he was not decisive enough. He did not fight for the country to the end.'[85]

Plan B

Yevgeny Primakov had always been a man of consensus, a consummate diplomat who did not like to rock the boat. Already in his seventieth year, he stepped for a while into the shadows, appearing to concede a temporary defeat. Yeltsin's Kremlin, it seemed, had won breathing space.

But if Primakov had been the KGB's Plan A to take back power, another opportunity was lying in wait. Whether by coincidence or by design, a combination of legal threats, fears, rivalries and pure political calculation came together, and led to the takeover of Russia by a far more ruthless generation of KGB men. The Family had been stuck in the mindset that Primakov could only be replaced by someone from the security services. 'After Primakov, it was not possible to appoint a liberal,' said Yumashev. 'It had to be someone that the Duma – and society – would see as a strong figure, like Stepashin, who was a general.'

But Sergei Stepashin was probably the most liberal of all the leaders of the Russian security services – he'd even joined the progressive Yabloko Duma political party. Despite a background serving in the interior ministry in Soviet times, he was a historian by training, and had long been close to Yeltsin. They'd been working together ever since Yeltsin entrusted him to lead a federal investigation into the KGB's role in the failed August coup. Yet for Yumashev and Pugachev, Stepashin had never been more than an interim candidate. Stepashin, Pugachev said, was *vyaly* – the Russian word for weak. He did not believe Stepashin was decisive enough to take the actions necessary to protect them: 'It seemed to me he was someone who would make compromises with the Communists.'[86] Yumashev said that he too began to entertain doubts about Stepashin. They were jealous of Stepashin's close relationship with Anatoly Chubais, the former Kremlin chief of staff and privatisation tsar who'd long been their rival for Yeltsin's affections. Until late June, part of the Yeltsin Family had been toying with the idea of another candidate, Nikolai Aksyonenko, the railways minister, who they believed would more strongly defend their interests. But Yeltsin soon took a strong dislike to him.[87]

In the background, said Pugachev, he'd long been advancing his own candidate, the man he believed to be the safest, most loyal pair of hands. He was backing Vladimir Putin, who he'd first seen as a potential successor when he handled the tape of Skuratov with the prostitutes so coolly. They'd first met briefly in St Petersburg in the early nineties, and had got to know each other better when Putin was appointed as Borodin's deputy in the Kremlin property department. There, they'd worked together every day, said Pugachev. Pugachev's Mezhprombank was involved in raising funds for the foreign property department Putin headed (though Pugachev declined to specify exactly what the bank did).[88] From his office in a small room of the former Central Committee's headquarters on Old Square, Putin was tasked with rooting through the vast foreign holdings Russia had inherited on the Soviet Union's collapse. There were the palatial buildings of the special trade representative offices through which the lifeblood of the USSR's export-based economy had run. There were the embassies and the strategic military bases, the arms depots and the secret safe houses of the KGB. Many of these holdings had been looted in the chaos of the collapse by the KGB and organised crime. They were meant to be on the balance sheet of the ministry of foreign affairs, but no accounting had ever been done. Putin's job was to bring these properties back onto the books, but it's not clear if he ever succeeded in doing so. The foreign property department was at the heart of the strategic interests of the KGB, and while Pugachev claimed that Putin had no inkling of the slush-fund machinations through Mabetex, or MES, the oil trader granted billions of dollars in export deals, it's far from clear whether that could have been the case.

They'd stayed close as Putin continued his dizzying rise through the Kremlin, first as head of the Control Department, and then when he was anointed head of the FSB in July 1998. All the while, said Pugachev, Putin had been his protégé. His charm lay in the fact that he knew him as someone he could give orders to: 'He was as obedient as a dog.'[89]

Initially, Yumashev claimed, he'd 'had no idea about Putin' as a candidate, and had pushed Aksyonenko instead.[90] But he had always been aware of Putin's abilities. As Kremlin chief of staff, he'd overseen and approved each of the key moments of Putin's rise, and they'd forged a close relationship. By March 1997 Putin was a deputy head of the Kremlin administration. Yet he'd always appeared modest, said Yumashev, and, unlike most other officials, uninterested in furthering his career: 'Among my deputies, he was one of the strongest. He always worked brilliantly. But at one point he came to me and said he wanted to step down. I asked him not to go. He told me, "I have sorted out this work. I would like to find something new."'[91] Soon after, in May 1998, Yumashev promoted Putin to the third most powerful post in the Kremlin: first deputy chief of staff in charge of the regions, a role that brought him into more frequent contact with Yeltsin. And then, just two months later, Yumashev moved Putin sideways to head the FSB.

This was the first sign of Yumashev's – and the Family's – absolute trust in Putin. In those days, just a month before the August 1998 financial crisis, clouds were already fast gathering over the Yeltsin administration. The country was besieged by a series of miners' strikes over unpaid wages, which were beginning to spread into the nuclear sector too. The miners were blockading the Trans-Siberian Railway, a vital artery of the Russian economy. Putin's predecessor as FSB chief had been seen as close to the Communists, and that summer, as the strikes began to spread and the threat of economic crisis loomed, while parliament was already beginning to speak of impeachment, it was of paramount importance for Yeltsin's Kremlin to have its own man in charge of the security services.[92] The fact that Putin was only a lieutenant colonel rather than a general was whitewashed, and he was dubbed the first civilian head of the FSB instead. In that summer of crisis and murk, they got away with it.

Yumashev insisted that he'd always been convinced of Putin's democratic credentials. What struck him most, he said, was his dogged loyalty to his former mentor and boss, Anatoly Sobchak, the former St Petersburg mayor. One incident in November 1997 stood out for him above all others: 'The reason why I so strongly recommended him [as head of the FSB] was because there was an episode when he worked as head of the Control Department and he came and said, "Sobchak is going to be arrested, and I have to save him." He said, "I have to take him out of the country because the *siloviki* – the prosecutors, the interior ministry and the FSB – should arrest him in the next two or three days." It was absolutely clear to him and to me that there was a 50:50 chance he would be caught. I told him Vladimir Vladimirovich, "You understand that if you are caught you will lose your position, and it's possible you will never find work again. You are going against the law."'[93]

Putin, however, held his ground. He insisted the case against Sobchak was fabricated, just part of the smear campaign launched by the old-guard security men in 1996 ahead of Sobchak's bid for re-election in St Petersburg because they hated him ideologically. Then Sobchak had been targeted by a criminal investigation over bribery allegations.[94] But what neither Putin – nor Yumashev when he recounted the tale – spoke of was the risk that the arrest of Sobchak could lead to Putin himself. There was no telling where it might lead if a rival faction had it in for him.[95]

Putin had arranged for Sobchak to be spirited away out of hospital on a national holiday, when no one was watching. He'd whisked him off on a private jet, which one insider said belonged to his close ally Gennady Timchenko, the alleged former KGB operative who'd won a monopoly on exports through the St Petersburg oil terminal. When Putin arrived back in the Kremlin after a brief absence, Yumashev was deeply relieved: 'For two or three days I was between worry and horror, because it would have been such a grandiose scandal if the FSB or the MVD [the interior ministry] had caught Putin and Sobchak when they were crossing the [Russian] border. For me it was important that a person was ready to sacrifice his career for justice, and when he returned I told Boris Nikolaevich [Yeltsin] of this.'[96]

Yumashev claimed that another event had also imprinted itself on his perception of Putin. In late 1998, during Primakov's tenure as prime minister, Putin had called Yumashev from his car and told him he'd just been with Primakov, and wanted to meet urgently. 'When he arrived, he told me, "There is a very strange situation." He said, "Primakov called me and asked me as head of the FSB to begin wiretapping Yavlinsky."' Grigory Yavlinsky was a leader of the liberal opposition in the Duma who had spoken out about corruption in Primakov's cabinet. Primakov had apparently told Putin he needed him to bug him because, he claimed, Yavlinsky was an American spy. 'Putin told me that he'd refused him, because this is absolutely unacceptable. He'd said that if we return the FSB to Soviet times when it went after dissidents in politics, then we will destroy the security services. He said that if Yeltsin shared Primakov's position, he was ready to resign over it.'[97]

None of these sentiments fitted in any way with Putin's activities as deputy mayor in St Petersburg, when a ruthless alliance of the

KGB and organised crime ruled the roost. Nor did they fit with Putin's activities in Dresden, running illegals against the West. But still Yumashev claimed to have taken him seriously. Even now, after everything that has followed in Putin's twenty-year rule, Yumashev said he has stuck to this view: 'I am 100 per cent sure he was not playing me. In this case Putin really would have resigned, because he was absolutely aggressively against this. But of course Boris Nikolaevich would never have given the go-ahead.'[98]

Yumashev believed there was no way that during Putin's time as deputy mayor of St Petersburg, Anatoly Sobchak's ardent proclamations for democracy could have failed to rub off on him. But he appeared not to know, or not to want to know, the details of how St Petersburg had been actually run.

Putin was a past master at recruiting. In the KGB it had been his speciality, according to one former close associate.[99] 'In KGB school, they teach you how to make a pleasant impression on the people you are speaking with. Putin learned this art to perfection,' said a senior Russian foreign-intelligence operative. 'In a small circle of people he could be extremely charming. He could charm anyone. And as a deputy, he was extremely effective. He carried out any tasks quickly and creatively, without worrying much about the methods.'[100]

If Yumashev was naïve, then in that year of intense pressure and attack on the Yeltsin Family from Primakov, so too perhaps was Boris Berezovsky, the wily, fast-talking oligarch who'd become the epitome of the insider dealing of the Yeltsin years, when a small coterie of businessmen bargained behind the scenes for prime assets and government posts. The former mathematician had earned his fortune running trading schemes for AvtoVAZ, the producer of the boxy Zhiguli car that symbolised the Soviet era, at a time when the car industry was steeped in organised crime. He'd survived an assassination attempt that decapitated his driver. Yet somehow he'd still found his way into the Kremlin. He'd hung out drinking tea in the office of Yeltsin's chief bodyguard, Alexander Korzhakov, and then found his way into the graces of the president himself and his Family. All the while he cultivated ties among the leaders of Chechen separatists. Berezovsky's LogoVAZ club, in a restored mansion in downtown Moscow, became an informal centre for government decision-making. At the height of his powers in 1996, the Yeltsin government's 'young reformers' and oligarchs would gather there through the night to plot counter-coups against the hard-liners.

By 1999, however, Berezovsky was politically toxic. His relations with members of the Yeltsin Family had come under target. Not only had the raid on the Sibneft oil major he'd helped to create threatened to expose dealings with the oil-trading company of Yeltsin's daughter Tatyana's then husband, Leonid Dyachenko, there was also a criminal investigation into his business operations through Aeroflot, the state's national airline, in which he held a significant stake, and where the husband of Yeltsin's second daughter, Elena, was president. The Family were seeking to jettison their relations with him. Rumours surfaced that his security company had been bugging the Family's offices, and he'd been ousted in April from his Kremlin post as executive secretary of the Commonwealth of Independent States, as the loose alliance of former Soviet republics was then known. Yumashev, for one, had tired of dealing with him. 'There was only so many times he could hear Berezovsky telling him he didn't understand,' said one close Berezovsky associate.[101] 'He began to get on his nerves.' Berezovsky seemed to have been abandoned by all. And so when Vladimir Putin turned up at the birthday party of his wife Lena early in 1999, he was deeply touched by the show of solidarity when everyone else had their knives out for him.

Putin's gesture helped Berezovsky set aside qualms about his KGB past.[102] Initially, he'd chiefly supported Aksyonenko, the railways minister, as Yeltsin's successor – his relations with Putin had chilled distinctly that year after Putin, as FSB chief, ordered the arrest and March 1999 jailing of the FSB officer closest to him, Alexander Litvinenko. But, faced with the constant threat of arrest, Berezovsky eventually fell in line behind Putin's candidacy. Later, always a myth-maker about the extent of his influence in Yeltsin's Kremlin, Berezovsky liked to claim that it was he who had helped bring Putin to power, by proposing him to Yumashev as FSB chief in the summer of 1998. He said he'd then held secret meetings with Putin in the lift of the FSB's imposing Lubyanka headquarters, where they'd discussed Putin possibly running for the presidency.[103] The two men had met only fleetingly prior to that, when Berezovsky visited St Petersburg in the early nineties and Putin assisted him in opening his LogoVAZ car dealership there. That was a business riven with the mafia, and Berezovsky must have known about Putin's links with organised crime there, said one Berezovsky associate: 'Putin helped him in all questions connected to the sale of LogoVAZ cars in St Petersburg. This business was a mafia business, a bandit business, and in Moscow Berezovsky organised this with the help of Chechens and the corrupt bureaucracy. In St Petersburg he organised this with Putin's help. Therefore he understood everything about his connections and his situation. He wasn't a child.'[104]

But although Berezovsky was undoubtedly to play an enormous role in helping secure the defeat of Primakov later that year, he had never known or worked as closely with Putin as Pugachev had. And according to one of his closest associates, Alex Goldfarb, he never claimed to have been the one to introduce Putin to Yeltsin's daughter Tatyana, or to suggest him as a replacement for Stepashin, or as Yeltsin's successor.[105]

*

The moment everything changed came in the middle of July, in the dog days of the Moscow summer, when the Kremlin was emptying and many, including Yeltsin, were away on vacation. It was then that the Swiss prosecutors presented the Yeltsin Family with another shock. They'd thought the Mabetex case had been dealt with – Skuratov had been suspended from his position for several months by then, as a result of the criminal case Pugachev had helped open. But the Swiss were still active – and so were Skuratov's deputies. On July 14, the Swiss prosecutors announced that they'd opened a criminal case into money laundering through Swiss bank accounts by twenty-four Russians, including Pavel Borodin and other senior Kremlin officials, and alleged that the funds may have been obtained through 'corruption or abuse of power'. When asked whether the list included Yeltsin's daughter Tatyana, one of the Swiss investigating magistrates answered, 'Not yet.'[106] It was clear that they were circling, and according to Pugachev, a fresh sense of panic set in.

The Geneva prosecutors said their Russian partners were still conducting a parallel inquiry. It was then, Pugachev said, that he decided to act: 'We needed someone who would be able to deal with it all. Stepashin wasn't going to do it. But there was Putin with the FSB, the Security Council, Patrushev. There was an entire team.'[107] Pugachev remembered Putin's coolness when he handled the Skuratov tape, and said he decided to introduce him to Yeltsin's daughter Tatyana, who in those days was still the main channel to the president. As if on cue, a day later Putin's FSB had taken action, opening a criminal investigation into the construction business owned by the wife of the Yeltsins' political opponent, the Moscow mayor Yury Luzhkov.[108] Pugachev had first sought to undermine Tatyana's view of Stepashin, demonstrating to her how, unlike Putin, he had failed to vigorously defend the tape of Skuratov and the prostitutes after it had been aired on TV. 'I told her, "Tanya, look. You need a person who will save you. Stepashin will make compromises with the Communists. He will compromise us in front of our eyes. Look at how he is now."'[109] Then he said he'd taken Putin from his office in the Kremlin's Security Council to her. 'I told her Putin was a much clearer person. He is young and listens attentively. Stepashin doesn't listen any more.' Pugachev claimed that Yumashev later persuaded her to go to her father and convince him to make the switch.

Yumashev insisted, however, that Pugachev played no role in Putin's rise, while the criminal case in Switzerland and the investigation in the US had never posed a threat at all: 'Of course, it was total rubbish that this was dangerous,' Yumashev said. 'The only thought I had – and Voloshin shared this view, and Yeltsin too – was that power was being given to a person who mentally, ideologically and politically was exactly the same as us. We'd worked together in the Kremlin as one team. There was an absolutely common understanding with Putin on how the world should work and how Russia should work.'[110]

But these were the days when everything was decided. Stepashin's world – and the chances for a more liberal administration – were to be swept away. There was no pressing reason to risk replacing Stepashin with Putin, a relatively unknown official, unless the Yeltsin Family needed someone they considered more loyal – and more ruthless – because of the risk presented by the escalating Mabetex probe. Yumashev tried to explain the switch with lame-sounding reasons, for instance that Stepashin was under the thumb of his wife. He liked to tell long, contorted tales of the many arguments he'd made in those days for why they had to act quickly, before it was too late to replace Stepashin, who just was not the right fit. But no explanation other than the rising panic over the Swiss probe made any sense. This was the motive the Yeltsin Family never wanted told, for it revealed how the Family's rush to save itself was the inadvertent cause of Putin's rise and its world's demise. They needed a tough guy to protect their interests, and got more than they bargained for. In his authorised narrative, Yumashev didn't want to give credence to any of this. Pugachev was the narrator who strayed from the Kremlin's official version, and appears to have told the truth.[111]

At first Yeltsin had hesitated. But in the last week of July, Chechen rebels began to mount armed attacks on the border with Dagestan, the mountainous region neighbouring the breakaway Chechen republic, and, Yumashev claimed, Stepashin appeared to struggle to deal with it.[112] Before he made his first trip as prime minister to Washington, DC, on July 27, he'd publicly vowed that there would be no new war against Chechnya. But almost every day in the week that followed his return, clashes on the border broke out. At the weekend, on August 8, there was a massive escalation in fighting as two to three hundred armed Chechen insurgents seized control of two villages in Dagestan. Yeltsin's efforts to retain him as prime minister were running out. Even then, at the last minute Anatoly Chubais, who worked closely with Stepashin, had nearly derailed Pugachev and the Yeltsin Family's plans when he'd got wind that a replacement was being lined up. Chubais tried to reach Yeltsin at his dacha the weekend before the announcement was to be made, and to talk him out of it. But he only reached the security guard, who promptly relayed his request to Pugachev.

Furious at this attempt to undermine his plans, Pugachev said he made sure the security guard never told Yeltsin about Chubais' call: 'I'd worked constantly for the last eight months to get Putin into power. I turned Putin from being a total nobody who'd been head of the FSB into this, a real pretender for power. I'd monitored and checked ceaselessly. And where was Chubais when we had to deal with the Mabetex scandal?' he raged. 'Where was he? What did he do? He'd completely disappeared.'[113]

Even then, when they all met in Yeltsin's office early that Monday, August 9, Yeltsin had still hesitated, said Pugachev. Stepashin refused to step down without a vote by parliament, and Yeltsin had left his office to think again. 'I remember the whole story,' said Pugachev. 'Stepashin told Yeltsin Putin was no one, that he would not stand for it. But everything had already been decided. It was a rare case when Yeltsin decided nothing himself. It was a matter of life and death.'[114]

When Yeltsin finally made the announcement later that day, the nation was stunned by the identity of their new prime minister. Putin was a little-known bureaucrat, a grey figure who rarely appeared on the news. The country's news outlets scrambled to put together biographies of him. What shocked the nation most of all was that Yeltsin openly named him as the man he hoped would succeed him as president, announcing in a televised address: 'I decided to name the person who in my opinion will be able to consolidate society based on the broadest political forces, to ensure the continuation of reforms in Russia. He will be able to unite those around him who, in the twenty-first century, have the task of renewing Russia as a great nation. This person is the secretary of the Security Council, the director of the Federal Security Service, Vladimir Vladimirovich Putin.'[115]

Putin had accomplished the most vertiginous leap of his dizzying career. The Russian parliament was in shock, although most believed he was a nobody who later could easily be defeated, and this helped squeeze his appointment as prime minister through a confirmation vote.[116] By that time, Primakov had re-emerged from the political sidelines to form a bold new alliance with Yury Luzhkov, the powerful Moscow mayor, for the upcoming parliamentary elections. By comparison, said Yumashev, 'Putin looked like a child.'[117] But many in the Kremlin still worried that Yeltsin had gone too far in naming him as his preferred successor. 'Many of our colleagues considered that Yeltsin categorically should not do this – because Putin was an unknown entity and Yeltsin only had 5 per cent political support. They thought that after such an announcement Putin would never win,' Yumashev said.

To the outside world, it seemed the Yeltsin Family were taking an enormous risk. But other plans were afoot. An escalation of a Russian military offensive against Chechnya had already been under discussion, Stepashin said later.[118] Most important for the bureaucrats and spin doctors inside the Kremlin was to transform the awkward-seeming candidate they'd been presented with into a force to be reckoned with. At first glance, the material didn't seem very promising. People still talked over Putin in meetings. The plan was to cast him in the image of one of the most popular fictional TV heroes from Soviet times. He was to be a modern-day Max Otto von Shtirlitz, an undercover spy who'd gone deep behind enemy lines to infiltrate the command networks of Nazi Germany. Putin would be the *kandidat rezident*, the spy candidate, a patriot who would restore the Russian state.[119] Their main task was to distinguish him from the Yeltsin Family – so that the public would see him as independent. His youth, cast against the ageing and ailing Yeltsin, was meant to give him an immediate advantage, while Kremlin-linked TV channels sought to portray him acting decisively against the separatist incursion into Dagestan. In the background, Berezovsky was perfectly capable of trying to organise a small victorious war to help spur Putin's vault to power, two of his close associates said.[120]

In the rush to help engineer his ascent, Pugachev had paid little attention to warning signs of Putin's duplicity. That July, when Pugachev had attempted to deal with the fallout of the Swiss prosecutors' case, holding talks in the Kremlin late into the night with Putin, Patrushev and Voloshin to try to persuade the acting prosecutor general, Yury Chaika, to step down in favour of an even more loyal ally, Putin had apparently played a double game. Chaika initially resisted, only to agree a few days later after separate talks with Pugachev, during which he warned him that Putin's allegiance to the Kremlin might not be clear-cut: 'With Putin you need to be careful,' he said. 'When you all met with me in the Kremlin and tried to persuade me for six hours to step down, Putin accompanied me out of the Kremlin after it was all finished. He told me I was right not to agree. He told me if I did it would be a crime.'[121]

But Pugachev promptly forgot Chaika's warning. The scandal over Mabetex was still refusing to die down despite all the manoeuvrings, and at the end of August calamity hit, when details of how the probe was linked to the Yeltsin Family finally broke into the open. The Italian newspaper *Corriere della Sera* published an article that disclosed how Mabetex's owner Behdjet Pacolli had issued the credit cards to the Yeltsin Family and covered the payments for them.[122] The paper said the Swiss prosecutors suspected the payments were bribes in return for the Kremlin renovation contract. It named Felipe Turover as the central witness for these claims.

The news hit Yeltsin's Kremlin hard.[123] Till then, only they – and the prosecutor – had known how far the probe might go. Pugachev once again scurried to assist. 'Tanya was totally flabbergasted when the press reports appeared,' he said. 'But I promised her I would make it go away.'[124] He invited the Yeltsin Family to open accounts at his own Mezhprombank, and then told the media that the credit cards in question had first been issued years ago, through his bank. The move was designed to confuse the press and remove questions over whether Yeltsin had broken the law by holding a foreign bank account.[125]

In Pugachev's eyes, the whole case was unfair. Yeltsin, he said, had never even understood what money was. On one occasion, drunk, he'd asked his chief bodyguard, Alexander Korzhakov, to buy him vodka, and had pulled a wad of notes out of a safe in his room. This, said Pugachev, was where he'd kept the royalties for the books he'd written with Yumashev. Yeltsin had pulled out $100. 'He asked Korzhakov if this was enough. He had no idea what money was, or how much things were worth. He never handled this himself.' Almost no money had ever been spent on the credit card issued in Yeltsin's name – only some for an official visit to Budapest. His daughters, however, had spent considerably more. 'Tanya could spend $100,000

a month on furs,' said Pugachev. But none of them understood
what a credit card was, or how it worked or what it signified: 'They
would just go out with this piece of plastic and use it to buy things.
They didn't understand that someone had to pay for it.'[126]

Yumashev said they'd been convinced that the cards were financed
by Yeltsin's royalties from his memoirs. Borodin, the Kremlin
Property Department chief, had told them so, he said: 'They absolutely sincerely spent this money believing it was from the royalties
of the books. But I don't doubt that this stupidity of Borodin could
be used by all kinds of forces against us, including Primakov and
Skuratov.'[127]

Clouds were looming ever larger on the horizon, and the money
trail had the potential to go further still. On the first anniversary
of the August 1998 financial crisis, the *New York Times* broke the
news of yet another Russian financial scandal.[128] US law-enforcement
agencies were investigating billions of dollars in suspected
money-laundering transactions through the Bank of New York by
Russian organised crime. A month later, reports of a link to the
Yeltsin Family emerged. Investigators had traced the $2.7 million
transfer to two accounts held with the Bank of New York in the
Cayman Islands, held in the name of Tatyana's then husband, Leonid
Dyachenko.[129] Later, documents from the Swiss prosecutors' office
showed that they were also investigating a much bigger transfer
through Banco del Gottardo to an account beneficially owned by
Tatyana.[130] No charges were ever pressed and Yumashev said any
suggestion that Tatyana had ever received such funds was 'absolute
lies'.

But amid the mounting tension and the scramble to save themselves from attack, Pugachev had brushed aside a warning from
Putin's former mentor Anatoly Sobchak, who'd told him he was
making a great mistake: 'I thought maybe he was jealous. But of
course he knew it all.'[131] He'd forgotten about Berezovsky's own qualms
when he told him, 'Sergei, this is the biggest mistake of your life.
He comes from a tainted circle. A *komitetchik* cannot change. You
don't understand who Putin is.'[132] He'd forgotten, too, about his own
deep hatred of the KGB, about how he'd run and dodged from them

long ago when he was trading currency as a teenager in the tourist
hotels of Leningrad. He'd forgotten Chaika's warning, and nobody
– not even Pugachev – noticed that Putin still met frequently with
Primakov, who was meant to be the arch-enemy, after he'd been fired
as prime minister. It turned out that Putin had taken the entire top
ranks of the FSB to Primakov's dacha, where they toasted him, and
in October that year Putin attended Primakov's seventieth birthday
celebrations and gave a speech lauding him.[133]

Pugachev and the Yeltsin Family had closed their eyes to all this.
They wanted above all to believe that Putin was one of them. That
summer of intensifying investigations had left them desperately
seeking a successor from among the security men who could protect
them. Somehow they came to believe that Putin was the only candidate capable of that. Increasingly impaired by illness, Yeltsin seemed
forced to go along with them. Ever since Primakov had been
appointed prime minister in the wake of the August 1998 financial
crisis, the Yeltsin Family had believed there was no alternative to
appointing someone from outside the *siloviki* as a replacement. In
the financial collapse, liberal ideals and the young reformers among
whom Yeltsin had once been searching for his successor had become
tainted. 'We swallowed so much freedom we were poisoned by it,'
Yumashev later said wryly.[134]

Putin's lip service to market and democratic principles had helped
the Family believe he would continue their course. But paramount
in their calculations had been his daredevil operation to whisk his
former mentor Anatoly Sobchak out of Russia and away from the
threat of arrest. 'This show of loyalty was counted . . . as a weighty
factor in choosing him,' said Gleb Pavlovsky, a Kremlin adviser and
spin doctor at the time.[135] The Family knew that, much more than
Stepashin, Putin was ruthless enough to break the law to protect his
allies if necessary.

Besides, Pugachev said, Putin seemed loyal and obedient. He still
thought of him as someone who followed him like a dog, and still
identified him with Sobchak's liberal and democratic beliefs: 'My
feeling was that if he was close to Sobchak then he should be a
person of liberal views. I didn't study closely what he represented.'

What's more, Putin had seemed reluctant to take on the post of prime minister. He had had to twist his arm, he said, and tell him it was not for long, only till the situation was stable.

What Pugachev didn't know was that Putin had once worked closely with one of the main players in the attempt to overthrow the Yeltsin regime. He wasn't aware that Felipe Turover, the KGB officer behind the leaks on Mabetex and the Yeltsin accounts, with connections to the top of the KGB's legendary black-ops department, had helped Putin set up the oil-for-food barter scheme in St Petersburg.

He'd never heard the story Turover told me, about how after Yeltsin's chief bodyguard had allegedly given the order to eliminate Turover when his name was leaked to the Italian newspaper that August, Putin had gone to see his old associate, who was then in Moscow, warned him about the order and told him he should leave the country, fast: 'He told me to leave because he had an order from the president to finish me off. He told me I could leave under his guarantee.'

Pugachev didn't know that all the while, Putin had played all sides. 'He always kept his promises,' said Turover. 'He never worked for the Family against Primakov. And he only worked formally against Skuratov.'[136]

Pugachev also had little inkling that Putin could represent anything close to a Plan B of the KGB, after the Primakov takeover failed. He always claimed he thought of Putin as someone he could control. He didn't realise that he might have been lying to the Family when he appeared to support them. Putin 'deceived them', said Turover. 'Warfare is based on deception. This is the strategy of Sun Tzu. He wrote *The Art of War* 2,600 years ago,' referring to the ancient Chinese military treatise. 'Putin learned his judo lessons well.'

5

'Children's Toys in Pools of Mud'

Instead of falling to what they believed was a coup by forces from the Communist past, what the Yeltsin Family had in fact succumbed to was a creeping coup by the security men. Under siege from all sides, they'd had little choice but to reach an accommodation with the KGB.

'They had to find a compromise figure,' said one former senior KGB officer close to Putin.[1] 'There was a huge army of former and current law-enforcement officers who were all still in position. They needed a person who could smooth relations with this force after Yeltsin's departure. Their regime was under attack from all sides. They didn't have any choice. It was a forced decision based on the fact that they very much feared that the departure of Yeltsin from power could lead to a real counter-revolution and the loss of everything they'd achieved with such effort. It was a question of security and agreements. They thought Putin was a temporary figure they could control. The only person who was strongly against it was Chubais. He feared that Putin's background – his service in the KGB – would mean that he would not be a manageable puppet in the hands of the Family. His intuition did not let him down.'

For a long time, Putin has been portrayed as Russia's 'accidental president'. But neither his rise through the Kremlin nor his vault to the presidency seem to have had much to do with chance. 'When he was moved to Moscow they were already beginning to check his suitability,' said the close Putin ally from the KGB.[2] If, to the outside world, Russia under Yeltsin was a country of epochal change where the power of the security services had long been smashed, then inside Russia, beneath the surface, the security men were still a force to be reckoned with. Inside Yeltsin's Kremlin, and in second-tier posts across the country's institutions and companies, were representatives of the KGB, some of whom ten years before had backed efforts to bring the market to Russia, understanding all too well that the Soviet Union could not compete with the West under the planned economy. They had watched from the shadows as the reforms they began spiralled out of their control under Yeltsin's rule. They'd been left largely on the sidelines as the freedoms of the Yeltsin era led to the ever faster rise of the oligarchs, who by the mid-nineties had outpaced their former KGB masters. The freedoms had created a robber-style capitalism under which, in the end, the security men had been able to compromise Yeltsin and his family. With the market crash, their moment had come. Yeltsin and his family were vulnerable over the Mabetex accounts and their close business ties to Berezovsky, while the men behind the scenes in the Kremlin had long been planning a statist revanche.

'The institutions the security men worked in did not break down,' said Thomas Graham, the former senior director for Russia on the US National Security Council. 'The personal networks did not disappear. What they needed simply was an individual who could bring these networks back together. That was the future. If it hadn't been Putin, it would have been someone else like him.'[3]

The broader caste of security men behind the scenes in the Kremlin were seeking only to secure the property and economic gains that had been made in the move to the market. Inside the Kremlin, the prevailing conviction was that after the chaos of the Yeltsin years the new president, whoever he might be, had to represent a statist revanche, a revanche of the losers from the Yeltsin years – when state workers – teachers, doctors and law enforcement – had suffered most. 'We were looking for the glue for the pro-Kremlin coalition,' said Gleb Pavlovsky, the Kremlin adviser and spin doctor at the time.[4] 'A different style politician had to come to power, and complete the post-Soviet transition.'

'It was the KGB in any case that was going to take over the regime,' said Andrei Illarionov, the former presidential economic adviser.[5]

If Primakov, as Plan A, represented the threat of a Communist-style revanche and the very real risk that a combined Primakov–Luzhkov ticket could result in Yeltsin and his Family spending the rest of their years behind bars, then Putin was the *silovik* who was meant to save them, the charmer who'd spent his time assuring the Family he was progressive, that he was one of them. 'Putin is an outstanding politician, and he carried out a very successful operation to win the trust of the Family,' said Illarionov. 'Primakov was seen as the main enemy for Yeltsin. The security men accurately calculated that Yeltsin would not hand over power just like that.'[6]

But in their rush to secure their position, the Yeltsin Family were handing over the reins to a faction of younger KGB men who were to prove far more ruthless in their bid to gain power than any among Primakov's elder, more statesmanlike generation might have been. In the hurly burly of Kremlin intrigue and warring clans – even within the security services – they were handing over power to a clan of security men who'd forged their alliances in the violent battles of St Petersburg, who were far hungrier for power and who would stop at nothing to demonstrate their loyalty.

The Kremlin spin doctors worked incessantly to portray Putin as acting decisively against the Chechen incursions into Dagestan. But in the first month of his premiership, Putin's approval rating barely grew. He was still frequently described as colourless. He remained a grey and obscure bureaucrat, while Primakov's newly announced alliance with Luzhkov was gathering in force – one by one, Russia's powerful regional governors were lining up to join it. All the while, the news about overseas investigations was setting alarm bells ringing. The revelations about the Bank of New York probe, and its potential to lead to the Yeltsin Family, were like a ticking time bomb, and the breaking news about the link between the Mabetex investigation and the Yeltsin Family credit cards intensified the pressure further still. Somewhere, locked in a safe inside the deputy prosecutor's office in the stately mansion on Petrovka Street, arrest warrants were lying, signed.

There was still one more crucial metamorphosis to come.

It was at this time, Pugachev told me, that he'd proposed the most audacious step yet. He began trying to convince Tatyana and Yumashev that Yeltsin should step down early, so Putin could succeed him before the next election. It was the only way to secure his vault to the presidency. 'We're not going to be able to hold on to power till the presidential elections the following summer,' he told them. 'The fact that Yeltsin said he wants him to be his successor is not going to help. We still have to get him there.' The discussions went on for hours. Yumashev, for one, was convinced that Yeltsin would not agree. 'I told him, this is a question of your personal safety, of the safety of his family, and for you and for all of us. It's a question of the future of the country. But he said, "You understand he'll never give up power."'

In the end, according to Pugachev, Yumashev said he would go to Yeltsin. They parted late in the evening, and the next day, when Pugachev was back in the Kremlin, he said he received a call from Yumashev: 'He told me the question has been decided.'[7] Yumashev, however, insisted that no such decision was made then. The official Kremlin line has always been that Yeltsin only decided to step down early much later, towards the end of the year.

But two other former Kremlin officials also indicated that the decision had been made earlier than that,[8] and one of Putin's close KGB allies noticed that something serious was afoot. Towards the end of August Putin had retreated with one of his closest comrades to his old dacha in the Ozero compound for a few days. He went there to be alone, the close ally said.[9] He was deep in thought, and something was clearly weighing on him.

It was only after three weeks of tragedy and terror that September that public perception of Putin was turned around. The headlines surrounding Mabetex were blown away, while Putin rose to take command and Yeltsin disappeared from sight.

*

Late in the evening of September 4 1999 a car bomb ripped through an apartment building in the Dagestani town of Buynaksk, killing sixty-four people, most of them family members of Russian servicemen. The blast was seen as a response to the escalation of the armed struggle with Chechen rebels, who had launched a new incursion into Dagestan that same weekend, seizing several villages just one day after Putin, the newly anointed prime minister, had declared victory for federal forces in Dagestan. It seemed yet another tragic twist in the sporadic clashes Russia had been forced to engage in ever since Yeltsin launched a war against Chechen separatists in 1994.

When, just four days later, another blast tore out the central section of an apartment building in a sleepy working-class suburb of southeast Moscow, killing ninety-four people as they slept in their beds, Russia's military struggle in the Caucasus seemed to have acquired a deadly new reach. At first, investigators said the blast might have been an explosion of natural gas.[10] Few of the families who lived in the building had anything to do with the breakaway Chechen republic. How could the blast have anything to do with a far-off military struggle? But one by one, without presenting any evidence, officials began to denounce the bombing as an attack by Chechen terrorists. Emergency workers had barely finished digging out the last few charred bodies from the wreckage of what had been number 19 Guryanova Street when, four nights later, another blast completely obliterated a drab nine-storey apartment building on Kashirskoye Shosse in the south of Moscow. One hundred and nineteen people died. The only evidence that seemed to remain of human life were children's toys left floating in pools of mud.[11]

Panic spread through Moscow. It was unprecedented for the near decade of on-off war against separatist rebels in the south to reach into the heart of the capital. As the national sense of emergency and fear grew, the financial scandals surrounding the Yeltsin Family were pushed far off the front pages, and Vladimir Putin was thrust to the fore. This was the pivotal moment at which Putin took over the reins from Yeltsin. Suddenly, he was the country's commander in chief, leading a bombastic campaign of airstrikes against Chechnya to avenge the attacks.

What happened that autumn, as the death toll from the apartment blasts rose to over three hundred while the Kremlin rolled out a meticulous PR campaign, has become the most deadly and central conundrum of Putin's rise. Could Putin's security men have bombed their own people in a cynical attempt to create a crisis that would ensure he took the presidency? The question has often been asked, but answers have been thin on the ground. Anyone seriously involved in investigating the issue seems to have died or been arrested unexpectedly.[12] Yet without the blasts and the concerted military campaign that followed, it's impossible to imagine that Putin would ever have garnered the support to pose a serious challenge to Primakov and Luzhkov. The Yeltsin Family would have remained mired in the Mabetex and Bank of New York investigations, and Putin by association, as Yeltsin's chosen successor, would have been ground down with them too. Now, as if on cue, he suddenly emerged confident and prepared. He was the all-action hero who by September 23 had launched airstrikes against the Chechen capital Grozny, while Yeltsin had completely disappeared from view. Putin spoke to the Russian people in the language of the street, vowing to 'wipe out' terrorists 'in the outhouse',[13] lashing out at the breakaway republic as a criminal state where 'bandits' and 'international terrorists' roamed free, enslaving, raping and killing innocent Russians.[14] To the Russians it seemed like a breath of fresh air. Compared to the sick and ailing Yeltsin, suddenly they had a leader who was in charge.

In a series of slick TV encounters with the military leadership in Dagestan, Putin was seen bounding from a descending military helicopter, dressed for action in khaki trousers and light jacket. He was shown solemnly raising a toast in a field tent with military commanders. 'We have no right to show a second of weakness, because if we do it means all those who died have died in vain,' he declared with firm conviction.[15] He was presented as the saviour of the country, a Russian James Bond who would restore order and hope.

The campaign was a shot in the arm for Russians' humiliated sense of national identity. It immediately distinguished Putin from the chaos and collapse of the Yeltsin years. The all-out air assault gave vent to a decade of pent-up nationalistic frustration that had escalated earlier that year when NATO forces had launched an incursion into Russia's traditional Eastern European sphere of interest, bombing Kosovo in the former Yugoslavia. As the airstrikes stretched into the autumn, demolishing more and more of Chechnya and indiscriminately killing thousands of civilians, Putin's approval ratings soared from just 31 per cent in August to 75 per cent by the end of November.[16] If it had been a plan, Operation Successor, as it later became known, was working: an enormous pro-Putin majority had been formed.

But nagging doubts over the Moscow blasts were expressed almost immediately. Communist deputy Viktor Ilyukhin was one of the first to raise the alarm, claiming that the Kremlin could be behind the bombings in an attempt to fan hysteria and discredit Luzhkov.[17] For months rumours had been rife in Moscow that the Kremlin might provoke some kind of crisis as a pretext for cancelling elections. The Duma's speaker, Gennady Seleznyov, had informed lawmakers that another bomb attack had taken place in the southern Russian city of Volgodonsk three days before it actually happened.[18] The biggest red flag appeared late in the evening of September 22 in the town of Ryazan, not far from Moscow, when a resident reported to the local police that he'd seen three suspicious-looking individuals carrying sacks into the basement of his apartment building. By the time the police arrived, the suspects had left in a car whose licence plates had been partially papered over.[19] The police searched the basement of the building, and emerged shocked and white-faced: they'd found three sacks, connected to a detonator and a timing device.[20] The entire building was swiftly evacuated, its terrified residents not allowed back to their homes until the evening of the following day. The police initially said that tests had found the sacks to contain traces of hexogen,[21] a powerful explosive that had been used in the other apartment blasts. The local FSB chief said the timer had been set to go off at 5.30 that morning, and congratulated the residents on escaping with just hours to spare.[22]

The Ryazan FSB and police mounted a huge operation to track down the apparent terrorists, cordoning off the entire city. A day later, on September 24, Russian Interior Minister Vladimir Rushailo reported to law-enforcement chiefs in Moscow that another apartment bombing had been averted. But just half an hour later Nikolai

Patrushev, the hard-bitten, salty-tongued FSB chief who'd worked closely with Putin in the Leningrad KGB, told a TV reporter that the sacks had contained no more than sugar, and that the whole episode had been no more than an exercise, a test of public vigilance.[23] Patrushev was as ruthless as he was relentless in manoeuvres behind the scenes,[24] and his new explanations not only contradicted Rushailo, but seemed to surprise the Ryazan FSB, which had apparently been on the verge of capturing the men who'd planted the sacks.[25] The local resident who originally contacted the police later said that the substance he saw in the sacks was yellow, with a texture more like rice than sugar – a description that, according to experts, matched hexogen.[26]

For months afterwards, the residents of the apartment building at 14 Novoselyeva Street were angry at, confused and traumatised by the conflicting accounts. Several insisted that they didn't believe it could have been a mere exercise.[27] A report later emerged that local law enforcement had intercepted a phone call they believed had been made by the apparent terrorists to an FSB-linked number in Moscow.[28] If this was true, it was starting to look as if Patrushev had declared the incident was just an exercise to make sure the investigation went no further. Local authorities involved in the investigation clammed up, refusing to comment to the press except to confirm the official line that it had all been an exercise. The police explosives expert who carried out the initial tests was transferred to a special unit whose employees are forbidden from speaking to the press.[29] The case files were immediately classified.[30]

A few years later, in 2003, a brave former FSB colonel, Mikhail Trepashkin, who stuck his neck out to investigate the Moscow bombings, was tried and sentenced to four years in a military prison. He had been arrested just days after telling a journalist that a composite sketch of one of the suspects in the first blast, at 19 Guryanova Street in Moscow, resembled a man he recognised as an FSB agent.[31] (The sketch, based on a description by one of the eyewitnesses, a building manager, had later been switched to a more suitable subject, a Chechen who claimed he'd been framed. The original sketch had been disappeared from police files.[32])

If this really was the deadly secret behind Putin's rise, it was the first chilling indication of how far the KGB men were willing to go. For years, questions have swirled over the bombings, while investigative journalists have penned exhaustive accounts of everything that happened then, only to be met by a wall of denial from Putin's Kremlin. But one of the first chinks in the Kremlin's version has recently appeared. A former Kremlin official has claimed he heard Patrushev directly speak about what actually happened in Ryazan. Patrushev had raged one day about how the interior minister Vladimir Rushailo, a holdover from the Yeltsin years with close ties to Berezovsky, had nearly exposed the FSB's involvement in the bombings: his officers had been close to catching the agents working for the FSB who planted the explosives. Rushailo had nearly blown the whole operation, seeking compromising information against the FSB and Patrushev. The FSB had been forced to backtrack and say the sacks contained no more than sugar to prevent any further investigation.[33]

Patrushev had apparently expressed no remorse, only anger at being threatened with the FSB's exposure. The former Kremlin official said he still could not quite fathom what he recollected hearing: 'There was no need for the bombings. We would have had the election all sewn up in any case.' The Kremlin propaganda machine was powerful enough to ensure Putin's victory in any case. But Patrushev, he said, 'wanted to tie Putin to him and cover him in blood'.[34]

The Kremlin's spokesman, Dmitry Peskov, dismissed the claim as 'total rubbish'. And to this day, Valentin Yumashev insists that there could never have been any FSB conspiracy behind the apartment bombings: 'I am absolutely sure this is not correct. The country categorically didn't want a second Chechen war.'[35] The first war had been so humiliating, Russia's once-great army losing so many lives in a tiny republic that barely even appeared on the map, that 'to be an initiator of war in Chechnya was suicide'. 'To organise explosions in apartment buildings so as to start a second war,' said Yumashev, 'would be to completely destroy the political future of the person you are trying to support.' But the campaign Putin conducted was vastly different to the war waged by Yeltsin that lost so many lives. It consisted mainly of airstrikes, rather than sending in ground troops, and Putin had made the distinction clear from the start: 'This time we will not put our boys under fire,' he said.[36] Pavlovsky, the Kremlin spin doctor, also denied that there could ever have been any plot: 'The apartment bombings . . . seemed to us to be electorally advantageous for Luzhkov. But all of a sudden he disappeared from view . . . That September of hexogen, the Moscow mayor lost the chance for leadership of Russia.'[37]

But Luzhkov, as Moscow mayor, had no power to command airstrikes on Chechnya in vengeance for the attacks. Though he was supported by the NTV channel of media mogul Vladimir Gusinsky, he was never going to be able to marshal a propaganda machine like that of the state-owned TV channel, RTR, and Berezovsky's ORT to slavishly promote his every action, as Putin did. All of the Kremlin's counter-arguments seemed weak. If the bombings were an FSB plot, they could have been undertaken without the knowledge or involvement of the Yeltsin Family. Putin's KGB men might have ruthlessly taken the initiative themselves. 'We all thought it was an act of terror. We had no idea it could be anything else,' said one person close to the Yeltsin Family.[38] But if there was an FSB plot, it went far beyond even the KGB playbook that since the 1960s had supported terrorist groups in the Middle East and Germany as a way of disrupting and dividing the West. German terrorist groups handled by the Stasi and the KGB had blown up American servicemen in Berlin nightclubs and German bankers on their way to work,[39] with Vladimir Putin – if the account of one former member of Germany's Red Army Faction is to be believed – handling members of these groups while stationed in Dresden.[40] It was another matter entirely, of course, to direct such tactics at Russia's own citizens. 'I couldn't believe it at the time, that any citizen of Russia would be ready to kill such a number of civilians for their own political aims,' said one Russian tycoon who'd been close to Berezovsky. 'But now, though I don't know whether they participated or not, I know only one thing: that they really are capable of more than this.'[41] 'Whichever way you look at it, he began the election campaign with the apartment bombings,' said a senior Russian banker with ties to foreign intelligence.[42]

Putin had emerged as a tough-talking leader from a new generation. 'The campaign acquired the stylistic mask of national
liberation revolution,' said Pavlovsky. 'Here was a simple guy from
a Leningrad communal apartment who in the name of the people
was taking the Kremlin . . . Putin's decision to go to war to avenge
the bombings was spontaneous, but it didn't destroy our model. It
fitted with the idea of a strong new regime.'[43]

*

For a long time in the years that followed, Boris Berezovsky, the
fast-talking mathematician who'd been the arch-insider oligarch of
the Yeltsin era, had been haunted by the apartment bombings. Later,
at odds with Putin's Kremlin and forced into exile in London, he'd
made repeated claims that the FSB was involved in them.[44]

But in those days Berezovsky was still on board, and as the parliamentary elections in December 1999 loomed, he put aside his qualms
about Putin's KGB past[45] and got firmly behind the Putin campaign.
Despite being hospitalised with hepatitis, he waged a devastating
media campaign that autumn through his ORT federal TV channel
that sought to destroy the reputations of Primakov and Luzhkov.
The two men had formed a powerful parliamentary alliance called
Fatherland-All Russia, and the Duma elections were to be a crucial
first test of its potency. From his hospital bed, Berezovsky would
call ORT late at night with instructions for Sergei Dorenko,[46] a
popular, deep-voiced anchor who savaged Primakov and Luzhkov
in weekly broadcasts that broke boundaries even by the standards
of Russia's mud-slinging media wars. In one, Dorenko accused
Luzhkov of taking $1.5 million in kickbacks from the corrupt mayor
of a Spanish seaside town, while his wife, Yelena Baturina, Moscow's
biggest construction tycoon, had allegedly funnelled hundreds of
millions abroad through a chain of foreign banks.[47] The sixty-nine-
year-old Primakov, Dorenko said in another broadcast, was unfit to
become president because of hip surgery he'd undergone recently in
Switzerland. Graphic footage of blood and bone in a similar operation being performed on another patient in Moscow was shown to

underline the argument. Sticking the boot in further, Dorenko claimed that while Primakov was Russia's foreign-intelligence chief he could have been involved in two assassination attempts against Georgian president Eduard Shevardnadze. The programme also played footage of Skuratov with the prostitutes almost on a loop, in an effort to discredit the regional governors who'd joined Fatherland-All Russia and given their backing to Skuratov.[48]

Berezovsky, high-octane as ever, said he was intent on destroying Primakov and Luzhkov. He left hospital one night in early autumn to visit an associate to organise logistics for the campaign. 'He was completely wrapped up. He looked like a crazy man,' the associate said.[49] 'He was carrying three mobile phones as usual and talking non-stop. He kept saying, "I'm going to break them into small pieces. Nothing will remain of them."' Though Putin's approval ratings were climbing steadily, the stakes were high. The criminal investigations launched under Primakov into Berezovsky's business dealings were still pending. He continued to face the threat of arrest.[50]

Dorenko was an extremely effective media attack dog, and slowly support for Fatherland-All Russia began to fall. But the allegations against Primakov and Luzhkov could seem tame compared to the financial scandals that faced the Yeltsin Family, which were aired in full on the rival NTV channel, which backed Primakov and Luzhkov. And although Berezovsky was helping cobble together a new pro-Kremlin parliamentary party, called Unity, in answer to Fatherland-All Russia, it looked like no more than an amorphous mass of obscure and faceless bureaucrats. In the middle of November, Unity's approval ratings stood only at 7 per cent, compared to nearly 20 per cent for Fatherland-All Russia.[51]

It was only when Putin issued a public statement of support for Unity at the end of November that the party's ratings began to surge. By then, the blanket TV coverage of Putin's decisive action against Chechnya had turned him into a political Midas, and within a week Unity's approval ratings had surged from 8 per cent to 15.[52] Fatherland-All Russia's had fallen to around 10 per cent, despite continuing strong support for Primakov personally, while the Communists led with 21 per cent. Putin's own ratings were sky-high at 75 per cent.[53] Even with Berezovsky's and Dorenko's Herculean efforts, the Kremlin might have lost parliament without Putin's backing for Unity.

On polling day, December 18, Unity's vote was unexpectedly high, at 23 per cent, just one percentage point behind the Communists. Even more importantly, Primakov and Luzhkov's Fatherland-All Russia had been trounced, with just 12.6 per cent of the vote.[54] Yumashev claimed that it was only then that Yeltsin had been sufficiently convinced of Putin's power as a rising political force to take the decision to stand down early to make way for him. He insisted that Yeltsin had taken the decision alone, and Pugachev's role was minimal.[55]

In the memoirs Yumashev ghost-wrote for Yeltsin, the Russian president told of how he'd summoned Putin to tell him of his decision to step down on December 14, four days before the election. According to Yeltsin, Putin had appeared reluctant to take power. Yeltsin wrote that he'd told Putin when they met that day, 'I want to step down this year, Vladimir Vladimirovich. This year. That's very important. The new century must begin with a new political era, the era of Putin. Do you understand?' Yeltsin said that Putin had remained silent for a long time before replying, 'I'm not ready for that decision, Boris Nikolayevich. It's a rather difficult destiny.'[56]

But neither the story of Putin's apparent reluctance, nor Yeltsin deciding to step down only at the last minute, matched the narrative that had already unfolded. Nor did it match Pugachev's or the two other Kremlin officials' tale, that the decision had been taken much earlier. In the months preceding the parliamentary elections, Putin had already essentially taken over the army and the entire law-enforcement system, including the security services, while Yeltsin faded from view. Putin couldn't have acted as decisively or as presidentially as he did in the military campaign against Chechnya if he hadn't already received some assurance that he was about to become president.

Even if Putin had been personally reluctant to take on the presidency, in those days he was just one member of a group of security men who were coming to power. When he addressed the

FSB in the final days of 1999 for the annual celebration of the Chekists, as the secret police were known, he made their ascendancy clear: 'The group of FSB operatives assigned to work undercover in the government have successfully accomplished the first stage of their task,' he said.[57] He made the comment with a deadpan expression, but he could not help but smirk as he reached the end of his speech. If it was meant as a joke, the deep shadows under Putin's eyes and his pale, gaunt appearance told a different story. Essentially, Putin was telling the security men that the country was finally theirs.

Putin's remarks slipped by unnoticed in the background. But the security men in the Kremlin backing him had been quietly preparing. Three days before the end of the year Putin had published an article on a new government portal that sounded like a manifesto for the security forces. Entitled 'Russia at the Turn of the Millennium',[58] it was the first time he had laid out his vision for the country.

The article signalled that Putin was planning to take on the mantle of Andropov's modern-day heir. He outlined a programme for a new era of state capitalism, in which Russia would fuse the strong hand of the state with elements of a market economy. The aim was to modernise and boost efficiency by encouraging economic growth and further integration into the world economy, but also to pursue stability and strong state power. It was on the one hand a resounding rejection of the dogma of Communism, which Putin called 'a road to a blind alley', that had cost the country an 'outrageous price' and doomed it to lag behind economically advanced countries. But it also signalled a rejection of the path Yeltsin had once sought for Russia as a liberal, Western-style democracy. The country was to seek a third way that would rely on its traditions of a strong state. 'It will not happen soon, if it ever happens at all, that Russia will become the second edition of, say, the US or Britain, in which liberal values have deep historic traditions,' Putin wrote. 'For Russians, a strong state is not an anomaly which should be got rid of. Quite the contrary, they see it as a source and guarantor of order and the initiator and main driving force of any change.'[59]

In the rush and preparations before the New Year holidays, the eve of a new millennium, barely anyone noticed. Only one national newspaper ran a comment on Putin's article.[60] Otherwise, it didn't register with anyone at all. Across Russia, families were dashing to buy last-minute presents. Fir trees were being sold in snowbound town squares. The streets were jammed with traffic as usual. In most homes, families would gather around the television for the Russian president's annual New Year speech. But this year, at the stroke of midnight, the turn of the millennium began with a shock. Unsteady, puffy-faced, yet speaking with dignity, Yeltsin announced to the nation that he was stepping down early, and anointing Putin acting president. He made the announcement with all the swagger and drama that had defined his tumultuous rule. His decision had been kept secret to the very last. 'I've heard people say more than once that Yeltsin would cling to power for as long as possible, that he would never let go,' he said. 'That is a lie. Russia should enter the new millennium with new politicians, new faces, new people who are intelligent, strong and energetic, while we, those who have been in power for many years, must leave.'

But Yeltsin also bowed out with an extraordinary expression of humility, and an apology for the near-decade of chaos that had unfurled as he sought to dismantle the Soviet regime, and for his failure in the end to fully bring his country freedom: 'I want to ask your forgiveness – for the dreams that have not come true, and for the things that seemed easy but turned out to be so excruciatingly difficult. I am asking your forgiveness for failing to justify the hopes of those who believed me when I said that we would leap from the grey, stagnating totalitarian past into a bright, prosperous and civilised future. I believed in that dream. I believed that we would cover that distance in one leap. We didn't.'[61]

It was a poignant cry for what might have been – and possibly prophetic of what was to come. He was handing over a country that had been blighted by one economic crisis after another. But he was giving it to a man who'd been helped to power by a group of security-services men who believed that the overriding achievement of the Yeltsin era – the establishment of basic democratic values – had brought the country to the brink of collapse. When Yeltsin handed the presidency to Putin, the values of democracy appeared strong.

Governors were elected. The media was largely free from interference from the state. The upper and lower chambers of parliament were a forum for criticism of government policy. But those who'd supported Putin's rise believed Yeltsin had taken the country's hard-won freedoms too far, and that under the influence of the West he had engendered a regime of lawlessness that had brought a corrupt oligarchy to power, and put the state itself up for sale. Instead of seeking to strengthen democratic institutions to tame the helter-skelter excesses of the Yeltsin years, they intended to dismantle democracy – purely to consolidate their own self-serving power.

If Yeltsin had any inkling that Putin was influenced by that strain of thought, that he was about to turn the dial back to a grim echo of the grey totalitarian past, he struggled not to let it show. But he was essentially handing over power to the *komitetchik* who'd become the anointed front man for the foreign-intelligence cadres who started the Soviet Union's move to the market in the first place, recognising the need to change in order to survive. For these men, Putin's vault to become Yeltsin's successor meant the revolution they'd embarked on to bring the market to Russia could be completed. The fragments of KGB networks they'd preserved following the Soviet collapse, as they followed the memos of the Politburo to create a hidden economy, were in position to be revived and restored. The financial collapse under Yeltsin had put them in a strong position to take back the leadership role. Putin's programme for a stronger state resonated with a population that had become deeply disenchanted with the free-for-all excesses of the Yeltsin era. People were exhausted from a decade in which they'd lurched from one financial crisis to another, while a handful of businessmen close to power had gained unimaginable wealth. With the right chore-ography, the way was open for them. 'The rise of Putin was a natural consequence of the nineties,' said one former senior government official with close ties to the security services.[62]

Primakov and Luzhkov melted into the background to cede the way to Putin as soon as Yeltsin announced he was stepping down to make Putin acting president. Following the defeat of Fatherland-All Russia in the parliamentary elections, neither of them ran for president. Instead, they cast aside their apparent former rivalry and threw their backing behind Putin. Primakov, the former head of the Russian foreign-intelligence service who'd been at the heart of the Soviet Union's efforts for *perestroika* and an end to the ideological standoff with the West, had stepped aside for a member of the younger KGB generation. In doing so, he was making way for a group that would be more adept at completing Russia's transition to a state capitalism that would reach far into international markets. Putin's men would not be tainted, as Primakov would have been by his Communist past, which still deeply coloured his views and his actions despite his role in Russia's initial transition. They were part of a far more commercial generation who initially liked to paint themselves as progressive. They were younger, and the elderly generals at the top of Russia's foreign-intelligence service still thought they could control them. Yet Primakov was passing the baton to a group that was far more ruthless than his own, that would stop at nothing to assure their own rise to power.

Though Primakov would just as surely have sought to restore the power of the Russian state and the power of the KGB, he hadn't had to climb through the crime-racked rubble of St Petersburg of the nineties. He hadn't been part of the fusion of KGB and organised crime that had ruthlessly taken over the city's sea port and fuel networks, sharing the spoils of the privatisation of the city's property with the Tambov organised-crime group and then laundering the cash. He hadn't been part of the younger KGB generation who'd made their way in the eighties funnelling cash and technology through the systems of the West, combining KGB networks with a ferocious capitalist grasp. He was an elder, more principled statesman of the Cold War, far above the asset grab of the nineties. He hadn't been like Putin's men, left out of the carve-up of the nineties and hungry to take a slice of the nation's wealth for themselves.

The consequences of the Yeltsin Family's decision to back Putin, to save themselves from Primakov's and the prosecutors' attacks, were to be felt in Russia, and across the world, for decades to come. We'll never know what would have happened had Primakov taken the presidency. But it is safe to say that his version of a KGB revanche

would never have lasted as long as Putin's, nor would he have ultimately acted as ruthlessly on the international stage. His attachment
to the Communist era would have made him a target for a backlash.
He would have seemed like a dinosaur from the past,[63] while a
Stepashin presidency would have been far milder, and less likely to
see the rollback of freedoms that Putin's regime led.

*

In agreeing to step down early, Yeltsin opened the way for an immediate unwinding of some of the democratic gains of his rule. He'd
made Putin's election as president almost a *fait accompli*. As acting
president, Putin had the entire might of the administration behind
him, and could almost spend the nation's budget at will. On the eve
of the election, which was to take place on March 26, he'd signed a
decree boosting wages for teachers, doctors and other state workers
by 20 per cent.[64] No one doubted that he would win.

He hardly even had to campaign, and treated the entire election
process with disdain. 'I could never in my worst dreams imagine I
would take part in an election,' he told journalists on election night.
'It seems to me an absolutely shameful business . . . You always need
to promise more than your opponent to look successful. I could
never imagine that I would have to make promises knowing before-
hand that such things could not be done. Thankfully the way this
presidential campaign was conducted helped me avoid this. I did
not have to deceive a huge part of the population.'[65]

He refused to take part in television debates with the other candidates – the stalwart Communist leader Gennady Zyuganov and the
firebrand nationalist Vladimir Zhirinovsky of the Liberal Democrat
Party – both of whom had already lost to Yeltsin in 1996, and stood
even less chance against Putin. He eschewed the Western-style TV
clips and boisterous events that had marked Yeltsin's campaign.
'These videos are advertising,' he told reporters. 'I will not be trying
to find out in the course of my election campaign which is more
important, Tampax or Snickers,' he sneered.[66]

The fact was, in those days Putin would have been unlikely to survive any televised debate. He'd never played a role as a public politician. But he was given an easy out. Instead of campaigning, his role as acting president meant that he was granted fawning blanket coverage on TV, which portrayed him as the nation's resolute leader. He was shown criss-crossing the nation on visits to factories, and swooping into Chechnya on a Sukhoi fighter jet. All of these activities, campaign staff insisted, were part of his working schedule and had nothing to do with the election campaign. The tactics chimed with an electorate disillusioned with the showmanship and political drama of Yeltsin. They just wanted someone to lead. Putin's rivals were left far behind, fringe figures irrelevant to an election that was rapidly becoming a foregone conclusion. Two days before the vote, Putin and Luzhkov appeared together on a Moscow construction site, displaying their truce for all to see.[67]

The Kremlin had been handed to Putin on a plate. 'It was like a Christmas present. You wake up in the morning and suddenly it's there,' said Pugachev. 'There were no real elections, and the entire system had already been built.'[68]

But in the rush to hustle Putin into power, a worrying omen had barely been noticed. He began his campaign with a farewell to the man who'd been his mentor, who'd defined him in the eyes of the Yeltsin Family as a progressive and a democrat. Anatoly Sobchak, the former St Petersburg mayor, had died suddenly just as the election campaign was due to officially start. He'd returned to Russia from his forced exile in Paris shortly before Putin was appointed prime minister the previous summer. The criminal case accusing him of bribery when he served as mayor had been dropped, possibly at Putin's instigation. And now that his former protégé was fast on the way to becoming the country's leader, he didn't have to worry about it returning to haunt him. To outward appearances, he threw his backing behind Putin's campaign. But according to Pugachev, Sobchak had warned him that he was making a mistake in forwarding Putin's candidacy, and in November 1999 he'd made a rare outburst against the St Petersburg FSB and other law enforcement for their aggressive takeover of the Baltic Sea Fleet, saying those behind its bankruptcy should be jailed.[69] It was the only time he'd ever publicly criticised the city's post-Soviet law enforcement, and he never did so again.

On the day he died, February 20 2000, he was accompanied by a figure from Russia's underworld, from the shadowy nexus between the security services and organised crime. This was Shabtai Kalmanovich, a KGB operative who'd been jailed for five years in Israel in 1988 for spying for the Soviets, and who on his release developed close ties with the leaders of Russia's most powerful organised-crime group, the Solntsevskaya. Kalmanovich had been a close partner of a businessman running South American fruit imports through the St Petersburg sea port, and according to one former city official he handled South American contraband too. To Sobchak's widow, Kalmanovich was a family friend.[70] But to the FBI he was 'a powerful associate of the Solntsevskaya Organisation . . . He is a millionaire Russian émigré . . . with ties to former KGB agents and high-level Russian, Israeli and other government officials throughout the world.'[71]

The St Petersburg sea port still seemed to haunt Sobchak wherever he went. When he lived in Paris, a close neighbour was Ilya Traber,[72] the leading member of the Tambov organised-crime group who'd controlled the sea port and had befriended the Sobchaks in the early nineties, when he dealt in antiques. And when he died, it seemed Kalmanovich had again brought the sea port to him. Complaining of chest pains, Sobchak had retired early that day to his hotel room in Kaliningrad, where he was staying while delivering a course of lectures at the local university. Half an hour later he was found unconscious by 'the person staying in the room next to him'.[73] His door had been unlocked. For some reason an ambulance wasn't called for another thirty minutes, and by the time it arrived another ten minutes later, Sobchak was dead.[74] It was Kalmanovich, Sobchak's widow later said, who had been the one to find him.[75]

At first, the local authorities had opened an investigation into suspected poisoning, but they later announced that Sobchak died of natural causes. He'd suffered a heart attack before. But some associates still question whether he knew too much for the comfort of Putin's men. Sobchak had been privy to some of the murkiest dealings of Putin's St Petersburg: the oil-for-food scheme, the laundering of cash for the Tambov group through the real-estate company SPAG, the privatisations and the break-up of the Baltic Sea Fleet that led to Traber's takeover of the sea port and the oil terminal. No one had been able to explain why an ambulance was not called immediately after he was discovered unconscious. 'I don't believe he died his own death,' one former Traber associate said. 'He knew too much about all this. Of course they got rid of him, but they are too clever to leave any trace.'[76]

Putin had comforted Sobchak's widow, Lyudmilla Narusova, as she wept in St Petersburg's Tavrichesky Palace, where his body lay in state. He publicly criticised those who had pursued Sobchak over the corruption allegations, claiming that in death he was a victim of persecution.[77] Narusova, a glamorous blonde who would later become a politician in her own right as a senator in the Federation Council, the upper chamber of parliament, appeared to cling to the belief that Putin had remained loyal to her husband throughout. But, just once, years later, she allowed herself to voice doubts about his death. It was in November 2012, shortly after her career as a senator had come to an abrupt end when she was suddenly removed as a candidate for re-election to her seat. As Putin's rule eradicated all remnants of parliamentary freedom, she'd become too outspoken and critical. The process of her dismissal, and the clampdown she'd seen imposed on the country's politics, had 'destroyed certain illusions', she told a reporter.[78] She insisted that she knew Putin as an 'absolutely honest, decent and devoted person', but she said she felt 'disgusted' by those who surrounded him. When her husband died, she'd had an independent autopsy conducted. It found that he had died because his heart stopped, she said. But she would not say how exactly that had happened – only that tests had found it had not been due to a heart attack. 'The scars on his heart were old scars from the heart attack he suffered in 1997. Why his heart stopped is another question,' she told the reporter. She claimed to know the answer, but said she could not disclose it because she feared for her daughter's life: 'I can see what these people are capable of, these people who don't want to hear a word of truth. All the documents are kept in a safe abroad. Even if something happens to me, they will still be there.' When asked who she meant by 'these people', she said, 'Some of them are in power.' She never repeated the allegation.[79]

*

Following his appointment as acting president, Putin slowly began to shed the skin of his St Petersburg past, and to adjust to his new life. For a time, Yeltsin and his family remained in the vast Gorki-9 presidential complex in the woods outside Moscow, and Putin, still living in the state dacha of the prime minister, needed a presidential residence. Pugachev drove him to look at three state residences from Soviet times that were free.[80] One was too close to the road, another was not suitable at all. But the third, a vast estate built before the Revolution in the nineteenth century, appeared to fit the bill. For Pugachev, the residence, named Novo-Ogarevo, had a historic and spiritual significance. It had been the home at the turn of the century of Grand Duke Sergei Alexandrovich, a son of Tsar Alexander II, and his wife Elizaveta Fyodorovna. In the tumult of those pre-Revolutionary years, a terrorist bomb had taken the life of the arch-conservative Grand Duke, who served as governor of Moscow. His wife had quietly gathered his limbs and other body parts from the street, and devoted the rest of her life to caring for the needy, eventually becoming a nun. After the Bolsheviks took power she was murdered by being buried alive in a mineshaft, and in 1981 she was canonised as a Russian Orthodox saint. To Pugachev's Orthodox believer's eyes, Novo-Ogarevo had significance as a religious relic of the tsarist past. For Putin, however, the house, built in the style of a neo-Gothic Scottish castle, with a vast lawn that stretched down to the Moscow river, had quite a different pull: it came equipped with a fifty-metre swimming pool. When he saw it, Pugachev said, 'his eyes went so big and round. I understood that he wouldn't need anything else in life. I thought this would be the limits of his dreams.'

Pugachev, still apparently believing that Putin was under his control, thought it would be easy to impress him with the trappings of presidential life: 'Before the collapse of the Soviet Union, he lived most of his life in communal flats. He was forty before he began to work in the mayor's office.' He'd been born and raised in a cramped communal flat in Leningrad, and before he was sent to Dresden by the KGB, he and his wife Lyudmilla had continued to live in a communal flat there. 'Lyuda was told she could only use the kitchen between three and five p.m.,' said Pugachev. 'Can you imagine coming to this after living like that?'[81]

The Novo-Ogarevo estate had been renovated in Soviet times as a guest house for visiting government delegations from abroad. A second house, a copy of the first, was built a short distance away, across an orangery, for holding Central Committee receptions. The heads of the Soviet republics had gathered there to work on Gorbachev's historic new Union agreement, the fateful reform of relations between the Soviet republics that was one of the causes of the August 1991 coup. Pugachev could see that beyond minor renovations, all that was needed for the Putins to move in was to build a high enough fence.

Pugachev still appeared to believe that Putin was a reluctant leader. Putin would often refer to himself as the 'hired manager' and seemed convinced that his term in power would only be for a few years. From the start of his career in St Petersburg, from the time of his very first interview with Igor Shadkhan, he had always portrayed himself as a 'servant of the state'.

As the results of the presidential election came rolling in on the evening of March 26 2000, Putin still seemed outwardly dazed by his sudden elevation. Even when his vote count passed the 50 per cent needed for victory in the first round, he appeared daunted by the task ahead. 'Everybody has a right to dream,' he told a room at his campaign headquarters packed full of journalists. 'But nobody should hope for miracles. The level of expectation is really very high . . . people are tired, life is tough and they are waiting for a change for the better . . . But I don't have the right to say from now on miracles are going to happen.'[82]

But behind the scenes, at Yeltsin's dacha outside Moscow, Yeltsin's daughter Tatyana was already celebrating. Footage shot for a documentary film by Vitaly Mansky shows the Yeltsin family gathering around a stately oak dining table.[83] When Putin's vote edges over 50 per cent, celebrations begin. Champagne is poured. Tatyana is leading the jubilation, almost hopping in joy. 'We can start having champagne – small sips!' she smiles. 'We won!' But Yeltsin himself seems to be struggling with the loss of power, and the potential loss of his legacy. Puffy-faced and impaired by illness, he seems to have trouble comprehending what is going on. 'Papa, why such a sad face?' Tatyana asks him at one point. 'Papa, are you glad? . . . You did everything. You looked at the person and saw he was fit.'

But when Yeltsin called to congratulate his successor that night, he received the ultimate insult. The man he'd handed the presidency to was too busy to take his call. Already he was no one, an old man left struggling to speak and fumbling with the phone. Tatyana's relief, by contrast, was clear. Later that evening she smiled and snuggled with Yumashev at Putin's campaign headquarters, where Yeltsin-era hold-overs – Voloshin, Pavlovsky, Chubais – were celebrating with some of Putin's St Petersburg security men. The victory was jointly theirs.

The Yeltsin Family still felt secure in the belief that Putin would protect their safety and their fortunes from attack. When Yeltsin had agreed to bow out ahead of time, behind the scenes they'd made a pact with his successor, according to a close Putin ally and a former senior government official.[84] One of Putin's first acts as acting president was to issue a decree granting Yeltsin immunity from prosecution. But a broader bargain had also been sealed behind the scenes. 'The negotiations that went on over Putin's rise and Yeltsin's departure were about property,' said Andrei Vavilov, first deputy finance minister at the time. 'The subject of these negotiations was about property, and not about the structure of society . . . Everyone forgot. Everyone thought that democracy would just be there. Everyone was just thinking about their personal interests.'

The bargain was to guarantee the Yeltsin Family immunity from prosecution and preserve the financial empires of their acolytes, chief among them the vast businesses owned by Berezovsky's associate Roman Abramovich, long labelled in the media as being close to the Yeltsin Family. The businesses involved included the Sibneft oil major and the aluminium giant Rusal, forged just before

Putin took the presidency and permitted to take control of more than 60 per cent of the Russian aluminium industry – a potent symbol of the Family's continued power.[85] The deal also granted the Yeltsin Family's appointees the right to continue to run the economy during Putin's first term in power, the close Putin ally said.[86]

Yumashev, however, denies any such deal was ever made. The decree issued by Putin granting Yeltsin immunity had made no mention of the Yeltsin Family, he said, while the Family had no businesses to be preserved. As for the make-up of the government, 'Putin was absolutely free in choosing whoever he wanted. He could have fired everyone.' The only reason behind Putin's rise to power, he said, was that Yeltsin believed in his adherence to democracy.[87]

Pugachev too told of a curious moment. He insists that he agreed with Yumashev and Tatyana that they would leave the country and allow Putin free rein to run things as he wanted. The only thing they still needed to secure was an immunity guarantee, he believed. But Putin had turned round at the last minute, when they met at his dacha soon after the election to celebrate the formal handover of power, and insisted that the Yeltsin Family and their people in the government stayed, said Pugachev: 'I didn't understand it. He'd been talking all the time about the need for a clean slate. But then he told them, "We should do all this together. We are one team."'[88]

Despite the apparent aboutface, Pugachev nevertheless understood that a regime change was under way. Putin's people, the KGB men, were coming to power, and he worked to ingratiate himself with them. 'In any case, it was clear that the men of force – the security men and spies known as the *siloviki* – were coming to power,' he said.[89]

To many, including Khodorkovsky's associate Leonid Nevzlin, after everything that followed it's still a matter of bewilderment that the Yeltsin Family could have made a pact with the likes of Putin: 'When they had all sources of information under their control, how could they have brought him into the Kremlin? He was already a mafia guy in St Petersburg. How could they have made him successor?'[90]

Putin's identity card as a Stasi officer would have given him direct access to Stasi buildings and made it easier for him to recruit agents.

Ministerrat der Deutschen Demokratischen Republik
Ministerium für Staatssicherheit

Bezirksverwaltung

Dresden

B 217590 ✳

Putin handled sleeper agents, otherwise known as 'illegals', while serving in Dresden as a liaison officer between the KGB and the Stasi.

Katerina, or Katya, the second daughter of Putin and his wife, Lyudmilla, was born while the family was stationed in Dresden in August 1986.

Sergei Pugachev (left), known then as the Kremlin's banker, worked closely with Pavel Borodin (right), the Kremlin property department chief, during the nineties.

In 1999, Russian president Boris Yeltsin (right) was facing a growing challenge from Yevgeny Primakov (left), the former spymaster he anointed prime minister.

Yeltsin's daughter, Tatyana Dyachenko, and her husband, Valentin Yumashev, Yeltsin's former chief of staff

In his 1999 New Year's Eve speech, Yeltsin (right) handed over the presidency to Putin.

Putin's election as president was good news for Pugachev (right), pictured here with Putin during an evening in St Petersburg together with close allies Vladimir Yakunin and Yury Kovalchuk.

Putin's war in Chechnya helped propel his vault to the presidency and ensured the rise of the St Petersburg *siloviki*, the 'men of force' led by Nikolai Patrushev, then Federal Security Service chief (right).

The free-for-all days of plenty for Yeltsin-era oligarchs such as Mikhail Khodorkovsky (left) and Boris Berezovsky (right) were numbered after Putin took the presidency.

Russia's onetime richest man, Mikhail Khodorkovsky (left), and his closest lieutenant, Platon Lebedev, facing trial in 2005 for fraud and tax evasion

The wealth at the command of Igor Sechin (left), chairman of state oil major Rosneft, and Gennady Timchenko (right), founder of oil trader Gunvor, grew rapidly following the Kremlin takeover of Khodorkovsky's Yukos oil major.

Yury Kovalchuk, the biggest
shareholder in Bank Rossiya

Martin Schlaff, the billionaire former Stasi
agent who allegedly smuggled embargoed
technology through Dresden in the 1980s

Konstantin Malofeyev,
the Russian Orthodox tycoon

Kremlin-connected tycoon Dmitry
Firtash was at the centre of a shadowy
gas-trading scheme between Russia,
Ukraine and Turkmenistan.

Putin comforted Lyudmilla Narusova, the widow of his former mentor Anatoly Sobchak, the St Petersburg mayor, who died mysteriously just a month before Putin was elected president in 2000.

The *kandidat rezident* striding into the glittering Andreyevsky Hall during his inauguration as president in May 2000

More than 115 hostages died in October 2002 after Russian special forces disbursed an unidentified gas into Moscow's Dubrovka theatre in a desperate attempt to break a siege by Chechen terrorists.

It was the first hostage crisis of Putin's presidency, and according to one insider account, Putin plunged into panic as events unfolded far from according to plan.

Times were good for Putin's close allies as Pugachev wined and dined the likes of Tikhon Shevkunov, Igor Sechin and Nikolai Patrushev.

Putin and Lyudmilla were welcomed with ceremony during a state visit to the UK in 2003. At home, however, Russian prosecutors launched a relentless legal campaign against Russia's richest man, Mikhail Khodorkovsky.

Mourners at the site of the gymnasium at the school in Beslan where 330 hostages died, more than half of them children, after armed Chechen terrorists seized the school and wired it with bombs.

The hostage crisis ended in a deadly conflagration when a series of explosions rang out in the gymnasium and Russian special forces began firing flamethrowers at the school. Questions remain over the initial cause of the explosions.

Semyon Mogilevich was jailed for eighteen months on charges of tax evasion. At the intersection of the Russian security services and organised crime, he'd been the brains moving money into the West for Russian organised crime since the eighties.

Moscow police raiding the dacha of Sergei Mikhailov, the alleged head of the powerful Solntsevskaya organised-crime group, in 2002. No charges were ever pressed.

Vladimir Yakunin was one of the first KGB men close to Putin to convert to Russian Orthodoxy after a career defending the atheist Soviet state.

Russian billionaire Roman Abramovich (top right) became a well-known fixture on the UK football scene after he bought London's Chelsea Football Club in 2003.

Putin could not help but shed a few tears when he declared victory in the 2012 elections. The news that he intended to return to power after four years of more liberal presidency under Dmitry Medvedev (right) had sparked the first serious protests of his rule.

The fortunes of close Putin allies such as Gennady Timchenko continued to surge during Putin's third term as president.

Donald Trump inside his Taj Mahal casino weeks before the glittering Atlantic City venture opened in April 1990. The casino became a favourite haunt of Russian mobsters and émigrés.

Donald Trump with Tevfik Arif and Felix Sater, the former Soviet émigrés behind the Bayrock Group, the New York-based real estate developer

PART TWO

6

'The Inner Circle Made Him'

As Vladimir Putin strode alone through the vaulted halls of the Grand Kremlin Palace, he seemed dwarfed by the majesty of the presidential inauguration. Solemn, with a slight smile, downcast gaze and light lopsided gait, he was dressed in a dark suit that differed little from the garb of an everyday office worker. He'd been trained to be bland and unremarkable, to blend in anywhere. But on this day, trumpeters dressed in an imperial uniform of white and gold heralded his entrance, while the state officials who thronged the gilded palace rooms applauded his every step down the endless red carpet into the glittering Andreyevsky Hall.

It was May 7 2000, and the *kandidat rezident* had arrived in the Kremlin. The former KGB officer who only eight months before had been just another faceless bureaucrat was about to take on the mantle of Russian president. The gold that dripped from the walls and the chandeliers was testimony both to the KGB men's plan for Russia's imperial revival and to the crooked Mabetex contracts that had restored the Kremlin far beyond its pre-Revolutionary grandeur – and had helped bring Putin to power.

Never before had there been such splendour at a Kremlin inauguration – it was the first time the newly restored palace halls had been opened for a state event – and never before in the history of the country had there been a peaceful handover of power from one president to another. It must have been a bitter pill for Boris Yeltsin to be surrounded by the glitter and gold that proved to be his own undoing. But he stood there bravely and stiffly, battling to contain his emotion as he lauded the country's hard-won freedom. 'We can be proud that the handover is being done peacefully, without revolutions or putsches, in a respectful and free way,' he said. 'Such a thing is possible only in a free country, a country that has stopped fearing not just others, but also itself . . . This is possible only in a new Russia, one in which people have learned to live and think freely. We wrote the history of the new Russia from a clean slate . . . There were a lot of challenging tests, a lot of difficulties. But now we all have something to be proud of. Russia has changed. It's changed because we took care of her . . . and strongly defended our main achievement – freedom . . . We didn't allow the country to fall into dictatorship.'[1]

Yeltsin's parting words almost sounded like a warning. But the man picking up the mantle that day was decisive and focused, and when he spoke, he spoke of a restored Russian state in which all of the country's history – no matter how brutal – was to be honoured and preserved. Though he paid lip service to respecting Russia's democratic achievements, the central thrust of his speech was as different from Yeltsin's as night from day: 'The history of our country has run through the walls of the Kremlin for centuries. We don't have the right to be "Ivans who don't remember their birth". We shouldn't forget anything. We should know our history as it was, and take lessons from it, and always remember those who created the Russian state and defended its values, who made it a great and powerful state. We will preserve this memory, and this connection through time . . . and all the best from our history we will hand over to our descendants. We believe in our strength, that we can really transform our country . . . I can assure you that in my actions I will be led only by the interests of the state . . . I consider it my holy duty to unite the people of Russia, to collect its people around clear aims and tasks, and remember each day and every minute, that we have one Motherland, one people, and that together we have one common future.'[2]

In the front rows of those who applauded him that day were the Yeltsin Family officials who'd helped bring him to power. First among them was Alexander Voloshin, the deft former economist who'd served as Yeltsin's chief of staff. Next to him was the gravel-voiced, barrel-chested Mikhail Kasyanov, another Yeltsin holdover who'd climbed through the ranks to head the finance ministry, handling the payments of Russia's strategic foreign debts, and had been appointed acting prime minister when Yeltsin handed over the reins to Putin on New Year's Eve. In a signal of the continuity pact Putin had made with Yeltsin's Family, his first act as president was to reappoint Kasyanov as prime minister, while later in May he reinstated Voloshin as Kremlin chief of staff.

But hidden and unnoticed in the mass of officials who thronged the golden Andreyevsky Hall were the KGB men Putin had brought with him from St Petersburg. In those days, they were seldom seen and rarely heard. But these were the *siloviki* who, first in union with Yeltsin's officials, and later on their own, were to flex their muscles and make their presence very well known. Within days of the inauguration they were to send a strong signal that the decade of freedom Yeltsin was so proud of was coming to an end.

Among them were KGB-linked businessmen such as Yury Kovalchuk, the former physicist who'd become the largest shareholder in Bank Rossiya, the St Petersburg bank created by the Communist Party in the twilight of the Soviet Union. There too was Gennady Timchenko, the alleged onetime KGB operative who'd worked closely with Putin to control the city's oil exports. These men had been hardened in the vicious struggle for cash in the St Petersburg economy, and they were now hungry for the riches Moscow had in store. Also hidden among the faceless crowds were a web of little-known allies with whom Putin had first served in the Leningrad KGB, and who he'd brought in as his deputies on his appointment as FSB chief in July 1998. Few had paid much attention to them.

Among them was Nikolai Patrushev, the gnarled and experienced operative who, according to one former Kremlin official, had fumed at being caught red-handed in the Ryazan apartment-bombing plot. Patrushev had replaced Putin as FSB chief the moment Putin was appointed prime minister, and he would remain in the post for the entirety of Putin's first two terms in power. He'd served in senior posts of the FSB in Moscow since 1994, long before Putin began his rise. A year older than Putin, he'd served with him in the Leningrad KGB's counter-intelligence division in the late seventies. When Putin was appointed as Sobchak's deputy mayor, Patrushev headed the contraband division of St Petersburg's newly created FSB, just as Putin's group of former KGB men were beginning to take over the main channel for the city's contraband goods – the Baltic Sea Fleet and the strategic sea port.

Soon Patrushev was transferred to Moscow, where he rose rapidly to the top of the FSB. A hard-drinking KGB man, he combined a strong capitalist ethic of amassing wealth with an expansive vision for the restoration of Russian empire. 'He's quite a simple guy, a Soviet person of the old school. He wants the Soviet Union, only with capitalism. He sees capitalism as a weapon' to restore Russia's imperial might, said one person close to him.[4] Another close Putin ally agreed: 'He's always had very strong independent views.'[5] Always, Patrushev had been a visionary, an ideologist for the rebuilding of Russian empire. 'He is a powerful personality. He is the one who really believes in rebuilding the empire. He is the one that got Vladimir Vladimirovich into all these ideas,' said the person close to him.[6] But while Patrushev was well-versed in the founding texts of Russia's geopolitical ambition,[7] he was a ruthless and relentless operator who would stop at nothing to get his way. He could not speak without swearing, and if you didn't swear back, he wouldn't respect you. 'He doesn't understand any other way,' the person close to him said. 'He can't speak or behave any other way. He will come into a meeting and say, "Well, you motherfuckers, what is it you've fucked up all over again?"' The other close Putin ally would only say that Patrushev had always been tough, while Putin had initially been more liberal than him. The person close to Patrushev said that he'd always considered himself cleverer and wilier than Putin: 'He never considered Putin was his boss.' Patrushev had waged a vendetta against the rebels in the breakaway Chechen republic – he hated the 'Chechy', and anyone who worked with them, with a vengeance.

Also among the little-noticed *siloviki* applauding Putin's inauguration in the Andreyevsky Hall was Sergei Ivanov, who'd served as a senior foreign-intelligence operative for the KGB. His urbane manner and fluent English masked a sharp tongue and an at times vicious manner. He too had worked closely with Putin in the Leningrad KGB. They'd operated out of the same dingy room in the Bolshoi Dom KGB headquarters, a monolithic block of granite on Liteyny Prospekt, for two years until Ivanov was promoted and transferred abroad – long before Putin made it to the Red Banner school. Ivanov had served in Finland, and possibly the UK, before being whisked away to serve as chief resident in the Kenyan embassy after a spy who defected to the UK blew his cover.[8] In the nineties, he'd served directly under Primakov as deputy chief of the European desk for the foreign-intelligence service, or SVR, becoming the youngest general since the Soviet collapse. When Putin became FSB chief he appointed Ivanov one of his deputy chiefs together with Patrushev, and after he took over as prime minister, Ivanov became secretary of Russia's Security Council, a post that became the second most powerful position in the Kremlin. He was to grow in influence during Putin's regime.

Also hidden in the grey mass of besuited men was Viktor Ivanov, a mustachioed KGB officer of the old school who viewed the world strictly through a Cold War lens. Two years older than Putin, he'd been a Party worker before being recruited by the Leningrad KGB. He'd begun service shortly after Putin, and worked his way up over nearly two decades through the KGB's human resources department to head the St Petersburg FSB's contraband division, taking over that important post from Patrushev at the time Ilya Traber's men were taking over the sea port. According to a former colleague from the FSB contraband division, Ivanov was notorious for never lifting a finger against smuggling: 'His favourite words were "later" and "not now".[9] One intelligence report written by a former senior KGB officer suggested that there might have been a very good reason for Ivanov's inactivity: he had helped the Tambov group (of which Traber was part) in its efforts to take over the sea port while it was being used to smuggle drugs from Colombia into Western Europe.[10] The report, which was later aired in a London court and drew strong denials from Ivanov, also claimed that Putin had supplied Ivanov with protection all the time he was operating in St Petersburg.

When Putin became FSB chief he immediately brought Ivanov in as his deputy, and when he rose to the presidency he appointed him deputy head of his administration. His job was to keep a close eye on everyone, and according to one person close to him he had 'a phenomenal memory', and knew everybody's idiosyncrasies.[11] Yury Shvets's report put it far less charitably. The job of human resources, he said, was to collect damaging information on colleagues and use it to destroy their careers: 'Anywhere Ivanov worked he deliberately set people against each other, thus creating an unfriendly environment in which he could dominate by resolving the conflict generated by him. He is masterful at understanding the balance of forces around him.'[12]

But perhaps the closest to the new president was Igor Sechin. Eight years younger than Putin, he had followed him like a shadow ever since his appointment as deputy mayor. He had served as his secretary, standing like a sentry behind a podium in the anteroom leading to Putin's office in the Smolny headquarters, a fierce gatekeeper to all. He controlled access to Putin and all the papers Putin saw. Anyone who needed Putin's signature to establish a business had to deal with Sechin first. When one St Petersburg businessman required Putin's signature to set up a joint venture with a Dutch company trading coal and oil product, his friends arranged for him to see Putin. After they'd discussed it, Putin told the businessman to go to his secretary, Igor Sechin, saying, 'He will tell you which documents to bring and I will sign.' 'I left the office and went to Sechin without thinking who he was,' the businessman, Andrei Korchagin, recalled. 'I was just wondering about how he was a guy, and not a girl like the secretary usually was. We were very dismissive of officials in those days. We began talking about which documents I'd need, and then Sechin suddenly began writing on a piece of paper. He said, "And bring . . ." showing me he'd written "$10,000" on the piece of paper. This made me very mad. I said, "What! have you lost it completely?!" But he said, "This is how we do business here." I told him where to go – but that was it: we never registered the business. Back then, it was an absolutely different time. I had no idea who Sechin was. This was how they collected petty bribes.'[13]

Sechin would always act as a barrier in front of his boss, and would organise meetings for those who wanted to see him, a former close Putin ally said. Even if a meeting had already been put in the calendar, Sechin would say it had to be organised through him: 'This is how he would take control of the connection. And if it would turn out that the person did not follow Sechin's orders, he would become his enemy, designated for destruction.'[14]

Sechin had long served in the KGB, according to two people close to him, not in military intelligence, as is often ascribed to him.[15] He'd been recruited in the late seventies, when he was studying languages at the Leningrad State University, and was asked to file reports on his fellow students, one person close to him said. Sechin's parents had divorced when he was young, and he had studied hard, driven by a relentless ambition to succeed, to escape the poverty of his childhood in the grim outskirts of Leningrad. 'He always had a chip on his shoulder. He always had an inferiority complex,' said a former Kremlin official who knew him well. 'He came from such a poor region of Leningrad, but where he went to university, in the language department it was filled with the children of diplomats.'[16]

Sechin had always served undercover for the KGB, and his time there was never mentioned in his official biography. Instead it said he'd been sent to work as a translator, first in Mozambique, where his knowledge of Portuguese was in demand as a civil war was raging and the Soviet military was training and equipping a national army. He'd then been sent, again officially as a translator, to Angola, where the Soviet military, still playing out a Cold War great game in Africa, was advising and equipping rebels in another civil war. When he returned, he took a post at the Leningrad State University, where he'd met and worked with Putin supervising foreign ties, and later in the city council, overseeing its work with foreign twin towns, but remaining an undercover operative for the KGB all along. He'd kept close to Putin ever since, always acting as his obsequious servant, carrying his bags whenever he travelled, following in his footsteps wherever he went. He'd been his deputy in the Kremlin foreign property department, working in the same small office in the former Central Committee headquarters, and then moving into higher posts in the administration as Putin's career soared. When Putin became president, he made Sechin deputy chief of his administration. But behind his subservient manner lay a relentless ambition for control and an endless capacity for plots. And, said two people close to him, he hated and resented his master.

While Sechin sought to quietly put thoughts into Putin's mind, Putin regarded him as a mere shadow, no more than a servant of his regime. 'He always saw him as the guy who carried his bags,' said the former Kremlin official close to both men.[17] In Putin's head, a petty insistence on rank and position always reigned. At the beginning of their Kremlin careers in the mid-nineties, Kremlin property chief Pavel Borodin provided both men with apartments in the centre of Moscow, but a problem arose when Putin realised that Sechin's was bigger than his. Sechin invited Putin over soon after they arrived, and showed him around, demonstrating the views across Moscow. Putin asked how large the flat was, and after checking the documents Sechin told him: 317 square metres. He immediately started. 'I have only 286,' he said. He congratulated Sechin, but then stepped away, as if Sechin had stolen something from him, or cynically betrayed him. 'Putin has a problem with envy,' the official familiar with the incident said.[18] 'You need to know him well to understand what this means. Igor told me that at this moment he understood that everything was up, that when Putin said "Congratulations," actually he wanted to shoot him, to shoot him with a controlled shot to the head. He said he couldn't speak with him for weeks after. It was such a banal, tiny matter . . . But Putin has such complexes. It is always better when you see him to tell him how badly everything is going. Igor learned to do this very fast.'[19]

It was a telling indication of Putin's mindset, of how quick he would be to take offence at perceived slights in the years to come. Like Sechin, he too had climbed to the top from a background of poverty, from the back streets of Leningrad, where he'd had to fight to win respect. A chip on his shoulder, the mark of an inferiority complex, was always there.

The last of the close-knit group of former Leningrad KGB men Putin brought with him to the Kremlin was Viktor Cherkesov, who had ruled the city's FSB ever since Putin had been appointed deputy mayor. Two years older than Putin, he'd held top posts in the Leningrad KGB for nearly eight years, and had been Putin's senior before Putin was sent to study in Moscow. In the final years of the Soviet regime, Cherkesov had headed one of the KGB's most vicious divisions, investigating the activities of dissidents. But after the regime collapsed he embraced the new shadow capitalism that ruled St Petersburg, acting as a vital link between the mayor's office, the security services and organised crime. He'd been a key player behind the Tambov group's takeover of the Baltic Sea Fleet and the sea port,[20] and Putin had always treated him with the utmost respect. 'He was a senior figure when Putin was no one,' a person close to both men said. 'He is from the closest circle. He is the elite.'[21] When Putin was appointed prime minister, he'd intended Cherkesov to replace him as FSB chief, but Patrushev had made sure he was appointed in his place. Yumashev had been told he shouldn't grant Putin his every wish, that there had to be some counterbalances. Cherkesov was appointed deputy chief instead.

*

For the first few years of Putin's presidency, these Leningrad KGB men, the *siloviki*, shared an uneasy power with the holdovers from the Yeltsin regime. They watched and learned as Voloshin, the wily Kremlin chief of staff who Putin retained in the role, helped ensure that Putin inherited 'a well-oiled machine'. Voloshin was the main Kremlin representative of the Family, a liberal in his economic views, but a statist in his political ones. He was among those who'd helped engineer the transfer of power to the KGB. An economist, he'd graduated from the Academy of Foreign Trade – which had always been associated with the First Chief Directorate, the foreign-intelligence division of the KGB[22] – and then served as the deputy head of its Centre for Competitive Research in the *perestroika* years. Putin later sent Voloshin, who spoke fluent English, as a special envoy to discuss military matters with top generals in the US. In the beginning he proved a vital ally for the *siloviki* as he assisted Putin in pushing out political enemies.

Voloshin had also worked in tandem with the other leading figure who remained from the Yeltsin era, Mikhail Kasyanov, who Putin had reappointed as his prime minister. Having been in charge of foreign debt in his previous post as first deputy finance minister, Kasyanov was steeped in the murky debt deals that were the core of the shadow financing of the regime. Although he was a pro-Western economic liberal, he was seen as a safe pair of hands. But he was in fact the personification of the Yeltsin years, a deep-voiced, avuncular type with a reputation – strongly denied – for greasing the wheels behind the scenes that had earned him the nickname 'Misha 2 Per Cent'.

In line with the relatively pro-market pitch he'd used to win the trust of the Yeltsin Family and then in his manifesto as president, Putin announced a series of liberal reforms that won him plaudits with economists across the globe and convinced investors of his market credentials. He introduced one of the world's most competitive income-tax rates, a flat 13 per cent that at one swoop eradicated many of the problems with non-payment that had plagued the Yeltsin regime. He embarked on land reforms that allowed private property to be bought and sold, lifting another major brake on investment. As his presidential economic adviser, he'd hired Andrei Illarionov, widely regarded as one of the country's most principled liberal economists. Amid the pro-market moves, oil prices – on which so much of the Russian budget depended – were finally starting to rise. And, buoyed by the surging inflows, Putin's government began paying down the vast debts on funds the Yeltsin administration had borrowed from the IMF. The instability and chaos of the Yeltsin years seemed, finally, to be coming to an end.

The world was also cheered by Putin's attempts to seek rapprochement with the West. One of his first acts as president was to close down the Lourdes listening station in Cuba, that Yegor Gaidar had fought so hard to maintain. He sought to build a close relationship with US president George W. Bush, and was the first world leader to call and express his condolences after the September 11 2001 attacks. He even defied the advice of his own defence minister – by that time Sergei Ivanov – and allowed the US access to military

bases in Central Asia from which it could launch attacks in neighbouring Afghanistan. Putin's KGB past was pushed into the
background, as George W. Bush said that when he looked deep into
his eyes he got a 'sense of his soul'.

But all of this was short-lived. The early days of Putin's presidency
now seem an era of wishful thinking and great naïvety. According
to Pugachev, the attempts at rapprochement with the West were
made not out of any sense of generosity, but because Putin expected
something in return.[23] So when in June 2002 George W. Bush, after
months of being courted by Putin, announced that the United States
was unilaterally withdrawing from the Anti-Ballistic Missile Treaty,
a key arms agreement dating from the Cold War, Putin and his
advisers felt betrayed. The withdrawal from the treaty would allow
the US to begin testing a missile-defence system that it proposed to
install in former Warsaw Pact states. The US claimed that it was
intended as a defence against Iranian missiles, but Putin's administration saw it as directly aimed at Russia. 'It's clear the missile-defence
shield can't be against any other country apart from Russia,' Voloshin
told reporters. American officials, he said, had 'Cold War cockroaches
in their head'.[24] At the same time, NATO was continuing a relentless
march east. Assurances given by a string of Western leaders to
Gorbachev that there would be no eastern expansion were being
ridden over roughshod. The final year of Yeltsin's rule had seen
NATO swallow Poland, Hungary and the Czech Republic. In November 2000, NATO invited seven more Central and East European countries to join.[25] It seemed to the Kremlin that the US was
rubbing the West's dominance in their faces.

From the beginning, behind the appearance of liberal economics
there was a strong undertow aimed at strengthening the control of
the state. Putin's early reforms were in fact intended to establish an
Augusto Pinochet-type rule, whereby economic reform would be
pushed through with the 'totalitarian force' of a strong state. Almost
as soon as he was elected, Pyotr Aven, the bespectacled economist
who'd trained first with Gaidar and then at a KGB-linked institute
of economics in Austria, had called on Putin to rule the country as
Pinochet had ruled Chile.[26] Putin, Aven was clearly hinting, was not

in a position to complete Russia's market transition in the way Andropov had intended, before the process spiralled out of control. Aven was the former minister for foreign economic trade who'd signed off on the St Petersburg oil-for-food schemes on behalf of Prime Minister Gaidar, and who'd been involved in the international investigations firm Kroll's attempt to track down the missing Party gold, before the Russian government denied the firm access to the information Russian prosecutors had. By this time, he had joined forces with Mikhail Fridman, one of the young Komsomol who became one of the country's first entrepreneurs. Aven was president of Fridman's Alfa Bank, which formed the core of one of Russia's biggest financial industrial conglomerates, with holdings in oil and telecoms. Within the Alfa Group's financial network sat the director of one of its main holding companies in Gibraltar, Franz Wolf, the son of Markus Wolf, the Stasi's ruthless former intelligence chief.[27]

The signs that Putin was seeking to carve out a different type of power were there from the start. Optimists hoped at first that he was carrying out a tightrope act, seeking to balance the relatively liberal, relatively pro-Western Yeltsin Family flank of his regime with the St Petersburg security men. But the influence of the KGB men began to far outweigh all else. Their world view was steeped in the logic of the Cold War, and gradually that came to define and mould Putin too. Seeking to restore Russia's might, they viewed the US as eternally seeking the break-up of their country and the weakening of its power. For them, the economy was to be harnessed as a weapon first to restore the power of the Russian state – and themselves as leaders of the KGB – and then against the West. Putin had, to some degree, retained some of the influence of the liberal Sobchak. But eventually, said Pugachev, 'the inner circle made him. They changed him into someone else. He got disappointed in the US and then he just wanted to get rich. It was the inner circle who pushed him to restore the state.'[28]

The FSB chief Patrushev, in particular, had sought to tie Putin to the KGB security clan and its Cold War views. He had been more senior than Putin within the FSB, holding top posts in the Moscow security services for most of the nineties, and when Putin was elevated first to FSB director and then to the presidency, he was sceptical and believed he could manipulate him. 'He was always the most decisive. Putin was nothing compared to him,' said a Kremlin insider.[29] Patrushev wanted to bind Putin to the presidency so he would not ever be able to step away. He'd begun to do so from the very beginning of Putin's run for the presidency. with the apartment bombings that led to the Chechen war. But for the first year, the Yeltsin Family seemed oblivious to this strand of Putin's background – or, believing that their own position had been secured, they did not want to know.

All the while, Pugachev moved in the shadows, watching over his protégé like a hawk, trying to balance the influence of the opposing forces – the Yeltsin Family and the security men – over the president. He attempted to shield Putin from attempts to bribe him, he said, instead paying for everything he needed himself. In Putin's first year in office, Pugachev said that he spent $50 million on meeting the Putin family's every need, down to buying the cutlery they used in their home. He bought apartments for prosecutors in order to make sure they were under the president's – and his – control. He insisted that this was essential to make sure the president and his prosecutors remained uncorrupted: 'There were always people proposing he take money for this, or for that. Mostly it was done through Yury Kovalchuk,' he said,[30] referring to the St Petersburg ally who'd taken over Bank Rossiya, the main cash pot for Putin's St Petersburg allies. Pugachev claimed that he was trying to bring an end to the era when the oligarchs of the Yeltsin years believed they controlled the Kremlin by giving 'donations' to Kremlin officials – not realising, perhaps, that essentially he was doing exactly the same.

'I was just trying to make sure this didn't happen. The rules had to have changed,' he said.

*

When Putin took over the presidency, the might of the Yeltsin-era oligarchs was still strong. The Moscow businessmen who'd been propelled through the first market experiments of the *perestroika* era with the support of the KGB had by then long broken free from their former masters to emerge at the top of Russian power. They'd taken over a considerable swathe of the country's economy when they took advantage of Yeltsin's vulnerability on the eve of the 1996 elections and persuaded him to hand over the crown jewels of the nation's industry. The loans-for-shares auctions had consolidated nearly 50 per cent of Russia's wealth in the hands of seven businessmen, while Yeltsin was left ever more dependent and weak. He'd depended, in part, on funds from the oligarchs to secure his re-election in 1996, and they'd grown used to a role where they not only supported but dictated some of the rules to the regime.

An estimated $20 billion in cash had flooded into bank accounts in the West every year since 1994, while the Yeltsin government coffers had been bled dry.[31] The funds that oligarchs like Khodorkovsky and Berezovsky had stowed abroad had weakened the Russian state to such a degree that Putin's KGB men argued the country was on the brink of collapse. In the nineties, wage arrears had mounted, while paying taxes was almost universally avoided. Russia had fallen deep in debt to Western institutions such as the IMF and the World Bank, and the $40 billion debt default, more than a third of which was to foreign creditors, had tarnished the country's finances even more. In the KGB men's view, the political freedoms Yeltsin had granted to the regions had brought the country even closer to the brink. Amidst the political tumult of Yeltsin's final year, some regional governors had refused to transfer part of their tax take to the federal government. 'We saw how the country was disintegrating,' said Sergei Bogdanchikov, a close Putin ally who served as head of the one remaining state oil company, Rosneft, and had also been close to Primakov.[32] 'What Putin took over was no more than fragments of the state. Things had gone so far that some governors were talking about introducing their own currency . . . If Putin had not come and another two or three years had passed we would not have had the Russian Federation. There would have been separate states like the Balkans. The collapse was absolutely clear to me.'[33]

The KGB men had long been looking at the situation intently.

Vladimir Yakunin, the bluff former senior KGB officer who'd served undercover at the United Nations in New York and then taken over Bank Rossiya on his return to Leningrad, had prepared a study on the ownership of the Russian economy, which found that in 1998–99 almost 50 per cent of the nation's gross domestic product was produced by companies owned by just eight families. 'If things stayed that way then they would soon control more than 50 per cent,' says Yakunin now, nearly twenty years later. 'All the profits were going into private pockets. No taxes were paid. It was looting, pure and simple. Without greater state involvement, it was clear to me it was a path to nowhere.'[34] Yakunin, who'd been close to Putin since they had shared the Ozero dacha compound, said he'd handed the report with his comments to Putin soon after he took the presidency.

But for Putin's security men, the Yeltsin-era oligarchs' sending of cash to the West provided a useful argument for shoring up their own power. They could claim that the dominance of the oligarchs was a threat to national security, though it was mostly a threat to their own positions. They saw themselves as the anointed guardians of Russia's restoration as an imperial power, and believed that the resurgence of the state and their own fates were inextricably – and conveniently – linked.

Soon after Putin's inauguration, Yakunin recalled, Zbigniew Brzezinski, the Cold War-era US national security adviser, had scoffed when discussing the cash held in overseas accounts by the Russian elite. If all that money was in accounts in the West, he said, then whose elite was it? Russia's, or the West's?[35] Brzezinski's comments had scalded the KGB men's ears. It was all the more rankling to hear them from a Cold War warrior like him, who they regarded as one of the architects of the West's efforts to dismantle the Soviet regime.

None of the oligarchs' arrangements had seemed more odious to the KGB men than the billions that ran through Valmet, the offshore fund co-owned by Khodorkovsky's adviser Christian Michel. With branches in London, Geneva and the Isle of Man, it managed the foreign bank accounts of Khodorkovsky's Menatep Group, as well as the Swiss oil trader Runicom, which exported oil from Sibneft, the Russian oil major created by Boris Berezovsky and Roman Abramovich. Khodorkovsky and Berezovsky were two of the most independent oligarchs, and in many ways Valmet had come to represent the new post-Cold War order, in which the US reigned supreme and Russian money from the by-then independent oligarchs fled to Western bank accounts. This status was underlined when one of the oldest and most venerable banks in the US, Riggs National Bank of Washington, bought a 51 per cent stake in Valmet. The bank, which for decades had held the accounts of US embassies across the globe, was seeking to expand into Eastern Europe and Russia, and Valmet was its vehicle for doing so. The symbolism of the West's Cold War victory ran deep. Riggs's chief of international banking was a former US ambassador to NATO, Alton G. Keel, who saw his mission as helping 'foster private enterprise in previously hostile climates'.[36] Christian Michel, meanwhile, an avowed libertarian, was convinced that Riggs Valmet's operations were contributing to an effort to free Russian entrepreneurs from the weighty hand of the Russian state. And when Khodorkovsky's Menatep took a stake in Riggs Valmet too, Michel believed that the investment represented 'a wonderful symbol of the new world order that President Bush senior was so proud of . . . The oldest US bank and an upcoming Russian bank sharing in the capital of Valmet. I thought it was a coup.'[37]

But in the eyes of the St Petersburg KGB men and the generals who backed them, the Riggs–Menatep tie-up was a symbol of the Yeltsin era: a Western-backed gangster capitalism in which oligarchs like Khodorkovsky had been able to dictate their will to power. They viewed Anatoly Chubais, the architect of Russia's privatisation programme, in particular as a stooge of the West.

In the Cold War mindset of the KGB men, for whom almost every action was part of a zero-sum game, the American economists who flocked to Russia to advise Chubais must have been agents of the CIA, bent on destroying what remained of Russian industry as, with their assistance, it passed into private hands, while the defence industry was dismantled piece by piece. The KGB had sought to retain control of industrial cash flows, but under Chubais' watch the nation's enterprises had been broken up and transferred to independent hands.

'The US sent senior CIA people to Russia to help to negotiate the privatisation process,' said one close Putin associate who, more than twenty years after Chubais' privatisation programme began, was still livid about it. 'They took advantage of this process and made money out of it. They had no right to make money in this privatisation.'[38]

For all his declarations about backing Russia's further transition to a market economy, Putin had in fact made his feelings about the oligarchs clear from the start of his election campaign. The first hint came at the end of February, when he answered a question from a campaign worker about when he was going to 'waste' the 'leeches' – meaning the oligarchs – that had attached themselves to power. He replied that his regime needed to do more than 'just destroy them': 'It is extremely important to create equal conditions for all so no one can fasten onto power and use these advantages for themselves . . . Not a single clan, not a single oligarch . . . all should be equally distanced from power.'[39] The next warning came a week before the election, when he told a Moscow radio station he wanted to eliminate the oligarchs: 'Such a class of oligarchs will cease to exist . . . Unless we ensure equal conditions for all, we won't be able to pull the country out of its current state.'[40]

Such statements, of course, were cheered by a population tired of the excesses of the Yeltsin years and fed a daily diet of corruption stories by a relatively free media that was being used by its independent tycoon owners as a means of battering their rivals. Putin was echoing the line first drawn by Primakov when he called for space to be freed in the country's jails for businessmen and corrupt officials.

But while Primakov's statement had sent a chill through the Yeltsin Family, when Putin made such comments, they seemed oblivious. He was their agent in the Kremlin, and they felt sure he would never touch them. 'The inner circle and the oligarchs thought he was a temporary figure, and they really thought they could take him under control,' said one person close to Putin. Ahead of the presidential election, one oligarch had apparently gone to see Putin in the White House, the seat of the Russian government where he still kept his office, and told him in no uncertain terms that he should know he would never be elected without their support, and that he should therefore understand how to behave. Putin barely batted an eyelid, and merely replied, 'We'll see.' 'He didn't throw anyone out of his office. But of course he was playing with them. They absolutely underestimated him.'[41]

Boris Berezovsky was probably the oligarch who went to see Putin. At the time he seemed to be the only one who was beginning to wonder if they'd made a fatal mistake. After completing his effort to destroy the Primakov–Luzhkov tandem, he'd been holidaying on Anguilla with a new girlfriend for most of the presidential election campaign. When he arrived back, he'd clearly been distressed by the changes he saw. 'He came back from his holiday and something happened he didn't like,' said one person close to him. 'He'd gone to see Putin to agree on who would be president in 2004. He proposed Putin would only be president for four years, while he, Berezovsky, would work on creating an opposition party. He wanted there to be a real democracy.'[42] But if this conversation took place, it evidently did not go well. Days before Putin's inauguration, Berezovsky's *Kommersant* newspaper raised the alarm with an article leaking what it said were plans to merge the Kremlin with the FSB, with the aim of muzzling opposition parties, all critics and the free press. Although such a merger never formally occurred, the plans the article described seem ominously prescient now. Putin's rise to power did of course amount to the takeover by the KGB of the Kremlin. The two entities really were to be fused. It was as if Berezovsky had suddenly realised the depth of his mistake. 'The new president, if he really wants to ensure order and stability, does not need a self-regulating political system,' the alleged Kremlin blueprint read. 'Instead he needs a political structure in his administration that can clearly control the political and social processes in the Russian Federation. The intellectual, personnel and professional potential of the FSB should be brought in to work on controlling the political process.' The FSB would be used for damage control when information surfaced that wasn't in the interests of the president or his inner circle.[43]

The Kremlin denied that any such proposals were under discussion. But just four days after Putin's inauguration, phase one of the plan seemed to be put into play. It was clearly aimed at bringing the media to heel. Masked police commandos with automatic weapons had swarmed through the offices of Vladimir Gusinsky, the tycoon who owned the Media Most empire, which included the television channel NTV, Putin's most vocal critic.[44] NTV was Russia's second most popular channel, and Gusinsky had never been afraid to use it for political ends, deploying it in support of Luzhkov's Fatherland bloc in the parliamentary elections. The channel had also been a strident voice of independence, probing Putin's Chechen war. On the eve of the presidential election it aired a prime-time discussion on the suspicious incident in Ryazan, and openly questioned whether the FSB was behind the apartment bombings. Its weekly satirical show *Kukly*, or 'Puppets', was a constant thorn in Putin's side. On more than one occasion it wryly portrayed him as an ungainly dwarf from an E.T.A. Hoffmann fairy tale named Tsaches, who inherited a ready-made kingdom of great riches through no effort of his own.

The raid on Gusinsky was not the only powerful signal from the Kremlin's new KGB masters in the first few days of Putin's rule. Ten days after his inauguration, Putin unveiled sweeping plans to rein in Russia's regional governors – measures clearly intended to ensure that the elected governors would never again unite against the Kremlin as they had on behalf of Luzhkov and Primakov. The proposed legislation would take away the governors' seats in the Federation Council, the upper chamber of parliament where they'd dug in for so long to block the removal of Skuratov as prosecutor general, essentially becoming an independent political force.[45] The removal of the governors' seats would take away their immunity from prosecution, while the proposed measures would also allow the president to dismiss any regional governor into whom a criminal investigation was opened, a move clearly aimed at making sure they never again departed from the Kremlin line. As a further element of Kremlin control Putin proposed seven Kremlin-appointed plenipotentiaries – sort of super-governors – who would oversee seven swathes of territory. Five generals from the army and the FSB, and two other Kremlin loyalists, were promptly anointed to the posts.

To Berezovsky, this legislation represented a dangerous disman-tling of the democratic achievements of the Yeltsin era. On May 31 he wrote an open letter to Putin protesting that the proposals were a 'threat to Russia's territorial integrity and democracy'.[46] The letter made the front page of almost all of Moscow's newspapers, while the Berezovsky-controlled TV channel ORT gave it first billing on the evening news. One of his friends, a business tycoon who'd always been close to the security men, in particular to Primakov, warned him he'd better pipe down: 'I said, "That's enough, Borya. What are you doing? Your guy became president. What more do you want?"' But Berezovsky had answered, 'He's a dictator.' 'He saw that he was a dictator before everyone.'[47]

But back then Berezovsky was the lone canary in the coal mine, warning about the demise of democracy. Officials close to the Yeltsin Family who were running the Kremlin, namely the chief of staff Alexander Voloshin and his baby-faced deputy Vladislav Surkov, had been among the chief architects of the project to bring the regional governors to heel. Behind the scenes, they'd also thrown their backing behind plans to rein in the media. It was as if they were taking revenge on the forces that had nearly had them jailed, and had caused them so much angst, just twelve months before. Yumashev insisted that when Putin raised the matter with him, he'd told him that any attack on NTV went against the grain of freedom of speech. But neither he nor Voloshin did anything to stop what was to become a campaign to bring the TV channels under the control of the state, while Voloshin actively participated in it. 'Putin told me that Yeltsin will be tainted in the history books,' Yumashev recalled.[48] 'He said all the books will tell of the Family, and it will be one lie after the other because of NTV. Putin said, "Why should I put up with this? Why should we allow them to discredit the regime? Why should I put up with this if they are going to lie every day?" I told him freedom of speech was the most important insti-tution of power. We need to remember this. But he said this should never be tolerated when the regime is weak. It can be tolerated when the regime is strong, but when it is weak it can never be stomached. And then he acted as he considered necessary.'

The way Putin steered the conversation was a typical KGB manipulation: he was stirring up the Yeltsin Family's visceral antipathy towards NTV after they'd been subjected to its unforgiving spotlight over the corruption scandals that had plagued and humiliated them the previous year, eventually forcing them into the hasty handover of power. He exploited their fears about how this would impact their legacy to manipulate them into giving their backing for an attack on the channel. 'He considered this was a TV company that was involved not in informing people but in lobbying for the interests of its owner,' said Yumashev. 'He said, "They've been caught. They took a loan from the state." He said, "If there was not this loan, I wouldn't have touched them. But they've been compromised, and therefore we need to use this."'[49]

The raid on Gusinsky's Media Most was the beginning of an all-out campaign by Putin's Kremlin, Voloshin and the officials of the Yeltsin Family included, against many of the oligarchs of the Yeltsin era. It was the launch of Putin's efforts to eradicate challenges to his power. All that was needed was for a target to be compromised in some way – and now that Putin's men had taken over the apparatus of law enforcement, it was not hard to find something to latch on to after the hurly-burly transition of the Yeltsin years.

What followed that summer was a well-planned series of coordinated raids aimed at scaring the tycoons out of politics that were carried out with KGB precision. First, less than a month after the raid on Media Most, Gusinsky was jailed. Though he was held for just three nights in Moscow's notorious Butyrka prison, charged with embezzling $10 million from the state, for the oligarchs who had grown used to their near-untouchable status during Yeltsin's rule, the unthinkable had happened. Gusinsky, a garrulous, larger-than-life figure, had always been able to use his media to criticise the authorities and get away with it. The tycoons united to fire off a joint letter in protest at Gusinsky's arrest, calling it 'an act of vengeance . . . against a political opponent'.[50] But if any of them were thinking of rebelling against the new regime, they were soon to get a new warning. A week later, Moscow prosecutors filed suit to contest the 1997 privatisation of Norilsk Nickel, the sprawling $1.5 billion nickel producer that had been sold for a mere $170 million in the controversial loans-for-shares auctions to Vladimir Potanin, the architect of the privatisation scheme. Igor Malashenko, the first deputy chairman of Gusinsky's Media Most, warned that the suit indicated that any businessman involved in privatisation 'could be thrown in prison tomorrow . . . A new order is being created in the country, which in the eyes of the new leadership means that everything has to be under the control of the Kremlin.'[51]

As if to further underline the arrival of a new regime under which none of the tycoons' empires was safe, in early July Putin's men launched three more raids in the space of two days. They first targeted Lukoil, the vast energy conglomerate owned and run by a wily Soviet-era official from Azerbaijan, Vagit Alekperov, accusing it of falsifying tax refunds. Then they raided Gusinsky's Media Most again, and for the first time its TV channel, NTV.[52] The next day it was the turn of another potent symbol of the capitalism of the Yeltsin era, the sprawling AvtoVAZ, the nation's biggest carmaker, which was controlled by associates of Berezovsky. The head of the tax police claimed that the company had evaded tax amounting to hundreds of millions of dollars.[53]

The panic in the business community was reaching fever pitch. On the same day that the tax police were swarming through AvtoVAZ, Putin gave a television interview justifying the raids and vowing to bring justice to those who had made their fortunes in the 'muddy waters' following the Soviet collapse. 'We cannot confuse a democracy with anarchy,' he warned.[54] 'In Russian, we have a saying about catching fish in muddy waters. There are fishermen who have already caught a lot of fish and would like to keep the system as it is. But I do not think this state of affairs is appreciated by our people.' The next day he gave a newspaper interview in which he claimed that the recent moves did not signal a return to a police state. But he added that business should observe 'the rules of the game' – particularly now that he'd tabled the new 13 per cent flat income-tax rate that was supposed to support liberalising efforts.[55]

It was a typical KGB tactic of bait and switch, and the well-oiled machinery of the Kremlin was being unfurled for Putin. The

Kremlin's propaganda machine and law enforcement were working in near-perfect tandem, and the tycoons, desperate to understand the new rules of the game, were begging for a meeting with him. Khodorkovsky warned quietly that any of them could fall foul of post-Soviet laws, as they'd been written in a contradictory way, and the judiciary was weak.[56] Berezovsky, again, was the lone voice of protest. He'd noisily resigned his post as a member of parliament, telling a packed press conference that he didn't want to take part in 'the dismantling of Russia and the imposition of authoritarian rule'.[57] His stance was a desperate rallying cry to the other Moscow tycoons. But it came far too late.

When twenty-one of the most powerful tycoons met Putin at the end of July, the encounter around the oval table of the Kremlin's ornate Ekaterinovsky Hall was a far cry from the cosy secret meetings they'd had with Boris Yeltsin. This was a formal affair, and it was a public dressing-down. Putin's comments were televised across the nation as he told the magnates that they had only themselves to blame for the wave of tax-police raids and criminal probes: 'You must remember that you formed this state yourselves through the political and quasi-political structures that you controlled.' Citing a Russian folk saying, he continued, 'It's no use blaming the mirror [if you have an ugly face].'[58] In the end, while he reassured them that he would not reverse the privatisations of the nineties, he exhorted them to support his economic programme, and to stop using their media outlets to 'politicise' the legal probes against big business. After the TV cameras had left, he made the new rules of the game clear to them. They should stay out of politics, or else. Two of the tycoons were conspicuous by their absence: Berezovsky and Gusinsky, both of whom had publicly railed against Putin's policies, and used their media empires to do the same.

But another was conspicuous by his closeness. To Putin's right hand, from time to time whispering in his ear, was Sergei Pugachev. While the others quaked, he seemed unperturbed. In those days, while Putin was adjusting to his new role, the two men spoke many times a day. Later that day, at Pugachev's suggestion, Putin hosted the oligarchs for another gathering, away from the TV cameras, that was rich in symbolism. Pugachev had persuaded Putin to meet them in more informal circumstances to demonstrate to them that he didn't want to go to war. But the setting Putin chose for the 'friendly' barbecue was also meant as a pointed signal. Hidden in the woods on the outskirts of Moscow, Stalin's dacha had been kept almost untouched since the day he died there in 1953. The telephones down which the dictator barked orders remained in place. The couch on which he preferred to sleep instead of retiring to bed still stood in his study. Time seemed to have stood still since Stalin had spent days and nights there drawing up lists of enemies among the country's elite. The oligarchs had been invited to the place from which Stalin had ordered thousands to be sent to their deaths in what became known as the Great Purge. Putin was dressed in T-shirt and jeans, and was trying to appear relaxed and approachable. He'd only ever seen many of the tycoons on TV, said Pugachev, and he was still anxious about how to behave in front of them. But if Putin was uneasy, the tycoons were even more so. No one was going to challenge the new president there. 'It was enough that he let us leave,' Pugachev remembered one of them saying.

All the while, Pugachev had been operating behind the scenes. In those days, while the other oligarchs faced raids and tax police, he believed that he commanded all he surveyed. He'd installed his man as president, and an ally as FSB chief. He'd personally brought in the new head of the Federal Tax Service, Gennady Bukayev, an associate from Bashkortostan where he had interests in the oil sector. He'd helped to appoint Vladimir Ustinov as Prosecutor General, as he sought to quash the investigation surrounding Mabetex. Pugachev liked to believe he controlled them all. Through his Mezhprombank, he doled out cash left and right. An apartment for Ustinov here, an apartment for his deputy there. Other tycoons lined up to work with him. 'They were coming to me constantly, saying, "Let's raid this guy and take over the business,"' he laughed, with a deep nostalgia for those days.[59] According to a source, even Roman Abramovich, the seemingly shy, stubble-faced oil trader who'd begun as a protégé of Boris Berezovsky, bowed to him: much later, Abramovich would reportedly complain to the same source that he'd had to agree everything with Pugachev in those days. A spokesperson for Abramovich denies that this conversation ever took place. One Moscow newspaper hailed Pugachev as the Kremlin's new 'favourite', while others called him the new grey cardinal, who together with Putin's KGB men from St Petersburg was taking over financial flows.[60] He was seen as an ideologue behind the new policy of keeping the oligarchs 'equally distant from power', an idea he'd never admit to now, but which then he seemed to subscribe to, as long as he was above everyone else.

While some oligarchs, like Pugachev and Abramovich, were clearly more equal than others, the chief threats to Putin's power were picked off one by one. Just days before Putin's Kremlin meeting with the Moscow tycoons, Gusinsky had been presented with an offer he couldn't refuse. He was told by Putin's new press minister, Mikhail Lesin, that he should agree to sell his Media Most empire to the state-controlled gas monopoly Gazprom for $473 million in debts and $300 million in cash; otherwise he would face jail.[61] The debts, which Putin had honed in on in his conversation with Yumashev, were mostly owed to the state gas giant, and Media Most was behind on its payments. Gusinsky had quickly agreed – he didn't want to risk any more nights in the decrepit Butyrka jail. By the time the tycoons gathered in the Kremlin, prosecutors had announced they'd dropped all charges against Gusinsky.

But soon after, Gusinsky fled the country, and later he re-emerged saying he'd been forced to sign the deal under duress, practically 'at gunpoint'.[62] Therefore, he said, he was reneging on it. When news first emerged of the deal, the country's elite had been shocked. It was the first sign of how far Putin's regime was willing to go to acquire control over the independent media networks. Putin's men were using the criminal justice system as a weapon of 'crude blackmail' to force through a takeover. For them, such tactics were par for the course.

But for Putin, the final showdown with the media tycoons was yet to come. From the beginning, the Kremlin focused its efforts on them. Putin had become obsessed with the media's power, knowing all too well how, with the help of Berezovsky's TV channel, he'd been transformed from a nobody into the country's most popular leader. He was aware that without control of the country's federal TV channels, that could change at any minute.

*

More than any of the other tycoons, Boris Berezovsky represented the archetypal oligarch of the Yeltsin era to Putin's men, by whom he was reviled, loathed and feared in equal measure. He was the epitome of the insider dealing of the Yeltsin years, when a small coterie of businessmen bargained behind the scenes for prime assets and government posts. The ties he'd cultivated with the separatist leaders of Chechnya made him invidious in the eyes of the KGB men – especially Patrushev, who hated anyone connected with the Chechens. Berezovsky had backed separatist leader Aslan Maskhadov and helped forge a peace deal following Yeltsin's disastrous first Chechen war, in which thousands of Russian soldiers – and many more Chechen civilians – had lost their lives. The deal granted Maskhadov broad autonomy for a republic that, in the eyes of Putin's KGB men, had become a black hole for people and cash. Berezovsky had been able to navigate the treacherous clans of Chechen warlords to make money not just out of negotiating the release of hostages, but also out of the business of war. 'He is a war criminal. He stole people,' one Putin associate claimed. 'All this: the war, the Chechen warlords, was Berezovsky's work.'

But most of all Putin's men feared the power of the media he ran. Even though his ORT TV channel was, on paper, controlled by the state, which held a 51 per cent stake, Berezovsky, who owned the rest and had stacked the board with his allies, was in fact in charge.

By early August, Berezovsky had moved into outright opposition to the new regime. The day after a terrorist bomb tore through an underpass in central Moscow, leaving seven dead and ninety injured, he held a press conference to announce that he was creating an opposition bloc to combat what he called Putin's rising authoritarianism. He warned that more such blasts could occur if the Kremlin continued its 'dangerous' push to destroy the rebels in Chechnya.[63]

With Berezovsky's ties to the Chechen rebels, it seemed he was laying down the gauntlet to the Putin regime.

When disaster struck later that month, leaving Putin facing the first major crisis of his fledgling presidency, it became more urgent for the Kremlin's men to push Berezovsky out of the media game. A torpedo on board one of the country's nuclear submarines, the *Kursk*, had somehow detonated, sending an explosion ripping through it, and sending it and its crew to the bottom of the sea. Berezovsky deployed the full force of his ORT TV channel to hurl criticism at how Putin handled the disaster. For six days confusion reigned as he failed to publicly address the tragedy, remaining hidden away in his summer residence near Sochi on the Black Sea coast, only appearing – in footage shown by ORT – to frolic on a jetski. Putin stayed totally silent while the navy obfuscated for days over what had happened, even after acknowledging that the submarine had sunk. The families of the crew were in despair, a rescue operation had only been haltingly mounted, and Russia had initially refused offers of international assistance, fearing the disclosure of secrets about the state of its nuclear fleet.

Still an inexperienced leader, despite his years of work handling illegals against the West and his decisive military action in Chechnya, Putin was initially paralysed by fear, one person close to him said. 'He was in a stupor. He went totally white. He didn't know how to deal with it, and therefore he tried to avoid dealing with it. We knew that it had exploded right away . . . We believed everyone was dead from the start. Putin just did not know how to deal with it, and so when everyone came and said, "What do you want us to do – launch a rescue operation, announce war against the US [one of the claims had been that the *Kursk* had collided with a US submarine]?" he played for time. Even though we believed all were dead we launched the rescue operation, and all the stories appeared about the plaintive cries of the submariners knocking on the walls. The Norwegians and others were calling in with offers of help. But he did not want them to uncover that everyone was dead, and so he just refused the help – which of course made everything worse. All the lies just made everything worse.'[64]

On the seventh day, Putin flew quietly back to Moscow. But it was only three days later that he emerged in public. After much prodding and cajoling from advisers, he flew to Vidyayevo, a closed military city above the Arctic Circle, where the *Kursk* had had its home port, and where the stricken relatives of the crew had gathered days ago, in vain hopes of good news that had long descended into grief, anger and despair. The day before, the Russian authorities had finally admitted that all 118 crewmen were dead, and Putin had already been taking a beating in the media over his inaction in handling the affair. Berezovsky's ORT led the charge, interviewing grief-stricken relatives who laid into Putin for his lack of leadership. Putin exploded in rage over the footage, and claimed that his security men had given him a report saying that the women who appeared on screen were not wives or relatives, but prostitutes hired by Berezovsky to discredit him.

But when Putin arrived in Vidyayevo he was faced with a tirade of real-life anger as wives and relatives tore into him. The fury portrayed on Berezovsky's channel was genuine: any suggestion that it had been staged was out of the question. Putin's initial reaction was another sign of his deep-seated paranoia and his lack of empathy. For three hours he spoke with them, trying to soothe their rage. Though he told them he was ready to take responsibility for everything that had happened in the country in the hundred days since he'd become president, he said he could not do the same for the previous fifteen years: 'For this, I am ready to sit down next to you and pose these same questions to others.'[65] He blamed the bungled rescue operation on the parlous, pitiful state of the military, which had been left to decay with little funding during Yeltsin's rule.

But most of all he laid the blame at the feet of the media tycoons. Clearly targeting Berezovsky and Gusinsky, he lashed out at them as the real cause of the military's plight, for stealing from the country even as they sought to score political points out of the tragedy: 'There are people on television today who . . . over the last ten years destroyed the very army and fleet where people are dying now . . . They stole money, they bought the media and they're manipulating public opinion.'[66]

Eventually, Putin appeared to have won the relatives round. But his comments singling out the media tycoons as thieves who'd undermined the state signalled that any hope for Berezovsky's or Gusinsky's continued ownership of their independent media channels was dead. Again, the Berezovsky associate who retained ties with the security services had scolded his friend and warned him to back off.[67] 'I said, "Borya, why are you undermining him and not giving him a chance? How can you blame him for this submarine?"' But Berezovsky was unrepentant; he feared the rise of the KGB state, and wanted to do everything he could to undermine it. After the *Kursk* episode, Voloshin told Berezovsky that his ownership of ORT was over, as he'd been found to be using the channel 'to work against the president'.[68] Then, according to Berezovsky, he told him he had to surrender his stake within two weeks, or follow Gusinsky into Butyrka. He regarded this as an ultimatum that would lead to the 'end of television information in Russia': 'It will be replaced by television propaganda controlled by [Kremlin] advisers.'[69] For a time he played an uneasy game of cat and mouse with the Kremlin, announcing that he'd handed his stake in ORT in trust to the channel's journalists, all the while proclaiming he would not allow the country to fall into an authoritarian abyss.

For all Berezovsky's prescience, the Yeltsin holdovers in the Kremlin were working in lockstep with Putin and law enforcement. The Kremlin machine was united against Berezovsky and Gusinsky, and there was never going to be any chance for them. Gleb Pavlovsky, the Kremlin spin doctor who'd helped engineer some of the propaganda behind Putin's election campaign, had helped to create a new Kremlin 'Information Security Doctrine' which, he said, would allow the government to remove 'shadow information brokers' like Gusinsky and Berezovsky, who posed 'serious threats to the country's national interests'.[70]

In mid-October, prosecutors reopened their case into allegations that Berezovsky had siphoned hundreds of millions of dollars through Swiss companies from Aeroflot, the Russian state airline he part-owned. The pressure became unbearable. When prosecutors announced on November 13 that they were calling him in for questioning, and that they were ready to charge him, Berezovsky fled Russia and said he would never return. 'They have forced me to choose between becoming a political prisoner or a political émigré,' he said in a statement from a location he would not disclose.[71]

The same tactics were used against Gusinsky. He'd also been called in for questioning on the same day. But he too was long gone, having fled out of the prosecutors' reach to his villa in Spain soon after he signed the deal to hand over his shares in Media Most in July. He'd then reneged on the deal, claiming it was signed under duress in exchange for a guarantee of his freedom. But he could not escape the long arm of the Russian prosecutors. They charged him *in absentia* with misrepresenting his assets in Media Most when he'd accepted loans from Gazprom, and fired off an Interpol warrant for his arrest.

Even in exile, the pressure became too much to bear for both men. In February 2001, following the insistence of Voloshin that he stop his involvement in ORT, Berezovsky sold his shares to Roman Abramovich. The Russian government remained the majority shareholder and took full control of the channel. (Eventually Abramovich sold most of his stake to one of Putin's closest allies, Yury Kovalchuk, and the remaining shares to the state.) In April that year Gazprom seized control of Gusinsky's NTV, launching a boardroom coup as it called in a $281 million loan it had lent to Media Most.

Putin and his men were flexing the tried and tested tactics of the St Petersburg days, when all they'd had to do to take over the city's port and Baltic Sea fleet was to have its director thrown in jail. But at that early stage of their rule they would have been able to do little without the assistance of the Yeltsin holdovers in the Kremlin. 'They [the Yeltsin Family] were the ones who thought up the schemes to bring all the media into the state's hands, that led to the practical destruction of all independent media,' said Leonid Nevzlin, the former Menatep tycoon who was closely watching the goings-on from the sidelines. 'They gave this to Putin . . . We should have concluded where this was all leading to in the first year of Putin's rule. But we wanted to continue looking through rose-coloured glasses, because everything else in the economy seemed to be fine.'[72]

Behind the wizard's curtain of Putin's Kremlin, behind the bombastic show of force, Putin had still been nervous, according to Pugachev. In January 2001, before the takeover of NTV by Gazprom, he'd invited the channel's top journalists to the Kremlin in an attempt to reassure them of the state's intentions. He was visibly fretful before he walked into the Kremlin library to greet them, Pugachev recalled: 'He was scared before the meeting. He didn't want to go in and speak with them. I had to tell him what to say. They were the cream of the Moscow intelligentsia, household names.'[73]

Putin was so anxious that he pulled one of the journalists aside into a separate room and asked her what she wanted to hear, said Pugachev. For the past four years Svetlana Sorokina had been the face of NTV's most popular political talk show, *Glas Naroda*, or Voice of the People. 'He told her, "You and I, we are both from St Petersburg, we have that in common, tell me how you would like it to be,"' Pugachev said. The other journalists, waiting outside, believed Putin had pulled Sorokina aside to wrongfoot them, to take the wind out of their sails. But Pugachev claimed it was because he had no idea what to say. It was also a classic tactic for recruiting allies. By the time Putin finally walked into the wood-panelled Kremlin library to greet the journalists, chameleon-like, he'd absorbed Sorokina's persona and was able to tell them exactly what they wanted to hear. It was another KGB operation. Over the next three and a half hours, he sought to assure them of the Kremlin's benign intentions. The fight, he told them, was only with Gusinsky. He didn't want the channel's editorial staff to change. He would welcome a foreign investor in the channel. He wanted them to preserve their editorial independence. Gazprom, he assured them, was not the state. As for the prosecutors, who were now turning their attention to individual journalists' financial relations with Gusinsky, he could not control them – they were beyond his command.

'We found out that day that the prosecutor's office is an absolutely independent organisation – Putin said it several times,' one of the journalists, Viktor Shenderovich, later recalled of the meeting, barely believing what he'd heard. 'He said he is ready to help us, and considers some of the prosecutors' actions excessive.'[74] Putin had told them: 'You will not believe me, but there is nothing I can do. Do you want me to return to the times of telephone law?'[75] – a reference to how the Soviet Politburo had dictated judgments from on high to the courts and prosecutors.

It was a command performance, typical of many Putin would later make in his insistence on observing the official, legal status of institutions while masking the real power games at play. He was at his most skilled when taking on the persona and concerns of others. It was a tactic he'd honed in Dresden. 'He was like a mirror,' said Pugachev. 'He just tells everyone what they want to hear.'[76]

Nevertheless, the journalists left the Kremlin uneasy. How could they believe what they had just heard? And when Gazprom installed new management in early April, on the grounds that Gusinsky had defaulted on his debts, they staged a sit-in to keep control of the station, and continued to air reports critical of the Kremlin, as if still half-hoping that Putin had meant what he said.

But early in the morning of the eleventh day of their sit-in, Putin's true intentions became crystal clear. He'd meant nothing of what he said about preserving the channel's editorial independence. Security men quietly entered the building at 4 a.m. and replaced the channel's security force. Journalists arriving to work that morning were only allowed in if they swore loyalty to the new management. The senior journalists resigned en masse in protest at the strong-arm tactics that had seized their hard-won independence away from them. 'A creeping coup is taking place in the country,' declared Igor Malashenko, a co-founder of the channel. 'This operation is along the same lines as the attempted putsch in August 1991, and it is being carried out by the same people, members of the secret service.'[77] 'We are all guilty, because we have let the KGB get back into power,' Sergei Kovalyov, a prominent human rights activist, told reporters.[78]

Putin's Kremlin had taken back control of the airwaves. The free-wheeling media of the Yeltsin years was no more.

7

'Operation Energy'

Far to the east of Moscow, beyond the Ural Mountains, where birch forest gives way to a taiga of fir trees and swamp, lies the vast flatland of the west Siberian oil basin. Ever since Soviet geologists discovered huge oil and gas reserves there in the sixties, the region had been the power behind the Soviet empire's global ambitions. It was the key to the country's imperial might.

The engineers, drillers and geologists who developed the near-deserted territory had been lauded as Soviet heroes. They'd battled the ice and plunging temperatures of winter to build drilling rigs and pipelines across terrain that turned into impassable lakes and mosquito-infested bog during the summer months. Their labours helped turn the Soviet Union, for a time, into an economic powerhouse that by the end of the eighties became the world's biggest oil and gas producer. Production was recklessly ramped up to meet the ever greater demands of the Politburo. Wells were being flooded with water to force out the oil that helped fuel the Soviet Union's voracious military-industrial complex. Two thirds of all Soviet oil output was produced there. It was the jewel in the Soviet system that overall held 40 per cent of the world's gas reserves and 12 per cent of oil reserves outside the Middle East.

Most of the oil and gas extracted was sold domestically at fixed low prices, subsidising the mass production of tanks and other weaponry to arm the Soviet empire against the West.[1] But the oil exports were more strategic: they were the black gold on which the Soviet empire's global reach was based. The economy of the East German republic was mostly funded through the sale of Soviet oil and gas at a fraction of the world market prices, and the rest of the eastern bloc was propped up by similar deals.[2]

Oil exports in particular were jealously watched over by the KGB. The profits the Soviet state monopoly oil exporter Soyuzneftexport made from the difference between the Soviet and world prices – six times higher – helped fill the hard-currency coffers of the Soviet empire, funding forays into the Middle East and Africa, stoking armed conflicts and uprisings, and financing active measures to disrupt the West.

When the Soviet Union collapsed and the oil ministry's chain of command shattered, the oil industry broke up initially into four separate vertically-integrated production companies: Lukoil, Yukos, Surgutneftegaz and, for a time, Rosneft. Though they were still nominally controlled by the state, they were mostly taken over by the directors, the oil generals, who had run them in Soviet times, while organised-crime groups, running amok in Russia's regional towns, tried to muscle their way in.[3] There was a widespread collapse in output, as the oilfields of west Siberia had been largely depleted by decades of Soviet mismanagement. But, unnoticed in the shadows, in the first half of the nineties, members of the KGB's foreign-intelligence arm kept control over the majority of oil exports. Producers had been ordered to sell up to 80 per cent of their output at the fixed low internal price to the state, which then allowed a system of *spetsexportery*, specially designated exporters allied closely with the KGB or with crony organised crime, to reap the difference from the global price.[4] Often the funds this brought in were siphoned for black cash for the KGB and the Kremlin – to fund election campaigns and make sure parliamentary votes went the Kremlin's way – or were simply looted.

When the most strategic and lucrative sectors of Soviet industry were sold off in the mid-nineties under the loans-for-shares auctions, many of these gold seams for KGB networks passed into private hands. Control of the likes of Yukos and Sibneft, a neighbouring west Siberian oil producer, were sold to the young bankers close to the Yeltsin government, including to Khodorkovsky and Abramovich with the assistance of Berezovsky, for just $300 million and $100 million apiece. The access to capital the young tycoons gained through their banks' management of government treasury accounts helped give them the upper hand in the battle for the country's resources. The KGB operatives were never going to be able to stump up such amounts.

The consequences were enormous. Oil – despite the low global prices at that time – still made up a large chunk of the country's export revenues.[5] Khodorkovsky's men, for instance, set up their own trading networks for Yukos as soon as they took over the company in 1996. The profits were stashed in the private offshore accounts of Khodorkovsky's Menatep group, far out of the reach of the Russian state, while Menatep found loopholes in the laws to minimise tax payments. The balance of power was decisively shifting towards the Yeltsin-era tycoons. Their privatisation of the oil-export cash flow changed everything. It turned the likes of Khodorkovsky and Berezovsky into full-blown oligarchs, able to bribe Yeltsin's men, and stack parliamentary votes in their own favour. According to former KGB officer-turned-oil-trader Andrei Pannikov, the break-up of the oil trade into independent ownership was a threat to the integrity of the Russian state that should never have happened: 'I would never have destroyed the state monopoly. I would have kept all the export trading in state hands.'[6]

For Putin and his KGB men, it was a matter that of course drew their immediate attention. Global oil prices began to surge almost as soon as Putin was anointed Yeltsin's successor in the summer of 1999. By mid-2002, Khodorkovsky, who'd started out as an intense, softly-spoken chemistry student running discos for the Komsomol, was announcing to the world a personal fortune of $7 billion through his ownership of a 36 per cent stake in the Menatep group.[7] It was a colossal leap in fortune since the days when Menatep acquired Yukos for $300 million in the loans-for-shares auctions of 1995, when Yukos itself was knee-deep in debt.[8] The disclosure officially made Khodorkovsky Russia's richest man, at a time when the entire Russian state budget was $67 billion, and the market capitalisation of Russia's biggest state-controlled company, Gazprom, was $25 billion.

Khodorkovsky and his partners in Menatep had been the first Russian tycoons to publicly disclose their business holdings. Most of the oligarchs hid their ownership behind a web of front companies, still fearing retribution from the state after the controversy of the nineties-era privatisations. Khodorkovsky was putting his head over the parapet partly because Putin's vault to the presidency was meant to signal a legalisation of the country's chaotic market transition, a securing of the gains of the nineties. It was one of the reasons Putin had won such broad support, most crucially from the Yeltsin Family. Even though he'd ruthlessly taken out the media tycoons, Putin had given no indication that he wanted to increase state ownership anywhere else. And while he'd made plenty of threatening noises about bringing the oligarchs to heel, he'd insisted that he would not overturn the privatisations of the nineties. It seemed that with Khodorkovsky's disclosure, Russia was further progressing on the way to a more mature and developed market economy. The move was lauded as a break-through for transparency, but it was also perhaps Khodorkovsky's bet on the power of the market to protect him. He was banking on oper-ating according to Western market rules of the game.

But for the *siloviki* who'd risen to power with Putin, Khodorkovsky's new status as the country's richest man – operating outside their control – was another red flag. They'd been waiting in the shadows since the Soviet collapse, harbouring ambitions to restore Russia's might. Putin's rise to the presidency, through his subtle deception and promises to the Yeltsin Family, was meant to be the first step towards achieving that. The KGB men had always seen the country's oil industry as currency in geopolitical power games. In their view, taking control of Russia's oil resources was going to be crucial in both securing their own position in power and in restoring Russia's standing against the West. It didn't hurt, of course, that they would be able to line their own pockets in the process.

The question was how they would go about it. Unlike the Communists, the new generation of *siloviki* – from the ranks of KGB, which had started the market reforms in the first place – were never going to announce a renationalisation campaign: they'd always declared themselves in favour of the market. But they aimed to use and distort the market as a weapon. They wanted to establish a form of quasi-state capitalism that would further their own – and as they saw it, Russia's – power.

The gas industry posed a much easier equation than the oil sector.

Unlike oil, it had been preserved almost in its entirety as a vast state-controlled monopoly. Gazprom, the state gas giant, was the country's most strategic asset. Straddling the biggest gas reserves on the planet, it was the world's number-one gas producer, and brought in the country's largest tax revenue stream. It not only provided Russia's homes with heat and light, it also supplied Europe with 25 per cent of its gas needs. Its role as the predominant supplier to much of Central and Eastern Europe, as well as Ukraine and Belarus, meant it could be used as a tool of political influence, while its vast cash pools and financial assets presented a wealth of opportunity for Putin's men. Under Yeltsin, Gazprom's senior management had largely taken control of the company, transforming it into their own fiefdom. But Putin made their replacement with his own allies one of his first priorities, launching a sweeping purge after shareholder investigations showed the Yeltsin-era managers had siphoned a string of gas fields and other assets out of Gazprom and into companies connected to them. The men he appointed in their place had all served in executive positions at the St Petersburg sea port, the strategic asset that Putin's *siloviki* had taken over, cutting their teeth joining forces with the Tambov organised-crime group. It was the first indication that the alliance forged then would take over assets on a federal scale. Gazprom's new chief executive was thirty-nine-year-old Alexei Miller, a short, mustachioed man who'd served as Putin's deputy on the Foreign Relations Committee of the St Petersburg mayor's office and then as a director at the sea port.[9]

The privately-owned oil industry was going to pose a far more difficult challenge. In St Petersburg, the *siloviki* had been able to easily bend the city's law enforcement to their will to push out rivals. But tackling the Moscow oligarchs was a different matter entirely. For all the power they wielded through the FSB, Putin's followers had not yet consolidated control over the entire system of law enforcement, and the Moscow tycoons were established figures, well known in the West, who'd built companies that were traded on Western markets. At stake was the country's ability to pull in outside investment, which the pragmatic Putin understood was still essential to speed Russia's economic recovery from the nineties collapse.

The *siloviki* began what became known as 'Operation Energy' quietly. The Yeltsin Family continued to feel secure in their belief that Putin was a man of the market. To them he was the president-in-training, still learning the ropes of government. In the first year of his rule he was taking intensive lessons in the English language, in how to speed-read stacks of documents, and in the administration and history of the Russian state, according to a senior KGB-linked banker familiar with the matter, who said: 'The system for preparing leaders had collapsed.'[10]

The Yeltsin Family still believed firmly in Putin's loyalty, and in his obedience to them. It seems they also believed they had the run of most of the economy for Putin's first term, while Putin appeared to indicate initially that he didn't intend to serve beyond that. The Family felt so comfortable, and were so unaware of any ambitions the St Petersburg KGB men might harbour towards the oil industry, that they began to hatch plans to privatise the last remaining state oil major, Rosneft. Roman Abramovich had long been eyeing the company – he and Berezovsky had hoped to merge it into Sibneft when it had first been slated for privatisation in 1997. Now that they believed they'd secured their future, said Pugachev, Voloshin had even prepared a decree for Rosneft's privatisation that was just awaiting Putin's signature. Behind the scenes, Abramovich had been quietly lobbying to smooth the way. A row of fine Italian suits and shoes had suddenly appeared hanging in the hallway of Putin's Novo-Ogarevo residence, courtesy of Abramovich, according to Pugachev. 'I said, "Volodya, what on earth do you want all this for? You are president of one of the world's biggest countries. Surely you can get your own suits! You don't want these bribes. They will ask for something in return."'[11] A spokesperson for Abramovich denies this ever happened.

For Pugachev, Abramovich's overtures had been the final straw. Pugachev believed it was essential to keep the state's last oil company out of the Family's hands. As his standing rose due to his role in propelling Putin to power, he had begun to move fluidly between alliances with Putin's St Petersburg KGB men and with the Yeltsin Family, depending on the political imperative, often keeping his real allegiances hidden. But on this occasion he began to shift decisively towards the *siloviki*. 'They'd invited the president to Voloshin's dacha. They called him to them. It was absolutely improper,' he recalled. 'I said, "Why are you going there? Why should it be privatised, what are you thinking about? There is no money in the budget. Without Rosneft, how do you intend to live, where are you going to get wages from?"'[12]

In the background, the St Petersburg *siloviki* were already building their own defences to keep Rosneft out of private hands. Behind the backs of the Yeltsin Family they'd been quietly putting a parallel system of government in place, according to a senior banker close to the security services.[13] Leading the process was Igor Sechin, Putin's loyal KGB colleague from St Petersburg, who'd been appointed deputy head of his administration, and, further behind the scenes, according to the senior banker, Gennady Timchenko, the alleged former KGB operative and close Putin ally from the St Petersburg oil terminal. In those days, the banker said, Timchenko was one of the most influential operators in Putin's entourage: 'He was immediately powerful as soon as Putin was appointed president.' But Putin kept him hidden from view. 'He was like the invisible man. He was never seen,' another person close to Putin said.[14] (Timchenko, through his lawyers, said any suggestion he was involved in any project to create a parallel system of government was 'utterly false to the point of being absurd'. Timchenko has 'simply never involved himself in political issues, nor discussed political issues with Mr Putin or any of his staff or ministers.')

One of the first tasks of this group was to make sure Putin was elected for a second term, regardless of whether he himself was yet convinced that that was what he wanted. To achieve this, they needed to bolster their position in power. 'Their task was to get their hands on more cash flow,' the banker said. 'They were concerned that the Family, Abramovich, were controlling certain sectors of the economy.'[15]

Meanwhile, in the background, a broader caste of KGB men had long been drawing up lists of targets in the oil sector.[16] Initially at the top of the list was Surgutneftegaz, the west Siberian oil producer run by Vladimir Bogdanov, who'd served as its director since Soviet times. But Bogdanov and Surgutneftegaz had already established a close relationship with Putin's KGB men through Timchenko, whose oil trader had a near monopoly on exports from Surgut's Kirishi refinery. 'Timchenko brought Bogdanov to the Kremlin to meet Putin for tea,' the senior banker tied to the security services said. 'There Bogdanov told Putin, "It's your company. I am for you in any case. Just tell me how to spend the money."'

The *siloviki* had then trained their sights on Lukoil – at the time Russia's biggest oil major, forged out of three west Siberian oil units by the former Soviet deputy minister of oil and gas, Vagit Alekperov, when the Soviet Union collapsed. Alekperov was a wily Azerbaijani who'd been one of the founding fathers of the carve-up of the Russian oil industry. He'd always been close to Russian intelligence networks – Lukoil had initially sold oil through Urals Trading, the oil trader set up by former KGB officer and Timchenko partner Andrei Pannikov – and it didn't take long before Putin's men had brought Lukoil to heel.

The opening volley against Lukoil was fired in the summer of 2000, amid the first wave of Kremlin probes into the oligarchs. The tax police declared that they'd opened a criminal investigation into alleged tax fraud by Alekperov, which they said was part of an industry-wide probe that was later claimed to have unearthed a total of $9 billion in tax avoidance through special offshore zones created inside Russia.[17] But it wasn't until September 2002 that the pressure on Lukoil really began to mount. Early one morning that month, Lukoil's first vice president Sergei Kukura was kidnapped by men dressed in police uniforms and wearing masks, who had apparently incapacitated him and his driver by injecting them with heroin, then thrown bags over their heads.[18] Kukura reappeared only thirteen days later, apparently at a loss about who was behind the attack. Four months later, Russian police mysteriously shelved their investigation into the kidnapping.[19] A week before, the government had announced that Lukoil had agreed to pay $103 million in back taxes – exactly the amount the government claimed it had lost through Lukoil's operations via the internal offshore zones.[20]

If Alekperov and Lukoil had reached some kind of compromise with Putin's new government, then, as with Surgut, there was no need for any formal takeover by the state. Later, a senior oil executive told me that Alekperov had agreed to hold some of his stake on Putin's behalf, part of a system of fronting for the Kremlin that was to become entrenched in Russia's most strategic industries.[21] (Lukoil denies any such system is in place.)

But while Lukoil appeared to quickly bend to the will of the new masters, a big chunk of oil output was still far out of the Kremlin's reach. Intent on rectifying that, the *siloviki* were heading towards a standoff that would become the defining moment of Putin's rule, changing the face of the Russian oil industry and shifting the country definitively towards a form of crony state capitalism in which strategic cash flows were diverted into close allies' hands. The power of Putin's KGB men would be cemented, helping forge their return as a force on the global stage. It was a conflict that would also take down Russia's richest businessman and subvert the entire Russian legal system.

Of all the Moscow oligarchs, Mikhail Khodorkovsky was the one most actively seeking to integrate his company into the West, most openly courting Western investors and leaders for support. He was leading the way in trying to instil Western corporate governance methods and transparency at his company, after years of being a bad boy of Russia's Darwinian business scene. The conflict that unfolded as Putin's *siloviki* fought to wrest away Khodorkovsky's control of Yukos's west Siberian oilfields was at once a clash of visions for Russia's future, and a battle for empire. It was to define Russia's imperial resurgence and Putin's efforts to restore his country as an independent force against the West. But it was also a clash that was deeply personal. It had its roots in a conflict at the end of the nineties, when Khodorkovsky had taken away one of the last remaining black-cash channels from Putin's closest allies, who'd formerly been at the heart of KGB operations to transfer Communist Party funds into the West.

Khodorkovsky's takeover of VNK, or Eastern Oil Company, was one of the last big oil-industry privatisations of the nineties – and seeing it seized from under their noses had been the final straw for Putin's men. 'It was the first conflict between Putin's group and

Yukos, and the most serious one,' said Vladimir Milov, a former deputy Russian energy minister. 'This is when it all began.'[22]

*

Far away from it all now, as we sit in the oak-panelled conference room of his London office overlooking the leaves of Hanover Square, after a ten-year jail sentence and in forced exile from home, Mikhail Khodorkovsky claims he wasn't aware back then of the ties between VNK and Putin's KGB men. 'Had I known how much VNK was a structure in which the FSB had interests, I probably wouldn't have risked going in there,' he said,[23] dressed now in a simple quilted shirt not unlike the padded jackets he'd been forced to wear in Siberian prison, as if it was a habit he couldn't break.

It was the end of the nineties when Khodorkovsky had made it to the top of Russia's hurly-burly transition to the market – and VNK was one of the Russian oil industry's last prizes. When it was put up for privatisation in 1997, the sale was heralded as a clean break from the controversial discount loans-for-shares deals. The company, forged out of the Tomskneft oilfields surrounding the genteel central Siberian university town of Tomsk and the Achinsk oil refinery, was slated to go on sale for as much as $1 billion, nearly ten times more than the loans-for-shares sales of Yukos and Sibneft had raised just one year before.[24] Anatoly Chubais, the steely privatisation tsar, was determined to show the world that Russia was transforming itself into a real rules-based market economy. He wanted VNK to be sold for its true market value.[25]

The only problem was that the men who ran the company appeared to think that Chubais had promised it to them. VNK was meant to be the consolation prize for the KGB men behind it, after they'd watched much of the rest of the Russian oil industry swallowed up by the independent tycoons. It had served as a source of cash, an *obschak*, for them ever since it was formed in 1994. Much of its oil exports had been directed through companies connected to a little-known Austrian company called IMAG, which was run by Andrei Akimov, a senior foreign-intelligence officer who'd headed the USSR's foreign banking arm in Austria, Donau Bank, right up to the Soviet collapse.[26] Akimov had been the youngest ever Soviet bank chief when he headed Donau Bank at the age of thirty-four, having been appointed just as the KGB began setting up schemes to siphon the Communist Party wealth through foreign bank accounts, while Vienna had long been a strategic gateway for Soviet funds into the West.[27]

Akimov's connections in Russia's foreign-intelligence networks ran far and deep.[28] Working as his deputy at IMAG was an economist who'd helped develop the early *perestroika* reforms under Primakov at the Institute for World Economy, the hive for foreign-intelligence operatives. This was Alexander Medvedev, and he was to become Akimov's closest confidant,[29] while IMAG was to become one of the earliest sources of financing for Timchenko's trading operations.

Akimov had been so convinced of victory in the VNK sell-off that he'd had Medvedev appointed as VNK's vice president in charge of finance ahead of the sale.[30] For IMAG, hundreds of millions of dollars in oil contracts were at stake. Almost ever since its creation, VNK had sold most of its oil through a trader called East Petroleum Ltd, registered near IMAG's offices and run by another close Akimov associate, Yevgeny Rybin.

When the state's 84 per cent stake in VNK was put up for auction and Khodorkovsky decided to bid for it, he was heading into a hornets' nest. With the help of an American banker named Charlie Ryan, who'd been associated with Putin since he'd done a stint at the European Bank of Reconstruction and Development in St Petersburg in the early nineties, Akimov was determined to win, no matter what the cost. The two men were aware from the start that Khodorkovsky was bidding against them. 'We decided we were going to buy VNK,' said Ryan. 'Sasha [Medvedev], Andrei and I were going to organise the bid with proper funds.'[31]

But the sale turned into a bruising standoff between Khodorkovsky and Akimov's men, and the outcome was almost as murky as the loans for shares. The state's 84 per cent stake in VNK was to be sold in two parts – one 50 per cent minus one share stake through a cash auction, and the rest through an investment tender. But the first part of the sale was held behind closed doors, without being open to any scrutiny, while the second ended up being cancelled because there was only one bidder, a shell company representing Khodorkovsky's Yukos.[32]

Instead of setting a new standard for transparency, the sale ended up looking just as rigged as the privatisations that had gone before. The government announced that Khodorkovsky's Yukos had won the cash auction with a bid of $775 million for a 45 per cent stake. It had already bought a further 9 per cent on the open market, making its stake a controlling one.[33] Yukos had agreed to pay far more than anyone had offered in any of the privatisations that had gone before, but according to Ryan, Khodorkovsky had still skewed the outcome in his favour, leaving Akimov's team without a chance. Ryan said that Khodorkovsky's men threatened Akimov and his team, and then, between the first and second auctions, paid off a section of the Russian security services to raid the Federal Property Fund, which was organising the sale.[34] During the raid they'd seized documents relating to Akimov's bid, and then rigged the outcome, Ryan claimed. 'They saw our information and they knew we'd bid more. They then tried to borrow more money, guaranteed by their own oil exports, including from the exports of VNK, before they'd even acquired control over the company.' Khodorkovsky and his team were able to raise more money than Akimov's, and emerged with the winning bid. They never had any intention of taking part in the second auction.

Khodorkovsky denied he was involved in any such actions. But what followed was a protracted battle over VNK's exports, which Akimov's team had pledged to sell through Yevgeny Rybin's East Petroleum for the next twenty years, as a further defence against the company's cash flow falling into outside hands.[35] Khodorkovsky refused to continue this contract, and the standoff escalated beyond the boardroom, into the courtroom and then onto the street. Two attempts were made on Rybin's life. The first came late on a snowy evening in November 1998, when a gunman fired at him on a Moscow street. The second came in March the following year, when a bomb exploded and killed Rybin's driver. Shaken to the core, Rybin fled Russia and went into hiding for the next five years.

Akimov and his men were bruised and deeply humiliated by Khodorkovsky's takeover of VNK. The story of the battle for the company was little-noticed during the chaos that followed the August 1998 financial crisis, but it was to define the future battle for Russia's oil sector. From then on, Akimov was set on revenge. And though he was in hiding in Vienna, Rybin began gathering compromising information on Khodorkovsky's Menatep group and feeding it to Russian law enforcement, most of all to friendly officers in the FSB.[36]

At first Rybin's efforts didn't seem to be getting anywhere. But after Putin came to power, the atmosphere changed. Sechin and one of Akimov's partners began a campaign to convince the president that Khodorkovsky posed a danger to his hold on power, according to a senior banker with knowledge of the matter. Rybin had also enrolled Egor Ligachev, a prominent member of the old guard of the Politburo, who served as a lawmaker in the Tomsk region of Siberia where VNK's oilfields were located.[37] Ligachev delivered Putin a stark message: Khodorkovsky was endangering the existence of his regime; his men had all the country's financial flows under their control, and soon they would have more money than the state itself – already he'd bought more than half the state officials in power.[38]

It was a message that resonated strongly with Putin as he sought to shore up his power against rival groups. But despite the manoeuvrings, he was at first reluctant to follow the calls to take Yukos on. The company was too big, and too well-entrenched in Western markets – it seemed too complicated a task, said a senior banker close to the security services.[39] It was the country's most recognisable, most widely traded company. It had become a symbol of Russia's market progress.

The takedown might never have happened had it not been for Khodorkovsky's own behaviour. Instead of bowing to the Kremlin's will, as Lukoil and Surgutneftegaz had before, Khodorkovsky kept raising the stakes until it *did* become a battle over who would rule Russia and the direction the country would take. He was willing to bet his life on Putin's men not daring to arrest him: he believed they weren't strong enough, and would not risk Russia's precarious transition to the market. In many ways, this was typical of him. 'He set about building his empire like a maniac,' recalled his adviser Christian Michel. 'He was stoppable only by a bullet.'[40]

*

Khodorkovsky himself admits now that he is an *adrenalinschik*, an adrenalin junkie, with a vastly reduced perception of risk. He'd first become aware of this many years before the battle for Yukos, when he was a chemistry student at the Mendeleyev Institute in Moscow, specialising in explosive materials. 'I am a person who for some reason unknown to me does not have the feeling of fear,' he told me with a wry grin in an underground bar in Zürich not long after his release from ten years in jail. 'I never had a feeling of danger from making a bomb, or from holding one. My favourite pastime was always rock-climbing without any safety equipment. This is not because I somehow overcame my fear, it's because I didn't have it. All those years in prison I slept absolutely soundly. Even though there were situations when I'd been attacked with a knife, I would go back to the bunk where I'd been lying and would peacefully go asleep. It was funny even for me to understand sometimes, when people asked me whether I knew that behind my back there could be a knife. I just wasn't afraid.'[41]

The first time Khodorkovsky heard that he could be in danger was towards the middle of 2002. Lukoil was already under fire, and the former KGB men he employed in his own security service warned him that the FSB had launched an operation, Operation Energy, to collect compromising information on the country's energy giants. In Yukos's case, they said, the target was the company's operations with the shares of VNK. But Khodorkovsky assumed it was no more than a run-of-the-mill operation to seek information that could bring the oil barons to heel. 'This was not the first such operation, and we didn't think it was so radical,' he said when we met in the safety of his office in Hanover Square.[42]

Back in 2002, Khodorkovsky was unveiling his $7.6 billion fortune through his ownership of a 36 per cent stake in Menatep. He'd become, relatively speaking, a beacon of transparency among the

Byzantine rules that still governed most of Russia's business climate then. He was staking his company and his future on Russia's integration with the West. It was only three years since he had represented the epitome of Russia's wild east robber capitalism, accused of violating the rights of Western minority shareholders. But now he was seeking legitimisation and protection for the future in Western markets, and in blazing a trail for better, Western-style, corporate governance standards at Yukos.

He was still as intense and driven as when he started out in business in the Komsomol. But he'd swapped his heavy thick-lensed glasses of the mid-nineties for light designer glasses that seemed in their clarity to represent his new drive for transparency. Although he still dressed simply in jeans and dark poloneck sweaters, the abundant black hair he had sported in the nineties was now cropped short and had turned a steely grey, while his moustache was long gone. He'd hired a string of Western executives to oversee finance and production at Yukos, leading an industry-wide turnaround that finally helped restore output at west Siberian oilfields to its levels before the Soviet collapse. Across the board, the privately-owned oil majors were hiring Western drilling-equipment makers, improving their techniques, investing in equipment and hiring Western accountants. Yukos was by then producing more oil than Kuwait.

As Khodorkovsky won plaudits in the West for his transformation, while Yukos's stock price continued to soar, he deepened his engagement with the West further still. He wined and dined the Washington elite and launched a philanthropic organisation, Open Russia, where Henry Kissinger and a former US ambassador to Russia sat on the board. He sent a pioneering tanker of crude to Texas, the first shipment of Russian oil ever sent directly to American shores, and began lobbying for a pipeline to be built, independent of the Russian state, from Russia's far north Murmansk port to the US.

All these activities only antagonised Putin's KGB men still further. Khodorkovsky's dalliance with the West was a direct challenge to their authority, while his lobbying of the other private oil barons to band together and build privately-owned oil pipelines was an even greater threat.[43] The oil-pipeline system had always been the preserve of the Russian state, and granting access to it was seen as one of the few strategic levers the government still had to keep the oil barons in check. By early 2003, as Putin's security men began to step up their plans for revenge, Khodorkovsky was admitting privately that he might have a problem. One gloomy morning that February we were sitting in the dim lamplight of his cavernous office in the fortress-like concrete hulk on one of Moscow's main thoroughfares that served as Menatep's headquarters. He spoke ever more quietly as he said it was becoming clear that there was 'a group of people in the Kremlin who want to take my company'. These men wanted to test once again whether state-owned companies could be more effective than private ones, he said. But he insisted – he was sure, in fact – that Putin would never let that happen, that he'd meant it when he'd pledged not to overturn the privatisations of the nineties. 'Putin keeps his word,' he said. 'I am absolutely not worried.'[44]

The mood that dark grey February morning belied the tension and the background preparations for the battle ahead. Khodorkovsky clearly still hoped that Putin, despite his background in the KGB, had another side to his personality, one that had been nurtured by his work in St Petersburg with the liberal and democratic Sobchak. And, just a few weeks later, it was as if Khodorkovsky was preparing to battle for Putin's better angels when he decided to make a direct appeal to him. He'd already warned the month before that Russia stood at a crossroads, that the country could either go down the road of state bureaucracy, like Saudi Arabia where half the budget was spent on the wages of state bureaucrats, or it could take the path of Western economies, of increasing productivity and post-industrial societies with rising service sectors.[45] When Russia's oligarchs gathered later that February for their by-now regular meetings with Putin around the vast oval table of the Kremlin's Ekaterinsky Hall, Khodorkovsky decided to frame the question of the gradually increasing state participation in the economy more starkly still.

He had decided to make a point about state corruption, and began with a PowerPoint presentation boldly titled 'Corruption in Russia: A Brake on Economic Growth'. He said that the level of corruption in the country had reached 10 per cent of GDP, or $30 billion a year, at the same time as the annual tax take was estimated at about 30 per cent of GDP.[46] Why was it, he asked, that students were racing to qualify as officials in the Russian tax service, where the official wage was only $150–170 a month, while far fewer wanted to become oil engineers, whose wages were four times higher.[47] 'This could lead one to certain thoughts,' he said, with a glance at the president sitting across the huge table. Then he raised the issue more pointedly still, turning his attention to a deal in which the state-owned oil giant Rosneft had made its first big acquisition of recent years, paying $600 million to acquire an oil company, Severnaya Neft, which sat on huge reserves in Russia's far north. The privately-owned oil companies had been eyeing it for months, but Rosneft had trumped them, paying twice the accepted valuation. The question was, Khodorkovsky suggested, where did the $300 million in overpayment go? An investigation should be mounted, he told the president, to pin down the reason for the overpayment.[48] Whispers had been circulating for weeks that the difference was a kickback pocketed by officials.

Khodorkovsky's gamble backfired badly. He'd hit one of Putin's rawest nerves. The discussion was being broadcast live on TV, and though Putin was smiling, he was clearly smarting. 'Rosneft is a state company that should increase its reserves,' Putin said. 'Some other companies, for example Yukos, have an excess of reserves, and how it acquired them is to be one of the subjects we will discuss today, including questions of non-payment of taxes . . . I return the puck back to you!'[49]

'When I saw this on TV I realised this was the end for us,' said Khodorkovsky's chief of analysis, former KGB general Alexei Kondaurov. 'We hadn't discussed it before. When he came out after the meeting, I said, "Mikhail Borisovich, why couldn't you give the corruption presentation to someone else?" He said, "How could I give this to someone else? There are so few fighters among us." And so we began to have problems. I knew he [Putin] would never forgive him for this. Putin's men had taken $300 million for themselves.'[50]

If Putin's KGB men had pocketed a $300 million kickback, it was the first major deal since he took the presidency in which they'd been able to enrich themselves. The deal had been structured through one of the initial owners of Severnaya Neft, Andrei Vavilov, a former deputy finance minister, who conceded he did not own all of it. (On paper, Severnaya Neft was owned by six obscure companies.) According to one person familiar with the deal, Vavilov had kicked the money back to Putin through Rosneft's president, Sergei Bogdanchikov.[51] When we spoke, Vavilov denied that any kickbacks were involved,[52] and the Kremlin hotly denied any irregularity too.

But judging by Putin's reaction, Khodorkovsky had hit a sensitive spot. For Putin, it was unthinkable for Khodorkovsky to openly challenge him over the deal. He deeply resented the allegation of corruption when, to his mind, Khodorkovsky had acquired his fortune, in particular Yukos, in a corrupt way.

Khodorkovsky had opened the door even wider for the Kremlin to attack his wealth. But he had laid down the gauntlet, in part, because he had no choice. The Severnaya Neft deal, which boosted Rosneft's reach, signalled that the rules of the game were significantly shifting in favour of the state, challenging Khodorkovsky's entire business model. 'He understood that to act in any other way was not possible,' said Kondaurov. 'He could not develop his business any other way. So he went for broke. He bet it all. He understood that in any case further ahead there could only be a dead end.'[53]

From that moment on, it was as if Khodorkovsky was putting all his chips on the table, and he accelerated the expansion of his empire, driving through a $36 billion deal that would merge Yukos with Abramovich's Sibneft, creating the world's fourth-biggest oil producer, and the second-biggest in terms of reserves.[54] The deal was announced without warning at the end of April, in a flurry of camera lights in the elegant lobby of Moscow's newest high-end hotel, the Hyatt, just around the corner from the Lubyanka headquarters of the FSB. It was as if Khodorkovsky believed the merger would provide him with an extra layer of protection, as he was joining his company with the Yeltsin Family. But to this day, his business partner Leonid Nevzlin believes Abramovich was setting a trap, seeking to take over Yukos through the merger and squeeze Khodorkovsky out.

Khodorkovsky continued regardless. He stepped up his drive for integration with the West, launching historic behind-the-scenes talks on the sale of a stake in the merged YukosSibneft to a US oil company, either ExxonMobil or Chevron.[55] This would be yet another layer of protection for Yukos, keeping it beyond the reach of the Russian state. Only three months before, another group of oligarchs led by Alfa Group's Mikhail Fridman, also a former Komsomol member, had agreed a groundbreaking $6.75 billion partnership with British Petroleum, under which the UK company would take a 50 per cent stake in their Tyumen Oil Company, known as TNK. It seemed only natural that YukosSibneft would follow. At first Putin seemed to humour the negotiations, harbouring grandiose ambitions, one person familiar with the matter said, that with the help of loans from Russian state banks, YukosSibneft would instead take control of one of the US energy giants.[56]

But while Fridman and his business partner Pyotr Aven, who'd once worked closely with Putin on the St Petersburg oil-for-food deals, kept a low profile and did everything they could to display loyalty to the Putin regime, Khodorkovsky began to step up his activities in the political field too. He'd been pouring funds through his Open Russia foundation into philanthropy, seeking to teach young Russian teenagers the principles of democracy at annual youth camps and at a school he'd established outside Moscow for the children of Russian servicemen killed in action. Shortly before the merger between Yukos and Sibneft was announced, he'd made his personal political ambitions clear, telling the world he wanted to step down from the helm of Yukos when he reached his forty-fifth birthday.[57] That would be in 2007, just before the presidential elections scheduled for 2008. It seemed he was signalling his intention to run.

Khodorkovsky had also long been in talks with parliamentary leaders about transforming Russia into a parliamentary republic, a move that would erase what many critics saw as the fatal flaw of the country's political system – the overconcentration of power in the hands of the president. The system, which allowed the president to essentially run the country by decree, had been tipped in favour of the president following Yeltsin's violent standoff with parliament in

1993. A move to a parliamentary republic would strip key executive powers from the president and transfer authority to the prime minister, elected by parliament. Khodorkovsky insists now that these talks went on within Putin's full view, and with his consent.[58] He says they were not aimed at reducing Putin's power, but at forging a more balanced system after he stepped down in 2008 after two terms in office, which in those days was seen as the constitutional limit. But many viewed Khodorkovsky as driven by a growing mega-lomania, and eyeing the role of prime minister for himself.

Like many of Russia's business tycoons, Khodorkovsky was funding political parties in the Duma. This was actively encouraged by Alexander Voloshin, the Kremlin chief of staff, and his deputy Vladislav Surkov,[59] in the hope that it would help to turn the Communists into more of a party of the left-wing bourgeoisie. But concerns were growing that Khodorkovsky was taking the practice too far. He was pouring tens of millions of dollars into funding the Communists and two liberal parties, Yabloko and the Union of Right Forces. Two of the top executives from his Yukos group headed the Communist Party candidates list, while one of his closest business associates, Vladimir Dubov, a founding partner of the Menatep group, had already won election in December 1999, and headed the powerful parliamentary committee on taxation.[60]

The clout Khodorkovsky wielded in parliament was beginning to pose a challenge to the Kremlin's power. The situation was all too strongly underlined in May 2003, when the tycoon managed to secure enough parliamentary votes to block Kremlin efforts for sweeping oil-sector tax reforms that for the first time aimed to restructure the Russian economy away from its over-reliance on oil income.[61] Fast-rising global oil prices – from $12 per barrel in 1998 to $28 in 2003 – had helped to rapidly boost government coffers and pay down foreign debt. But the increasing oil price was also further heightening Russia's dependence on oil and gas revenues to fill its budget and for economic growth. In 2003, oil and gas output accounted for 20 per cent of Russia's GDP, 55 per cent of its entire export earnings and 40 per cent of total tax revenues.[62] The International Monetary Fund had produced a report which showed that Russia had become five times more dependent on world oil prices by 2003 than it was before the August 1998 default – when the precariousness of the country's reliance on the global oil price had become all too disastrously evident.[63] If oil prices dropped back down to the $12 per barrel level last seen in 1998, Russia could lose $13 billion, the equivalent of 3 per cent of its GDP, in budget revenues, the IMF said.

Russia's overarching dependence on global energy prices outside its control had long had the more liberal wing of Putin's government searching for ways out. In the Yeltsin years, the government was too busy lurching from crisis to crisis to reduce Russia's reliance on oil and gas revenue – it needed every source of income it could get as it scrambled to collect taxes. But now that oil prices were surging, the liberal faction in government – led by Alexei Kudrin, the finance minister who'd served under Sobchak with Putin in St Petersburg, and German Gref, the economy minister, who'd also worked in St Petersburg as the Federal Property chief – could finally seek to use the more stable situation, and the burgeoning revenue, to restructure the economy. As early as February 2003, Gref had announced measures to further increase the tax take from the oil industry's windfall gains, in order to then plough state investment into high-tech and defence sectors.[64]

The government was seeking to raise taxation on the oil industry both through levying greater export taxes and a royalty tax. But Khodorkovsky was resisting the royalty taxes all the way. When, in May, his men in parliament were able to defeat one of the first government attempts to impose it, the liberals in Putin's government – Gref and Kudrin – took it personally. Till then, according to one senior banker close to Kudrin, they'd been seeking to defend Khodorkovsky from the growing appetite of the statist security men to attack him. But he'd not only undermined their plans, he'd also undermined their arguments in his defence. 'He'd become a major investor in the Duma,' the banker said. 'He was bankrolling half the Duma. It had become clear that to say he wasn't a threat was utter rubbish. The deal he put together to pull the vote on the increase in the tax burden was backed not just by a coalition of pro-business deputies, but by diehard Communists, rabid anti-Semite nationalists, liberals and conservatives. It was the most bizarre mix of people voting against a tax increase. Kudrin called him and said, "Misha, you're fucking up. You're not supposed to buy the organs of the state. There are people out there who want to increase taxes to 90 per cent. You should have taken the deal." But you know what he told Kudrin? He said, "Who do you think you are? Go fuck yourself. I will have you removed."'

The situation, Gref and Kudrin believed, was becoming untenable. Khodorkovsky, the banker claimed, made things even worse when, jubilant after the vote, he began calling future candidates for the post of prime minister and telling them they would have to agree their agenda with him. 'He was telling them the vote was an objective demonstration of his control of the Duma. He said he now had the right to pick the next PM.'[65]

Khodorkovsky denies ever making any such calls. But a few weeks later a report was published in the media claiming that he was the leader of a 'dangerous' group of pro-Western oligarchs who were seeking to undermine presidential rule. Their aim, the report said, was to purchase majority power in parliament and transform the country into a parliamentary republic where the president would play no more than an honorary role. The report, which described Khodorkovsky's recent actions almost exactly, was clearly intended to further justify the paranoia among Putin's men. It called the actions of the group of oligarchs 'anti-national'. Their property was registered in offshore zones in order to protect it against the Russian state: 'It's possible to say the oligarchs . . . appeal to the resources of other states as a guarantee of their political and economic interests in Russia. Having achieved the privatisation of the main assets of the national economy, they are now moving on to privatise political power in Russia.'[66]

The report exactly reflected the mindset of Putin's men, and, according to its author and a senior banker close to the security services, it also reflected what they'd heard when they'd tapped the phones and offices of Khodorkovsky and his associates. 'Many of those who are in jail today are there because the security men heard exactly what they thought of them. They'd heard the insults in their name,' said Stanislav Belkovsky, a well-known political analyst who co-authored the report.[67]

Soon Putin also began to make his feelings clear. Later that May he called Khodorkovsky, Abramovich and several of their key lieutenants to a private dinner in the oak-panelled reception room of his Novo-Ogarevo residence. According to one of those present, over the meal they'd discussed the Exxon/Chevron deal, but when they moved on to the fine cognac, Putin ordered Khodorkovsky to stop funding the Communists. He objected, saying he'd agreed the funding with Voloshin and Surkov, the chief and deputy chief of staff, but Putin told him, 'Leave it. You have a big company, you have a lot of business to complete. You don't have time for this.' Khodorkovsky continued to dig in his heels, saying he couldn't prevent the other Yukos shareholders from funding whomever they wanted, even if he himself stopped funding the Communist Party. 'He said, "If we are an open and transparent company then I can't stop shareholders and employees from following a certain political line." He tried to explain to Putin that social projects and the support of democracy in Russia were just as important to him as the business.'[68]

The conversation ended abruptly, and the guests left. But Putin wasn't going to leave the matter at that. As he prepared to leave Russia later that June for the honour, pomp and ceremony of a state visit to the UK, his first as president, where he was to be fêted by prime minister Tony Blair and the Queen, he gave the first hint of trouble ahead. In an annual press conference, he lashed out at the business barons for blocking reforms in parliament to raise the tax take on the energy industry. Although he didn't mention Khodorkovsky by name, his reference was unmistakable. 'We must not allow certain business interests to influence the political life of the country in their group interests,' he said.[69] For the first time, Putin had also spoken out publicly against reform of the political system to transform the country into a parliamentary republic. It was out of the question, he said, even 'dangerous'.

It was clear to everybody who Putin's statements were aimed at.

And while he was out of the country, attending a glittering banquet in Buckingham Palace and signing off on the accord between BP and TNK, which Blair hailed as a sign of the UK's 'long-term confidence in Russia', the machinery of state rolled into action. Orchestrated to look as if it had nothing to do with Putin, Russian prosecutors were quietly taking the first, fateful step in the attack on Yukos. They arrested the company's security chief, Alexei Pichugin, and then, on his boss Khodorkovsky's fortieth birthday, charged him with the murder of a married couple who they claimed had tried to blackmail him over his orders to assassinate another Menatep employee.[70] The threat from the Kremlin couldn't have been stronger. But Pichugin's arrest might have passed unnoticed had it not been for a much more high-profile arrest that followed a week later. Platon Lebedev, Khodorkovsky's wisecracking, long-standing right-hand man, the chairman of the Menatep group and the man behind much of its business, had been arrested. Suddenly Khodorkovsky's world was on fire.

Lebedev had been hauled from his hospital bed in handcuffs, charged with embezzling a 20 per cent stake in Apatit, the fertiliser giant that was the first big enterprise privatised by Menatep.[71] News of the arrest was splashed over newspapers everywhere, and $2 billion was wiped from Yukos's market capitalisation in the space of a day.[72] In the background another criminal case, related to the privatisation of VNK, was opened, another senior Yukos executive was sought for questioning. The onslaught against Yukos had begun.

That summer the headlines continued relentlessly. Yukos's stock was pummelled as prosecutors stepped up their investigations. At the end of July, four days after Khodorkovsky had returned from a trip to the US to drum up investor support, prosecutors announced four more separate criminal inquiries into murder and attempted murder by Pichugin.[73] The announcements dredged up all Khodorkovsky's worst nightmares. Under examination were not only the attacks on Yevgeny Rybin over the VNK shares, but also the killing in June 1998 of the mayor of Nefteyugansk, the west Siberian oil town where Yukos was headquartered. The mayor, with whom Khodorkovsky had been locked in conflict after Menatep took over

Yukos, had been shot dead on his way to work on the morning of Khodorkovsky's birthday, and rumours had fast spread that he'd been killed by a zealous underling wanting to present Khodorkovsky with a birthday gift.[74] Yukos had been preparing to spin off the service companies that employed nearly 30,000 workers from Nefteyugansk at its main production unit as it sought to streamline its cash flows, and the mayor had personally protested in a letter to Yeltsin about the city's plummeting tax take after the Yukos takeover. Thousands of the town's citizens took to the streets to openly accuse Khodorkovsky of ordering his death. But Khodorkovsky, according to a *Financial Times* journalist who spoke to him not long after, appeared genuinely disturbed by the killing.[75]

Khodorkovsky vehemently denied any involvement by him or any of his associates in the murders and attempted murders. In the case of the mayor of Nefteyugansk, his lawyers pointed to dangerous Chechen criminal groups which had had a grip on some of Yukos's exports until Khodorkovsky's men forced them out.[76] And later, when the backgrounds of the KGB men Khodorkovsky had fought over VNK became clear, one person close to him suggested that the killings had in fact been organised by VNK's KGB backers, in an attempt to tarnish Khodorkovsky's name.[77]

Khodorkovsky sought refuge and protection from the United States. Immediately after the arrest of his key lieutenant Lebedev, he'd headed directly for the US embassy, where, among the bunting and the stars and stripes on display for Independence Day, he'd insisted to reporters that he didn't think the conflict between himself and the government could last.[78] Soon after, he attended a conference in Sun Valley, Idaho, where he hobnobbed visibly with the likes of Bill Gates and Warren Buffet.[79] On his return to Moscow he again sought to raise the stakes, declaring on national TV that any continuation of the attack on his organisation would lead to an upsurge in capital flight from Russia that would ruin the investment climate and turn the clock back to the totalitarian past.[80]

But Khodorkovsky's overtures to the US had only antagonised the Kremlin further. In September, as Putin prepared for a major visit to the US where he was to hold talks at Camp David with

President George W. Bush, he had a stark message for anyone who thought he could hold the prosecutors back. These cases involved murders, he pointedly told US journalists. 'In such a case, how can I get involved in the prosecutors' work?' he asked.[81]

If Khodorkovsky had ever had any chance of escaping the full force of the Kremlin campaign, the final straw for Putin came during his visit to America. He had been invited to the New York Stock Exchange, where he addressed dozens of leading US executives and assured them of Russia's commitment to a market economy in which no privatisations would be overturned. On the sidelines, he'd met privately with the chief executive of ExxonMobil, Lee Raymond, the towering Midwesterner who'd led Exxon through its merger with Mobil to become the world's biggest company, worth $375 billion. Known for his aggressive style, Raymond had not minced his words with Putin, telling him he wanted to eventually buy control of YukosSibneft, after the first stage of a deal in which Exxon would buy a minority stake.[82]

Putin was totally taken aback. He'd never discussed any scenario in which a US energy giant could take control of Russian reserves with Khodorkovsky or with Abramovich. He'd been under the impression that the idea was for Exxon or Chevron to take a minority stake, while YukosSibneft took a stake in one of the US energy giants too. 'For Putin, the exchange of shares was important,' said one person familiar with the negotiations. 'It would have been an energy bridge between Russia and the US.'[83] But as the pressure on Yukos had grown that summer, shareholders had pushed to hurry a sale. They wanted to cash out completely, rather than swap shares.

For Putin, the sale of a controlling stake in YukosSibneft to ExxonMobil was absolutely out of the question. He couldn't possibly approve the sale of control of Russia's strategic reserves to the US. It went against everything the KGB men stood for in their bid to restore Russia's imperial might. Fridman and Aven might have been allowed to clinch a 50:50 partnership with BP, but they, unlike Khodorkovsky, had remained absolutely loyal to the Kremlin, and did whatever they could to stay in the driving seat of the joint TNK–BP venture.

Lee Raymond arrived in Moscow just a week later, apparently hoping to seal the deal. That day the *Financial Times* splashed on its front page the news that Exxon was deep in talks to acquire a 40 per cent stake in YukosSibneft for $25 billion, and the stake could later rise above 50 per cent.[84] But instead of handshakes and toasts, Raymond was greeted by the news that more than fifty investigators bearing machine guns and wearing bulletproof vests were raiding Yukos-related locations across Moscow, including the homes of some of Khodorkovsky's closest partners, the other main shareholders in Menatep – who lived together in a guarded compound behind a high metal fence outside Moscow in the elite village of Zhukovka – among them Lebedev, who was already in jail.[85] When Khodorkovsky received a call from his wife that the police were swarming outside the door, he hurriedly made his excuses to Raymond and left.

The signalling from the Kremlin could not have been clearer. ExxonMobil was never going to get its deal. When Khodorkovsky received the call from his wife, he and Raymond had been attending a conference hosted by the World Economic Forum, at which Putin was due to make a keynote speech. But while Khodorkovsky rushed home to secure his house against the raids, all Raymond could do was warn the conference that Russia should not 'arbitrarily' restrict any investor if it wanted to participate in world markets.[86] Putin, as if blissfully unaware of the raids, continued to insist to investors that he was doing everything he could to remove hurdles to investment.[87] It was typical of the double-speak he had employed ever since he'd begun his rise to power. He spoke in praise of the market, while behind the scenes his security men were doing everything they could to seize control for themselves.

Still Khodorkovsky refused to back down, announcing to the world that he was ready to go to jail, if that was what it took to defend his company.[88] He would not leave the country and give up the fight. Privately, however, he'd been desperately seeking a way out, even visiting Pugachev, his old rival from the nineties who was by then close to the St Petersburg security men, to ask him about the Kremlin's motivations. Pugachev, after making enquiries, had an unambiguous message for him. If he wanted to remain free he should leave the country. Otherwise, he told him, he was going to jail.[89] Khodorkovsky said he did not believe it. The Kremlin would not dare to arrest him – and if it did, the United States would step in to defend him.

It was a sign of his hubris, his overestimation of the lengths the US would go to to protect an oligarch who'd sought to build bridges with it.

*

Khodorkovsky was defiantly touring Siberia on a business trip when it happened. The prosecutors had called him in for questioning the previous day, but he was far from Moscow. Shortly before dawn in the morning of Saturday, October 25 2003, his private jet had landed at an airstrip in Novosibirsk to refuel when a squad of armed FSB commandos forcefully came on board. Khodorkovsky had been in a first-class compartment when they broke in on him, shouting, 'FSB! Put your weapons on the ground! Don't move or we'll shoot!'[90] He was arrested on charges of large-scale fraud and tax evasion, and by the evening he was in Moscow's notorious Matrosskaya Tishina jail.

This was the moment when Russia's political and economic course turned irrevocably away from a Western-led global integration, and took a course of its own that was heading for collision with the West. It was the point of no return for the group of statist security men who had lobbied and plotted and eventually convinced Putin that there was no other way to ensure the Russian state's resurgence – and their own financial clout. But it was uncharted territory as much for them as it was for the country. While few had expected things to go so far, many in the business community hoped there was a way back, that Khodorkovsky could be freed, and the two sides could settle. Even Pugachev said the expectation had long been, even among some of the *siloviki*, that Khodorkovsky and his associates would agree to pay Putin and his men a significant sum of cash to make the charges go away. 'Everyone was waiting for the kickback,' he said. 'No one was really prepared. No one knew what to do with the company. They had no experience of running things then.'

Khodorkovsky's arrest sent the entire business community into a state of shock. He was the country's richest man, the most prominent proponent of the market, the man who'd been on the brink of pulling off the deal of the century – the sale of his company for $25 billion just seven years after he'd acquired it for $300 million. If he could be taken down, it could happen to any of them. The day Khodorkovsky was arrested, leading members of the Russian Union of Industrialists and Entrepreneurs, which had become the main official representative organ of the oligarchs, gathered for an emergency meeting in Moscow's Baltschug Hotel. Many were too fearful to speak directly to the press, but collectively they wrote a muted and hesitant letter to Putin condemning the arrest and calling for an audience with him: 'Only the clear and unambiguous position of the Russian president Vladimir Putin can improve the situation. Its absence will make the worsening of the investment climate irreversible and will turn Russia into a country unfavourable to those developing their businesses.'[91] Anatoly Chubais, the privatisation tsar and author of Russia's liberal reforms, took the message a step further. In a TV interview that weekend, he warned that Khodorkovsky's arrest, and the lack of clarity over whether other business leaders might be next, could lead to an 'uncontrollable' split in the elite that could draw in the whole of society.[92]

But Putin was not going to step back now. Though he consistently denied having anything to do with Khodorkovsky's arrest, such things did not happen without a clear nod from the top. Above all, Khodorkovsky's arrest showed that he'd failed to grasp a basic tenet of Putin's rule that later other oligarchs – through his experience – came to understand all too well. 'When you buy in Russia a large oil company for $150 million with the help of deposits from the finance ministry then you have to play according to Russian rules,' said Dmitry Gololobov, a lawyer who once worked for Khodorkovsky but ended up turning on him. 'You can't say you are the legitimate owner. Privatisation didn't create legitimate property. The other oligarchs understood this well. None of them claimed they were actually owners of the business. They understood they were just holders.'[93]

This way of thinking went against everything Putin had claimed to stand for when he ran for the presidency. It was a deception rooted in the KGB's belief that they had made the tycoons when Russia began its transition to the market, that everything the new billionaires had won was owed to them. What happened to Khodorkovsky was revenge for the nineties, when the KGB had been forced to wait on the sidelines, pushed aside by the growing reach of the Western-leaning Moscow tycoons. 'What's happening now with Putin is the revanche of the KGB,' said one former senior-level military-intelligence officer at the time. 'The KGB created the oligarchy, and then they had to serve it. Now they are having their revenge.'[94]

The battle had reached a point where the KGB felt they could justify their asset grab by telling themselves they were preventing the handover of the country's richest oil assets to the West. 'Yukos had the intention to hand over the largest part of its assets to the West,' said one of their number. 'The capitalisation that [Khodorkovsky] built like lightning, all these assets would have floated abroad through fake offshore companies. If we had not stopped this, then we would not have kept control of our oil and gas industry. We would have become the servants of Western industrialists for a long time.'[95]

And so, over the days that followed Khodorkovsky's arrest, the rest of the nation's billionaires watched in horror as prosecutors seized his $15 billion stake in YukosSibneft. Putin firmly told them there would be no dialogue over the arrest, and the stock market went into freefall. On the Monday immediately after the arrest, Putin issued a brusque and unequivocal response to the oligarchs' call for clarity: 'There will not be any meetings or bargaining over the activities of law enforcement agencies, as long as these agencies stay within Russian law. Everyone should be equal before the law, irrespective of how many billions of dollars a person has on his personal or corporate account. Otherwise, we will never teach and force anyone to pay taxes and defeat organised crime and corruption.'[96]

It was a new era. Putin had cast off much of the hesitancy that had marked the first two years of his presidency. The Kremlin's new masters were ready to carve up the country's strategic assets for themselves. There was no way back, either for Putin or his men.

8

Out of Terror, an Imperial Awakening

'It's like a knot with three elements'

Vladimir Putin had seemed to begin his presidency as a reluctant leader. When he was catapulted to power he'd told Boris Yeltsin he hadn't been ready to take the job on, and described himself to members of the Yeltsin Family as the hired manager, suggesting he would serve only a few years. When disaster struck, such as the sinking of the *Kursk* submarine, he had a habit of withdrawing, paralysed into inaction, sometimes as white as a sheet. But now that he'd ordered the arrest of Russia's richest man, there was no going back. Even if he'd wanted to, he didn't feel he could. His inner circle in particular, the *siloviki* he'd brought with him from St Petersburg, pressed him to stay on. 'They would frighten him,' said Pugachev. 'They told him, "No one will forgive you for Yukos, for the takeover of NTV. If you go to the West, they will arrest you at once."'[1] Now that they'd tasted power, the KGB men were not about to step aside. They were preparing a further takeover of the country; following Putin's re-election in 2004 they would be freed from some of the agreements he had made with the Yeltsin Family when he took over from them.[2]

Putin had eliminated the media tycoons Vladimir Gusinsky and Boris Berezovsky. Early reforms launched by his administration had drastically reduced the power of regional governors through the creation of 'super-regions' ruled over by Kremlin-appointed pleni-potentiary leaders. Such measures – led by Dmitry Kozak, a former military-intelligence officer and prosecutor from St Petersburg – had reversed the policies of the Yeltsin years, when the president had commanded his governors to 'grab as much freedom as you can'. Liberals and the former media tycoons warned darkly of the revanche of the KGB, of the Kremlin's increasingly authoritarian grip. The arrest of Khodorkovsky and the seizure of his stake in YukosSibneft had sent tremors through the stock market and the business community. But Putin and the Kremlin sought to portray it as an isolated case, punishment for one rogue oligarch who had gone too far. The rest of the country was revelling in the benefits of a surge in oil prices, which had climbed from $12 to $28 per barrel since Putin came to power. Reflecting public approval of the end of the chaos of the nineties, and of his efforts to put the oligarchs in their place, Putin's ratings throughout his first term were consistently at around 70 per cent.

All the signs were good for him to sail into a second term. But the takeover of NTV and the arrest of Khodorkovsky were not the only events that had scarred his first term with controversy – and according to one inside account, never before revealed, some leading members of the *siloviki* were seeking to leave nothing to chance. On the evening of Wednesday, October 23 2002, at least forty armed Chechen fighters filed into the Dubrovka musical theatre in a Moscow suburb south of the Kremlin, firing assault rifles into the air just as tapdancers trouped across the stage for the opening of the second act of a popular new Russian musical, *Nord-Ost*.[3] The theatre was packed with a nearly nine-hundred-strong audience, members of a middle class that was beginning to thrive in Putin's Russia, there to see a show that paid homage to the bravery of the Soviets during the siege of Leningrad in the Second World War. The Chechens proceeded to wire the building with explosives, while some of the hostage-takers, women known as 'Black Widows' dressed in black hijabs, who appeared to have belts of explosives strapped to their bodies, stationed themselves among the terrified audience as the fighters sealed off the auditorium.

The siege that played out over the next three days appeared to be Putin's worst nightmare. The Chechen fighters, led by Movsar Barayev, the nephew of one of Chechnya's most renowned rebels, were demanding an end to Russia's war in the republic, which had been going on ever since the 1999 apartment bombings that spurred Putin's rise to power. They gave Russia seven days to withdraw its troops or they would blow the building up.[4] The evening the news of the siege broke, opposition politicians and security officials alike gathered outside the theatre in the dark and the cold rain, shocked that this could have happened a mere three and a half miles from the Kremlin. How had so many rebels, armed to the teeth with explosives, been able to enter the theatre, apparently in plain sight?

For the next three days, Putin did not stir from his office on a top floor of the Kremlin, seized by panic at the events spiralling out of control in the world below. As he cast about for a way out of the crisis, he cancelled a planned trip to Mexico, where he'd been due to meet world leaders including US president George W. Bush. The hostage-takers had allowed some prominent individuals into the theatre to negotiate, including member of parliament and well-known singer Iosif Kobzon, liberal opposition politicians, and a journalist, Anna Politkovskaya, renowned for her fearless reporting on the war in Chechnya. Although they secured the release of a number of hostages, including some of the children and foreign citizens, the attackers refused to back down on their demand for an end to the war.

On the third evening of the siege, a crew from NTV was allowed in to record an interview with Barayev. 'Our goal – which we have declared more than once – is to stop the war and get the troops out,' he said.[5] A female hostage-taker apparently wearing an explosive belt told the reporter: 'We are following Allah's path. If we die here, that won't be the end of it.'

Again, Putin was paralysed by fear. The attackers had made it clear that they would kill the hostages and blow up the building if the security forces sought to intervene,[6] and already there'd been deaths: two civilians and one FSB colonel seeking to enter the theatre had been shot dead.[7]

The Russian security services finally acted just before dawn broke on Saturday, October 26. In order to avoid the hostage-takers setting off the explosives, a gas was released into the auditorium through the theatre's ventilation system. But although it knocked out the hostages and some of the Chechen fighters, it also left many of the hostages dead, while the emergency services were ill-equipped and unprepared to deal with those still alive, who were laid on the roadside, some vomiting, some unconscious, others choking on their tongues.[8] Ninety minutes passed before they were taken to hospital for treatment.[9] Expecting to find a bloodbath from explosions and gunfire, 80 per cent of the ambulances that arrived on the scene were equipped only to deal with trauma wounds, not the effects of gas.[10] By the end of the following day, the death toll among the hostages was at least 115. Only two had been killed by gunfire. The rest had died from the gas.[11]

For a time, Putin faced an outcry over the handling of the siege. How had it happened in the first place? Why weren't the emergency services adequately informed of the nature of the gas? According to several witnesses who survived the attack, the gas had seeped into the auditorium from under the stage, knocking out the captors nearest to it but filtering into the hall slowly enough for some of them to notice a caustic smell and a green-looking gas.[12] Facing mounting pressure to identify the gas, Russia's health minister eventually claimed it was an aerosol derivative of the anaesthetic fentanyl, a potent opioid widely used as a painkiller, which he said 'cannot in itself be called lethal'.[13] The reason the hostages died, he claimed, was that they'd been weakened by three days of severe stress, dehydration and hunger. In the final report by Moscow prosecutors, which eventually emerged a year later, the gas was labelled only as an 'unidentified chemical substance'.[14]

What took place in the Kremlin on the night the theatre was stormed has been locked ever since behind a wall of secrecy. But now, one insider who said he was involved in the Kremlin discussions back then has begun to open a window. He claimed that what happened was the deadly unravelling of a plot that had not gone according to plan. In his account, the attack on the theatre was planned by Nikolai Patrushev, the gnarled FSB chief, to further cement Putin as president. It was intended as no more than a fake exercise that would boost Putin's authority when he successfully brought it to an end, and increase support for the war in Chechnya, which was beginning to flag. Patrushev, this person says, told Putin that the terrorists-for-hire were not armed with real bombs, and that when the siege was over they would be flown to Turkey under FSB protection, while Putin would emerge as a hero, as the one world leader who'd ended a hostage crisis without any civilian deaths – and then he could tighten control in Chechnya.

But everything unravelled on the very first day of the siege, when one of the Chechens shot dead a civilian trying to enter the theatre. Putin plunged into panic, the insider said: 'Everything spiralled out of control. No one knew who or what to trust.'[15] By the time the security forces prepared to storm the building, the hostage-taking was being treated as if it were a real act of terror. Igor Sechin, Putin's closest KGB colleague from St Petersburg, was brought in to help deal with the situation, and knowing of Sechin's tendency for over-zealousness, Patrushev encouraged him, the former official familiar with the discussions said. 'He told him, "Here, Igor you have military experience. Help us take care of this."' It was Sechin's idea to use the gas, according to this account. He had spoken with a former commander of Russia's chemical-warfare troops who'd told him the gas was old, and there was a chance it would not be effective. 'Sechin told me he'd therefore ordered them to use ten times the usual dose,' said the former official, who claims that, horrified at how events had played out, Putin had signed a resignation letter. But by then he was too deeply involved, and was told he had to stay. Patrushev, it seemed, had left the planning of the attack, and the security forces' response to it, deliberately ambiguous. Bloodshed and loss of life would also tie Putin to the presidency. 'It was organised so Putin would have to stay for a second term.' If anything went wrong, he would have to be dragged in deeper still. 'If Putin was replaced then it would have been the end for Kolya [Patrushev]. So he arranged this to cover him in blood.'[16]

Dmitry Peskov, the Kremlin spokesman, dismissed the insider's account as 'total rubbish', saying this person 'doesn't know anything'. It may be impossible ever to fully verify it. Only a very small circle at the top of power know how these events unfolded, but the former official who gave me this version of events was close enough to know. Were it not for a little-noticed Moscow prosecutors' report that appeared a year after the siege, his account could easily be dismissed as just another of the wild conspiracy theories that typically emerged about closed-door Kremlin decision-making, especially after the murk of the apartment bombings. But when the prosecutors finally completed their investigation, they found that the two main bombs placed inside the auditorium were essentially fakes. At least one part of the insider's story was ringing true. 'The bombs had not been prepared for use: the detonators had nothing to fuel them,' said the report. 'There were no batteries . . . The bombs turned out to be safe blanks.'[17] The same went for the suicide belts worn by some of the women, as well as other explosive devices. Many of the women who wore the belts had been with the hostages in the auditorium, but rather than setting off the devices as they'd threatened, they passed out from the gas. Then, instead of taking them in for questioning to get to the bottom of the terrorist plot, the Russian security services shot each and every one of them dead.[18]

Even though it had taken five to ten minutes for the gas to take effect, the prosecutors found, the terrorists hadn't detonated any of the bombs. Could it really have been the case that they had never intended to blow anything up at all, and the use of the gas had led to a needless loss of life? Unnamed sources in the FSB and the interior ministry told *Kommersant*, seemingly the sole Russian newspaper that reported on the prosecutors' findings, that the terrorists themselves had ordered the detonators to be removed, because they feared accidental explosions.[19] But the liberal politician Irina Khakamada, who'd entered the building for negotiations, also voiced doubts about the siege: 'I came to believe that it had not been in the plans of the terrorists to blow up the theatre centre, and that the authorities were not interested in the release of all hostages. But the head of the presidential administration ordered me in a menacing tone not to mess with this story.'[20]

Questions also arose about some of the terrorists involved. Their apparent leader, Movsar Barayev, had reportedly been arrested by the authorities just two months before.[21] How did he get from jail to taking part in the attack? The same went for one of the supposed female suicide bombers, whose mother identified her from television footage of the siege.[22] Could the authorities have been involved in moving them from jail to the theatre?

It was not the first time a terrorist attack in Russia had left lingering questions about security service involvement, the most notable previous examples being the apartment bombings that helped spur Putin's rise to power. But in this case, the attack caused far less controversy. Most questions revolved around the use of the gas, and the prosecutors' findings about the bombs being dummies were buried at the end of the *Kommersant* report, which led on the round-up of an alleged terrorist group preparing other attacks.[23]

In the aftermath of the siege, questions over how it unfolded were largely brushed aside, and most of the population simply breathed a sigh of relief that the death toll had not been higher. Putin was praised by international leaders and local politicians alike for his handling of the situation.[24] His ratings surged to their highest since he was elected.[25] Instead of facing a shake-up for allowing a group of armed terrorists into the centre of Moscow, Russia's security services were rewarded with an increase in funding.[26] And the attack enabled Putin's men to ramp up their military action in Chechnya, cancelling plans to reduce troop numbers.[27] Countless Chechens began disappearing from their homes in night raids and the pressure that had been rising on the Kremlin to begin peace talks with the Chechen leader Aslan Maskhadov fell away overnight. Once again there was public backing for the war, and Maskhadov had been totally discredited. The Russian authorities accused him of being behind the attack,[28] but they never presented any evidence, apart from an old videotape of threats of a new offensive, and Maskhadov himself denied any involvement.

The siege also presented the Kremlin with an opportunity to paint its war in Chechnya as akin to the West's war on terror. An effort to establish links between the Chechen rebels and Islamic militants from abroad had already begun in the months before the attack,[29] and the siege further heightened that perception: Al Jazeera broadcast video of people it claimed were accomplices of the Chechens in front of banners proclaiming 'God is great' in Arabic, while Putin called the attack a 'monstrous manifestation of terrorism' planned by 'foreign terrorist centres'.[30] In the months that followed, the US began to change its view of the Chechen rebel forces, naming three groups it said were involved in the siege as terrorist organisations linked to Al Qaeda,[31] while Maskhadov was no longer seen as a moderate. 'Our policy on Chechnya has moved closer to Russia,' a senior US diplomat said soon after the attack. 'This attack has substantially damaged [the Chechen] cause.'[32]

*

If Putin's KGB men sought to tie him to the presidency, the truth was that, barring terrible events like the Dubrovka attack, he was in any case becoming accustomed to the role. 'He'd begun to like it – all the ceremony, the G8, the recognition,' said Pugachev.[33] He was lauded by his inner circle as the saviour of Russia. He'd saved the country from certain collapse, they said, from the thrall of the oligarchs and the destructive power of the West. Even those who'd once served above him in the KGB now bowed down before him. On one occasion, early on in his first term, when Putin gathered a small circle of friends for his birthday, one of his former bosses in Dresden, Sergei Chemezov, toasted his rise to power. 'This was a very close person who in a previous life, before Putin had become president, was older and more senior in rank than him, and who Putin respects,' said Pugachev. 'He told him, "Vladimir Vladimirovich, I want to raise my glass. You know a lot of time has passed since I first heard that you were the president, but the feeling that I had then remains with me still. I thought it was like the sun rising over Russia . . . now I understand that 100 per cent of the population share that feeling with me."' For Pugachev, the speech was cringeworthy. He'd interrupted, wanting to get on with discussing the political situation, all the monumental tasks ahead. But Putin, he said, glared at him and told him to let his friend finish his speech. 'He looked straight into his eyes and he told him he was a gift from God. He told him God had given the country a ruler who is ending the great suffering of the Russian people. This was a guy who knew him for fifteen years, and used to be his boss . . . I saw this for the first time . . . this was how it was from the very beginning, almost from the very first day. He's an extremely vain person.' In order to ask Putin a question, it became customary to flatter him at length first. 'Sechin knew how to do this very well. He would tell him with a deep bow, "Vladimir Vladimirovich, I remember how you did this and you transformed the world." When I first heard all of this I thought I was in the mental hospital. They would say to him things like "You have shaken the essence of humanity. You are a stunning person."'[34]

Gradually, the constant kowtowing went to Putin's head. Beginning to believe in his powers as the new tsar, he was emboldened to take tougher and more authoritarian decisions, including to take on Khodorkovsky and his men. 'The entire oligarchy in essence was bowing down before him and offering him this and that and coming to him for permission for the slightest thing,' said Pugachev. 'And he really did like this. And somehow it entered his head. It was a creeping process. He'd always had these tendencies, but at some point he changed, and this grandiose belief in himself as the tsar took over.'[35]

If at first Putin had shared the machinery of state with the Yeltsin Family's representatives, once Khodorkovsky had been arrested, the state apparatus really became his own. In shock at the turn of events and at being kept in the dark, Alexander Voloshin, the wily Yeltsin holdover who had served as Kremlin chief of staff since March 1999, stepped down. Voloshin had spoken several times with Putin about the legal onslaught against Khodorkovsky, but right up to the last he'd considered that it could be contained: 'I honestly did not think they would put him in jail. I thought it was some kind of misunderstanding. It was clear that it was a campaign, and it was bad. I considered it was harmful for the development of the country.'[36] Putin replaced him with his own man, a colleague from St Petersburg: Dmitry Medvedev, a quietly spoken lawyer who'd worked on legal issues for Putin, including on containing the fallout of the oil-for-food scandal. He had a reputation for zealous precision, but also for timidity. Most importantly of all, he'd been virtually brought up by Putin when he entered the St Petersburg administration aged only twenty-five. 'Putin reared Medvedev,' said Valery Musin, who also acted as a legal adviser to Sobchak's City Hall. 'Medvedev always looked up to Putin as someone he could learn from.'[37]

The most influential holdover from the Yeltsin era had been replaced by a St Petersburg yes-man, with little more than three years' experience in the Kremlin as deputy chief of staff. On the same day Medvedev's appointment was announced, the St Petersburg *siloviki* signalled their intentions more loudly than ever before. Prosecutors announced that they had frozen $15 billion in Yukos shares, the 44 per cent Khodorkovsky held indirectly in the combined YukosSibneft, to prevent him from selling them.[38] Shell-shocked, the market perceived the move as a clear sign that the *siloviki* were intent not just on Khodorkovsky's arrest, but on seizing Yukos itself. In addition, the move was seen as the end for the Yeltsin-era oligarchs, for the Family, whose interests had been carefully balanced against those of the *siloviki* for nearly four years. Just in case anyone was still wondering, Alexei Kudrin, Putin's comparatively liberal-minded finance minister, made it even clearer, publicly hailing Voloshin's departure as marking the end of the Yeltsin era. 'Byzantium is over!' he proclaimed. 'With all due respect to Alexander Voloshin, I want to stress that his departure coincides with the end of the Yeltsin epoch . . . [The oligarchs] have been returned to a business environment in which you can only be successful if you play fair.'[39]

It was as if the machinery of the parallel government on which Sechin and others had been working quietly behind the scenes was slowly being rolled out, and a PR campaign was being launched. On the same day the Yukos shares were seized and Medvedev was appointed Kremlin chief of staff, Putin held an intimate meeting with the heads of some of the largest financial institutions in the world, including CitiGroup, Morgan Stanley and ABN Amro.[40] Helping to relay his intentions was the US-born head of local brokerage United Financial Group, Charlie Ryan, who'd worked with Putin since his days in St Petersburg in the early nineties. From the start, Ryan had been a vital conduit for Putin's Kremlin's messaging to the global finance community and the wider world. Putin told the investors that the Yukos campaign in no way presaged a broader onslaught against private business,[41] and the seizure of the shares was not a confiscation, but was only about covering liabilities. The campaign was no more than imposing the rule of law. To some degree, the global banks – some of which, including CitiBank, held billions of dollars in exposure to Yukos debt – were persuaded. They did not pull in the loans. If they had, Khodorkovsky's direst predictions about the resulting collapse of the economy could have come true. Power had tilted in the Kremlin, and Putin's men were already building a system of communication with global finance, the titans of which would one day be on bended knee for the hundreds of billions of dollars' worth of assets under Putin's control.

If Voloshin's departure signalled a transfer of power from the Yeltsin Family to Putin's St Petersburg *siloviki*, the parliamentary elections just over a month later further cemented their political power. The pro-Western liberal parties had kept a vital foothold in parliament throughout the Yeltsin era, through Anatoly Chubais' Union of Right Forces and Grigory Yavlinsky's Yabloko. But they were routed in the election of December 2003.[42] The TV channels now monopolised by the state kicked them off the air, while the Kremlin threw its backing behind a party of the new Putin generation, the nationalist group Rodina, which was given extensive coverage on state TV. Its leaders, Sergei Glazyev and Dmitry Rogozin, pronounced a firmly statist course that chimed with the new mood in the Kremlin to take the oligarchs' profits and hand them back to the state: 'Return the wealth of the nation to the people!' was one of the party's slogans.[43] This fitted exactly with the mood of the moment, as the state TV channels endlessly replayed news of Khodorkovsky's arrest. The liberal Union of Right Forces and Yabloko didn't stand a chance. They failed to get past the 5 per cent barrier to holding seats in the Duma, while Rodina emerged from nowhere to take 9 per cent of the vote.[44] The pro-Kremlin party United Russia, which had been created just four years earlier as a vehicle that would help sweep Putin to power, secured an outright parliamentary majority, even though it had run on a campaign that was almost devoid of any content apart from loyalty to the president.[45] The Communists, in the meantime, the great foe of the Yeltsin era, ambled in with a mere 12.6 per cent of the vote.

It was clear that Putin's hands were going to be freed to conduct whatever policies he wanted from then on. There would be no countering force from the liberals. Pro-Kremlin parties had a clear and resounding majority. Russia had entered the era of a rubber-stamp parliament. In such an environment, Putin's election for a second term as president seemed almost a foregone conclusion. His ratings stood at over 70 per cent. But even then, he and his men did not leave anything to chance.

*

Ever since Khodorkovsky's associate Platon Lebedev had been arrested in July, tension had been rising between Putin and Mikhail Kasyanov, the gregarious prime minister and the last remaining Yeltsin holdover in power. Kasyanov had been a Yeltsin-era Finance Minister, and his ties to the Family ran long and deep. When Putin came to power, Roman Abramovich had insisted on his appointment as prime minister, as their representative, a senior Russian banker close to the security service claimed.[46] A spokesperson for Abramovich denies this. Kasyanov had had little appetite for taking on the role, which he considered dangerous. He'd become used to his comfortable position in the finance ministry, where he served as deputy minister in charge of foreign debt. To be thrust into the centre of what seemed like a precarious transition of power, answering to both the Family and to Putin, was not among his ambitions. But he was persuaded, and gradually he'd grown accustomed to his new role. 'For three and a half years I considered that we were the right people in the right place doing the right thing,' he said. 'But when they threw Lebedev in jail and a number of other scandals began, I understood that was it.'[47]

Kasyanov's government had led the liberal-seeming economic reforms of Putin's first term – the income-tax cut to a flat rate of 13 per cent, and the ambitious land reforms to finally allow the privatisation of land. As prime minister he'd also spearheaded the talks with Exxon's Lee Raymond over the potential sale of YukosSibneft to ExxonMobil. 'In those days,' he said, 'we lived in friendship with the US. There were great relations with Bush and with [vice president] Cheney. I was speaking with Cheney all the time about energy assets. We had great cooperation after the tragedy of September 11, and over transit into Afghanistan we had a cooperation channel between the two governments . . . If there had been an exchange of assets between Yukos and ExxonMobil the entire energy sector would have been different. It would have been much more liberal.'

But by 2003, frequent clashes began to break out between Kasyanov and Putin's KGB men. In the beginning, the conflicts had centred around Gazprom. Putin had installed his own man, Alexei Miller, at the helm of the state, gas giant, and was starting to use it as a way to flex the Kremlin's muscles and exert control over the former Soviet states, which Russia liked to possessively call its 'near abroad'. Under Putin's orders, Gazprom was becoming much tougher about payment for its gas supplies to Belarus and Ukraine, as the Kremlin sought to force the former Soviet republics to toe the line.

Kasyanov, however, had been pursuing a reform of Gazprom that had been pushed for by liberals in government ever since the Yeltsin years: to liberalise the gas market and break Gazprom up into production and transportation units, splitting its gas production companies from its pipeline network. This had long been seen as a reform vital to boosting competition in the economy. But now that Putin's men were cementing their grip, it was pushed off the agenda indefinitely – at the very moment Kasyanov had believed he was about to announce the momentous reform.[48] That September the press had gathered for a cabinet meeting, at which the gas reform was the first item on the agenda, when Kasyanov received a call from Putin. 'He told me, "I insist you remove this item from the agenda,"' Kasyanov recalled. 'We'd been so close. We were even ahead of Europe on this. We were ready. But Putin called me just minutes before.'

Kasyanov's position was becoming untenable. When Khodorkovsky was arrested a month later, Kasyanov was one of only two senior Russian officials who dared to speak out against it. But at a cabinet meeting, in front of everyone, Putin told him directly to 'stop the hysterics'.[49] 'It was a sort of warning to me,' said Kasyanov.[50]

Undaunted, however, he spoke out publicly again when, in January 2004, the tax ministry went public to confirm long-rumoured claims that it was charging Yukos retroactively with $3 billion in back taxes for 2000. Kasyanov told the *Vedomosti* newspaper that it was unfair for tax laws to be retroactively applied.[51] None of it looked good for the rule of law, he said.

Kasyanov was almost the sole voice in power speaking out against Putin's grab for the energy sector. They were still on speaking terms, but Putin spoke to Kasyanov with ever greater coldness and suspicion, as if he could hardly bear to look at him. Then, in the middle of February, when temperatures stood at minus 24, Gazprom took its first ever step to cut off gas supplies to a neighbour, in this case, Belarus,[52] and the tension between the two men escalated to outright confrontation.[53] Gazprom had been locked in tough negotiations with Belarus over ending subsidised gas prices to the former Soviet republic and on taking a stake in its gas transportation network. The Russian gas giant had long been threatening to cut off supplies to strongarm the negotiations, but Kasyanov had stubbornly resisted the move. 'I had forbidden Miller [the Gazprom CEO] to turn off gas to Belarus. In Minsk, it was minus 25. But in the morning in the middle of February I was called by the Prime Minister of Poland and the Prime Minister of Lithuania, and they said, "We have no gas." Nobody had even told me. We had a public scandal.' Miller told him he had acted on Putin's orders. 'We just shouted at each other, and at Putin. All the other ministers were ready to crawl under the table.' Putin had had enough. Just over ten days later Kasyanov was fired.[54] 'It had built up with him,' said Kasyanov. 'Khodorkovsky, Exxon, gas reform, Belarus and Ukraine. And I was starting this scandal. He couldn't bear me any more.'[55]

It was just two weeks before the presidential elections, and it was expected that Putin would make changes to his cabinet after the vote. But he and his men were leaving nothing to chance. Now that they were making moves to cement their grip on power, they could not afford any accidents. According to the constitution, if something happened to Putin, the prime minister would take over the rule of the country.

In an election race that was barely a contest at all, Putin had removed the final element of risk, the last holdover from the Yeltsin years in power capable of challenging him. To replace Kasyanov, he appointed Mikhail Fradkov, a little-known technocrat who'd worked in the shadows of the security establishment for decades.[56] Before his appointment he'd been serving as Russia's special representative to the EU, and few people had ever heard his name. But he'd proven himself a trusted ally to Putin's KGB men, working since the early eighties as a key cog in strategic operations in foreign trade, including with the so-called friendly firms supporting the Soviet regime from abroad. During the time of the St Petersburg oil-for-food scheme, he'd been deputy minister of foreign economic relations. As Pyotr Aven's man in St Petersburg, he'd approved the contracts Putin handed out to the small circle of allies and friendly firms that ultimately created a strategic black-cash store for Putin and the city's security men.

Even after his unceremonious dismissal, Kasyanov still thought Putin's path could be changed. It was difficult for him to comprehend that the entire course Russia had set out on since the Soviet collapse was being reversed. 'Even after I left government, for another six months I believed Putin was mistaken, and that all this could be corrected, and that it would be corrected. It was only later – after the terrorist attack in Beslan – that I understood that all this was planned to change the entire political system.'[57]

*

The presidential elections that March barely registered on the public consciousness. Putin won with ease, with more than 71 per cent of the vote. The chief political adversaries of the Yeltsin era, Gennady Zyuganov, the head of the Communist Party, and Vladimir Zhirinovsky of the nationalist Liberal Democratic Party, could not even muster the enthusiasm to stand. They appointed proxies to run in their place, and the Communist candidate, the little-known Nikolai Kharitonov, came a distant second with 13 per cent of the vote.[58] It was not even a contest. But even so, the Kremlin had left little to chance. State TV granted next to zero airtime to the opposition candidates: Kharitonov calculated that his meetings with voters had been broadcast for a mere four minutes and fifty seconds, compared to the blanket coverage Putin received. Putin's KGB men soon filled all the most powerful posts in the cabinet. They were embarking on a second term in power without the checks and balances of the Yeltsin-era powerbrokers.

The only person who voiced any objection to Putin's second term was his wife, Lyudmilla. She'd been raised in a rundown village in Kaliningrad. Her father had drunk heavily, and it had been hard for her to adjust to the scrutiny and the trappings of presidential life. 'She wanted to leave him when he told her he was running for a second term,' said Pugachev, who'd become close to her, often sitting in the kitchen of the presidential residence for hours on end as they waited for Putin's return. 'She said she had agreed to four years, no more than that. He had to persuade her to stay. It would be bad for the polling. He could not be running for president at the same time she was trying to divorce him. Always, she drank a lot.'[59]

It had been difficult for Lyudmilla to adjust to Putin's constant absences. Throughout his career he'd spent long hours away at work, but now they stretched ever more endlessly. As if embarrassed by her, Putin kept his distance, taking her with him on official visits and trips less and less. When he did return home, often in the dead of night, he would sit in his slippers watching bland comedy shows on TV rather than spending time with his wife.

All the while, Pugachev had been watching the rising power of the KGB men with a faint sense of unease. Back in the eighties, he'd fought against the KGB in his hometown of Leningrad. Back then, he'd been a black-market currency trader whose sworn enemy was the KGB, which sought to cut him off and threatened him with jail. But he'd also learned how to buy KGB officials off. And now he hobnobbed with the new men in power, inviting them often to his home, on familiar laughing terms with Vitya (Ivanov) and Igor (Sechin). He'd become a senator in the Federation Council. But he was still considered a behind-the-scenes powerbroker. For a time he'd kept his office in the Kremlin, across the way from the chief of staff. And for a time, Putin remained a constant companion.

But all the while, Pugachev says now, he was worried about the statist direction things were heading in, about the clampdown on freedom, about the events that had cemented Putin's grip on power. Though he says he frequently raised these concerns, he chose not to do anything about them, saying he believed he could exert more influence from the inside than by objecting and stepping away. He thought that he could better act as a brake on the more authoritarian tendencies of Putin and his men if he remained close to them. But in fact he enjoyed his power and status as much as any of them. And in any case, he believed he didn't have much of a choice: 'It's a story when you get in the car and the doors are closed and you can see the driver is on the edge of sanity,' he said. 'But the doors are closed and the car is already moving fast. And you have to decide whether to stay in or whether to jump is more dangerous. The moment when you can calmly get out of the car has passed.'[60]

A new ideology propounded by the KGB men to restore the greatness of the Russian state and bolster imperial ties with the former Soviet republics was emerging. One of Putin's first acts as president – to the great dismay of Yeltsin holdovers such as Pugachev and Voloshin – had been to restore the Soviet anthem 'The Unbreakable Union of Freeborn Republics'.[61] The powerful score of Alexander Alexandrov's music was more than nostalgia, it was a call to revive the empire of the Soviet past, born as a hymn to Stalin and to the feats the country achieved as a global superpower – as well as to the great and terrible sacrifices it made along the way. Along with this call to the Soviet past, a new fervour for the Orthodox Church appeared to grip the ruling elite. Putin had broadcast his religious belief to the world in a book of interviews published just months before his first election as president, proudly telling how his mother and a neighbour in their communal Leningrad apartment had baptised him in secret, keeping it hidden from his father, who was a Party member and could not condone religious belief.[62] He'd told how in the early nineties, when he was due to visit Israel as the St Petersburg deputy mayor, his mother had given him his baptismal cross so he could have it blessed at Jesus's Tomb. 'I have never taken it off since,' he said. Then, during his first meeting with George W. Bush in 2001, he'd charmed the US president with the story of how he'd saved his cross from the fire that destroyed his dacha in the mid-nineties. Bush said afterwards he got 'a sense of his soul'.[63]

It seemed odd for a KGB officer who'd spent his career serving a state that outlawed the Orthodox Church to profess religious belief. But one by one, the KGB men who came to power with Putin, and who stood behind his rise, followed suit. From the beginning, they were searching for a new national identity. The tenets of the Orthodox Church provided a powerful unifying creed that stretched back beyond the Soviet era to the days of Russia's imperialist past, and spoke to the great sacrifice, suffering and endurance of the Russian people, and a mystical belief that Russia was the Third Rome, the next ruling empire of the earth. It was ideal material with which to rebuild a nation out of hardship and loss. According to one oligarch who viewed the surge in religious belief with scepticism, it was conveniently designed to make serfs out of Russians again, and keep them in the Middle Ages, so that Putin the tsar could rule with absolute power: 'The twentieth century in Russia – and now the twenty-first – has been a continuation of the sixteenth century: the tsar is above all else, and this is a sacred and heavenly role . . . This sacred power creates around itself an absolutely impenetrable cordon of guiltlessness. The authorities cannot be guilty of anything. They serve by absolute right.'[64]

According to Pugachev, who'd been a devout Orthodox believer since his teenage years, Putin understood little of the true Orthodox faith. Pugachev often blamed himself for the turn things took, because it was he who had introduced Putin to Father Tikhon Shevkunov, the priest who became known as Putin's 'confessor'. But the alliance, said Pugachev, had been one of convenience on both sides. For Shevkunov, it had allowed him to bring prominence to the Orthodox Church and its teachings, and riches and funding to his Sretensky monastery. For Putin, it was part of his appeal to the masses, and no more than that. 'I would never have introduced Putin to the Church if I'd known how it would all end up,' said Pugachev.

On one occasion, when Putin and Pugachev attended a service together on Forgiveness Sunday, the last Sunday before Orthodox Lent, Pugachev told Putin he should prostrate himself in front of the priest, as was the custom, and ask for forgiveness. 'He looked at me in astonishment. "Why should I?" he said. "I am the president of the Russian Federation. Why should I ask for forgiveness?"'[65]

In their search for a new idea to bind the nation together after a decade of collapse, it had long been clear to Putin and his supporters that Communism had failed. 'Communism vividly demonstrated its inaptitude for sound self-development, dooming our country to steadily lag behind economically advanced countries. It was a road to a blind alley, far away from the mainstream of civilisation,' Putin had said on the eve of his ascent to the presidency. And so, in the first years of his rule, when teachers and other experts were brought in to inculcate the new president in the history of the Russian state, they drew on Russia's imperial Orthodox past. Putin was taught about the White Russian émigrés who had fled Russia at the time of the Bolshevik Revolution, and had spent their time in exile trying to craft a new ideology for the country's revival should the Soviet Union ever collapse. There were, for instance, the writings of the religious philosopher Ivan Ilyin, who believed that Russia's new national identity should be based on the Orthodox faith and patriotism, tenets that Putin would refer to in speeches in his second term. In addition, there were the writings of linguist Nikolai Trubetskoi and of Lev Gumilev, the Soviet historian and ethnologist who propounded Russia's unique nature as a fusion of Slavic, European and Turkic cultures after centuries of invasion by Mongolian hordes. These thinkers stressed Russia's unique Eurasian path, promoting the philosophy of Eurasianism as an alternative to the Atlanticism of the West. Putin referred to this philosophy again and again as he sought to create first a Eurasian common economic zone that would draw in Belarus, Ukraine and Kazakhstan, and then a greater empire based on the alliances of the former Soviet states that, he hoped, would one day reach into Europe too.[66]

The aim was to forge an identity for the Putin regime that would

fortify it against internal collapse and outside attack. Direct descendants of the White Russian émigrés, many of whom had become
closely connected with the KGB, were brought into Putin's inner
circle to lead the effort to build a bridge with Russia's imperial past.
One of them described the philosophy of Putin's rule as being 'like
a knot with three elements. The first is autocracy – strong government, a strong man, a papa, an uncle, a boss. It is an autocratic
regime. The second element is territory, the fatherland, love of
country and so on. The third element is the Church. It is the element
to put everything together. It is the cement, if you like. It does not
matter whether this is the Church or this is the Communist Party.
It doesn't make much difference. If you look at the history of Russia,
you always had these elements put together. Putin is very careful in
bringing the three elements together. It is the only way to keep the
country whole. If you take away one of the elements, it collapses.'[67]

This philosophy was a direct copy of the state doctrine of
'Orthodoxy, Autocracy and Nationality' of Nicholas I, one of the
most reactionary tsars, known for his brutal suppression of one of
Russia's first democratic uprisings. Now Putin's KGB men were
seeking to recycle his ideology to define their rule and justify their
clampdown on any opposition.

But these were merely the germs of a transformation. It was only
towards the end of 2004, when they were faced with a challenge to
the Kremlin's hold over the vital former Soviet republic of Ukraine,
and when Russia was then struck by another horrific terrorist attack,
that Putin and his allies doubled down. Only then did Putin, relying
on the writings of Russia's imperial Orthodox past, set a path that
subverted what remained of the country's democracy, and sought
to unite the country by pitting it against the West.

The causes of the crisis in Ukraine were all too clear in the minds
of Putin's men: they believed the West was plotting to steer Kiev
away from Moscow. But what was not clear were the causes of yet
another horrific terrorist act – an act that left over three hundred
hostages dead, galvanising Putin's Kremlin to further tighten its grip.

*

On the morning of September 1 2004, children all over Russia were preparing for their first day of school. The girls were in their finest dresses, with enormous coloured bows in their hair. The boys had been armed with flowers for their teachers, and the parents were flocking around the school gates, clucking and proudly taking pictures of their young. But in Beslan, a small town in the North Caucasus about seventy miles from Chechnya, the traditional start-of-school ceremony was disturbed. Although Putin's devastating war in Chechnya was officially over, Russian troops still occupied the republic, and the entire region was a tinderbox. Violent skirmishes with Russian troops continued on a near daily basis, and armed incursions into neighbouring republics were still taking place.[68]

At approximately 9.10 a.m., as the children of Beslan milled around the school gates for the start-of-school ceremony, dozens of armed terrorists drove up in a police truck, firing at the handful of policemen guarding the school. They seized the school, taking more than 1,100 parents, children and teachers hostage. Several of the hostages later described how the terrorists had retrieved stacks of munitions from under the floorboards of the school, which a senior police official said had been hidden there by a group of workers during renovations ahead of the school year.[69] The terrorists herded the hostages into the gym, and wired the entire school building with explosives. Bombs were hung on a line stretched between two basketball hoops at each end of the gym, while two others were attached to a pedal mechanism at the feet of two seated terrorists. Tripwires were placed around the school to deter rescue attempts. In order to avoid being taken out by gas as in the Dubrovka siege, the terrorists were equipped with gas masks, and knocked out all the windows of the gym. For the next two days, the hostages were refused food and water despite the terrible heat. Children begged to drink each other's urine, and ate the flowers they'd brought in for their teachers.[70] From time to time gunfire broke out, and on the second day the terrorists fired grenades at two cars they thought had approached too near the school.[71] The terrorists were again demanding an immediate Russian troop withdrawal from Chechnya, recognition of Chechnya's independence, and an end to armed activities in the republic.[72]

Negotiations soon began – the hostage-takers allowed Ruslan Aushev, the former president of the neighbouring republic Ingushetia, into the school on the second day, and he promptly secured the release of twenty-six mothers and babies.[73] The presidential adviser on Chechnya, Aslambek Aslakhanov, an ethnic Chechen, said he'd reached an agreement to enter the school at 3 p.m. the following day.[74] He was proposing that seven hundred well-known Russian volunteers go into the school as hostages in return for the release of the children, and he was flying from Moscow to Beslan in the hope that he could pull the plan off. It later emerged that the local authorities had even reached out to Aslan Maskhadov, who'd been Chechnya's president in the mid-nineties, when it was a separatist state.[75] For the Kremlin he was still persona non grata, the arch foe they'd declared a terrorist and branded responsible for the Dubrovka siege. But the situation was so desperate that an aide to the deputy head of the local North Ossetian regional parliament had called Maskhadov's closest associate in London, who said he'd agreed with Maskhadov that he would come to the school to negotiate with the hostage-takers. Maskhadov's only condition was that he be granted safe passage there. At noon on the third day, this message was relayed directly to the North Ossetian president.

But just an hour after they spoke, an explosion suddenly rang out in the gymnasium. It was followed by a second, and then by a series of blasts.[76] Gunshots and rocket fire broke out as Russian special forces began launching rockets known as Shmel flamethrowers at the school.[77] Soon the roof was on fire. At about 2.30 p.m., according to eyewitness accounts, at least one Russian tank advanced and fired at the school's walls.[78] As the fire spread, the terrorists ordered many of the hostages out of the burning gym to the cafeteria, where they were forced to stand at the windows as human shields.[79] An independent investigation later found that as many as 110 hostages had died there.[80] The fire was meanwhile still raging through the gymnasium, but firefighters arrived only two hours after it began.[81] By then the roof had collapsed. Many of the hostages, including children, were burned alive, while others who tried to run out of the school were shot in the crossfire. Only a few ambulances were in attendance to transport the wounded to hospital.[82] The gunfire continued into the night.

Aslambek Aslakhanov arrived in Beslan in time only to witness the deadliest ever end to a terrorist attack.[83] 'When I was going there, I was in anticipation of this great joy over the fact that we would be setting the children free now,' he said. 'And when I got off the plane, I was simply at a loss. I thought to myself, how could this happen?'[84]

In all, 330 hostages died, more than half of them children. To this day, questions remain over how the deaths were caused, why the Russian special forces had begun attacking the building with rocket and gun fire, and most importantly, what had triggered the first explosion in the gymnasium. No one knew whether it had been deliberately set off by the terrorists, or accidentally by the Russian troops. Was the fire that caused so many deaths started by the explosion inside the school, or by the troops' flamethrowers?

Putin reluctantly agreed to a parliamentary investigation, but it was led by a close ally, Alexander Torshin, a senator with long-standing ties to the FSB. It could scarcely be described as independent, and when its work was eventually done over two years later, it found that one of the terrorists had caused the destruction of the school by intentionally detonating one of the bombs.[85] He was 'acting according to a plan developed earlier', it was claimed, while the federal authorities had acted completely in line with the law.[86] 'As the tragic events unfolded, all possible measures were taken to save the lives of people,' said the report, which claimed that the tanks and flamethrowers had only been deployed once all the hostages were out of the building. This was completely inconsistent with eyewitness accounts,[87] while the conclusion that the first explosion had been intentionally set off by a terrorist jarred with the findings of other independent investigations. One such investigation was led by the deputy speaker of the North Ossetian parliament, Stanislav Kesayev, who'd been present at the siege. It cited testimony from a captured hostage-taker that the first blast was triggered when a sniper took out one of the terrorists whose foot had been on a detonator.[88]

It was relatively easy for Torshin's commission to cast doubt on that claim, because the windows of the school were opaque, making it nearly impossible for a sniper to see inside.[89] But it was much harder to dismiss the findings of a third investigation led by a weapons and explosives expert, Yury Savelyev, an independent Duma deputy, who found that the initial explosions could only have been caused by rockets fired from outside the school.[90] His report concluded that the special forces had fired rocket-propelled grenades without warning, even as the negotiations were still going on.[91] In essence, he found, it was the Russian forces' intervention that led to the string of explosions that caused so many needless deaths.

Savelyev was highly respected in his field. He'd initially served on Torshin's panel, on which he'd been the only ballistics and weapons expert, but had stepped down when it became clear that the official findings were going to diverge widely from his own. His conclusions chimed with a video that was released nearly three years after the events at Beslan, apparently of army engineers talking to prosecutors when the siege was over.[92] The engineers were examining several of the home-made explosive devices rigged by the terrorists that lay undetonated on a table in the school. They were plastic bottles filled with shrapnel and ball bearings. 'The holes inside [on the walls of the school] could not have been caused by these explosives,' says one of the engineers. 'As they keep saying, all of these [ball bearings] would have been scattered around, but there was no evidence of these sort of injuries on the children we brought out. And all around, too.' 'So there was no explosion inside the building?' asks another of the engineers. 'Inside the building there was no explosion,' replies the first.

The extent of the carnage that broke out that day meant it was difficult to present the evidence as absolutely conclusive. But the claim that the first shots had been fired from outside the school was repeated by surviving hostages interviewed by the *Los Angeles Times*. One of them told of the shock on the hostage-takers' faces when the explosions began: 'They didn't expect this explosion. And that phrase – I'll never forget it – "Your own people blew you up." One of the hostage-takers repeated this several times in this very deep voice. I'll never forget it.'[93] Could it be, as one former Kremlin insider suggested, that the Russian authorities had ordered the firing that set off the attack on the school because they did not want to risk the arrival of Maskhadov, the former rebel leader and their sworn enemy, for talks?[94] The first explosions had rung out just one hour after his aide conveyed the message that he would come to negotiate. It was a rumour too terrible even to contemplate.

Putin faced a tidal wave of anger over the handling of the siege. Instead of the praise he'd won for the resolution of the Dubrovka theatre attack, questions mounted not only over the bloodbath that broke out when the Russian forces stormed the school, but over how the terrorists had managed to travel there in the first place – again armed to the teeth, and again in plain sight. Questions were being asked by the few remaining independent members of parliament in the Duma about whether he could ensure the security of the nation. One of the key planks of the social contract Putin had offered to the Russian people when he came to power had been an end to the terrorism that had brought the apartment bombings, through his war against Chechnya. But his security services had failed to learn the lessons of the Dubrovka siege, said the critics. The well-known political commentator Sergei Markov, seen as close to the Kremlin, called it 'a colossal crisis'.[95] Even the Communists, long cowed and silent as an opposition force, began to claim that Putin's clampdown on the political opposition had distracted his regime from tackling the bigger problem of terrorism. 'They've built a vertical of power that's proved useless in the face of these terrorist threats,' said Ivan Melnikov, the Communist Party's deputy leader.[96] Putin's ratings had been steadily sinking ever since his re-election, as fatigue over the endless Chechen war set in, and after Beslan they sank to a four-year low of 66 per cent.[97]

But the answer that Putin emerged with, pale-faced and determined when it was clear that the death toll had reached catastrophic proportions, was that the attack had been staged by forces outside Russia, who wanted to undermine the country's territorial integrity and bring about its collapse. In a direct address to the nation the day after the siege had ended, he called the tragic events 'a challenge to all of Russia, to all our people. This is an attack against all of us.'

'We are dealing with the direct intervention of international terror against Russia, with total and full-scale war, which again and again is taking away the lives of our compatriots,' he said. Instead of pointing the finger at terrorists in Chechnya, he claimed the attack was part of a broader plot that, it seemed he believed, emanated from the West: 'Some would like to tear from us a "juicy piece of pie". Others help them. They help, reasoning that Russia still remains one of the world's major nuclear powers, and as such still represents a threat to them. And so, they reason this threat should be removed. Terrorism, of course, is just an instrument to achieve these aims.'[98]

The attack, he argued, followed on directly from the collapse of the Soviet Union – which he and his KGB men believed had been engineered by the West. Russia, the core of what had been a 'vast and great state', had been unable 'to fully understand the complexity and the dangers of the processes at work in our own country and in the world. In any case, we proved unable to react adequately. We showed ourselves to be weak. And the weak get beaten. We simply cannot and should not live in as carefree a manner as previously. We must create a much more effective security system . . . Most important is to mobilise the entire nation in the face of this common danger.' At an annual meeting with Western academics he took the claims further, drawing direct parallels between the Beslan attack and the Cold War standoff with the West: 'It's a replay of the mentality of the Cold War . . . There are certain people who want us to be focused on internal problems, and they pull strings here so we don't raise our heads internationally.'[99]

Despite the fact that the subsequent investigations appeared to show that most of the deaths at Beslan had been caused by the Russian forces' own intervention, what happened next was the start of a sea change in Putin's Russia as his KGB men further sought to strengthen their grip. The response, he declared, would be the biggest constitutional change in the country's post-Soviet history. Russia, he announced ten days after the Beslan attack, was abolishing elections for regional governors. This went much further than the attempts to control the regional governors' powers already imposed by the Kremlin. Now, instead of being elected, they would be installed by

Kremlin appointment, and confirmed by regional parliaments. The move would strengthen the system against external threats, Putin said: 'The organisers, the perpetrators of the terror attack are aiming at the disintegration of the state, the break-up of Russia . . . The system of state power needs to not only adjust to the Beslan tragedy, but also prevent a repeat of such a crisis.'[100]

Independent political commentators like Nikolai Petrov, and independent Duma members, warned that this was a return to Soviet practices, tantamount to a return to a single-party system in which the Kremlin ruled supreme.[101] It was a complete reversal of one of the most important freedoms won in the Yeltsin years, and removed a system that had provided voters and regional elites alike with one of the most important lessons in local democracy. But the Kremlin argued that it was removing a system that had been corrupted, that had allowed elections for regional governors to be bought by those who could throw the most cash at them. Russia's young democracy was too weak to afford the risk of direct elections. The external threat to its unity was too great. Putin's men were building a fortress Russia, presenting the country as under siege from an external threat. But in reality they were intent only on preserving their own power. Putin's foreign policy establishment had long lashed out at the West for harbouring some of those it believed backed Chechen terrorists – Akhmed Zakayev in the UK, and Ilyas Akhmadov in the US.[102] It had questioned whether the Chechen rebels had been using the Pankisi gorge, a narrow valley that ran between Georgia and the North Caucasus, as their route through which to launch terrorist attacks on Russian soil. But till that moment, Putin's men had rarely publicly alluded to the idea that the West was intent on breaking Russia apart.

The evidence of Western involvement in the Beslan attack had, according to a Kremlin insider, been presented to Putin by Patrushev, and had of course been accepted unquestioningly: 'Putin believed it because it suited him. The main thing was to create a myth, to blame it on the West. This is how they were able to cover it all up. It was only after it happened they decided it was a good excuse to cancel elections for governors too.'[103] In fact, the move had long been on the agenda. The security men had just been waiting for a moment to bring it into force.

Putin had made no similar assertions about Western involvement after the Dubrovka siege. What's more, no evidence was ever presented that any Western forces had been involved in the Beslan attack. A report leaked by Russia's security services claimed that three UK residents, one an attendee of a well-known radical mosque in London's Finsbury Park, the other two Algerians living in London, took part in the siege.[104] But soon there was no more mention of this, and it was never confirmed.

What *was* happening at the same time, however, was a mounting threat to Russia's influence over its most vital near neighbour. In Ukraine that autumn, presidential elections were approaching. The constitutional term of Leonid Kuchma, a former Communist Party boss who'd balanced the country between East and West since 1994, was coming to an end. The pro-Kremlin candidate, Viktor Yanukovych, the then prime minister and a former convict and industrial boss who hailed from the pro-Russian stronghold of Donetsk in east Ukraine, was facing a mounting challenge from a candidate who favoured much closer integration with the West. This was Viktor Yushchenko, who'd also served a spell as prime minister, and everything he stood for was anathema to Putin's plans for Ukraine.

Of all the former Soviet republics, Moscow had always felt the loss of Ukraine following the Soviet collapse most keenly, as if it were a phantom limb of empire that Russia still believed was attached. Ukraine was the third-biggest former Soviet republic, after Russia itself and Kazakhstan. Nearly 30 per cent of its population spoke Russian as their native language, and its economy had been closely linked with Russia's since Soviet times. The Politburo had invested heavily in the industrialisation of Ukraine, once an agricultural region, transforming it into a major defence manufacturer vital for supplying Russia. Its steel plants had been joined with Russia's in the Soviet command economy, while its factories were still key suppliers of raw materials for Russia's aluminium industry. Most importantly of all, Ukraine was a vital transit zone for Russia's most strategic export. Eighty-five per cent of Russian gas exports to Europe were shipped through Ukraine's pipeline network, arteries of empire built in Soviet times, while Ukraine's Crimean peninsula on the Black Sea was still home to a strategically important Russian naval base.

As Putin sought to assert a Russian imperial revival, the last thing he needed was for Ukraine to turn to the West. But the country had long been divided, a crossroads between East and West since pre-Revolutionary times. Poland and Lithuania had controlled vast swathes of western Ukraine ever since 1686, when Russia and Poland divided the country between them after thirty years of war. Though Soviet rule put an end to any remnants of that, Western influence remained indelibly imprinted on the west of Ukraine, and the pro-European independence movement there was strong. During his rule, Kuchma had skilfully carried out a balancing act between the country's pro-Western and pro-Russian forces. But now Yushchenko had emerged to challenge Putin's plans for a tighter union through the creation of a Eurasian common economic zone. Both countries' parliaments had ratified the common economic zone's creation in April. But in Putin's mind Yushchenko was being backed by governments in the West determined to foil Russia's resurgence.

Yushchenko strongly supported Ukraine's integration into the European Union and NATO – Kuchma had fired him as prime minister for his Westernising bent. His Ukrainian-American wife had been raised in Chicago, and had gone on to serve in the US State Department. They had first met when they were seated next to each other on a plane – which Putin regarded as suggesting that Yushchenko had been recruited by the CIA.

Putin and his men were horrified at what they perceived as a clear incursion on their turf, a direct threat to the closer Eurasian integration they had been plotting. Putin had already voiced his first warning about Ukraine to the West that summer, several months before the Beslan attack. At stake were Kremlin plans for the first step in the resurrection of Russian empire, the so-called Common Economic Space between Russia, Ukraine, Belarus and Kazakhstan. 'By getting closer we are increasing our competitiveness. And this is understood not only by us, but by serious people, our partners abroad,' Putin had declared during a meeting with Kuchma in July.[105] 'Their agents, both inside our countries and outside, are trying everything possible to compromise the integration between Russia and Ukraine.' Putin chose the setting for this statement carefully: the meeting with Kuchma took place in the same historic Livadia Palace in Yalta where Stalin, Roosevelt and Churchill had divided Europe into spheres of influence between East and West towards the end of the Second World War. Putin was laying claim to a renewed historic right, a Russian sphere of influence over its near abroad.

But his warning appeared to have no impact. Yushchenko's popularity continued to rise by the day, despite a deployment of Kremlin spin doctors to Kiev to rally Yanukovych's vote. By September 5, just one day after Putin claimed in his speech about Beslan that outside forces were trying to tear juicy chunks out of Russia, Yushchenko's opponents went on the offensive. Yushchenko went for dinner at the dacha of the head of Ukraine's security service, General Ihor Smeshko. The next day he felt ill, and terrible cysts broke out on his face in the days that followed. Doctors in Austria, where he flew for treatment, concluded that he'd been poisoned by a highly toxic dioxin. But still the juggernaut of his campaign went on. Although Yushchenko had been temporarily sidelined, Yulia Tymoshenko, a formidable political operator and Ukrainian nationalist, continued the campaign in his absence. Their campaign was catchy and slick. The slogan was no more than a simple *Tak* – Yes – and their orange banners and placards seemed to be everywhere. Putin's attempts to intervene – even visiting Ukraine's capital Kiev just days before the poll to call on people to vote for the pro-Kremlin candidate Yanukovych – only seemed to backfire.[106] The blanket backing by Russian state TV for the gruff Yanukovych, the Party boss and ex-convict from the Russian stronghold of east Ukraine, who at times seemed as if he could barely string a sentence together, grated on an electorate anxious for independence after decades of Soviet hegemony. Yanukovych paled in comparison to the erudite Yushchenko, who'd become a hero for surviving the poisoning attempt that had left him disfigured and might still threaten his life.

When the nation went to the polls late in November, Putin's intervention again appeared to backfire. He congratulated Yanukovych on his victory even before the results had come in, although exit polls pointed towards the opposite result.[107] The official count was being overseen by a close Putin ally, and when it eventually tallied with Putin's early call, the opposition claimed that the vote had been rigged. Tens of thousands of Yushchenko supporters took to the streets, including legions of young people, many of them united by the youth group Pora!, who built a tent city in Kiev's main square, Maidan.[108] Despite the freezing cold the protests swelled, with up to a million people gathering on Maidan Square, and Kuchma was eventually forced to agree a new vote. This time the poll, held in December under the intense scrutiny of local and international observers, ended in victory for Yushchenko. The West's candidate had won.

For Putin and his supporters it was a devastating defeat that many have not forgotten to this day. The fallout from what became known as the 'Orange Revolution' was so great, the blow to the Kremlin's plans so devastating, that, according to two people who were close to him, Putin tried to resign.[109] But the fact was that no one in his inner circle wanted to take his place, no one was willing to take on the immense responsibility. This was the second pro-Western revolution in Russia's backyard. Just a year earlier, the Columbia-educated, pro-Western Mikheil Saakashvili had swept to power in the former Soviet republic of Georgia. To Putin and his allies, the forces of the West seemed to be activating all around them, encroaching on Russia's sphere of influence and threatening to reach into the country itself. It was the worst nightmare of Putin's KGB men that, inspired by events in neighbouring countries, Russian oppositionists funded by the West would seek to topple Putin's regime too. This was the dark paranoia that coloured and drove many of the actions they were to take from then on.

Again, the response of Putin and his inner circle was to double down, presenting Russia as a nation under siege. What had happened in Ukraine and Georgia would influence the actions of Putin's Kremlin for many years to come. Seeing themselves as being engaged in both a battle for empire and a battle for self-preservation, they could not allow the emergence of any outside influence – a factor that had surely coloured their decision to abolish elections for regional governors.

In December, just days before the second vote in Ukraine, Putin used his annual press conference to rail against the West, which he claimed was trying to isolate Russia by fomenting revolution in its near abroad. Again he linked this to the turmoil in Chechnya: 'If this is the case, then the West's policy towards Chechnya becomes more understandable . . . as a policy aimed at establishing elements that would destabilise the Russian Federation.' The revolutions in the former Soviet republics, he claimed, had been 'planned in other places', adding that the American billionaire George Soros was bankrolling the salaries of the new Georgian government.[110]

By the time Putin gave his annual state of the nation address the following April, the themes he had learned from the White Russian émigrés of the imperial past were clearly coming to the fore. Quoting liberally from Ivan Ilyin, the religious philosopher who'd fled the Bolshevik Revolution, and citing Sergei Witte, the reforming prime minister of Russia's last tsar, Putin said that Russia was following a unique path, its own destiny. Its form of democracy would not follow the models of the West. The collapse of the Soviet Union, he told the nation for the first time, had been the greatest tragedy of the twentieth century. 'Many thought or seemed to think at the time that our young democracy was not a continuation of Russian statehood, but its ultimate collapse, the prolonged agony of the Soviet system. But they were mistaken,' he said. Now the country was reaching a new stage of development: 'Our society was generating not only the energy of self-preservation, but also the will for a new and free life . . . We had to find our own path in order to build a democratic, free and just society and state.'[111]

Before then, Putin's state of the nation addresses had focused almost entirely on the economy, on measures to double GDP, to create a 'comfortable' life for Russia's citizens, and on the closer integration of the country into the global economy and Europe. 'The expansion of the European Union should not just bring us closer geographically, but also economically and spiritually,' he had said in his address just a year before.[112] But this year's speech had a different twist: 'Russia should continue its civilising mission on the Eurasian continent. We consider international support for the respect of the rights of Russians abroad of major importance, one that cannot be the subject of political and diplomatic bargaining.'[113]

Russia was marking out its sphere of influence, albeit belatedly, in the former Soviet republics. It was on a new trajectory – building a bridge to its imperial past.

9

'Appetite Comes During Eating'

When Mikhail Khodorkovsky was led in handcuffs into a cramped Moscow courtroom in June 2004, a trial began that would change the course of the Russian economy and subvert the country's justice system to the benefit of Putin's men. Khodorkovsky hadn't been seen since his dawn arrest on a Siberian runway. But now he was there, behind the bars of the metal cage in which Russia's draconian courtroom rules dictated defendants sat, his fall from grace apparent to all. A trio of female judges with bouffant hair looked down, stern-faced, from a plywood tribune, while armed guards surrounded the cage.[1]

The heat in the tiny courtroom that summer day was stifling. Power-suited lawyers were squashed shoulder-to-shoulder on make-shift wooden benches with reporters and members of Khodorkovsky's family, including his elderly parents. Dust hung in the air. From time to time, the cries of a handful of protesters shouting 'Freedom!' wafted in hopelessly through an open window. Dressed simply in jeans and a brown jacket, Khodorkovsky looked calm and intense as ever as he requested to be freed on bail. His detention for the past eight months in Moscow's notorious Matrosskaya Tishina jail, he said quietly, was an illegal abuse of power that would embolden the state to persecute others: 'My case is a precedent for justice in general; it will lead to hundreds of people being held in detention before their trials.'[2]

What emerged from the eleven-month-long proceedings, the hundreds of hours of cross-examination and courtroom testimony, was the case that created the foundations for Putin's state capitalism.

It opened the way for his KGB men to take control of the strategic 'commanding heights' of the country's economy, and created a precedent for the country's judiciary to be turned into an extension of the long arm of Putin's *siloviki*. The trial helped transform the entire law-enforcement system – the police, prosecutors and the courts – into a predatory machine that took over businesses and removed political rivals for Putin's ruling elite. By the time it was over, thousands of businessmen were being held every year in pre-trial detention, many of them released only when they agreed to hand over their businesses.[3] It was the crudest weapon the *siloviki* had in a legal arsenal that was eventually systematised for FSB and law-enforcement officers across the country on a scale large and small. The takedown of Khodorkovsky would give carte blanche to Putin's security men to such a degree that by 2012 more than 50 per cent of Russia's GDP was under the direct control of the state and businessmen closely linked to Putin, a huge and rapid turnaround since the time of the Khodorkovsky trial, when more than 70 per cent of the economy was in private hands.[4] It also fuelled a vast shadow economy of black cash for the resurgent security services, partly won from bribes in shakedowns that afforded a legion of FSB and other law-enforcement officers with tricked-out Humvees and palatial apartments far beyond the purchasing power of their official salaries. It gave the security men unfettered access to insider deals that won them trillions of roubles in cash to be stashed away and later laundered into accounts in the West.

The trial, to put it mildly, changed everything. It took place at the same time that Putin's men were digging in for what they believed was the resurrection of their country against the forces of the West, against the backdrop of Beslan and the Ukrainian and Georgian revolutions. In their view, the takeover of Yukos was a crucial element in restoring the country's imperial glory, in tightening control over the nation – and over its financial flows. At least, that was how they justified it to themselves then. 'The KGB saw that they had created a Frankenstein's monster which had a life of its own, called capitalism,' said Khodorkovsky's former adviser Christian Michel. 'They saw how the oligarchs they'd helped create were now making billions,

and they weren't getting any of it. And so they began to take back
the resources in the name of the country. They told themselves,
"We're taking back the resources which belong to the nation.
Otherwise the Americans will buy control."[5]

This convenient myth-making was not only a driving motivation
– it also allowed them to act as they wanted. In their view, they were
the guardians of Russia's restoration; they told themselves they
were the saviours of Russia, and deserved to build their own fortunes.
Like the Soviet leaders before them, they were the personification
of the state, their interests were fully aligned. But whereas previously
the state had been synonymous with the Party, they were about to
create an era of state capitalism, in which the lines between the state's
strategic and their own individual interests were to be almost indistinguishable. 'They painted it all in terms of a higher cause. But it
was also for personal greed, and this is where the problems began,'
said Michel.

The idea that the state would take back the commanding heights
of the economy had found ready support among a population that
was as resentful of the Yeltsin-era billionaires as were Putin's KGB
men. Putin summed up the widespread ill-will when, just a week
before Khodorkovsky's arrest, he'd again lashed out at the nineties-era
tycoons for trying to create a system of 'oligarchic rule': 'We have a
category of people who have become billionaires, as we say, overnight.
The state appointed them billionaires. It simply gave out a huge
amount of property, practically for free. Then as the play developed,
they got the impression that the gods themselves slept on their heads,
that everything is permitted to them.'[6] The Kremlin had even sought
to portray the battle against Yukos as part of the fight against
terrorism. Three weeks after the Beslan attack, by-then state-
controlled NTV aired a curious hit job alleging – without presenting
any evidence – that Khodorkovsky and his partners had financed
Chechen terrorists.[7]

Sergei Ivanov, Putin's close KGB ally from St Petersburg who now
served as defence minister, had been the first to openly signal what
was to come. 'The state should not lose control over strategic sectors of the economy,' he said in November 2003, a month after

Khodorkovsky's arrest. 'We should have control over the level of oil extraction and over exploration . . . The Soviet Union invested huge resources in the exploration and development of fields, and now the heads of the oil companies are getting huge profits from this. In any case, oil wells and resources are state property, not private. So the state has the full right to control this process.'[8]

But though the signalling was clear that there would be a turnaround in how Russia was run, Western governments didn't seem to think it was going to be as far-reaching as it was to prove. Initially, US officials struggled to understand whether it was a campaign that targeted Khodorkovsky alone, or whether it signalled a broader effort to take control of the energy sector.[9] They didn't realise that it was the beginning of a takeover of the entire legal and political systems, or that the resources Putin's KGB men were to accumulate would eventually be turned against the West. Though Sergei Ivanov had strongly indicated their desire to strengthen the control of the state, he and the rest of Putin's men took care to insist that this did not signify an overturning of the nineties-era privatisations, that the case against Khodorkovsky was about one rogue oligarch, that property rights would be respected, and that Russia was still a market economy, set on integration with the West.

The sharp response to his arrest from the US administration that Khodorkovsky had been counting on, and had believed would lead to his swift release, never came. Instead, the reaction was muted. Individual politicians like Republican senator John McCain, as well as George Soros, the billionaire currency-trader-turned-philanthropist, called for Russia to be turfed out of the elite G8 group of industrialised nations, which had only expanded to include it after Putin took the presidency. But only McCain seemed to recognise the potential consequences of the state onslaught against Yukos: 'A creeping coup against the forces of democracy and market capitalism in Russia is threatening the foundation of the US–Russia relationship and raising the spectre of a new era of cold peace between Washington and Moscow,' he told the US Senate in response to Khodorkovsky's arrest. 'The United States cannot enjoy a normal relationship, much less a partnership, with a country that increasingly

appears to have more in common with its Soviet and tsarist prede-
cessors than with the modern state Vladimir Putin claims to aspire
to build.'[10]

But for the administration of George W. Bush, it was mostly
business as usual. In those days, in the wake of the September 11
terrorist attacks, the focus was on counter-terrorism cooperation. It
was thus important to keep the lines of communication with Russia
open, especially now that Russia had begun to convince the West
of the links between Chechen rebels and the global terrorist cause.
The US was also becoming ever more dependent on Moscow's assistance in Afghanistan, including through the provision of a transport
route through Russia for war materiel. 'At a minimum the administration didn't want Russia to get in the way of what the US wanted
to do,' said Thomas E. Graham, the then director for Russia on the
US National Security Council. 'For instance, there were disagree-
ments over Iraq, and at best it wanted assistance in counter-terrorism,
as we saw in Afghanistan.'[11]

Nevertheless, the administration raised concerns about
Khodorkovsky's jailing and the state takeover of Yukos in several
communications with the Kremlin, said Graham. 'But the administration wasn't focused on domestic developments inside Russia that
much then.' It hadn't seemed at the time that Russia was stepping
back from democracy, he said, while Putin's efforts to rebuild the
power of the state apparatus was not seen as a bad thing, after the
chaos of the Yeltsin years. The forced departures of the media tycoons
Vladimir Gusinsky and Boris Berezovsky, and the handover of their
TV channels to the state, were seen as an internal affair. Neither was
viewed as a supporter of democracy, said Graham. They'd used their
media empires to peddle their own agenda.[12] Khodorkovsky, however,
had risen to become a different class of oligarch ever since he'd begun
to cast off his robber-baron image and started to pursue better corporate governance – as well as the sale of his oil company to the US.
'But from the standpoint of the administration this was not a big
deal that was going to cause us to step back and change policy towards
Russia.'[13] Essentially, for all his efforts to cultivate ties in America, the
US government had thrown Khodorkovsky to the wolves.

For global investors who'd bought into Russia's market transformation, however, the arrest of Khodorkovsky and the subsequent takeover of his company was much more significant. From the moment of the arrest and the state's freezing of Khodorkovsky's 44 per cent stake in Yukos, investors' eyes had been trained on the company, and whether the state would seek to use Khodorkovsky's trial to dismantle it. Yukos was Russia's number-one oil producer, extracting more oil than Kuwait. It had become the country's most well-known company, a flagship for Western investment, and any state move on it could portend a broader overturning of market reforms. Investors feared that the longer Khodorkovsky stayed in jail, the greater the risk that the *siloviki* would seize his company, which would ruin the investment case for the entire Russian market.[14] They feared a repetition of Gusinsky's treatment over NTV, and Khodorkovsky's detention being used to force him to hand over his shares, tactics first honed by Putin's KGB men in St Petersburg. Despite high global oil prices and a resurgent economy, the Russian stock market was one of the world's worst-performing that year, and Yukos shares had lost more than half their value since their peak the autumn before.[15] Khodorkovsky's closest partner Leonid Nevzlin had already proposed that Menatep shareholders cede control of Yukos to the state in return for the release of the 'hostages', explaining that he was making public what he heard from intermediaries offering backroom deals every day.[16]

But in this case, such proposals went down like a lead balloon with Putin's Kremlin, which was still desperate to keep Western investors – and the West in general – on side. The KGB men understood that every step they took had to be considered carefully. The process of jailing Khodorkovsky on charges of fraud and tax evasion had to look legitimate, part of a process that justified the state's break-up and takeover of Yukos and that, from a certain viewpoint, could be seen as acceptable in the eyes of the West. In those days, Putin's circle still feared the consequences of international court cases. They were keen to ensure Russia's deeper integration into global markets, and they knew they needed Western investment to continue the country's economic recovery, and to build a brand of state capitalism whereby they could expand – and infiltrate – into the West without being perceived as a threat.

So instead of crudely seizing Menatep's holdings in Yukos, they embarked upon an elaborate legal campaign in which the trial of Khodorkovsky was just one element of death by a thousand cuts. What emerged was the beginnings of a sophisticated process whereby tightly-controlled judicial orders and the court system were used as cover for the *siloviki*'s expropriation.[17]

It was a process made altogether easier by the no-rules transition of the nineties, when the oligarchs, including Khodorkovsky, had been able to skew the environment in their own favour, riding roughshod over the rights of minority investors and others, while privatisations had been rigged. Most businessmen then had operated almost in a legal vacuum, the state having become so weak it could barely enforce any laws. The court system and law enforcement were essentially up for sale. But now that Putin's KGB men had taken over the Kremlin, they began to reverse the situation entirely. In the Khodorkovsky case, the bottom line was the court rulings were essentially dictated by the Kremlin. The hearings were full of procedural violations, laws were applied retroactively and selectively. Instead of seeking to strengthen institutions in order to erase the abuses of the past, Putin's allies simply took them over, giving themselves the monopoly on abusing power.

They were assisted by the fact that many Russian laws were full of loopholes, making it easy for anyone to be accused of transgressing them. In such an environment, laws were open to interpretation, and meant far less than a system of mafia-type 'understandings', or agreements between friends, under which you had to stay on the right side of the Kremlin if you wanted to survive.

By the time Khodorkovsky faced the first day of his trial, Yukos had warned that it was on the brink of bankruptcy. Prosecutors had embarked on a parallel attack to besiege the company, retroactively levying $3.4 billion in back taxes for the year 2000 against it. Investors feared that the intention was to deliberately bankrupt Yukos, so the state could take control of it. Foreign creditors already feared that the company would be unable to pay a $1 billion loan.[18] Government officials led by the finance minister Alexei Kudrin, a liberal-leaning technocrat, had long been frustrated by the oil companies' use of domestic offshore zones to minimise tax payments. But Yukos was far from the only company to use such schemes, which had been legal under Russian law at the time. The effective tax rate Yukos paid was on a par with that of other privately-owned oil companies, such as Roman Abramovich's Sibneft and TNK-BP.[19] While investors feared that similar back tax claims could be deployed against others, the Kremlin and subservient Western bankers were anxious to insist that the case was about Khodorkovsky alone.

It was a measure of the Kremlin's sophistication that, the day after Khodorkovsky's first appearance behind bars in the Moscow courtroom, Putin went public with rare reassurance for investors about the case. On an official visit to the neighbouring former Soviet republic of Uzbekistan, he played the magnanimous leader, further underlining the turn in Khodorkovsky's fate. 'The official authorities of the Russian Federation, the government and the country's economic authorities are not interested in the bankruptcy of a company like Yukos,' he said. Relieved investors sent Yukos's stock price surging 34 per cent in the space of a day. But Putin left himself a get-out clause, by which the pretence of due process in an independent court system gave cover for the state asset grab: 'The government will do all it can to prevent the collapse of the company. But what happens in the courts is a separate matter. The courts should speak of this themselves.'[20]

He didn't mention, of course, that everything that happened in the courts was by then directly under the control of his closest associate, Igor Sechin, his deputy chief of staff, who had overseen and propelled the legal attack on Khodorkovsky since its start. As if to ensure close coordination, Sechin had even become part of the family of the prosecutor general, Vladimir Ustinov: his daughter had married Ustinov's son in November 2003, just as the legal attack was launched. From his perch overseeing the campaign, the stooping former KGB officer had seen nothing but opportunity.

For Sechin, the Yukos case was a unique chance to raise his standing from that of Putin's ever-obsequious servant. For years he had carried Putin's bags and stood guard over access to him; now he could turn the position to his own advantage. A Kremlin insider once complained to me that Sechin had deliberately lost a directive he'd agreed with Putin: 'Everyone was asking where it was. It hadn't been published. Putin said he'd signed it and given it to Igor . . . I went out to Sechin and he said, "Oops, it must have fallen behind the cupboard. I have so many papers here." And so it went on. He was doing it to show he was the one who makes decisions, and who decides whether things get done or not, and that I should go to him to decide things.'[21]

With the Yukos case, Sechin had an opportunity to expand his power base and create a fiefdom of his own. 'He understood that it was a chance for him to kill two birds with one stone,' said Alexander Temerko, one of Yukos's former significant shareholders. 'To take the asset and to use the case to take control of law enforcement.' When Sechin's daughter married the prosecutor general's son, 'it became a family business'.[22]

Temerko was the sole Yukos shareholder who remained in Moscow to try to seek a way out of the impasse. All Khodorkovsky's other remaining business partners with whom he'd founded the Menatep empire, including Nevzlin, had fled Russia, mostly for Israel, fearing arrest. But Temerko was different. Three- and four-star generals had once worked under him, and essentially he was untouchable.[23] Early in Yeltsin's presidency he'd served as head of a state military committee. He'd become close to a series of Yeltsin-era defence ministers and run a strategic state arms conglomerate. He'd known Khodorkovsky since his days in the Komsomol, and he helped Yukos win a major contract to supply the army with fuel.[24] Temerko was the ultimate lobbyist. He was charming and irascible, with a round belly and a thick moustache. If anyone was going to be able to negotiate a solution to the standoff with the Kremlin, it was him. He straddled the world between Khodorkovsky and the murky security men who ran Putin's Kremlin – his business partners said he was close to Nikolai Patrushev, the hawkish FSB chief.

Western investors were placing their hopes for negotiations in the two American oilmen who remained as Yukos's senior executives:

Steven Theede, formerly of ConocoPhilips, and Bruce Misamore, a Texan from Marathon Oil. Both were well-versed in Western management techniques, hardworking Americans who took the Moscow subway to the office. But they were far out of their depth in the Byzantine labyrinths of Kremlin negotiations. Temerko was the only person fit for that. Behind the scenes, he took on the mantle of backroom broker, sometimes sitting for eight hours on end in Sechin's Kremlin anteroom waiting for a chance to talk. On one occasion he tried to get around Sechin and take his case directly to Putin, agreeing with a senior Kremlin official that he could sneak out of the back entrance of a meeting of the Security Council to intercept the president. But Sechin found out about the plan, and angrily blocked his way. 'It was Sechin's job to personally hand over sensible proposals to the president,' said Temerko. 'But he was always saying, "This is not correct, this is not sensible." And we would go back to the drawing board.'[25]

From the beginning, Khodorkovsky's men were fighting a losing battle. Early in July, less than three weeks after Putin's reassuring comments, the pressure on Yukos was raised further. The system the president was building showed its true face. Dozens of government agents raided Yukos's headquarters in one of Moscow's shiniest new office towers, seizing computer servers and then freezing the company's bank accounts.[26] As if for good measure, tax officials carrying guns personally delivered a new back tax bill for $3.4 billion for 2001 to Steven Theede. This doubled the tax charge facing the company at a time when it hadn't been able to pay the previous one, and the deadline was about to run out. 'This will kill it,' said Igor Yurgens, a senior member of the oligarchs' lobbying group.[27]

In the days that followed the raid, Khodorkovsky went public from his jail cell with another offer to hand over Menatep's share in Yukos in order to pay down the tax debt.[28] Yukos's senior management team, led by Theede and Misamore, had proposed a restructuring plan that would allow the company to pay off $8 billion in back taxes over three years – if only the government would unfreeze Yukos's accounts to allow it to do so.[29]

All of these efforts came to nought. The negotiations continued throughout July, when all of a sudden the government side announced that, instead of accepting any of the restructuring plans, it intended to sell off Yukos's main production unit, Yuganskneftegaz, to cover the tax bills.[30] It alone produced 60 per cent of Yukos's total output, more oil than Libya. The decision sent shockwaves through the market once again. The break-up of Yukos had become reality. Just days after the announcement, Sechin, who was coordinating the attack behind the scenes, tipped his hand. He'd been appointed chairman of the state-owned oil company, Rosneft,[31] and rumours that Rosneft was pursuing Yukos's assets for itself suddenly gained weight.

With each coordinated blow against Yukos, Sechin had been growing in power. He was turning from trusty Putin deputy, fierce gatekeeper and controller of information and access to the president into a powerful player in his own right. Throughout the negotiations he'd played the servile assistant, offering to speak to the tax ministry and the justice ministry, and to funnel proposals to Putin, in order to help Menatep's negotiations along. 'In the beginning he would try to distance himself. He never said he was leading the process,' said Temerko. 'But each time we thought we were reaching an understanding, they would arrest another account so that we wouldn't be able to pay.' Sechin would shake his head regretfully and tell Temerko how sorry he was that they hadn't been able to agree. 'He would tell us we weren't capable of agreeing. But actually his position was to push us into more and more compromises and disclosure of information.'[32]

Still the government sought to keep Western investors on side. It promised a sale of Yukos's main production unit, Yugansk, at a fair market price; but the task of conducting the valuation was entrusted to the Moscow branch of Dresdner Bank, headed by one of Putin's closest allies, Matthias Warnig, the former Stasi agent who'd worked with him in Dresden.[33] Amid the drip-drip of information and the steady stream of new attacks, the Western market was becoming accustomed to the idea that Yukos would be broken up, and by the time the government announced the Yugansk sale, Western oil majors were offering to help take it off Khodorkovsky's hands. These offers undermined the US administration's warnings to the Kremlin about the Yukos case. 'The problem was, every time we told the Russians that what they were doing would have a negative impact on the investment climate in Russia, one of the Western companies would come forward and make an offer to buy Yukos,' said Thomas Graham. 'There were two or three proposals that went to the Kremlin then offering to buy up Yukos shares and help alleviate the problems Russia would have with its image.'[34]

The offers also served to confirm Putin's long-standing cynical view that anyone in the West could be bought, and that commercial imperatives would always outweigh any moral or other concerns. And soon the Kremlin was launching a major new charm offensive to win Western investor support for the state's asset grab.

*

By this time the Kremlin had begun to operate fairly slickly. Behind the scenes, Western investment bankers were advising the government on the Yukos takeover. (Later, one Moscow investment bank, Renaissance Capital,[35] that had been initially advising Yukos, participated in a government auction for part of the spoils.) When Putin announced in mid-September that he was overturning one of the biggest achievements of Russia's transition to democracy, the election of governors, in response to the Beslan tragedy, the news might have looked ominous against the backdrop of the state's increasingly clear efforts to break up and take over Yukos.

But Putin had a pleasant surprise for foreign investors. The day after the Kremlin announced the end of elections for governors, it told the market it planned to create the world's biggest energy major, merging the state-controlled gas giant Gazprom with the state's last remaining oil major, Rosneft, to create a behemoth that would control the world's second-biggest reserves, behind only Saudi Arabia's Aramco, and five times larger than its nearest counterpart in the West, ExxonMobil. Unlike Aramco, it would be open for Western investors to take a stake in.[36]

The proposed deal was testimony to the audacious global ambition of Putin and his circle at a time when Western interest was growing in Russia's role as an energy supplier, due to the turmoil in the Middle East. It was a big turnaround from only six months previously, when prime minister Mikhail Kasyanov had wanted to break up Gazprom under liberal reforms to reduce its monopoly hold over the gas sector. Putin had rejected that out of hand, and the new plan to merge the gas monopoly with Rosneft was a stark symbol of the government's intentions for state domination of the energy sector.

Yet for Western investors, the news was good. The strengthening of state control over the economy, which they'd long feared, was paired with the enticing prospect of a slice of a huge new energy giant. The deal would increase the state's stake in the merged GazpromRosneft to a controlling 51 per cent, automatically lifting restrictions on the amount of stock foreign investors could hold in Gazprom. Plans to lift these restrictions – known as the 'ring fence' – had long been contemplated by Putin's government; now it appeared that they had finally got the green light, immediately boosting the share price. Western investors salivated at the money they could make trading the proposed new state behemoth. 'This will be the largest oil-and-gas company in the world that foreigners can invest in, at a time when oil and gas prices are going through the roof,' said William Browder, the head of Hermitage Capital Management, which held a significant chunk of Gazprom shares,[37] adding that it was 'some sort of sugar to help the Yukos medicine go down'.[38] Ian Hague, head of the New York-based Firebird Fund, described the Kremlin's proposal more directly: 'They are buying off the loyalty of the foreign investor community as they create what looks like a political dictatorship. And it's working.'[39]

It was the beginning, for some, of a beautiful friendship, as the Kremlin signalled that foreign investment was welcome as long as Putin's men were in control. The unease about the takedown of Yukos died away as investors lined up to join the new state giant. The only person who didn't seem pleased by the prospect was the Rosneft chairman Igor Sechin, as the planned tie-up between Rosneft and Gazprom threatened to bring down the curtain on his dreams for a state energy giant of his own.

Even as Sechin seethed, the drama surrounding the proposed Yugansk sell-off was far from over. A leaked report said Dresdner Bank had valued the production unit at between $15.7 billion and $17.3 billion, which seemed in line with what the market believed was a fair price,[40] and led Yukos's Western managers to believe that there would be cash available to keep the rest of the company together after the sale of Yugansk. But at the end of November that year, any hope of that was irretrievably dashed when the justice ministry not only announced an opening price for the government auction of Yugansk of $8.65 billion, well below the Dresdner range, but also presented Yukos with two more enormous tax claims for 2002 and 2003.[41] These brought the tax bill facing Yukos to a monumental $24 billion, more than four times the company's battered market capitalisation. For Yukos's management it was all too clear that this was game over, and that the rest of the company was going to be broken up and sold for a knockdown price.

If the message hadn't been resounding enough already, the night before the new tax charges were announced, armed police raided the homes of dozens of Yukos managers, who said the move recalled Stalin's purges of 1937. They were 'afraid of being at their home at night, afraid for their relatives', said one of the managers.[42] The point was also driven home to the Western oilmen Khodorkovsky had brought into Yukos as a symbol of its move to better governance. Bruce Misamore, the affable chief financial officer from Texas, had been in London that day. As he weighed whether or not to risk flying back to Russia, he received a call from Temerko, who warned him that he would be arrested on arrival.[43] Misamore never returned. The same went for Steven Theede, who'd served as Yukos's president since June 2004. He too was out of the country on business that day, but a police raid on his office sent a clear signal that he should not go back to Moscow. The low sale price announced by the government for Yugansk, he said, represented 'government-organised theft to settle a political score'.[44]

For Bruce Misamore it had become clear that all the management's efforts to reach a settlement had been in vain. The last-minute flurry of tax claims, taking the total to over $24 billion, would allow all of

Yukos's assets to be sold off piece by piece to state-controlled companies. Misamore believed this had been the Kremlin's goal from the start. The asset and bank-account freeze ensured that the company would never be in a position to pay down the debts. 'At first we thought that if we paid the money, they would maybe go away,' he said. 'We used many different ways to try to access the right people in the Kremlin to negotiate a settlement. They would lead us on, and we would think that we were very close to a settlement, but then someone would meet Putin and the whole thing would get dropped.'[45]

For Alexander Temerko too, it was finally apparent that the negotiations had been a road to nowhere, that Sechin, Putin and his men had been using them as cover for the takeover, as they'd needed to lull the market and foreign leaders into a belief that due process was being observed. But ultimately, said Temerko, 'We were being lied to. They sent all these false messages. Some senior people in Putin's circle had told me, "This is all a game." They said, "If they have started gnawing at the company, they will gnaw at it to the end, till they have gotten down to the bones." They probably thought they should show some process, some readiness to negotiate. But when everyone got used to what was going on, they took the view, "Why should we agree? It's all ours anyway."' The Dresdner Bank valuation, the constant dangling of potential deals, were 'typical Chekist manoeuvres. They gave out false information and then got on with their own business on the side.'

It was a tactic that was to be repeated by Putin's Kremlin again and again, right up to Russia's seizure of Crimea from Ukraine many years later in 2014. Then, they would claim at first that the sudden appearance of troops on the ground in Crimea had nothing to do with them. But once the annexation of Crimea had been secured, Putin admitted that they were Russian forces. 'They lied to Western heads of state,' said Temerko. 'They told them we were criminals, but that they were not going to take the company from us, they just wanted to find a common language. Putin said many times, "We don't want to bankrupt Yukos." But then they did. Yukos is when they first learned how to lie. The lies are professional by now.'[46]

As Russia prepared to sell off Yugansk, a fight was breaking out between the two main factions within Putin's security men for the spoils. Emboldened by Putin's backing for a merger with Rosneft, Gazprom, the country's state gas giant, had become intent on acquiring Yugansk too. It had the backing of the more liberal-leaning technocrats in Putin's government, led by Alexei Kudrin, the finance minister, who were keen to ensure that the power of Sechin, as chairman of Rosneft and their biggest rival and the leading and most hawkish member of the security bloc, increased no further. They were pushing for Yugansk to be sold at a fair market price, and wanted Gazprom to have a Western stamp of approval for the acquisition through the backing of Western institutions providing billions of dollars in loans.[47] They believed such an outcome would produce a more palatable version of state capitalism, and the West was more than willing to engage on those terms. By the time the auction was due to be held, Gazprom had lined up the biggest loan in Russia's corporate history – more than $13 billion from a syndicate of banks led by Germany's Deutsche Bank and Dresdner Bank.[48] It had also won the backing of the same US energy majors, Chevron and Exxon, which had once been on the brink of a deal with Khodorkovsky but were now ready to turn on him. Now they were discussing taking a slice of the Yugansk sale in a consortium with Gazprom, according to two people with knowledge of the matter,[49] while the UK's Royal Dutch Shell was also in talks for a stake.

To Putin this was yet another example of how, for the West, commercial considerations outweighed concerns over the direction of democracy. But for Khodorkovsky's partners there could never be even a patina of respectability to the sale, and Kudrin's attempts to lend it legitimacy through the participation of Western institutions and companies represented nothing more than a cover-up, and a sellout of principles by the West. In their view the Yugansk sale was outright theft, and they had to do everything in their power to stop it going through.

Everything had been prepared for what promised to be the sale of the Kremlin's new century, the auction whereby one of the biggest prizes in the oil industry was to be returned to the hands of the state – with the approval and participation of Western banking institutions and oil majors to boot. But just four days before the Yugansk sale was due to be held, Yukos's senior management, still led by Theede and Misamore from exile in London, dug in for a final act of defiance. The blow came without any warning: they'd quietly filed for Chapter 11 bankruptcy for Yukos in a Houston court, and won a temporary stay to halt the sale.[50] All of a sudden, Gazprom's Western backers fell away.[51] The Yukos managers had argued that the company fell under the protection of the US legal system because US minority investors held a 10 per cent stake, while the oil major itself had 'significant business' in the US.[52]

The last-minute move sent Putin into a vituperous rage. 'I'm not sure [the judge] even knows where Russia is,' he snapped.[53] Insisting that the US courts had no jurisdiction over what happened in Russia, the Kremlin pressed ahead with the sale. But for Gazprom, the risks of bidding in the auction had become too high. Its ownership of a web of assets in the West – storage facilities, trading hubs and joint ventures for gas distribution in Europe – left it open to lawsuits should it seek to bid in the sale and violate the US order. Instead, the way was cleared for Igor Sechin, the *silovik* many in the banking community had begun to name 'the dark lord' for his propensity for scheming and his ruthless ambition, to make another bid for Yugansk. His Rosneft oil major had no assets in the West.

The sale of Yuganskneftegaz was meant to mark the opposite of the backroom loans-for-shares auctions that had transferred the .crown jewels of Soviet industry into the hands of a handful of well-connected tycoons at discount prices. Though Yukos had decried it as theft, the Russian government was seeking to present the sale as obeying the normal rules of the market. As if to underline the difference from the closed-door sales of the nineties, journalists had been invited to observe the auction, broadcast live on two screens in the plush red conference room of the Russian Federal Property Fund.[54] It was meant to set a new precedent for transparency. But the last-minute bankruptcy filing in the Houston court meant the sale ended in farce. It was still broadcast for the journalists, but there was only one bid, and no one knew who was behind it. Of the two sets of besuited executives sitting behind desks in a small wood-panelled room, only one was identified. They were from GazpromNeft, the oil arm of Gazprom created just weeks before. The other two executives – a tall man in a grey suit and a thickset woman wearing glasses – were completely unknown. Their company had registered to take part in the auction only three days before, yet they were the only ones to bid. The tall man solemnly raised his paddle to bid $9.37 billion, just $500 million above the opening price, while the executives from GazpromNeft made a telephone call and then did not bid at all. The much-anticipated sale was over with a sudden bang of the auctioneer's gavel almost as soon as it had begun.

The oil-production unit that produced more oil than Libya had been sold to an outfit, later named as Baikal Finance Group, that no one had ever heard of. Even the chairman of the Federal Property Fund, Yury Petrov, had no idea about it at all. 'We know nothing about this company,' he said.[55] It turned out that Baikal Finance Group had been founded just two weeks before, in a pre-Revolutionary building above a bar named 'London' in the provincial Russian town of Tver.[56] No one seemed to know who the owners were.

But Putin knew exactly who was behind the winning bid, and told everyone not to worry. The individuals behind the company had 'years of experience in the energy sector', he said.[57] It turned out that they were connected to two of his closest allies, one of whom Khodorkovsky had trampled on when he took over Eastern Oil company, or VNK, in the nineties: Gennady Timchenko, the oil trader who'd worked with Putin in St Petersburg, and Andrei Akimov, the former Soviet state banker who'd financed Timchenko's oil trader and launched a rival bid for VNK. The executives who had actually bid for them at the auction were identified as mid-level managers from Surgutneftegaz, the Kremlin-loyal oil major.[58] Surgutneftegaz was the chief supplier to Timchenko's oil-trading company, and by the time of the Yugansk sale he controlled a significant stake in it, according to Vladimir Milov, the former deputy energy minister, a former Timchenko partner, and a senior Russian banker who worked with Timchenko.[59] Timchenko has said he only ever owned less than a 0.01 per cent stake in Surgutneftegaz.

His lawyers said he had no connection to or ownership interest in Baikal Finance Group.

Putin's KGB allies had finally taken revenge on Khodorkovsky for squeezing them out of VNK. They'd landed the first and biggest piece of Yukos after more than a year of behind-the-scenes manoeuvring persuading Putin to take Khodorkovsky on. They seem to have hastily cobbled together Baikal Finance Group as a front company to minimise transparency over its participation in the sale and avoid legal consequences from the US court order. Within four days of the sale, Baikal Finance Group sold Yugansk on to Sechin's Rosneft.[60]

Overnight, Rosneft grew from being a minnow worth no more than $6 billion to an oil giant of global stature with assets worth nearly $30 billion, strengthening Sechin's hand along the way. Instead of bringing a halt to the sell-off, Yukos's bankruptcy suit had resulted in creating a new powerhouse for the *silovik* who'd orchestrated much of the legal campaign to bring down Yukos.

If Gazprom had been able to acquire Yugansk cleanly, without legal risk, then Rosneft would most likely have been merged into Gazprom too, removing a key asset from Sechin's sway. Though powerful, Sechin would have remained a bureaucrat. But now the company he chaired had become a new state oil champion, and he had gone from backstage Kremlin player to a real economic force in his own right. His increased stature heralded problems for the much-vaunted merger of Rosneft into Gazprom. Sechin wanted Rosneft to remain an independent power.

For one of the Western bankers who'd worked closely with Gazprom on raising funds to acquire Yugansk, the Houston court filing was nothing less than a calamity that had skewed the process towards strengthening the *siloviki*. To him, the liberal technocrats, led by Kudrin, who had backed Gazprom were a more benign force who would have ensured a more investor-friendly climate in Russia in future. 'We were preparing a deal that might have improved transparency and increased Western influence,' he said. 'We were going to have one of the original firms that were planning to come, like Exxon, Chevron or Shell, take a slice of the deal. We were going to bring in one of these firms to be a strategic partner. But then there was the injunction, and the bad guys rushed back in. The power, influence and career path of Igor [Sechin] was to be dramatically curtailed. This was one of the crazy things about that stupid US judge.'[61]

If the Western banker truly believed the sale of Yugansk to Gazprom would have improved due process, he was probably deluding himself. What mattered was that its sale was effectively a state expropriation, triggered by the government selectively applying tens of billions of dollars in back tax charges for schemes that had been legal at the time. Any participation by Western banks would have been no more than window-dressing, while the disappointment of the technocrats was probably no more than Kremlin infighting over the spoils. A sale to Gazprom might have looked more palatable to the West, but the end result would have been the same.

For Sechin, however, it was without doubt a victory. For transparency – and for the Russian budget – it was undoubtedly a further loss. The sale that was to be financed by Western banks ended up being paid for through a murky deal that involved funding from the Russian budget. Although the Yugansk sale had ostensibly been forced through to pay off billions of dollars in back taxes to the Russian budget, central bank data showed that the federal treasury ended up transferring $5.3 billion through the state-owned Vneshekonombank to Rosneft to help pay for the purchase.[62] One of the biggest scandals of the loans-for-shares sales of the nineties was the widespread belief that the oligarchs had dipped into federal treasury funds held in accounts in their banks to finance them. Now it appeared that Rosneft had done almost exactly the same. But this time there was barely the whiff of a scandal. Only one newspaper, the business daily *Vedomosti*, reported the scheme, and only one state official raised his voice. The funds were only paid back to the treasury in 2005, when Rosneft and Vneshekonombank clinched an emergency funding deal for $6 billion from Chinese banks as part of an oil-supply deal whose terms were never disclosed.[63]

The sole official within the Kremlin to protest against the sale, which he described as 'daylight robbery',[64] was Andrei Illarionov, a liberal economist who'd been Putin's economic adviser since the earliest days of his presidency. The funding for the acquisition from the federal treasury, he said, laid bare the pretence that it was all about collecting back taxes. Illarionov, who was widely respected for his principles, was growing increasingly uneasy. He didn't know how long he could remain in his post when the country was turning definitively away from any version of a liberal market, and the emerging state capitalism looked so corrupt. He'd already been demoted from one of his main roles because of his criticisms. The official explanations for the legal attack against Yukos 'didn't have a leg to stand on', he said. 'At issue is not the existence of tax arrears, because nobody was interested in tax arrears in this case. The company had started to pay down the tax arrears when it had not even admitted them . . . They were prepared even to pay these fantastic amounts, but no one was interested in that.' The entire campaign of back tax bills against Yukos had, he believed, been cooked up to seize its assets. Putin's Kremlin 'gave up receiving additional tax payments in order to obtain property. This is the most dramatic and the most candid statement of their genuine interest in the Yukos affair.'[65]

In the months and years that followed, the institutions of the West bowed to Putin's new economic order. The way had eventually been cleared thousands of miles from Moscow in a courtroom in Houston, Texas, where in February 2005, two months after the sale, a judge finally dismissed the merits of Yukos's case for bankruptcy protection following strong arguments from Gazprom's legal representatives, the powerful Texas law firm Baker Botts. Though a temporary stay had been issued in time for the sale, after considering all arguments, the judge ruled that Yukos did not have sufficient presence in the US to receive the protection of the US courts.[66] The decision had essentially given the all-clear for the break-up of the rest of Yukos. The way was opening up for Western companies, hungry for a piece of the action, to participate in the further bankruptcy sell-off of Yukos assets.

When the ruling came, said Temerko, 'it became clear to me that the battle was over, that the US was not going to stand in the way'.[67] Till then, he said the Kremlin had been nervous that the US might retaliate. But although the US State Department had continued to quietly condemn the sale, the prospect of further Western outcry that Khodorkovsky and his partners hoped for gradually fell away. Instead, the oil giants of the West began to line up with ever greater zeal to take part in Putin's new order, to become investors and partners in the newly endowed Rosneft. Deutsche Bank and Gazprom's Western lawyers, in particular, were helping ease the way. A key player remained Charlie Ryan, the head of the Moscow brokerage United Financial Group, in which Deutsche Bank had bought a 40 per cent stake in late 2003. He'd worked to help Gazprom line up Western loans, and then introduced the state gas giant to Baker Botts, which fought strongly against the petition for bankruptcy protection in Houston on its behalf.

Ryan had taken Russia's campaign to gain the approval of the West to one of the US's most prestigious law firms, at the heart of the Republican establishment. Baker Botts's backing for the Kremlin, and for its energy giants Gazprom and Rosneft, followed a model it had already honed in many of the world's autocratic regimes, where for decades it had been a supporter of major US oil company interests. The firm's main partner, former US secretary of state James Baker, had been introduced to Alexei Miller, the close Putin ally who served as Gazprom's chief executive,[68] and over breakfast in the grand dining room of the Hotel Rossiya, just across the way from the Kremlin, he had been convinced to take on Gazprom's defence. 'I told him Khodorkovsky was a murderer,' said one of the Western intermediaries involved in the process. 'Baker is very sophisticated.' He'd immediately understood.

A bit of moral relativism had helped win the Texan law firm over. The men they were dealing with in Russia seemed mild in comparison to some of the leaders they'd worked with in the Middle East. 'Of all the places in the world where God in His infinite wisdom decided to put oil, Russia seemed one of the more civilised regions compared to the rogues' gallery they were dealing with in Gaddafi and Saddam Hussein,' said the Western intermediary. 'Up against that crew, Alexei Miller looked like a schoolboy.'[69]

But Miller, a bureaucrat who'd served in the foreign relations committee in the St Petersburg mayor's office, was no more than a deputy for Putin. Even if he did look a bit like a schoolboy, it didn't matter, because at Gazprom Putin called the shots. For Baker Botts, however, the new relationship was to prove lucrative. It was to work closely with Gazprom and then Rosneft for more than a decade, eventually opening the way for Exxon to form a strategic $3.2 billion tie-up with Rosneft to jointly explore the Arctic and the Black Sea in the search for new oil reserves.[70] It assisted Rosneft's defence against lawsuits filed by Yukos managers and by Menatep over the state expropriation. Emails show that it even appeared to help Rosneft in the subversion of the rule of law, assisting in the preparation of rulings drafted by Rosneft's lawyers for an Armenian court as the state oil giant defended itself against litigation filed by Menatep.[71]

The fallout from the Yugansk sale had helped Putin find a crucial weakness in the West's armour: ultimately, financial interests would outweigh concerns about his regime's abuse of the law and democracy. It was part of a widespread complacency – and to some degree arrogance – in the West that Russia no longer represented any danger, that after the break-up of the Soviet Union the collapse had been so deep that all that remained for the West was to find a way to take a share of its energy wealth, while the country's integration into Western markets would mean that, with time, it would become part of a Western-dominated globalisation where it would abide by the same rules as other nations. But for Temerko, the US looked to have agreed to a non-aggression pact with Russia that had given the green light for Putin and his men to act as they liked.

The way was being opened for the Kremlin to control ever greater cash flows, which one day would enable it to challenge the West. Its takeover of the oil sector received a further Western stamp of approval in the summer of 2006, when Rosneft launched a $10.4 billion initial public offering of its shares on Western markets. By then the company had been valued at nearly $80 billion, a huge increase on its $6 billion valuation before the Yugansk acquisition. BP took a slice worth $1 billion, and other international oil majors also bought significant shares.[72] Investors worldwide were betting on continued Kremlin backing for the state oil giant's takeover of the rest of Yukos, as well as soaring global oil prices. All of this

served to legitimise the Putin regime and enable its further integration into Western markets, expanding the Kremlin's reach. The
possibilities were potentially limitless. 'Before, they only thought
about coffee and maybe a bit of salad,' said Temerko. 'But when they
brought the salad, it turned out they could eat the entire buffet.
Appetite comes during eating,' he sniffed. [73]

When the rest of Yukos went under the hammer in a series of
bankruptcy auctions in 2007, Western oil majors and financial institutions facilitated the process. In fact, they provided convenient
cover for Putin's men. First, a consortium of Western banks led by
France's Société Générale – and not the Russian state – filed a petition for bankruptcy on Yukos in 2006, over $482 million in
outstanding loans.[74] Though the Western banks had filed the bankruptcy petition, it was Rosneft – and the Kremlin – that was in
the driving seat. The London lawyer representing the interests
of the beleaguered Menatep Group, Tim Osborne, said he believed
the Western banks were acting at Rosneft's behest.[75] Sure enough,
three days after they filed the suit, Rosneft bought out the Western
banks' outstanding debt.[76]

When the time came for the gavel to fall on Yukos's remaining
assets, another Western banking consortium provided Rosneft with
a record-setting $22 billion loan,[77] while three Western energy majors
provided legitimacy for the process, despite Menatep's protests that
the sales constituted outright theft. At the first bankruptcy sale, for
a 9.4 per cent stake Yukos had wound up owning in Rosneft, TNK-
BP, the Russian energy venture half owned by BP, bowed out after
just ten minutes to allow Rosneft to make the winning bid.[78] Then,
when Yukos's gas assets were up for sale, the Italian energy majors
Eni and Enel made the winning bid of $5.6 billion, then promptly
handed control of the assets to Gazprom as part of a broader deal
they'd struck with the state gas giant.[79] In both cases, the foreign
participants were seen by market analysts to be seeking the Kremlin's
favour at a time when, in order to gain a toehold in the Russian
energy sector, it was crucial to win the state's backing. 'The Kremlin
would like to have the likes of Eni and BP participating because they
want to show that despite the damage of Yukos . . . the reality is

international oil companies are queuing up to enter the Russian energy sector,' said Chris Weafer, then chief strategist at Russia's Alfa Bank.[80]

By the end of the Yukos break-up, the state had taken control of 55 per cent of the nation's oil output, a huge turnaround from the 80 per cent in private hands when Putin came to power.[81] Some Western lawyers and bankers had privately struggled to justify assisting the Kremlin in a campaign that had provided such riches. 'Khodorkovsky was extremely aggressive on the tax front,' said Frank Kujilaars, who then headed global oil and gas at ABN Amro, the now defunct Dutch bank which led the financing for Rosneft's take-over of Yukos. 'He was trying to maximise the returns in terms of using every loophole. It wasn't illegal, but it was very much on the edge.'[82]

*

While Western lawyers and bankers lined their pockets in the Kremlin's Yukos takeover, the reality Khodorkovsky was dealing with was far grimmer. Almost every day for eleven months he'd been taken in handcuffs to the same Moscow courtroom, forced to sit through hours of evidence as the Kremlin, intent on demonstrating the legitimacy of its case against him, laid out its accusations. But the allegations were deeply flawed – as even the foreign bankers who assisted the Kremlin in its expropriation seemed to acknowledge. One set of charges related to Khodorkovsky's 1994 privatisation of Apatit, a large fertiliser plant in Russia's far north, as well as a research institute attached to it that he acquired the following year – they were the first big privatisations Khodorkovsky's Menatep Group had participated in. While Khodorkovsky's defence lawyers argued that these charges had no basis in fact or law, they related to events that were rapidly reaching the end of a ten-year statute of limitations. The second set of charges related to Yukos's use of tax shelters inside Russia in 1999 and 2000, which the prosecution alleged was illegal. But the same schemes had been widely used by other oil majors, and were in line with the Russian laws of the time.

Khodorkovsky was being targeted retroactively and selectively, his lawyers said.

When Khodorkovsky was finally allowed to present his case in closing arguments, he launched into a tirade as he detailed each charge one by one. There was 'not a single document – let me emphasise – not a single one – that would point to my illicit activities', he said. 'Two years of inhuman labours by the Prosecutor General's office – and a zero result!'

The whole case, he claimed, had been launched as a show trial to provide cover for the expropriation of Yukos by state officials driven by greed: 'The entire country knows why I was locked up in jail: so that I wouldn't interfere with the plunder of Yukos. In doing so, the people who organised the persecution of me personally tried to frighten the authorities and society with my mythical political ambitions. When they say that the "Yukos case" has led to a strengthening of the role of the state in the economy, this evokes bitter laughter from me. Those people who are busily plundering Yukos's assets today do not actually have anything to do with the Russian state and its interests. They are simply dirty, self-serving bureaucrats and nothing else.'

He ended his impassioned speech with a direct appeal to the judges' sense of justice, arguing that surely such a 'direct, barefaced deception' of the court by the prosecutors could not pass: 'I have faith that my country, Russia, will be a country of justice and law. And this is why the court must rule on the basis of justice and on the basis of the law.'[83]

But though the trio of judges appeared to listen intently, scribbling down notes as he spoke,[84] their verdict had already been determined. An eyewitness account has emerged that details for the first time how Sechin and one of his deputies had tightly controlled the process every step of the way.[85] To remove any doubt about how the judges would rule, the Kremlin had arranged for them to be put up in a sanatorium fifty kilometres outside Moscow, all expenses paid, while they wrote their verdict. In those days, the Kremlin could still not be completely sure of the judges' loyalty, but this was the moment when the Russian court system fell under the Kremlin's sway. The

Kremlin had been anxious to ensure that Khodorkovsky's business partners could not bribe the judges to rule in his favour. And at the sanatorium, security service agents could keep a close eye on them.

Sechin and his deputy in the presidential administration, a stern and pale-faced FSB general named Vladimir Kalanda, who happened to be married to the chief general counsel at Rosneft, had closely monitored the situation. When one of the judges refused to go to the sanatorium under police guard, Kalanda paid a visit to the chairwoman of the Moscow City Court, a doughty blonde named Olga Yegorova who'd climbed to the top of the court system since Soviet times, to make sure her subordinate complied.[86]

After a month at the sanatorium the three judges had still failed to finish writing the verdict, finding it difficult to complete more than a fraction of it in line with the Kremlin's wishes. So Yegorova took on the task, telling a colleague to write it blindly, suspending all doubt. According to the eyewitness account, the colleague had told her the charges made no sense, but Yegorova had known exactly what the verdict should be from the start. 'When I've made my mind up, I never change it,' she told her colleague.[87]

The Moscow city court dismissed the eyewitness account as no more than 'invention' that did not require any comment. But when the verdict was finally read out in court, it differed little from the charges the prosecutors had presented, at times appearing as if it had simply been copied from the prosecutors' case, with reams of witness testimony for the prosecutors cited verbatim. The judges dismissed the defence's arguments one by one, apart from the charge related to the privatisation of the Apatit fertiliser plant, for which the statute of limitations had run out. 'I have the impression that this is the same as the prosecution's charges, just a little bit edited,' said Khodorkovsky's elderly father, shaking his head, after the first day of the delivery of the verdict.[88] 'The judge has completely taken the side of the prosecution,' one of Khodorkovsky's lead lawyers said.[89]

The sentence the judges handed down after twelve long days of reading out the judgment in a rapid, monotone voice was severe. Khodorkovsky was sentenced to nine years in prison for the retroactive tax fraud charges, and one count of fraud related to the 1995 privatisation of the Apatit research institute for which the statute of limitations had not run out.[90]

Though the ruling had always seemed preordained, it still came as a shock. Sobs were heard across the courtroom as Khodorkovsky's slight, blonde wife crossed her arms over her chest, struggling to hold herself together.[91] Khodorkovsky too went pale, as if he had not been expecting this, as if he'd thought the Kremlin machine might still exercise some leniency, or had even hoped that justice would somehow prevail. Though he remained slumped against the bars of the cage while the rest of the ruling was read out, he mustered the strength to register one last protest. When everyone began filing out of the courtroom, as if leaving him to his fate, he clambered on a bench to shout 'This is lawlessness!' to a reporter, even as armed guards tried to stop him. 'There is no legal basis for this.'[92]

If Khodorkovsky still hoped for leniency, by the time his appeal came around just four months later, in September 2005, the Kremlin had tightened the screws even more. Sechin had piled the pressure on Yegorova to rush through the appeal, as the Kremlin was worried that the statute of limitations on the remaining fraud charge related to the privatisation of the Apatit research institute, which carried a maximum sentence of seven years, was about to run out. The other charges related to tax fraud carried sentences of only four, three, and one and a half years, and although there was one more fraud charge, with a seven-year sentence, related to the use of promissory notes in one of the tax schemes, the Kremlin – which in those days still worried about the appearance of due process – was concerned that it was far from solid.[93] The case against Khodorkovsky had to look legitimate, to strengthen Rosneft's takeover of Yugansk. Yegorova had to issue the appeal verdict before the statute of limitations on the Apatit charge ran out, otherwise the Kremlin feared a challenge in the European Court of Human Rights.

Once the appeal trial started, Sechin called Yegorova to his Kremlin office every day – she went there so often the guards knew her by sight.[94] There, Sechin and one of his closest associates, Viktor Ivanov, the Kremlin head of personnel who'd closely watched over the Yukos case, anxiously needled Yegorova to make sure the verdict on the fraud charge was handed down on time. They feared that if the statute ran out they would have to reduce the sentence, and Khodorkovsky could be at liberty before the next presidential elections, scheduled for 2008. In that case, the entire Yukos takeover might be overturned. They'd been so taken aback by the events in Ukraine the previous year that they feared they could face their own Orange Revolution if Khodorkovsky was freed in time to organise a rebellion. 'In three years,' Sechin told Yegorova according to the witness account, 'it will be a madhouse here. The prisoner needs to stay in jail.'[95]

Sechin's nerves had been stretched to breaking point on the first day of the appeal, September 14, when none of Khodorkovsky's defence team turned up. Khodorkovsky told the court the only lawyer authorised to defend him had been hospitalised, so Yegorova had no choice but to postpone the hearing till the following Monday, September 19. A furious Sechin called her in to the Kremlin and ordered her to begin the trial without the defence. When Yegorova dug her heels in, they called her in for a second time, and Ivanov and the deputy prosecutor general piled the pressure on her to speed things up. A rumour was going around Moscow that Yegorova had taken a $1 billion bribe from Khodorkovsky's partners in Menatep to delay the hearing and make the sentence go away.

It was the rumours and the whispers that did the trick. Yegorova couldn't bear the thought that the Kremlin thought she was corrupt. Though she continued to insist on Khodorkovsky's right to a defence, she told Sechin and the Kremlin chief of staff, Putin's ally Dmitry Medvedev, that she was going to hand down a sentence of eight years – a one-year reduction – no matter what happened. 'I'll take the entire responsibility for this on myself,' she said. 'And if I somehow disappoint you, I'll resign. I'm sick of this.'[96]

The proceedings continued amid further tension and delays over the absence of Khodorkovsky's main lawyer, Genrikh Padva, with the pressure on Yegorova mounting as whispers continued that she had taken a bribe. 'Let them arrest me,' she'd retorted. 'Let them do what they want. I've never been so offended . . . so that you don't think I took anything, it will be eight years,' she told Sechin and Medvedev. When at the very last minute Khodorkovsky agreed to replace Padva with another lawyer who'd been working on the case, the hearing was rammed through in the space of a single day, September 22, to make sure the statute of limitations did not run out.

Khodorkovsky's defence team repeatedly protested during the hearing at the speed with which it was proceeding. 'What we're dealing with here is not the prosecutors or the judges, it is the full weight of the state machine,' said his main lawyer.[97] 'The political authorities are dictating what's going on here.' The record of the initial trial had stretched to six hundred pages, and the defence complained that they hadn't been given sufficient time to study it. But the judges ploughed relentlessly on. When Khodorkovsky made a closing speech in his defence, they tried to close him down after an hour. 'We have all the documents. We're actually ready to give the ruling,' one of them said.[98] It was already 7.20 p.m., well past the hour when the court usually closed for the day. Though the judges let Khodorkovsky continue for another hour, it didn't matter what he said. They'd already decided. They were only out of the courtroom for a matter of minutes before returning to deliver their verdict: eight years – exactly as Yegorova had promised. It was 9 p.m. on September 22. The statute of limitations on the fraud had not yet expired.

Khodorkovsky and his business partner Platon Lebedev were to be sent to as-yet undisclosed prison camps. Pale and exhausted, this time Khodorkovsky had no parting shot as he was led out of the court. His parents, Boris and Marina, waved to him with tear-filled eyes. Just over three weeks later he was transported in a windowless railway carriage across the Russian steppe to the end of the earth, a prison camp in the bleak uranium-mining town of Krasnokamensk in the far-east region of Chita, where almost two centuries before the political prisoners of the tsarist age, the Decembrists, had been sent.[99]

*

It was the trial that changed everything in Putin's Russia. The pressure Sechin had brought to bear on the judges, the speed of the appeal process, the lack of substance to the charges, had brought the court system irrevocably under the *siloviki*. If, previously, the judges' pitifully low wages had left them open to bribery by powerful oligarchs, now the Kremlin was taking over. 'This was a matter of state,' Putin told Yegorova when he greeted her in the Kremlin after the trial to thank her for the work she'd done, according to the eyewitness account.[100] He defended the haste with which Khodorkovsky was put behind bars by explaining: 'Foreign capital has been ruling the country, that's why there has been all this chaos.' Putin and the Kremlin justified their power grab by painting Khodorkovsky and his allies as agents for the West. Khodorkovsky's men had lined up $10 billion to interfere in the process, he told her. No one would ever check this claim. It was just part of the elaborate system of lies that was being constructed.

Putin's Kremlin moved swiftly to stamp its control. This was the beginning of what was to become widely known as *ruchnoye upravleniye*, or the manual regime, in which the mechanics of every process were to be tightly controlled by the Kremlin's men. Putin had always insisted that the Yukos court case had nothing to do with him or the Kremlin. But from the start every decision, every move, had been closely overseen. The takeover of the court system had begun with accusations and whispers that judges were taking bribes from the Kremlin's opponents. The judges would seek to counter such allegations and display their loyalty by producing verdicts exactly in line with the Kremlin's orders, in a pattern that harked back to Soviet times, when colleagues had spied and reported on each other, when everyone was under suspicion and closely watched.

That paranoia had never really gone away. And now the country was falling back into the times when everyone was divided between 'us and them', when there were fears of an outside enemy working to corrupt the system. But, in a new twist, the judges would now be tainted by the Kremlin instead. The husband of one judge, for instance, was picked up by the security services outside his home on his birthday, driven to a Subaru salesroom and told to choose a vehicle for himself.[101] Everyone knew the car was above his pay grade. Everyone knew what his wife did for a living, and which high-profile case she had just overseen. Everyone would assume it was a bribe, no matter how much the husband protested that he had had no choice. By such means were people tainted, tied to the Kremlin and kept under control. As time passed and the Putin regime further cemented its power, the size of these 'gifts' grew dramatically.

For Yegorova, married to an FSB officer who became a general, the trial was also a turning point. She became known as the 'Iron Lady' of the Russian legal system, the chairwoman who established a rigorous hold over the courts, threatening judges with loss of their jobs and housing if they failed to toe the line.[102]

The country was turning back to the times of the gulag. The Soviet system of 'telephone law' was being restored. The Kremlin had taken control of the legal system. The power of the secret services was being cemented. Khodorkovsky, the country's onetime richest man, was languishing in a prison camp in Krasnokamensk. And the West had been complicit in the process.

PART THREE

Obschak

While all of Moscow was gripped by the attack on Yukos in the summer of 2004, a series of transactions on the city's stock exchange slipped by under the radar. Shares in Sogaz, a little-known insurance company belonging to Gazprom, had been sold in three tranches – first 49.9 per cent, then another 26 per cent and then another 12.[1] It seemed unremarkable at first. The shares, it turned out, had been acquired at a discount by three obscure companies connected to Bank Rossiya, the St Petersburg bank that was once a vehicle for Communist Party funds and then for Putin allies connected to the KGB.

The transactions had taken place quietly, far from the din of government discussions and edicts that would normally accompany such state-asset sales. For years the government had debated what to do with Sogaz and the other financial assets Gazprom had accumulated. But instead of an auction, a pumping and priming of assets by Western investment banks which Kasyanov and others in his government had discussed, the sale had taken place unheralded on the stock exchange. 'The fact that Sogaz was sold so quickly and so cheaply was a new development,' said Vladimir Milov, a former deputy energy minister in Kasyanov's cabinet. 'We'd never discussed this. Kasyanov's firing opened the way for this kind of deal . . . There had never been the question it would be sold to allies. It was all so unexpected . . . But back then I didn't understand the Sogaz sale was the beginning of a massive new process. It was just an insurance company, that's all.'[2]

The Sogaz sale, it turned out, marked the beginning of a series of transactions, similarly unnoticed, that siphoned tens of billions of dollars in financial, industrial and media assets once held by Gazprom to Bank Rossiya, the stronghold of Yury Kovalchuk, the Putin ally from the St Petersburg days. It was the start of the forma- tion of an *obschak* on a grand scale for Putin's strategic – and personal – needs. It also heralded the rise of a new caste of oligarchs, all of them Putin's KGB-connected associates from St Petersburg – and, in the case of Bank Rossiya's main shareholders, most of them mem- bers of Putin's Ozero dacha cooperative.

While Putin was squeezing the independence out of the Yeltsin-era oligarchs, jailing Khodorkovsky and threatening to eliminate the others as a class, Kovalchuk was at the centre of a group of loyal KGB allies rising fast to replace them in the second term of Putin's presidency. At first quietly and then ever more noticeably, they began to benefit from insider deals. The transfers from Gazprom trans- formed Bank Rossiya, for instance, from a regional banking minnow few in Moscow had ever heard of into a new financial powerhouse with tentacles across Russia. Its assets mushroomed forty-fold after 2004, to reach $8.9 billion within eight years.[3] The transfers also led to the handover of control of the country's third-biggest bank, Gazprombank, the Gazprom financial arm that held assets worth tens of billions of dollars, to Bank Rossiya.

None of the transfers would have happened had Putin's men not taken over Gazprom at the start of his presidency. Ever since Putin made the replacement of its management with his own allies from St Petersburg one of his first priorities, its vast cash pools and finan- cial assets had presented a wealth of opportunity for his inner circle. The asset sales would also never have gone through if the more liberal Yeltsin-era holdovers such as Kasyanov and Voloshin had remained in government. 'Before, everyone had to agree,' said Vladimir Milov. 'But in Putin's second term there was a very clear moment when the St Petersburg group took what the Moscow group hadn't wanted to give.' One by one, Putin's men were being put in charge of swathes of the economy, while the *siloviki* were taking over the court system, the federal tax service and other branches of government previously out of reach to them.

It was part of a process that became known as 'Kremlin Inc.', whereby Putin in his second term appointed key loyalists in charge of strategic sectors of the economy. The process was most visible as he installed his closest KGB allies not only in charge of the state-controlled energy majors Gazprom and Rosneft, but of a host of state companies.[4] First there was Aeroflot, the airline that had once been the fiefdom of the Yeltsin Family. Viktor Ivanov, Putin's KGB comrade from St Petersburg who now served as deputy head of the administration, was installed as its chairman at the end of 2004. Then there was Russian Railways, a vast empire of 1.3 million employees and revenues totalling nearly 2 per cent of Russia's GDP, where Vladimir Yakunin, the bluff former senior KGB officer who'd been a leading Bank Rossiya shareholder and a member of the Ozero dacha cooperative, was appointed president in June 2005.

Andrei Akimov, the former Soviet state banker with ties to foreign intelligence, was repatriated from Vienna and promoted to oversee Gazprombank. Andrei Kostin, a former Soviet diplomat once based at the embassy in London, took over the reins at Vneshtorgbank, or VTB, the direct descendant of the Soviet bank of foreign trade. Putin appointed his closest colleague from the Dresden years, Sergei Chemezov, as head of the state arms export agency, Rosoboronexport, in 2004.

'The people from the KGB and the financiers of the KGB are the ones who run the show now,' said one leading participant in this process triumphantly. 'Finally, they are taking over from the first layer of capitalism.'[5] 'The 1990s oligarchs have ceased to be oligarchs and just become businessmen again. Now we have a Chekist oligarchy,' said leading opposition politician Boris Nemtsov sardonically.[6]

But it was the shareholders of Bank Rossiya who were accumulating wealth most silently and rapidly. Among their number, for a time, was Gennady Timchenko, the low-profile alleged former KGB operative-turned-oil-trader who'd worked closely with Putin in St Petersburg. After Khodorkovsky was jailed and Sechin's Rosneft began taking over Yukos, Timchenko focused more on his oil-trading operations. His latest venture, Gunvor, was sinking roots deep into Switzerland. Quietly, almost imperceptibly at first, it began picking up the barrels of oil once traded by Khodorkovsky's Yukos.

The Bank Rossiya shareholders were the elite of Putin's inner circle. And as the bank grew in size during the second term of Putin's presidency, so did the residences of the shareholders. They moved en masse to a leafy island in the delta of St Petersburg's Neva river that had once been home to the chancellors of the tsars.[7] The gated compound of palatial townhouses on Kamenny Ostrov, or Stone Island, was surrounded by an ornate moat, sweeping stone bridges and heavy security. The new inhabitants of the renovated compound, the financial courtiers behind the Putin regime, took on the mantle of modern-day noblemen. They would dress in tailcoats for secret parties at palatial estates, their wives and girlfriends in ballgowns from the era of Catherine the Great. The starlets hired to perform for them would not be told who their audience was, and would be paid in diamond rings, wristwatches and icons – anything valuable, as long as it didn't leave any trace.[8]

More than any other, the story of the rapid expansion of Bank Rossiya in Putin's second term casts light on the formation of a Kremlin *obschak* that could be used both for Putin's personal needs and to bolster the rule of his KGB clan. As with the slush funds created in Liechtenstein and other havens for Putin and his St Petersburg allies in the early nineties, the lines between cash taken for strategic and personal needs were always blurred. The Sogaz share transfers, for instance, were the start of a process by means of which a vast national media empire was transferred into Kovalchuk's loyal hands, helping cement the Kremlin's strategic media monopoly. But they also allowed a palace fit for a tsar to be built for Putin on the Black Sea. Some of the hundreds of millions of dollars stashed in the network of companies behind Bank Rossiya appeared to lead directly to Putin. They were part of Putin's personal wealth, according to a financier who worked on the schemes.[9]

The man who drew open the curtain on how the system worked was Sergei Kolesnikov, a member of the tight-knit circle of financiers closely involved in Bank Rossiya's operations. He'd become increasingly concerned at how the bank's precipitous growth was symptomatic of the increasing lack of checks and balances on Putin's regime. 'When Putin first came to power, I viewed his arrival with great gladness,' he said. 'We all connected it to the bringing of order to the country. In the first three years, I supported him and saw that everything he did was good, and even when he threw Khodorkovsky in jail I thought it was good. But then, after the second election in 2004, this understanding that he could rule forever began to appear . . . They'd taken control of the media and then business through the Khodorkovsky case. But then they cleared the political field. They cancelled the elections for governors and for the mayors in the biggest cities. This was the main task. There was no chance for independent people to appear and develop themselves.'[10]

It was a process, said Kolesnikov, shaking his head, that had left Putin ruling like a tsar, presiding over what was becoming a near-feudal economy. The Yeltsin-era oligarchs were cowed by Khodorkovsky's trial, fearing that any one of them could face a similar fate. Kolesnikov saw that, instead of eliminating oligarchs as a class as Putin had pledged, the men behind Bank Rossiya had become part of a new oligarchy.

Kolesnikov himself had been one of their number. He knew intimately how the Putin system worked. He'd lived among the Bank Rossiya shareholders on Kamenny Ostrov. But he became ever more horrified as he observed the escalation in asset-siphoning from Gazprom: 'As soon as you take control of financial resources, it is not possible to stop. This is a law of business.'[11] By the autumn of 2010, he was unable to bear it any longer. Taking only a small bag that contained, among other things, USB sticks with a trove of documents on all the transactions he'd conducted for Putin's men, he slipped out of his townhouse on Kamenny Ostrov and hurried to the airport, where he bought a one-way ticket to Turkey, and then to the US. The documents he carried out with him were a roadmap of the creation of a presidential *obschak*.

The earnest and bespectacled Kolesnikov had started out as a physicist, working in Soviet times at a top-secret research institute developing medical and other devices.[12] The two men he was later to go into business with were involved in the same field. One of them was Dmitry Gorelov, then the chief KGB *rezident* in Denmark, with whom Putin had worked closely in Dresden, when Putin was involved in operations to smuggle technology through Western embargos.[13] The other was Nikolai Shamalov, the St Petersburg representative of the German technology giant Siemens, which had long been infiltrated by Soviet agents seeking to supply dual-use equipment to the KGB,[14] and another old friend of Putin's. 'It was clear that they had known each other since before the nineties,' said Kolesnikov. 'But to go into the history of these things was not correct.'[15]

Kolesnikov, Gorelov and Shamalov joined in business in the early nineties to form Petromed, a medical-supplies company that sold Siemens equipment to St Petersburg's hospitals. They were among Putin's closest friends, Shamalov in particular, who joined the Ozero dacha cooperative. Through their activities old KGB networks were being preserved. 'Fragments of the system remained,' said a former KGB officer who worked with Putin in St Petersburg. 'Putin and his team were one of them.'[16]

When Putin took over the presidency, Petromed became a centre for collecting hundreds of millions of dollars in donations, ostensibly to buy medical equipment from Siemens and General Electric to upgrade St Petersburg's Military Medical Academy.[17] The donations were seen by some as essentially tributes paid by oligarchs to the new Russian tsar, and according to Kolesnikov some of the donations later became part of a slush fund for Putin's rule. A large percentage of the money was used to fund Bank Rossiya's rapid expansion. It provided the cash for Bank Rossiya to acquire Gazprom's Sogaz insurance company – and for Gorelov and Shamalov to acquire stakes in Bank Rossiya. By that time Matthias Warnig, the former Stasi officer with whom Putin had also worked closely on technology transfers, had become chairman of Bank Rossiya. It was a sign that Putin's former KGB networks were more than being preserved: they were being resurrected, and then provided with tens of billions of dollars of siphoned Gazprom cash.

The story Kolesnikov was to tell me, years later, when he emerged from it all, still wide-eyed at the secrets he was daring to reveal, described how he worked with Shamalov and Gorelov to funnel the Petromed donations through a web of offshore companies that stretched from Liechtenstein to the British Virgin Islands to Panama. Thirty-five per cent of one such donation – of $203 million from the Yeltsin Family oligarch Roman Abramovich in July 2001 – was transferred by Petromed to a BVI company, Rollins International, and $50 million of that then made its way to a Panamanian company called Santal Trading, which Kolesnikov liked to call the 'safe'.[18] A spokesperson for Abramovich says that the money was donated for the purchase of medical equipment, for charitable reasons. Kolesnikov himself has confirmed in interviews that Abramovich did not have any knowledge of any later unauthorized use of funds. The 'safe' was the cash store that funded the Bank Rossiya expansion, while Rollins International financed Gorelov and Shamalov's acquisition of 12.6 per cent stakes apiece in Bank Rossiya on the eve of the bank's rapid growth. First, said Kolesnikov, Rollins paid out $22.3 million and $21.8 million in dividends to Gorelov and Shamalov respectively, and they used the funds to acquire the stakes.[19] Then, in the summer of 2004, Santal quietly transferred $18 million and $41 million in loans and guarantees to two obscure companies – Aktsept and Abros – connected to Bank Rossiya, which used the cash to acquire 13.5 per cent and 51 per cent stakes in Sogaz respectively.[20] A further 12.5 per cent stake was acquired through another investment group, Lirus, which was run by Kolesnikov.

The amounts involved might seem small compared to the tens of billions of dollars now wielded by Putin's circle. But those transfers were the first steps towards building a far greater pool of assets. The acquisition of Sogaz was the start of a remarkable process. Once it had been acquired by Putin's men, its bottom line began to boom. The country's biggest state companies were racing to join its client roster. It was no longer the insurance company of choice solely for Gazprom, but also for the Russian state railways monopoly and Rosneft. Adding to its weight as an outfit for the Putin clan, the son of Sergei Ivanov, Putin's defence minister, another close ally from the St Petersburg KGB, was installed as head of the Sogaz board. As top-level clients streamed in, by 2006 its net profits had more than tripled. Then, with business booming, Sogaz was used as a springboard for a much bigger prize. In a series of deals in August 2006 it acquired a 75 per cent stake in the aptly named Leader Asset Management for an undisclosed sum.[21] This was the company that managed the assets of Gazprom's vast pension fund, Gazfond, containing more than $6 billion (167.7 billion roubles), one of the country's biggest pension pots as well as a 3 per cent stake in Gazprom, then worth $7.7 billion.[22] For good measure, Shamalov's son Yury was appointed Gazfond's head.

Once these pieces were in place, Gazfond was used for Bank Rossiya to take over a bigger target – Gazprom's banking arm, Gazprombank, then the country's third-largest bank and, most importantly, a vault in which Gazprom had parked tens of billions of dollars of its biggest assets. The deal, once again, happened under the radar, barely noticed. Instead of a cash auction with competing bids and Western investment banks, as Kasyanov's government had once discussed, it was handed over in a simple asset swap towards the end of Putin's second term.[23] Gazfond exchanged the stake it held in a Moscow electricity utility called Mosenergo, then worth $1.8 billion, for Gazprom's controlling stake in Gazprombank, and then transferred this to Bank Rossiya's Leader Asset Management, giving Bank Rossiya direct control of the country's third-biggest bank with barely anyone noticing.[24] 'Gazprom had given it all away for nothing, just like that,' said Milov, the former deputy energy minister in Kasyanov's cabinet.[25]

It was as if control of the country's third-largest bank had been transferred through a set of Russian nesting dolls, or *matryoshki*, into Bank Rossiya's hands. The deal was layered in complexity, as if to hide its ultimate results and to attract the minimum scrutiny. Gazprom later argued that the asset-swap deal had been in line with a market valuation given by Dresdner Bank. But Gazprom itself had valued Gazprombank at $8 billion just a few months after the $1.8 billion deal – a valuation that later nearly doubled as the bank's profits continued to soar during Putin's rule.

The deal had also seen Gazprom hand over tens of billions of dollars' worth of industrial and media assets for nothing in return. First, there was the federal media empire Gazprom had accumulated, which included NTV, Gusinsky's once fiercely independent television channel. A year before the asset swap was completed, Gazprom had sold its media assets to Gazprombank for $166 million. Barely two years later, once this media empire was firmly under Kovalchuk and Bank

Rossiya's control, Dmitry Medvedev, Putin's chief of staff from St Petersburg, estimated the value of the same media assets at $7.5 billion, transforming Kovalchuk into the nation's most important media tycoon,[26] at the head of the country's biggest so-called 'privately-held' media conglomerate. The empire expanded to include the once Berezovsky-owned Channel One and two smaller channels, Ren TV and STS, as well as one of the country's most respected newspapers, *Izvestia*, and its most widely-read tabloid, *Komsomolskaya Pravda*, and the radio station most beloved of the intelligentsia, Ekho Moskvy. Gradually, its operations became a crucial cog in the Kremlin propaganda machine.

Then there was Sibur, Russia's biggest petrochemicals company, in which Gazprombank held a 75 per cent stake, while Gazfond held the remaining 25 per cent. The year after Gazprombank was transferred to the control of Bank Rossiya for $1.8 billion, Sibur was valued at $4–5 billion: its revenues totalled $6 billion, its operating profits were $1.2 billion. Yet its transfer to Bank Rossiya went unnoticed and unremarked. In 2011 Gazprombank would flip Sibur to two businessmen close to Putin, Timchenko and Leonid Mikhelson, for an undisclosed price. At the same time, Gazprombank said it valued the company at $7.4 billion.

The share shuffling had stealthily drained as much as $60 billion in assets from state-controlled Gazprom into Bank Rossiya's hands, according to an estimate by Vladimir Milov, some of which had then been handed to Putin's closest cronies.[27] Yet none of this had faced any independent oversight from government, shareholders or parliament. Gazprom was meant to be the Russian state's largest and most important company, its biggest generator of revenues, yet its carve-up had taken place without discussion, behind closed doors. 'This was a total giveaway of all the financial and other assets. And Gazprom got nothing. It's a fantastic tale,' said Milov.[28]

Milov, then in his early thirties, with thick dark hair and a frank, inquisitive air, had been one of the brightest young officials in the Putin government during his first term. But he left after less than a year, disappointed by the lack of reforms to break up monopolies like Gazprom, and became one of the rare voices criticising government policy. Having set up an independent think tank commenting on government energy policy, he gained a reputation as an astute, liberal-minded expert. In 2008, as Putin's government began more and more to resemble a kleptocracy, Milov joined the liberal opposition movement led by former deputy prime minister Boris Nemtsov. He co-authored a series of reports that delved into the failings of the Putin regime, including one he wrote himself on the asset-siphoning from Gazprom called 'Putin and Gazprom'.

In those days, Milov was a lone brave voice pointing out the scale of the asset-draining. As Putin's men increasingly dominated all levers of power, few investment banks or investors investigated the transfers. When we spoke, Milov would often mention the irony of how Putin's men claimed to have taken over Gazprom in an attempt to root out asset-siphoning by its Yeltsin-era executives, making it even more cynical that the asset-siphoning took on an even grander scale once Putin took control of the gas giant. 'The previous Gazprom management were doling out assets that they had some reason to do,' said Milov. 'They gave to others at a discount price the assets that Gazprom was not capable of developing itself. But when Putin's men were in charge they just gave away assets for no reason, almost for free.'[29]

After Sergei Kolesnikov fled to the West, he joined in explaining that there was a simple reason for that. Putin had made Gazprom his personal fiefdom, his property to direct both as a geopolitical instrument to project Kremlin power, and as a source of cash for his circle. 'Do you know who the real owner of Gazprom is?' Kolesnikov asked me. 'The one who tells its CEO Alexei Miller what to do, who tells him whom to give what contract to and at what price, what price to work with Sogaz at, who to sell it to, and who to sell Gazprombank to? This is all Putin's.'[30]

Kolesnikov was privy to highly sensitive information. He understood exactly how the slush fund system worked, and beyond the asset-siphoning from Gazprom, what disturbed him most of all was how more and more of the cash in the network he oversaw began to be diverted for Putin's own personal comfort. One of the funds Kolesnikov ran was intended to funnel part of the 'donation' cash into investments in the real Russian economy, including St Petersburg shipyards. In the beginning, this had made some of the donation-siphoning palatable for Kolesnikov – at least some of the wealth was being distributed into creating jobs and growing the economy. Another part, however, was to be spent on the building of an opulent palace for the president on the Black Sea coast. The project had originally been intended as a comparatively modest thousand-square-metre house. But it snowballed into a four-thousand-square metre Italian-style palace with three helipads, a summer amphitheatre, a marina and a teahouse with swimming pools, at a cost of $1 billion.[31] When, after the 2008 financial crisis Putin issued instructions that all the remaining funds in the Petromed slush fund should be spent on his palace instead of on the shipyards and other projects in the real economy, Kolesnikov began making plans for an exit. 'It turned out that I'd been working every day for fifteen years for ten hours a day to build a palace for the tsar,' he said. 'I could never be in agreement with this. But when I objected they told me, "Who are you speaking against? You are going against the tsar."'[32]

The diversion of the funds for the president's palace was the clearest sign that the network of companies Kolesnikov had helped oversee was closely linked to Putin's personal fortune – that this was a slush fund that could be dipped into for his own use. Kolesnikov alleged that it was Shamalov, Putin's closest friend, whom Putin personally instructed to spend increasing amounts on the palace instead of on the investments in the real economy. Indeed, it was through a company belonging to Shamalov that the palace was owned.[33] 'Shamalov represented Putin,' said one insider.[34] 'He was the one who got the orders on where the money was to go.' The activity raised an interesting question. If Shamalov was representing Putin's interests in the building of the palace, did his shareholding in Bank Rossiya also represent Putin's personal interest? Shamalov declined to comment. But when Kolesnikov emerged to tell his story, Dmitry Peskov, Putin's spokesperson, derided any such claims as 'nonsense': 'Putin never had and does not have any connection to Bank Rossiya, nor to any transactions or deals through any of the offshore companies or companies that are mentioned. He has no connection to the growth of the bank.'[35]

If it hadn't been for the funds being spent on Putin's personal comfort, any link to his own interests would have been impossible to trace. 'There are no documents or papers showing Putin's owner-ship' of anything, said Kolesnikov.[36] 'Putin was a person who was taught specially not to leave any trace.' Those who handled the Bank Rossiya network had also been instructed to conduct their affairs in secrecy. When they met to discuss business, they invented a system of nicknames so that – in case of eavesdropping – no one would know who they were talking about. Putin was 'Mikhail Ivanovich' – the name of an omniscient police chief in a classic Soviet comedy film.[37] Kovalchuk was strangely named 'Kosoi', or cross-eyed. 'When they decided to give everyone a nickname he had a sore eye, and therefore they decided to call him this,' said Kolesnikov.[38] Shamalov chose 'Professor', after the character who experiments on a stray dog in Mikhail Bulgakov's satirical novel on the state of Soviet man, *Heart of a Dog*. Gazprom's Alexei Miller, meanwhile, was 'Soldat', or soldier, a nod to his standing as a loyal yes-man who followed orders. Putin's close ally Timchenko became 'Gangrena', or gangrene, because at the time his oil-trading business was developing so fast.[39]

When Kolesnikov fled overseas, he took with him not only docu-ments on transactions, but also tapes of conversations between members of this group. One of them appeared to be of a meeting he'd had with Shamalov in St Petersburg. In it, they tot up whose cash is whose in the stash they manage in Rollins International, the BVI part of the Petromed network. 'The money of Mikhail Ivanovich is $439 million. This is Mikhail Ivanovich's money,' Kolesnikov says.[40]

What was being created was an elaborate system of fronts that could act on behalf of Putin and his regime of *komitetchiki*. If the Yeltsin-era tycoons had sought to manipulate a weakened Kremlin into parcelling out assets at a discount price, Putin was creating a loyal network of trusted, KGB-connected custodians. This process was extending westwards into Europe, into Liechtenstein and Monaco, and then to Panama and the BVI. Timchenko had long moved from his St Petersburg base and was sinking roots deep into Geneva. Surrounded by the snowcapped Alps and the Jura moun-tains, the city had long been a natural destination for Russian money.

Part of a neutral buffer zone between East and West since the end of the Second World War, the financial secrets of the world's great powers were securely buried within its walls. 'It was a haven for both blocs,' said a former KGB officer who operated there.[41] 'It's like a restaurant in the middle, between Chinatown and Little Italy, where the two mob bosses can go and eat and discuss business. It's the most secure restaurant in the world.' KGB money had long been stashed in the city's vaults: bankers would whisper stories of how, in the days of the Cold War, Soviet businessmen carrying suitcases stuffed full of cash would call them from telephone boxes.[42] Those were days of numbered accounts, of code words and business conducted on a nod and a wink. Now, with the Cold War long pronounced over, Geneva was once again becoming an important outpost for the oil wealth commanded by Putin's KGB men.

From a prime spot overlooking Lake Geneva, Timchenko's oil-trading company Gunvor became the most immediate beneficiary of the Kremlin takeover of Yukos. For a time, its rise was one of the industry's great mysteries. At first, few noticed when, after Sechin's Rosneft acquired Yuganskneftegaz, the new state oil champion began redirecting the bulk of its exports through Gunvor. Then, when state-controlled Gazprom took its own chunk of the oil industry, acquiring Roman Abramovich's Sibneft in 2005, its oil arm Gazpromneft also began awarding large contracts to Gunvor. Cowed by the Kremlin's growing might, other oil majors, anxious to curry favour, followed suit. Within four years Gunvor was trading 30 per cent of all seaborne exports from Russia.[43] Its rise had been so meteoric that it could no longer be hidden from view: by 2008 it had become the world's third-biggest oil trader, with revenues of $70 billion.

One by one, the other independent Russian oil traders that flourished in Geneva in the Yeltsin years had shut up shop. When Yukos had sold oil through its Geneva-based Petroval, the billions of dollars it netted from the difference between the domestic and global oil prices had been a big issue for the Putin regime. But now that the oil flows had been redirected through a trader owned by one of Putin's closest allies, the concern seemed to die away. Bereft of oil,

Petroval, which had been based just around the corner from Gunvor, on Geneva's central rue du Rhône, was forced to close down.[44] Gunvor 'took over all our barrels', said one former Petroval trader.[45]

Putin's government seemed to have clamped down on the worst excesses of the so-called transfer-pricing trading schemes of the nineties, by which commodities were sold through middlemen and traders at lower domestic prices, netting the difference from the global price. But Gunvor never disclosed its profits, and for a long time both it and Rosneft, its main supplier, Gunvor avoided any scrutiny. Before late 2007, Rosneft didn't sell any of its crude exports to traders through an open tender system. In the beginning 'the margins were unbelievable', said one person involved in Gunvor's trading operations.[46] Timchenko, through his lawyers, said all contracts with Rosneft were awarded entirely on merit, reflecting Gunvor's 'market leading status and depth of expertise and experience'.

For a time, part of Gunvor's ownership seemed as much of a mystery as its finances. On paper it was owned by Timchenko and his Swedish business partner Torbjorn Tornqvist, but also by a third shareholder whose name, the oil trader said, could not be revealed.[47] Of all Putin's close KGB cohorts who were now rising in business, Timchenko had kept the lowest profile. He operated in a world shrouded in secrecy, shuttling between Moscow and Switzerland, where he lived anonymously in a mansion surrounded by manicured gardens and a high guarded fence in the salubrious suburb of Cologny, overlooking Lake Geneva. The business he handled was so sensitive that he never used email.[48] If he spoke by mobile phone, he did so in the full awareness that he was being listened to.[49] He'd never given an interview until 2008, when Gunvor's meteoric rise forced him into the light.[50] At that point only one photograph of him had ever been seen.

In the early days Timchenko was kept almost invisible even to those closest to Putin. Sergei Pugachev often spent time with the likes of Yury Kovalchuk, but he'd seen Timchenko only once. 'Putin had always hidden him from me,' he said.[51] One wintry evening he'd arrived at Putin's Novo-Ogarevo residence outside Moscow to find Timchenko in the kitchen. Putin had immediately ordered Timchenko to wait outside in the snow while they discussed business. It was as if he was trying to demonstrate to Pugachev that he wasn't important to him. But to Pugachev, it revealed the sensitivity of the relationship between the two men.

The reason for the apparent secrecy became clear to Pugachev when a banker flew in to see him from Switzerland towards the end of 2003. The banker asked him about Timchenko, and said he'd been told that he was a holder of funds for the president: 'He told me, "There's a guy named Timchenko, and he's brought us a huge amount of money." He told me all this money is Putin's,' Pugachev said.[52]

*

Ever since Gunvor's rise began attracting speculation about financial ties to Putin, Timchenko had always strongly denied that the company's success had anything to do with the president, insisting it was down to his own business savvy. After the well-connected political analyst Stanislav Belkovsky dared, towards the end of Putin's second term, to publicly claim that Putin was an ultimate beneficiary of Gunvor,[53] Putin swatted the allegations away with more than his usual disdain. They were nonsense, he told reporters, 'picked out of someone's nose and smeared on bits of paper'.[54]

But for Pugachev the sensitivity and secrecy surrounding Timchenko could only mean one thing: more than anyone else in Putin's inner circle, at the beginning of Putin's presidency he was the first business ally to hold funds for him. This, he said, must have been why Putin seemed shocked when Pugachev asked him about Timchenko after he'd visited Berezovsky, by then in exile in London, and told him his arch-rival was threatening to unleash a scandal involving Timchenko. 'He went absolutely white,' said Pugachev. 'He shut the conversation down immediately. He didn't even ask what the scandal would be.'[55]

For two of Timchenko's former KGB associates and two close Putin allies, the root of Gunvor's success could only lie in financial connections with the Russian president. 'Putin's money, of course it's there,' said one of them. 'How else do you think Timchenko became such a billionaire?'[56] 'When Gunvor was created it was 100 per cent Putin's company,' said a Russian tycoon close to Putin.[57]

'Timchenko is just the holder of a purse which has $10 billion in its account. He might differ over how much of it is his and how much of it is Putin's. But really it is all the same.' Later, the US Treasury Department flatly said that 'Putin has investments in Gunvor and may have access to Gunvor funds.'[58]

Timchenko has repeatedly denied any connection between Gunvor and Putin and called the sanctions no more than an attempt to put pressure on the Russian regime. But in Geneva, a network of money men, some of whom worked with Timchenko, also laid a trail of connections to the Russian president. They also offered an indication of a greater strategic aim. Among them were descendants of White Russian aristocrats who'd fled in the wake of the Bolshevik Revolution, who dreamed of restoring Russia's empire and had long had ties with the KGB. Almost by definition, they supported the restoration of Russia's imperial might, and as Putin's men took control over the economy, they backed him every step of the way.

One of them was a banker whose appointment as head of Russian private banking at HSBC in Geneva in 2007 was closely followed by the arrival of Timchenko and his daughter as its clients.[59] The banker, Jean Goutchkov, had worked closely with Timchenko at a succession of top private banks in Geneva, according to two people familiar with the situation.[60] (Timchenko, through his lawyers, said he knew Goutchkov but had no business relationship with him. He repeated there was no connection to Putin.)

Goutchkov was the grandson of a White Russian aristocrat who'd served as chairman of one of the first Dumas, and had been a leader of the Octobrist movement that desperately pushed for reforms of the constitutional monarchy before the Bolsheviks swept to power.[61] Goutchkov maintained the stately presence of his illustrious ancestor. He kept his hair swept back over a high forehead, his eyes were cold and blue. For years he'd worked closely with the Putin regime, sweeping in and out of Moscow in style, cultivating wealthy Russian clients as he worked first for Intermaritime Bank of New York, then for Julius Baer and then HSBC. But for most of his colleagues in Moscow, his movements were a mystery. 'He would never tell you when he was in Moscow, and he would never tell you who he was meeting with,' said a former asssociate at HSBC.[62] 'He would arrive and leave without leaving a trace.' Those who know him say the secrecy was well-founded. 'This guy is at the nerve centre of Russian power,' said one of his Geneva associates.[63]

In the 1990s Goutchkov played a key role in introducing Timchenko to his Swedish business partner Torbjorn Tornqvist, according to two of his Geneva associates.[64] Back then Goutchkov and Tornqvist had worked in the business empire of a controversial Swiss financier, Bruce Rappaport, who'd long been dealing with the Soviets – Goutchkov at his Intermaritime Bank, and Tornqvist at his Petrotrade oil trader.[65] (Timchenko has claimed his meeting with Tornqvist came several years later, when the Swede was working at a trading outfit in Estonia.) Goutchkov denied ever knowing Putin. But three of his associates said that after Putin became president, Goutchkov had grown close to him.[66] When Goutchkov's wife died in 2010, he travelled with Putin and Timchenko to an ancient monastery on Lake Ladoga, near the border with Finland, a spot long revered by Russian Orthodox believers,[67] one of these close associates said, and he would return there with them two or three times afterwards. In thanks for his services, Putin had given Goutchkov a Russian passport, two people close to him said.[68] When one of Goutchkov's Geneva associates was asked if Goutchkov's friendship with Putin extended to providing him with financial services, he offered a tightlipped reply: 'It is much more of a friendship. But it is strategic. If Putin wants anything, Goutchkov can do it.'[69]

The proximity of Goutchkov was an indication that, as with Kovalchuk and Bank Rossiya, Timchenko's rise was about a lot more than the president's personal finances. It was about creating a slush fund for Putin's KGB clan, aimed at preserving and projecting their power. Timchenko and Goutchkov appeared to be part of a strategic network that, like the underground KGB financial networks that had promoted Communist Party interests during Soviet times, would manage and disburse cash for the strategic needs of the Putin regime. 'Of course, in Timchenko's activities there are some interests of Putin,' said a former senior KGB officer, an associate of the Geneva money men.[70] 'But this is not necessarily in the form of some personal money. This can be black cash for funding party activities or a charity fund that can influence the electoral situation. It can be strategic resources.' 'Timchenko implements what is necessary to implement,' said a close Putin former KGB ally. 'He is a source of resources for the realisation of a certain policy for certain interests.'[71] Two senior US officials said they shared this view.[72]

It was a way of operating that was integral to the KGB – as if it didn't know how to survive without the non-transparent financial networks it had deployed in Soviet times to smuggle embargoed technology, to fund the influence campaigns of the Communist Party and clandestine operations abroad. Putin's people were replicating the KGB-run systems of the past, in which oil exports had been a key source of black cash. Russia had shed the rules of the command economy, and become a full-blown participant in the global market economy. But now that Putin and his KGB men had taken power, they were transforming the way Russia interacted with it, exercising a form of state capitalism under which, just as the KGB memos for the transition to the market had recommended so long before, trusted custodians like Timchenko acted on behalf of the regime. They were extensions of the Kremlin, not independent companies that only followed the maxims of self-interest inherent to standard Western economies.

The KGB blueprint had called for companies to be established abroad to 'take part in all forms of information and intermediary activity: traders, brokerages, service companies and representative offices', of which 'the shareholders would be the trusted custodians'. Most particularly, the memos had indicated that such operations be based 'in one of the capitalist countries with a mild tax regime like Switzerland'.[73]

For Putin's men, it was only logical that the country's biggest and most strategic cash flow, from the oil trade, should be put in the hands of a close ally. In their view, the political challenge they believed Khodorkovsky had posed demonstrated the need for this. 'You could say all [Gunvor's] money is Putin's,' said Andrei Pannikov, the former KGB officer who was one of Timchenko's first partners in the oil trade. 'But it is much more complicated than that: if the market is in loyal hands, then this means control over prices. And it also means the profits do not go towards financing terrorism.'[74] Pannikov was a pioneer in operating through the Western financial system.[75] In the eighties he'd studied offshore finance at the Soviet Academy for Foreign Trade just as the KGB began preparations for a new phase in its struggle against the West.

The off-book system originally proposed by the KGB appeared to be being put into operation under Putin, and it bypassed the usual systems of modern-day state accounting such as a federal budget, in which spending on intelligence, elections, the legal system and politics is approved by parliament. Instead, vast slush funds were being created, where the lack of any transparency or accountability suited a regime intent on authoritarian rule and on restoring Russia's geopolitical might.

Jean Goutchkov grew up in a tight-knit White Russian community in Paris alongside another member of the Geneva group of money men. Serge de Pahlen, a tall, stooping man with thick commanding eyebrows and a lofty forehead, had long been close to Putin.[76] 'De Pahlen is one of the closest friends of Putin. He is from one of the noblest families of Russia,' said a Geneva associate.[77]

When Goutchkov's grandfather settled in Paris after joining the hundreds of thousands fleeing the 1917 Bolshevik Revolution,[78] his family and de Pahlen's had lived as part of a close diaspora bound by grief at losing their empire, and by their devotion to Russian culture and the Orthodox Church. For the most part, the White Russians in Paris lived very modestly: the city was filled with tales of grand dukes and princes driving taxis or waiting on tables. It was a community that was always riven by intrigue, double agents and plots. While many continued to rail against the Bolsheviks, and attempted to organise opposition cells from abroad, others had taken to informing on their compatriots. The Soviet secret services had long sought to infiltrate the White Russian diaspora – firstly to penetrate the opposition movements, and then to recruit agents to further their own power. For those they recruited, it was a source of much-needed cash, and for some, a window to a Russian empire they still believed in, no matter who had taken the reins of power.

According to a former senior Russian foreign-intelligence officer, Serge de Pahlen and Alexander Trubetskoy, the son of a White

Russian prince, were among the imperial believers recruited by the KGB in the eighties.[79] They became been part of a network run by Igor Shchegolev, later Putin's communications minister, who at the time served undercover for the KGB as Paris correspondent of the Soviet state news agency TASS.[80] At a time when the smuggling of embargoed technology was at its height, Trubetskoy worked at Thomson, a semiconductor and microelectronics firm that had long been infiltrated by Soviet agents. De Pahlen, meanwhile, shuttled between Paris and Moscow for a French company supplying Soviet oil refineries with equipment, part of the network of friendly firms that appeared to help fund Soviet influence operations. In 1981 he made an invaluable connection when he married Margherita Agnelli, daughter of the head of the Fiat family,[81] and was promptly made Fiat's vice president for international relations. From there, he continued to pay frequent visits to Moscow, hobnobbing with Party bigwigs and foreign bankers supporting the Soviet regime.[82] Fiat had always been a key Soviet partner, and according to two former KGB intermediaries it became a supplier of dual-use technology through a myriad of friendly firms.[83] Meanwhile, Goutchkov was working in Moscow, overseeing a group of French banks providing financing for the Soviet oil industry.[84] The two men were part of a network of operatives assisting the Soviet regime.

De Pahlen first met Vladimir Putin in November 1991, when Putin was St Petersburg's deputy mayor and de Pahlen helped organise the return of the last heir of the tsars, the Grand Duke Vladimir, to Russia.[85] He already knew St Petersburg's mayor Anatoly Sobchak through the White Russian community in Paris, and he and Putin struck an immediate rapport. De Pahlen 'picked out Putin', said another member of this imperial-minded group, Konstantin Malofeyev: 'He said, "This guy thinks like us."'[86] Neither of the two could think of Russia as anything other than a great power. They were both shocked by the collapse of the country, and the chaos that was unfurling after the failed August coup. They kept in close contact: whenever Putin was in Paris he would visit de Pahlen, and Sobchak and his family remained close to him too.

When Putin became president, de Pahlen immediately gave him

his support. On the eve of his first meeting with his French counterpart Jacques Chirac, Putin turned to de Pahlen for advice.[87] They dined together in a private room in a Paris restaurant, where de Pahlen told him he should rule for thirty years, as long as Catherine the Great. It was the only way to restore order, he told him. It was the only way to restore Russia as a global power.

Goutchkov and de Pahlen were leading members of a network of White Russian descendants who helped propel Putin on a mission to restore Russia's global position following the Soviet collapse. Putin had drawn on the writings and philosophies of exiled White Russians who'd written of the country's unique path as a Eurasian empire, its destiny as a counter to the West, as he sought to forge a new Russian identity and build bridges with the pre-Revolutionary imperial past. Their words seemed to make a deep impression on him, and Goutchkov and de Pahlen supported him wholeheartedly as he sought to curb the power of the Yeltsin-era oligarchs after taking the presidency. They approved the emphasis on building a new system of Kremlin loyalists. 'When you are in strategic sectors you are part of the state,' said one of the Geneva associates. 'Oil, gas, telecoms – by definition these are strategic sectors. If you are in this sector, you serve. You are not independent from the state.'[88]

Putin 'had a sacred mission to save the country', one person close to Goutchkov said.[89] For de Pahlen, when we met in his book-strewn Geneva office, Putin was key to Russia's revival: 'He stopped the disintegration of the country and started the restoration of a new Russia. It's very important for America, which doesn't want a multipolar world. They don't want a strong Russia.'[90] The privatisations of the nineties, he said, were 'barbaric'.

Goutchkov and de Pahlen didn't seem to particularly care that Putin's KGB men were engaging in their own barbaric methods, trampling on legal rights as they asserted control over the economy. They told themselves the Kremlin subversion of the legal system was part of a historic mission to restore Russian power as a counter to the West. 'Everyone was stealing,' said one of their Geneva associates. 'But then Putin came and said, "Enough is enough. Now it is the time when Russia is a great power of the twenty-first century . . .

You received a lot from Russia's resources. Now it is time you should give back." I understand that from the point of view of the rule of law maybe it should have been done differently. But Putin didn't have time. He had to take short cuts. Maybe Khodorkovsky suffered, but Putin had to do what he had to do . . . Patriotism is more important.'[91]

They didn't seem to particularly care either that Putin's KGB men were stealing – and in ever greater quantities as oil prices began to soar. The most important thing was reasserting the power of the Kremlin. It didn't matter how they got there. 'Money and power have gone together since the time of the ancient pharaohs,' said the Geneva associate. 'There has always been a higher sphere where money and power meet. The people in Russia are not stupid. Of course Putin has some personal interests. But the important thing is there is no other leader so popular. The normal population wants to have a fridge, a TV, a house, children, a car. For the rest, more or less, you don't care, as long as your material situation isn't impacted.' The aim was to restore Russia's position as a geopolitical power: 'What we have seen over the last twenty to thirty years with the arrival of Gorbachev, it was a moment of temporary weakness. Like any big power might have . . . Now that the economy is being restored, Putin wants to take back the sphere of interests.'[92] Another KGB associate of the Geneva money men railed against the undue influence he believed the US had wielded over Germany ever since the end of the Second World War, and spoke of one day breaking that.

But at the beginning these were goals they could only dream of, and in Putin's second term there was still a long way to go. Efforts to restore Russian influence were to begin, first of all, a lot closer to home.

*

It was November 2005, about a year since the Orange Revolution had sent Ukraine spinning out of Russia's orbit into the arms of the West, and Oleh Rybachuk, Ukrainian president Viktor Yushchenko's chief of staff, was nervously heading to Moscow.[93] The purpose of his visit was to hold talks on a new agreement on the supply of gas from Russia to Ukraine, and the signs were not good. Ukraine depended on Russia for most of its gas, and its economy was already starting to slow. Ever since the summer, Kremlin officials had been warning that they would impose a significant hike in prices, and now that the pro-Western Yushchenko was installed, they made it clear they did not want to effectively subsidise the Ukrainian economy, especially since, they claimed, the country's leaders 'receive salaries from the Americans either directly or covertly'.[94]

Gazprom's position at the centre of the gas trade between the former Soviet republics, with its enormous gas reserves and its extensive pipeline network traversing Russia, had long made it a key lever of Russian influence over its near neighbours. While the Central Asian republics had gas reserves of their own, Georgia, Belarus and Ukraine were dependent on supplies from Gazprom and companies connected to it. For the most part Gazprom had doled out gas at heavily discounted prices, just as it had when they were part of the Soviet empire. Ukraine, above all, stood out as a vital transit corridor for Russian gas to Europe, where it supplied 25 per cent of the continent's needs. But now that its leadership had taken a Westward tilt, the Kremlin indicated that it intended to put an end to any more subsidies.

When Rybachuk reached the Kremlin, Putin made his intentions clear. Russia wanted to substantially hike prices, and Ukraine would have to agree to 'certain conditions', otherwise the gas would be cut off.[95] But in a subsequent meeting, Dmitry Medvedev, then the Kremlin's chief of staff and chairman of Gazprom's board, opened the window for a compromise deal. If Ukraine agreed to purchase more gas through a certain trader of the Kremlin's choice, instead of from Gazprom, then the overall price could remain cheap. Medvedev said he could go into more detail once Rybachuk had secured Yushchenko's full agreement, but as a taster he told him such a deal would earn each side $500 million a quarter – or $2 billion a year, while ensuring a continued cheap supply of gas. 'He told me this is the share that would be ours – meaning the Ukrainian government,' said Rybachuk.[96]

Rybachuk could scarcely believe his ears. What he was being offered sounded like a kickback scheme: 'It was a deal to corrupt the whole government.' The gas trader on which Medvedev and the Kremlin was insisting on as a middleman was named Rosukrenergo, and its ownership was shrouded in secrecy.

What Medvedev was describing was the latest incarnation of a series of shadowy schemes operated by the Kremlin to trade gas between Russia and Ukraine, and with Turkmenistan. Large quantities of cheap gas from Turkmenistan could be routed through Russia's pipeline network and mixed with Russian gas, and then sent on to Ukraine, making the overall price to Ukraine lower, even if Russia hiked its own prices. Instead of trading the gas directly through Gazprom, via a transparent system of pricing, it would be sold through a shady intermediary, opening the way for billions of dollars in profits to be siphoned out – and potentially handed out as kickbacks.

The way in which this was done was uncovered by the American-born William Browder, the dark-haired and determined manager of the biggest foreign-investment fund in Russia, Hermitage Capital. The grandson of long-time US Communist Party leader Earl Browder, he was a devout capitalist, and had become one of the most aggressive advocates for Russian corporate transparency, making it a cornerstone of his fund's investment strategy to scour Gazprom's books for signs of asset-siphoning. Late in 2003 his researchers stumbled across an obscure trader, Eural Trans Gas, to which Gazprom had granted the rights to transport billions of dollars' worth of gas from Turkmenistan to Ukraine through its pipeline network a day before the company had even been created.[97] It was a deal that would siphon out nearly $1 billion in pre-tax profits for Gazprom, said Browder. Eural Trans Gas had been registered in a Hungarian village, and its four owners seemed almost uniquely unsuited for the task ahead. They were three Romanians with no business experience – an actress hoping to earn money to pay her phone bill, a nurse and a computer programmer – and an Israeli lawyer who counted one of Russia's biggest mobsters among his clients. There was no reason, said Browder, why Gazprom should have handed over this trading channel to any independent outfit, never mind to one whose ownership looked to be clearly a front.[98] Gazprom had then gone on to grant Eural Trans Gas nearly $300 million in loans and guarantees. The US ambassador to Ukraine, Carlos Pascual, openly expressed concern about the firm's apparent links to Russian organised crime.

In the ensuing scandal, Gazprom quietly wrapped up Eural Trans Gas, replacing it with Rosukrenergo. Ostensibly, Rosukrenergo was far more respectable than its predecessor – it was 50 per cent owned by Gazprom. But although it was held through Austria's Raiffeisen Bank, the ultimate ownership of the other 50 per cent was initially unknown, and its participation in the trading scheme with Ukraine would still cost Gazprom more than $1 billion in lost revenues in 2004 and 2005, said Browder. Browder railed for a while against Rosukrenergo, briefing the press on the apparent corruption, but the scheme he was targeting represented a lot more than straight-forward profit-skimming for personal enrichment: he was wading into the minefield of Russia's efforts to exert influence over its near abroad. Rosukrenergo was essentially a slush fund that could be deployed as a tool of political influence to buy off and corrupt offi-cials, to undermine democracy in Russia's neighbouring states. It was central to the operations of Putin's KGB regime, where an economy of smuggling was being rebuilt, and where influence, and not just profit, was a driving motivation. It was the first black-cash operation by Putin's men to become visible to the West.

By the time Rybachuk was heading to the Kremlin to negotiate the new gas-supply deal, Browder's outspokenness had landed him in hot water. He was being barred from entering Russia – because, the Russian foreign ministry said, he posed a national security threat. Ukraine's new pro-Western leadership, meanwhile, had pledged to turn away from such murky gas-trading schemes. 'Always it was a corrupted mechanism that allowed both sides to take tons of cash,' said Rybachuk.[99] He added that the KGB was always behind these traders, and that Rosukrenergo, registered in the wealthy Swiss town of Zug, with two of its three directors former KGB officers, was no different.

But now it seemed the Kremlin was proposing a new gas deal, in which the role of Rosukrenergo would be boosted further still. Rybachuk returned to Kiev fully expecting that Yushchenko, who was meant to be turning Ukraine on a new course, away from the murky dealings of the past, would reject the scheme. What was more, Ukraine's current gas-supply contract with Russia, which set the price at a low $50 per thousand cubic metres, was meant to be in force until 2009. When Rybachuk reported back, Yushchenko asked him to ask Ukraine's Western allies – the US State Department and the German foreign ministry –whether they could provide alternative supplies should Russia cut off the country's gas. Within two weeks, Rybachuk had received assurances of Western support. 'They told us we would not be under pressure,' he said. Rybachuk and his family left for a New Year holiday trip to Slovenia, convinced that the leadership was not going to cave to Russian pressure. It seemed unlikely to him, in any case, that Russia would risk going ahead with such a drastic measure as cutting off the gas supply.

But when he switched on the television on New Year's Day, the headlines on CNN showed that crisis had struck. Russia had turned off gas supplies to Ukraine. And as Ukraine was a vital transit corridor for Russian gas, the pressure was also dropping at a succession of utilities across Europe. The winter that year was unusually cold, and Western leaders were in shock. That very same day, Russia was taking over the presidency of the G8 group of industrialised nations. This was supposed to herald a big step forward for the country's integration with the global economy, and the theme of its leadership was meant to be energy security. Instead, the gas cut-off that day was the first clear signal of how Russia was defining its global integration in its own interests, how it would seek to undermine the global system to suit itself rather than adapt to the rules of the West. The cut-off, said the US State Department, 'raises serious questions about the use of energy to exert political pressure'.[100]

Rybachuk was still expecting the West to step in with support. He knew that Russia could not leave the gas turned off for longer than three days, otherwise it would damage its own pipeline network. But at 3 p.m. the following day, the gas supply was suddenly turned back on.[101] Without Rybachuk's knowledge, Yushchenko had agreed to the deal Medvedev had hinted at. The terms were surprising. Rather than losing the share of the trade it already had, Rosukrenergo was to be granted a monopoly on all gas supplies to Ukraine, as well as access to half its domestic distribution market. This agreement would allow Russia to save face and say it was selling gas to Ukraine at the vastly hiked price of $230 per thousand cubic metres. But that gas would be combined with cheaper Central Asian gas, allowing Ukraine to pay only $95 per thousand cubic metres overall.[102] Yushchenko declared the deal a 'healthy compromise', while Putin praised the 'mutually beneficial decisions'.[103] But to Rybachuk, it stank: 'I didn't understand. There was the government of Russia and the government of Ukraine. Why did we need an intermediary?'[104] None of it fitted with the ideals of the Orange Revolution, that sought to turn Ukraine into a more transparent, Western-style economy. What's more, Gazprom's insistence that it was merely applying a market formula to the price of the gas was nonsense, said Rybachuk: 'Gazprom was never using any market formulations. It was always using political components to determine the gas price.' Belarus was still paying Gazprom $49 for every thousand cubic metres of gas, while Rosukrenergo was going to walk away with potentially billions of dollars in profits.[105]

Rybachuk said he'd never forget the words the US ambassador to Ukraine said to him when he returned to Kiev: 'Welcome to the corruption club.'[106] The deal sent the Ukrainian government into chaos, sowing deep division between Yushchenko and his Orange Revolution prime minister Yulia Tymoshenko, who was bitterly opposed to Rosukrenergo and its gas-trading schemes. But Yushchenko and his fuel and energy minister, and the head of the state energy company Naftogaz, were resolutely behind it. It turned out that even before he dispatched Rybachuk to Moscow, Yushchenko had been holding talks of his own, meeting secretly with a man named Dmitry Firtash, a forty-year-old Ukrainian gas trader who secretly, with the Kremlin's blessing, held most of the other 50 per cent stake in Rosukrenergo.[107]

Precisely how it happened Rybachuk still doesn't know, but it seems that somehow Yushchenko had been compromised in the deal. Rybachuk's suspicion fell on the close relations Firtash had cultivated with Yushchenko's brother and with a Syrian businessman close to the Yushchenko family: 'We can't prove it. But it is the only logic for this deal being approved.'[108] Prime minister Tymoshenko, whose firebrand air and peasant-style blonde braids had symbolised

Ukraine's revolution for many, also railed against the deal. 'Without corruption it was impossible to sign such an agreement,' she said.[109]

From the moment of the deal's signing, Ukraine's pro-Western coalition became ever more divided, and the country was thrown into political chaos. Parliament passed a vote of no confidence in the government, and with parliamentary elections looming in March 2006, the pro-Russian presidential candidate Viktor Yanukovych, the former prime minister ousted by the Orange Revolution, and his Party of Regions were once again on the rise. Already weakened by infighting and an economic slowdown, Yushchenko was further undermined by the allegations that he'd been corrupted in the Rosukrenergo gas deal. By August, after months of political wrangling, Yanukovych, Russia's man, was installed as prime minister.[110] Ukraine's Orange Revolution dream of building closer political and economic ties to Europe seemed to be over, barely more than a year after it began.

To Rybachuk, the Rosukrenergo deal seemed a typical Russian influence operation: 'To make sure that Ukraine was not led by a pro-Western alliance they tried to corrupt with all measures. Yushchenko was the first Ukrainian president who was not cleared by Moscow, which made Putin furious. The idea was to break the Orange coalition and to get back the pro-Russian candidate.'[111]

The deal was also an indication of how Putin's KGB men were continuing to team up with organised crime to conduct their influence operations. Firtash, the Ukrainian who quietly held almost 50 per cent of Rosukrenergo, had always claimed that it was through his business savvy and connections with the Turkmenistan leadership that he'd been able to take over the Turkmen–Ukraine gas trade when Putin's men kicked out the Yeltsin-era bosses. But in reality he would never have been able to accomplish that without the Kremlin's backing. 'He was 100 per cent Putin's man,' said one person who knew both Firtash and Putin.[112] He'd also never have been able to do it without the assistance of the major Russian organised-crime figure whose Israeli lawyer had originally registered Eural Trans Gas.

The mobster lurking behind Eural Trans Gas had many different passports and two different dates of birth. Sometimes he went by the name 'Shimon', sometimes he called himself 'Sergei Shnaider'.

But mostly to those who knew him he was 'Seva'.[113] His real name was Semyon Mogilevich, a chain-smoking three-hundred-pound former wrestler who'd done time for arson, with hands like dinner plates and a pockmarked face, who'd become the brains behind moving money into the West for Russian organised crime. He'd started out in the seventies, helping the first wave of Jewish émigrés permitted to leave the Soviet Union sell their possessions to fund their trips. Mostly he'd helped to screw them over, said a former associate and a former Western official.[114] Later he became the go-to man for Russian mobsters laundering their funds into the West.[115]

Mogilevich himself had always insisted that he was no more than a businessman. He'd been so sure of himself that he told people that one day he wanted to make the *Sunday Times* rich list of the most wealthy people in Britain.[116] 'He is just the bogeyman the West likes to connect to everything,' his lawyer Zeev Gordon told me.[117] But according to the FBI and two of his former close associates he'd worked with the most powerful organised-crime group that emerged in those days. This was the Solntsevskaya group, a vast organisation whose tentacles extended across Russia and then into Ukraine, Central Asia and Hungary. It was headed by Sergei Mikhailov, otherwise known as 'Mikhas', a chubby gangster with a cherubic face and an angelic grin, and his partner Viktor Averin, or 'Avera'. Mikhailov also liked to say he was just a businessman. But the two men were considered among the most dangerous in Russia. They'd made their first money running prostitution rings, and had then gone on to selling arms and drugs. 'Who was Mikhas? Between us, he was a waiter and a pimp,' said one of his former associates.[118] 'As a waiter he had access to hard currency, and as a pimp he had access to even more hard currency from the whores.' Mikhas and Avera had reputations as fearsome fighters: some called them 'psychopaths'.[119] But they had little idea what to do with the dollars they were rapidly making. With a degree in finance from a university in western Ukraine, 'the only one who knew how to invest was Seva', said the former associate. 'Avera and Mikhas were supplying the money. Seva was doing the logistics.'[120]

But Mogilevich had also always represented the interface between the KGB and organised crime as the KGB sought to move money out of the Soviet empire using organised-crime networks to act as fronts. Putin had continued this practice when he aligned himself with the Tambov group in St Petersburg, and further entrenched it under his presidency. Mogilevich had been recruited by the KGB in the seventies: 'In return for informing on the Jewish community, he was allowed to flog the valuables of émigrés,' said a former Western official.[121] As his business activities with organised-crime leaders expanded, so did his cooperation with the KGB. 'Seva was always working for the security services,' one person who worked with him said. 'He was the criminal part of the Russian state.'[122]

Mogilevich's presence behind Eural Trans Gas and in other dealings had been useful for the Kremlin, said people familiar with the matter. He could be brought out during the more heated parts of negotiations with Kiev over the price of gas: his connections with local organised-crime networks served to remind Ukrainian officials of the power of the people they were dealing with. In addition, 'His role was to remind the Ukrainians that at the end of the day they'd been bought,' said a former Western official.[123]

But the open involvement of Mogilevich's lawyer in registering Eural Trans Gas had become too much of a political hot potato for Gazprom. Even though the state gas giant denied that he had anything to do with it, his fingerprints on the operation had become too evident. In those days Mogilevich was on the FBI's Top Ten Most Wanted List: he and his associates had been charged with stock fraud by the US Department of Justice for bilking American investors out of $150 million in investments by falsely representing the business of a magnet manufacturer, YBM Magnex, they'd listed on US and Canadian stock exchanges.[124] What's more, the FBI alleged that he was involved in weapons trafficking, contract murders, extortion, drug trafficking and prostitution on an international scale.

Firtash had come in as a replacement, a more acceptable face. He always insisted he'd severed all ties with Mogilevich as soon as he took over the Turkmen-Ukraine gas trade, buying out a shareholding held by Mogilevich's wife in one of the companies he took control of in 2003,[125] and that he'd never had any business dealings with Mogilevich himself.[126] But traces of linkages in the network of companies behind Rosukrenergo remained.[127] Later, Firtash would admit to the US ambassador to Ukraine that he'd received Mogilevich's permission to set up businesses.[128] In those days, in the explosion of crime that followed the break-up of the Soviet Union, it was impossible to meet a member of the Ukrainian government without also coming into contact with figures from organised crime, he said. But others said the ties went deeper. 'Without Seva, Firtash would be nothing,' one of Mogilevich's former associates told me. 'Whatever Firtash has, he has from Seva.'[129]

Like the Russian organised-crime networks that began to stretch into Europe via Austria and then into the US, the Firtash and Mogilevich connection was part of the underbelly of Putin's influence operations. But as Rosukrenergo's accounts filled with cash, Firtash rose in respectability. He became a powerbroker in Ukraine whose influence stretched across the political divide. First he'd worked with Yushchenko. Then, as Yushchenko faded, tainted by the gas deal scandal, he worked closely with the Kremlin's candidate, Yanukovych, who began to stage a political comeback almost immediately.[130]

Later, Firtash was among a handful of Ukrainian tycoons who worked with Paul Manafort, the suave American political lobbyist brought in to groom Yanukovych's image as an anti-corruption candidate.[131]

The cash Firtash's group made in Ukraine began flooding into Europe. Rosukrenergo was reporting a net annual income of about $700 million, while the vast chemicals group Firtash also owned was making billions of dollars more. He based his empire in Vienna, a major gateway for Russian cash into the West since Soviet times, registering his half of Rosukrenergo there as part of a broader company he named GroupDF.

Firtash was making a base in a city that was laden with secrets. Vienna's location at the crossroads between the great powers fighting the Second World War, and then on the dividing line between East and West during the Cold War, had long made it the spy capital of the world. Since 1955 Austria had been a neutral country, and the laws governing spying there were notoriously lax. Once filled with starving refugees ready to give away their country's secrets for a slice of bread and a glass of beer, its historic streets were still home to thousands of spies. But while some had written off political espionage as irrelevant in the days of the West's post-Cold War domination, many failed to note the Russian operations quietly taking root in Vienna, such as those connected to Firtash through Rosukrenergo and another shadowy Gazprom gas-trading intermediary called Centrex. These companies were on the front line of a different type of political operation – an extension, perhaps, of how Putin's men had operated in Ukraine. At the interface between Russia's burgeoning economic clout and Putin's ambition to restore the country's geopolitical standing, they represented layer upon layer of non-transparent ownership structures in which opportunities for cash-siphoning and influence-peddling were rife.

In Vienna Firtash was joining forces with Andrei Akimov, one of the top financiers of the Putin regime. A KGB banker who'd funded Gennady Timchenko, Akimov had set up an investment outfit, IMAG, in the city in 1990. Akimov, who of all Putin's men had kept the lowest profile, became connected to many of the Gazprom-linked intermediaries. Soon after Putin took over the presidency, he'd been appointed head of Gazprombank, which held tens of billions of dollars in assets and became a financial nest for Putin's men through its transfer to Bank Rossiya. Gazprom's stake in Rosukrenergo had been held through a Cyprus offshore company associated with Gazprombank, and Akimov had taken a seat on Rosukrenergo's coordination committee. There he was joined by Firtash and his associates, as well as by his own long-standing deputy Alexander Medvedev, who by then was head of Gazprom's most strategic unit, Gazexport, which controlled all the state gas giant's exports. Together they oversaw the billions of dollars that were transferred from Gazprom's coffers to Rosukrenergo, as it began independently exporting excess gas from Ukraine into Europe.

Old networks from the Cold War past were being reconnected as Rosukrenergo became one of dozens of Gazprom-connected trading intermediaries springing up across Europe. In Berlin there was Gazprom Germania, which was staffed by many former Stasi agents.[132] Gazprom's foreign operations had always been 'a nest for Russian intelligence', said a senior banker with connections at the top of the Kremlin.[133]

In Vienna, Akimov's associates and others behind Rosukrenergo also intersected with another member of the old KGB and Stasi networks, and one who was directly connected to Putin's Dresden past. This was Martin Schlaff, the former Stasi agent who'd worked in Dresden to smuggle embargoed technology from the West, siphoning hundreds of millions of Deutschmarks through fake contracts to preserve Stasi networks after the fall of the Berlin Wall.[134] Schlaff had entrenched himself in Vienna as one of the nation's most powerful businessmen. By the time Putin was in power he was in his fifties, and had expanded the pulp and paper trader in which he'd employed Herbert Kohler, the Dresden Stasi foreign-intelligence chief, following the collapse of the Soviet Union.[135] A billionaire with a penchant for Cuban cigars reportedly brought to him personally by Fidel Castro's envoy, he owned casinos across Central and Eastern Europe, and in Israel. He had ties at the top of the Austrian banking system, and deep into its political system, while his connections to Russian organised-crime networks appeared to run deeper still.[136]

When Gazprom, via Akimov, set up another European intermediary, Centrex, for supplying gas to Austria, Switzerland, Italy and Hungary, Schlaff and one of his close business partners took stakes in its Vienna-based arm, Centrex Europe Energy and Gas AG.[137]

The Centrex operation was another outpost of Gazprom's trading empire that was soon making hundreds of millions of euros through murky trading schemes and opaque ownership structures.[138] It had been set up by the same Cyprus offshore company through which Gazprom's stake in Rosukrenergo was meant to be owned. Yet it filed no financial reports for 2005 and 2006.[139] The trading outfits were structured through Byzantine layers of complexity – and most of them seemed to bypass Gazprom. For some experts, the complicated ownership structures sent alarm bells ringing. 'The lack of transparency, the practice of hiding the names of the beneficiaries, the use of offshore nameplate companies, and the secretive nature of Gazprom's contracts with its clients bode ill for the EU,' wrote energy expert Roman Kupchinsky in an in-depth report on the schemes. 'Such elaborate layers . . . are an indication of money laundering and possible kickbacks to officials involved in their creation.'[140]

In those days, few policymakers, it seems, paid much heed. Schlaff's presence, however, was an indication that the gas-trading schemes, like Rosukrenergo, were about more than cash-siphoning. He was a representative of the Cold War networks of the past, an influence-peddler who'd been investigated by the Israeli police for the suspected bribing of Israel's prime minister Ariel Sharon.[141] His influence ran far and deep, not just in Austria but across the Middle East, where he'd cultivated senior Israeli and Arab politicians, including the Palestinian leader Yassar Arafat, Libya's Muammar Gaddafi and Syria's Bashar al-Assad.[142] He appeared to be an integral part of an influence network that had been preserved since Soviet times. The leaders of the Arab world he'd built ties with were the same men cultivated by Soviet foreign-intelligence agents during the Cold War.

In 2005 Centrex became mired in scandal when Italy's parliament uncovered its involvement in an operation to funnel funds to a close friend of the Italian prime minister Silvio Berlusconi. Gazprom had agreed with the Italian energy giant Eni to sell gas to Italy through yet another murky company, owned 41 per cent by Centrex and 25.1 per cent by Gazprom's export arm Gazexport, while the remaining 33.9 per cent was held by two companies owned by Berlusconi's friend. When they discovered the connection, Italian lawmakers were outraged that some of the firm's expected $1 billion in annual revenues would be heading to this friend, who they believed was no more than a front for the president himself.[143]

They were able to block this particular deal. But members of Berlusconi's political party later told the US ambassador to Italy that they believed he was still profiting 'handsomely' from other undisclosed energy deals.[144] Putin's men were again building on connections forged long ago in Soviet times, when Berlusconi had been one of the intermediaries working closely with the Soviet Politburo.

The initial intention of such operations was to create a platform from which Russia could seek to influence European policy, a former Austrian security chief who'd once worked closely with Akimov told me.[145] By 2009 the US ambassador to Italy, for instance, complained that Berlusconi's pro-Russian public statements were undermining

Western unity on US security initiatives such as the missile defence shield in Eastern Europe and NATO expansion. Putin's men were laying down deep roots in Europe. London became a particular target: Firtash took up a place at the heart of the the city's establishment, and his chief London minion funnelled hefty donations to Conservative Party grandees. If, in the beginning, the aim had been to seek to undermine Western unity on security initiatives counter to Russian interests, things were later to take a more sinister turn. To Oleh Rybachuk, the former chief of staff to Ukrainian president Viktor Yushchenko, Firtash's investments in London seemed to follow a previously-trodden path. 'Ukraine was a training ground for Russia's undermining of the EU,' he said.[146]

The black-cash operations of Gazprom's web of intermediaries were just the beginning of Putin's efforts to restore Russia's global influence. In Russia itself, a gradual transformation was still under way, with Putin's KGB men taking over greater swathes of the economy. By the end of Putin's second term as president, the economy was increasingly resembling a feudal one. For the Geneva banker Jean Goutchkov and his associates, it was only natural that Russian businessmen should feel they owed everything to a modern-day tsar. 'It is an oriental people. They have a different understanding of life, of existence,' said one of the Geneva money men. 'Because of the scale of the territory, the understanding of ownership is absolutely different. Ownership of people was part of this central culture. They were owned by masters for centuries, and then they were owned by the Party. They need to have an owner, a strong tsar.'[147]

Cowed by the legal attack on Khodorkovsky, the remaining Yeltsin-era tycoons were, one by one, beginning to vow fealty to the Putin regime. The unruly media tycoons Gusinsky and Berezovsky had been exiled, their assets taken over by the state. A consolidation of assets was occurring across industry – in particular in the strategic-metals sector – and the new leaders who emerged all bowed to the Kremlin's might. But it was Roman Abramovich, the billionaire oil trader described as close to the Yeltsin Family, who appeared to some to have performed the first and most overt act of fealty of all.

Londongrad

When Roman Abramovich headed out to serve as governor of the far east region of Chukotka, a remote, ice-locked area across the Bering Strait from Alaska, it was still the first year of Vladimir Putin's presidency. His destination was a godforsaken place at the ends of the earth, 3,700 miles from Moscow, where trees rarely grew and the winds howled so viciously they swept dogs from their feet and hurled them across the street. Chukotka had always been sparsely populated, but its inhabitants had all but deserted the region following the Soviet collapse. The population had plummeted from 153,000 to 56,000 by the time Abramovich arrived, and those who remained were struggling to survive, ground down by poverty and alcoholism. He'd gone there, he said in a rare interview, because he was 'fed up' with making money all the time.[1] He always presented the move as his own decision, claiming that he wanted to drive 'a revolution towards civilised life'.[2] Promising to change things for the better, he won the December 2000 election for governor with 92 per cent of the vote.

The local population of Chukotka worshipped the ground Abramovich walked on. The stubble-faced tycoon with a shy smile had grown up an orphan, raised by his grandparents in a bleak, hardscrabble northern Russian oil town. But now he was acting as benefactor to the region's residents, shipping in a team of executives to work on improving living standards. They built new television and radio channels, a bowling alley, a heated indoor ice-rink and a movie house. He spent tens of billions of his own roubles in the process.[3] It was as if he was bowing immediately in an act of fealty to Putin's calls for big business to take on more social responsibility after the excesses of the nineties.

Some claimed he hadn't been given much choice. According to a tycoon close to him, he was sent to Chukotka on Putin's orders,[4] because Putin wanted the fortune Abramovich had made through his stakes in the oil major Sibneft and in Rusal, the aluminium giant that controlled more than 90 per cent of the nation's output, to be at his command. It wasn't enough that Abramovich's charitable foundation Pole of Hope was ready to later donate $203 million to Petromed, the medical-equipment-supplies company connected to Bank Rossiya.[5] Putin wanted to be able to access the rest of Abramovich's cash too, and the laws of the time made it easier to jail officials than businessmen. 'Putin told me that if Abramovich breaks the law as governor, he can put him immediately in jail,' said the Abramovich associate.[6] Abramovich's investment of large amounts of his own fortune in Chukotka seemed to reduce his risk. But the threat of back tax charges similar to those levied against Yukos seemed always to hang over his Sibneft – especially as Abramovich's personal investment in Chukotka seemed to some to be part of a two-way process that left him yet more firmly on the Kremlin's hook. Soon after he became governor, Sibneft transferred a large portion of its oil sales through trading companies registered in the far east region, which were promptly granted hundreds of millions of dollars in tax breaks.[7] A spokesperson for Abramovich challenges this theory and notes that Abramovich was elected to the State Duma as the representative for Chukotka prior to Putin becoming president.

These tax schemes were remarkably similar to the ones that had landed Khodorkovsky in jail – and they provided Sibneft with an opportunity to pay even less tax than Yukos did.[8] As if in warning, just a few months into his governorship Abramovich was hauled in to the Moscow prosecutors' office for questioning.[9] The alleged tax fraud in question seemed comparatively tiny: $350,000 in underpayments. But three years later, in March 2004, just after the Russian tax ministry levied the first of a series of back tax claims that would eventually bankrupt Yukos and see it taken over by the state, the sum suddenly grew. Sibneft was now being probed over $1 billion in alleged underpayments for the year 2001.[10]

Nothing happened as a result of the investigation, and Sibneft always insisted its tax schemes were in line with the law.[11] But the ever-present threat of tax fraud charges was part of a process that put pressure on the Yeltsin-era oligarchs to become more subservient to the Putin regime. It seemed to some that Abramovich, long before the others, had been first among them. As if to underline that, when, after eight years' hard service his term as governor of Chukotka was finally up, Putin reportedly told him his next destination would be another impoverished and desolate region in Russia's far east. 'He is a young guy. Let him work,' Putin had said.[12] 'He was meant to go to Kamchatka, and spend even more of his resources,' one person close to Abramovich said. Eventually, and only after long bargaining, was Abramovich finally let off the hook.

After Khodorkovsky's trial, Russia's businessmen were all too aware that a criminal case could be opened against them at any time, in which, guilty or not, the odds would be stacked against them from the start. A feudal system was being resurrected, where the owners of the country's biggest companies, especially those in the strategic resource sector, were beginning to operate as hired managers, working on behalf of the state. They were no more than the guardians, and they kept their businesses by the Kremlin's grace.

This mentality had its roots in the tsarist system, in the beliefs of men like Jean Goutchkov and Serge de Pahlen. Putin's KGB men were the new imperialist rulers of the country, the rightful owners of its resources, and its assets were to be parcelled out to Kremlin favourites who would work for the state and of course pay tributes to their masters. 'By 2003 the first stage of Russia's transition – the stage of oligarch capitalism – had finished, and the second stage – of state friendly capitalism – began,' said Yevgeny Yasin, an influential economist who'd been a leading figure in that transition. The KGB men who'd come to power, he said, considered that they had every right to regard the country's wealth as their own: 'They believe they held the country back from total collapse. But in fact, they just seized power, and the country is being run for the preservation of the ruling elite.'[13]

*

The signs should have been troubling. But for a long time, it seemed the West didn't understand the depth of Russia's transformation. The rise of Putin's KGB men was evident as they asserted control over the country's strategic energy sector, and the boards of the biggest state companies. But to Western eyes, the rest of the nation's business still appeared to be largely independent. Yeltsin-era tycoons like Abramovich were seen as symbols of modernising, pro-Western forces in the Russian economy. Most importantly, it seemed, for once the economy was booming, and hopes grew that an emerging middle class would one day demand a greater say in the political process.[14]

Ever since Putin had been anointed Yeltsin's successor, oil prices had surged, fuelling an economic recovery. By 2005 they'd tripled, and Russia's disastrous $40 billion debt default and the rouble devaluation of 1998 seemed a distant memory. By then the country had $150 billion in hard-currency reserves, the world's fifth largest.[15] Under the guidance of the liberal-minded finance minister Alexei Kudrin, the government had created a stabilisation fund out of the windfall oil-tax revenues it had reaped since it made the tax-code changes so resisted by the oil barons. In 2005 this fund, which was meant to act as a buffer for the economy in case of a sudden oil-price drop, stood at $30 billion.[16] By the following year it was at $70 billion, while foreign reserves had soared to $260 billion.[17] Oil prices by then had climbed to more than $60 per barrel, compared to $17.4 in 1999, when Russia was barely emerging from its latest economic crisis and Yeltsin had anointed Putin his successor. The oil-price surge had changed everything. The economic turmoil that had helped convince Yeltsin's Family to cede power to the security men seemed a world away.

While Roman Abramovich toiled to improve living standards in Chukotka, in Moscow and in other regional capitals a more spontaneous transformation was under way. Slowly at first and then ever faster, bright European-style shopping malls were being built in city centres. The likes of Mango, Benetton, Diesel and Adidas replaced the dingy food and Soviet-style department stores of the not-too-distant past.[18] Swanky restaurants in cities in the depths of Siberia served lamb from New Zealand, veal from Australia and wine from France.[19] Consumer spending was soaring. Russia was suddenly starting to grow a middle class. People finally had money to spend

after a decade in which their savings had twice disappeared overnight. With the oil price climbing, economic growth averaged 6.6
per cent in the years after Putin was elevated to the presidency, while
the average monthly wage quadrupled.[20]

These were days of plenty and stability. And although the oil-price
surge driving it was entirely unconnected to him, these were the
days when Putin's godlike status as the tsar who saved Russia was
established. It was part of an unwritten pact that the people of Russia
seemed to have made with their president. They chose not to notice
the increasing state corruption, the growing arbitrary power of the
FSB and all branches of law enforcement over businesses large and
small. They didn't care about the clampdown on media freedom as
long as their incomes were growing, as long as there was finally
stability. They were beginning to live like their European neighbours.
Putin and his KGB men, it seemed, could jail whoever they wanted,
as long the emerging middle class could afford an annual holiday
in the likes of Turkey.

In any case, the tales of the KGB takeover at the top, of the asset-
siphoning and the subversion of the legal process, didn't reach most
of the population, as Putin's Kremlin had taken over the media and
eradicated all political competition. The Kremlin takeover of all
levers of power meant the population had been alienated from the
political process. But in what one analyst, Masha Lipman, later called
the Russians' 'Non-Participation Pact',[21] they were content to let the
Kremlin monopolise political and economic decision-making, as
long as it didn't intrude into their own lives. This was an altogether
different model from that of Soviet times. Then, the overweening
power of the Party and the KGB had infringed on almost all aspects
of daily life. Now, as long as the security services' interests weren't
encroached on, they stayed well out of it. Most of the population
readily accepted the new system, which further cemented the manner
of governing prevalent in Russia since the time of the tsars. It was,
Lipman wrote, 'the perennial Russian order – the dominant state
and a powerless, fragmented society'.[22]

The KGB-connected businessmen I spoke to often referred to this
mindset to justify their actions and their rule. It was, they said, the

tragedy of Russia that its people did not want to participate in politics – indeed, they didn't know how to. This had been deeply ingrained in the national mentality since Russia began, they would say, sadly shaking their heads. But in fact they were merely seizing on a convenient excuse to convince themselves that they were right not to allow the people to participate in democracy. The KGB had learned well the lessons of the Soviet past. Instead of an overbearing state, capitalism had become the instrument that allowed them to act as they wanted. Indeed, they believed that, just as the Geneva associate of Jean Goutchkov had cynically put it, people were content if they had 'a fridge, a TV, a house, children, a car. For the rest, more or less, you don't care, as long as your material situation isn't impacted.'[23]

Some Western policymakers, however, continued to believe in a different dream for Russia's rising middle class. Their hope was that eventually, as their incomes and ability to access Western countries grew, people would demand more political rights.[24] Emboldened by the apparent Cold War victory, and the expansion of the European Union into the countries of the former eastern bloc, the West believed in Russia's global integration and opened its markets ever wider to it. Belief in the power of globalisation, in liberal markets and democracy was at its zenith. Europe's eastward expansion was 'the most important contribution to peace, stability and prosperity in Europe in recent years', said the EU Commissioner for Enlargement, Gunter Verheugen, in the heady days of 2004.[25]

Russian companies were rushing to list their shares on Western stock exchanges, in particular in London. In 2005 alone they raised more than $4 billion in share sales in London, compared to $1.3 billion in all markets in the thirteen years after the Soviet collapse.[26] It was firmly believed in the West that these companies, and the mostly Yeltsin-era tycoons behind them, represented Russia's future. Despite fears aroused by the state's takeover of Yukos, the conviction was that the growing number of offerings was a sign that Russia was maturing as a market economy.

The businesses heading to London had to have three years of audited accounts to international standards under their belts, as well as at least six months of shares being listed in Moscow, to qualify for being listed on the London Stock Exchange.[27] Many in the Western policymaking world believed that the more Russian companies listed in the West, the more they would have to adapt to Western rules of transparency and governance. 'The belief was that the oligarchs who were listing would have to abide by corporate governance rules, that they would become part of the global system,' said Nigel Gould-Davies, a former economic attaché at the UK embassy in Moscow and later the UK's ambassador to Belarus.[28] Instead of the aggressive behaviour of the nineties-era transition, he said, 'they would change their behaviour because they had to'. A listing in London was also seen as offering an extra layer of protection from attack by Putin's *siloviki*, and a prized symbol of respectability.

Western bankers and policymakers rested their hopes on the growing army of Russian companies in London contributing further to the growth of Russia's middle class. The developing generation of businessmen, it was thought, would one day bring pressure on Putin's government for a liberalisation of the political and economic environment. 'The chances are high that things will keep moving in the right direction, because of the changes in society,' said Stephen Jennings, the New Zealand-born head of one of Moscow's biggest investment banks, Renaissance Capital. 'At some point these conditions will demand a much more liberal and modernising leader. We just don't know whether that is going to be the next one or the one after.'[29]

Western bankers flocked to Moscow in search of fees – some in the firm belief that they were doing 'God's work' by bringing the markets to the people and freeing them from the heavy hand of the state. Delegations flew in to Moscow regularly from the City of London, touting for business, stressing the benefits of London's 'light-touch regulation'.[30] At a time when emerging markets across the world were booming – most notably in China and in India – Russia had become the biggest source of international offerings on the London Stock Exchange.[31]

It was perhaps because the City of London had become so enthralled by the flood of cash that bankers and investors often chose not to worry that the next wave of Russian offerings was entirely different. The companies coming to London were now mainly the new behemoths of Putin's state capitalism, which had zero interest in liberalising the Russian economy. The City also chose to ignore the fact that there were large gaps in the transparency of the ownership structures and the financial accounts of some of these companies. One of the reasons Russian companies were heading to London in droves was that the standards required for listing there were far less stringent than those in New York. In the US, regulations required the chief executives and finance directors of companies seeking a stock exchange listing to sign off on the accuracy of the financial accounts.[32] If anything turned out to be not true or misleading, it was treated as a criminal offence. 'No Russian company was ready for this. We needed another five years to clean up, maybe more,' said Dmitry Gololobov, a Russian lawyer who worked on a US listing of global depositary receipts for Yukos, which dropped the plans due to the risks.[33] In London, however, companies listing global depositary receipts were welcomed by a system that allowed a much lower level of due diligence, and left investors responsible for checking whether the information provided by the company was correct or not.[34]

London's *Financial Times* wryly noted that the pages of the share prospectus for one upcoming London offering, Novolipetsk steel, contained 'more drama than a Dostoevsky plot'.[35] It revealed a wilderness of insider dealing and opaque transactions. Tens of millions of pounds were being given in interest-free loans to obscure companies later acquired by Novolipetsk's controlling shareholder. Millions more were being handed out in 'consultancy fees' to the same person. Most notably, Novolipetsk's privatisation had taken place in Russia's Darwinian wild-east 1990s, and the company admitted that its ownership and title to any other company it had acquired could be challenged at any time. But still investors piled in. Tony Blair's government seemed to have given the order for London to throw open its doors to Russian money, regardless of its provenance.

Russian listings were providing London with a huge stream of income for armies of bankers, lawyers, consultants and PR firms.

The city was awash with Russian cash. But instead of Russia being changed through its integration into Western markets, it was Russia that was changing the West. The tycoons coming to London, who the West hoped would become independent driving forces for change, were instead becoming more dependent on the Kremlin. They were becoming hostage to Putin's increasingly authoritarian and kleptocratic state. Instead of bringing Russia into line with its rules-based system, slowly the West was being corrupted. It was as if a virus was being injected into it.

*

The path had been smoothed in part, it seemed, when Roman Abramovich bought London's Chelsea Football Club in the summer of 2003. The £150 million ($240m) purchase was something of a PR coup. London newspapers marvelled at Abramovich's private Boeing 767 as he swooped into London to inspect his new club. They devoted copious column inches to his luxury yachts, including the world's biggest, the *Eclipse*, a 168-metre floating palace kitted out with two helicopter pads and its own submarine. The secretive oligarch, stubble-faced and dressed simply in jeans, was lauded as he spent lavish funds buying world-famous players for Chelsea, and upgrading its Stamford Bridge stadium. Few asked where his money came from. 'It's very good exposure,' one former Abramovich associate said. 'With Chelsea, he'll get three pages in the back of the papers, and there's nothing bad. No one questions him.'[36]

According to Sergei Pugachev, Putin's Kremlin had accurately calculated that the way to gain acceptance in British society was through the country's greatest love, its national sport. In Pugachev's view, from the start the acquisition had been aimed at building a beachhead for Russian influence in the UK.[37] 'Putin personally told me of his plan to acquire the Chelsea Football Club in order to increase his influence and raise Russia's profile, not only with the elite but with ordinary British people,' he said, referring to a meeting he claimed to have had with Putin a year before Abramovich made the purchase.[38] For another Russian tycoon and a former Abramovich associate, it also looked like

Putin may have asked Abramovich to buy the club. The purchase made Abramovich an instant celebrity in Britain. An invitation to watch a match from his private box was one of the hottest tickets in town. For Abramovich, 'it was . . . an entry ticket into UK high society', the Russian tycoon said.[39]

The former Abramovich associate also suggested that Abramovich's move into Premier League football appeared to have been aimed at increasing Russia's clout with FIFA, the International Football Federation, which later chose Russia to host the 2018 World Cup. 'Roman was asked by Putin to go into football', said the former Abramovich associate. 'He thought they should do it to win influence in FIFA, which was well-known as a corrupt organisation.'[40] 'Through Chelsea, he got an entry ticket into the football world', said the Russian tycoon. 'He was able to use it to lobby for the World Cup, which meant a lot for Moscow. They wanted to win the hosting to show to people that Russia was not in isolation. It was very important for them.'[41]

There is no evidence, beyond the statements of the individuals themselves, supporting the claims made by Pugachev, the former Abramovich associate and the Russian tycoon about the purchase of Chelsea Football Club, and a person close to Abramovich strongly denied the tycoon was acting under Kremlin direction when he bought the club.[42] This person said Abramovich had first looked at clubs in Italy and Spain, but they were all 'problematic', and then considered four different clubs in the UK before settling on Chelsea because it was a 'distressed asset'. He added that the president may have been informed about the deal. Abramovich himself has said that throughout his ownership of Chelsea he has invested with two ambitions: 'to create world-class teams on the pitch; and to ensure the club plays a positive role in all of its communities'. A spokesperson for Abramovich has also pointed out that Pugachev has been regarded as an unreliable witness in previous UK court proceedings.[43] This spokesperson said that the purchase of Chelsea FC was not aimed at increasing Russia's clout with FIFA and that the club was purchased many years before Russia announced its intention to bid for the 2018 World Cup. Abramovich used his box at Chelsea for family and friends and never invited British politicians, the spokesperson said.

At the time of the deal, others suggested Abramovich bought the club as part of a plan to secure at least part of his fortune against potential Kremlin attack. Regardless of his motivations for the purchase, Abramovich's choice of Chelsea became a symbol of the Russian cash that was flooding into the UK, and his ready acceptance helped Russian money become part of the fabric of London life.

The reason few questions were asked about Abramovich was partly that he appeared to have nothing to do with Putin's KGB men. He'd continued to maintain close ties with the Yeltsin Family – with Valentin Yumashev and with Alexander Voloshin, the Yeltsin-era Kremlin chief of staff. He was seen as the acceptable face of Russian business, a representative of the more liberal wing of the Russian elite the UK was so anxious to cultivate. But Alexander Temerko, the former Yukos shareholder who by the end of 2004 had fled Russia for the UK, claimed that this perception was in fact no more than a convenience for Putin. 'Putin likes people like Abramovich and Yumashev to travel the world and tell people he's not such a crocodile. He needs them to do this for him. They are voluntary unpaid ambassadors for him.'[44] A spokesperson for Abramovich denies this claim.

KGB capitalism was becoming turbocharged as it extended its reach into the West while energy prices continued to soar. The acquisition of Abramovich's Sibneft oil major was part of that transformation. In September 2005 it too was swallowed up by the state as the Kremlin continued its drive to take control of the strategic energy sector. But instead of winding up in jail like Khodorkovsky, his company bankrupted over billions of dollars in back tax charges, Abramovich was able to sell Sibneft to the state for $13 billion – cash. Instead of merging with Yukos and selling the company to the US's Exxon or Chevron as he and Khodorkovsky had once planned, it appeared to some that Abramovich had bowed instead to the Kremlin's new order. Once again, he had little choice. The sale of Sibneft to Gazprom at the end of 2005 was another stage in the process by which the Kremlin's energy takeover gained international legitimacy, further fuelling the Russian stock market boom.

The deal was done in a multi-step process that began barely two weeks after a Moscow court finally pronounced the guilty verdict against Khodorkovsky in May 2005. It was then that the Russian government sought to boost foreign investors' mood with the ultimate enticement, announcing that it was going to borrow $7 billion from international banks to raise its stake in Gazprom to a controlling 51 per cent.[45] This was the move foreign investors had long been waiting for. It might have seemed counter-intuitive that more government control over Gazprom would be good for them, but for years they'd been locked out of freely trading shares in the world's biggest gas producer, because the Russian government didn't officially own a majority stake in it. In effect, of course, the state controlled the gas giant, but on paper it only owned 38 per cent, and the government feared that, without restrictions on the amount they could own, foreign investors could take over Russia's most strategically important company. The previous year, when it announced plans to merge Gazprom with Rosneft, the government had dangled the prospect that it could raise its stake to a controlling one, and lift the restrictions, thereby creating the world's biggest energy major accessible to foreign investors. But these plans fell apart when Yukos filed its last-ditch suit for bankruptcy protection in Houston, and Rosneft acquired Yukos's Yuganskneftegaz instead of Gazprom, because of the legal risks. Rosneft's takeover of Yugansk fuelled the ambitions of its chairman Igor Sechin to build his own state energy giant, independent of Gazprom, and infighting between the two state titans scuppered the merger plan.

Now that the dust had settled, the government was announcing a much simpler deal. It was going to borrow $7 billion from international banks to buy the shares it needed to boost its stake in Gazprom, and it was going to buy the shares from the company itself. The announcement sent ripples of cheer through the stock market after the gruelling Khodorkovsky case. Now that Khodorkovsky's trial was over, investors believed a corner had been turned. Lifting the so-called ring-fence restrictions on foreign ownership had always been seen as a way for the Kremlin to buy the favour of foreign investors after the toxic forced sale of Yugansk. Now the foreign investors hoped that the Khodorkovsky verdict would be the end of the state onslaught, that his trial was an isolated case, and the Kremlin wasn't going to seize any more assets. The stock market boomed, the Russia RTS index doubling in six months. The growth that had been stunted during the Khodorkovsky affair had been fully recovered, driven by Gazprom shares, which soared more than 100 per cent.[46] It was part of a wilful blindness to the state's growing reach: that didn't matter, as long as stock prices were going up.

Gazprom, in turn, announced that it was going to use the cash it received from the government for its shares for an acquisition of its own: rather than bankrupting Abramovich's Sibneft and then seizing control, it was going to buy it. This was a compromise amid the infighting with Sechin that would give Gazprom an oil operation of its own. In the end, Gazprom purchased Sibneft from Abramovich for $13 billion, in a deal that seemed to underline how much Abramovich's fate differed from Khodorkovsky's.[47] The deal handed over yet another oil major from the private sector into the hands of Putin's men. But Abramovich appeared to have walked away with a fair market price for his company, without the forced sale, bankruptcy and back tax charges of the Khodorkovsky case – despite the fact that Sibneft paid an even lower effective tax rate than Yukos ever had. It was lauded as the biggest takeover deal in Russian history, and was seen by the market as a sign that the Kremlin had moved on from the Yukos affair, and that further expropriations would not occur.

But in fact it was just another evolution of an emerging KGB capitalism. Boris Berezovsky was the public source of rumours that Abramovich would have to split the lion's share of the $13 billion he'd received with Putin's men. 'I've been saying for a long time that Putin is a business partner of Abramovich's,' said his former business associate Boris Berezovsky at the time. 'I have no doubt that the profits from the sale of Sibneft will be shared between Abramovich and Putin as well as among several other individuals.'[48]

When asked for this book about such claims, a spokesperson for Abramovich responded by saying that he's 'never seen any evidence of that'. Later another spokesperson for Abramovich strongly denied this claim and noted that Berezovsky had failed to provide any evidence supporting his claim during the legal proceedings he brought against Abramovich.

It was becoming a system in which all businesses of any scale were dependent on the good will of the Kremlin, where tycoons had to serve the state in order to preserve their standing and wealth. But it was also a system that, by stealth, was gaining ever greater international acceptance and legitimacy. While the West had immediately accepted what it believed were liberal-minded tycoons like Abramovich, it had also begun to reconcile itself to the Kremlin's new energy order. The following year, in the summer of 2006, it waved aside concerns over the de facto confiscation of Yukos's main production unit, Yugansk, and allowed Rosneft to conduct an initial public offering on London's stock exchange. It was then that the first real blow to the integrity of Western markets occurred.

The share sale of Igor Sechin's Rosneft that year had been hailed as one of the world's biggest. Initially the company said it planned to raise $20 billion, a sum that would have broken records.[49] Though it later reined in the amount to half of that, the volume was still eye-watering for Western bankers, who rushed to take a slice of the $120 million in fees.[50] The IPO, still the third-biggest in the world that year, was essentially an investor referendum on the Kremlin's takeover of Russia's energy sector. The Western executives who continued to run what remained of Yukos from exile railed against the sale, claiming that it would be tantamount to abetting the sale of stolen property, and appealed to the UK markets regulator, the Financial Services Authority, to halt it.[51] Everything about Rosneft's takeover of Yugansk, they said, had been illegal – from the selective and retroactive back tax charges that led to the forced sale, to the discount sale itself, which was in breach of a temporary injunction issued by the Houston court.

For those who'd watched in horror as Putin's KGB men had subverted the legal process to seize control of Yugansk just over a year before, the listing raised deep moral and ethical questions. George Soros, the billionaire investor-turned-philanthropist, wrote to the *Financial Times* questioning whether the IPO should be allowed to go through at all: 'To argue that it will improve transparency ignores the fact that Rosneft is an instrument of state that will always serve the political objectives of Russia in preference to the interests of shareholders.'[52] For other defenders of Yukos, it seemed that a successful IPO would be seen by the Kremlin as a seal of market approval. 'Western leaders must take a realistic and long-term view of the implications of appeasing the Russians on such issues of fundamental human rights and the rule of law,' wrote Robert Amsterdam, an attorney for Khodorkovsky, by then well into his first year in prison camp in Russia's far east. 'If not, those presently in power in Russia will take Western double-standards as a licence for impunity. To deny, dismiss or discount the gravity of the consequences is to turn a blind eye to the lessons of history.'[53]

Although what Amsterdam wrote now sounds like a warning of what was to come, Putin's men had accurately calculated that, for the West, money would outweigh all other concerns. 'At the end of the day, everyone's out to make money and the Kremlin knows it,' said Harvey Sawikin, the head of the New York-based hedge fund Firebird Management.[54] Despite all the protests and the threat of lawsuits, the IPO went ahead, presented as a triumph for Putin as he played host to the G8 group of developed nations in St Petersburg that summer. Rosneft was valued at $80 billion, an enormous transformation since before its acquisition of Yugansk for a mere $9.4 billion,[55] when Rosneft was estimated to be worth no more than $6 billion. The vaulting valuation was testimony to the power of Putin's KGB cohort, and the knowledge that their backing for Rosneft was a guarantee of its future expansion: the Kremlin's support meant it was certain to pick up the rest of Yukos's assets for a song in bankruptcy auctions to come.

But the IPO had in fact not really been an IPO at all. Instead, it was more like a private placement. Foreign oil majors including BP, Malaysia's state oil company Petronas, and China National Petroleum Corporation, anxious to curry favour with the Kremlin, had bought up almost half the total offering, while KGB-connected Gazprombank bought $2.5 billion in shares.[56] It was widely reported that the Kremlin, which couldn't allow the sale to fail, had pressed tycoons like Abramovich to take part in it. Abramovich was reported to have bought as much as $300 million worth of shares.[57] A spokesperson for Abramovich clarified that the investment in Rosneft shares was made strictly for financial purposes, based on an assessment of the financial prospects of Rosneft at the time of IPO. BP had made no secret of the fact that it was seeking to use the offering to buy its way into the Kremlin's favour, that it was an exercise in 'relationship-building'. 'We think it's a good strategic investment for our position in Russia and our relationship with the Russian oil industry and with the Russian authorities,' said a spokesman for the company.[58] But other investors complained that the sale was a typical KGB operation, while US investors and oil companies stayed away out of fear over the legal risks. 'This was a major extortion exercise,' said one fund manager, claiming that the sale was way overpriced. 'They leant on investors in true KGB fashion to make sure the offering was successful.'[59]

But it seemed to matter little to investors that they were legitimising the state takeover by Putin's KGB men. Nor did they appear concerned that the funds raised would bypass the Russian budget, going instead towards paying down the $7 billion loan a murky state special-purpose vehicle called Rosneftegaz had taken on from international banks when the state increased its stake in Gazprom the previous year. It was part of what former deputy energy minister Vladimir Milov called 'a three-card monte trick' aimed solely at avoiding the transparency normally required of state privatisations: 'This is very characteristic of the current regime. They work through non-transparent schemes where Putin's men are personally the beneficiaries and can divide the money between themselves without being accountable to anyone.'[60]

For Andrei Illarionov, the Kremlin economic adviser who by then had stepped down in disgust at the changes that were going on, the Rosneft sale was 'a crime against the Russian state and the Russian people'.[61] In taking part in and facilitating it, he said, 'Western companies are actually building long-term relations with those forces in Russia that are destroying the very pillars of modern society: a market economy, respect for private property, democracy.'[62] But for the KGB men behind Rosneft's transformation, it was the stamp of approval they'd been working for, and allowed them to deepen their infiltration of international markets.

As Rosneft hoovered up Yukos's remaining assets in bankruptcy sales, Western investors began to pile further into the Kremlin's order. Two other behemoths of the Kremlin's state-run system fast followed suit with equally enormous share offerings. But neither of them was a beacon of transparency. Rather they were representative of a fast-emerging system in which the Kremlin dominated everything. First there was an $8.8 billion offering in February 2007 by the state-owned savings bank Sberbank that drew in foreign and domestic investors alike.[63] Though investors worried about transparency, the bank was seen as a proxy for Russia's booming consumer economy, and the state's control of it was regarded as an advantage. It would never be allowed to fail. Then, just three months later, Russia's second-largest bank, VTB, the former Soviet trade bank, also owned by the state, took itself to London for an $8.2 billion initial public offering, the world's biggest that year.[64] VTB's reputation as a pocket bank for Kremlin 'special projects' closely connected with the KGB did little to dampen investor enthusiasm. Its avuncular chief executive Andrei Kostin, a former Soviet diplomat in London, had displayed little talent as a banker apart from his ability to win billions of dollars for the bank in state support. Just two years before, a former central bank chairman had called VTB 'a sinking *Titanic*'.[65] But when it listed that spring investor demand for shares was eight times the actual offering. 2007 was the year global investor interest was reaching its peak. Oil prices were nearing a record $70 per barrel, and even the chairman of Goldman Sachs, Lloyd Blankfein, a titan of Wall Street, wrote to Putin requesting a meeting – a fact that was proudly displayed on the Kremlin's website for all to see.[66]

Enticed by the billions of dollars in deals that were sloshing around, global investment banks were piling back into Moscow – some for the first time since being burnt in the August 1998 crisis. Mergers and acquisitions in 2006 alone reached $71 billion.[67] But the tycoons the foreign investors partied with in Moscow's increasingly upscale clubs and restaurants were by then often proxies for Kremlin interests. There was the forty-one-year-old Suleiman Kerimov, a quicksilver native of Dagestan, the volatile region neighbouring Chechnya. He'd first hit the headlines in 2006, when he wrapped his Ferrari around a tree on Nice's Promenade des Anglais and nearly died from burns,[68] after which he retreated to the lowlit air-conditioned cool of his office on the top floor of a heavily guarded Moscow townhouse, his burned hands protected by thin fingerless gloves. Once he recovered he became notorious again for his lavish parties, where the likes of Beyoncé crooned to senior bankers from Morgan Stanley and Goldman Sachs at his villa in Cap d'Antibes. By early 2007 Forbes was estimating his fortune at $14.4 billion, making him Russia's second-richest man after Abramovich.

Kerimov was part of a new generation of financial tycoons emerging out of Putin's KGB capitalism whose fortunes were totally dependent on access to resources of the state.[69] If the nineties-era Yeltsin tycoons initially made their fortunes by holding the treasury accounts of the government in their banks before graduating to taking over the country's biggest industrial assets, Kerimov's wealth was almost entirely paper. In 2004 he had benefited from $3.2 billion in loans from Sberbank, which he used to build a 6 per cent stake in Sberbank itself, as well as a 4.2 per cent stake in Gazprom.[70] As the value of Sberbank soared tenfold and that of Gazprom sixfold, Kerimov's fortune rapidly expanded to reach $17.5 billion. The globally-traded Gazprom and Sberbank stock enabled Kerimov to parlay his fortune into establishing ties deep in Western financial markets, building significant stakes in Morgan Stanley, Lehman Brothers, Fortis and Credit Suisse, among others.[71]

The problem was that no one was sure if the fortune he'd amassed could really be described as his own. Kerimov had always operated in a murky realm closely associated with the interests of Russia's foreign-intelligence service.[72] Formerly he had been little-known, but now that he'd come out into the light, thanks to billions of dollars in loans from a state bank, even the Western bankers who worked with him weren't exactly sure who they were dealing with. 'There were times when I wondered whether he was a front for the Kremlin,' said one.[73] 'Nobody would be surprised if he was,' said another.[74] 'There is always speculation that he's a custodian for Kremlin cash,' said a third. 'But how could you prove it? There is no real money, so there's nothing to manage. It's all leverage.'[75]

The fortunes being made under Putin were many times larger than those of the Yeltsin years, and the way the tycoons built their wealth was very different. Everything was dictated by the Kremlin. Opportunities in business hinged on Putin, to whom tycoons and their underlings referred in whispers as 'the papa', or 'the number one', pointing to the ceiling to indicate him. (Many were the meetings I went to where I'd be told to leave my phone on a desk outside the office of the person I was interviewing, such was the fear that everything was bugged.) At once fearing and revering Putin, they depended on his favour to win access to loans from state banks or to state contracts, by then the main ways of making money in Russia. It was a mafia system in which business was done on informal 'understandings' like those that ruled mafia groups. When the entire system was built on corruption, on kickbacks and access, every participant could be controlled. Putin and his men would have *kompromat* on everyone – from businessmen to state officials receiving bribes. It was a way to keep everyone on a hook, fully aware that at any time, if they stepped out of line, they could go to jail. State authority had turned into big business, and every government official was expected to use his position to earn cash, said two former Kremlin insiders.

Oleg Deripaska, a young metals tycoon who'd emerged at the top of the nation's aluminium industry after vicious nineties-era battles for control, was the first to make a public nod to the changing climate. 'If the state says we need to give it up, we'll give it up,' he told me in 2007, referring to his Rusal aluminium giant. 'I don't separate myself from the state. I have no other interests.'[76]

The dependency on Putin's Kremlin became further entrenched when the 2008 financial crisis hit. The collapse of Lehman Brothers ricocheted through the Russian stock market, erasing $230 billion of its $300 billion value in September and October that year alone.[77] Russia's billionaires had borrowed heavily from Western banks to fund the rapid expansion of their business empires. A practice known as margin lending had become widespread, whereby the tycoons would pledge stakes in their businesses as collateral for billions of dollars in loans. Now that the value of those shares was plummeting, the foreign banks were calling in the loans. Significant stakes in Deripaska's Rusal and Mikhail Fridman's Vimpelcom, the country's second-largest mobile-phone operator, were in danger of being seized by Western banks.[78]

When Putin's government stepped in to save the country's billionaires, it didn't renationalise their assets. A subtler game was afoot. Instead of seizing the shares for the state, state banks such as Sberbank, VTB and Vneshekonombank provided billions of dollars in bailout loans to the troubled tycoons, leaving them even more on the hook of the regime.[79] Countless others had been saved by the state banks agreeing to roll over billions of dollars in loans the businessmen owed them. 'It was a very careful policy,' said one tycoon who'd been saved in one of the state bailouts. 'Putin wanted people to be grateful to him. He saved such big companies. If the government gave you $2 billion or $3 billion in loans, and then you get a call from the Kremlin saying please give $1 billion for a project, you can't just reject it. You have to comply.'[80]

It became a cornerstone policy of the Putin regime. 'Putin sees it this way,' said the tycoon. ' "I gave you loans. You have to be loyal to me." It's a very oriental approach. It's a feudal system.' The circle of Kremlin custodians was expanding far beyond Putin's St Petersburg allies.

*

For the Western bankers who'd been working so intently to integrate the Russian billionaires into the global economy, dependency on the Kremlin always seemed a secondary matter. They'd been blinded by the flood of cash flowing into the City of London from the former Soviet Union, and increasingly they'd come to depend on it, especially as the Western banking system hurtled towards the 2008 financial crisis. In those days, one senior Western banker told me how he and his colleagues would order due diligence reports on new clients that would conveniently self-destruct on their computers once they'd been read, erasing anything that might have rung alarm bells.[81] For good measure, a whole industry grew of corporate investigations firms producing background reports that conveniently whitewashed the colourful histories of Russian tycoons.

Data on the total inflows of Russian cash into London is scarce. Most of it comes into the City via offshore shell companies in the likes of Cyprus, the British Virgin Islands and Panama, or through the British Crown Dependencies of Jersey, Guernsey and the Isle of Man, all well-known for hiding beneficial ownership through layers of inscrutability. One of the Geneva money men described to me how most Russian clients first directed their funds into Cyprus or Austria, both of which had a treaty with Russia that prevented it from being taxed twice.[82] From there they would go to the UK, and then to an anonymous trust in Panama. This system exploited a loophole between the continental and Anglo-Saxon tax systems, which almost eliminated taxation altogether. Most of the cash flooding into London in the past ten years or more has been of unknown origin. As an example, in the second quarter of 2009 alone, the three Crown Dependencies brought in $332.5 billion in net financing to the City of London.[83] Much of that was believed to be foreign money, its initial origin impossible to identify. But London real-estate brokers were well aware that their biggest clients, splashing millions on the capital's finest property, were from the former Soviet Union, while the city's lawyers and bankers queued to service the billions of dollars at the command of the Russian tycoons. This money's provenance, and who really controlled it, were of little concern.

There was scant awareness that the British lords paid lavish salaries to sit on the boards of Russian companies had been granted little oversight of the corporate activities. 'In London, money rules everything,' said one Russian tycoon. 'Anyone and anything can be bought. The Russians came to London to corrupt the UK political elite.'[84] 'The Russians know very well how to play the game,' said a former senior London banker with ties at the top of Kremlin power. 'They manipulate lots of people with money. There are fifty people here I could name. What do you think all those lords are doing on the boards of Russian companies? They are being paid £500,000 a year.'[85]

As London became known as Londongrad, or *Moskva-na-Thames* (Moscow on the Thames), two of Russia's richest billionaires, Roman Abramovich and Alisher Usmanov, an Uzbek-born metals tycoon whose business had always gone hand in hand with the Russian state, set up residence in the city and took prime positions in the top ten of the *Sunday Times* rich list. It was strongly denied on behalf of both tycoons that either had ever sought to corrupt or infiltrate the British political elite in any way. For one Russian tycoon, the process reminded him of an old Soviet anecdote from many years before.[86] In those days, when the Soviet Union was careening towards bankruptcy, the KGB was preparing to send an agent to the US. The agent had thought up an attractive cover story for himself: he would arrive in America as a rich man, with a fleet of yachts and a prestigious mansion. The whole of US high society would come to him. He'd told his KGB boss how effective this plan would be, and the chief wholeheartedly approved. But when it came to seeking approval from the KGB finance department, the concept had to be changed. The agent was told there was no money for such a scheme. Instead, he would have to head to the US as a homeless person without money. 'This was the situation,' the tycoon said. 'And now the dream has come true. They have the big yachts and the private planes. And here they have their big houses . . . It's a whole group that have descended into the West. The infiltration of the UK has succeeded.'

The Battle Begins

None of this would have mattered if the KGB men who ran Russia had sought to use the country's wealth to strengthen market and democratic institutions, rather than to preserve and project their own power. It wouldn't have been an issue had the hardcore *siloviki* around Putin seen the West as a possible partner, and not increasingly as the enemy, intent on weakening Russia as a global power.

But they came from a world where the Cold War had never really ended, where the only thing that mattered was restoring Russia's geopolitical might. Theirs was a world in which, from the start of Russia's transition to the market, factions of the KGB had seen capitalism as a tool for one day getting even with the West, a world in which Putin believed he could buy anyone. For Putin's people, the encroachment of the West, through NATO, ever closer to Russia's borders was an existential threat, while the democracy movements that overturned pro-Russian governments in Ukraine and Georgia were seen as US-funded revolutions, not as an expression of the people's free will.

These paranoias were born of the collapse of empire, grounded in the bitter defeat of the Communist system. The problem was that they were held by a group of KGB men who became ever more ruthless in their pursuit of power.

Putin had staked out the position most clearly when he addressed world leaders for the first time at the annual Munich Security Conference in February 2007. Many believed this to be the final year of his presidency. He would soon reach the end of his second term, and according to the constitution he would have to step down. But he began right away with a combative warning that some might not like what he had to say. For the next twenty minutes he railed against the post-Cold War world order, where the US dominated as the sole superpower: 'The United States has overstepped its borders in all spheres. It is imposing its will on other states in the economy, in politics and in the humanitarian sphere. And who likes this? Who likes it?' he said.[1]

He attacked the expansion of NATO into the countries of the former Warsaw Pact. The West, he said, had ridden roughshod over guarantees it extended to the Soviet Union after the fall of the Berlin Wall. Most of all, he condemned American plans to build a missile-defence shield in Poland and the Czech Republic. The US claimed this was necessary to guard Europe against missiles from Iran and North Korea, but it was Russia's long-held view that the shield could only be aimed at undermining Russia's capacity for a nuclear strike. Neither North Korea nor Iran had the capacity to reach Europe, Russia believed, and even if North Korea did try to launch missiles targeting the US, it would not route them via Europe. 'This is clearly against the laws of ballistics,' said Putin. Building a missile-defence shield on Russia's borders, he threatened, was only going to lead to a new arms race.

Putin's tirade ended with a warning for the West. The Cold War had left behind a minefield that had yet to be cleared, he said. The ideological stereotypes, the double standards, the patterns of 'bloc-thinking' had all remained, while the unipolar world in which the US dominated everything was bound to fail: 'This is a world of one master, one sovereign. And this in the end is ruinous not just for everyone who is part of this system but also for the sovereign itself – because it will destroy it from the inside.' The world, he noted quietly, was changing rapidly. The so-called BRIC countries – the emerging markets of Brazil, Russia, India and China – were rising fast, and challenging the economies of the developed world.

But in those days the West had other troubles. It was still grappling with the hangover from the September 11 terrorist attacks, and its military incursions into Iraq and Afghanistan. The threat of terrorism still loomed large. The last thing it wanted to hear was an upstart Russia laying claim to a place at the top of the global security architecture. The firm belief was that those days were long over, and Russia was finished as a global power. This attitude was summed up succinctly by the US's then defence secretary Robert Gates, who on hearing Putin's speech sighed, 'One Cold War was quite enough.'[2]

Instead, by the end of that year, the West was placing its hopes in the man Putin had anointed as his replacement as president: Dmitry Medvedev, the softly spoken, diminutive lawyer who'd served as his deputy since the St Petersburg days. With dark curly hair and a stilted, tightly-wound air, Medvedev was a self-proclaimed liberal. He'd grown up in a suburb of Leningrad as a bookish boy who queued for volumes of classic literature and underground recordings of Western rock music. The forty-one-year-old Medvedev had launched his presidential bid with a sweeping declaration that 'Freedom is better than non-freedom,' and pledged to cut back the role of the state in the economy. The West set store in the hope that with his presidency Russia would move back to the path towards becoming a normal market economy, and that the country's further integration into the global system would help spur the development of a politically active middle class. Medvedev's anointment was seen as an encouraging sign that the more liberal wing of Putin's administration was ascendant, and that the worst excesses of the *siloviki* – including the takeover of the court system and the growing clampdown on political opposition – would be curbed. Russia, it was hoped, would follow the same rules as everyone else. Soon after the Obama administration took office in January 2009, the US announced a 'reset' in relations, even after Russia's military conflict with its Western-leaning former Soviet neighbour Georgia in August 2008.

Early that month, fighting between the Georgian military and separatists in the breakaway republic of South Ossetia deploying heavy Russian weaponry had escalated into a five-day war. Georgian tanks bombarded the separatists, who were shelling Georgian villages, and then entered the regional capital, Tskhinvali, where dozens, perhaps hundreds, of civilians lost their lives.[3] Russia and Georgia blamed each other as the fighting spiralled out of control.

Russian planes bombed the positions of Georgian troops, while Russian tanks moved into Georgian territory. The Georgian president, Mikheil Saakashvili, maintained that he ordered the assault on Tskhinvali only after he learned that Russian forces had invaded through the Roki tunnel from Russia to the north, while Russia claimed its forces only entered after the Georgian attack had begun. The truth seemed clouded in the fog of war. But several independent military experts believed Russia had long laid a trap for Saakashvili, deliberately escalating the separatists' military action and planning the incursion well in advance.[4] The standoff led to a big chunk of territory being torn out of Georgia, and ended any hope it might have had of joining NATO, talks on membership having been held earlier that year. Russia unilaterally recognised South Ossetia's independence, rendering it a zone of 'frozen conflict'. Few were in any doubt that Russia's aggressive response indicated a new assertiveness in seeking control of its near abroad. 'Russia is claiming a whole new role, and it will have repercussions everywhere,' said Dmitry Trenin, then a political analyst at the Moscow Carnegie Center. 'Russia will start taking on the US around the world more actively. This attitude wasn't there a month ago – we're in a different environment now. Russia wants to assert regional hegemony.'[5]

Despite these aggressions, the new US administration of Barack Obama signalled that it wanted to start relations with Russia with a clean slate. There was to be an end to the bickering; instead the emphasis would be on engagement, cooperation and partnership. Medvedev had played a part in that, hailing Obama's election as creating a 'very good chance' to build 'good cooperative relations',[6] and signalling Russia's desire to further integrate into the global financial system, outlining a plan for reforming international financial markets: 'Russia is ready to engage in efforts in full cooperation with EU member states and other partners and would like to participate in the creation of a new world financial architecture.' One of the big themes of his presidency was a push to transform Moscow into an 'international financial centre'. He offered to rein in plans to station nuclear-capable missiles in the Russian enclave of Kaliningrad, wedged between Poland and Lithuania, in response to the US missile-defence system.[7] For top US foreign policy strategists such as Strobe Talbott, the Clinton-era deputy secretary of state, the belief was that the global financial crisis had weakened Russia, rendering it no longer a danger as a 'petro superpower'.[8] Talbott also believed in a future in which Russia's integration further into the global system meant it would follow the 'rule-based international order'.

What emerged was mutual back-slapping between Medvedev and Obama, who praised the Russian president as a 'thoughtful, forward looking individual'.[9] Discussions were launched on a slowdown of the US's missile-defence plans in return for Russian assistance in halting Iran's capacity to build long-range missiles.[10] 'Joint understandings' were reached on cuts to both countries' nuclear arsenals, and deals were made to strengthen cooperation in Afghanistan.[11] During Obama's first visit to Moscow in 2009, he and Medvedev seemed to strike a rapport. And when Medvedev headed to the US for a reciprocal visit the following year, the focus was on deepening business ties. He sought to portray himself as a moderniser, an all-new iPad-twirling, tweeting Russian president. He made a point of visiting Silicon Valley, expressing hopes for cooperation that would help Russia's efforts for high-tech development.[12] The bonhomie continued, with Obama and Medvedev visiting the US president's favourite burger joint.[13] The US was investing heavily in Medvedev, in hopes he would lead Russia's further integration.

But after stepping down as president, Putin had taken Medvedev's place as prime minister, and behind the scenes he was mostly running the show. Medvedev took few decisions independently, and his reforms to try to roll back the role of the state in the economy were little more than window-dressing. In many ways, he was no more than a cipher. Putin had picked him as his successor precisely because, of all of his inner circle, he was the least likely ever to gain the stature to challenge him. From the start, the plan had been for Putin to return as president after Medvedev had served out a term. 'You understand all this with Medvedev was based on finding a way for him to return,' said Sergei Kolesnikov, the former physicist who'd been one of the Bank Rossiya-connected financiers of Putin's regime.[14] One of Medvedev's first actions as president was to extend the term of whoever succeeded him from four years to six, as if in preparation for Putin's return.[15]

Instead of easing the political climate, the US's attempts at cultivating Medvedev only deepened Putin's suspicion of the West, and would later prompt a much stronger crackdown on dissent. When Putin announced in September 2011 that he was, after all, going to stand for re-election as president, the West's hopes for its policy were dealt a near-fatal blow. The Medvedev experiment seemed over – if it had ever begun.

Still, for one moment that winter, it did look as if Russia could face a turning point as hopes that the Medvedev presidency might have made an impact were briefly revived. When Putin announced that he was returning to the presidency, for the first time since his vault to power, he faced a real political backlash. The signs that all was not well came soon after he made the announcement, when he was booed as he stepped into the ring to congratulate the winner of a televised wrestling match.[16] The whistles and jeers the crowd directed at him were the first he'd experienced in his near twelve years – eight as president and nearly four as prime minister – in power. Although the bout was being shown live, the editors at the state TV channel had been able to fade out the sound of the boos. But when, six weeks later, on December 10 2011, tens of thousands of protesters carrying placards calling for 'Russia Without Putin' headed to a small island on the Moscow river to demand an end to his regime, their shouts were much harder to edit out.

The demonstration that day was the biggest since the Soviet fall. As snow fell on Bolotnaya Square, the protesters, shouting slogans such as 'Putin is a thief!' and 'The thief should sit in jail!', were just the width of the river away from the Kremlin's red walls. The most immediate cause of the demonstration was widespread vote fraud uncovered during the parliamentary elections the previous week.[17] Increasingly active members of Moscow's civil society had caught the Kremlin red-handed, ballot-stuffing and falsifying results in favour of the United Russia party, which was by then widely disdained as a mass of grey bureaucrats whose loyalty to Putin's state was driven by nothing other than corruption and a desire for personal advancement. But behind the cries of exasperation over the vote was a much deeper dissatisfaction, shared by those who'd jeered Putin at the wrestling match. People felt cheated by Putin's return to power. Although most recognised Medvedev as part of his clan, four years of his more liberal rhetoric really had stirred hopes for a political thaw, in particular among Moscow's urban elite. They felt mocked. Putin had kept the entire nation on tenterhooks over whether Medvedev might stay on for a second term, or he himself would return. But when he announced his decision at a party congress for United Russia in September, he indicated that he and Medvedev had decided it between themselves years before. It was as if Putin had come out and told them that everything they'd heard for four years had been a ruse. His decision 'really really humiliated the country', said Yevgenia Albats, editor of the *The New Times*, one of the few independent magazines critical of the Kremlin.

Bankers and businessmen joined pensioners and teenagers in outcry and disappointment, while left-wing anarchists mixed with liberals and ultranationalists. As the demonstrations continued deep into the Moscow winter, Russia's opposition finally found a charismatic leader who united them for the first time since Boris Yeltsin had stood up against the Soviet system: Alexei Navalny, a likeable, slightly gangly thirty-five-year-old former lawyer, who had long been seeking a way into politics. He had gained a big internet following as an anti-corruption blogger during Medvedev's presidency, and many believed he bore more than a passing resemblance to Yeltsin in his younger years. He'd been one of the few brave voices calling out the country's biggest state corporations over contract-rigging and kickbacks. But during the protests that winter he took on the electrifying presence of a rock star, shouting, 'Who is the power here? We are the power here!' as the crowds roared the same words back at him. He made ardent speeches denouncing the corruption of the Putin regime, which he dubbed the rule of 'swindlers and thieves'. As the protests continued past the New Year and into the presidential election season in March, talk even began of a battle between the more liberal and hard-line forces in the Kremlin.[18] For some of the more progressive members of Russian big business, news of Putin's return had felt like a blow. 'It's like if one of your relatives is terminally ill,' said one of them. 'When they die, you knew it was going to happen, but it doesn't stop you from grieving.'[19]

But though for a time the frenzied atmosphere that winter made it feel that there was hope for a political spring, in reality the protesters never stood a chance. They were a small urban minority, while Putin's KGB men controlled the whole of law enforcement. Putin had appealed to the Russian heartland, to the country's so-called 'silent majority', the blue-collar workers who prized stability above all else and still lauded Putin for ending the chaos that had marred the Yeltsin years. And Putin, most of all, couldn't believe that the wave of protests was a genuine outpouring of frustration and disappointment that all Medvedev's promises for greater openness had turned out to be no more than a charade. Instead, he saw the hand of the US State Department. How else, he thought, could it have been possible that crowds of nearly 100,000 had marched in protest? For Putin, if before the US had sought to stoke uprisings in Ukraine and Georgia, now it was interfering in Russia itself.

'We will not allow anyone to interfere in our internal affairs!' he told a stadium packed for a presidential election rally in February. 'We will not allow anyone to force their will upon us, because we have our own will . . . We are a victorious people! It is in our genetic code. It is transferred from generation to generation, and we will have victory!'[20]

This was a message that resonated with most of the population, still aggrieved by the collapse of the Soviet empire and just as deeply suspicious of the West. It helped Putin win re-election with 64 per cent of the vote.[21] But when on election night he took to the stage to declare victory to supporters massed outside the Kremlin, Putin couldn't help but shed a few tears. Though aides claimed it was only the wind, it was as if he was haunted by the spectre of the Arab Spring that had toppled authoritarian regimes across the Middle East in 2010 and 2011. The Kremlin had been as convinced of the US's hand in sponsoring those pro-democracy movements as it was of its presence in the Moscow protests. (It probably hadn't helped that John McCain, the Republican senator and arch Putin critic, had taunted him that winter in a tweet: 'Dear Vlad, the Arab Spring is coming to a neighbourhood near you.'[22]) It seemed he was caught up in the emotion of his own self-declared battle to reassert Russia's global position, as if he truly believed he'd succeeded in defeating a US plot.

From the moment Putin returned as president, a political clampdown began that underlined the powerlessness of Russia's liberal elite. First, in June, dozens of protesters who'd taken part in a demonstration that turned violent on the eve of Putin's inauguration were arrested and jailed, charged with participating in mass riots and attacking police. Then, the homes of opposition leaders including Navalny were raided and searched, while a month later Navalny was charged with large-scale embezzlement, which carried a penalty of up to ten years' imprisonment.[23] There was a new law that imposed significant restrictions on any non-governmental organisations receiving foreign funding. The impact was chilling. Instead of any loosening of control of the political system under Medvedev's much-promised thaw, Putin's KGB men had maintained – and strengthened – their grip on power. They still controlled the court system and the whole of law enforcement. They could jail anyone who crossed their path. Even if they'd wanted to, Russia's Yeltsin-era tycoons couldn't resist the country's new trajectory. They were too deeply invested. 'All of them depend on the number one,' said a close associate of one of them. 'Russia is the only place they make money. So they all depend on Putin's nod for that.'[24] 'How can we work against them, when they have all the power?' said one of the billionaires.[25]

And instead of Medvedev's vaunted liberalisation, what emerged from his four-year rule was in fact a system under which the state's grip on the economy was stronger than before. This was not just because of the state bailouts that saved the tycoons from Western creditors following the 2008 financial crisis, but also because under Medvedev's presidency billions of government dollars were poured into flagship state projects in the name of modernising the economy. First there was Rosnano, a corporation created as an incubator for developing nanotechnology, a field Putin's men had identified as being crucial in competing with Western advances in military technology and artificial intelligence. There was Skolkovo, a high-tech hub created by Medvedev in 2010 aimed at stimulating the development of tech startups. Both ventures turned into enormous black holes for government money, with little oversight over or transparency about how it was spent. When Rosnano invested more than $1 billion in US tech firms and Skolkovo deepened its cooperation in Silicon Valley and with the Massachusetts Institute of Technology, US law enforcement became concerned that Russia was reverting to the old ways of the Cold War. The FBI warned tech leaders in Boston that in reality the Russian state projects were sophisticated fronts aimed at accessing American dual-use and military technology.[26]

The rapprochement with the US under Medvedev's presidency, and the steady inflow of Western investment it encouraged, had only helped support the KGB men's grip on power. 'The West was very naïve,' said Lilia Shevtsova, a political analyst with Chatham House. The assistance given by the Obama regime was like financial and technological 'Viagra' for Putin's existing system, she said.[27] Resurgent oil prices had provided additional support. By the time Putin returned to the presidency they had soared to nearly $100 per barrel, almost three times the $35 that accompanied the 2008 financial collapse. Russia's hard-currency reserves were back at more than $500 billion, the world's fourth biggest.

The feudal system under which wealth depended on Kremlin favours had only deepened. Despite all Medvedev's talk of cracking down on corruption, two senior western bankers claimed several billionaires acted as fronts for him, while at least one tycoon devised a deal which both needed Kremlin approval and sought to make sure Medvedev would get a cut. Medvedev has previously dismissed corruption claims. Even as he preached about reducing the state role in the economy, the wealth held by Putin's closest business allies surged.[28]

*

While the fortunes of Putin's KGB cohort were rising, men like Sergei Pugachev were on the outs. Pugachev had become an anachronism, a symbol of a different era, of the Yeltsin years and the transition to

Putin, when business was much more free. Following the attack on Khodorkovsky, Pugachev had gradually been sidelined. 'After this takeover of power by the KGB I couldn't influence things any more,' he said.[29] 'They'd taken over like a tsunami.' Some time in Putin's second term, he let go of his office in the Kremlin. He didn't seem to need it any more, and it felt too conspicuous. He'd remained close to some degree with Putin, helping organise a vacation for him and Prince Albert of Monaco in the summer of 2007 in the Siberian wilderness of Tuva, the region near the border with Mongolia which Pugachev represented as senator. There, surrounded by the splendour of the Siberian mountains, the two men fished in the Yenesei river and Putin, famously, first posed topless, portraying himself as a macho hero dressed only in green khaki trousers and wielding a fishing rod.

But Pugachev had been unable to kowtow to Putin like the yes-men around him. Always irreverent, he'd often told him what he thought. There'd always been a friction between them, as if Putin resented knowing he was in debt to Pugachev for helping bring him to power. And gradually the friction grew. Even before the financial crisis hit and Medvedev was anointed Putin's successor as president, clouds had been gathering over Pugachev's business empire, which spanned the country's two largest shipyards in St Petersburg, a vast coking-coal deposit in Siberia and property development.

Pugachev had resigned as chairman of Mezhprombank soon after Putin came to the presidency in 2001, handing over its ownership to a New Zealand trust. But despite his personal irreverence towards Putin, Pugachev had financed anything he asked him to. He'd still been known as the Kremlin's banker.[30]

In the first year of Medvedev's presidency, Putin asked Pugachev to finance the rise of another tycoon, considered more loyal and closer to Putin. As Russia headed towards the global financial crisis in 2008, tycoons with access to cash were becoming harder to come by. But Pugachev was still among them. In the summer of 2008 he received a call from Putin asking him to stump up $500 million in loans to help out his friend Arkady Rotenberg. 'He told me, "It's only a loan. It will be paid back to you in six months,"' said Pugachev.[31]

Pugachev met often that year with Rotenberg, who'd grown up with Putin scrapping on the streets of Leningrad, and then training together at the same judo gym. Although Rotenberg's business interests had grown after Putin took the presidency, establishing with his brother Boris a bank in St Petersburg called SMP, he wasn't widely known. But Pugachev was helping groom him to expand the role of his bank as another financier of the Putin regime, while Rotenberg was in line for a deal that would grant him billions of dollars in state contracts. That spring Rotenberg acquired a series of construction companies from Gazprom,[32] and just weeks later Gazprom awarded the holding company Rotenberg had created, Stroigazmontazh, a multi-billion-dollar pipeline contract to build the Russian part of a major new strategic gas pipeline under the Baltic Sea to Germany.[33] The only problem was that by summer Rotenberg still hadn't been able to come up with the cash to pay Gazprom for the construction companies.[34] It was then that Putin called Pugachev, who said he'd readily assisted. But Putin's direct interest in the matter made it clear to Pugachev who was really behind Rotenberg's construction business. 'Putin wanted to bring Rotenberg in because he really could control him,' said Pugachev. 'He was absolutely his.' Unlike Putin's other business allies from St Petersburg, 'Rotenberg had no real business before then.'[35] The deal transformed Rotenberg into a billionaire. Rotenberg has denied his rising fortune had anything to do with his friendship with Putin. But he fast joined the ranks of Timchenko, Sechin and Kovalchuk as one of the close Putin allies taking over ever greater swathes of the Russian economy.[36]

This was the final favour Pugachev did for Putin before he was suddenly thrown out in the cold. When the financial crisis ripped through Russia's banking system just months after he lent Rotenberg the money, Mezhprombank, which he co-founded (but claimed no longer to be a direct owner of) was left, like many other Russian banks, deeply in the red. But compared to other over-leveraged banks, the central bank was less keen to roll over or restructure bailout loans issued to it as life support. At first it had stepped in swiftly, as it had across the entire crisis-hit Russian banking system, providing $2.1 billion in bailout loans to keep Mezhprombank afloat.[37]

But by summer 2010, when Mezhprombank had still not paid down the central bank's support, the outstanding debt became a mechanism by means of which Putin's government sought to seize control of Pugachev's two shipyards, Northern Shipyard and Baltisky Zavod.

Despite the enthusiastic noises being made by Medvedev about cutting back the state's role in the economy, Putin wanted to create a state shipbuilding corporation that would be chaired by Igor Sechin, the close KGB ally who'd engineered the state's attack on Yukos. Pugachev's shipyards, located across the wharf from the St Petersburg sea port, were to be crucial assets. Northern Shipyard and Baltisky Zavod were Russia's biggest military shipyards, the producer of the Russian navy's military frigates and corvette-class warships. Pugachev had invested heavily in modernising production, and the shipyards were the leading contenders to win a groundbreaking contract between Russia and the French defence ministry to build two of France's Mistral-class warships for the Russian navy. When Putin visited the yards for the first time, for the launch of Russia's first nuclear icebreaker, the *Fifty Years of Victory*, he couldn't believe his eyes. 'I remember his amazement,' said Pugachev. 'There was a swimming pool, gardens, an orangery on board. This was an icebreaker worth more than $1 billion. But for him, it was incomprehensible. In his view, a private owner can make buns, but he can't make icebreakers and military ships. It was as if Putin had understood for the first time what Pugachev did. 'It didn't suit Putin that I owned a military shipbuilder. He didn't consider I should own it. He is a Soviet person, a Chekist. I think he decided then he would take it from me.'[38]

When Putin called Pugachev for a meeting in November 2009 and told him the government was going to create a state shipping corporation, Pugachev immediately understood his shipyard business was up. Putin told him Sechin was to chair it. 'He told me, "Look, you will have big problems with him. Don't you want to sell?"' But in those days, Pugachev believed he could reach agreement. The shipyards were worth a lot. They had tens of billions of dollars' worth of government contracts. He asked for $10 billion. But after some negotiation he was told by the finance minister Alexei Kudrin that the government could pay $5 billion, no more. Pugachev had agreed.

But somewhere along the way, he said, Sechin decided he wanted to take the yards for a fraction of their value. It was the year after the crisis, and the newly created state shipping corporation didn't have any cash. Even though Pugachev claimed he no longer had anything to do with the management of Mezhprombank, he said he agreed to hand over his stakes in the shipyards as collateral for the central bank's $2.1 billion in bailout loans. The independent auditors BDO had valued them at $3.5 billion, while the Japanese investment bank Nomura had put them at between $2.2 billion and $4.2 billion. Their sale should have raised more than enough to cover the debt.[39]

But instead of continuing with preparations for the sale, in October 2010 the central bank suddenly revoked Mezhprombank's licence after it missed an interest payment. It then filed suit to seize the shipyard stakes, triggering a chain of events that led to their forced sale in 2012. The proceedings followed the same route as the forced Yukos sales. A Moscow court agreed behind closed doors to the sale of Northern and Baltisky for a fraction of their value – they went to Sechin's state-controlled United Shipbuilding Corporation for $415 million and just $7.5 million respectively.[40]

Instead of raising enough funds to pay down Mezhprombank's debts, the state had acquired Pugachev's shipyards for a minute fraction of their value. Once again, the court system had been tightly controlled to acquire strategic assets for Putin's men. 'When they revoked Mezhprombank's licence this had become a raid on my business, and then anything was possible,' said Pugachev.[41] As if open season had been declared on him, Pugachev was soon facing the expropriation of the rest of his assets. His property project at 5 Red Square, one of Moscow's most prestigious landmarks, which Putin had assigned him the rights to develop years earlier, was simply transferred back to the Kremlin Property Department without any compensation at all. Then, rivals moved in on EPK, the coking-coal company he'd created. Although Pugachev believed he'd reached agreement to sell it to a consortium led by Ruslan Baisarov, a close ally of the Chechen president for $4 billion (the buyers had even announced the deal in the Russian press), once he'd sold the first tranche of the company for $150 million, the Russian government revoked EPK's licence to develop the vast Elegestskoye coking-coal field, and granted it to a new company owned by Baisarov.

Even as Medvedev was preaching the need to reduce the state's grip on the economy and calling for law enforcement to stop 'night-maring' business, Putin and Sechin had launched an elaborately coordinated attack.[42] It was an example of how sophisticated Putin's state takeovers had become. Instead of raising enough funds to pay down Mezhprombank's debt to the central bank through the sale of the shipyards, Pugachev was blamed for the collapse of the bank. Soon he was facing criminal investigation alleging that he had caused Mezhprombank's bankruptcy when he transferred $700 million of his own funds from an account he held at the bank into a Swiss account at the height of the crisis in 2008.[43]

The man who'd manoeuvred to bring Putin to the Kremlin had become expendable. Pugachev no longer fitted the regime's objectives; he was no longer judged to be sufficiently loyal. The KGB had listened and watched as he met Yumashev, Pyotr Aven, Finance Minister Alexei Kudrin and the heads of Russia's biggest state banks in the dining room of his Moscow office. They'd heard his irreverent tone in discussing Putin and how the system now worked. 'He was a victim of his own tongue,' said another tycoon.[44] Most of all, KGB hard-liners had disapproved of Pugachev's efforts to gain citizenship in France, where he'd kept a villa since the early nineties, and where he was later to flee.

*

When we met, it was already September 2014 and we were sitting in Pugachev's office in Knightsbridge, the wealthy area of London which had become a playground for Russia's rich. Next door was the Mandarin Oriental, a palatial hotel where two years before Igor Sechin, by then renowned as the hard man of the Kremlin, had delivered his first speech to global investors on the eve of Rosneft's latest incursion into what remained of Russia's privately-owned oil sector. Across the road was the leafy Lowndes Square, where Roman Abramovich had bought up two stucco mansions around the corner from London's two most exclusive shopping emporiums, Harrods and Harvey Nichols. A little further away on Eaton Square was the $25 million residence of Oleg Deripaska, the metals tycoon who'd married the daughter of Yeltsin's son-in-law, Valentin Yumashev, and then publicly pledged his loyalty to Putin's state. Pugachev said he wished he'd never rented an office there. 'It's disgusting,' he said. The concentration of Russian cash in the square mile around him was a bitter reminder of how deep Russia's reach into the London elite had become.

By then Pugachev was battling an order freezing his assets issued by London's High Court as the Kremlin expanded its legal campaign against him. It didn't seem to matter that of the two main witnesses against him, one of them, Mezhprombank's former president, had completely disappeared, while the other, the bank's former chief executive Alexander Didenko, had done a deal with prosecutors by which, in return for testifying against Pugachev, his own sentence would be cut. (Later Didenko would get a job with a bank run by the same Russian government agency targeting Pugachev.) The Kremlin was pursuing Pugachev over the $700 million transfer, but Pugachev could only see the case as part of the Putin regime's broader campaign to take over his business empire. Boxes of documents on the government's actions against him included a note from Sechin discussing how to take over the shipyards that had been copied to the FSB, the prosecutor's investigative committee and the Moscow arbitration court, naming the precise criminal case to be opened against Pugachev.[45]

As Sechin's note shows, the Kremlin was not above issuing direct instructions to the country's law enforcement in order to seize an asset. But seizing an asset was not always the best way to truly build state power – or an effective economy. As Putin's men extended their reach, the Russian economy began stalling. After Sechin's ship-building corporation took over Pugachev's shipyards, production of warships there came to a halt.[46] One by one, the new management were arrested on charges of corruption and embezzlement as infighting over cash flows escalated.[47] And after the Chechen president's ally Ruslan Baisarov took over the coking-coal project that belonged to EPK, all development ended. When it was owned by Pugachev, production was at ten million tonnes, and work on plans for a $1.5 billion railroad from the coalfield to China were proceeding at full pace. Now it wasn't producing at all.

The same thing was happening at Sechin's Rosneft. After the state oil giant took over Yuganskneftegaz at the end of 2004, output mostly flatlined. Rosneft's production growth was based almost entirely on its acquisition spree, while its debt soared beyond $80 billion.[48] Executives would complain in private about how Sechin would seek to involve himself in every decision, down to signing off on management's business trips.

All of this pointed to a broader problem. The economic growth of Putin's first two terms in power, which had rebounded briefly following the crisis during the Medvedev years, was starting to sputter. In Putin's first two terms, surging oil prices had fuelled average growth of 6.6 per cent, but in 2013 it was slowing to 1.3 per cent, and many economists were forecasting a recession. The Putin regime's original sin – the subversion of the judicial system to secure the takeover of Yukos – had finally caught up with it. Fear of raids by the authorities had stymied investment. Putin's men were abusing the legal system to take over businesses with impunity, and the state behemoths they were building were becoming so large they didn't know what to do with them. 'The Yukos case was an additional impulse for corruption in the law-enforcement agencies,' said one former senior Kremlin official. 'After this, they began to expand as they understood they had carte blanche to actively encroach into the economy. Everyone was frightened, and they cut back investments.'

The economic woes were also eating into Putin's ratings, which were flagging at 47 per cent, the lowest since he became president.[49] His regime seemed to be on a road to nowhere, and the only way to kickstart growth would have been to launch reforms to unpick the state takeover of the economy – and the power of Putin's circle – which was stifling initiative. Only corruption flourished.

But by the time Pugachev and I were sitting in his Knightsbridge office trying to figure out how things had got so far, instead of tackling the economic problems, Putin had dramatically changed the narrative. Gone were the nagging worries about the economy and his own sagging popularity that had dogged most of the first two years after his return to the presidency. The fear of protests had totally evaporated.

Instead, Putin was staking everything on a new phase in Russia's imperial revival. He'd launched a huge gambit to reassert the country's place in the global order. That March, Russia had annexed Crimea, the Ukrainian peninsula on the Black Sea coast where Russia had long kept a naval base. For the first time since the end of the Cold War, Russia had invaded and taken over another country's territory, instantly plunging the Putin regime into a deepening standoff with the West.

In London, the Western bankers who'd assisted what they believed was Russia's global integration were struggling to understand how it had all gone wrong. Events seemed to have spiralled out of control. But parts of the military action appeared to unfold with precision. Few had doubted that Russia and the West had long been on a collision course over Ukraine's future – either close to the European Union or in Russia's common Eurasian economic space. But had Putin, as one senior Western banker suggested, 'dusted off a plan'? 'He had to do something to get himself on the front foot. The only way he could boost the economy would have been to decentralise power. But when push came to shove, the need to control and the need to stay in power got the better of him . . . What we're seeing now seems part of an age-old strategy to deflect from problems and mobilise support.'[50] Could Russia's own economic difficulties have made Putin's men all the more determined to dominate Ukraine, setting off the crisis that led to Crimea's annexation? When and how did it begin?

*

The first time the Kremlin signalled that Russia could be heading towards a deep conflict with Ukraine came much earlier, in September 2013. By that time the pro-Kremlin Viktor Yanukovych had – with the help of Firtash and Paul Manafort – vaulted to the Ukrainian presidency, after the Orange Revolution coalition and Yushchenko's presidency had foundered as a result of conflict and corruption allegations following the 2006 gas deal. Yanukovych had been gaining in independence and wealth since he came to power in 2010. Despite his pro-Kremlin leanings, encouraged by other independent-minded Ukrainian oligarchs, he'd been holding talks on signing a trade and cooperation agreement with the EU that would strengthen Ukraine's political and economic ties with the West. These talks revived an age-old bugbear for Russia, and they couldn't have come at a more sensitive moment. Any Westward move by Ukraine, especially so soon after the political backlash that greeted Putin's return, posed a serious threat to Putin's KGB men. It threatened the entire model of Russia's statist development under Putin, and was likely to strengthen the resolve of his liberal opponents. Yanukovych was due to sign the EU deal that November, and as the date neared, Putin's regime began piling pressure on him. That September, a firebrand Kremlin envoy, Sergei Glazyev, publicly warned that Ukraine faced catastrophe if it signed the deal, as Russia would impose punitive tariffs that would cost it billions of dollars and could lead to default on $15 billion in loans.[51] What's more, Glazyev raged even more ominously, it could lead to the collapse of the Ukrainian state, as Russia would no longer be obliged to observe a treaty delineating its border with Russia. The Kremlin could intervene if pro-Russian regions in Ukraine appealed directly to Moscow. 'Signing this treaty will lead to political and social unrest,' said Glazyev. 'The living standard will decline dramatically . . . there will be chaos.'[52]

Yanukovych had taken Glazyev's threats so seriously that he suddenly backed off that November from signing the agreement with the EU. But though events would take a very different course, Glazyev's warning of Russian action was to prove chillingly prescient. Yanukovych's step back ignited a powderkeg. Long-cherished expectations that Ukraine was finally on a Westward tilt were shattered all over again, kindling pro-EU protests that spiralled into hundreds of thousands of people taking to the streets. Students, backed by Ukrainian oligarchs fed up with the craven corruption of the

Yanukovych regime, once again set up a tent city on Kiev's symbolic Maidan Square, site of the 2004 pro-Western uprising that led to the Orange Revolution.[53] For almost three months a core group of protesters stuck it out through the ice and snow, from time to time clashing with riot police as the administration sought to clear the square. Violence escalated when Yanukovych imposed draconian legislation banning demonstrations and threatening protesters with heavy fines and jail sentences.[54] Protesters seized buses in defiance, setting one on fire and driving others into columns of riot police. Some tore down metal fences and used the bars as weapons against the police. The protesters were being infiltrated by a radical right-wing force that was becoming more and more organised, led by nationalist groups who manned the barricades surrounding the square. Armed even with catapults, they were on the front lines of clashes with riot police.[55] The protests seemed within a knife-edge of spinning out of control. And then, one day, they did.

Early in the morning of February 20 2014, sniper fire rang out. To this day, no one knows precisely how it started, or where the first shots came from. Within two hours, forty-six protesters were dead.[56] By the end of the day the death toll had reached seventy, and Yanukovych was in crisis talks for his political survival with the French, German and Polish foreign ministers. The negotiations ended with the Ukrainian leader agreeing to call presidential elections before the year was out, and to change the country's constitution to curb presidential powers. But still Russia was ratcheting up the rhetoric. One senior Russian government official told the *Financial Times* that day that if Ukraine continued on a Western tilt, Russia was ready to go to war over Crimea to protect its military base there and the ethnic Russian population: 'We will not allow Europe and the US to take Ukraine from us,' a foreign policy official said. They think Russia is still as weak as in the early nineties, but we are not.'

The world woke on February 22 to the news that Yanukovych had fled in the middle of the night, deserting his administration despite the agreements he'd seemed to reach on stepping down early from power. It seemed he believed he was no longer safe. His presidential guard had abandoned him, and the more radical leaders of the opposition had refused to recognise his compromise deal, pledging to continue the protests till he was gone. In the vacuum, a temporary pro-EU government took power.

But in less than a week, the apparent breakthrough for Ukraine took a new turn. Russia had made good on its threats. Before dawn broke on February 27, masked troops wearing no military insignia stormed the Crimean parliament, hoisting a Russian flag over the Soviet-era building, while an emergency session named a new regional prime minister and called for a referendum on joining Russia.[57] Meanwhile, 150,000 Russian troops massed near the Ukrainian border. Events were unfolding with incredible speed, almost exactly as Glazyev had warned. Later, Western officials wondered at how meticulously prepared the operation seemed.[58]

The West was reeling from the audacious actions of the Putin regime. Russia justified them by claiming that it had been forced to react to protect its interests in response to a US-backed coup in Kiev. 'We are witnessing a huge geopolitical game in which the aim is the destruction of Russia as a geopolitical opponent of the US or of the global financial oligarchy,' said Vladimir Yakunin, a close Putin KGB ally since the St Petersburg days. America, he told me when we met in the midst of the military tension, was continuing to follow a doctrine that the CIA had been pursuing ever since the sixties – the separation of Ukraine from Russia.[59] The former US national security adviser Zbigniew Brzezinski had written in 1996 that with Ukraine Russia was a great power, but without it, it was not: 'This was not a new idea,' said Yakunin. 'More than forty years ago, when the US developed plans for the destruction of the Soviet Union, CIA documents said it should be accompanied by the separation of Ukraine from Russia. Somewhere on the shelves of the CIA's leaders there are such files with these projects, and they activate them maybe every three years.'[60]

Without ever offering any proof or evidence, Russian officials and state media launched an unprecedented propaganda campaign claiming the US was behind the protests that had buffeted Yanukovych's regime. 'Neo-Nazis' had led the protests, they said – despite the fact that the vast majority of the protesters were the same Western-leaning educated Ukrainians who'd led the Orange Revolution in 2004, while most of the Ukrainian elite was fed up with the corruption that had distinguished the Yanukovych regime.[61] According to the Russians, it was neo-Nazi 'armed fighters' who'd fired the shots on the fateful day in February that left more than seventy dead on Maidan Square.[62] No mention was made of the fact that members of the Berkut, a unit of the Ukrainian security forces who'd manned the protest barricades that day, had then mostly fled to Russia or Russian-controlled parts of Ukraine, their weapons later being found at the bottom of a lake.[63] The Berkut had been notoriously infiltrated by Russian agents, especially during Yanukovych's rule; later, Ukrainian prosecutors would allege that Russian security services were involved in the killings.[64] Following a forensic investigation of video footage, the prosecutors accused an elite squadron of the Berkut, clad in black, of killing thirty-nine of the protesters. An official from the prosecutors' office and a source in the Ukrainian security service told the *Financial Times* that an unidentified force had sparked the gunfire by firing at both protesters and police from rooftops surrounding Maidan Square.[65]

But none of this fitted with the Russian propaganda that was saturating the airwaves. When Yanukovych fled two days after the shootings, again, according to the Russian state propaganda, it was because of the US-backed coup, and nothing to do with the fact that his own security detail had deserted him.

Russian officials insisted that the final straw that had spurred them to action had come when the Ukrainian parliament hurriedly repealed a 2012 language law that had improved the rights of Russian-speakers in Ukraine.[66] But the hastily assembled Western-leaning new Ukrainian government had swiftly conceded that this was a mistake, and had vetoed the move. The Russian campaign, however, carried on regardless.

When I met Yakunin, Putin was ratcheting up the tension still further by calling for the deployment of Russian troops in Ukraine. Yakunin said he hoped this threat was 'a cold shower' for Western leaders: 'It would be great if they understood it is not decent to stamp around in your boots in someone else's house.'

The rhetoric, and the state propaganda that accompanied the military action, appeared to reflect the deep paranoia that had haunted Putin and his men since the days of the Orange Revolution in 2004, and from long before when Putin had watched the Soviet empire crumble around him from his perch in the KGB villa overlooking the river Elbe in Dresden, that they were surrounded by a Western plot to undermine Russia's power. But it also seemed no more than a feint to justify the Kremlin's actions. It was as if all the talk of Russia's global integration, the need to bring in foreign direct investment, to modernise the economy and reach accommodation with the US, had been cast aside, and Putin's regime had suddenly shown its true face. One former aide to the last Soviet leader, Mikhail Gorbachev, said the atmosphere in those days was as if someone had flung open the cellar doors of the Kremlin and the ghosts and the stench of the Soviet past had come flying out.[67]

For Putin, Crimea's annexation was the moment to triumphantly declare a new post-Cold War world order, the moment when Russia defiantly began to turn the tables on the US, refusing to bow to its dominance. After Crimea voted overwhelmingly in favour of joining Russia, Putin was greeted by a rapturous standing ovation from officials gathered under the vaulting arches and golden chandeliers of the Kremlin's Georgievsky Hall to hear him speak. 'What happened in Ukraine reflects the situation that unfolded across the entire world,' he said. 'After the world of two superpowers broke down, the US decided it could use strongarm politics. They think they have been entrusted by God.'[68] The West had been trying to corner and contain Russia for centuries, he told them. 'But everything has its limits . . . If you press the spring too hard, it will spring back . . . Russia, just like any other country, has national interests which you need to respect.'[69]

By the end of his speech, some officials were wiping tears of pride from their eyes, while others chanted 'Russia! Russia!' Putin was tapping into a deep-seated longing for the glory days of the Soviet imperial past that was shared by many Russians. It was the same nostalgic longing that had helped elect him – as the *kandidat rezident*, the KGB man in the Kremlin – three times. Only now, in many

Russians' eyes, it was finally being acted on. Crimea had been lost many years before the collapse of the Soviet empire, in 1954, when Nikita Khrushchev, then Communist Party leader, signed it over to Ukraine. But most Russians blamed Boris Yeltsin for confirming it when, with the stroke of a pen in December 1991, he and the leaders of the other Soviet republics signed the Soviet Union out of existence, leaving Crimea firmly within Ukraine's borders.

When the Soviet Union collapsed and Crimea wound up in a different country, 'Russia felt that it had not just been robbed, it had been pillaged,' Putin told the officials gathered that day. 'Millions of Russians went to bed in one country and woke up across a border; in one moment they became minorities in former Soviet republics . . . But then Russia just dropped its head and swallowed the shame.'[70]

Now that he was taking steps for the first time to restore Russian empire, Putin's popularity surged to more than 80 per cent. He'd never had to demonstrate any proof of US involvement in the popular uprising against Yanukovych – the propaganda chimed too well with a population still convinced of Russia's humiliation following the Soviet collapse. It was enough to show pictures of US assistant secretary of state Victoria Nuland handing out cookies to pro-European demonstrators in the freezing cold on Kiev's Maidan Square. Later, the propaganda grew increasingly sophisticated. Cyber units working for Russia's military-intelligence agency, GRU, flooded Facebook and a Russian social media network with fake stories that justified Russia's invasion and condemned the revolution as being led by neo-Nazis, while Ukraine had become a hotbed for Chechen terrorists.[71] When the conflict spread into east Ukraine, Russian TV broadcast allegations that the Ukrainian army had launched a 'genocide', even reporting that soldiers had crucified a three-year-old child.[72] Slowly, the constant barrage brainwashed most.

The West was having to wake up to Russia's assertiveness in a way it hadn't during Moscow's brief victorious war against Georgia in 2008. The fear was that Russia's proxy war could spread into Europe. No one understood how far Putin would go. His manoeuvring in Ukraine called 'the whole of the peaceful European order into question', said German chancellor Angela Merkel.[73]

Across Europe and the US, governments were scrambling to find a response. When the Kremlin pressed ahead in March with holding a referendum in Crimea on its accession into Russia, the US government fired back with economic sanctions that targeted Putin's innermost circle. The twenty Russians facing asset freezes and visa bans included senior figures in the administration such as Sergei Ivanov, who'd served as defence minister and now as Putin's chief of staff, and Viktor Ivanov, the mustachioed former deputy chief of staff, another former KGB ally from St Petersburg who now served on the Russian Security Council, and the head of the military-intelligence service, Igor Sergun.[74] It also blacklisted the allies who'd become well-known as Putin's closest business partners, the trusted custodians in the system of Kremlin fronts: Gunvor oil trader Gennady Timchenko, Bank Rossiya's main shareholder Yury Kovalchuk, and Arkady Rotenberg, Putin's former judo partner to whom Pugachev had lent $500 million only four years before to set him up as a contractor for Gazprom with billions of dollars in deals.

For the first time, the US government was naming and shaming these men as Putin's cashiers. Putin, it said, 'has investments in Gunvor and may have access to Gunvor funds', while Kovalchuk was 'the personal banker for senior officials of the Russian Federation including Putin'.[75] Rotenberg, it continued, had benefited from billions of dollars in state contracts, including most recently $7 billion in construction projects for the 2014 Sochi Winter Olympics. The US government was going public with the system of Putin's closest front men. A senior administration official said they would be unable to access any US financial services, and would find it difficult to transact in the dollar: 'These individuals will find their ability to continue to act in the world economy in any fashion severely constrained.'[76]

The European Union also sanctioned members of the Russian parliament, and the recently installed Russian leaders of Crimea – and then, to add insult to injury, Europe joined the US in suspending Russia from the G8 group of developed nations, whose membership the country had so keenly sought as a sign of its integration into the global economy. But, after fearing even tougher economic measures, similar to those that had crippled the Iranian economy, the

Russian stock market soon rebounded, and Russian troops, unde-terred, continued to mass near the Ukrainian border.

The conflict escalated. Proxy fighters – who Russia insisted were 'volunteers' – began heading into east Ukraine, where they joined with a considerable contingent of local pro-Russian militants equipped with Russian military hardware. By April they were taking over administrations in the east Ukrainian regions of Donetsk, Lugansk and, for a while, Sloviansk.[77] To Western governments and the Ukrainian administration, the situation looked remarkably similar to the way in which unidentified Russian units had taken over and annexed Crimea.

The threat of much harsher economic sanctions averted a full-scale invasion into east Ukraine. But what unfurled instead was a hybrid war in which Russia's proxies battled Ukraine's ragtag army as the Kiev government struggled to fight back against the incursion into its territory. The Russian troops still stationed in the tens of thousands on the border acted as a form of psychological warfare to intimidate the Ukrainian army, while Russian heavy weaponry and so-called 'Russian volunteers' continued to slip into east Ukraine unchecked.[78]

In July the US and the EU struck back with more sanctions in an attempt to force Russia to back off. This time the US targeted the biggest Russian state companies, cutting off the titans of the state banking sector – including Andrei Akimov's Gazprombank, Andrei Kostin's VTB and Vneshekonombank – from accessing long-term US financing.[79] It also blacklisted Russia's prized state oil champion, Rosneft, as well as Timchenko's gas producer, Novatek, limiting their ability to access funds. The EU followed two weeks later with similar measures. The standoff had been exacerbated still further by the downing on 17 July of a Malaysia Airlines passenger plane as it crossed the territory held by the pro-Russian separatists, killing all 298 people on board.[80]

As Russia continued to fuel the proxy war that was devastating east Ukraine, slowly Western governments began to wake up to the under-standing that the hopeful policy they'd pursued ever since the Soviet collapse – that Russia would inevitably converge with the Western world – was no more than an illusion.[81] They were having to contend with a regime that appeared to be aggressively pursuing its interests regardless of the consequences for its standing with the West. Putin's was a regime for which the restoration of the country's global position was the only priority. Russia didn't wish to be part of the Western-dominated order. It wanted to set its own rules instead.

It was becoming clear to the West that this was a regime of many masks that would resort to subterfuge to get its way. The tactic had finally become obvious when Putin first denied that Russian troops were in Crimea, and then, once the process of annexation was completed, admitted that the unidentified troops who became known as 'little green men' were Russian after all. It was a regime for which the pursuit of empire was becoming all-consuming, no matter what sanctions the Western world threw in its way. By the time a tentative ceasefire was reached in September 2015, Russia's proxy war had claimed more than eight thousand lives, while the pro-Russian separatist strongholds in Donetsk and Lugansk remained in place.[82] Russia had succeeded in splitting Ukraine, and despite the so-called ceasefire, to this day sporadic fighting continues, with 13,000 now dead, more than a quarter of them civilians.[83]

We may never know exactly how it all started, who it was who fired the first shot. But it seems Russia had long been preparing for several contingencies. If the revanche was in any way planned, the groundwork had been laid down long before – in the days when the KGB had quietly plotted its survival through the preservation of networks and friendly firms, siphoning cash in the final years before the Soviet fall. The process had been strengthened when Putin took over the presidency, enabling the KGB men to take over strategic cash flows, beginning with Yukos and then stretching into the rest of the economy.

If any of the Yeltsin-era oligarchs were still in any doubt about whether they could act independently, they were given the final signal soon after the annexation of Crimea. Then even one of the most loyal tycoons, Vladimir Yevtushenkov, was forced to hand over his Bashneft oil major to the state. He was arrested, and his controlling stake in Bashneft was first nationalised and then taken over by Sechin's Rosneft.

It was a sign that Russia's market economy was no more than a simulation. Instead, behind the scenes there was an incessant sharing of revenue streams. Funds were to be funnelled into the common Kremlin cash box, the *obschak*, and every deal, almost no matter how small, had to be agreed with the number one. 'Yevtushenkov thought that Bashneft was his and that he'd paid money for it,' said a senior Kremlin official. 'But it turned out that it wasn't his, and that at any second it could be taken from him. For Russian business, it is absolutely clear today that the Kremlin can take everything from any one of them. Property in Russia today is not sacred, especially property won in the nineties. It is only defended by Putin's authority.'[84]

The Russian economy was now on a war footing, with everything subsumed to the Kremlin's will, said Pugachev: 'Now there is only Putin and his lieutenants who carry out his orders. All cash generated is put on the balance of Putin. The country is in a state of war. Big business cannot live as before. It has to live under military rules.'[85]

Almost the entire economy was now at Putin's command to deploy as he saw fit. 'It's all Putin's money,' said one senior banker with connections to the security services. 'When he came to power, he started out saying he was no more than the hired manager. But then he became the controlling shareholder of all of Russia. First they gave him a stake and then he took control. It's a shareholder company of the closed type.'[86] 'Putin is the tsar, the emperor of all the lands,' agreed another tycoon.[87]

For one of Putin's closest allies, Vladimir Yakunin, the former KGB officer who'd been one of the first shareholders of Bank Rossiya and who now served as head of Russian Railways, being on the US sanctions list was a badge of honour. But as far as he was concerned, the US government was behind the times in claiming that only Timchenko and Kovalchuk were cashiers for Putin: 'The Russian president has access to the funds of the entire country,' he said.[88]

It was a sentiment echoed in warning by another close former partner of Timchenko. When we met one rainy day in November 2014, he warned me that the US sanctions might be too little too late. By then a vast web of money men and tycoons were acting as proxies for the Putin regime. 'You'd have to sanction every one of them,' he said.[89]

Though the rouble plummeted in December 2014 under pressure from the sanctions and the lack of refinancing for Russian corporate debt, ultimately the country's economy was proving resilient. The government had suspended the rules of the normal market economy. State banks did not call in loans when Russian companies broke their terms. Most debts were rolled over and restructured, part of an endless refinancing pyramid. The government dug into part of the stabilisation fund it had been collecting from windfall oil revenues for most of the previous decade to bail out the state-linked companies in most need of refinancing. Most of all, one Russian financier smiled to me, the West had underestimated the extent of the informal Russian economy: the vast web of slush funds that were off-book and unrecorded in official GDP figures that contained large pools of cash.

While the West continued to threaten further sanctions unless Russia agreed a ceasefire, Putin demanded a rewriting of the rules of the global security architecture, giving Russia a more prominent role. Angela Merkel walked out of one set of talks, declaring that Putin was out of touch with reality.[90] But for Putin's former economic adviser Andrei Illarionov, it was the West that was out of touch: 'People in the West think Putin is irrational or crazy. In fact, he's very rational according to his own logic, and very well-prepared.'[91]

The signs of the power of the Russian cash that had poured into Europe over the past decade were becoming visible in the rifts that appeared between the countries of the European Union over how far economic sanctions should go. In the UK, a Foreign Office official was photographed with a briefing paper arguing that Britain must not 'close London's financial centre to Russians', while a law firm lobby group warned of the potential impact to London's status as a centre for settling legal disputes.[92]

For Pugachev, the danger was clear. The system of black cash to corrupt and buy off officials had long gone beyond the first custodians of the Putin regime, beyond Timchenko, Kovalchuk and

Rotenberg, and had extended to all the Russian billionaires who acted as fronts at the Kremlin's command. 'They all get calls to send money for this and for that. They all say, "We'll give it. What else do you need?" This is the system. It all depends on the first person, because he has unlimited power. All are ready to work under those rules. And those who aren't are either in jail or abroad.'[93]

If the Soviet Union had run influence operations deep into the Middle East and Africa, now Putin's KGB capitalism had penetrated deep into Europe. 'This black cash is like a dirty atomic bomb,' said Pugachev. 'In some ways it's there, in some ways it's not. Nowadays it's much harder to trace.'[94]

For the Ukrainian government, what the Kremlin was doing to their country was a warning that Russia could seek to expand its activities into disrupting and dividing the West. 'Russia is trying to create turbulence in the EU through supporting far-right political movements,' said Ukraine's Western-leaning prime minister Arseny Yatsenyuk in early 2015. 'This is a copycat case of what they did in Ukraine.'[95]

13

Black Cash

When a mysterious whistleblower calling themself 'John Doe' leaked an unprecedented amount of data from a Panamanian law firm, the world caught a close-up glimpse into the operations of a Putin regime slush fund.[1] The data trove became known as the Panama Papers, and it opened a window onto a secret world. There were the offshore nominee directors, the layers of shell companies that stretched through the Seychelles, the British Virgin Islands and Panama, the secret system of codenames invented for clients to hide their wealth.[2] The leak from the world's fourth-largest offshore services provider, Mossack Fonseca, unveiled the machinery of a financial system operating above the laws that governed most.

Among the gigabytes of data searched by the International Consortium of Investigative Journalists (ICIJ) were documents related to a Russian named Sergei Roldugin. Since 2005 he had been a shareholder of Bank Rossiya, the St Petersburg bank owned by Putin's KGB-connected allies which the US Treasury had called 'the personal bank for senior officials of the Russian Federation, including Putin'.[3] The documents showed that Roldugin played a central role in a network of companies connected to Bank Rossiya that extended from the British Virgin Islands to Panama. More than $2 billion had been funnelled through it between 2009 and 2012.[4]

Roldugin was far from being one of the grey and anonymous offshore operators on whom most of the document trove cast a spotlight. He was an acclaimed cellist, the lead soloist at St Petersburg's Marinsky Theatre. He was rector of the St Petersburg conservatory. He was one of Putin's closest friends. The two men had first met in the late seventies, when Roldugin's brother Yevgeny served with Putin in the KGB. They'd cruised around Leningrad together in a tiny, scrappy Soviet car known as a Zaporozhets in the days when even to own a car was considered a luxury. They'd sung songs together and gone to the theatre. Sometimes they got into fights. And then when Roldugin began dating an Aeroflot flight attendant from Kaliningrad he introduced Putin to one of her colleagues, a doe-eyed blonde named Lyudmilla. After a long courtship Lyudmilla became Putin's wife. When their first child, Maria, was born, Roldugin became her godfather.

This particular slush fund appeared to be one of the more personal ones exposed in the Panama Papers. Of all the close Putin allies who'd held shares in Bank Rossiya, Roldugin was the one who'd stayed most under the radar: he'd remained unnoticed long after the others – Shamalov, Gorelov, Timchenko and Kovalchuk – had been exposed as closely tied to Putin. He was also the most incongruous, a professional musician who, unlike the others, didn't have a business of his own. He'd served, one tycoon close to Putin said, as one of the president's fronts of last resort.[5] He was part of 'Putin's golden parachute'.[6]

Before his exposure, Roldugin had rarely faced any questions about how he'd become a shareholder in Bank Rossiya. When he was first asked about it by the *New York Times* in 2014, he responded vaguely that he'd taken the stake because he 'needed to have some money'. 'There was no money for art anywhere,' he said, adding that he'd managed to come up with funds for the shares by raising loans and through 'a lot of manipulations'.[7] But he'd never disclosed when exactly he acquired his stake, or how much it cost. Later, Bank Rossiya documents were published which showed he'd taken it as late as 2005, in a share issue for $13.5 million.[8] It was never made clear how a cellist could have had access to that type of cash. By 2014 Roldugin's stake was worth nearly $350 million. Yet he always insisted he lived modestly. 'Look, even my cello is second-hand,' he told one reporter after the Panama Papers exposé.[9]

The network revealed in the Panama Papers showed that offshore companies connected to Roldugin had received hundreds of millions of dollars in indirect payments from tycoons close to Putin.[10] The Roldugin-connected offshores also benefited from a series of back-dated share transactions that looked to have generated tens of millions of roubles a day.[11] One of the companies, Cyprus-registered Sandalwood Continental, received a $650 million credit line, unbacked by any collateral, from the Cyprus subsidiary of VTB, the state bank for 'special projects' run by a former Soviet diplomat.[12] VTB's Cyprus subsidiary was notorious among bankers and tycoons for being a funnel for kickbacks, while VTB, since its 2007 London IPO, had become the place of employment for the sons of Russia's most senior security service officers.[13]

One of Roldugin's companies – International Media Overseas S.A., or IMO – secretly held a 20 per cent stake in Russia's biggest TV advertising agency, Video International, which generated annual revenues of more than $800 million.[14] In documents leaked as part of the trove, Roldugin was disclosed as being IMO's beneficiary, a position that gave him access to assets worth £19 million ($26.6 million) in cash.[15]

The Panama Papers revelations had blown Roldugin's cover and unveiled a $2 billion offshore scheme. Later Putin revealed the extent of his displeasure at the leaks, claiming they were a plot orchestrated by 'opponents' to destabilise Russia through fabricated allegations of corruption. 'They are attempting to rock us from within, to make us more pliant,' he said.[16] Other Russian officials were more direct, claiming that the ICIJ was staffed by former members of the US State Department and the CIA. The scheme the ICIJ uncovered looked at first glance to provide a close-up glimpse into one of the crony slush funds that had become endemic to the Putin regime, a money machine by which tycoons paid 'donations' or tributes into the Putin *obschak*, sometimes in return for deals.[17]

The documents also showed how some of the cash in the network was funnelled into projects for the comfort of Putin and his men. The ICIJ journalists uncovered how millions of dollars were trans-ferred to a Russian company which owned Putin's favourite ski resort, Igora, not far from the Ozero dacha compound where he and the Bank Rossiya shareholders started out. The Roldugin-connected

Sandalwood Continental had made $3 million in virtually interest-free loans to the Russian company Ozon in 2011, just before it acquired the resort.[18] Soon after, Ozon began developing a luxury hotel complex at Igora, complete with state-of-the-art spa complex and ice palace.[19] By 2013 the once-rundown resort had been transformed into the venue for a very special occasion, a lavish wedding at which all the guests were sworn to secrecy.[20] The bride who'd swept off in a horse-drawn sleigh that day was Katerina, Putin's second daughter. She'd married Kirill, the son of Nikolai Shamalov, the Bank Rossiya shareholder who'd been closest to Putin. A year after the wedding, Kirill received a 17 per cent stake in Russia's biggest petrochemicals company, Sibur, from Putin's closest ally, Gennady Timchenko. He was assisted in the acquisition by a $1 billion loan from Kremlin-friendly Gazprombank.[21]

The scheme traced in the Panama Papers looked similar to the offshore system for 'donations' first described by Sergei Kolesnikov. The companies Kolesnikov oversaw provided the seed money for Bank Rossiya's expansion, enabling its shareholders to become fabulously wealthy, and later became a source of funds for the construction of Putin's lavish palace on the Black Sea. The Panama data revealed the next stage in the slush funds' evolution as Putin's close allies benefited from ever greater financial flows directed their way. A vast web of offshore companies had been created on a far more sophisticated and complex scale.

The offshore system exposed in the Panama Papers was not only a way to accumulate personal wealth: it was also connected to a broader system of black cash, a slush fund that had become so vast that it could now move to the next stage, and be used to buy influence abroad. In the thickets of information in the hundreds of thousands of documents were traces of the broader gambit at play. One of the two Swiss lawyers running much of the Roldugin and Bank Rossiya-connected companies turned out to have a sideline connected to Czech politics. It emerged that the lawyer, Fabio Delco, owned a string of companies in the Czech Republic whose employees provided more than half of the total donations to the political party of Czech president Miloš Zeman, long considered a close Putin ally.[22]

The Roldugin slush fund was indicative of a broader process. Across Russia, the scale of capital flight into Western bank accounts had become mind-boggling. One estimate by the US National Bureau of Economic Research, whose authors included the French economist Thomas Piketty, found that $800 billion had been stashed offshore since the Soviet collapse, more than the wealth held by the entire Russian population in the country itself.[23] Those making use of this system included not only criminals, but also ordinary businessmen seeking safer havens for their wealth, a sign of deep internal risks in the economy. The high oil price and the increasing stability under Putin should have slowed the rate of capital leaving the country, but in the second half of Putin's rule the flood of money leaving the country multiplied many times over the rates seen in the Yeltsin years.[24]

These outflows lowered the tax take, weakened the currency and hit investment in the entire economy. But Putin had done little to stop any of it. He'd launched a campaign, and then rubber-stamped legislation, urging businessmen to bring their wealth home. But in reality these measures had no real bite. Instead, his circle of trusted custodians were an integral part of the siphoning. It was a system whereby the KGB men who ruled Russia exploited a dizzying array of offshore firms to disguise their wealth, and in which systemic looting from state companies and kickbacks allowed them not only to live as Russia's new nobility, but also to create strategic stores of black cash to undermine Western democracies. Even the offshore wealth held by the Yeltsin-era tycoons could be directed at the KGB men's command.

In the beginning, it looked to Western eyes like banal cronyism and kleptocracy. Palaces were being built not only for Putin, but for his courtiers too. There was the one based on the splendour of the tsarist-era Peterhof, replete with ornamental gardens and a stately canal, alleged to have been built for the Gazprom chief executive Alexei Miller.[25] There was the seventy-hectare estate outside Moscow with a marble mansion, a fifty-metre pool, a garage for fifteen cars and a storage room for fur coats that apparently belonged to Vladimir Yakunin, the former senior KGB officer and Bank Rossiya shareholder who since 2005 had been president of Russian Railways, the state monopoly whose annual revenues totalled $42 billion, or nearly 2 per cent of GDP.[26]

Access to billions of dollars from over-bloated state contracts had become another new path to enrichment – reserved almost exclusively for Putin's men. This was underlined when Russia embarked on a series of showcase infrastructure projects. They included the Sochi Winter Olympics, whose costs nearly quintupled from the $12 billion first announced in 2007 to more than $50 billion by the time they were held in early 2014, making them the world's most costly Olympics, outstripping the $40 billion Beijing spent on the Summer Games in 2008. Most of the contracts for it had been handed to Putin's closest allies.[27] The most expensive was the construction of a forty-eight-kilometre road and rail track from the main Olympic Park, near Sochi's Black Sea coast, winding through tunnels and bridges high up into the mountains to the ski complex. It cost an astronomical $9.4 billion, a sum that, as opposition politician Boris Nemtsov pointed out, was three and a half times more expensive than NASA's project to send a Rover to Mars.[28] One of the main companies that won the rights to build the rail track and road without a tender, SK-Most, became part-owned by Putin's close ally Gennady Timchenko when he expanded into the construction business in 2012.[29] Putin's former judo partner Arkady Rotenberg was granted 235 billion roubles', or $7.2 billion, worth of construction projects.[30] By comparison, rather than winning multi-billion-dollar state contracts, the Yeltsin-era tycoons racked up losses. The likes of Oleg Deripaska, Vladimir Potanin and Viktor Vekselberg, once among the biggest winners in the nineties-era privatisations, were ordered by the Kremlin to invest billions of dollars of their own money instead.[31]

Putin's closest business allies were being elevated above all. 'The people from the inner circle live on a different planet,' said a senior Russian banker. 'They have their own banks. They even travel on different roads from us. There are roads for everyone else, and when they break the rules they get caught. But people like the Rotenbergs have their own roads, and they can't break the rules there.'[32] The former KGB men who'd attained this wealth regarded it as no more than they deserved. They told themselves they'd saved Russia from collapse and the grip of the Yeltsin-era tycoons: they were resurrecting the country as a power against the West. They awarded themselves medals in recognition of their accomplishments. Rotenberg, who'd once struggled to get by in the nineties, was even ordering himself a family coat of arms.[33]

But the takeover of cash flows by Putin's men reached such a scale that it couldn't have been motivated only by self-enrichment. The smuggling economy on which KGB operations had always been built was being resurrected. Accessing bloated state-contract cash was one way of forming parallel budgets, far removed from any democratic oversight, that could be used to influence elections, to buy off officials at home and abroad, participants in this process said. It was a mechanism for authoritarian control at home, and for undermining institutions in the West.

The Moldovan Laundromat

When a Russian banker was gunned down in the street as he was about to enter his home in the shadow of London's Canary Wharf in March 2012, one of these schemes began to be exposed. The banker, German Gorbuntsov, was a co-owner of a network of banks through which major contractors with Yakunin's state Russian Railways had siphoned billions of dollars in contract cash and then laundered the proceeds.

Gorbuntsov had been caught in the crossfire between powerful state officials and organised-crime groups warring over cash that went missing in the 2008 financial crash.[34] He survived the attack. But the story he began to tell when he eventually emerged from an induced coma led to an enormous money-laundering scheme, that became known as the Moldovan Laundromat, through which more than $20 billion had been illicitly transferred out of Russia through Moldovan, Latvian and Estonian banks into offshore havens in the West between 2010 and 2014.[35] The cash flow that washed through the Moldovan Laundromat was linked to the same group of Russian

Railways contractors led by Andrei Krapivin, a close Yakunin associate since the 1990s, and Valery Markelov.[36] Alleging that they were behind the attempt on his life, Gorbuntsov handed over a database on some of the transactions to Scotland Yard.[37]

In 2014, Moldovan prosecutors started investigating the scheme. It took another four years before Russian law enforcement began examining it: by that time the contractors had fallen victim to warring factions in the Kremlin. When a rival group in Russian law enforcement raided the apartment of a colonel in the interior ministry, they found a custom-built vault containing more than $124 million in cash stuffed in wine boxes and plastic bags – part of it payoffs from the railway contractors to turn a blind eye to the scam.[38] The police colonel's testimony led to more than $3 billion that these men had siphoned from Russian Railways and then laundered through the Moldovan scheme into the West.[39]

That $3 billion was hidden among layers of much bigger illicit outflows of cash, mostly from Russian businessmen using the scheme to avoid paying customs duties or taxes. The bankers behind the Moldovan laundering scheme had thought up an ingenious way to spirit funds out of Russia, setting up a web of shell companies registered in the UK that signed large fake loan agreements between themselves.[40] These fictitious loans were guaranteed by a separate web of Russian companies and Moldovan citizens, which were then forced to pay out cash to the UK companies after the bankers rigged rulings against them with complicit judges in Moldovan courts. More than $20 billion had been siphoned out of Russia into offshore havens in this way before the Moldovan prosecutors cottoned on to the scheme and shut it down. Because the cash stolen from the Russian Railways was mixed in with the even bigger outflows from entrepreneurs seeking to funnel their money away from the long arm of the Russian state, it was almost impossible to trace, most of it lost in a web of offshore companies whose real ownership was obscured.

All of it was part of a much bigger outflow, spirited away out of the reach of the Russian state and invested in luxury apartments and goods. 'The total capital flight covers trade. It's necessary to reduce customs and tax payments,' said the senior banker. 'Every day a huge number of goods come into Moscow. Let's take a television set as an example. To reduce customs and taxes, it could come in with an artificial reported cost of $100. But the production price is $300. So $100 is paid directly in Russia and the other $200 is paid outside Russia, abroad. The funds need to be taken out of Russia to pay for the goods. This is what the entire flow is. Traders are the main clients.' But Moldovan prosecutors investigating the scheme feared that hidden within it was also black cash linked to the Russian security services for influence operations abroad – for funding political parties on the extreme left and right to disrupt and undermine institutions in the West.[41] The resistance the pro-Western Moldovan prosecutors encountered from the Russian security services when they began investigating the scheme was an indication that it had top-level protection. When one of the Moldovan investigators travelled to Russia to investigate the scam in 2017, he was detained and searched at the border, while Russian prosecutors ignored requests for assistance.[42] Another indication that there was a lot more to the transfers than mere cash-siphoning was that the network of Russian banks behind the scheme led to Igor Putin, a cousin of the Russian president, as well as to high-placed officials in the security services.[43]

Journalists at the Organised Crime and Corruption Reporting Project traced one of the transfers directly to a small Polish non-governmental organisation run by the pro-Kremlin political activist, Mateusz Piskorski, who has publicly called for the 'de-Americanisation' of Europe as well as backing other key items on the Russian agenda.[44] Piskorski was later arrested for spying for Russia and for accepting payments. Later in 2018, when Russian law enforcement finally began rounding up some of the participants in the scam, a senior official involved in the Russian Railways contracts admitted to me that the siphoning had been a way to create a parallel black-cash budget for the Kremlin's strategic operations. Without rules or oversight, this person said, it was easy to blur the lines between the strategic and the personal. But it was also a system where if you fell out of favour you could be targeted by Russian law enforcement at any moment: 'What was permitted and approved before, suddenly is not,' he said.[45]

One of the main Russian banks funnelling cash through the Moldovan scheme was an indication of an even bigger gambit in play. Russian Land Bank, or RZB, was part-owned and controlled by a pugnacious former boxer with ties to organised crime, St Petersburg businessman Alexander Grigoryev. For a long time, he'd had protection from the very top.[46] When he and his men acquired RZB in early 2012, the then prime minister's cousin Igor Putin came in as chairman of the board.[47] Later that year, after Vladimir Putin returned to the presidency, Grigoryev and Igor Putin, together with another banker, Alexei Kulikov, joined the board of another mid-sized bank, Promsberbank, which soon launched another major illicit money-transfer scheme.[48]

The Mirror Trades

Promsberbank was part of a web of financial institutions being deployed by the same tight-knit network of security service officials and organised crime to flood the West with illicit cash. Between 2011 and 2014 it became a major conduit for the transfer of more than $10 billion out of Russia.[49] These funds were funnelled through what must have seemed the perfect cover: one of the West's biggest financial institutions, Deutsche Bank. And the transfers didn't involve fraudulent court rulings as in Moldova, but a system of stock trades. From 2011, an interconnected network of Russian companies and brokerages began placing securities trades with Deutsche Bank's Moscow arm. They would place orders to buy large blocks of blue-chip Russian stocks in roubles, while at the same time what seemed like unconnected companies based in the UK or offshore zones like the BVI would place orders to sell the same amount of the same stock through Deutsche Bank in London. They'd be paid for the shares in dollars or euros.[50] Later, regulators found that many of these companies were connected through common directors, addresses or owners. The trades, which became known as 'mirror trades', weren't about making money, but about bypassing the Russian regulations on transferring funds out of the country.

Many of the brokerages making the trades were connected in

some way with Promsberbank. There was IK Financial Bridge, a shareholder of Promsberbank that became one of the main players placing orders for shares with Deutsche in Moscow.[51] There was Lotus Capital, another Moscow brokerage, which according to the Russian central bank paid for its shares from a rouble account at Promsberbank, and held its shares through a depositary called Laros Finance, also owned by Promsberbank. One of Promsberbank's owners, Alexei Kulikov, met executives at Deutsche Bank in Moscow to persuade them to continue the schemes, according to Kulikov's later testimony.

The bankers seemed to have found an ideal conduit. Deutsche Bank's Moscow arm had always maintained a special relationship with the Putin regime. For most of the 2000s it was the fiefdom of Charlie Ryan, the American banker who'd first met Putin in the St Petersburg days, and had then co-founded United Financial Group, the Moscow brokerage Deutsche Bank eventually bought. It had always handled sensitive top-level clients for the Putin regime. Igor Lojevsky, who replaced Ryan when he stepped down as chief of Deutsche in Moscow, was equally well-connected. He had served in senior positions in Russian state banks, and had briefly replaced Putin's closest ally from the Stasi, Matthias Warnig, as head of Dresdner Bank in Moscow. He was believed to have close links with Russian foreign intelligence.

The young Western bankers who worked for Deutsche in Moscow led happy-go-lucky expat lives. Theirs was a world where the night-clubs were filled with hookers and money poured freely, as if from a tap. The equities traders had few qualms or questions about carrying out the mirror trades. 'Half of the daily trading volume was on the mirror trades,' said one trader who worked with them then. 'It wasn't a big deal. It was something they openly talked about.'[52]

But their world came crashing around them when a compliance officer in Moscow finally decided the trades were suspicious, and warranted further scrutiny.[53] Some of the Russian outfits placing the orders had their licences revoked for violating securities and money-laundering laws, and in February 2015 Moscow police visited the Deutsche Bank Moscow office as part of a fraud probe into one of the brokerages.[54] The internal investigation Deutsche Bank launched as a result placed the blame squarely on the shoulders of a comparatively low-level employee: Tim Wiswell, the clean-cut and gregarious thirty-six-year-old head of the equities desk. Conveniently, perhaps, for Deutsche's more senior executives, $3.8 million in unaccounted-for funds had been found in an offshore bank account belonging to Wiswell's wife – and $250,000 of it came from a company that took part in the mirror trades.[55] Some of Wiswell's colleagues were aghast. Of course more senior executives had been aware of the trades. 'You can't just move $10 billion offshore without someone knowing it was going on. And over four years,' said one. 'Tim had plenty of conversations about these guys with London . . . Everyone knew these guys would call, and they would buy and sell every day for four years. It's pretty hard to keep that a secret. The guy in London – even if he claims to know nothing about it – had to know who the clients were when for four years they were a top-five client.'[56]

When Moscow regulators finally clamped down on the scheme, they too settled on lower-level players. Kulikov, the thin and bookish Promsberbank shareholder who'd tried to arrange some of the trades with Deutsche, was put on trial for allegedly embezzling 3.3 billion roubles from Promsberbank, while Grigoryev, the owner of both Promsberbank and RZB, was later charged with running a criminal organisation for his role in the Moldovan scheme.[57] But both Kulikov and another senior banker with close knowledge of the scheme indicated that the real masterminds were much higher up.[58] The Moldovan and the mirror-trade scams were interlinked, and were on such a large scale that they couldn't have taken place without the oversight and participation of the FSB. 'This was an industrial-scale operation,' said former Deutsche banker Roman Borisovich.[59] 'It wouldn't have happened on such a scale without the involvement of the FSB,' said another senior banker from Deutsche Bank with ties to the security services.[60]

The funnelled cash had entered front companies in London and the US via schemes so layered in complexity that no one understood how it was spent. To the former senior Deutsche banker, the mirror-trade scheme, for instance, did not look like an operation aimed at avoiding taxes or customs, but like a scheme to create stashes of black cash to corrupt officials, whether at home in Russia or abroad.[61] By means of a process known as *obnalichivaniye*, cash from company books was converted into untraceable black cash.[62] 'In the nineties,' said the banker, '*obnalichivaniye* was used to avoid taxes. Now it is used for corruption, for the purchase of state officials. It is only needed by criminals and the FSB.'[63]

After Kulikov was put on trial over the embezzlement charges, he and another Promsberbank executive pointed the finger at another hidden shareholder – Ivan Myazin, a slender figure in his early fifties who liked to dress in expensive clothes, who was at the centre of the nexus between organised crime and the FSB funnelling the illicit cash.[64] Myazin, they said, was the real mastermind of both the Moldovan Laundromat and the Deutsche Bank mirror-trading scheme. 'This is a very interesting personage,' said a senior Russian banker with close knowledge of both schemes. 'This is the real person who developed these schemes. He is friends with very respected people in the FSB.'[65]

Behind Myazin, however, there was another level that went higher still – to the top of the FSB and Russian organised crime.[66] When Myazin too was eventually arrested in 2018, another victim of vicious infighting within Russia's security services and the interior ministry, still these higher-level players danced away. An indication of the powerful group behind him lay in Myazin's onetime friendship with one of Russia's most notorious mobsters, Vyacheslav Ivankov, otherwise known as 'Yaponchik', Russian slang for Little Japanese. Short and skinny, with a ragged beard and ice-cold eyes, what Yaponchik lacked in stature, he made up for in vicious energy. He'd been widely feared for his violent temper, and for a time in the early nineties he'd lived in New York running operations there for Russia's biggest organised-crime group, the Solntsevskaya. The FBI branded him 'one of the most powerful international Eurasian crime bosses'.[67] In 1995 he'd been indicted by US law enforcement for extorting $3.5 million from two Russian businessmen, threatening their lives and organising a violent attack on the father of one of them that led to his death.[68] But for Myazin he was 'a quiet, smart, simple man' with whom he used to celebrate the New Year 'together with our families'.[69]

While Yaponchik was being held in a US jail, he'd made a very close friend: Yevgeny Dvoskin, a Russian bandit from Brighton Beach doing time for a fraudulent fuel-trading scheme.[70] He turned out to be Yaponchik's nephew. When the two men returned to Moscow together in 2004, with the help of Yaponchik's connections and the close friendship Dvoskin subsequently made with Ivan Myazin, Dvoskin became the driving force behind many of the biggest money-laundering schemes,[71] the shadow banker who became known as the king of Russian black cash.[72] 'There turned out to be such a connection: Myazin, Yaponchik and Zhenya [the diminutive for Yevgeny],' said a former senior Russian banker who worked with all three men. 'And together they decided to take over the world.'[73]

Yaponchik was gunned down in Moscow in 2009. But Dvoskin was a survivor, who always managed somehow to escape scot-free from investigations into the money-laundering scams. He developed a powerful source of protection, working closely with the FSB general Ivan Tkachev, who became the head of the security service's all-powerful Directorate K.[74] This was the department supposedly charged with investigating economic crimes, but in essence it did almost the opposite of that: it oversaw and controlled Russia's biggest money-laundering channels into the West, according to two senior Russian bankers with direct knowledge of the matter.[75]

The first hint at how systemic these schemes had become to Putin's rule – and how deeply the security services were involved in them – came when the onetime chairman of the Russian central bank, Sergei Ignatyev, dared to publicly hint at it. In a valedictory interview with the Russian newspaper *Vedomosti* in 2013, the thin and earnest Ignatyev spoke about the $49 billion that had illegally left the country in the previous year alone.[76] He said that more than half that amount appeared to have been siphoned by firms that were linked to each other: 'The impression is created they are all controlled by one organised group of individuals.' A former FSB officer and a senior Russian banker both said they were sure Ignatyev was talking about the FSB.[77]

Later, Ignatyev complained to a colleague that every time he had tried to shut the schemes down, he faced strong opposition from the FSB: 'He told me he would have closed them all down long ago if the FSB didn't come and bang on his door and try and stop him,' this person said.[78]

Diskont Bank

Ignatyev had every reason to be cautious. Two weeks after a crusading deputy central banker named Andrei Kozlov had sought to shut down an early version of these cash-siphoning schemes by revoking the licence of a Russian bank named Diskont Bank in 2006, he was shot dead on the street.[79] Shortly before, Kozlov had paid an urgent visit to his colleagues in Estonia, warning the head of anti-money-laundering there that the Estonian branch of Sampo Bank was laundering billions of roubles in dirty Russian cash and demanding that several accounts be closed.[80] According to a report in the investigative journal *The New Times*, a later Russian police investigation into Kozlov's death found that the money-laundering scheme was linked to senior Kremlin officials and the deputy head of the FSB.[81] But the connections to anyone in authority were swiftly covered up, and officially the trail – and the buck for the killing – stopped with a lower-level Moscow banker who was jailed for the murder.[82] Other individuals involved in setting up the money-laundering scheme were connected to Dvoskin and Myazin, but again they escaped scot-free.[83]

While Austrian and Russian prosecutors moved to shut down the Diskont scheme, other schemes took its place, and the route for Russian black cash through Estonia only expanded. When the Danish Danske Bank took over the Estonian Sampo Bank in 2007, despite repeated warnings from the Russian central bank, it became one of the central channels for funnelling the Moldovan Laundromat cash and the Deutsche mirror trades into the West.[84] In all, investigators later found, more than $200 billion in black cash had been transferred through the Danske accounts. The same bank also funnelled out $200 million in fake tax rebates granted by the Russian tax ministry, part of a separate 2007 scam uncovered by Russian tax lawyer Sergei Magnitsky, who died in a Moscow jail after he blew the whistle on it.[85] Further investigations showed that a total of more than $800 million was siphoned out of the country in fraudulent tax rebates between 2006 and 2010, using part of the same web of companies and banks.[86]

The number of common denominators between all the schemes – the fake tax rebates, the Moldovan Laundromat and the mirror trades – were astonishing, and for one banker in the middle of it, they proved deadly. Alexander Perepelichny was an owner of IK Financial Bridge, which was in turn a shareholder in Promsberbank and a large placer of orders with Deutsche Bank Moscow in the mirror-trade scam. After he began sharing information with investigators about some of the transfers through the fraudulent tax rebate schemes, which he'd also participated in, he died of a heart attack in suspicious circumstances while jogging in a park near London.

Though all of the schemes were eventually shut down after they attracted too much scrutiny, each time it was too little too late. By the time Russian regulators moved in on them, tens of billions of dollars had already moved illegally into the West. Dvoskin and his top-level handlers in the FSB remained unpunished, safely above the fray. In the case of the Moldovan Laundromat and the Deutsche mirror-trade scheme, the president's cousin Igor Putin stepped down from the boards of the banks involved just before the regulator took action, while the money-laundering channels merely replicated themselves through other bankers at other banks. When the mirror-trade scheme was shut down, for instance, it was replaced by other mechanisms for moving money, such as through fraudulent court orders or reinsurance scams. 'There's only a number of times you can use an object,' said a senior Russian banker familiar with the schemes. 'You can't watch the same TV for a hundred years, for example. It's the same thing with the banks. When there is a framework and the people involved begin to go beyond the bounds of that, they begin to undermine everything. They begin to be noticed.'

Myazin, he said, for example, 'liked to dress well and travel in style. This was not fitting for his position. In Russia, there are two types of schemes. There are the ones with Vanya Myazin, who has connections with all the groups and who are talking too loudly. And then there are the structures which are half military, and work with discipline, that no one knows about.' The schemes were forever morphing. As soon as one channel was closed down, a new channel opened. 'That scheme you saw – you can't trace it. The money is taken and mixed. It's useless to try and trace,' the senior Russian banker said.[87]

The Bank of New York

The first sign that the Russian security services and organised crime were deeply involved in funnelling billions of dollars into Western markets had come back in the summer of 1999. When the news broke that US investigators were probing whether one of the pillars of the American banking system, the Bank of New York, had laundered more than $7 billion in potentially mob-linked Russian cash, the alarm bells had rung loudly. Initially, the scandal seemed breathtaking: as we've seen, the front-page headlines helped speed Yeltsin's handover of power to Putin after the investigation threatened to extend to the Yeltsin Family accounts. The whole of Washington DC was on high alert about the potentially corrosive power of the Russian black cash. Two days of congressional hearings raked through the possible links between the money-laundering operation, organised crime and the KGB.[88] The congressmen heard from the former CIA director James Woolsey, as well as other former CIA Russia specialists. Yury Shvets, the former senior KGB officer stationed in Washington, was blunt about the origins of it all: 'Wide-scale infiltration of the Western financial system by Russian organised crime started right on the eve of the collapse of the Soviet Union . . . The main players of the game were high-ranking officials of the Soviet Communist Party, top KGB leadership and top bosses of the criminal world.'[89]

The Bank of New York operation had been startling in its audacious simplicity. It was far less sophisticated than the later Moldovan and mirror-trade schemes. Two Russian bankers from little-known, mid-sized banks had wired funds for Russian clients, often through offshore shell companies and a shell bank registered in Nauru, Sinex Bank, into accounts held by two obscure companies, Benex and Becs, at the Bank of New York.[90] The funds had then been instantaneously transferred into other third-party accounts. Investigators found that the Benex account was moving an average of 'one wire transfer every five minutes, night and day, twenty-four hours a day, for eighteen months'.[91] By 1998 the volumes had reached as much as $200 million a month.[92]

What disturbed investigators in the US and UK most was that some of the Benex transactions led back to one of Russia's most notorious mobsters, Semyon Mogilevich. British investigators had first stumbled across Benex when they were sifting through boxes of documents related to another case – a stock fraud investigation into a Mogilevich front company.[93] Then the FBI found that a connected Benex travel agency had sponsored US visa applications for a number of known Mogilevich associates.[94]

Western law enforcement began to suspect that Mogilevich could be the mastermind behind the entire laundering scheme. The connection alone had 'stunning implications', said former deputy assistant secretary of state for international law enforcement Jonathan Winer, when he testified to Congress about the case: 'It suggested as a serious possibility that Benex was a multibillion-dollar money-laundering business operated by a couple of Russians, including one insider at a major United States money centre bank, and that Benex was among other things laundering funds in New York City for some of the worst elements of the Russian mob. My jaw literally dropped when I was provided this information.'[95]

Mogilevich, the chain-smoking three-hundred-pound mobster with a pockmarked face who Putin's KGB men had used as a middleman in the shadowy gas-trading schemes between Turkmenistan, Russia and Ukraine, had always been linked with the Russian security services.[96] Even when he started out in business in the seventies, helping Jewish émigrés leave the Soviet Union – often fleecing them of their possessions in the process – he was working with the KGB.[97] His university education in finance helped turn him into the point man for funnelling the funds of Russian organised crime into the West,[98] and according to three former Mogilevich associates and an FBI dossier on him, he worked most closely with the Solntsevskaya organised-crime group, which became Russia's most powerful, and developed close ties with the Moscow city government.[99] 'They had a lot of hard currency, and they didn't know what to do with it . . . Seva was investing for them,' said one former associate. 'He is their banker,' said another. 'They make the money, but they don't know what to do with it.'[100]

The FBI believed Mogilevich had long since progressed to running a criminal empire of his own that extended to running prostitution rings and weapon and drug smuggling.[101] His operations had always gone hand in glove with the KGB. 'Half of Seva's business was always with the security services,' said one former associate. 'He was always working for them. The KGB is never going to turn against him. He is the criminal part of the Russian state.'[102] The Bank of New York money-transfer scam looked to be no different from that. It seemed a continuation of the process whereby, just before the Soviet collapse, the KGB joined with organised crime to begin funnelling the Communist Party's wealth into bank accounts abroad. None of the outflows through Benex and into accounts at the Bank of New York would have been possible without coordination with the FSB and the foreign-intelligence service – and New York prosecutors believed that increasingly Russian organised crime was using sophisticated offshore mechanisms previously used by cocaine traffickers, including through manipulation of publicly traded stock, said Jonathan Winer.[103]

While much of the architecture of the scheme looked to be run by an alliance of the KGB working with organised crime, those who used it included anyone who wanted to move money out of Russia into a safe haven in the West. Just as with the later Russian black-cash schemes, such as the Moldovan Laundromat and the Deutsche Bank mirror trades, the majority of the money that went through Benex was from Russian businessmen seeking to avoid customs duties and tax. But the beneficiaries also included mobsters, Italian organised crime and, apparently, members of the Yeltsin Family. The

KGB and organised-crime money men worked in loose affiliation: they created the schemes, and then they promoted it to everyone. 'Once you have such a vehicle you market it,' said Mark Galeotti, an expert on Russian black-cash schemes. It was like going to a grocery store said Jonathan Winer: 'You may go to the same grocery store ten times a week. It doesn't mean you're part of the organisation.' The people behind it were part of a network of ad hoc 'jobbers'. 'They get together to move money,' said Winer. 'They are people who can get things done. But none of them are employees.'[104]

Even though the alarm bells over the Bank of New York scheme had initially rung loudly, the noise began to die down when it turned out that far from all of the transactions were connected to organised crime. Instead of a full-scale investigation, the scandal was papered over, and soon forgotten. Two American citizens – both Russians who'd emigrated to the US – Lucy Edwards, who headed the Bank of New York's East European division, and her husband Peter Berlin, who ran Benex out of a small office in Queens – were sentenced for money laundering.[105] But no one more senior at the Bank of New York suffered any consequences. The bank eventually settled with prosecutors, agreeing to pay $38 million in penalties.[106] To Yury Shvets, this was a fatal error: 'The investigation didn't go anywhere. It was blocked. [President] Clinton did not have time for it. He knew Yeltsin was a son of a bitch. But they thought the main thing was he was their son of a bitch. The US was giving money to Russia and it was being stolen. But they didn't care. Clinton just gave more. He had too much else going on. But the Bank of New York case was an operation run by the Russian foreign-intelligence service through Mogilevich. It was absolutely an operation of the Russian security services, and the US never acknowledged this. As a result we got what we have now. In the US we have Trump, and in the UK it's the same.'[107]

The way was being paved for the later schemes, including the Moldovan and Deutsche Bank mirror trades, that would funnel tens of billions of dollars in Russian black cash into the West. Some of that money went to acquire luxury apartments and mansions, or into private bank accounts. Some went back to Russia for reinvestment. But part of the funds looked to be invested, through a web of organised-crime-linked funds and brokerages, in the US stock market.[108] Slush funds were being created that one day could be used to buy influence. And Mogilevich stood at the root of it all. In the early nineties he'd worked with the KGB to secure the early release from Russian jail of Yaponchik, the fearsome thief-in-law who'd later joined forces with Yevgeny Dvoskin, helping him to set up the new generation of more sophisticated laundering schemes after Mogilevich was exposed in the Bank of New York scandal, as well as in the gas-trading schemes. In those days, Mogilevich had become too visible. He'd landed a short jail term in 2007 as Putin's security men asserted their primacy, and according to one former associate he had been forced at the same time to hand over part of his business to the FSB.[109] 'Dvoskin is definitely part of a new generation,' said Mark Galeotti, the expert on the Russian mob. 'He could have been granted some of the accounts Mogilevich dealt with.'[110]

In the wake of the Bank of New York scandal and the September 11 terror attacks, the US introduced tougher banking regulations that at first glance made the path for Russian black cash into America more difficult. These measures – part of the Patriot Act – required US banks to identify the beneficial owners of accounts and prohibited the use of shell banks. Simple schemes like those used by Benex were no longer going to be so easy. But the more sophisticated schemes soon found routes in. In London, the doors were being opened ever wider to Russian cash. The Moldovan Laundromat, the Deutsche mirror trade and the Danske Bank scam showed that the Russian shadow bankers took particular advantage of a form of UK company called a Limited Liability Partnership, or LLP, which afforded next to zero transparency.[111] The UK LLPs were created in the early 2000s, following the Enron scandal and the collapse of Arthur Andersen, as a way for partners in the big four accountancy firms to avoid personal liability for the debts of their companies.[112] It appears that no one realised their creation might have far-reaching consequences. But by the mid-2000s the British LLPs were the money launderers' vehicle of choice, and London had gained a reputation as the world's laundromat, washing hundreds of billions of pounds of dirty cash every year, according to estimates by the UK's National

Crime Agency.[113] The LLPs not only allowed shell companies to acquire the label of being UK-registered without conducting any business in Britain, they also made it possible to file completely fake accounts. LLPs were not taxable, so there was no way of checking whether accounts filed with the official UK registry, Companies House, were accurate or not. Ownership of such companies was mainly through notoriously impenetrable offshore jurisdictions like the Marshall Islands or the Seychelles. 'We have no idea what happens next with the cash,' said Graham Barrow, an independent expert on money laundering.[114] Western banks were becoming ever more susceptible as the looming 2008 financial crisis left financial institutions desperate for cash flow.

The depth of the problem was recognised only when it was already much too late. The crusading journalist Daphne Caruana Galizia, renowned for her investigations into corruption in her native Malta, had warned of the possible consequences when she spoke to a British Member of Parliament shortly before she was killed in a bomb attack in 2017. 'She came to see me in my office,' said the MP, 'and told me Russian and Azeri money had bought the whole of [the Maltese government], and they were sending it all to London. She told me, "There's a wall of cash heading to London." But I didn't get involved. I'm a family man. I have kids.'[115]

In many ways, the West's 'light touch regulation' had created the mechanism for its own destruction. The way had been opened for the KGB to create a vast web of black cash, far larger and far more sophisticated than the networks it had utilised for black ops and influence-peddling in the battle for empire of Soviet days. These networks had been preserved when the KGB made preparations for the transition to the market economy in the twilight of the Soviet Union. But they had become so complex that Western law enforcement, underfunded and understaffed, is still struggling to trace any of them.

For one former senior KGB officer, who has spent years studying offshore systems, in the black-cash operations Russia has developed a weapon more powerful than anything it has ever possessed before: 'You can't use nuclear weapons every day, but you can use this black cash every day. It can be deployed to dismantle the Western system from the inside.'[116]

The senior Russian official who oversaw the Russian Railways at the time contract cash was being siphoned through the Moldovan scam had long been active in the West, creating a network of think tanks and alliances that reached high into the security services in Germany, the British Parliament and the top circles of French politics. Vladimir Yakunin, the former senior KGB officer from Putin's inner circle, had stepped down as chief of Russian Railways two years before the son of his close ally, Andrei Krapivin, was found with $277 million from the Moldovan Laundromat on his bank accounts.[117] Yakunin claims he had no knowledge of any of the financial machinations.

Soft Power in an Iron Fist:
'I Call Them the Orthodox Taliban'

The influence operations began quietly in Ukraine, long before Russian agents infiltrated regional administrations in the east of the country, helping pro-Kremlin separatists take them over with ease. Ukrainian politicians had by then long been warning of the corrosive power of Russian black cash, the influence of which had been felt in the shadowy gas-trading schemes believed to have corrupted and undermined a succession of Ukrainian presidents. Its presence was perceived in Russia's growing investment in the activities of the Russian Orthodox Church, whose roots stretched historically deep into Ukraine. Long before the region was taken over by the pro-Kremlin militants, Russian Orthodox priests would call during prayers for Moscow to save 'Holy Rus', the name for the cradle of Russian empire founded centuries before in Kiev, which united Russia, Ukraine and Belarus. Increasingly, Russian Orthodoxy was being promoted as a counterpoint to Western liberal values, its reach funded by deep-pocketed Russian Orthodox oligarchs, first in Ukraine and then deeper into the West.

Among these Orthodox oligarchs were Vladimir Yakunin, the former KGB Russian Railways chief, and Konstantin Malofeyev, the cherub-faced associate of the Geneva network of money men, a protégé of Serge de Pahlen and Jean Goutchkov, the imperialist-minded Geneva-based White Russians who were close to Putin and his oil trader ally Gennady Timchenko.

When he first met de Pahlen in the dim and spectral light of St Petersburg's St Peter and Paul Cathedral, Malofeyev was a seventeen-year-old monarchist.[1] The last direct heir of the Russian tsars, the Grand Duke Vladimir Kirillovich, was praying for the first time at the burial place of his ancestors, and the Soviet Union was entering the final month of its existence. The relationship Malofeyev forged with the tall and stooping de Pahlen that grey November 1991 day, like Putin's before him, turned into an enduring one. De Pahlen 'played a big role in my personal fate', said Malofeyev. 'He's a unique person. The whole of Russian history flows through him.'[2] Malofeyev was to become an integral part of a network of KGB men and imperialists that sought to restore Russia's imperial power after Putin took the presidency. His supporters liked to boast that he was Russia's version of George Soros, the billionaire financier who'd dedicated much of his fortune to encouraging liberalism in the countries of the former Soviet bloc. But of course Malofeyev was also the antithesis of him.

In 2005, at the tender age of thirty-one, Malofeyev became the founder of an investment fund, Marshall Capital, that quickly grew to hold more than $1 billion in assets in telecoms, children's food manufacturers, hotels and real estate.[3] He never disclosed who his investors were,[4] but at around the same time, together with de Pahlen, who served on the board, he established a Russian Orthodox charity, the Foundation of Saint Vasily the Great, ostensibly to support the spread of Orthodox values and conservative ideals across Ukraine, Europe and then into the US.[5] He soon gained high-level backing from the inner circle of Putin's KGB men, and by 2009 he had gained an inside role as an independent director on the board of state telecoms giants Svyazinvest and Rostelecom, just as they were undergoing a sweeping restructuring.[6] While Malofeyev's partner from Marshall Capital took over the role of Rostelecom's president,[7] the Bank Rossiya-controlled Gazprombank began quietly buying a 7 per cent stake in Rostelecom on Malofeyev's behalf.[8] It was a creeping takeover that helped Malofeyev's close partners, just like Yakunin, benefit from billions of roubles in Russian state contract cash. Rostelecom disbursed over 12 billion roubles in contracts, more than 80 per cent of the total, to a company headed by another Malofeyev ally from Marshall Capital.[9] 'Malofeyev became the centre for siphoning cash out of Rostelekom,' said Yevgeny Yurchenko, the former head of Svyazinvest, which was later subsumed into Rostelecom.[10]

The state support rapidly turned Malofeyev into a billionaire, while the funds under management by his Marshall Capital grew faster still. It turned out there was a reason for this. Malofeyev's St Vasily the Great Foundation was to become an integral player in the Kremlin's growing political project to expand Russian influence; and Malofeyev would be a front man in Russia's battle for empire against the West. He was part of a process that began soon after Ukraine's pro-Western turn in the Orange Revolution, when the Kremlin started creating a network of Russian non-governmental organisations and state proxy groups that first sought a toehold in Ukraine, and then expanded into the West. Their mission was to counter US-funded non-government organisations such as the National Endowment for Democracy, Freedom House and George Soros's Open Society, which was despised most of all by Putin and his cronies.[11] Putin's KGB men believed that these groups had conspired with the US State Department to diminish Russian influence in Ukraine. In the Kremlin's eyes, their focus on human rights, civil liberties and supporting democracy was no more than a cynical pretext to pull the former Soviet states, which Moscow always considered its own backyard, into the West's orbit.

Unlike Soros, a public figure, Malofeyev operated in the shadows. He never disclosed his budget or what he was up to. And instead of the liberal openness Soros's Open Society sought to promote, Putin's men wanted to advance an ideology, based on the shared Slavic values of Russian Orthodoxy, that preached almost the opposite of Western liberal values of tolerance. Russian Orthodoxy saw itself as the one true faith, with everything else considered a heresy. Individual rights, it preached, must be subordinate to tradition and to the state, and homosexuality was a sin. Putin's KGB men had chosen an ideological rationale for the drive to restore Russian empire that resonated with those who felt left by the wayside in the tumult of globalisation, as well as with base innate prejudice. They turned to once-marginalised philosophers such as Alexander Dugin, a long-bearded political thinker straight out of the pages of a Dostoevsky novel, to propound theories of Russia's destiny as a Eurasian empire that would take its rightful place as the world's one true power, as the Third Rome. They had been grasping for an ideology that would unite their allies against the liberal West, and Putin had long been discussing these ideas, and those of other exiled White Russian imperialists, with de Pahlen and the other Geneva money men. Their words, it seemed, made a deep impression on him. 'We were very lucky with this group,' said Malofeyev. 'This civilisational project arose because of their background and their understanding of the past and the future of the country. Putin spoke a lot with them.'[12] The KGB had dabbled in cultivating Russia's far-right nationalist and imperialist groups ever since the Soviet collapse. But after Ukraine's Orange Revolution in late 2004, gradually, almost imperceptibly at first, they were pulled in from the fringes, slowly gaining access to a steady stream of financing.

Malofeyev and Yakunin – through the Russian Orthodox charity he founded, Andrei the First-Called, named after the Apostle St Andrew – were far from the only ones mobilising. Russia's growing official, and unofficial, wealth meant that increasing amounts of cash were poured into a web of state agencies created to promote Russian 'soft power' abroad. These included Rossotrudnichestvo and Russky Mir, or Russian World, created in 2008 and 2007 respectively.[13] They ran cultural and language programmes for the Russian diaspora and beyond, pouring millions into promoting the Kremlin's version of events. As Russky Mir put it, they were providing 'objective information' on contemporary Russia and its citizens. But their budgets were always murky, and according to a former senior Soviet foreign-intelligence officer, they were essentially fronts for Russian intelligence.[14] Neither Rossotrudnichestvo nor Russky Mir ever published financial reports, and while state support for such operations was estimated (based on a government website listing state contracts) at about $130 million in 2015, that figure was not a reflection of the total funding, because support was also procured by the Kremlin from oligarchs.[15]

A myriad of other proxy organisations also went into action.

Russian Cossack groups ran paramilitary youth camps. A gang of motley bikers known as the Night Wolves, that served alternately as propaganda and paramilitary group, won Putin's express support. Four years before his 'little green men' appeared to take over the Crimean peninsula, Putin rode triumphantly into Crimea with a leather-jacketed, bandana-wearing gang of Night Wolves on an enormous three-wheeled Harley Davidson, kicking up clouds of dust as they roared in.[16] No one has ever been able to calculate the total funding for such groups. The Night Wolves, for instance, were granted eighteen million roubles in Kremlin funding in 2014, one of the largest such grants, for 'the patriotic education of youth'.[17] But as the Kremlin – and the FSB in particular – could turn to any businessman or illegal slush fund for support, unofficial sources of cash were also readily on tap.

The Ukraine operation began almost imperceptibly. When a ragtag group of pro-Russian separatists established the 'Donetsk Republic' political movement in eastern Ukraine in 2005, shortly after the Orange Revolution, no one took them particularly seriously. Its leaders were seen as 'three crazy guys',[18] and none of their biographies seemed to amount to much: one of them, Andrei Purgin, a thickset Russian nationalist with a wiry beard, appeared to have had seventy different jobs, including a stint in the circus, before he settled for a life as a separatist.[19] The group held sparsely-attended rallies calling for Donetsk to be granted a special federal status closer to Russia. They handed out forlorn-looking pamphlets condemning Ukrainian nationalists as fascists. And they began to forge loose affiliations with the newly-created Kremlin-sponsored Russian nationalist groups, attending Kremlin youth camps and joining a Eurasian Youth movement founded by Alexander Dugin, with whom Malofeyev also worked.[20] For a time, Ukraine's pro-Western government banned the Donetsk Republic, but it continued operating underground. 'They travelled to Moscow and took part in the programmes of Rossotrudnichestvo,' said Konstantin Batozsky, an aide to one of Donetsk's former governors and leading industrialists, Sergei Taruta. 'They were never taken seriously.'[21] Even the pro-Kremlin administration of Viktor Yanukovych mostly ignored them.

At some point, however, things changed. By 2012 the Donetsk Republic movement had enough wherewithal to open its own 'embassy' in the headquarters of Dugin's Eurasian Youth movement in Moscow, where they handed out passports to the Donetsk Republic, unrecognised by anyone.[22] And then, one day, according to Batozsky, as Ukraine tumbled towards chaos during the Maidan Square protests in January and February 2014, several unidentified Russians appeared at the self-styled embassy and told the leaders of the Donetsk Republic they had to work now, and that Russia would be behind them.[23]

When Yanukovych fled soon after the killings on Maidan, the political goals of the fringe group became reality. They joined the storming of Donetsk's administration buildings, briefly hoisting the Russian flag.[24] Though their first attempt at a self-proclaimed Donetsk People's Republic lasted only a matter of days before they were removed by riot police, they were at the forefront of what the Kremlin liked to call 'the Russian Spring', Russia's first real answer to pro-democracy movements across the globe. The Donetsk Republic movement led demonstrations which grew rapidly from a few hundred people in the early days of March 2014 into the thousands, as Russian nationalists poured across the border to join them.[25] Ukrainian officials claimed that some were bussed in dressed as tourists, among them military-intelligence officers smuggling in weapons.

By April the demonstrations had become a military insurrection, as hundreds of masked armed men stormed and took over government buildings across Ukraine.[26] Though local public support still seemed to number only in the hundreds, somehow by May, as Ukrainian troops fought to take back control of the regional governments, what began as the protest of a few dozen 'crazies' had become an army of suddenly very well-organised and very well-armed pro-Kremlin separatists.[27] The leaders of the Donetsk Republic movement were not forgotten: Andrei Purgin, who'd never before been able to hold down a job, became the first vice prime minister of the self-proclaimed Donetsk People's Republic,[28] and the military leaders who'd arrived from Moscow joined them to take over the reins of the new separatist republic.[29] The Russian government insisted they were all volunteers, but the ties of some of them to pro-Kremlin oligarchs ran long and deep.

The war in Ukraine, which claimed more than 13,000 lives and became a major crisis for the West, would never have happened without Russian black cash. Some of it was the product of complex laundering schemes, some of simple siphoning. It was a key element in a proxy war in which everything was unofficial: from the Russian military men leading the fight to the weapons they smuggled in. Everything was to be deniable. Nothing was to be traced. Some of the cash for the pro-Kremlin separatists' insurrection that spring appeared to have been funnelled across the border into Ukraine by the rebels. There had always been a large amount of unofficial trade between Ukraine and Russia, and there was a substantial shadow economy between the two countries, while the border was extremely porous, making any attempt to track the cash movements near-impossible. 'It was all black cash. It was brought in in suitcases,' said Batozsky. 'We weren't able to catch anyone by the hand.'[30] Ukrainian officials believed much of the early funding for the uprising had been brought in by the Russian secret services, who arrived in the region soon after the annexation of Crimea.

Malofeyev was in the middle of it all. His central Moscow office was not only home to an extensive collection of antique icons and rare tsarist maps, it had also been the workplace of the men who became the leaders of Russia's covert Ukrainian invasion: Malofeyev's former security chief, a military-intelligence officer with a pencil moustache known variously as Igor Strelkov, 'Strelok', or Igor Girkin,[31] led the ad hoc Russian forces arriving in east Ukraine from Crimea; his burly public relations adviser was the new leader of the Donetsk's People's Republic.[32] In November 2013, before the fighting broke out, Malofeyev cashed in his stake in Rostelecom, selling it back to the state company for $700 million so he could concentrate on 'human-itarian projects'.[33]

Malofeyev's security chief Igor Strelkov had previously fought in covert wars for Russia in Chechnya and Bosnia,[34] and he ended up being denounced as a 'monster and a killer' by Ukraine's interior minister.[35] In the month before the situation in Ukraine spiralled into chaos, he accompanied Malofeyev on a triumphant tour he organised for the Russian Orthodox Church, bringing the Gifts of the Three Wise Men from an Orthodox monastery in Greece to Moscow, then to Kiev and on to Crimea.[36] Strelkov was ostensibly in charge of security for the ancient gold, frankincense and myrrh as thousands of Orthodox believers flocked to see it. But in Crimea, the two men also had another mission. There they met Sergei Aksyonov, who one month later was to become Crimea's new pro-Russian leader,[37] raised from obscurity as leader of a tiny pro-Moscow Russian Unity Party almost as suddenly as the unmarked Russian troops appeared on the peninsula.[38] 'At these exhibitions Malofeyev and Strelkov got to know each other well,' said Batozsky. 'There are no witnesses to what happened later on.'[39] At least one former Russian Orthodox Church leader believed the tour of the holy relics was no more than a cover for a reconnaissance mission for everything that lay ahead. 'The Gifts were brought to Crimea to prepare the ground and collect intelligence,' said Valery Otstavnykh, who later stepped down from the Church because he feared it was being used as an arm of Putin's state.[40]

Malofeyev was believed to be the linchpin in funnelling cash to the pro-Kremlin separatists, working through a network of charities connected to his St Vasily the Great fund. Later, the Ukrainian security services leaked what they said were wiretapped phone calls between him and Strelkov, in which the two men discussed successes in fighting the Ukrainian army. According to a transcript of one call, Strelkov tells Malofeyev, 'From our side, not one position was dropped. All positions in Kramatorsk were held on to. But Konstantin Valerevich, could you tell me who it was exactly we hit?' Malofeyev responds by saying he'll pass the news of Strelkov's successes to the Crimean leader Aksyonov, who is visiting him.[41]

Malofeyev denied that he was involved in the conflict at all, apart from providing funding for refugees fleeing the fighting, and said his ties to the rebel leaders were no more than a 'coincidence'.[42] But even the EU found that he was involved up to his neck, sanctioning him over his links to the separatists,[43] while the Ukrainian government opened a criminal investigation, claiming he financed terrorists.[44]

For the Kremlin, however, Malofeyev was an ideal foil. His participation gave the Russian government a degree of deniability. They could claim he was a hothead imperialist acting independently. Certainly, in interviews, Malofeyev often couldn't help himself. 'I'm sorry for my lack of political correctness,' he told Bloomberg, 'but Ukraine is part of Russia . . . It is an artificial creation on the ruins of the Russian empire.'[45] 'For Russia this is a battle for historical survival,' he told me. 'Russia in its nature is an empire. When the US was only being born it was an empire. And we can't exist in another quality.'[46] But behind the scenes, his ties to the top of the Kremlin ran long and deep. Besides his friendship with de Pahlen, he'd also built connections to Putin through the Orthodox priest who'd become the president's confessor, the increasingly powerful Tikhon Shevkunov.[47]

As Malofeyev helped expand Russian influence into east Ukraine, the KGB-connected Geneva money men, who behind the scenes worked with Putin and Timchenko, looked on approvingly. 'It's really a religious war,' said one of them. 'People from Donetsk and Kharkov, if you look at their ancestors, they've always been Russian. They've been Russian forever.'[48]

From the start, Malofeyev's operations seemed connected to Russian intelligence. The telecoms sector, in which he built the bulk of his fortune, had always been the realm of military intelligence. The Kremlin's support for far-right Russian nationalist groups aiming to fracture Ukraine and prevent it from joining the EU was starting to look like a flashback to Putin's Soviet days in Dresden. Back then, the KGB (Putin included, according to the two former associates we met before) had run agents deep in German neo-Nazi groups and in the far-left Red Army Faction, which murdered American military officers and titans of West German industry to sow chaos and instability.[49] The Kremlin's foray into Ukraine seemed like a passage torn from an old KGB playbook to divide and disrupt, to funnel weapons and cash through a series of fronts and middlemen, at a time when the economy of strategic operations was based on smuggling, and nothing seemed to matter to the Soviet leaders apart from the projection of power and the battle for supremacy against the West. Putin's men were dusting off the tactics they'd used then, when, just as now, Russia was unequal to a direct ground war, and had to resort to feints, proxies, agents of influence and front organisations, to propaganda and outright lies, in order to unbalance its opponent and undermine it from within.

In Soviet times, such tactics were known as 'active measures'. And by 2014, with Russia having completed the transition to its own distorted version of state capitalism, the Kremlin was ready to take on the West anew. Some of the tactics it honed in Ukraine were fast being expanded first into Eastern Europe and then further into the West. Old networks were being awakened, and new fronts were being put into play.

The Ukrainians had been the first to warn that a resurgent Russia was seeking to sow division in the West. 'Everyone thought the Russians were just stealing,' said Konstantin Batozsky, the aide to the former Donetsk governor. 'But they're working to create their own circle of corrupt politicians. This has been going on for a long time, and Russia will undermine Europe. Russia is laying a huge bomb in the foundations of the European Union. Russia is looking for vulnerable points to split Europe. This is a gigantic risk today. Russian NGOs are working very actively, giving grants to groups on the ultra left and ultra right.'[50]

In the West, some experts were also becoming increasingly aware that Russia's black-cash influence operations weren't limited to Ukraine. 'Russia is funding the National Front in France, Jobbik in Hungary, the Liga Nord as well as the Five Star movement in Italy,' Michael Carpenter, then adviser on Russia to US vice president Joe Biden, told me in September 2015. 'They've funded Syriza in Greece and we suspect die Linke in Germany. They're going after all these anti-establishment parties on the left and right. They are totally promiscuous in that respect, and they use these slush funds to do it. Their goal is to target the European countries to weaken the EU and to break consensus on sanctions. It's very serious. They've spent a lot of time and money on this.' But such fears were drowned out amid other threats that seemed more immediate and real to policy-makers less well-versed in Russia. 'They told us we had default bias,' said Carpenter. 'They said, "You work on Russia, so of course you think Russia is a threat."'[51]

Exhausted from the Ukraine conflict, the mounting strife in the Middle East and the growing tide of refugees, there was widespread disbelief in the West that Putin's Russia could penetrate its political and economic institutions. Despite its apparent success in splitting Ukraine, this was largely seen by the West as a Pyrrhic victory. Russia's economy had long been viewed as a basket case, and its foreign-intelligence service was believed to be emasculated following the Soviet collapse. The money flooding into the West was seen only as stolen cash, not as a vast slush fund that could be used for any strategic agenda.

But across Europe, old KGB networks were being resurrected. While Konstantin Malofeyev was still a child growing up in a Moscow suburb, Serge de Pahlen had been serving undercover in Paris for the KGB as part of a network cultivated by Igor Shchegolev,[52] and had worked with Jean Goutchkov for friendly firms helping equip Soviet industry,[53] while another close White Russian ally, Alexander Trubetskoy, had been part of Shchegolev's network supplying the Soviets with French computer technology.[54] Now they'd all moved to support Malofeyev: de Pahlen sat on the board of the St Vasily the Great Foundation, and Goutchkov on that of a Malofeyev-linked company.[55] In 2011 Trubetskoy was anointed chairman of Svyazinvest, the state telecoms giant that was subsumed into Rostelecom, which was part-owned by Malofeyev.[56] He also sat on the management board of the St Vasily the Great Foundation, while Shchegolev, as Putin's minister for communications, oversaw Malofeyev's business progress.

Without their patronage, Malofeyev might never have got anywhere. They seemed at first to keep a distance as his St Vasily the Great Foundation expanded into Eastern Europe. In the Czech Republic, Malofeyev appeared to run a chaotic campaign to cultivate anti-Western politicians of any political stripe, handing out at least 100,000 euros to a Belarus-born political fixer who attempted to orchestrate the rise to power of pro-Russian groups there, according to leaked emails between the two men.[57] But the leaks exposed only the surface of what was already a sophisticated operation, in which Malofeyev was just one of a web of players. Yakunin, for example, had courted the politician Miloš Zeman long before his election as Czech president in 2013, while Martin Nejedly, the head of the Czech branch of Lukoil, a major Russian oil company loyal to the Kremlin, was a key adviser to Zeman, and a co-founder of the political party that funded Zeman's presidential campaign.[58] The employees of companies owned by one of the Swiss lawyers in the Bank Rossiya/ Roldugin slush fund were also major backers of Zeman,[59] who became a consistent supporter of Putin's Kremlin: he was one of the first EU leaders to publicly call for EU sanctions against Russia to be rolled back.

In Hungary, Kremlin interests were being supported in the rapid rise of the far-right Jobbik Party, whose fortunes had been transformed since it was struggling on the fringes in 2005. The leaked emails showed that Malofeyev's political fixer was working with Jobbik as well.[60] But the catalyst that turned it into Hungary's biggest opposition party was the arrival, apparently out of nowhere, of an enigmatic Hungarian businessman named Béla Kovács, who after years working in Russia joined the party and then promptly saved it from the brink of bankruptcy.[61] Kovács insisted he'd bailed it out with his own funds, but in 2014 Hungarian prosecutors began an investigation into whether he was an agent of the KGB, and the European Parliament was sufficiently convinced to strip him of his immunity as an MEP. The investigation, however, went nowhere: the Hungarian president Viktor Orbán had also become a close ally of the Kremlin.

By supporting political groups on both the far left and right, the Kremlin was latching on to and stoking a rising wave of discontent in Eastern Europe. Now that the former countries of the eastern bloc had been EU members for almost a decade, the lustre of the West and liberalism was beginning to wear off. The yearning for consumer goods after the shortages of the planned economy had long been sated, and Eastern Europe was filled with shining shopping malls and the latest-model iPhones. But the consequences of joining the EU's liberal order of free movement were deeply felt, and the ghosts of the Soviet past – the network of agents who once worked with the KGB – still pervaded society.

When Russia, fresh from helping to split Ukraine, waded into the Middle East, launching a bombing campaign in Syria in 2015 to protect the regime of long-time Kremlin ally Bashar al-Assad, Europe's problems only deepened. The bombing further fuelled an already substantial tide of hundreds of thousands of refugees seeking safe haven in Europe. In 2015, more than a million fled Syria to Europe. For Putin's Kremlin, this presented an opportunity to stoke unrest, hatred and opposition to the ruling liberal order. The Kremlin's tactics found especially fertile ground in Eastern Europe, where the spread of economic wealth was extremely uneven, and the conservative call of the Russian Orthodox Church against the liberal freedoms of the West found a ready ear.

In Geneva, the Swiss banker close to Timchenko, Jean Goutchkov, openly dreamed of the creation of a Slavic Europe that would merge Poland, the Czech Republic, and Bulgaria with Russia and Ukraine, extend to Hungary, and splinter away from the French- and German-dominated EU.[62] In May 2014, at the height of the Ukraine crisis, Goutchkov claimed that the European Union was doomed and that the French and German leaders wanted to create a new Europe without the troublesome new members from the east. It was only the start of a process that Putin's men hoped would fracture the EU.

Expanding the tactics it had begun in the East, the Kremlin began sinking resources deep into the West. The Geneva money men, for instance, had long forged ties to the top of the French elite, in particular with the aristocracy. When Gennady Timchenko began to build a relationship with France's most important energy major, Total, the way was open to further entrench Russian influence at the top of French society. In 2009 Alain Bionda, an avuncular Geneva lawyer who worked closely with Goutchkov and Timchenko, had wined and dined two of Total's top executives just as Timchenko was buying into Russia's second-biggest gas producer, Novatek, while in early 2013 Goutchkov attended a breakfast meeting with François Hollande on his first visit to Moscow as French president.[63]

With the help of his Geneva associates, Timchenko cemented these ties by selling a 12 per cent stake in his Novatek and a 20 per cent stake in the company's liquefied natural-gas project to Total for $4 billion. Two years later, Timchenko was awarded France's highest honour, the Légion d'honneur. He had also been elected to chair the economic council of the Franco-Russian Chamber of Commerce, a trade body that soon became filled with France's most senior industrialists as well as the top members of Putin's KGB capitalism, including Andrei Akimov, the KGB-connected head of Gazprombank, and Sergei Chemezov, Putin's KGB comrade from the Dresden days who now headed Russia's state arms monopoly.[64] As the West moved to sanction Russia following its incursion into Crimea, Timchenko and Akimov remained off the EU sanctions list, despite being targeted by the US, while Chemezov somehow remained on the board of the economic council despite facing EU sanctions. Total called for sanctions to be lifted, full stop.

Russia's efforts were not based only on forging business ties, or on attempts to split Western unity on sanctions. Through state agencies like Rossotrudnichestvo and Russky Mir, a network of think tanks had begun putting down roots deep into Paris. Russia's Institute for Democracy and Cooperation set up shop on a quiet street in the 7th Arrondissement in 2008. It was meant to be Russia's answer to the US's Carnegie Endowment for International Peace, countering negative Western views of Russia and ending what one of its founders said was 'the Western monopoly' on defining human rights and Russia's observance of them. This was part of a PR offensive that began when Putin's government set up Russia Today, the global English-language TV network aimed at challenging the hegemony of Western channels such as CNN and the BBC.[65] But there was nothing on the stately stone building the institute supposedly occupied to indicate its presence, while its head was a barely concealed Russian intelligence agent – a high-ranking former Soviet-era United Nations diplomat named Natalia Narochnitskaya, who according to one former senior Russian intelligence officer had been working for the KGB since Soviet times. The sharp-suited, bird-like brunette had been a protégée of the spymaster Yevgeny Primakov at the Institute for World Economy in Moscow during the time of the *perestroika* reforms.[66] While her institute did its bit for propagating the world view of Putin's KGB men, it also had a sideline in targeting and recruiting future agents of influence.[67] Its funding was obscure – one of its founders could tell the US ambassador to Moscow no more than that it would be supported by, among others, 'ten businessmen'.[68]

Narochnitskaya was close to Vladimir Yakunin, who through his Russian Orthodox charity, the Foundation of Andrei the First-Called, and his think tank 'The Dialogue of Civilisations', was building ties deep into European political circles, including to the top of France's Republican Party, with which Serge de Pahlen was also connected. In May 2014 de Pahlen and I spoke in his office in Geneva, on the desk of which were strewn a few books from the publishing house he ran (behind which stood an impenetrable investment fund). He told me the days of US hegemony were over. 'US soft power is failing,' he said, a gentle giant as he stooped over his desk. 'They already don't have it. The days when it dominated the EU are over. Now Russia is big, as is China. The US has no credibility today. What they did in Libya, they are doing the same now in Ukraine. Maybe it is not clear to America that they are a power in decline.' When I asked whether he was trying to recreate the European influence networks of the Soviet past, he looked at me incredulously before breaking into a wide grin. 'If you're talking about lobbying, then yes. Everyone does this.'[69]

Just as the Soviet Union had run financing for political allies and parties across Europe through a network of friendly firms to seek to undermine Western unity in the Cold War days, Moscow was now deploying a new web of front men and proxies to fund political parties on the far left and far right across the West. Parts of the old networks, and some of the money men, Goutchkov and de Pahlen among them, remained, and now were receiving a new influx of cash. In France, Moscow's focus was mostly on funding political parties on the far right. Though it found a willing advocate on the far left in Jean-Luc Melenchon (he was already avowedly anti-US and anti-NATO without much prodding from Moscow), it was quick to open credit lines for the Front National of Jean-Marie le Pen and his daughter Marine. This source of funding was again made through proxies to give the Kremlin plausible deniability, but some of them were becoming easier to spot. In November 2014, for example, it emerged that Front National had borrowed 9.4 million euros from a Czech bank with links to Gennady Timchenko.[70] (Timchenko's lawyers said he played no role in the bank's decision and had never been involved in the bank's management nor had he ever been a beneficiary of it.) Konstantin Malofeyev, meanwhile, helped set up a further deal to lend 2 million euros to Jean-Marie le Pen.[71] In another instance, a French documentary film-maker shot footage of le Pen entering Malofeyev's Marshall Capital office in Moscow, and later leaving with an aluminium case. The presumption was that it had been stuffed full of cash, an allegation le Pen (and Malofeyev) hotly denied.[72]

The activity was becoming dizzying. Moscow had long been securing support across Europe. In Germany, Putin had a staunch ally in former chancellor Gerhard Schröder, who was richly rewarded for his labours defending Putin's actions in Ukraine and Syria, and his clampdown on democracy at home. Together with Matthias Warnig, Putin's close ally from the Stasi, Schröder was on the board of the Nord Stream gas pipeline consortium, a Russia-led 14.8-billion-euro project to export gas directly from Russia under the Baltic Sea, bypassing Ukraine. In Italy, Putin had long had a friend in Silvio Berlusconi. The two men holidayed in Sardinia together, and Berlusconi was a frequent guest at Putin's Sochi residence. Berlusconi was also a member of a financial and influence network that had existed back in Soviet times. In the late eighties his Fininvest publishing house won air time from the Soviet state television corporation to broadcast Italian films.[73] He also worked closely with the banker Antonio Fallico, who knew the Communist Party's foreign funding operations intimately, and whose Intesa Bank continued to be a major financial backer of Putin's KGB capitalism. When an apparent attempt by a Gazprom-linked intermediary to funnel money Berlusconi's way was uncovered by the Italian parliament, politicians in both Berlusconi's party and the opposition told the US ambassador in Rome that they believed it was not the only Kremlin scheme intended for Berlusconi's personal benefit.[74]

While these relationships had long been known about, Russia's activities in the West were clearly entering a much more active phase. Across Europe, Malofeyev was promoting a right-wing populist agenda, a rebellion against the liberal establishment. In June 2014 he hosted a conference for right-wing forces in Vienna at which Marine le Pen's niece Marion had mingled with the leaders of Austria's right-wing Freedom Party and Bulgaria's far-right Ataka party, as well as with Serge de Pahlen.[75] Malofeyev always insisted he was promoting a religious agenda, as a supporter and protector of Christians, not a political one.[76] But the fingerprints of his allies were also everywhere in the rise of Syriza, the radical left-wing party that swept to power in Greece in January 2015: leaked emails revealed that the Eurasianist Alexander Dugin, who worked with Malofeyev, had assisted it on strategy and PR. Malofeyev also developed close ties with the right-wing Independent Greeks headed by Panos Kammenos, a firebrand nationalist who became Greece's defence minister.[77] Kammenos had been a frequent visitor to Moscow, forging a close friendship with Malofeyev, while his Athens-based Institute for Geopolitical Studies had signed a 'memorandum of understanding' for cooperation with the influential Russian Institute for Strategic Studies, which also worked closely with Natalia Narochnitskaya's outfit in Paris and essentially was an arm of Russian foreign intelligence.[78]

None of these activities stopped when the US and Europe imposed sanctions against Russia in March 2014. Instead, Russia only accelerated and intensified its efforts to split the West. Alliances were deepened in Italy, for instance, where another Malofeyev associate worked closely with Gianluca Savoini, a top aide to the head of the far-right Liga Nord party, Matteo Salvini.[79] Together they created the Lombardy Russia Cultural Association, which began promoting Kremlin-friendly right-wing views and then aimed to 'change all of Europe'.[80] Along the way, Savoini explored Kremlin-linked oil deals to fund Liga Nord's election campaign, first discussing sales via a little-known oil company, Avangard – which, according to an investigation by the Italian magazine *L'Espresso*, happened to have the same address as Malofeyev's downtown Moscow office.[81] Savoini then discussed a deal to channel tens of millions of euros to the party through oil sales from Rosneft, via an intermediary, to Italy's Eni.[82] These deals were to be structured in the same way as the KGB-led Communist Party foreign financing deals of old. The oil was to be sold through a middleman at a discounted price, allowing the intermediary to keep the difference and funnel the proceeds (about $65 million over the course of a year) into the coffers of Liga Nord, BuzzFeed reported. 'This is just the same as the financing deals we did through the friendly firms,' said one former senior KGB officer involved in Soviet-era oil trading deals.[83]

Salvini denied that the deal had ever gone ahead. But according to a transcript of the discussions published by BuzzFeed, his aide Savoini had made it clear that the alliance being forged as a result of the proposed deal should become a fulcrum for a pro-Russian coalition across Europe. 'The new Europe must be close to Russia because we want to have our sovereignty,' he said. 'We must not depend on the decisions made by the Illuminati in Brussels or in the US. Salvini is the first man who wants to change all of Europe ... Together with our allies,' he continued, listing other far-right pro-Kremlin parties such as Austria's Freedom Party, the Alternative für Deutschland in Germany and Marine le Pen's Rassemblement National in France. 'We really want to have a great alliance with these parties that are pro-Russia.'[84]

Instead of trying to remove the sanctions by adhering to the Western liberal-dominated, rules-based order, Putin's Russia was going to try and buy its way out of them. But the aim also went much deeper than that. Putin's men were seeking to forge their own bloc within Europe, and subvert the political landscape of the entire continent. And politicians from many far-right political groups were only too willing to receive the Kremlin's black cash and influence. In Austria, the head of the Freedom Party, Heinz-Christian Strache, was forced to resign after a video was leaked of a booze-fuelled meeting at a villa in Ibiza at which he sought political support from a woman who said she was the niece of a Russian gas tycoon.[85] Strache had offered lucrative government contracts in return for support in elections, including via a Russian takeover of Austria's biggest newspaper, the *Kronen Zeitung*. All objections to Russia's rebellion among Western-leaning tycoons had been overridden by Putin and his men long before. In the immediate aftermath of the March 2014 sanctions, Putin met behind closed doors with leading titans of Russian industry. One of them tried respectfully to explain to him that having such sanctions when Russia now existed in a global world was not a good outcome. This opinion was met with fists banged on the table. Putin told them he didn't care whether they liked it or not. 'It will be,' he said, according to a Geneva associate of one of the oligarchs who'd been present.[86] The tycoons might have been personally disappointed, but they had no choice but to accept it. In the euphoria that followed the takeover of Crimea, patriotism trumped everything.

Timchenko, for one, was said by friends to be devastated when he found himself on the US sanctions list. He'd always dreamed of being an international businessman. He packed his bags in Geneva, leaving his ornate mansion in the salubrious lakeside suburb of Cologny. Fearing what he called 'provocations' from the US, perhaps even arrest as the Department of Justice reportedly launched a money-laundering probe into Timchenko's operations,[87] he didn't dare venture westward out of Russia into Europe, even though he'd avoided being on the EU sanctions list. Instead he flew east, to China, where with the help of Alain Bionda, the Geneva lawyer who worked with Timchenko and Goutchkov, he began cultivating ties with the leadership.[88] His Gulfstream private jet had been grounded by the sanctions due to its US make. (Its pilots weren't able to use the built-in navigation maps, and the US Gulfstream corporation annulled its contract to service the plane.)[89] But business otherwise continued largely as usual.

Timchenko's reach into Western policy circles was such that, it seems, he may have found out about the US sanctions ahead of time. A few days before they were announced, a small group of people worked late into the night in Bionda's office in Geneva's financial district, urgently restructuring the holding company of one of Bionda's Russian clients. 'The entire team was here,' said one of those present. 'The room was filled with cigar smoke. One of the clients was getting very worried about the sanctions. He was told he was on the expanded list.'[90] Bionda denied that this activity had anything to do with Timchenko, but when the sanctions were announced the following day, Timchenko's Gunvor oil trader was prepared. It announced that Timchenko had sold his stake in the company to his Swedish business partner Torbjorn Tornqvist, allowing Gunvor to continue operating despite the sanctions. According to one of Bionda's associates, the deal was 'a fronting operation': 'The banks had stopped all credit lines until they made the announcement. The problem was, all their trading is in dollars. But as soon as they announced they'd sold the stake, the problems went away.'[91] (Timchenko said Bionda had no involvement in the transaction and that negotiations on the sale had begun 'long before' the sanctions were announced. Any suggestion the sale was no more than a 'fronting operation' was completely false, he said.)

The sanctions made life more difficult. Bank accounts were opened in China and Hong Kong. Restructurings were undertaken. Jean Goutchkov quietly retired from his post as head of private banking at Société Générale in Geneva, apparently concerned about scrutiny of his ties to Timchenko.[92] 'Today these type of connections put you in jeopardy,' said one of his associates.[93] But the sanctions didn't stop business, or the Geneva money men's influence-peddling. Bionda, for example, had always liked to schmooze titans of the global energy industry through the stake one of his companies owned in the Lotus Formula One racing team. 'If you're in Shanghai or Singapore, it's great for the oil industry executives to come with their mistresses. It's good in this respect,' said one of the Geneva money men.[94] After the sanctions, one of Bionda's connections funnelled money to Britain's Conservative Party.

Through his connections with Timchenko and Goutchkov, Bionda had long been at the nexus between Russian money and power. From his office at No. 1 Place du Port, the gateway to Geneva's financial district, he owned a stake in a company called Genii Energy. His partner in Genii, and in the Lotus Formula One team, was a Spaniard named Gerard Lopez, who'd made his first billion through investment in Skype and who then became close friends with the Russian president, spending time with him at his summer residence, feeding apples to his pets and listening to piano music.[95] Another company Lopez invested in, Rise Capital, soon began receiving billions of dollars in Russian state contracts. As the UK hurtled towards its referendum on membership of the EU in June 2016, Lopez made a surprising donation of £400,000 to the Conservative Party. No questions were asked.[96]

It was part of a flood of Russian cash that had been entering British politics, including from two prominent men with close connections to the KGB who'd also been donating heavily to the Tory Party. One of them was Alexander Temerko, the garrulous onetime Yukos shareholder who'd started out in business at the top of the Russian state-owned arms industry. After remaining in Russia to negotiate with the Kremlin while the other Yukos share-holders fled, he'd acquired British citizenship in 2011, and poured more than £1 million into Tory coffers. Portraying himself as a dissident critic of the Putin regime, in private he continued to praise senior members of the Russian security establishment, including the powerful Security Council chief Nikolai Patrushev. He wined and dined Tory Party grandees, forging a close relation-ship with Boris Johnson, who spearheaded the campaign to leave the EU. In public he claimed to be against Brexit, but privately, from time to time, he would laud it as 'a revolution against bureau-cracy', while all his closest allies were leading Brexiteers. Former business partners said he had long-standing ties with the Russian security services. Leonid Nevzlin, the former leading Yukos share-holder, said Temerko had originally been brought into Yukos for his ties with the Russian 'Federal Security Service and the Defence Ministry', adding that Temerko knew Patrushev 'well'.[97]

But mostly the Russian activity seemed directed at British busi-nessmen who'd appeared out of nowhere to lead funding for the campaign pushing for Britain to leave the EU. One of them was Arron Banks, a brash millionaire who initially made his wealth in the insur-ance business and then expanded into diamond mines in South Africa.

Banks's wife had arrived in the UK in the late nineties as a young Russian woman on a student visa, and had narrowly avoided deportation after suspicions were raised by her first marriage, to a retired merchant seaman more than twice her age.[98] (After being briefly investigated by Special Branch she'd bought the car number plate 'XMI5 SPY'.) Banks was the biggest funder of the Leave.EU campaign, donating £8.4 million. But a parliamentary committee investigating the referendum said he'd never made it clear where this money had come from. The Electoral Commission referred a case to the National Crime Agency, believing it had reasonable grounds to conclude that Banks was not the 'true source' of the funds. But the NCA came back empty-handed, saying it had not found any evidence any laws had been broken.[99] Banks had raised the funds by borrowing £6 million from an Isle of Man company he majority-owned, Rock Holdings Ltd, a loan that the NCA said Banks was legally entitled to take. But both the Electoral Commission and Transparency International slammed the investigation as demonstrating a 'weakness' in UK laws that opened the way for overseas funding into UK politics.[100] Banks has repeatedly and vehemently denied any business connections with Russia. Speculation had first begun to swirl after leaked emails revealed that he met senior Russian diplomats in the months before the referendum, and was offered a series of lucrative Russian business deals, which Banks said he never acted on.[101] While the ultimate source of the Rock Holdings cash may remain unidentified, Banks's closest business partner had his own connections. Jim Mellon, the co-owner with Banks of the sprawling Manx Financial Group (owned by Banks through Rock Holdings), was a founder of an investment fund that made hundreds of millions of dollars investing in the Russian stock market in the nineties. More recently, Mellon continued to hold a near 20 per cent stake in another Russia-focused fund, Charlemagne Capital, that worked closely as a co-investor with the Kremlin's sovereign wealth fund right up until the end of 2016.[102]

The stakes were being placed for division as Europe was heading into its most turbulent time since the end of the Cold War.

*

When we met – in St Petersburg and Moscow, and later in London, where his son had acquired British citizenship – Vladimir Yakunin liked to portray himself and the Putin regime as fighters for conservative values that had been abandoned in the West's pursuit of globalisation. He was the avuncular patriot who just happened to disagree with much of the West.

One of our first meetings was in June 2013, just after the Kremlin-ruled Russian parliament passed legislation banning the distribution of 'propaganda of non-traditional sexual relationships' among minors. The law provoked widespread criticism in Europe for reinforcing Russia's already deep homophobia: gay men were regularly subjected to beatings, and later in Chechnya they would be rounded up, imprisoned and tortured. But Yakunin was proud of the law, and claimed that many European politicians had privately told him they wanted similar legislation. 'Representatives of French social organisations who demonstrated against the same-sex marriage law told me they are looking at Russia as if it is the only stronghold that can stop this depravity,' he said. 'They were not expecting that their words would be conveyed to Putin. They were not counting on any reward. They were just speaking of their despair. I am very often in Greece. Today practically there is not one Greek who if he knows you are Russian would not say, "We are counting on you from the point of view of defence of Orthodoxy." And when I meet with Western partners and politicians they say we objectively understand that today Russia is the leading positive force that can stop humanity from falling into the abyss. This is not flattery of Putin. It is just statement of fact.'[103]

This so-called defence of 'family' values against the tolerance and liberalism of the West was becoming the Putin regime's leitmotif in shoring up support among far-right nationalists and conservatives across Russia, Europe and the US. Yakunin was one of the first of the KGB men close to Putin to make a display of converting to Russian Orthodoxy after spending most of their career defending the officially atheist Soviet state. His charity, Andrei the First-Called, lavished money on restoring Russian Orthodox monasteries and outposts of the Church's empire. Konstantin Malofeyev also claimed to be defending Christian values against Western depravity, and he and Yakunin joined forces to hold an event in Moscow in September 2014 for the World Congress of Families, an obscure US-based anti-gay organisation that was forging close links with America's powerful evangelical movement.[104] Malofeyev told the gathering, which took place despite the new US sanctions regime, and included prominent members of France's Front National and Austria's far-right Freedom Party, that the world was witnessing 'an unprecedented triumph of Orthodoxy', and that Russia was a bastion defending Christian values against the secularism of the West.[105]

Most of this newfound religious zeal was in fact no more than cover. Inside Russia, the joining of Church and state was just another element of the erosion of any remnants of democracy; the swerve to Orthodoxy by the ruling elite enabled them to crack down further on anyone operating outside their system. 'I call them the Orthodox Taliban,' said Lyudmilla Narusova, the widow of Putin's onetime mentor Anatoly Sobchak. 'It's a return to some kind of Middle Ages. They are using religion to undermine the constitution, and the fundamental rights of Russian citizens.'[106]

For Yakunin and others in Putin's inner circle, this tactic had been long ingrained. When Yakunin started out in the KGB, he joined the department fighting against dissidents, against gays, against anyone who thought differently.[107] Now they were using the same tactics to infiltrate Western politics. The link with the World Congress of Families was one of the vehicles that allowed Putin's people to make the leap into the US conservative right. Yakunin was also forging close ties with Dana Rohrabacher, a Republican member of Congress who became well known for his pro-Putin views,[108] while Malofeyev and Serge de Pahlen were building a relationship through the pro-life movement with Rand Paul, the Republican senator whose libertarian father Ron Paul had been an inspiration to the Tea Party.[109]

These tactics were, once again, pulled from the playbook of Soviet times, when the KGB had infiltrated the US anti-nuclear movement and the protests against the war in Vietnam. But now Putin's allies were appealing to base populism, to prejudices against immigrants and minorities. It was a seductive message to many who felt left behind by the rush of globalisation and multiculturalism, and were nostalgic for what seemed like simpler days – a contingent that had been growing in number ever since the 2008 financial crash increased the divide between rich and poor.

But even Yakunin had to admit that what he called a 'battle of civilisations' was in reality no more than a new ideological cover for the same old geopolitical battle for supremacy that Russia had been waging against the West since the onset of the Cold War: 'If before it was a battle of two ideologies – the Communist versus the capitalist . . . today it is the conflict of ideas of a humanist society of traditions versus absolute consumerism. I'm not going to argue with you,' he said, 'that this battle is used by Russia to restore its global position. Of course the battle of ideas is always a form of state policy and should follow a concrete aim. But I should return to Putin's Munich speech,' he said, unable to help referring to the moment in 2007 when Putin first reeled off the deep grievances of his KGB clan against the West: the expansion of NATO to Russia's borders, the anti-missile defence system in Romania and Poland, and the string of colour revolutions that turned former Soviet republics in a Westward direction. 'Putin spoke openly then of what was worrying Russia. He didn't hide it. He didn't send the Russian secret services anywhere . . . He came out and said, "Guys, this is what we're worried about. This is unjust." And after that they made him an outcast. They rejected him. You understand?'[110]

This was the explanation for Russia's increasing activity, the motivation behind the Kremlin's efforts to divide and disrupt the West, to shatter the post-Cold War order. Putin had asked for a seat for Russia at the top table of global security, and felt he'd been resoundingly ignored. While Barack Obama made overtures to Dmitry Medvedev during his term as president, the US administration had kept its distance from Putin and his security men, as if hoping to relegate them to a past era. Putin believed the US had a hand in stirring up the protests against him when he returned to power.

Putin had warned in his Munich speech that the West should take note of the rise of the emerging economies of Russia, India and China. The West had always viewed Russia's economy as a resource-based basket case, incapable of the productivity gains of the West. But to see Russia through that prism was to miss the short-term ambitions of Putin's security men. They didn't particularly care about the economic well-being of their country's people, as long as the economy was secure enough to allow them to hold on to power – and to project power globally. Russia's GDP was now $1.6 trillion, and Putin's KGB men had half as much, or more, stashed away in offshore bank accounts.

This was a point that Yakunin liked to make from time to time, although he was careful to do so a little more subtly. He would tell a story of how in the early days of his presidency Putin and his inner circle met with Zbigniew Brzezinski, the Cold War-era US national security adviser, who mentioned, with a sorry shake of his head, the billions of dollars held in overseas accounts by the Russian elite. Brzezinski asked, if all that money was in accounts in the West, then whose elite was it anyway? – suggesting that they were now under Western control. The Russians had been furious at such comments from a Cold War warrior. But now, Yakunin said quietly, 'the backdrop has changed'.[111] This money was now mostly under the control of Putin's men.

Some commentators have suggested that the leaking of the Panama Papers, with their details of Putin's crony bank accounts, was the reason Putin began meddling in Western politics. But that was to miss the point. The battle of Putin's KGB men with the West had been brewing long before. It was being prepared even before the Soviet Union collapsed, when parts of the KGB sought to preserve their networks after the transition to the market economy, helping factions to later plot and assist Putin in his ascent to power.

'Bush announced victory in the Cold War, and that was it,' said Yakunin. 'If they are the victors, they decided they can dictate. But suddenly it turned out that not everyone is ready to live according to this order. Putin's efforts were rejected out of hand. Now today we are all reaping the fruits of this short-sighted policy of the West.' The sanctions imposed by the West in the wake of Russia's incursion into Ukraine had only deepened and accelerated the standoff, he said. 'You know Russians well. We can be lazy, we can be drunk. We can pierce ourselves until blood comes out. But as soon as there is an external threat, then this is written in our genetic code, independent of whether we are young or old: we fight back. Sanctions did more for unifying Russian society than any information campaign of the Kremlin. Why should we just sit back and wipe ourselves when we are being spat on? Imposing sanctions was like a declaration of war.'[112]

*

As Russia hurtled deeper into standoff with the West, some in the Obama administration became increasingly alarmed about the Putin regime's capacities. One of the most vocal at the time was vice president Joe Biden, who warned of how the Kremlin had generated the ability to direct loyal oligarchs to carry out geopolitical strategic operations, and was using corruption as a power to undermine democratic regimes. 'Corruption is the new tool of foreign policy,' said Biden. 'It's never been as handy and as useful in the hands of nations who want to disrupt and oligarchs that respond to them. It's like the kryptonite of a functioning democracy . . . The stakes are strategic as well as economic, because Russia and others are using corruption and oligarchs as tools of coercion.'[113]

For Western experts on Russia there was a gradual reckoning. Inside the US Department of Justice and the FBI, the first real wake-up calls about the true nature of the Putin regime came first in November 2006, with the excruciating death by polonium poisoning in London of Alexander Litvinenko, a former FSB officer close to Boris Berezovsky, and then with the investigation into the Russian mafia Litvinenko had been working on in Spain. There, with his assistance, prosecutors had rounded up a Russian money-laundering ring that involved leading members of the Tambov organised-crime group, which Putin had worked closely with in the St Petersburg years. What they uncovered, including from wiretaps of the mobsters' phone calls, was flabbergasting. The heads of the group, who included Gennady Petrov, a former shareholder in Bank Rossiya, were in regular contact with leading members of Russian law enforcement. One call to them could deflect a Russian investigation that was getting too close, another could help put pressure on customs officials to allow shipments through the St Petersburg sea port, still a gateway for drug supplies into Europe. Payments to senior law enforcers would get rivals arrested and remove incriminating evidence from government databases, while Petrov was in regular communication with the Russian defence minister, who also hailed from St Petersburg.[114]

Russia, the Spanish prosecutor leading the investigation told his counterparts in the US Department of Justice, was a 'virtual mafia state'.[115] The alliance that began in the St Petersburg mayor's office had extended its power across the whole of Russia, with organised crime entwined with the highest levels of the security services. The Tambov group's activities in Spain included drug running and weapons smuggling: its outpost there, said former military-intelligence officer Anton Surikov, was key to overseeing black channels of arms sales into Syria and Iran.[116]

The growing concerns about the fusion of Russian organised crime with the highest levels of government coincided with an increasing awareness of Russian intelligence activity in the West. In 2010, the FBI rounded up ten Russians it accused of acting as agents for Russian foreign intelligence, including a flame-haired *femme fatale* named Anna Chapman who'd run an online real-estate broker in New York, all the while seeking top-level political contacts. Eight of them were accused of acting under deep cover as 'illegals', assuming fake identities and appearing to live normal American lives. The activities of the spy ring were dismissed by many commentators as demonstrating no more than how much Russian foreign-intelligence capacities had degraded since the end of the Cold War. But for former Western intelligence officers the affair was a sign that the networks of Russia's foreign intelligence were far from moribund. The group they'd arrested was just the 'tip of the iceberg', said one.[117] 'The number of Russian intelligence operatives in the US is much higher than anyone thought,' said another.[118]

But the Obama administration, still intent on the reset of relations with Russia that it had embarked on under the Medvedev presidency, chose to wave aside many of the experts' concerns. 'There was a real interest in the reset,' said Frank Montoya Jnr, the then head of the FBI's counter-intelligence division. 'It was partly based on the thought they could try to influence through Medvedev, and it would be a different world.'[119]

By the time vice president Biden sounded his warning in 2015, the world was soon to discover that the threat posed to Western unity went far deeper than he suggested. The weaknesses of the Western political system had left a deep imprint in society. Increasing inequality and the politics of austerity that followed the 2008 financial crisis had left the West wide open to Russia's aggressive new tactics of fuelling the far right and far left. 'We were seeing a new boldness in Georgia, Crimea and the Baltics,' said Montoya. 'There was a lot of concern that they could turn against us. But that was dismissed, because they'd never done that. But then all of a sudden it exploded.'

When the UK woke up on June 24 2016 to the shock referendum result that put a majority in favour of leaving the European Union, the post-Cold War order entered uncharted territory. In the US, the forthcoming presidential election was also shaping up to be a referendum on the established order. A widespread feeling that the ruling elite had abandoned and forgotten the American heartland and the working class had left the way open for a celebrity real-estate mogul to become the leading Republican candidate. 'If Donald Trump wins, then he'll bury the EU,' said Alexander Temerko, the former Russian arms tycoon who'd cultivated close ties to leading members of the Leave campaign in Britain. 'That will be it for the Transatlantic alliance.'[120]

15

The Network and Donald Trump

*

'You in the West, you think you're playing chess with us. But you're never going to win, because we're not following any rules.'

A Russian mobster to his lawyer

*

'One time, a Soviet agent was sent to the UK and he ran out of money. He was introduced into a poker-playing circle and he decided to play to save his situation. He noticed that when you play poker in the UK, your cards are not normally checked or shown. Everyone takes you at your word as a gentleman. He began to win, because no one was checking his cards. He was winning big money. It's the same situation here.'

A Russian tycoon who'd been among the first wave of illegals sent into the West in the perestroika era

*

When Shalva Tchigirinsky first met Donald Trump at the Taj Mahal casino in Atlantic City in November 1990, he'd been in the West for more than three years.[1] He'd left Russia before the Soviet Union fell, permitted by the government to join his wife, a Spanish citizen who'd been brought up in the Soviet Union and then allowed to leave in a wave of repatriation in the early eighties. But this supposed marriage, by Tchigirinsky's own admission, was a fiction. Long before he left the Soviet Union he'd been befriended by two leading lights of Soviet foreign intelligence. He told people that he'd been hounded by the KGB over his black-market business to such a degree that for five years he never used the telephone. But in fact the Russian spymaster Yevgeny Primakov was like a father to him, while the former head of Soviet military intelligence in the United States, Mikhail Milshtein, was known to him as 'Professor', and he went often to his home. 'He was a general and he was also my friend,' Tchigirinsky told me. 'He loved me very much, and I loved to debate with him on history.'²

Tchigirinsky, an ethnic Georgian with a thick mane of dark hair and a distinguished air, had trained as a doctor in Moscow, but his business was antique-smuggling: he sold ancient icons, paintings and other valuables into the West. While one branch of the KGB pursued him for his black-market activity, top minds in foreign intelligence encouraged and cultivated him, and then helped send him to the West. The dichotomy reflected the broader split in the Soviet security services as, beginning from the time of former KGB chief Yury Andropov, progressives pushed and prepared for a transition to the market as the only way to survive the rivalry with the West, while the old guard fought any sign of change. The progressives cultivated a network of agents in the black market, and funnelled out antiques and then raw materials through them. They turned to organised-crime networks, which sent out representatives in the wave of emigration permitted in the late seventies and early eighties who opened trading businesses in Austria and Switzerland, and then deeper into the West. Security men like Primakov at Moscow's Institute for World Economy, and Mikhail Milshtein at the Institute for USA and Canada, had led in pushing for reforms.³ When the Soviet Union collapsed under the frenetic force of change and the flood of assets into the West, the KGB progressives were to some degree prepared. Their agents were already embedded, the cash networks they'd created – at least in part – still under their control.

Tchigirinsky would never directly admit that he was part of this process. But the story about him leaving Russia to join his wife was no more than a cover, and the identities of the men he hobnobbed with as he made his way in business on the other side of the Iron Curtain, were indications that he had high-level backing.[4] He claimed he lived in poverty for the first few months after his departure from the Soviet Union in 1987: 'I slept on the floor for two months in the flat of my friend.'[5] But that same year he'd set up one of the Soviet Union's first joint ventures from his base in Berlin on the Western side of the Wall, which he began to criss-cross smuggling cigarettes and alcohol to Soviet military bases in the East. He rented a small flat above a casino run by Soviet émigrés just off the Kurfürstendamm, West Berlin's main thoroughfare, and was soon frequenting the grand halls of the Hotel Bristol, near which he set up an office. On the West side of Berlin he had high-level protection, having become friends with the Soviet consul, Rudolf Alexeyev. The year the Wall fell, Tchigirinsky attended the May 9 victory celebrations in Berlin's Spandau Castle with Alexeyev and other Soviet dignitaries.[6]

By the time he met Donald Trump in November 1990, Tchigirinsky had made it. The joint venture he'd set up – almost exactly following the KGB memos for the transition to the market economy – had expanded into trading computers, and then into construction. His contract to build the first business centre for foreign companies in Moscow, which was to house the French energy major Elf Aquitaine, made the eyes of his partners in the Soviet foreign ministry water with joy. Not only could they keep close watch on their foreign tenants, they would receive huge sums from them too. Tchigirinsky was already rich enough to be what the casino industry calls a high roller, and when he entered Trump's Taj Mahal in Atlantic City, he liked what he saw. The Taj Mahal was a vast palace of thirty-nine storeys dripping with chandeliers and gold, and covered with an onion dome. There were hundreds of gaming tables, and elegant lounges, restaurants and bars. 'I saw him for the first time around 3 a.m.,' Tchigirinsky recalled. 'Suddenly there was Trump, and around him were forty people. We were there for three or four days, and every night he would appear at 3 or 4 a.m. It was an unrepeatable project. It was a huge operation. He spent huge money on this. Trump was such an attractive man. He was very polished and full of energy. We were playing in the casino. We already had money by then. We had big money by then. Trump showed us the Taj Mahal, where the cash room was, where the safe was, where the computers were and everything. He lived there, and around him there were many beautiful girls.'[7]

The relationship Tchigirinsky began to forge with Trump that night would form the roots of a network of Russian intelligence operatives, tycoons and organised-crime associates that has orbited Trump almost ever since. The people tied to Tchigirinsky included a Georgian, Tamir Sapir, his business partner Sam Kislin, and an Azeri, Aras Agalarov, who set up some of the first Soviet–American joint ventures and US trading operations before the Soviet fall. They were part of an interconnecting web of figures that became testimony to the enduring power of the black-cash networks created in the final years of the Communist regime. Some of them later joined Trump in real-estate ventures, helping bail him out when he fell into financial difficulty, offering the prospect of lucrative construction deals in Moscow, while Agalarov organised the 2013 Miss Universe pageant in Moscow for him. They were among those who, according to Yury Shvets, later helped 'save Trump from bankruptcy'.[8]

The money flows that went through part of this network to Trump's business operations are yet to be fully uncovered – they remain at the centre of a legal standoff between the Trump Organization and Congress over what records can be disclosed. But some of the contours of Moscow's influence over Trump can be traced. Tchigirinsky, Agalarov, Sapir and his business partner Kislin were among those in the vanguard of the first KGB experiments at funnelling money into the West. They operated in the half-light between the Russian security services and the mob, with both sides using the other to their own benefit. Tchigirinsky faced rumours that he was connected to the Solntsevskaya organised-crime group, which was emerging at the end of the eighties as Russia's most powerful, with ties to the top of the Moscow city government, and which Semyon Mogilevich had worked with as he ran money into the West for the KGB and the mob.[9] Tchigirinsky always denied any links to organised crime ('There is no such thing as organised crime,' he said. 'There's just a group of people who support and protect each other'). But he admitted he knew Mogilevich, as well as another of his close associates.[10] Others in the same network were also closely tied to the group.

Tchigirinsky had been invited to meet Trump that evening by a leading player in the Atlantic City casino industry – a lawyer named Martin Greenberg, who'd drafted New Jersey's casino laws in the early eighties, and had then become president of one of the state's biggest casinos, the Golden Nugget.[11] Greenberg had first met Tchigirinsky a year earlier, in 1989, just as progressives in the KGB's foreign-intelligence arm were stepping up plans to transfer the Communist Party wealth into havens abroad.[12] Together with Alfred Luciani, an assistant attorney general who'd also worked on New Jersey's casino laws, and had then become the Golden Nugget's executive vice president, Greenberg had been drawn to talk business with Tchigirinsky by rumours of the fabled Communist Party wealth.[13] The three men met in the fading glory of the Soviet resort town of Yalta, on the Crimean peninsula, and discussed potential investments, including possibly building a Soviet casino there. But the Americans were also 'looking for investments in their casinos', said Tchigirinsky. 'They'd heard the myth of the Party money, and they decided the casinos would be a good home for it.'

Tchigirinsky denied that the talks resulted in any investment. ('US business is too transparent. It's not possible to do anything,' he said.) But shortly after, he travelled to Atlantic City with one of his foreign-intelligence friends, and Greenberg took him to the Taj Mahal and introduced him to Trump.[14] By that time Tchigirinsky had joined in a business partnership with the son of the man he called 'Professor', the former head of Russian military intelligence in the US, Mikhail Milshtein, who'd taught generations of future intelligence officers. His son Vadim was officially an economist,[15] but he'd also set up a translation agency that looked like a front, where his business partners included a former member of the KGB's elite Alfa special forces and the former Soviet envoy to the UN.[16]

At the time he met Tchigirinsky, Trump had poured so much money – more than $1 billion – into building the Taj Mahal, which he liked to call 'the eighth wonder of the world', that he was deep in debt and facing bankruptcy.[17] Tchigirinsky recalled him saying that the casino business was 'an uphill struggle'. Trump later told *New York Magazine* that in 1990 he was $5 billion in debt, with $980 million in personal guarantees. 'I was worth minus 900 million,' he said. The real-estate market had entered into a downturn, and he told the magazine of how he'd pointed to a blind beggar outside Tiffany's in New York when he was out walking with his wife of the time, Marla Marples, a glamorous blonde beauty-pageant winner, and said to her: 'How would you like to know he's worth $900 million more than me today?'[18]

But by 1992 Trump had achieved a remarkable turnaround. He'd reduced his personal guarantees to $115 million by selling off a string of yachts and planes, and had somehow reached a restructuring on the rest of his debts.[19] In July 1991 the Taj Mahal had entered pre-packaged bankruptcy, but Trump was bailed out by bondholders who agreed to extend his debt payments as long as he gave them 50 per cent of the casino.[20] He'd been helped in the process by two titans of Wall Street: hedge-fund owner Carl Icahn, and Wilbur Ross, who headed the bankruptcy division at the investment bank N.M. Rothschilds.[21] Together, they were reported to have helped herd the bondholders into agreeing the deal. The same Martin Greenberg who'd introduced Tchigirinsky to Trump also had a connection: he represented the bondholders in the restructuring; Tchigirinsky, for his part, admitted he knew Icahn.[22]

Whether Tchigirinsky was involved in the Taj Mahal bondholders' pact we may never know. (He insisted he'd never invested in the Taj Mahal, but at one point when we were speaking of the financial difficulties that were facing the casino at that time, he spoke of the business almost as if it were his own. 'We'd never been in this business,' he said. 'We didn't understand everything about this business then.'[23]) In any case, business at the Taj Mahal soon began to boom again. By September 1992 Trump was boasting of record profits for the house three months in a row, with more than $80 million being reaped in the two preceding months.[24] Russian émigrés had been going there in droves almost ever since it opened, attracted by its bling, the Trump name and the Russian pop stars brought in to perform there. Russian high rollers would plunk down $100,000 a visit, and receive the special treatment reserved for favoured customers,[25] including plush hotel rooms, free food and alcohol, and chauffeur services in stretch limousines or even helicopters. The Taj Mahal was also a place where few questions were asked, and it became a favoured venue for laundering cash. The US Treasury's Financial Crimes Enforcement Network later found that it had regularly failed to report suspicious transactions and file the reports it was required to make whenever a customer gambled more than $10,000 in a twenty-four-hour period.[26]

It became a favourite haunt of Vyacheslav Ivankov, or 'Yaponchik', the feared associate of the Solntsevskaya group with the ice-cold eyes and the violent temper who'd landed in New York in March 1992 after Mogilevich, in partnership with the KGB, helped win him early release from the Russian jail where he'd served ten years for forgery and drug trafficking.[27] The FBI believed Yaponchik was leading an international criminal organisation out of his base in Brighton Beach, dealing in drugs, extortion and murder, and overseeing the US interests of the Solntsevskaya.[28] Agents eventually tracked him down to a luxury condo in Trump Tower in Manhattan, and then to the Taj Mahal, to which he made nineteen visits while under surveillance between March and April 1993, gambling $250,000 there.[29]

Trump had survived his first threat of bankruptcy, and the Russians were among those who had helped him do so. The Taj Mahal became such a popular spot for Russian émigrés that part of a Russian movie was filmed there, a comedy that featured a casino owned by the Russian mob.[30]

While Trump climbed out of near-bankruptcy, Tchigirinsky stayed close by. He grew close to the Sotheby's owner Alfred Taubman and his son-in-law Louis Dubin, a New York real-estate developer who was friends with Trump.[31] He hired one of Trump's top executives, Louise Sunshine, who'd served as the Trump Organization's executive vice president, and he nearly bought Mar-a-Lago, Trump's palatial estate in Palm Beach, Florida – he decided against it, he said, because Taubman warned there were too many low-flying planes. He hobnobbed with Steve Wynn, the Golden Nugget casino owner who was in turn a rival and then a close friend of Trump.

The hundreds of millions of dollars the charming and debonair Tchigirinsky made as he expanded his businesses in Moscow had won him easy entrée into US high society.[32] He was working in close cooperation with Yury Luzhkov's Moscow city government, even sharing an office with senior officials of the city's new construction department. Together with Milshtein and Yelena Baturina, the wife of Moscow's mayor, he became an owner of the Moscow oil refinery, which supplied most of the city and the surrounding region through a lucrative contract with BP.[33] The refinery was contracted to sell at least $800 million worth of oil-product exports through Tchigirinsky's enigmatic fellow Georgian associate Tamir Sapir in New York.[34]

Sapir had emigrated from the Soviet Union to New York in 1975, becoming a pioneer in the first KGB-backed oil trade operations there.[35] He'd worked first as a taxi driver and then providing an exclusive clientele of Soviet officials and KGB officers with the latest in American electronic goods. In those years he'd operated from a store called Joy Lud in the centre of Manhattan, whose customers included Soviet foreign minister Eduard Shevardnadze and Yevgeny Primakov. But the shop became a front for a much bigger operation, which granted Sapir lucrative licences to trade large amounts of Soviet fertiliser and oil products. Soon he became a billionaire. His partner in the business was Sam Kislin, a barrel-chested émigré from the Ukrainian port of Odessa who also traded in metals with Mikhail Cherney, one of the first alleged mobsters to transfer Soviet wealth through KGB-linked firms. Neither of them would have been able to run such operations out of New York without the explicit support and involvement of the KGB.[36] Kislin had met Trump as long ago as the seventies, when he gave Trump a loan for seven hundred television sets, he later said.[37]

Later, Sapir and a business associate of Kislin, a former Soviet trade official named Tevfiq Arif, were to join forces to bankroll the construction of a Trump Tower in Manhattan, SoHo, just at the time when Trump most needed cash. Kislin, meanwhile, went on to forge a close relationship with the New York mayor Rudy Giuliani, later Trump's personal attorney.

Agalarov

The Moscow billionaire who was later to invite Trump to hold the 2013 Miss Universe beauty pageant in Moscow – and would set up a fateful meeting between Trump and a mysterious Moscow lawyer promising dirt on Hillary Clinton's presidential candidacy – was Tchigirinsky's protégé, the construction tycoon Aras Agalarov. An imposing former Communist Party official born in the Soviet republic of Azerbaijan, Agalarov had been chosen to set up another of the first Soviet joint ventures under the KGB memos for the transition to the market economy. He'd been among the few allowed by the KGB to leave for the US, where in 1989 he founded the US–Soviet joint venture Crocus International. 'He is my pupil,' said Tchigirinsky. 'I've known him for a long time.'[38] Tchigirinsky went on to hastily explain that he meant he'd taught Agalarov everything he knew about the construction business. But for most of the nineties, before he'd gone into construction in Moscow, Agalarov remained in the US, running an import-export business out of a small office in midtown Manhattan and then in New Jersey.

Agalarov appeared to be another of the agents recruited by the KGB in the twilight years of the Soviet Union to funnel cash into the West, according to Yury Shvets.[39] 'In those days, any Soviet–American joint venture could be established only with KGB approval,' said Shvets. 'My professional analysis from the point of view of the modus operandi of the Russian security services shows that he was recruited.' Like many joint-venture operators at that time, Agalarov and his partners started out by importing much-needed computer technology into the Soviet Union. They then expanded into trading consumer goods, including from China, into Russia, after the Soviet fall.[40] Agalarov had also acquired a stake in Europe's biggest outdoor market, the Cherkizovsky Rynok, a vast warren of plywood shacks on the outskirts of Moscow that gained a reputation as a Mecca for Chinese imports and smuggled goods, and as a 'state within a state' with its own 'police, customs service and courts', and legions of migrant workers.[41] Agalarov's co-owners of the market included other Azeri associates of Tevfiq Arif, the former Soviet trade official who later bankrolled the construction of the Trump Tower in SoHo.[42]

As Agalarov's US-based import-export business began to grow in the nineties, one of his closest partners in the US became the subject of a money-laundering probe. American officials were becoming aware of the Russian black cash that was starting to flood into the country, and suspected Irakli Kaveladze of being involved. According to Yury Shvets, the dapper ethnic Georgian was an 'illegal' – an agent the Russian intelligence services were seeking to infiltrate into America, where it was intended that he gain US citizenship.[43] If initially the KGB had mostly focused its efforts on developing an elaborate programme for its 'illegal' operatives to take on the stolen identities of real Western citizens, once emigration from the Soviet Union began to grow from the seventies onwards, it also sought to cultivate agents among the emigrants. Kaveladze was one of them, said Shvets. In 1989, at the age of twenty-eight, after graduating from the prestigious Moscow Finance Institute, he was allowed to travel to the US, where he became close to an American family in Gettysburg, Pennsylvania. Two years later, he acquired US citizenship: apparently he'd been 'adopted' by the mother of the family, Judith Shaw. (When she died in 1993, at the age of forty-nine, her obituary described Kaveladze as her 'adopted son'.[44]) 'He was sent there under the immigration line,' said Shvets. 'Soviet intelligence had always envied the Chinese and Mossad. You could go to any country, and there would always be a big contingent of Chinese and Jewish diaspora. They could always go to their countrymen. Before the collapse of the Soviet Union, there was a huge wave of emigration that was under the control of the KGB. Kaveladze was sent out as an émigré.'[45] (Kaveladze, himself, failed to respond to requests for comment.)

For nearly a decade, Kaveladze served as the vehicle for transferring more than $1.4 billion in Russian and East European black cash into US bank accounts.[46] After graduating, he'd fast been hired as a vice president at Agalarov's Crocus International joint venture, and in October 1991 his newly acquired US citizenship allowed him to start opening a web of US bank accounts. He set up his own venture, International Business Creations, which shared a midtown Manhattan address with other Agalarov outfits, and through which US investigators later found he had opened accounts for more than a hundred suspicious Russian clients at a pillar of the US financial system, Citibank, and a hundred more at the Commercial Bank of San Francisco, which was part-owned by a Latvian also alleged to have links with the KGB.[47] Citibank later admitted to investigators that Kaveladze had opened these accounts without his Russian clients ever having to appear in person, or provide evidence of their business activities.[48] Kaveladze also registered about two thousand corporations in Delaware for Russian clients he claimed to know little about – not even their true identities.[49]

According to a former Kremlin official, part of the cash flow stemmed from a billion-dollar slush fund created by an outfit known as the Russian National Sports Fund,[50] which in the mid-nineties was given the right by Yeltsin to import alcohol and tobacco into Russia tariff-free. The fund became a black hole for smuggling, and was linked to senior security service officials of the Yeltsin era, including Yeltsin's bodyguard Alexander Korzhakov. What most troubled one of the US investigators examining the Kaveladze-created accounts was that no cash had ever been transferred through some of them, while other companies were used to make transfers only once. It was as if cells were being set up for future operations, said a person familiar with the investigation. 'He was setting up so many goddamn corporations. He uses them when he needs them – just like they were burner phones.'[51]

The Kaveladze accounts were just the tip of the iceberg. Some of the transfers through the Commercial Bank of San Francisco were found to be connected to a much bigger operation: the $7 billion Bank of New York money-laundering scandal.[52] Essentially, the funds Kaveladze handled were part of the flow of Russian black cash that had been flooding into the US since before the Soviet collapse – and much of the architecture of the transfer system appeared to be run by the KGB and the Russian mob.

The Bank of New York cash channel was linked to the Russian mobster Semyon Mogilevich, whom Shvets described as an 'especially important agent for Russian foreign intelligence', and who'd long been running money into the West for the Solntsevskaya and the KGB. But after the scheme had been exposed in the summer of 1999, the scandal had soon been forgotten. There was no real criminal investigation, and the scheme was brushed aside as mostly tax and customs evasion by everyday Russian business. The architects of the scheme's connections to Mogilevich and the Russian security services were papered over, as were possible links with US brokerages, and stock-fraud scams. To Shvets, this was a fatal mistake. The West had been blinded by what it believed was its victory in the Cold War: 'They thought Russia was finished forever . . . They didn't care about stealing, just as long as it wasn't too visible. When Bush Senior said the Cold War is over and a new era of cooperation is beginning, that was it. But the Russians used cooperation to deceive the US. The Americans, they're like children. If you're cooperating, you're cooperating. That's it, and no questions are asked – even if the Russians are holding a brick behind their backs.'[53]

The way had been left open for the Russian intelligence services and their partners in organised crime to find other ways to funnel money into the US. Later, a new generation of shadow bankers linked to the same mob and the KGB invented the Moldovan Laundromat and the mirror-trade schemes. But before that, according to Shvets and a former Mogilevich associate, it seems one of the channels they focused on were the business operations of Donald Trump.[54] 'They needed to find more subtle ways to launder cash through businesses and not directly through US banks,' said Shvets. 'And there was Trump and his financial problems – it was a solution that was very much on time.'[55]

There's no evidence that Trump was aware there might be any issues with the former Soviet businessmen who began to line up in the early 2000s to offer him lucrative business deals. The Trump Organization's chief counsel, Alan Garten, said he'd had no reason ever to question the source of funds.[56] But in those days Trump was still mired in debt. He'd already escaped personal bankruptcy in the early nineties, but had been forced to sell prized properties like the Plaza Hotel and a prestigious development project on the Upper West Side of Manhattan, as well as part of the Taj Mahal casino.[57] The ownership of the rest of his vast real-estate empire was murky at best, and he was still wrestling with nearly $2 billion in bond debts owed by his casino and hotels group, Trump Hotels and Casino Resorts.[58] Western banks – apart from Deutsche Bank – had become wary of lending money to him. Instead, one by one, a string of former Soviet businessmen came to him with proposals to build a succession of Trump Towers. For the first time, Trump was being offered handsome licence and management fees just for the honour of featuring his name on the buildings. In at least one case, he would receive an 18 per cent equity stake without making any investment at all. The deals could not have been more serendipitous for Trump. And few questions were asked. 'Donald doesn't do due diligence,' a former senior Trump Organization executive, Abe Wallach, said later.[59]

Most of the businessmen who came to Trump then were connected to the same nexus of KGB-linked money men, some with ties to the Solntsevskaya group. There was Shalva Tchigirinsky's Georgian associate Tamir Sapir. There was Tevfik Arif, a former Soviet trade official with connections to Aras Agalarov, backed by a trio of Kazakh metals tycoons who'd earlier joined in business with an alleged associate of the Solntsevskaya group. There was Alex Shnaider, the metals-trading son-in-law of an alleged Solntsevskaya associate who'd funnelled out Communist Party cash in the twilight years of the Soviet regime.

The charm and the cash offensive of this network started with the son of an associate of Semyon Mogilevich, who'd grown up in Brighton Beach, the New York enclave that was home to Russian émigrés and mafia gangs.

Sater

When Felix Sater first approached Donald Trump sometime in 2001, he'd already lived several lives, and by his own admission he'd long

been working with senior figures in Russian intelligence.[60] The pugnacious former stockbroker with the face of a boxer had left the Soviet
Union with his family at the age of eight, part of the wave of Jewish
emigration permitted in the early seventies. They set up home in
Brighton Beach, where according to two former Mogilevich associates, Sater's father, Mikhail Sheferovsky, became an 'enforcer' for
some of Mogilevich's interests there.[61] Sater was brought up in a
world where gangland shootings and turf wars between mafia groups
were commonplace. It was also a world where Russian organised
crime was expanding into white-collar crime, forging alliances with
Italian crime families – first to sell bootlegged petrol, then into the
diamond industry in Sierra Leone, then into stock manipulations,
fraud, and elaborate commodity-trading schemes, as well as the
more standard gun and drug trafficking.

Sater would claim he'd never been involved in any of that. But
when we spoke, he could not disguise his pride in his background.
'Me and my friends grew up in Brooklyn, and being afraid was not
something that was the first thing on your mind,' he told me, puffing
up his chest. 'I would say it's a pretty unique group of people.'[62] Not
long after starting out as a stockbroker at a series of Wall Street
firms, he ran into problems with the law. In 1991 he wound up in
jail for fifteen months for stabbing a commodities broker in the face
and neck with the broken stem of a cocktail glass. Then he escaped
charges for running a $41 million 'pump and dump' stock-fraud
scheme in collusion with members of the Gambino and Gravese
Italian crime families, contacts he had made through his father's
connections.[63] Through two New York brokerages he co-founded,
Sater and his partners had secretly acquired large blocks of stock,
and then artificially inflated their price by paying off brokers to issue
false statements and deploying the muscle of the Italian crime families.[64] Some of the brokerages involved had been investigated for
links to the Bank of New York money-laundering scheme.[65] When
that scheme collapsed in 1996, Sater left New York for Moscow,
where his Brighton Beach connections helped him make friends at
the top of Russian intelligence. He claimed he'd gone to Russia as a
consultant for the US telecoms firm AT&T, to negotiate a $100

million deal to rent out a transatlantic cable to the United States, and that it was through this proposed deal that he came into contact with high-level officers from Russian military intelligence, who controlled the country's telecoms.[66] But he would never have gained such access so fast had it not been for his connections in Russian organised crime. Those connections included Mogilevich, who collaborated with Russian foreign intelligence, according to Yury Shvets and a former close Mogilevich associate who knew Sater then.[67]

In January 1998, soon after the FBI in New York uncovered a stash of documents revealing his involvement in the stock-fraud scheme, Sater contacted US intelligence officers in Moscow and offered his cooperation.[68] He would supply top-grade information on the activities of the Taliban and the Northern Alliance in Afghanistan, where Russian intelligence operatives and organised crime had long been active. For Sater – and for Russian intelligence – it was the beginning of a beautiful friendship. Sater first provided information on lost Stinger missiles the US government had long been trying to trace, even providing their serial numbers, and relaying the information that they were in the hands of the Northern Alliance, who now wanted to sell them.[69] Then, after providing further information including the coordinates of Al Qaeda camps and what he said were five satellite-phone numbers belonging to Osama bin Laden, he returned to the US to give himself up. On his arrival he made a deal with the FBI that enabled him to avoid the charges – and a potential twenty-year jail sentence – for the stock-fraud scam. Instead, he won plaudits for what became ten years of fruitful cooperation with the FBI.[70]

But Sater was also following a time-honoured tradition. Ever since Soviet times, Russian mafia associates from Brighton Beach had offered themselves as FBI informants in exchange for criminal charges being dropped.[71] But Sater's organised-crime and Russian intelligence contacts should have set alarm bells ringing. He'd even helped the FBI uncover the stock-fraud scheme, leaving a stash of documents in a safety deposit box he failed to pay for and then helping agents decipher them.[72] When we met in May 2018 he told me his Russian intelligence contacts, including in military intelligence, the GRU, agreed to provide him with information because they were desperate for cash. 'The GRU weren't worried about spying on America then. They worried only about making money. They weren't exactly financially savvy, and I was someone who worked on Wall Street, spoke fluent Russian and English and understood finance – and I was talking to them about a deal that would make $100 million.' That deal never came off, and Sater could not explain what – if any – money he ever paid them.

According to Yury Shvets, Sater's top-level contacts in Russian intelligence were following a time-honoured tradition, dating back to Soviet times – funnelling information through an asset in order to raise his standing and influence. It would have been impossible for Sater to gain access to such information without the active co-operation and assistance of high-ranking members of Russian intelligence and organised crime. Shvets said he believed Sater's connections stemmed from an alliance with Mogilevich and Shabtai Kalmanovich, another KGB-linked Solntsevskaya associate, who'd been jailed by the Israelis in the eighties for spying for the Soviets: 'Kalmanovich decided everything for Sater.'[73] Mogilevich and Kalmanovich were at the centre of an arms-smuggling empire that traded weapons with all sides – with the Taliban and their opponents the Northern Alliance – and carried out tasks for Russian intelligence. According to a former Mogilevich associate who knew him then, Sater had never set foot in Afghanistan, and the information on bin Laden's phone numbers and the missing Stinger missiles 'would have most likely come from Seva'.[74]

Ever since childhood, Sater had been part of a vicious world in which to survive was to play a double or even triple game, changing one's mask according to the circumstances. 'Everyone has many faces, and it is very difficult for us to know which is true and which is not,' said another former associate of Mogilevich. 'They had to be like this to survive.'[75] Theirs was a world of backroom deals and an underground economy which had operated in the shadows since Soviet times, where a single misstep could land you a lifetime in jail, or more likely a bullet in the head.

Sater insisted he'd never had any contact with Mogilevich, nor had the mobster ever assisted him in his dealings tracing weapons and Al Qaeda camps for the FBI. Any suggestion he was connected to Mogilevich: 'I am telling you it is complete and utter bullshit. It's a complete fucking lie. I wouldn't know him if he came and sat down next to us.'[76] However, he could not help bragging that his connections went higher than that: 'Any claim I'm associated with Mogilevich is kind of insulting. I am active on a much higher level than him.'[77]

In fact, Sater's ties extended into the new generation of Russian mobsters who took over some of the illicit black-cash transfer schemes after Mogilevich was exposed in the Bank of New York scandal. His closest friend since childhood was Yevgeny Dvoskin, the shadow banker who'd worked in close cooperation with a senior FSB general to become an architect of many of the new money-laundering schemes of the 2000s –the Moldovan Laundromat and the Deutsche Bank mirror trades – that funnelled tens of billions of dollars of illicit transfers into the West.[78] The two had grown up together on the same block in Brighton Beach, Brighton Twelfth Street.[79] 'I knew him very well,' said Sater. 'I knew his first wife and then I knew his second wife. I grew up with him. He is an old and dear friend of mine.'[80]

Sater was proud of his connection to Dvoskin, who, he said, 'wouldn't even piss on Mogilevich if he was on fire'. He told of how Dvoskin had worked closely with Ded Hasan, another powerful Russian mobster, who was later shot dead in a Moscow restaurant. When I naïvely asked if he hadn't been worried when his best friend was doing business with Ded Hasan, Sater snorted scornfully, 'Look at what happened to Ded Hasan. They were the ones who should have been worried doing business with [Dvoskin].'[81]

*

By the time he met Donald Trump in 2001, Sater had joined forces in business with the former Soviet trade official Tevfik Arif.[82] Arif had made his money trading chrome from Kazakhstan as an agent for Mikhail Cherney's metals trader, TransWorld Group. He'd then forged a close partnership with a group of Kazakh metals tycoons known as 'the trio', led by Alexander Mashkevich, who started out in business working for Boris Birshtein, an alleged Solntsevskaya associate.[83] (Mashkevich did not respond to requests for comment.) Arif 'was doing business with Mashkevich. They've known each other for twenty or thirty years,' said Sater. 'It was Transworld . . . and Mikhail Cherney. He was working with Cherney in the beginning.'[84]

Sater claimed he'd known Arif for only three months before he agreed to go into business with him. They'd met, he said, because Arif was his neighbour in Sands Point, an exclusive Long Island enclave, once home to William Randolph Hearst and the Guggenheims, that had been the model for *The Great Gatsby*'s East Egg.[85] Together they set up a real-estate development firm called the Bayrock Group, and moved into an office one floor below the Trump Organization head-quarters in Trump Tower at 725 Fifth Avenue, staffed with 'eye-catching' women from Eastern Europe.[86] One of Trump's managers started stopping by, and soon he was providing an introduction for Sater to Trump.[87] The way Sater tells it, the meeting was spontaneous and on his initiative: 'I walked into his office and told him, "I'm going to be the biggest developer in New York City." He laughed. I think he enjoyed my Trumpesque approach. We started working together right away.'[88]

Sater and Arif offered Trump a deal he could hardly refuse. The Bayrock Group would take on the financing and construction of a series of luxury developments, paying Trump a licence fee for the honour of using his name.[89] A luxury condominium-hotel resort at Fort Lauderdale in Florida was announced at the end of 2003.[90] There would be the $200 million Trump International Hotel and Residence in Phoenix, Arizona, purchased by Bayrock at around the same time.[91] Then, in 2005, Bayrock bought a site on an up-and-coming street in Manhattan's SoHo that would become Trump SoHo, a $450 million forty-six-storey glass tower of luxury and excess, of condos, a hotel and Fendi furniture.[92] Trump was to be given an 18 per cent equity stake in the project, and a steady stream of manage-ment fees, despite not having to contribute a cent.[93] The deals couldn't have come at a better moment for Trump. By 2004 the casino and hotels branch of his empire was filing for Chapter 11 bankruptcy protection and another restructuring deal.[94]

The tie-up also provided potential benefits for Bayrock. Real-estate developments offered a way around the stricter US banking regulations imposed following the Bank of New York scandal and the September 11 terror attacks. 'They couldn't easily bring money in through shell companies any more,' said Jack Blum, a Washington lawyer specialising in white-collar financial crime. 'But the money then flowed into real estate in Miami, New York and London. Real estate was exempt from any kind of reporting of suspicious activity. All of a sudden you had these luxury condos springing up. No one asked where the money was coming from. If I'm a crook and looking around for someone to help cover things up, then the whole deal was how about I invest in your real estate. "I'll do the building and you provide the cover. You'll even make some money from it." It became a model for the Trump Organization all over the world.'[95]

It took almost two decades for US Treasury officials to warn that premium US real estate was becoming a vehicle for corrupt foreign officials and transnational criminals to launder dirty money. An investigation by the Treasury in 2018 found that one in three cash buyers of high-end property were suspicious, while most sales at the top of the market took place through companies whose ownership was hidden.[96] And even if those behind the schemes sold apartments at a loss, said a US investigator, they could make a profit by taking a cut for laundering the cash.

For Bayrock's former finance director Jody Kriss, the source of the company's funding became an alarming question. He later claimed in a racketeering lawsuit against Bayrock that its backers included 'hidden interests in Russia and Kazakhstan', and that the company was no more than a front for laundering cash. 'Tax evasion and money laundering are the core of Bayrock's business model,' the lawsuit filed by Kriss initially stated.[97] Bayrock, he claimed, was 'largely a mob-owned and operated business' which had 'access to cash accounts at a chromium refinery in Kazakhstan'.[98] Bayrock denied the claims.

The refinery Kriss was referring to was the sprawling Aktyubinsk

Chromium Chemicals Plant, the world's second-biggest producer of chromium-based chemicals, which belched smoke into the bleak Kazakh steppeland and leaked toxins into the local water supply, making it undrinkable.[99] It was owned by Arif and his brother, who'd served as a senior official in the Kazakh industry ministry in the nineties. In a sign of the close ties that bound this network, the chromium mine that supplied the plant was owned by the Kazakh metals tycoons known as 'the trio', or more officially Eurasian Natural Resources Corporation (ENRC).

The town that surrounded the plant was no more than an impoverished hub for migrant workers. Clearly all the profits were sent elsewhere. Bayrock itself never seemed to run out of cash. Arif and Sater, Kriss alleged, would come up with funds 'month after month, for two years, in fact more frequently, whenever Bayrock ran out of cash'.[100] Every time cash flow started getting tight, according to the lawsuit, the owners 'would magically show up with a wire from "somewhere" just large enough to keep the company going'.[101] But Trump never seemed to ask any questions. In fact, he later admitted in court proceedings that he 'never really understood who owned Bayrock'.

At the same time, Trump began signing similar deals with a string of other former Soviet outfits. In early 2002 an Israeli Soviet émigré, Michael Dezer, and his son Gil signed a licensing deal with Trump for the $600 million Trump Grand Ocean Resort and Residences on a stretch of prime beachfront in Sunny Isles, near Miami.[102] A Reuters investigation estimated that Trump made tens of millions of dollars from the deal, in which the Dezers took on all the costs and risks.[103] In total, more than $98.4 million worth of property in south Florida was bought by Russians in seven Trump-branded luxury towers. Six of them were developed by the Dezers. A third of the more than 2,000 apartments in the seven Trump buildings had been bought through anonymous ownership vehicles – limited liability companies or LLCs. A number of politically-wired second- and third-tier Russian businessmen, or 'minigarchs', including three former state officials, paid out millions of dollars for condos in the Trump developments.[104]

Then there was Alex Shnaider, a thirty-six-year-old Russian-born metals trader who'd made a $2 billion fortune by acquiring a Ukrainian steel mill and then expanding across Eastern Europe into Serbia, Montenegro and Armenia, where he owned the country's electricity grid.[105] Built like a boxer, with close-cropped hair and a square, determined jaw, Shnaider just happened to be the son-in-law of Boris Birshtein, who according to the FBI was an associate of the Solntsevskaya group.[106] In 2003, Shnaider's Midland Resources became the developer for the $500 million Trump International Hotel and Tower in Toronto, a sixty-five-storey block of condos and hotel rooms behind a shining glass façade.[107] In Soviet times his father-in-law had set up Seabeco, the commodities trader which was among the first wave of vehicles set up by the KGB for funnelling Communist wealth into bank accounts in the West.[108] Along the way, he'd also become a key operative for the Solntsevskaya group. According to an FBI report, in October 1995 Birshtein hosted a meeting for Solntsevskaya bosses at his office in the diamond centre in Tel Aviv.[109] Among them were Semyon Mogilevich and the Solntsevskaya chief Sergei Mikhailov. The subject under discussion, the FBI reported, was 'the sharing of interests in Ukraine'.

The FBI was not the only arm of Western law enforcement examining links. Swiss intelligence in a 2007 report also mentioned Birshtein's 'close connections' with the Solntsevskaya,[110] while Swiss police noted that when Birshtein left Seabeco later in the nineties to set up his own operation in Antwerp, Belgium, he established at least one company there, MAB International, with Mikhailov.[111] Birshtein, however, through a lawyer, has denied ever working with the Solntsevskaya.[112] He also established a close connection with the trio of Kazakh metals tycoons who worked closely with Arif and Bayrock. One member of the trio, Patokh Chodiev, founded a branch of Seabeco in Brussels in 1991, while another, Alexander Mashkevich, who started out in the late eighties as a Seabeco vice president, also set up another Brussels-based company with a separate Seabeco associate.[113] Shnaider claimed to be estranged from his father-in-law, but his closest business partner testified in London's High Court that he owed his career to his relationship with Birshtein.[114]

Trump was soon being courted by others who would help him expand further afield. In 2005 a Lebanese importer-exporter with no experience in the property industry, Roger Khafif, approached him with an offer to build the Trump Ocean Club International Hotel and Tower in Panama.[115] The gleaming seventy-storey building was to bring Trump $75 million in fees. The broker brought in by Khafif to sell apartments in the tower was a Brazilian former car salesman named Alexandre Ventura Nogueira, who would later be charged with money laundering.[116] Nogueira, who'd been caught on tape by a former business partner talking about laundering 'drug money', in turn worked closely to sell the Trump Ocean Club apartments with two former Soviet Canadian émigrés, Alexander Altshoul and Stanislau Kavalenka, despite the fact that both faced accusations from Canadian law enforcement of being linked to organised crime.[117] Altshoul had been charged with participating in a mortgage-fraud scheme, while Kavalenka was accused of kidnapping and pimping Russian prostitutes.[118] In both cases, the charges were later dropped.

Alan Garten, the Trump Organization's chief legal counsel, has told Reuters that no one at the company could recall ever having any dealings with Nogueira, nor any involvement in the sale of the apartments. Trump, he said, was merely licensing his brand and providing management services. But for Trump, regardless of who or what was behind them, the deals looked like no-brainers. They became a totem signifying his financial health. When the US was hurtling into the credit crunch at the end of 2007, Trump brandished them as proof that his empire was firmly afloat. 'In an environment when no developers are getting financing for their jobs,' he wrote in a letter to the *Wall Street Journal* in November 2007, 'we have successfully secured financing within the last three months for our Trump International Hotel & Tower in Toronto, Trump SoHo, and Trump International Hotel & Tower in Panama. Those facts are a testament to the strength of the Trump name and brand within the financial community.'[119]

The men who joined Trump in business then were all interconnected, and by the time he was writing the *WSJ* letter they'd indeed taken steps to bring in more financing. In 2006 Tamir Sapir, the denizen of New York real estate who'd made his fortune trading Soviet oil, joined Bayrock in the development of Trump SoHo. And in early 2007 the Kazakh trio, through their holding company ENRC, officially came in as strategic partners to Bayrock who could provide equity financing.[120] Without access to Bayrock's finances, it's not clear what, if any, funding they could have provided. But the network was becoming complete. Shalva Tchigirinsky too was among them. He, Mashkevich, Sapir, Arif and Sater were all friends and associates. They attended the weddings of each other's offspring[121] and all at some point conducted business with Trump.

As the financial crisis came ever closer, Bayrock continued to seek support. In May 2007 it signed off on a $50 million 'loan agreement' with a murky Icelandic financial company, FL Group. This loan would turn into a controlling stake in a new joint venture comprised of Bayrock's interests in four of its projects, including Trump SoHo, just before the projects were expected to pay out to shareholders more than $500 million profits over the following two years.[122] In fact, according to the initial version of the racketeering lawsuit later filed by Bayrock finance director Jody Kriss, the arrangement was intended as a way for Sater and Arif to 'strip' tens of millions of dollars in earnings out of the projects, leaving other creditors high and dry.[123] But this claim was later withdrawn and it's not clear whether cash and assets were transferred into this new venture, leaving the main Bayrock development firm an empty shell, or whether Trump received any share of these profits from the 18 per cent stake he was granted in the Trump SoHo venture. The Icelandic outfit's ownership was part of a tangled web of companies that were persistently rumoured to be connected to Putin's Kremlin, and that were soon to collapse in the financial crisis amid allegations of financial crimes. Jody Kriss, the former Bayrock financial director, later testified that he'd been told by Arif and Sater that FL Group was 'close to Putin'. But the truth seemed buried in the financial crash.[124]

When the cash crunch tightened further, another Russian tycoon appeared on the horizon to help Trump out. In July 2008, on the eve of the crisis, fertiliser magnate Dmitry Rybolovlev agreed to buy a Palm Beach mansion from Trump for $95 million, more than twice what Trump originally paid for it. (Rybolovlev never lived in the property. He eventually demolished the mansion and parcelled up the land for sale.)

Then, when many of these projects went belly-up after the financial crisis, it didn't seem to matter much to any of them. First, Bayrock's development in Fort Lauderdale, on which more than $140 million had been spent on construction, teetered into bankruptcy.[125] In 2009, with the tower still an empty concrete shell, Trump pulled his name from the project, while Bayrock stiffed scores of buyers out of the millions of dollars they'd put down in deposits – as well as the main lender bank. By that time, in any case, Bayrock would appear to essentially transfer a controlling interest in this and other projects to the new FL Group-backed venture.[126] The glitzy development Bayrock had promised in Phoenix, Arizona, had never even got off the ground, locked in conflict with a local investor who alleged Felix Sater had skimmed cash from it.[127] Trump SoHo opened with great fanfare in 2010, but Bayrock and Trump faced lawsuits from buyers alleging they'd been tricked into purchasing units by means of artificially inflated sales figures.[128] Three years later, Trump SoHo went into foreclosure.[129] Four years after it opened in 2012, Alex Shnaider's Trump Tower in Toronto was still three-quarters empty. By 2016 it was bankrupt, while the development company Shnaider founded to build it had gone bankrupt in 2015, defaulting on a $300 million loan from Raiffeisen Bank, the Austrian bank known for its close connections with the Kremlin's ruling elite, and earlier with the black-cash transfers involving Diskont Bank.[130]

If it was all a mirage, Trump had nevertheless benefited massively from undisclosed licence payments and management fees, while the likes of Bayrock and Shnaider had been able to funnel money through the projects and, potentially, still make a killing. 'In a lot of places bankruptcy was very profitable,' said the white-collar-crime lawyer Jack Blum. 'You borrow money from banks for the project and then put it in bankruptcy. You still walk off with the construction money.'[131]

The Dangle

Evan as the US property deals came together, the same network dangled a series of proposals for a grandiose Trump Tower in Moscow, where Trump would again make a hefty percentage for lending his name without putting up any of the construction costs. None of these deals would ever get off the ground, but they were enough to keep Trump's interest – and to keep him and his family travelling to Moscow. In 2005 Sater, through Bayrock, promised a Trump Tower on the site of an old pencil factory on the Moscow river.[132] The land was owned by two bankers, one of whom was on the board of Diskont Bank, the same Moscow bank which had been at the heart of the money-laundering scandal that led to the killing of the deputy central banker Andrei Kozlov.[133] The deal fell apart when the banker fled Russia after the scandal, claiming he'd been forced to conduct financial operations under threat from the security services.[134] But by that time Sater had escorted Trump's daughter Ivanka and his oldest son Donald Jnr on visits to Moscow. On one occasion, in the icy grey of a Moscow winter in February 2006, he leveraged his connections to arrange a tour of Putin's Kremlin office for Ivanka.[135]

Soon Tchigirinsky stepped into the fray. The Georgian-born businessman frequently schmoozed with Ivanka and Donald Trump Jnr in Moscow and Mayfair, and proposed an elaborate glass skyscraper designed by Norman Foster, planned to be Europe's tallest and costing $2–2.5 billion, in Moscow's upcoming financial district.[136] He said he was willing to give Trump 20 per cent of profits just for the honour of using his name. That project went south in the 2008 financial crisis, when Tchigirinsky's business empire – leveraged to the hilt – collapsed.

Aras Agalarov, the former Communist Party official who'd been Tchigirinsky's protégé, was fast to take over. By then Agalarov had long graduated from his roots running one of the first Soviet–American joint ventures, becoming one of Moscow's biggest construction tycoons, noted for Crocus City, a huge luxury shopping mall and concert hall he'd built on the outskirts of Moscow. In

November 2007 he invited Trump to the Millionaire Fair, an annual luxury-goods exhibition he hosted there. Trump ostensibly attended this festival of extravagance and bling, where luxury yachts, diamond-encrusted mobile phones and entire islands were up for sale, to market the launch of his Trump-branded '24K Super Premium Vodka', which came in a bottle decorated with 24-carat gold. This effort at launching a vodka venture in Moscow was about as successful as bringing coals to Newcastle, but it seems that in Agalarov, Trump made a new and fateful acquaintance.

In November 2013 Agalarov again hosted Trump in Moscow, this time for the Trump-owned Miss Universe beauty pageant. Agalarov was legendary for his hospitality – and, according to one Western banker, for the beautiful girls who worked for him. Trump stayed two nights in the penthouse suite of Moscow's luxurious Ritz-Carlton hotel overlooking Red Square, and emerged beaming. The fact that he hadn't met Vladimir Putin, as he'd hoped, did nothing to dampen his mood. 'I had a great weekend in Moscow with you and your family,' he tweeted to the Agalarovs. 'TRUMP TOWER – MOSCOW is next.' The project for a Trump Tower in Moscow had been revived, and Agalarov began talking about plans for a major new business development. Irakli Kaveladze, who'd worked with Agalarov to open hundreds of US bank accounts, led the discussions. Plans were under way to build twelve properties near the Crocus City Mall, a project that would be called 'Manhattan', with two towers at the centre of it – one to be named after Trump, the other after Agalarov.[137] Sberbank, the Russian state bank, was meant to be lining up financing.

This was yet another project that failed to materialise. Nevertheless, while Agalarov deepened his relationship with Trump, he was fast climbing up the ranks in Moscow. Putin's government selected him for a series of prestige state infrastructure projects: first for a 73-billion-rouble contract for a new university in the far east, and then for the construction of two football stadiums for the 2018 World Cup, for 18 billion roubles apiece.[138]

In 2015, when Trump decided to run for the US presidency, Shalva Tchigirinsky was close by. He told me he was with Trump's close friend and ally Steve Wynn, the casino owner who was to become a major donor for the Trump election campaign and subsequently the Republican Party's finance chairman, soon after the decision was announced. Tchigirinsky remembers shaking his head with joy, but also with disbelief: 'Wynn told me, "Shalva, it's going to last maximum two months, then he will be done. He knows about that. But then in three months he didn't give up. He was more and more popular, making speeches all over the US. He had so much energy. When I spoke with him, I was surprised by his determination, energy and self-confidence.'[139]

Even as Trump ramped up his bid for the presidency, the same Russian network stepped up its courtship of him. Felix Sater reappeared on the scene almost as soon as the decision was announced. He began working with Trump's personal lawyer, Michael Cohen, who he'd been close to since his teenage days in Brighton Beach, and whose father-in-law Yefim Shusterman, a Ukrainian-born taxi-fleet owner, kept close ties at the top of the Moscow city government.[140] Together, they began to seek another Moscow Trump tower project, this time even grander than all the proposals that had gone before. Sater boasted that the tower, a hundred-storey glass-encased obelisk that would be Europe's tallest, would bring Trump $100 million under a licensing deal.[141] In a letter to Cohen in October 2015, he promised to leverage all his Kremlin connections to get it done: 'I will get Putin on this program and we will get Donald elected,' he wrote. 'We both know no one else knows how to pull this off without stupidity or greed getting in the way . . . I will get all of Putin's team to buy in on this.'[142] Sater had turned to VTB, the state bank for special Kremlin projects, and then to Genbank, an obscure sanctioned Crimean bank part-owned and run by his childhood friend Yevgeny Dvoskin, the shadow banker behind so many black-cash schemes, for funding. It was as if all scruples about potential conflicts of interest had been flung to the wayside. But for Sater – and for Russian intelligence – that may have been the point. In this analysis, they needed to continue to compromise the candidate. As if to underline that, Sater even proposed that a $50 million penthouse in the tower would be gifted to Putin. This suggestion had zero chance of ever coming off, but it was one that would compromise a future US president. Emails about the proposed tower were still flying back and forth in June 2016, when Trump was officially announced as the Republican Party's presidential candidate.

At the same time as Michael Cohen and Sater were scheming, Agalarov was working another angle. He set up a meeting between a Moscow lawyer he was close to, Natalia Veselnitskaya, and Donald Trump Jnr. The meeting had been pitched by Agalarov's son Emin, who'd become a well-known pop star across the former Soviet Union, via Emin's publicist, a squat former journalist from the north of England named Rob Goldstone, who told Donald Trump Jnr that Veselnitskaya was offering dirt on Trump's Democratic rival Hillary Clinton. Details of the meeting, which took place at Trump Tower in New York on June 9 2016, emerged after Paul Manafort, the Kremlin-linked American lobbyist who for a time had headed the Trump campaign, and who was present at the meeting, testified to US congressional investigators. Leaked emails later showed that Goldstone had written to Donald Jnr stating boldly that Aras Agalarov had met the 'crown prosecutor of Russia' and was offering 'to provide the Trump campaign with some official documents and information that would incriminate Hillary and her dealings with Russia and would be very useful to your father . . . It is part of Russia and its government's support for Mr Trump – helped along by Aras and Emin.'[143] 'If it's what you say I love it,' Donald Jnr wrote back.[144]

If the accounts of most of those who attended are to be believed, however, the meeting turned out to be a bust. Veselnitskaya had merely lobbied to lift the Magnitsky Act, a set of punitive sanctions against Russian law enforcers for human rights abuses, pushed through Congress by the activist American investor Bill Browder following the death in a Moscow prison of his lawyer Sergei Magnitsky. The only dirt Veselnitskaya seemed to have on Trump's rival for the presidency was some documents showing that a hedge-fund backer of Browder had donated a few million dollars to the Clinton campaign. Even Goldstone seemed embarrassed by the meeting. But the next day Goldstone had a new message from the Agalarovs for Trump, telling Trump's assistant that Emin and Aras Agalarov 'have a fairly sizeable birthday gift for Trump', whose birthday was a few days later, on June 14. A painting, accompanied by a note that no one apart from Trump seems to have read, was delivered shortly afterwards.[145] A few days later, news broke that the Democratic National Committee's computer servers had been hacked earlier that spring, apparently by a Russian group calling themselves 'Guccifer2.0'.[146]

The rest is history. One month before the election, WikiLeaks began releasing a series of emails hacked by the Russians from the account of John Podesta, the chairman of Clinton's campaign. Those leaks seem trivial now, in comparison to what's been revealed about the workings of the Trump Organization. But the spin that surrounded them bolstered Trump's populist claims that Washington was a swamp, from which the United States was run by and for the benefit of an insider elite. Ahead of the leaks, close Trump ally Roger Stone tweeted twice that WikiLeaks was about to destroy Clinton.[147]

When Trump won the presidential election in November 2016, at first the Russians couldn't seem to believe their luck. The scenes in the Russian parliament were uproarious: when a lawmaker ran into the parliamentary session that morning to shout the news that Trump had won, the entire hall leapt to their feet in raucous applause. That evening, champagne was poured. 'Tonight is a night of Trump for all Americans and the world', declared Boris Chernyshev, a member of the nationalist LDPR. 'Tonight we can use the slogan with Mr Trump: Yes we did', he said, citing Barack Obama's 2008 slogan.[148] 'This is a great day for American democracy', crowed Sergei Markov, one of the Kremlin's main ideologues. 'We have to respect American democracy'. In New York ostensibly for a chess tournament, Putin's spokesman Dmitry Peskov could barely disguise his exuberance. Putin and Trump, he said, 'set out the same main foreign policy principles, and that is incredible. It is phenomenal how close they are to one another when it comes to their conceptual approach to foreign policy'.[149]

*

Had Russia pulled off a monumental operation to install its man in the White House? If not, what had been the point of all the cultivation, the dangling of deals by those with links to Russian intelligence ahead of Trump's vault to the presidency? Was it all meticulously planned, or sheer opportunism? Could they really have a hold on him? According to Yury Shvets, Trump had long been of interest. Approaches were made in July 1987, when he'd first visited Moscow at the invitation of Yury Dubinin, the then Soviet ambassador to the US.[150] He had been wowed by the spectacular architecture, the generous hospitality, and particularly by the women. 'His interest in Russian girls, in Slavic girls, was always without question very big,' one senior former KGB officer close to Putin told me with a chuckle.[151]

According to Shvets, the KGB at least believed it had recruited Trump then. Whether Trump was aware of any of this is another question. But soon after his return from Moscow he ran a full-page ad in three US newspapers declaring his opinion that America should withdraw its support for and defence of key strategic allies in Japan and the Persian Gulf. 'It's time for us to end our vast deficits by making Japan and others who can afford it, pay,' he wrote. 'Our world protection is worth hundreds of billions of dollars to these countries, and their stake in their protection is far greater than ours.' It was a policy that appeared designed to unravel the US's position as a global superpower. And according to Shvets: 'It was a total collection of views and interests forwarded by the KGB.'[152]

We may never know if Russia was providing Trump with cash that long ago. Trump himself has consistently denied ever receiving any funds of Russian origin. 'I HAVE NOTHING TO DO WITH RUSSIA – NO DEALS, NO LOANS, NO NOTHING!' he tweeted in January 2017. But what's clear is that ever since Tchigirinsky first appeared at the Taj Mahal in 1990, a network of Moscow/Solntsevskaya money men and intelligence operatives surrounded him, and that they stepped up the business connection after 2000, when Bayrock appeared on the scene.

Agreement was never finalised for a Trump Tower Moscow. But it didn't matter whether Trump sealed a deal there or not: it was enough for it to be constantly dangled before him. The US property deals arranged by the same network of Solntsevskaya-linked former Soviet businessmen provided cash flow instead. The same principle applied to the Trump Tower meeting in New York in June 2016. For the Russians, it was enough for Don Jnr to full-throatedly approve the idea of receiving dirt on his father's opponent from someone sent by the 'crown prosecutor' – i.e. a representative of the Russian government. In Yury Shvets's view, the meeting was all about intelligence games. By then it was an opportunity to further compromise the future president.

We still don't know how much the Trump Organization may have made from the licensing deals and the 18 per cent equity stake in Trump SoHo, or whether Trump had any other hidden stakes in the Bayrock development projects, or in Alex Shnaider's Trump Tower Toronto. In one legal deposition in 2008, Sater said the Trump Organization was receiving 'ongoing' monthly payments from Bayrock for 'development services' for the Trump Tower in Phoenix, even though it never got off the ground.[153] But he did not disclose how much those payments were for, apart from one $250,000 transfer for 'services rendered'.[154] Without access to Trump's financial records, for now it's impossible to know how much Bayrock paid him.

In an interview with the US ABC network, Sergei Millian, a former Soviet émigré who said he had worked as an agent for Trump properties in Florida, bringing in Russian buyers, and to have met Trump and Michael Cohen along the way, claimed to know some of the answers. He said Trump had done 'significant business with Russians', and had received 'hundreds of millions of dollars as a result of interaction with Russian businessmen'. He spoke most of all about Tamir Sapir, the Georgian-born businessman who'd partnered with Bayrock to finance Trump SoHo. Some of the Russians Trump dealt with, said Millian, had lost 'tens of millions of dollars' as a result. But while they lost out, 'Donald Trump made a lot of money doing business with Russians.'[155]

Rumours persisted of further financial support from Moscow via Deutsche Bank, which offered Trump more than $4 billion in loan commitments and potential bond offerings in the years after he faced personal bankruptcy in the early nineties. The German bank became Trump's lender of last resort when other Wall Street banks shunned him as too great a financial risk. After 2011 its private banking arm provided more than $300 million in loans to Trump projects, including for the Trump International Hotel and Tower in Chicago and the Doral Golf Resort and Spa in Florida. This caused great controversy within the bank, because Trump had already defaulted on a $334 million payment on a $640 million loan from Deutsche's commercial banking arm for the Trump Tower in Chicago. Deutsche had always maintained a special relationship with Putin's Kremlin. Under Charlie Ryan, who'd first met Putin in St Petersburg in the early nineties, its Moscow arm was home for the corporate accounts of Putin's closest allies – Timchenko, Rotenberg and Kovalchuk – while it had cultivated close relations with the powerful Russian state bank VTB, employing the son of its head, Andrei Kostin. Josef Ackerman, the then Deutsche Bank chief, hobnobbed with Kostin and frequently consulted him. Deutsche Bank Moscow later became the vehicle for the more than $10 billion in illicit transfers through the mirror-trade scheme of which Felix Sater's close friend Yevgeny Dvoskin was an architect.

In the beginning, Trump's business was probably no more than a convenient vehicle through which to funnel funds into the US. 'I don't think this was a long-planned strategic operation,' said Yury Shvets.[156] But at some point Trump became a political opportunity.

Revenge of the KGB

Putin's security men revelled in Trump's victory. To many, it seemed like revenge for the Soviet collapse. 'While the West was playing James Bond . . . we turned our attention to gaining respect,' said Konstantin Zatulin, a prominent Russian lawmaker. 'When the West thought the Cold War competition was over, they lost respect for their opponent. Now they are waking up to this again.'[157]

After the dust had long settled, Putin could not help expressing his delight. Populist leaders were also rising across Europe, and with

Trump's election and Britain's looming departure from the EU, the post-Cold War order was unravelling. 'The liberal idea has become obsolete. It has come into conflict with the overwhelming majority of the population,' Putin told the *Financial Times* in June 2019. Liberals, he said, 'cannot dictate anything to anyone just like they have been attempting to do over the recent decades'. Even before Trump's victory, Vladimir Yakunin for one had tried to draw parallels between the rising tide of populism in the West and the demands for the dismantling of the Communists' political monopoly that heralded the Soviet collapse. In fact, the two processes could not be more different, but Yakunin tried to argue that the Western elite was almost as ageing and distant from the population as the Soviet elite had been in its last days. 'Brexit and Trump should be useful in that they should cause concern in the political elite and show them that they have gotten too fat,' he said in the summer before Trump's election. 'They have lost the ability to react to political situations, and they have separated themselves from the masses . . . It is a natural process. When the elite ages, new forces arrive to replace them.'[158] After Trump's election, Yakunin delighted in what he saw as the defeat of the liberal world order: 'The neocons who thought they controlled the whole world, that they had the whole world by the balls, suddenly got hit in the face so hard that everything shook for them. This system they have built is not able to exist when there is an alternative. The worst thing for them is an alternative. Putin is an alternative. The appearance of Trump is an alternative. The shaking Europe is an alternative.'[159]

Russia, he eventually admitted, had, like any other world power, used its secret services to take advantage of existing weaknesses in the West. 'All intelligence services carry out active measures,' he said. 'I know what I'm speaking of. Of course, whenever there are conflicts each side tries to find an advantage. The Germans do this. The French do this. The Russians do this. There was never the aim to influence anyone. There was the aim to raise Russia from its knees. This can be done through conducting an independent policy . . . For this you need to have a circle of friends.' This, he said, was a process not dissimilar to Cold War times, when the Soviets funded the peace movement in the West. 'When there was the Soviet Union, you remember how powerful the peace movement was. The Soviet Union financed this movement. Now we have an absolutely different configuration. The problem is, our politicians have not yet understood that there will be no victors in this battle,' he reflected, slowly shaking his head.[160]

Such 'active measures' had led to a backlash. In the US, allegations that Russia had a hand in Trump's rise were under investigation. The unwitting disclosure by a Trump foreign policy adviser that he knew in advance that the Russians had access to Hillary Clinton's emails led the FBI to open an investigation, while Trump's firing of FBI director James Comey only exacerbated the situation. It led to the appointment of a special counsel to investigate Russia's efforts to interfere in the election, including whether Trump had obstructed justice when he fired Comey, and possible collusion between Russia and the Trump campaign. The US intelligence community concluded overwhelmingly that Russian military intelligence had hacked the Democratic National Committee's servers, and had sought to sway public opinion in Trump's favour through a social media campaign – findings that led the more hawkish members of Trump's administration to impose increasingly stringent sanctions on the Russian economy and its tycoons. For more than two years, allegations of Russia's involvement dominated the headlines. Decades of operations were being slowly unpicked.

For Yury Shvets, the Putin regime's campaign had been a disaster, a heavy-handed, flat-footed and opportunistic operation that, he sniffed disdainfully, was about as subtle as a *kolkhoz*, a giant Soviet collective farm filled with peasants. 'How could this be a success?' he exclaimed. 'They turned the whole of Russia into a global pariah!'

*

But despite the new sanctions imposed by his administration, Trump was still a president who answered many of Putin's KGB men's dreams. He was driven by his own long-standing America-first sensibilities, as well as his chaotic decision-making style. But he'd also immediately made clear his deference to Putin and his circle. In an unprecedented Oval Office meeting at the start of his presidency he told Russia's foreign minister, Sergei Lavrov, and Russia's ambassador to the US, Sergei Kislyak, that he was not worried about the US intelligence community's claims of Russian interference in the presidential election, since America did the same elsewhere.[161] Soon he began to pick away at the Western order, at the stable alliances that had dominated since the end of the Cold War. During his campaign he'd argued that NATO was obsolete, while suggesting that he might recognise Crimea's annexation by Russia. Following his election, he actively encouraged Britain's prime minister Theresa May – and then her successor Boris Johnson – to deepen the UK's split from Europe, threatening to withhold a trade agreement with the US unless they did so. He constantly badgered NATO member states with complaints that they were not paying their dues. His relations with German chancellor Angela Merkel, a bastion of the global liberal order, were testy at best, and he criticised her over her immigration policy. In 2019 he would withdraw US troops from Syria, a devastating move that abandoned the US's Kurdish ally and left Russia and Iran to fill the resulting power vacuum. He was erratic, unpredictable, and his every statement seemed to undermine American leadership. Under his watch US democratic institutions were eroded, and US society became ever more divided. Foreign policy was deployed as an instrument to trade Trump's own political interests. The former US ambassador to Ukraine, recalled from her post by Trump, said the State Department was being 'attacked and hollowed out from within'.[162] By 2019 Trump was even publicly lobbying for Russia's reinstatement in the G8.

Shalva Tchigirinsky, for one, was delighted by Trump's effectiveness. 'Everything he's promised he's doing,' he said when we met in May 2018. He found it almost impossible not to gloat. An old Soviet dream that Europe, left without US military support, would dissolve into battle between its nation states, could even become reality. 'Then there will be nothing left but for the Russians to come and take all the women,' he laughed.[163]

Tchigirinsky, who remained in contact with senior Russian

foreign-intelligence figures such as former foreign minister Igor Ivanov, seemed to be joking, of course. But there was an edge to his laughter. The world was suddenly in a dissonant new reality, where everything seemed to be turned on its head. When Trump finally met Putin, for their first summit in Helsinki in July 2018, many who'd dismissed as media hoopla the allegations that the Putin regime had some kind of hold over him were confronted by a stark picture. There was the US president before the whole world, apparently scraping to Putin, full of praise for how he'd conducted the recently-concluded football World Cup, kowtowing to the Russian leader as a 'good competitor'. There was Trump directly contradicting the conclusions of his own intelligence agencies about Russian interference in the 2016 presidential election, preferring what he called Putin's 'extremely strong and powerful' denial.[164] Facing a packed press hall, a smiling and at times smirking Putin took the lead in almost everything. Questioned about Russia's attempts to influence the US election, he shrugged them off as the actions of 'private individuals', pointing in particular to the indictment by US prosecutors of a close ally of his, a former caterer nicknamed 'Putin's chef', Yevgeny Prigozhin, and his Concord Management company. Prigozhin was accused of running an internet troll factory that had been behind a sweeping online effort to influence American voters to support Trump. 'They do not represent the Russian state,' Putin claimed. 'This is a matter of private individuals, not the state . . . You have many people, including those with fortunes worth billions, Mr Soros, for example, and they are meddling everywhere. And is this the position of the American state? No. It is the position of a private individual. It's the same here.'[165]

Putin was being facetious. The use of the term 'private individuals' was a typical KGB tactic that allowed plausible deniability for any Kremlin involvement, and it went to the heart of how Putin's regime operated. By then under his KGB capitalism, all of Russia's significant so-called 'private' businessmen had become agents of the state. Since Mikhail Khodorkovsky's arrest in 2003, their independence had increasingly been taken away from them. The financial crisis of 2008 had deepened the process, with many of the country's billionaires dependent on state bailouts. In 2014, as Russia headed for a standoff with the

West, they were given the final signal, with even a loyal billionaire being forced to turn over his business to the state. The tycoons once known as powerful oligarchs were now the vassals of Putin's Kremlin, their every move closely followed, most of their telephones bugged. The collection of *kompromat* to keep them on a tight leash had become big business for law enforcement. Many tycoons sought to stay in Putin's favour by carrying out tasks for him. 'These are cats that like to bring dead mice to the Kremlin,' said Mark Galeotti, an expert in Putin's influence operations at the Institute of International Relations in Prague.[166] They needed Putin's approval to get ahead in business, and also to survive attacks from law enforcement and rival oligarchs. 'All of them depend on the number one,' said a close associate of one billionaire. 'Russia is the main place they make money, and they all depend on the nod from the number one for that.'[167]

They had become part of a feudal system in which Putin's role as the ultimate arbiter between rivals fighting for business was the source of his power. Almost any deal above a certain level – some said over $50 million – required Putin's approval to go ahead, although one senior Western banker said that sometimes he intervened in deals worth less than that: 'What absolutely floored me is that Putin got involved in a deal in the $20 million range.' That particular case involved a businessman who wanted to sell up and leave the country. 'But he was told he wasn't going anywhere, and had to keep his company,' said the banker.[168] Under such a system, it is not difficult to imagine Russian businessmen volunteering to cultivate foreign politicians on the Kremlin's behalf, in return for Putin's nod for a piece of land or a development licence, or merely to stay out of jail.

And it was a system where, especially after the annexation of Crimea, Putin's men had given a clear signal about where they wanted things to go. 'The idea is very clear,' said one senior Russian businessman. 'The West is going to destroy Russia because we are Orthodox . . . We have reserves that they want to take from us. We have the most talented sportsmen, artists and ballerinas, and we are envied. We have the most advanced people, the most intelligent. By now each part of the machinery deals with its own business, and the machine works by itself. Everyone does what they can.'[169]

Putin and his KGB men had gone far. The networks created on the eve of the Soviet collapse to funnel assets into the West had been preserved, and filled with new cash. The alleged organised-crime associates like Boris Birshtein were still active and within reach, while the ostensibly more respectable businessmen who'd followed them, like Shalva Tchigirinsky, were also still deeply aligned with the Russian state. If, for a brief period under Yeltsin, there had been a risk that some of these networks might spin out of control, under Putin the security services had reasserted their primacy. In Tchigirinsky's case, for instance, Putin's security men had a hold over him. His brother Alexander remained in Moscow after Tchigirinsky left Russia again following the 2008 financial crisis. Tchigirinsky told everyone that he was in exile, and that he no longer spoke with his brother, with whom he had fallen out. But he showed me a set of messages they'd recently exchanged, which included photos of the retirement ceremony of a senior Moscow city official which Alexander had attended, and Alexander's property business depended almost entirely on maintaining good relations with the Kremlin.[170] The black-cash networks laid down so long ago through Mogilevich and his associates, through the Solntsevskaya, and through Sam Kislin, Tamir Sapir, Aras Agalarov and Tchigirinsky were still being deployed. Such security service networks, said Thomas Graham, the director for Russia on the US National Security Council under George W. Bush, 'are never abandoned. They always remain in place.'[171]

Even beyond this network of Moscow money men that had expanded to include the new generation from Brighton Beach (Sater and Dvoskin), Putin had developed other levers of influence. There was Dmitry Rybolovlev, the fertiliser tycoon who overpaid for Donald Trump's Palm Beach mansion. Then there was Viktor Vekselberg, the mandarin-like head of the Skolkovo high-tech hub who spent some of the fortune he'd acquired in Russian oil buying up American assets, including control of CIFC, one of the US's largest managers of collateralised loan obligations, which managed $14 billion in private debt, making it a vehicle of potentially untold leverage and influence over indebted American businessmen. 'Each one of the top ten Russian businessmen is doing something,' said a former close associate of one Russian billionaire. 'They have so much cash. They can buy anyone. The US was swanning around about how they have Bill Gates and how they have Mark Zuckerberg, and Russia came along and just destroyed [the illusion]. The Russians are always cleverer. On a cold level, Putin is doing a fantastic job for Russia. Any way they can get around the rules, they do. They always have three or four different stories, and then it all just gets lost in the noise.' Putin's people, he said, had long been active on multiple levels. 'For them, it's not big money if you give $3 million to Idaho for a health centre and help get a guy elected. It's cheap.'[172]

Dmitry Peskov, Putin's powerful press secretary who'd previously served abroad as a diplomat, had once boasted that the efforts of Robert Mueller, the special counsel appointed to investigate Trump's ties to Russia, would never get anywhere. 'In Russian, it's called passing water through a sieve,' he said. 'That's exactly what the process looks like.'[173] He turned out to be pretty much right. Former KGB officer Yury Shvets had nothing but scorn for the published results of the Mueller investigation. 'It was no more than a collection of interviews,' he said. What was published contained zero counterintelligence. 'How can you investigate Trump without this?'[174]

The Mueller investigation, in the public pronouncements of Trump and the Republican Party, appeared to have fizzled out. But it became clear that parts of the same network of Moscow money men were continuing to operate. As the 2020 US presidential election approached, some of them appeared still to be attempting to steer things Trump's way. Sapir's business partner and Tchigirinsky associate, Sam Kislin, had forged close relations with Rudy Giuliani, the former New York mayor who by that time was acting as Trump's personal attorney. Kislin liked to boast of his friendly relations with Trump, and he'd funnelled substantial donations to Giuliani's mayoral campaign in the nineties.[175] By 2019 he was urging Giuliani to investigate allegations of corruption in Ukraine,[176] and was calling for Trump's administration to investigate the former Ukrainian president Pyotr Poroshenko, who'd led the country through its bitter war with the Kremlin-backed separatists and Russia's annexation of Crimea. He was doing so at a crucial time, when Giuliani was actively seeking dirt in Ukraine against

Trump's potential Democratic rival in the 2020 presidential race, Joe Biden – and Kislin appeared to be opening doors for him there.[177]

Then there were two Soviet-born businessmen, Igor Fruman and Lev Parnas, eventually arrested on charges of conspiring to circumvent laws against foreign influence, who had also befriended Giuliani and – one of them claimed – Trump.[178] They'd acted as middlemen, introducing Giuliani to three current and former Ukrainian prosecutors with information about corruption allegations surrounding a Ukrainian gas company, Burisma, on the board of which Joe Biden's son Hunter had sat.[179] At the same time, they also began trawling for anything that might amplify a pet theory peddled by Trump that Ukraine had worked with the Democrats in 2016 to stir up the Kremlin–Trump campaign collusion claims.[180]

The two men, who splurged tens of thousands of dollars on limousine services and stays at Trump hotels, and funnelled hundreds of thousands into Trump-aligned super PACs, turned out to have been working for Dmitry Firtash,[181] the gas tycoon who'd taken over the Turkmenistan–Russia–Ukraine gas trade with the backing of the Kremlin and Mogilevich, creating a slush fund that corrupted a series of Ukrainian presidents. By then, Firtash had been under house arrest in Vienna ever since 2014 as the US sought his extradition on bribery charges. But still his reach stretched far – first into Europe and then into the US, where Parnas had begun working in 2019 as an interpreter for him. The two men boasted Firtash was funding their lavish lifestyle[182] while federal prosecutors in Chicago had noticed Parnas and Fruman during their investigation into the Firtash bribery case.[183]

The Russian black-cash networks seemed to be digging in ever deeper. Their activities, combined with Trump's disregard for the institutions and codes of US democracy, were leading to a systemic standoff. When Trump was caught on a July 27 2019 telephone call asking Ukraine's new president, Volodomyr Zelensky, to meet Giuliani and press ahead with an investigation into Biden, to many his actions represented an abuse of office. Trump was directly requesting a foreign power to assist him in the 2020 election. Trump appeared to suggest that US military assistance for Ukraine could be contingent on compliance with his request. For many, such actions represented a degradation of democracy, and an undermining of everything US diplomats had sought to stand for ever since the Soviet collapse. The US government had long sought to bolster democracy in Ukraine and protect it from Russian domination, seeking to eliminate the corrupt schemes that had undermined its governance. This 'irregular policy channel was running contrary to the goals of longstanding US foreign policy', said William Taylor, the top US envoy to Ukraine at the time of the call.[184] The only way to deal with it was through an impeachment probe.

The Russians appeared delighted with the chaos, yet also fearful about where impeachment might lead. The scandal exposed both the fragility of the American political system and how it had been corroded from within. 'It looks like the whole of US politics is for sale,' said a former senior Russian banker with ties to the security services. 'We believed in Western values . . . But it turned out everything depended on money, and all these values were pure hypocrisy.'[185]

But from the beginning the Russian black-cash networks had, in part, been embedded to erode the system, and exacerbate corruption in the West. For one senior Russian businessman, Putin's Russia posed an increasing threat to Western liberal democracy. In the impeachment probe and the 2020 US presidential race, the clash between liberal values and a Putin-style corrupt authoritarian order was reaching a denouement. 'Putin understands that Russia can spend any amount of money it wants [on sowing chaos in the West]. The *obschak*, the black-cash box, has become the size of the budget, and they can give orders to the oligarchs as well. It is a mafia that has seized power, and the state is acting as the mafia.'[186]

The system of KGB capitalism was still working. The networks were still in place.

Epilogue

Sistema

If, beyond its borders, Putin's Russia was posing an increasing threat to the Western liberal order, internally the system of KGB capitalism appeared to be calcifying and perhaps becoming unsustainable. The mafia system of tight control and corruption was penetrating every crevice of society, every political decision and every business deal. After the takedown of Yukos and Mikhail Khodorkovsky, the power of the security men had expanded to such a degree that the FSB had leverage over almost every businessman, and every regional politician, no matter how low in the food chain. It was a system of warring clans – including even different branches of law enforcement – fighting over slices of the country's wealth, in which to survive meant you had to cooperate. Those who rebelled found themselves in jail. The story of one comparatively lowly bureaucrat exemplifies the system's workings. Unlike the thousands of others who disappeared without trace after being thrown in pre-trial detention, this bureaucrat published damaging documentary evidence that revealed the corrupt intertwining of the security services and organised crime determining even the minutest questions of regional power. The trail he disclosed led to the FSB general who worked with Felix Sater's friend Yevgeny Dvoskin on the black-cash schemes.

Alexander Shestun was the head of the Serpukhov district, a small slice of countryside about a hundred kilometres south of Moscow. In Russia's rough-and-tumble capitalism of the nineties his success as a hard-bitten seller of construction materials made him one of the area's richest businessmen, a big fish in a small pond.[1] Ever since his election as the region's head in 2003, he had made every effort to demonstrate his fealty to Putin's state. He joined the pro-Kremlin Unity Party, and worked closely with the FSB. Shestun was what the FSB called a 'torpedo'. He agreed to secretly record conversations with local businessmen and officials to provide the FSB with compromising information that could sink their rivals. It was almost a replication of the Soviet system of informants, when citizens told tales on their neighbours in order to stay on the right side of the authorities and out of prison – only now it was a hundred times more sophisticated.

Shestun's work had proved extremely valuable to the FSB; he helped it maintain its ascendancy when he informed on a ring of regional prosecutors running an illegal casino business.[2] But when a powerful new governor of the Moscow region was appointed in 2013, his days as head of the district were numbered. The new governor was a former deputy to the defence minister, Sergei Shoigu. Putin's close ally Gennady Timchenko had invested in his family's business, and he wanted the slice of prime real estate Shestun controlled for himself. As Shestun's term as district head drew to a close, the FSB opened a criminal investigation into his purchase of the land on which he had built his home. But instead of bowing to the inevitable, Shestun dug in his heels. When Ivan Tkachev, the FSB general he'd formerly cooperated with, began blackmailing him over the case, Shestun taped their conversations, and later downloaded some of them on YouTube.

Tkachev was the head of the FSB's powerful Department K, which was ostensibly meant to investigate financial crimes, but actually oversaw many of the black-cash schemes. According to a former senior banker who knew Yevgeny Dvoskin, he had worked closely with Dvoskin and Ivan Myazin to run many of the black-cash transfer schemes.[3] Shestun later said he'd often seen Tkachev in the company of Dvoskin, as well as with another banker who'd run connected money-laundering schemes that funnelled tens of billions of roubles into accounts in the West.[4] Tkachev had also used his position to prevent an interior ministry investigation into some of these schemes.

When two police investigators, Denis Sugrobov and Boris Kolesnikov, got too close in 2014, Tkachev organised their arrest. Kolesnikov fell to his death from a balcony while he was in custody.

In one of the tapes Shestun downloaded, Tkachev and a senior official from the Kremlin administration referred to the police officers' fate as he tried to force Shestun out of his post. 'You won't be left in peace,' Tkachev threatened. 'The matter has been taken to the president. The head of the FSB, the head of the presidential administration have all spoken about this. If you mess about they will run you over with a steamroller. Didn't you see what happened to Sugrobov? . . . Why do you need this? Why do you, or your wife or your children need such problems? They will put you in jail anyway, and you will sit there for as long as they keep you there. You must understand this.' He then told him he'd already jailed a string of far more powerful regional governors who dug in their heels over being replaced, and listed them one by one. 'Show me Udmurtia – he was the tsar and god there. Show me Mari El, also the tsar and god. Sakhalin, Vladivostok – he was the coolest, but I carried him out with my bare hands. I worked with all the governors, with all the regional chiefs.'[5]

Tkachev told Shestun he would stand a better chance of surviving if he was in conflict with organised crime, and not with Putin's state: 'You're a normal guy. You're not a traitor. You always knew how to take a blow. But now you really really have fallen under the steamroller. It would be better for you if you were tangling with bandits.'[6] In any case, he told him, Putin was in touch with the head of one local organised-crime group, Sergei Lalakin, otherwise known as Luchok. 'The president speaks with him. He received a medal. How could he not speak with him? Life is such, you understand.'[7]

It was a system, one Kremlin insider said, that was becoming unsustainable.[8] The success of Putin's foreign policy exploits had long propelled the president far above the rest of his inner circle. But among Putin's security men infighting was escalating. The economic slow-down resulting from Western sanctions was leading to an ever more bitter struggle to control resources and wealth. Igor Sechin, the Kremlin insider whispered, was rapidly gaining power. Swiftly, and without fanfare, he'd attained one of the highest ranks in the FSB, that of general colonel, and had appointed his own followers, who carried out his orders, to senior posts in the FSB. The once-mighty former Russian Railways chief and close Putin ally Vladimir Yakunin, for one, seemed to be struggling. His close associates were being rounded up and arrested. One Russian tycoon speculated that they were just a signature away from testifying against Yakunin himself.[9] At the same time, corruption pervaded every part of the system, right down to crony deals at inflated prices for supplies of sausages and other food-stuffs to Putin's elite personal security force, the national guard.[10]

Amid the intensifying struggle and Russia's increasing isolation, 'those that used to worry about what the West might think have long forgotten about all that,' said a Russian tycoon. 'Now it's only a battle for survival.' One senior Moscow judge, who'd once cared about at least the appearance of following the rule of law, had long been swallowed into the system. Her daughter was earning an enormous salary at Rosneft, the state oil champion, and she wouldn't do anything to jeopardise that. 'These people, they have changed,' said the tycoon. 'It's like she's drunk blood. She is totally part of the system. Now they only think about how they can be tougher and crueller than the rest.'[11]

Russian officials seemed to care so little about Western investment following the sanctions that they even arrested one of the few Western investors remaining in Russia, Michael Calvey, in February 2019, freezing his fund's assets, ready for takeover by Putin's security men.

But the sanctions, the infighting and the near monopoly reach of Putin's men were proving an incessant drag on the economy. Before the Crimea campaign, one Western lawyer wryly noted, Russia had been on track to be the world's fifth-largest economy by 2020.[12] Now, he said, it was going to be lucky to make number thirteen, and no one seemed to care. Growth was stagnating at just over 1 per cent. If, before, most of his clients had been private businessmen, now they all seemed to be acting in some capacity on behalf of Putin's state, he said.

'This is what happens when the KGB come to power. All they know is how to run black operations,' said a former senior govern-ment official.[13]

The surge in patriotism and pride after Russia's annexation of

Crimea had remained in force just long enough to carry Putin through to re-election in March 2018, with 77 per cent of the vote. But soon afterwards inside Russia public support for Putin finally began to fall. The unwritten pact that had allowed him and his circle to rule as they wished, as long as incomes were rising, was fraying.

Just as in Soviet times, Putin's Russia was focusing on influence operations and restoring the country's clout abroad, while neglecting to develop the domestic economy. Putin's government was ever more openly increasing spending on displays of military power in the Middle East, and on political support for friendly nations as it sought to fracture Western alliances. A report by the independent TVRain put the cost of the country's expenditure on its military campaign in Syria at $3 billion, while a further $1 billion was pledged for restoring Syrian infrastructure.[14] At the same time, Russia was wheeling out new generations of missiles. Loans were being handed out to developing countries – Venezuela had received more than $20 billion – in hopes that they would support Russia's cause against the liberal West. All this was on top of the untold amounts of black cash being siphoned out of the country to spend on covert operations to buy foreign politicians and influence.

But at the same time, in 2018 the government told the population that the funds to pay pensions were dwindling, and it would have to raise the retirement age. 'People understand the regime has a lot of money,' said the former deputy energy minister and now opposition politician Vladimir Milov, 'and against this background, for the government to say we have no money for pensions is a big mistake. Pensions are one of the main guarantees that the state is meant to give the population. People have built their entire life strategy around this. The Kremlin thought the people's support for Putin was unconditional, like for a great tsar. But they are not going to forgive him for everything.'[15]

As Moscow headed towards local elections in September 2019, the first signs that one day there could be a critical standoff between the tsar and his people appeared. That summer, riot police forcibly detained hundreds of protesters as they took to the streets to demonstrate against the barring of opposition candidates, threatening some with fifteen-year jail sentences under draconian new laws, while opposition leaders were rounded up and held for weeks in jail. The heavy-handed responses to the peaceful protests meant only one thing: fear was setting in among Putin's security men. Public trust in Putin fell to a low of 31.7 per cent – until the Kremlin hastily ordered a revamp of the polling methodology.

The unrest soon died down, and, steadied by a constant diet of state propaganda and budget handouts, Putin's ratings started to climb again. But Putin and his security men took the warning signs seriously. Putin would soon be running into another constitutional limit on his hold on power: this time in 2024 – the end of his second consecutive term as president since his return in 2012 – when the constitution dictated he step down. Increasing uncertainty over who would replace him was already deepening infighting among the elite, and Putin's people understood all too acutely the dangers of any transfer of power. They'd seen the jeopardy the Yeltsin Family faced as it entered the final year of Yeltsin's rule. And with each year that passed of Putin's own twenty-year rule, the potential threats he – or any of his security men – could personally face went far beyond anything that had confronted the Yeltsin Family. Any handover, even within the ruling elite, was fraught with peril. There were the apartment bombings, the Dubrovka theatre siege, the handling of the Beslan terror attack, the takedown of Russia's one-time richest man, and then the subversion of the country's legal system and economy, and the hundreds of billions of dollars they'd seized command of as they shored up their own power and then projected it abroad. There was no telling where a backlash might lead. The lengths they'd gone to to forge their own fortress of power had dragged Putin and his security men so deeply into a web of compromise and criminality that the only way to secure their position was to find a way to prolong Putin's rule – or at the very least a way to drag out the transition.

They'd already tightened their hold over the country's political system to such a degree that any outside challenge appeared a remote possibility. But the uncertainty and infighting within their own ranks were creating vulnerabilities, while flailing support for the Kremlin's ruling party United Russia was posing an ever greater risk. On January 15 2020, Putin stepped forward with a surprise announcement: he was proposing changes to the constitution that would leave the way open for him to maintain his grip on the political system. The powers of parliament would be boosted, giving it greater oversight over government, but more importantly, so would those of the president. Future presidents would be able to fire judges, ministers and the prime minister at will. Most importantly, the announcement left the way open for Putin to stay on as president, should growing social unrest or mounting infighting make it impossible for him to secure a safe exit from power. Under a new constitution, he could run for another two terms as president, allowing him to essentially rule Russia for life. Alternatively, the proposed amendments also allowed for Putin to continue to oversee policy-making from a great height: as a father of the nation-type figure heading up a newly empowered State Council. This had at first seemed the more likely route, but eventually seemed ruled out. It could only be taken should Putin believe it was safe to start gradually withdrawing from more active politics. Putin, however, began clearly signalling he didn't believe that was the case, portraying the constitutional amendments as necessary in order to stabilise the country in a time of 'extreme turbulence.'

In one swoop, Putin seemed to be seeking to pre-empt any potential political challenge. Never before had he dared to entertain formally tinkering with the country's constitution. Though in essence his men had already ridden roughshod over its contents, it had always been guarded as the bedrock of the country's stability. What's more, as if foretelling potential external threats, Putin also boldly stated that Russia would no longer abide by the rulings of international courts, further deepening his country's isolation – this time through his regime's own choice.

The rule of his men looked to be calcifying. But now that he'd opened a Pandora's box of constitutional change, it was also in danger of becoming more brittle by the day.

Reckoning

When Vladimir Putin agreed in December 2013 to the early release of Mikhail Khodorkovsky after ten years in a Siberian prison camp, it was the last grand gesture of a magnanimous tsar. It was the eve of the Winter Olympics in Sochi, in what now looks like a different world. This was the era before sanctions, before the world had woken up to the corrosive power of Russian black cash and the revival of Russia's ambitions on the global stage. But even then, perhaps as a symbol of all that was to come, Khodorkovsky's release was an echo of a Cold War-era prisoner swap.

For ten years Khodorkovsky had survived on a diet of thin gruel and potatoes, assembling paper folders in a vast, draughty hangar in Russia's icebound far north while surveillance cameras whirred above his head, watching his every move. Without warning he was bundled into a prison van that rattled through snow-covered forest to a small icy airstrip where a twin-engined plane was waiting for him. He was flown to Schönefeld, the drab airport south of Berlin that was once the westernmost outpost of Soviet rule, where he was greeted by Hans-Dietrich Genscher, the former German foreign minister who'd once been at the centre of negotiations on reunifying Germany. The next morning, after a brief rest and an emotional reunion with his parents, he headed for the Checkpoint Charlie museum, on the site of the notorious Cold War crossing point between East and West.

There he greeted a select group of journalists he'd known before his imprisonment. With his slight smile, immaculate shave and crisp Armani suit, he looked at first glance as if he'd just walked straight out of a boardroom. But his pale-grey pallor and anxious eyes betrayed the gruelling path that had led him there. His hair was neatly cropped, but it had turned white in the years that had passed. 'I last saw most of you ten years ago,' he said. 'For me, this meeting is a kind of bridge to freedom. I want to speak first to the people that I know.' He answered questions about his time in jail and the events that had led him there. The question that gave him most pause was about the West's reaction to his arrest. He stumbled over his answer, reddening and saying he'd been disappointed by the actions of some.

When we spoke almost four years later in the comfort of his office in London's Hanover Square, the question of the Western banks' and energy majors' participation and facilitation of the Yukos takeover still deeply irked him. I asked if the West, by these actions, had to some degree prepared the ground for Russia's subsequent attempts to undermine Western institutions. 'It was a strategic mistake of some Western institutions to think they could live without principles,' he replied. 'They thought it was great – "We will work with Putin, because we can make money from this." But it turned out to be not such a good idea. This lack of principles has brought the West to the consequences it is experiencing now. This constant changing in saying what is good and what is bad has caused society to lose these principles for itself. And now we have a situation where populists are coming to power. Everything is being turned on its head. They point to the example of Putin, and say, "Look he deceived everyone, but he still had political success."'[16]

Though Khodorkovsky is no saint, and makes an unlikely freedom fighter, the West's backing of the Kremlin's takeover of his company and its usurping of the rule of law facilitated the domination of Putin's security men, and furthered their integration into Western financial markets. The weakness of the Western capitalist system, in which money ultimately outweighed all other considerations, left it wide open for the Kremlin to manipulate.

In Russia, the West's willing complicity had helped produce a KGB simulation of a normal market economy. Institutions of power and the market that were meant to be independent were in fact no more than Kremlin fronts. The rulings handed down by Russian courts looked, on paper, as if they could be legitimate. In the Khodorkovsky case, the oil tycoon went through more than two years of court hearings and two sets of criminal charges, the second of which accused him of stealing all the oil Yukos had ever produced, the same oil that he'd previously been charged with evading taxes on. But in reality, the court's rulings were not rulings, but Kremlin directives. The court system was not a court system, it was an arm of the Kremlin. The same went for the parliament, for elections, and for the oligarchy. Putin's KGB men controlled all of them. It was a phantom system of phantom rights, for both individuals and businesses. Anyone who crossed the Kremlin could be jailed at any moment on rigged or trumped-up charges. Property rights were conditional on fealty to the Kremlin.

In a system where stealing was pervasive, where property was constantly being divided up on a nod and a bribe to the relevant person in the Kremlin and in law enforcement, Putin's men had compromising information on everyone. The country had returned to the time of informants. Everyone was taping each other. Everything was known to be bugged. In December 2017 the economic development minister Alexei Ulyukaev, caught on camera receiving a $2 million bribe from Sechin in a sting operation to remove him as a political rival that had been set up by Sechin himself, was sentenced to eight years in prison. The Magomedov brothers, once prominent oligarchs at the top of the strategic port industry, were jailed in March 2018, ostensibly for racketeering and stealing state funds. But their real crime, according to a senior Russian banker, had been outstaying their welcome: 'They went too far. It's all very simple: when the film ends you need to get out of the cinema hall. You don't stay and wait for the next show.'[17] 'They can make anyone disappear now,' said another tycoon. 'Oligarchs, ministers. No one knows what's happening in the Magomedov brothers' case. They were super oligarchs, and now no one knows where they are.'[18]

Everyone was hostage to the system, including the Yeltsin-era powerbrokers who opened the way for the rise to power of Putin's security men. Former Kremlin officials like Alexander Voloshin and former prime minister Mikhail Kasyanov would never be free to speak or act freely. Putin had told them clearly when they stepped down from power that he knew where their money was.[19]

Putin and his security men were the most tightly locked of all to the system. After everything they'd done to shore up their own power, they couldn't trust anyone, even within their own circle, while Putin, by steadfastly eliminating all political rivals and concentrating power in his own hands, had also boxed himself in to such a degree that there was almost no way out for him.

Even those who'd fled Russia, like Sergei Pugachev, knew they could never truly escape the system's reach. For Pugachev, his manoeuvring and manipulation to help propel Putin to power twenty years ago are now a constant source of remorse and regret. 'I've learned an important lesson,' he said when we talked at his home in France amid the latest legal onslaught against him. 'And that is, power is sacred. When you believe the people are stupid, and that if you don't act they will vote in the Communists, that was a big mistake. We all thought the people weren't ready, and we would install Putin. But power comes from God. And if power comes from God, then there is no need to interfere . . . The people knew nothing about Putin. And in three months he became president. Of course, we thought it was cool. We thought we'd saved the country from the Communists, from Primakov and Luzhkov. But now it's not clear which outcome would have been worse. It would have been better had Primakov come to power. He would have been ousted in a year. When I left Russia I thought I'd left all that behind me. But still this follows me everywhere. My fate is attached to Putin's . . . We are tied to each other, no matter what.'[20]

In the rush to help install his man in power, and to save the Yeltsin Family from arrest, Pugachev had ignored warnings from Boris Berezovsky that appointing someone from the KGB was 'to enter a vicious circle. They can't change anything.' He ignored the shocked reaction of Putin's former mentor Anatoly Sobchak, who on hearing that Putin was to be appointed prime minister said, 'Don't frighten me!' 'I thought maybe he was jealous,' said a crestfallen Pugachev, his cheeks still reddening at the memory. 'But of course he knew everything. I'm in horror now myself.'[21]

But in many ways the recent history of Russia had been written long before him. The die had already been cast. The KGB were still everywhere in Russia's ruling elite. The idea of lustration – a ban on official posts for anyone who'd worked with the KGB – had been raised by Yeltsin, but had been swiftly set aside by the senior officials in his administration, all of them KGB men of differing experience and rank. 'They told him this would be impossible,' said Pugachev. 'There would be no one left to work. It would have hit 90 per cent of the ruling elite. People who didn't cooperate in some way were very few.'[22]

Russia's revolution had come full circle. The reformers who

declared to the world with such great promise nearly thirty years ago that the country was on a new market path towards global integration were either soon compromised, or had been working with the KGB on Russia's transition all along. Those who believed they were working to introduce a free market had underestimated the enduring power of the security men. 'This is the tragedy of twentieth-century Russia,' said Pugachev. 'The revolution was never complete.' From the beginning, the security men had been laying down roots for revanche. But from the beginning, it seems, they'd been doomed to repeat the mistakes of the past.

Acknowledgements

This book would never have been written had it not been for the tremendous friends and family who helped and supported me as what began as a two-year project became an odyssey of writing and investigation. Research started long ago in Moscow and St Petersburg where this book was spurred and made possible by hours of conversations I had with Vladimir Milov, the former deputy energy minister whose relentless tracking of the business dealings of Putin's inner circle provided a roadmap for the asset-siphoning of the Putin regime; as well as with Andrei Illarionov, the former presidential economic adviser, whose powers of forensic analysis and insights provided an early spark for part of the book's thesis. Pavel Voshchanov, the former Yeltsin spokesperson and investigative reporter at *Komsomolskaya Pravda*, opened a window onto a long-forgotten world of asset-siphoning by the KGB at the Soviet fall. Outside Russia, Sergei Kolesnikov, the brave whistleblower who fled Putin's tight-knit inner circle, shared documents and spurred further research, while Felipe Turover, the former KGB operative who was the informant sparking the investigation into the Mabetex Kremlin reconstruction contracts, was a source of revelatory insights. Tommy Helsby, the former Kroll chairman of investigations who died too soon in 2019, was a generous source of inspiration and valuable investigative leads. He is missed.

Vladimir Yakunin generously spent many hours explaining the point of view of the tight-knit clique of St Petersburg security men surrounding Putin, first in St Petersburg and then in London over many pots of tea. Valentin Yumashev, Yeltsin's former chief of staff and son-in-law, also spent hours explaining his version of how it was Putin came to power, while in Moscow Yury Skuratov, the former prosecutor general at the centre of the investigation that partly led to Putin's rise, shared the dramatic story of his probe and the Yeltsin Family's counterattack. Mikhail Khodorkovsky met with me soon after his release from ten years in a Siberian prison camp and then continued to do so as he helped me make sense of his standoff with the Russian state.

Many other current and former Russian state officials – including former senior Kremlin officials, as well as Russian tycoons, former senior KGB operatives, and senior Moscow bankers – and the current and former associates of Gennady Timchenko generously shared dozens of hours of their time explaining how the Putin system worked. Most of them did so anonymously because of the obvious sensitivities – and I am eternally grateful for the risks they took. My deep thanks too to N. and G.

It would of course also have been impossible to put this together without the faith shown in me by the *Financial Times*, for which I was Moscow correspondent for six years. My time with the *FT* enabled me to further deepen contacts with Russia's oligarchs, as well as with current and former Kremlin and government officials, forming the foundations for my reporting in this book. It was then that I was first able to meet and interview many of those closest to Putin, including Igor Sechin, Arkady Rotenberg, Viktor Ivanov and Sergei Chemezov. For the great opportunity to write for the *FT* and take this ringside seat, I am grateful most of all to Lionel Barber, Neil Buckley and John Thornhill, who hired me and then continued to support me, as well as to my colleagues in Moscow and then in London – Charles Clover, Courtney Weaver, Cynthia O'Murchu and Michael Stott – who all guided and inspired me and brightened my day. In addition, I am deeply grateful to the *FT* for partly funding a reporting project that became part of this book after I departed on book leave, while I owe a great deal to the warm insights of Elena Kokorina and Ekaterina Shaverdova of the *FT*'s Moscow bureau who continued to help craft interview requests even after I went on book leave.

It would also have been impossible to understand any of these Russian influence and cash networks without the trailblazing and fearless work – and the assistance – of my Russian comrades at the country's few remaining investigative outlets. Roman Anin of *Novaya Gazeta* generously shared documents on the operations of the St Petersburg sea port and provided a crucial contact. Anastasia Kirilenko at the *Insider* led the pack in reporting on the organised-crime networks connected to Putin, sharing documents and crucial contacts, while Roman Shleynov of *Novaya Gazeta* and then *Vedomosti* shared documents on a probe into Putin's activities as St Petersburg's deputy mayor and produced some of the most important early work on the business dealings of Putin's inner circle. The uniquely well-connected Irina Reznik, formerly of *Vedomosti* and currently of Bloomberg in Moscow, also generously shared invaluable contacts. Without the pioneering investigative articles of these four journalists long before me, it would have been impossible to even begin to put the pieces together. The late Vladimir Pribylovsky, who maintained a database of the connections of Putin's men, was also a crucial source of information.

In addition, the late Jürgen Roth, the German investigative journalist, long ago provided valuable documents and a heap of inspiration. Steven Lee Myers of the *New York Times* through his former book research assistant Almut Schoenfeld in Berlin shared another crucial contact. I benefited, too, initially from conversations with colleagues in the US, including Andrew Weiss and Eugene Rumer at the Carnegie Endowment for International Peace, and Thomas Graham, the former senior director for Russia on the National Security Council. In the UK, Christian Michel was an early source of inspiration, while it would have been impossible to even embark on a career in journalism in Moscow without the grounding I received in Russian politics while studying for an MA at the School of Slavonic and East European Studies at University College London.

Felicity Bryan MBE believed in the book's potential and agreed to become my agent, securing a deal with William Collins in the UK and Farrar, Straus and Giroux in the US. I am grateful for her efforts and for the great patience and belief in the project demonstrated by my editors – Arabella Pike, publishing director at William Collins, and Alex Star, executive editor at Farrar, Straus and Giroux. Fainter-hearted editors would have long given up! I had the immense fortune to have Alex Star's sharp observations and editing advice that helped improve this book many times over. Arabella's drive and patient understanding of the sensitivities propelled the book from manu-script into reality, while I am also extremely grateful to her team at William Collins – Jo Thompson for her wise read and suggested cuts, to Robert Lacey for a careful smoothing of the copy, and to Iain Hunt for his patient work on the final text. A deep bow too to the legal team.

Along the way, I was extremely fortunate and honoured to receive encouragement and endless patient advice from David Hoffman, the contributing editor and former Moscow bureau chief of the *Washington Post*, who carefully read chapters and whose 2002 book *The Oligarchs* stands not only as inspiration but as a model for the art of narrative non-fiction and the foundation for all future reporting on Russia's troubled transition to a market economy.

Even with all this superb professional assistance, I would never have made it to the end without the great friends who supported me all the way. Some, including Brad Cook, Miriam Elder, William Flemming, Gina Skilbeck and Emma Wells, not only offered friend-ship but also shared their homes when I needed a place to stay for reporting trips. Others, including Ellen Barry, Catherine Bell, Richard and Charles Emmerson, helped me maintain sanity through this marathon.

I'll always be grateful to Chris for his moral support. My deepest thanks go to my parents, Marjorie and Derek, as well as to Richard and to Catherine Birkett. Without their indefatigable support, none of this would have been possible.

Notes

Prologue

1 The valuations for the assets listed are based on documents seen by the author filed as part of a $12 billion Bilateral Investment Treaty Claim by Pugachev over the alleged expropriation of his assets. They show that Western accounting firm BDO had valued the shipyards at $3.5 billion, while Nomura had estimated them at between $2.2 billion and $4.2 billion. Ernst & Young had valued the coking-coal company EPK at $4 billion. Indeed, the buyers of EPK, Ruslan Baisarov and Igor Altushkin, had initially announced to the Russian press that they bought it for $4 billion.

2 Copies of correspondence between creditors represented by Nomura investment bank and the Russian central bank show that the stakes in the shipyards had been held as collateral for a central bank bailout loan. A sale at a market price would have guaranteed that all creditors' demands could be met, the correspondence says.

3 Author interview with Richard Hainsworth, June 2014

4 A tape of this conversation has been filed with the French interior ministry as part of a criminal investigation into the threats. The author has reviewed the evidence.

5 Jane Croft and Neil Buckley, 'Kremlin Critic Loses $6.5 Billion Lawsuit Against Fellow Oligarch', *Financial Times*, September 1 2012; Konstantin Kagalovsky, the former representative of the Russian government to international financial institutions and an architect of the loans-for-shares privatisation schemes, later told me that he understood that Berezovsky was an owner of Sibneft and that he'd seen documents testifying to that when he was working on the Sibneft privatisation. These documents, however, had later been destroyed, he said. (Kagalovsky also served as first deputy head of Khodorkovsky's Menatep Bank, and was working on merger plans between Khodorkovsky's Yukos and Sibneft in early 1998.) He also told Russian newspaper *Vedomosti* that Berezovsky was a shareholder in Sibneft in an interview on March 24, 2013: 'I knew this 100 per cent. Everyone in Russia knew that Berezovsky was a shareholder in Sibneft. Though those who were familiar in some way with this matter preferred to stay quiet. The decision of the English court about this was, in my view, incorrect.' Amid the 1998 merger plans, Khodorkovsky had also stated publicly that Berezovsky would be a shareholder in the merged

Yukos Sibneft through 'his previous investments in the Sibneft group'.

6   'Roman Abramovich wins Court Battle against Berezovsky', BBC News, August 31 2012; David Leppard, 'Berezovsky Cries Foul Over £3.5bn Abramovich Trial Judge', *Sunday Times*, September 22 2012. Mrs Justice Gloster declined to comment, while the Judicial Office, which represents judges, said she had declared the matter and that Berezovsky had raised no objection at the time.

7   Ablyazov claimed he was the victim of a political witch-hunt. He was Nazarbayev's only real political foe. The bank's collapse, he claimed, was caused by the fact that Nazarbayev had seized it from him.

8   Author interview with Pugachev, May 2014

9   The coroner recorded an open verdict in the inquest into Berezovsky's death, despite the protestations of the Thames Valley Police. A forensic expert acting on behalf of Berezovsky's family testified that examination of the post-mortem photographs led him to believe Berezovsky did not kill himself. There was no v-shaped mark round his neck, which there should have been if he'd hanged himself. Police had been unable to find a match in FBI and Interpol databases for the fingerprint found on the shower-rail. (Jane Croft, 'Open Verdict Fails to Dispel Mystery Over Death of Kremlin Critic Berezovsky', *Financial Times*, March 28 2014)

10 In March 2018, then home secretary Amber Rudd said the UK police and MI5 would reopen investigations into a string of Russian deaths on British soil, apparently including that of Berezovsky. ('Russia Spy Poisoning: Rudd Says Inquiry Widened to Other Deaths', BBC News, March 13 2018)

11 Documents from Swiss Prosecutors' office obtained by author. Russia's Investigative Committee, however, claims the funds transferred were not from Pugachev's company OPK Development, but from the central bank bailout loan. The Russian prosecutors claim that OPK deposits in Mezhprombank, holding funds from a commercial loan from Russian state bank, VTB, since June 19 2008, long before the central bank bailout loan, had been falsified and backdated. However, their evidence relied on testimony from two senior Mezhprombank executives who agreed deals with the prosecutors under duress. One of the executives, Dmitry Amunts, agreed to say the deposits were falsified after prosecutors promised him he would be freed from detention, according to transcripts of taped conversations between Amunts's wife and a lawyer, Marina Yarosh, citing senior officials from the FSB. (He gave the testimony, but was not freed.) The other executive, Alexander Didenko, also agreed to cooperate with prosecutors, and was freed early. He currently holds a senior position at a bank under the management of the state deposit insurance agency, i.e. the government body that is spearheading the case against Pugachev. For more on all this, see Ilya Rozhdestvennsky, 'Sbezhavshie Milliardy: kak Bankir Pugachev Vyvodil Dengi iz Rossii', *RBK*, November 14 2016

12 Author interview with person close to the Russian state legal team, February 2018. The bankruptcy case against Pugachev was also based on claims that he ordered another senior bank executive to lift pledges holding shares in his coking-coal company EPK in preparation for its sale, which also allegedly worsened the bank's financial position.

13 Author interview with person close to the Russian state legal team, February 2018

14 Author interview with senior Russian banker, March 2018

Chapter 1: 'Operation Luch'

1 Igor Shadkhan, Vlast, 1992

2 Author interview, Igor Shadkhan, June 2013

3 Vladimir Usoltsev, Sosluzhivets, p.239

4 Author interview with Lieutenant Colonel Horst Jehmlich, special assistant to Dresden Stasi chief, Horst Böhm, March 2018; Mark Franchetti, 'Germans Flush Out Putin's Spies', Sunday Times, January 16 2000

5 Andreas Forster, Auf der Spur der Stasi Millionen: Die Wien-Connection, pp.20–2

6 John O. Koehler, Stasi: The Untold Story of the East German Secret Police, p.75

7 Author interview with Jehmlich, March 2018

8 Kristie Mackrakis, Seduced by Secrets: Inside the Stasi's Spy-Tech World, p.116

9 Author interview with Franz Sedelmayer, April 2018

10 Author interview with Jehmlich, March 2018

11 Forster, Auf der Spur, p.111

12 Forster, Auf der Spur, pp.50, 51, 68–71

13 Ibid., pp.23–5

14 Deutscher Bundestag, Beschlussempfehlung und Bericht, May 27 1994, pp.97–102, 117–28, 137–41, 176–211

15 Koehler, Stasi, pp.74, 76, 79–80

16 Christopher Andrew and Vasily Mitrokhin, The Mitrokhin Archive: The KGB in Europe and the West, pp.598, 285 (The authors also state the HVA was a chief source of intelligence on Western technology.)

17 Author interview with Jehmlich, March 2018

18 https://www.youtube.com/watch?v=9PAQ_Y5ins8, Putin answering students' questions at the Sirius education centre for gifted children in Sochi

19 Author interview with former member of Red Army Faction, March 2018

20 Michael Wines, 'Putin Was Once Decorated as a Spy. Few Agree on his Deeds', New York Times, January 10 2000. See also author interview with Franz Sedelmayer, April 2018

21 Guy Chazan and David Crawford, 'In From the Cold: A Friendship Forged in Spying Pays Dividends in Russia Today', Wall Street Journal, February 23 2005

22 Ibid.

23 Warnig was recruited by the Department of Rocket Science and Technology. By 1989, Warnig had become deputy head of the Stasi's information and technology unit. See Mackrakis, Seduced by Secrets, p.50; Karen Dawisha, Putin's Kleptocracy: Who Owns Russia, pp.51-2

24 Author interview with former member of Red Army Faction, March 2018

25 Mark Franchetti, 'Germans Flush Out Putin's Spies', Sunday Times, 16 January 2000; Geoffrey York, 'Putin Brings Spies in From the Cold', Globe and Mail, 8 May 2000

26 Author interview with Jehmlich, March 2018

27 Natalia Gevorkyan, Natalia Timakova, Andrei Kolesnikov, In the First Person: Conversations with Vladimir Putin, p.69

28 Forster, Auf der Spur, p.111

29 Author interview with Western banker, February 2018; the princess later appeared in St Petersburg, her home town, when Putin was its deputy mayor. She'd led the Order of St Lazarus, a charitable order that sent humanitarian assistance and food to St Petersburg in the months following the Soviet collapse. Putin was later said to hold her in 'high esteem'. (This taken from Tatiana von Metternich's obituary, Daily

Telegraph, August 19 2006. Also, Putin signed a letter of thanks to von Metternich as head of the Charitable Order of St Lazarus of Jerusalem: 'Putin Tenders Thanks to Leader of German Charitable Order', ITAR-TASS, February 25 2003)

30 Forster, *Auf der Spur*, p.31

31 Koehler, *Stasi*, p.411

32 Forster, *Auf der Spur*, p.29

33 Ibid.

34 Ibid., p.31

35 Ibid., pp.29–31

36 Stasi archives Dresden, BSTU number 10448. The document dated December 22 1988 lists the birthdays of the Soviet comrades in Dresden. Putin is listed as a Liaison Officer and as the Party Secretary. Putin himself in *In the First Person: Conversations with Vladimir Putin*, p.73, claims he did not interact with Modrow apart from a few times at official receptions. 'In general, we didn't work with party functionaries, including our own by the way. It was prohibited.' – a claim that is belied by his official role as party secretary.

37 Forster, *Auf der Spur*, p.33

38 Leonid Nikitinsky and Yuriy Shpakov, 'Putin v razvedke', interviews with Vladimir Kryuchkov and Markus Wolf, *Moskovskie Novosti*, January 20 2000, http://flb.ru/info/3508.html

39 Ibid.

40 Author interview with Jehmlich, March 2018. Again in *In the First Person: Conversations with Vladimir Putin*, pp.72–4, Putin claims he wasn't involved in Operation Luch. 'I'm baffled to read that western countries are looking for agents I recruited. It's all baloney. Our friends as we called the GDR security agents have copies of everything we produced. It is all preserved in their archives . . . Everything is transparent and understandable.' Putin himself and his own colleagues however have described how they destroyed all their files, including the ones kept by the Stasi, while officials at the Dresden Stasi archive and Jehmlich confirm the Russians managed to destroy almost everything.

41 Forster, *Auf der Spur*, p.26

42 Ibid., pp.9–10 (The senior German official was Dr Klaus-Peter Wild, then in charge of 'special assets' in a state agency set up to reprivatise East German assets.)

43 Ibid., p.36; see also Deutscher Bundestag, 2 Untersuchungsausschuss 'DDR Vermogen', Protocol of witness statement of Herbert Kohler, Bonn, 27/2/1997

44 Report of Schalck commission, Beschlussempfehlung and Bericht des 2. Untersuchungsausschusses nach Artikel 44 des Grundgesetzes. Drucksache 13/10900, 1998, pp.221–3. Also Andreas Forster, *Auf der Spur*, pp.98–107; see also Kristie Mackrakis, *Seduced by Secrets*, pp.130–2

45 Forster, *Auf der Spur*, p.131. When questioned by the federal authorities of the reunified Germany in 1997, Kohler claimed that the plans to create a network of operative firms in case of collapse had never been put in motion, as the speed of the GDR's fall had taken everyone by surprise and rendered them obsolete. But documents from the Stasi archive appear to show that the Dresden Stasi, under Kohler's watch, signed off on a string of deals for the import of components for the hard-disc plant following the collapse of the Berlin Wall, while the components seem never to have shown up. Hundreds more millions of marks disappeared into Schlaff front companies in

Liechtenstein, Switzerland and Singapore in a series of deals. Schlaff's companies in turn made a series of unsecured loans to companies staffed by former Stasi members, including to a chain of travel agencies and to a Stasi collaborator who bought an elite guesthouse overlooking the Elbe, which was often visited by Markus Wolf. Kohler, meanwhile, went to work as an adviser to Schlaff. Precisely what happened to the hard-disc plant remains a secret. The German government filed suit against Schlaff in Switzerland in the late nineties for the siphoning of tens of millions of marks intended for the hard-disc plant. In 2002, a Swiss court rejected the claim. Schlaff has denied ever working for the Stasi. He didn't respond to an interview request for this book.

46 Author interview with Jehmlich, March 2018

47 See Chapter 11

48 Forster, *Auf der Spur*, p.91

49 Author interview with Sven Scharl, Stasi Archive Dresden, March 2018

50 Putin's Stasi file, Dresden, BSTU MfS BV Dresden 1.Stellvertr. d. LTR. 3, BSTU 000004, September 7 1989

51 Christoph Seils, 'Was tat Putin in Dresden?', *Cicero Magazin*, November 2004; see also Leonid Nikitinsky and Yuriy Shpakov, 'Putin v razvedke'

52 Vladimir Usoltsev, *Sosluzhivets*, pp.61–2; Putin first admitted his work with the illegal sleeper-agent division in an interview with Russian state television channel Rossiya on the ninety-fifth anniversary of the infamous Upravleniye S, June 24 2017, https://ria.ru/politics/20170624/1497226538.html

53 Vladimir Usoltsev, *Sosluzhivets*, pp.69–70, 109–10. The book mainly describes the everyday lives of the KGB officers serving in Dresden and their families, including the tourist trips they took, the Christmas fairs and other attractions of Dresden, the beer they drank and the many formal celebratory events they had to attend for 'protocol' with their Stasi 'friends'. It takes care to go into almost no detail on their operative work, stressing only its mundanity. See also 'Intervyu s byvshim sosluzhivtsom Vladimira Putina', Radio Svoboda, November 11 2003

54 Putin, *First Person*, p.70

55 Author interview with former RAF member, March 2018

56 From Politburo archives retrieved by Soviet dissident Vladimir Bukovsky. www.bukovsky-archives.net, document numbers 0903, 0911, 0912

57 Koehler, *Stasi*, p.359

58 Dr Marian K. Leighton, 'Strange Bedfellows: The Stasi and the Terrorists', *International Journal of Intelligence and CounterIntelligence*, Volume 27, 2014 (According to this paper, Leighton worked in the US intelligence community from 1980, first as a Soviet analyst at the CIA, then as a counter-terrorism specialist with the Defence Intelligence Agency, and then again with the CIA as an independent contractor.)

59 Koehler, *Stasi*, p.360

60 Ibid., pp.361–2, 368–71; see also Leighton, 'Strange Bedfellows'

61 Leighton, 'Strange Bedfellows'

62 Koehler, *Stasi*, p.333

63 Ibid., p.344

64 Oleg Kalugin, CNN interview, February 6 2007

65 Ion Mihai Pacepa, 'Russian Footprints: What does Moscow have to do with the recent war in Lebanon?', National Review Online, August 24 2006

66 Ibid.

67 Koehler, *Stasi*, p.389

68   Author interview, April 2018

69   Koehler, *Stasi*, p.392

70   Butz Peters, 'Dresden Vergessen', *Sächsische Zeitung*, August 1 2017, https://web.archive.org/web/2017080204 5025/http://www.sz-online.de/sachsen/ dresden-vergessen-3739077.html; see also Leighton, 'Strange Bedfellows'

71   Koehler, *Stasi*, p.392; see also Steven Kinzer, 'Spy Charges Widen in Germany's East', *New York Times*, March 28 1991

72   Jeffrey Steinberg, 'Arrests Prove Stasi-KGB Control of Baader-Meinhof Terrorists', *EIR*, Volume 17, Number 27, June 29 1990

73   Author interview with former RAF member, March 2018

74   Koehler, *Stasi*, p.370

75   Leighton, 'Strange Bedfellows'

76   Koehler, *Stasi*, p.392

77   Author interview, March 2018

78   Lally Weymouth, 'East Germany's Dirty Secret', *Washington Post*, October 14 1990. The defector interviewed for this article is described by West German officials as 'one of the most important eastern bloc intelligence agents to have emigrated'.

79   Author interview with former Red Army Faction member, March 2018

80   Koehler, *Stasi*, p.392; see also David Crawford, 'The Murder of a CEO', *Wall Street Journal*, September 15 2007

81   Author interview with Western intelligence expert, March 2018

82   Koehler, *Stasi*, p.392

83   Author interview, March 2018; other attacks the Red Army Faction was implicated in while Putin was in Dresden include bombings at the USAF Rhein-Main air base and the assassination of the chief technology officer at Siemens.

84   Author interview with Horst Jehmlich, March 2018

85   Author interview with Putin ally, October 2018

86   David Crawford and Marcus Bensmann, 'Putin's Early Years', *Correctiv*, July 30 2015

87   Ibid.

88   Putin, *First Person*, p.76

89   Ibid., p.79

90   Ibid.

91   Ibid., p.80

92   Vladimir Usoltsev, *Sosluzhivets*, p.253. 'All the documents that had anything to do with us were collected by Thomas Muller, and he handed them over in their entirety to Volodya Putin, carrying out the orders of Böhm. Within a few hours nothing was left of them apart from a pile of ash.'

93   Vladislav Kramar, 'Gruppa v Dresdene byla nebolshaya, no moshchnaya', *Voenny-Promyshlenny Kurier*, December 14 2005

94   Ibid.

95   Masha Gessen, *The Man Without a Face: The Unlikely Rise of Vladimir Putin*, p.97

96   Author interview with Jehmlich

97   Zuchold, however, had defected to the West almost immediately, and according to Thomas Schade, 'Verbrannte Vogel', *Sächsische Zeitung*, October 15 2015, he had allegedly exposed fifteen agents in Berlin, Leipzig, Dresden and Erfurt.

98   'Putin Rasskazal o nelegalnoi razvedke i svoei rabote v KGB', RIA Novosti, June 24 2017

99   Weymouth, 'East Germany's Dirty Secret'. The defector is cited as saying that Modrow was designated as successor to Egon Krenz, then leader of the SED, at a secret conference at the Soviet embassy in East Berlin on November 12 1989, attended by Valentin Falin, the head of the Soviet Communist Party's International Department, Markus Wolf, Krenz and Modrow

100   Forster, *Auf der Spur*, p.122

101 Weymouth, 'East Germany's Dirty Secret'

102 Oleg Blotsky, *Vladimir Putin: Doroga k Vlasti*, pp.281–86

103 Author interview with Andrei Illarionov, former presidential economic aide to Putin and a friend of Starovoitova from Leningrad, September 2014

104 Author interview with Franz Sedelmayer, April 2018

105 Archive footage in *Delo Sobchaka*, film by Ksenia Sobchak and Vera Krichevskaya, 2018, shows Putin entering the TV tower with Sobchak ahead of the speech

106 Author interview with Alexander Belyayev, then deputy head of St Petersburg's city council, and eyewitness to these events, June 2013

107 Ibid.

108 Author interview with Sedelmayer, April 2018

Chapter 2: Inside Job

1 Sovershenno Sekretno, *Taina Zolota Partii*, 2007. Interview with Valentin Falin.

2 Valentin Stepankov, *Kremlyevsky Zagovor: Versiya Sledstviya*, pp.238–9. This account by the Russian prosecutor general in charge of investigating the missing Party funds is based on testimony by Kruchina's wife and the KGB watchman who found his body. See also Sovershenno Sekretno, *Taina Zolota Partii*

3 Ibid., pp.235–6

4 Ibid., p.236

5 Author interview with Gerashchenko, September 2013

6 Author interview with Leonov, September 2013

7 'Soviet Turmoil; New Suicide: Budget Director', *New York Times*, August 27 1991

8 Sergei Pluzhnikov and Sergei Sokolov, 'Kak KGB Svodil Schety c KPSS', *Komsomolskaya Pravda*, January 1 1992

9 Peter Torday and Tony Barber, 'Communists Pillaged Party Gold – Officials Investigate Flight of Soviet Billions', *Independent*, March 27 1992; John Rettle, 'Russian government Launches Investigation into Missing Communist Party Billions', *Guardian*, September 10 1991. Nikolai Ryzhkov later told a parliamentary hearing that when Gorbachev came to power the Soviet Union's gold reserves had stood at 1,200 tonnes, but by the time he stepped down they were close to zero. One Russian newspaper *Komsomolskaya Pravda* cited documents apparently showing the Party had transferred 280 billion roubles ($12bn) into hard-currency accounts in foreign banks. The original article has since disappeared from the internet. Sovershenno Sekretno, *Taina Zolota Partii*

10 Stephen Handelman, 'How Man's Conscience Overcame His Fear', *Toronto Star*, February 14 1992

11 Stepankov, *Kremlevsky Zagovor*, pp.313–14

12 Ibid., p.284; Handelman, *Toronto Star*, February 14 1992

13 Stepankov, pp.286–7

14 Ibid., p.290

15 Handelman, *Toronto Star*, February 14 1992

16 When later questioned, many of the Party's top operatives believed they were in the right, and that the Party's interests were synonymous with those of the state. In fact, the Party *was* the state, and had been since the Bolshevik Revolution. 'There is nothing unusual about this practice,' the Party's former deputy secretary general, Vladimir Ivashko, later told prosecutors. 'The support of social

forces . . . to influence public opinion has always been one of the most important functions of the state.' Testimony from Ivashko, *Kremlevsky Zagovor*, pp.295–6

17   Stepankov, p.285; Smirnov however also said at least $200m per year had been transferred out of the Soviet Union to fund Communist-linked parties between 1977 and 1989: Handelman, *Toronto Star*, February 14 1992

18   Stepankov, p.301; Vadim Belykh and Valery Rudnev, 'Dengi Partii: Milliardy Obnaruzheny, no sledstvie, pokhozhe, v tupike', *Izvestia*, 10/02/92, https://old.flb.ru/info/4896.html

19   Author interview with Antonio Fallico, June 2013. Fallico named three friendly firms that Italian business had to work through in order to do business deals in the Soviet Union. One was named Restital, and   even if it did not participate directly in a deal, he said, Italian firms would have to pay a percentage to it. The two others were Italimpec and Esteuropa, while any tourists seeking to go to the Soviet Union would have to go through a Communist Party-owned firm, Italtourism.

20   Mary Dejevsky, 'Maxwell's former firm on List of Soviet Favourites', *Independent*, November 9 1991; Peter Pringle, 'Soviets to Conduct Inquiry Over Friendly Firms', *Independent*, November 11 1991

21   Author interviews with former senior KGB operative, May 2013, and with an intermediary who ran one of the friendly firms supplying dual-use medical/military equipment, March 2013. Christopher Andrew and Vasily Mitrokhin, *The Mitrokhin Archive: The KGB in Europe and the West*, pp.597–8, however, describes a more realistic explanation: that Thyssen, Siemens and others were infiltrated by Soviet agents stealing Western technology.

22   Author interview with former Gorbachev aide, June 2014

23   Vadim Belykh and Valery Rudnev, Izvestiya, 'Dengi Partii: Milliardy Obnaruzheny, no sledstvie, pokhozhe, v tupike', February 10 1992, https://old.flb.ru/info/4896.html; author interview with Tommy Helsby, a former Kroll chairman, March 2013. For more information on the work of the friendly firms and the looting of the Party funds by the KGB operatives see also the excellent testimony of Richard Palmer, former CIA station chief in the Former Soviet Union, on the Infiltration of the Western financial system by elements of Russian Organised Crime, before the House Committee on Banking and Financial Services, September 21 1999

24   Stepankov, p.301

25   Author interview with Vitaly Shlykov, September 2006

26   Stepankov, pp.301–3

27   Stepankov, p.236; Belykh and Rudnev, 'Dengi Partii: Milliardy Obnaruzheny, no sledstvie, pokhozhe, v tupike', *Izvestiya*, February 10 1992; Sokolov and Pluzhnikov, 'Zoloto KPSS: Desyat Lyet Spustya', *Moskovskie Novosti*, September 18 2001, http://kompromat.flb.ru/material1.phtml?id=566

28   Sokolov and Pluzhnikov, 'Zoloto KPSS: Desyat Lyet Spustya', *Moskovskie Novosti*, September 18 2001

29   Stepankov, p.296; Sokolov and Pluzhnikov, 'Zoloto KPSS: Desyat Lyet Spustya', *Moskovskie Novosti*, September 18 2001; Richard Palmer, House Banking Committee Testimony, September 21 1999; author interview with Yury Shvets, May 2018

30   Sokolov and Pluzhnikov, *Moskovskie Novosti*, September 18 2001

31   Ibid.

32   Author interview with Shvets, May 2018

33 Sokolov and Pluzhnikov, *Moskovskie Novosti*, September 18 2001. The criminal investigation by the Russian prosecutors into the missing Party wealth was later classified – all two hundred tomes of it. Only fragments of information have been released.

34 Sovershenno Sekretno, *Taina Zolota Partii*, interview with Oleg Sheinin, former Politburo member, who says Gorbachev ignored the Ivashko memo and nothing was done

35 Stepankov, p.303

36 One of the joint ventures Seabeco set up in Toronto was the Soviet Central Council of Trade Unions, to 'build resorts, a department store and even a car rental agency' ('Soviet Organisation, Toronto Group of Firms Join Forces in Projects', *Globe and Mail*, October 12 1988); another was between Seabeco and Georgy Arbatov, director of the Institute of Canadian and American Studies in Moscow, believed to be a front for Russian intelligence (Canada Newswire, November 15 1988).

37 Sovershenno Sekretno, *Taina Zolota Partii*. Interview with Kryuchkov

38 Sovershenno Sekretno, *Taina Zolota Partii*. The taped conversation is apparently between Dmitry Yakubovsky who worked for Seabeco in the early nineties, and Yury Kotov, a former colonel in the SVR, the foreign-intelligence service, who worked closely with Primakov in the seventies.

39 'Ex-Aide to Gaidar Targets Rutskoi in business scandal', Agence France-Presse, August 12 1993. The Swiss intelligence service later named Seabeco as being one of the firms believed to be at the centre of transfers of Soviet state and Party wealth by the KGB, while it claimed Birshtein was a former KGB officer.

40 Sokolov and Pluzhnikov, 'Zoloto KPSS: Desyat Lyet Spustya', *Moskovskie Novosti*, September 18 2001. Sovershenno Sekretno, *Taina Zolota Partii*, reports that the prosecutors were able to find six hundred banks and firms inside the Soviet Union, as well as a further five hundred abroad, including dozens of German, Swiss and offshore firms.

41 Andrei Illesh and Valery Rudnev, 'Poisk deneg KPSS: Pessimistichesky Konyets', *Izvestiya*, April 1 1993, https://old.flb.ru/info/4910.html

42 Author interview with Pyotr Aven, May 2015

43 Author interview with Helsby, March 2013

44 Ibid. Rich was indicted for fraud and racketeering, and later controversially pardoned by US President Bill Clinton. A chief investigating magistrate in Bologna Italy, Paolo Giovagnoli, has said Marc Rich worked closely with a Vienna-based trading firm owned by Grigory Loutchansky, an alleged Russian mobster. Giovagnoli said Nordex was another outfit set up to funnel out Communist Party funds before the Soviet collapse. (P.K. Semier, 'US Fugitive Rich Linked to Money Laundering; Russian-Mafia Prosecutors May Subpoena Him', *Washington Times*, June 21 2002)

45 Author interview with Pavel Voshchanov, March 2013

46 Author interview with senior Russian businessman, May 2018

47 David Remnick, 'Soviet Union's Shadow Economy – Bribery, Barter, Black Market deals are the Facts of Life', *Washington Post*, September 22 1990; for further reading on the shortages of the skewed Soviet economy see David Hoffman's excellent *The Oligarchs: Wealth and Power in the New Russia*, pp.11–20

48 Author interview with former black-market currency trader

49 Author interview with Shvets, May 2018

50 Author interview with Milshtein associate, May 2018; Vesti, Programma 60 Minut: 'Mikhail Milshtein: Genialny Razvedchik I Borets s Kholodnoi Voinoi', September 15 2010, http://www.vesti.ru/doc.html?id=392836

51 Author interview with Rair Simonyan, November 2013

52 Author interview with Vladimir Yakunin, August 2018; see also Vladimir Yakunin, *The Treacherous Path*, p.21

53 Author interview with Christian Michel, June 2004

54 Author interview with Anton Surikov, February 2005

55 A report by the Swiss intelligence service, obtained by the author and written in June 2007, stated Luchansky and Birshtein had been recruited by the KGB to transfer the state and Party wealth into private hands on the eve of the Soviet collapse: 'The money should have partly been used for financing political operations, but partly the cash was stolen to finance private economic activity.'

56 Mikhail Khodorkovsky and Natalya Gevorkyan, *Tyurma I Volya*, pp.91–2

57 Author interview with former Khodorkovsky partner

58 Khodorkovsky and Gevorkyan, p.94

59 Author interview with Khodorkovsky, May 2014

60 Hoffman, *The Oligarchs*, pp.107–10; author interview with Khodorkovsky, May 2014; Khodorkovsky and Gevorkyan, pp.75–82

61 Hoffman, *The Oligarchs*, pp.107–8; author interview with Khodorkovsky, May 2014

62 Author interview with Christian Michel, January 2014

63 Author interview with Thomas Graham, June 2014

64 Author interview with Michel, September 2013

65 Author interview with Khodorkovsky, May 2014

66 Chrystia Freeland, *Sale of the Century*, p.108

67 Author interview with former government official, June 2014

68 Author interview with Khodorkovsky, May 2014; Khodorkovsky and Gevorkyan, pp.82–6

69 Author interview with Artyom Tarasov, November 2013; see also the autobiography by Artyom Tarasov, *Millionaire: The Sermon of the New Russia's First Capitalist*, Chapter 5

70 Author interview with Michel, January 2014

71 A key intermediary in talks with the KGB on holding off any storm was Arkady Volsky, a former economic adviser to KGB chief Yury Andropov who'd built close ties with the KGB and later was seen as the grandfather to Russia's new class of tycoons as head of the powerful Russian Union of Industrialists and Entrepreneurs. Volsky had also participated in the gold rush: his Simako company had been permitted to convert roubles into dollars at a special Party rate of 1.8 roubles to the dollar, as well as export large quantities of arms.

72 Author interview with Andrei Illarionov, September 2015

73 Author interview with Simonyan, November 2013

74 Author interview with Graham, June 2014

75 Author interview with former senior KGB operative, May 2013

76 Richard Palmer, testimony before the House Committee on Banking and Financial Services, September 21, 1999;

see his testimony too for a clear-eyed account of the various stages in the KGB plans to transfer the Party wealth out of the country into the West.

77 Ibid.

78 See Chapter 15; Author interview with Yury Shvets, May 2018

79 Pete Earley, *Comrade J: The Untold Secrets of Russia's Master Spy in America After the End of the Cold War*, pp.285–8

80 One of the biggest conduits, a company named Fimaco, had been quietly set up on Jersey by senior Soviet banking officials just months after Ivashko's decree on the creation of the 'invisible economy'. A Russian prosecutor later claimed it had been used to funnel up to $50 billion in central bank reserves in the nineties, including billions of dollars in loans from the International Monetary Fund. ('Eight metric tons of platinum, 60 metric tons of gold, hoards of diamonds and an estimated $15 billion to $50 billion in cash were . . . transferred to unknown hands by the KGB's espionage branch between 1989 and 1991,' Palmer later testified to US Congress.)

81 Yevgenia Albats, *KGB: State Within a State*, p.303

82 Author interview with KGB intermediary, March 2013

83 Author interview with Andrei Illarionov, September 2015. The $200 million payment came out of the difference in price between the oil products supplied and the sugar imports received. For a full description of this scheme see Illarionov, 'Trudny Put k Svobode' Part II, *Zhurnal Kontinent*, No 146, May 4 2011, pp.13–17

84 Author interview with Illarionov, September 2015. The missing $1 billion IMF loan had troubled Illarionov's

associate Boris Fyodorov, then finance minister, since 1992. Illarionov had only been able to find out what happened to it after he was appointed Kremlin economic adviser in 2000. Then, as a member of the central bank's supervisory council, he was able to access the accounts of the Russian foreign state banks, including Eurobank: 'We were studying the accounts after the Eurobank network had been sold on, and I said, "Where does this $1 billion come from? We need to pay attention to this sum it received at the end of 1992." It turned out the IMF loan had been transferred to save Eurobank. It was the KGB bank, and Gaidar had been able to save it all.' The government had first transferred the loan from the central bank to the state bank for foreign economic operations, Vneshekonombank, from there to Eurobank, and then to Fimaco on the offshore haven of Jersey, which used the funds to buy up Eurobank's bad debts. For more detail on this see Illarionov, 'Trudny Put k Svobode' Part II, *Zhurnal Kontinent*, No 146, pp.150–6

85 Author interview with Michel, January 2014

86 Filip Bobkov, the former head of the KGB's fifth directorate for minorities, went to work with his close protégé Vladimir Gusinsky at Most Bank, as head of its analytical department. Leonid Shebarshin, the head of the KGB's foreign-intelligence directorate in the final years of the regime, served as head of security for the first bank to be given a hard-currency licence, the All Russian Exchange Bank. Nikolai Leonov, the powerful head of the foreign-intelligence service's analytical department, took a post as its vice

president. On paper, the bank was headed by a twenty-three-year-old finance whizz, Alexander Konanykhin. But in reality it was a front for the KGB. Leonov had worked closely too with a man who was then one of the country's most under-the-radar bankers, Sergei Pugachev, whose Mezhprombank had also been one of the first to receive a hard-currency licence.

87 Author interview with Shvets, May 2018

88 Hoffman, *The Oligarchs*, pp.120–1

89 Jeffrey D. Sachs, 'Russia's Failure to Reform', Project Syndicate, August 30 1999

90 Janine R. Wedel, 'The Harvard Boys do Russia', *The Nation*, May 14 1998 (Wedel refers to one of these Harvard economists, Andrei Shleifer, noting in his book *Privatising Russia* that 'Aid can change the political equilibrium by explicitly helping free-market reformers to defeat their political opponents'.)

91 Author interview with Yavlinsky, February 2014

92 Author interview with Pavlovsky, May 2014

93 Chrystia Freeland, *Sale of the Century*, p.169

94 Ibid., pp.173–4

95 Chrystia Freeland, John Thornhill and Andrew Gowers, 'Moscow's Group of Seven', *Financial Times*, November 1 1996. Tellingly, Khodorkovsky, for instance, had first secured a pact with the management of Yukos, including two former senior KGB operatives, agreeing to later pay them 30 per cent of the company's worth. One of the privatisation officials in charge of the Yukos auction later admitted that Khodorkovsky had used his connections there to pledge future oil sales from Yukos to raise the cash for the auction.

96 Author interview with Michel, December 2012

97 Author interview with Simonyan, November 2013

98 Author interview with Shvets, May 2018

Chapter 3: 'The Tip of an Iceberg'

1 Author interview, February 2014

2 Author interview, June 2014

3 Author interview with former senior KGB officer, May 2013

4 Author interview with former local FSB officer, June 2014

5 Marina Salye, 'V. Putin – "President" Korrumpirovannoi Oligarkhii!', The Glasnost Foundation, March 18 2000

6 Anastasia Kirilenko, 'Pochemu Marina Salye Molchala o Putine 10 Lyet?', interview with Marina Salye, Radio Svoboda, March 2-4 2010; for more information see also the excellent article by Vladimir Ivanidze, 'Spasaya Polkovnika Putina: Vtoraya Popytka', Radio Svoboda, March 16 2010

7 Vladimir Ivanidze, 'Spasaya Polkovnika Putina: Vtoraya Popytka', Radio Svoboda, March 16 2010. According to documents on the deals collected by the Salye foundation and seen by the author, Putin sends a letter to Aven on December 4 1991 asking for the city to be granted quotas for the export of $124m worth of raw materials in exchange for imports of food, as the only way to ensure food supplies to the city in the first two months of 1992. In the letter, Putin asks for his Committee for Foreign Relations to be granted the right to issue export licences to firms working on the deals. The signature of Yegor Gaidar, the Russian prime minister, saying he agrees, is apparently dated December 5 1991 (some commentators have cast doubt on the signature, saying they believe it is a forgery). But the government order

agreeing the scheme is issued only January 9 1992. However, a February 3 1992 letter from the head of St Petersburg's representative for the ministry of foreign economic relations A. Pakhomov to Aven indicates another barter scheme had been approved for St Petersburg earlier in November, but had also failed. This letter says the first quota for the sale of 100,000 tonnes of diesel fuel was issued by Gaidar on November 21 1991 and granted to Kirishinefteorgsintez, which it said sold the diesel fuel but had not given any of the revenues to the city for the purchase of food. Pakhomov's letter says a new set of quotas were then issued by the Gaidar government.

8   Author interview with Alexander Belyayev, former chairman of St Petersburg City Council, June 2013

9   Marina Salye, 'Nastal Chered Putina – 'Presidenta' Korrumpirovannovo Klana', February 29 2012; Ivanidze, 'Spasaya Polkovnika Putina: Vtoraya Popytka'; Letter from Belyayev to V Putin calling on him to address the city council on January 14 1992 and produce all documentation on the deals.

10   Ivanidze, 'Spasaya Polkovnika Putina'; Marina Salye, 'Nastal Chered Putina – 'Presidenta' Korrumpirovannovo Klana'; the two pages of notes Putin handed over can also be found in the documents of the Salye Commission: Prilozhenie 16 'O sostoyanii del po Vydache Litsenzii pod obespechenie goroda prodovolstviem', V. Putin; Tablitsa No 1 'Prodovolstvie, poluch-aemoe v schet Vydannoi Litsenzii'

11   Ivanidze, 'Spasaya Polkovnika Putina'

12   Salye, 'V. Putin – "President" Korrumpi-rovannoi Oligarkhii!'

13   Ibid.

14   Ibid.; Salye, 'Nastal Chered Putina – "Presidenta" Korrumpirovannovo Klana'

15   Documents from Salye Commission: January 27 1992 letter from the head of St Petersburg's Customs, V.T. Stepanov, to Putin, saying cargo of timber cannot be passed because the export licence is not in line with the laws governing such barter schemes: only 50 per cent of the revenue from the sale is to be used to purchase food, licence has not been signed by the correct person, the value of the goods is artificially low; February 12 1992 letter from Fyodor Shkrudnev, deputy representative of the president in the St Petersburg region, to Putin saying licences contain serious miscal-culations on the value of exported goods and on the sanctions to be levied if the intermediary fails to meet the terms; February 3 1992 letter from Alexander Pakhomov, the St Petersburg representative for the foreign trade ministry, to Aven pointing out that the quotas issued to Putin have not been confirmed by the ministry of economy and finance, the licences have been handed out to obscure firms not specialists in foreign trade operations, the 50:50 split in the revenues with half going to the city for food imports and the rest going to the intermediaries is not in line with laws governing barter schemes.

16   Salye Commission; Expert Opinion, Prilozhenie 12

17   Salye Commission: Copies of contracts and licences; Salye, 'V. Putin – "President" Korrumpirovannoi Oligarkhii!'

18   Salye, 'V. Putin – "President" Korrumpirovannoi Oligarkhii!'

19   Ibid.; Salye Commission documents: December 4 1991 letter from Putin to Aven asking for his Committee for Foreign Relations to be granted the right to issue export licences to firms

working on the barter deals. The signature of Yegor Gaidar, the Russian prime minister, saying he agrees, is apparently dated December 5 1991 (some commentators have cast doubt on the signature, saying they believe it is a forgery). But the government order agreeing the scheme was issued only on January 9 1992. Gaidar later apparently overrules Putin's authority to issue such licences, writing to the head of the Customs Committee that according to a government decree of December 31 1991 only the ministry for foreign economic trade and its regional representatives have the right to do so. But Aven writes an order dated March 25 1992 instructing A. Pakhomov, the St Petersburg representative for the foreign trade ministry, to hand over authority for foreign economic activity to Putin's Foreign Relations Committee – i.e. Putin's committee is to keep its sphere of authority over licences.

20   Salye Commission documents: Prilozhenie 3, date 20/12/91

21   Salye Commission documents: Prilozhenie 30, 59, date 14/1/92

22   Salye, 'V. Putin – "President" Korrumpirovannoi Oligarkhii!'

23   This was an Azeri named Dzhandir Ragimov. 'He was very close with Putin,' one former employee of the firm said, author interview with former employee of Dzhikop, March 2014. On paper the firm was owned by a German named Peter Bachmann who has never been heard of since – Ivanidze, 'Spasaya Polkovnika Putina'

24   Salye, 'V. Putin – "President" Korrumpirovannoi Oligarkhii!'; Ivanidze, 'Spasaya Polkovnika Putina'

25   Irena Pietsch, *Pikantnaya Druzhba*, p.171

26   Author interview with Belyaev, June 2013

27   According to documents obtained by the author from the Salye Commission [Prilozhenie 44, date 31/3/1992], quotas for the export of 150,000 tonnes in diesel and fuel oil were granted under the oil-for-food scheme to Kirishineftorgsintez, the Kirishi refinery which at the time owned Kirishineftekhimexport where Timchenko worked as a senior manager. (Andrei Korchagin, a former official in the St Petersburg city government, told me Timchenko also worked as Kirishineftorgsintez's finance director in 1991–92.) According to these documents, however, unusually the licence to sell these exports was given to an outfit named Nevsky Dom, not to Timchenko's Kirishineftekhimexport, which normally handled all exports for the Kirishi refinery. However, one of Timchenko's former partners in Kirishineftekhimexport told me the company participated in the oil-for-food scheme, and met its obligations in full (see note 34), while Belyaev is a senior official who had broader oversight of the scheme than Salye (Salye's commission did not have access to all the documents in the scheme) and his claims that Timchenko and co also took part in the scheme are credible.

28   Author interview with former Timchenko partner in Kirishineftekhimexport, June 2013. 'We decided to create an external trade firm for the refinery,' the former Timchenko partner said. 'This is how we began . . . We went [to the heads of the refinery] and got to know them. It was our initiative.'

29   Author interview with former Western intelligence source, July 2013

30   Author interview with former senior KGB, officer, March 2014; Author interview with another former senior KGB

officer and former Timchenko partner, September 2013

31 Irina Mokrousova and Irina Reznik, 'Chelovek s Resursom', *Vedomosti*, January 21 2013

32 Author interview with senior KGB officer, March 2014

33 Author interview with senior Russian banker with ties to the security services, September 2017; see also Alexander Levinsky, Irina Malkova and Valery Igumenov, 'Kak Matthias Warnig stal samim nadezhnym "ekonomistom" Putina', *Forbes*, August 28 2012

34 Author interview with former Timchenko partner, June 2013. In the interview, the former Timchenko partner said the following about their firm's participation in the oil-for-food deals: 'We sold oil products – diesel and fuel oil – in return for food. They were barter deals under a special decree of the Gaidar government . . . Of course we did not choose ourselves. We came to the city and said what do you need – we will sell for you – and what to buy for the city we didn't know. For this, of course, we were given orders from the city administration . . . 100 per cent of the earnings went to buy food. We were asking what was necessary. I don't remember now what we bought. I think we bought children's food for example.' The former Timchenko partner also said the firm's founders met with Putin then. 'Part of his authority was external economic trade. Of course we came across him.' In an earlier interview with *Russian Forbes* (Irina Malkova and Igor Terentyev, 'U menya vezde yest optsiony', November 2012), Timchenko had denied Kirishineftekhimexport, otherwise known as Kinex, took part in the oil-for-food deals. 'Kinex never had any relation to this story. For a long

time I didn't understand where all this came from. We were checked all the time. And recently I finally got documents which showed that Kinex had no relation to the story with this diesel. There was just a company with a similar name.' In addition, lawyers for Timchenko said in a comment for this book that any allegation Kinex was involved in any form of illegal or otherwise improper or unethical conduct in that regard – and that Mr Timchenko was thereby also complicit in any such misconduct – would be 'entirely untrue. All of Kinex's activities were fully transparent and legitimate.'

35 Author interview with Salye associate, March 2014

36 Author interview with Felipe Turover, over three days, May 2013

37 Ibid.

38 Second author interview with Felipe Turover, March 2014

39 Ibid.

40 Author interview with Viktor Gerashchenko, September 2013

41 Author interview with Turover, March 2014

42 Others who delved into these deals had been frightened, or worse. Yury Gladkov, a St Petersburg deputy who'd worked closely with Salye on the parliamentary investigation, refused for years to give any interviews on the subject. When he died in 2007 after a long illness, one associate said he believed he'd been poisoned: 'When I saw him a year before his death, he was shaking. It was as if he'd been pumped with something.' Another former Sobchak aide, Yury Shutov, who'd been Putin's sworn enemy, died in one of Russia's harshest and most remote penal colonies, having been arrested in 1998 as Putin moved up the Kremlin ladder.

The many secrets he'd dug up on Putin's time as deputy mayor disappeared with him forever.

43 Author interview with Illarionov, September 2015

44 Author interview with Kharchenko associate, November 2013

45 S. Ochinsky, 'Vozrozhdenie Flota – Zalog Stabilnosti Razvitiya Rossii. Konkurentskiya I Rynok', 2013, No. 4 (60). In 1991 the Baltic Sea Fleet's net profits reached $571m from transport services alone.

46 Ibid.

47 Author interview with Kharchenko associate, November 2013

48 Author interview with two associates of Kharchenko, November 2013 and March 2014; 'Vmeste rabotali, vmeste I syadem', Kommersant, October 24 1996

49 'Ubistvo Gendirektora Parokhodstva', Kommersant, October 4 1995

50 Author interview with Kharchenko associate, March 2014

51 Ibid.

52 Author interview with Kharchenko associate, November 2013

53 Documents from the Spanish court: Protocols from Initial Investigation no 321/06, Central Court of First Division No. 5, Fiscalia Especial Contra la Corrupcion y la Criminalidad Organizada; also a note from Interpol Monaco, dated July 3 2006, obtained by the author, which says that Traber was barred from the territory of Monaco from April 2000 due to his 'activities connected with Russian organised crime'; and in a note to Prince Albert's chief of staff, Jean-Luc Allavena, dated 10/04/2006, of which the author also has a copy, Robert Eringer, then head of the Monaco intelligence service, writes that Traber has 'ties to the Tambov Russian organised crime

group' and has been 'active in trading drugs, oils and metals on their behalf'.

54 Author interview with former Traber associate, November 2015

55 Author interview with former Traber partner, November 2015; DozhdTV, 'Minstr Porta: Kak Peterburgsky Avtoritet Ilya Traber Svyazan s Vladimirom Putinym I yevo okruzheniem', August 25 2017

56 Author interview with former St Petersburg FSB officer, June 2014

57 Author interviews with two former Traber associates, September 2015, and March 2013 and November 2015; and with former St Petersburg city official, March 2014. Documents obtained by the author show that in May 2001 Traber held a 52.5 per cent stake in the St Petersburg oil terminal via three Cyprus companies: Hellman Holdings Ltd, Myra Holdings Ltd and Almont Holdings Ltd.

58 Author interviews with two former Traber associates, September 2015 and March 2013 and November 2015

59 Interview with Lyudmilla Narusova, June 2014, in which she confirmed that her husband had stayed in close touch with Traber after he fled Russia for Paris in 1996, and that they were neighbours there

60 Author interview with former St Petersburg city official, March 2014

61 Author interview with former St Petersburg officer from FSB contraband division, June 2014

62 Kumarin became vice president of PTK in 1996, while his close partner Vladimir Smirnov became chairman of the board, as Kumarin's control over PTK came out into the open. Among the co-founders of PTK in 1994 was Bank Rossiya.

63 Documents from the Spanish court:

Protocols from Initial Investigation no 321/06, Central Court of First Division No. 5, Fiscalia Especial Contra la Corrupcion y la Criminalidad Organizada

64 Roman Anin, 'Druzya – Ne Razlei Neft', *Novaya Gazeta*, April 15 2011; author interview with Maxim Freidzon, former owner of the Sovex oil trader, September 2015; 'It was all one structure and at the top there was Putin. It would not have been possible to create PTK without him, while [Viktor] Cherkesov provided cover as head of the FSB,' said Andrei Korchagin, a former official in the St Petersburg city government.

65 German prosecutors opened a criminal probe into money laundering for the Tambov group by SPAG in 2003. At the time they were very specific about its suspected links: 'SPAG is Kumarin. All orders come from Kumarin,' said one of the prosecutors then. A founding shareholder of SPAG was a Liechtenstein financier named Rudolf Ritter, who in 2003 was arrested and charged with fraud and laundering millions of dollars in drug-trafficking funds for the Colombian Cali cartel, and transferring funds through SPAG for Russian organised crime. A Liechtenstein court found Ritter guilty of fraud in October 2003. The overarching investigation into SPAG ended in 2009 when the statute of limitation expired following resistance to the probe from Russian counterparts. The Kremlin has dismissed Putin's role on SPAG's supervisory board as no more than one of many such 'honorary' positions on companies' supervisory boards in his capacity as St Petersburg deputy mayor in charge of foreign economic affairs. One document seen by the author, however, appears to indicate a more active role: a December 1994 affidavit signed by Putin gives Vladimir Smirnov, Kumarin's business partner in PTK, or the St Petersburg Fuel Company, and a close Putin associate, 'voting rights in our absence' to 200 SPAG shares, then worth about 20 per cent of the company. In addition, another SPAG co-founder, Klaus-Peter Sauer, told me in 2003 he met with Putin five or six times in Frankfurt and St Petersburg to discuss SPAG's subsidiaries in St Petersburg.

66 See for instance Irina Malkova and Igor Terentyev, 'Tot samy Timchenko: Pervy Interview Bogateishevo iz Druzei Putina', *Russian Forbes*, October 26 2012

67 Irina Mokorusova and Irina Reznik, 'Chelovek s Resursom', January 21 2013

68 This French intelligence report, of which the author has a copy, was cited by Robert Eringer, then head of the Monaco intelligence service, in a note to Prince Albert's chief of staff, Jean-Luc Allavena, dated 10/04/2006, which the author also has a copy of.

69 Author interview with former Timchenko partner, August 2019

70 Ibid.

71 St Petersburg registration documents provided by Vladimir Pribylovsky

72 Author interviews with senior Western banker involved in the process, May 2014, and with former Timchenko partner involved in the process, May 2014 and August 2019

73 Ibid.

74 Author interview with former Timchenko partner, May 2014 (the senior Western banker said the talks foundered because the project was under attack from organised crime)

75 Ibid.

76 Author interview with two senior Western bankers, May 2014 and June 2013. According to them, the man who'd guaranteed Putin's daughter's safety in

Germany was the German banker Matthias Warnig – the former Stasi officer who had worked with Putin in Dresden as part of a KGB cell. Warnig took over legal guardianship of Putin's daughters, one of them said. 'Putin was afraid.' Warnig had arrived in St Petersburg soon after Putin's appointment as deputy mayor, as head of the new St Petersburg office of Dresdner Bank, which opened in December 1991.

77 Author interviews with two former Timchenko partners, June 2013, March 2014 and May 2014, August 2019

78 Author interview with former Traber associate, November 2015

79 Author interview with former KGB officer who worked in St Petersburg with Putin, May 2013

80 Roman Anin, 'Druzya – Ne Razlei Neft', *Novaya Gazeta*, April 15 2011

81 Alexander Levinsky, Irina Malkova, and Valery Igumenov, 'Kak Matthias Warnig stal samym nadezhnym "ekonomistom" Putina', *Russian Forbes*, August 28 2012

82 According to former Timchenko partner interviewed by the author in June 2013 and March 2014

83 According to Maxim Freidzon, the former Skigin partner in Sovex who the author interviewed September 2015

84 Ibid.

85 Ibid.

86 Anastasia Kirilenko, 'On Prosto Pisal Summu vo vremya besedy', interview with Freidzon, Radio Svoboda, May 24 2015

87 Author interview with former Traber associate, March 2013

88 Robert Eringer, then head of the Monaco intelligence service, note to Prince Albert's chief of staff, Jean-Luc Allavena, dated 10/04/2006

89 Author interview with two former Traber associates. According to

Freidzon, Putin's interest in the oil trading business extended to payment for his logistical support. At least, that's what he said had happened with the much smaller oil trader, Sovex, he co-owned with Skigin. Sovex bought fuel from Timchenko and sold it to the city's Pulkovo airport. Putin had granted Sovex everything it needed to operate: a licence to trade fuel, the right to use storage facilities at the airport, as well as the right to use its pipeline terminal. Freidzon claimed Putin had been granted a 4 per cent stake in the venture in return for his efforts. He said the stake was held via two of Traber's closest business partners, Alexander Ulanov and Viktor Korytov, a former KGB officer who'd worked closely with Putin in the Leningrad KGB. He was convinced the same arrangement must extend to other business such as the port and the oil terminal, but he never had any proof. The money Sovex made was funnelled through Liechtenstein where Skigin had registered the outfit. (Documents show that Nasdor Incorporated, the vehicle through which Traber and Skigin controlled the sea port, was registered there, while Hassler represented Skigin's interests in the oil terminal and the port into 2000 and beyond.) The same went for Skigin and Traber's stakes in the sea port and the oil terminal. The controlling stakes were held and managed by an outfit called Fibeko Treuhandstalt, where two financial managers who'd distributed Communist propaganda in Western Europe during Soviet times ran an antique bookstore as a front. Some of the financial intermediaries deployed in Soviet times had remained in place. 'These networks didn't go anywhere,' said one former intermediary for the KGB who'd worked with the Liechtenstein money men. (Author interview with former KGB intermediary, November 2015) 'The connections remained. When people have established trusted contacts, they don't like to experiment with new ones.'

90 The report cited by Yury Shvets said that Viktor Ivanov, a close associate of Cherkesov and Putin, who'd served as head of the FSB's contraband division in those years, had developed close links with the head of the Tambov organised-crime group, Vladimir Kumarin, and through him acquired an interest in the port. It also asserted that Putin was complicit in these dealings. Litvinenko Inquiry, Report into the Death of Alexander Litvinenko, Chairman: Sir Robert Owen, Jan 2016, pp.100–1, https://assets.publishing. service.gov.uk/government/uploads/ system/uploads/attachment_data/ file/493860/The-Litvinenko-Inquiry-H-C-695-web.pdf; https://www. litvinenkoinquiry.org/files/2015/03/ INQ006481.pdf

91 Olbi-Dzhaz, a company co-owned by a Russian businessman once under investigation by the FBI for importing cocaine into St Petersburg in the early nineties, ostensibly imported bananas. According to Vedomosti, the company had links with Shabtai Kalmanovich, the Russian mobster who according to the FBI worked closely with the KGB and the Solntsevskaya.

92 Author interview with former Traber associate, November 2015; DozhdTV, 'Minstr Porta: Kak Peterburgsky Avtoritet Ilya Traber Svyazan s Vladimirom Putinym I yevo okruzheniem', August 25 2017

93 Author interview with former Traber associate, November 2015

94 Konstantin Alexeev, 'Zavety Ilyicha,

Versiya v Pitere', September 28 2009, quoting newspaper article from Sovershenno Sekretno-Versiya, October 9 2001, which cites Shevchenko's testimony in full. As well as Nadezhda Ivanitskaya, 'Namyvnoe delo', Russian Forbes, November 2 2012; Dmitry Matveyev, 'Tsapki Ministra Levitina', Versiya v Pitere, December 20 2010; Arkady Butlitsky, 'Rokovaya Druzhba', Moskovskaya Pravda, August 16 2003; Anton Grishin, 'Vorotily "Zolotykh Vorot"', Versiya, October 9 2001. This article cites this testimony as being given by Shevchenko February 19 1999 to the deputy head of investigations of the St Petersburg prosecutors office, N. A. Litvinova.

95 In an email sent by his Moscow lawyer, Traber refused to answer a series of questions connected with the findings of this chapter, saying only 'It is not possible to comment on fantasy, slander, invention and stupidity.'

96 According to sea port documents obtained by author, which also show that 50 per cent of OBIP was owned by Nasdor. Author interview with former Traber partner, November 2015. See also: Anastasia Kirilenko, '4% Putina. Kak blizkie k Kremlyu kriminalniye avtoritety otmyvayut neftyaniye dengi v Monako', The Insider, December 19 2017; and Roman Anin, 'Zavody, Tsisterny, Offshory, Sosedy', Novaya Gazeta, April 20 2011. The new St Petersburg property chief who replaced Manevich and signed off on the deal was German Gref, a close Putin ally who became a senior state official under Putin and was apparently to keep close ties with Traber.

97 Anatoly Sobchak, 'Kak Rossiya Poteryala Flot na Baltike I Kto v Etom Vinovat?', Moskovskie Novosti, October

6 1998, retrieved from https://web.archive.org/web/20131029211741/http://datarhiv.ru/51/85

98 Interview with former Kharchenko associate, March 2014. For Sobchak's death, see Chapter 5

99 Author interview with former KGB officer, May 2013

100 Author interview with Yakunin, June 2013

101 Author interview with Yakunin, June 2013. 'Everything connected to rare earth metals was connected to the Ioffe Institute,' said Alexander Belyayev, the former head of the St Petersburg City Council. 'They were specialists,' he said.

102 Author interview with Yakunin, June 2013

103 Ibid.

104 According to copy of finance ministry audit of Twentieth Trust for the years 1993-1996, conducted December 12–April 7 1997, and obtained by author. For more information, see Roman Shleynov, 'Ugolovniye Dela, v kotorykh upominalsya Vladimir Putin, obyasnyayut kadrovuyu politiku prezidenta', *Novaya Gazeta*, October 3 2005; Ilya Barabanov, 'Ptentsy gnezda Petrova. Delo XX Tresta', *The New Times*, March 23 2009

105 Information provided by Lt Col Andrei Zykov, a former senior investigator in the interior ministry leading the criminal investigations into Putin and the funnelling of St Petersburg budget funds through Twentieth Trust. Author interview, March 2014

106 Author interview with former Putin associate, January 2013

107 Author interview with Ozero dacha cooperative neighbour, June 2014

108 Author interview with former Putin associate, January 2013

109 Author interview with Ozero dacha cooperative neighbour, June 2014

110 Alexander Bondarenko, 'Ob etom, mozhet byts, kogda-nibud rasskazhut', *Krasnaya Zvezda*, January 10 2002, interview with Gennady Belik

111 Author interview with Putin ally, August 2018

112 Author interview with Yakunin, June 2013

113 Author interview with former KGB officer, May 2013

114 Author interview with Sobchak's widow, Lyudmilla Narusova, June 2014

115 Author interview with Narusova, June 2014; *Delo Sobchaka*, film by Ksenia Sobchak and Vera Krichevskaya, Moscow, 2018

116 Author interview with Putin ally, August 2018

117 Ibid.

118 Author interview with Yumashev, October 2017

119 Author interview with former Putin associate, January 2013

120 Author interview with Andrei Korchagin, former St Petersburg official, January 2015

121 Author interview with Linkov, November 2013

122 Mariya Kaluzhskaya, Desyat Lyet bez Starovoitovy, Valeria Novodvorskaya on Starovoitova, grani.ru, November 20 2008, https://graniru.org/Politics/Russia/m.144242.html.

123 Author interview with former Traber associate, November 2015

124 Author interview with former FSB officer, June 2014; St Petersburg prosecutors finally charged the former leader of the Tambov group, Vladimir Kumarin, with organising Starovoitova's murder in April 2019. By that time, Kumarin was already serving the twelfth year of a 24-year prison sentence for charges including running an organised-crime group, after having fallen out with the Kremlin authorities, his

position as leader of the Tambov group long taken over by Gennady Petrov.

125 Author interview with Eringer, June 2016; Eringer has published a photo of this meeting; in an open letter to Putin, Prelin wrote of how at a press conference in spring 1999 he'd forecast that Russia's next president would be someone little known who was not part of the current political elite. Prelin wrote that after his prediction came true, the foreign press claimed that he knew ahead of time who would be president and he'd even taken part in a special operation of the secret services to bring 'their person' to power. Prelin writes: 'However strange it might seem, after these silly publications, I felt a certain personal responsibility for your actions as president of Russia, as if in fact I did have a direct role in your election to this high post.' Prelin said he hoped he'd been an inspiration to Putin and suggested the fact that Putin wore his watch on his right wrist even though he was right-handed could be a sign of that. 'I have some hope of that because as far as I know after you met me you began wearing your watch on your right wrist as I have done for my whole life,' he wrote. (Prelin wore his watch on his right wrist because he was left-handed.) A copy of the letter can be found at krasvremya.ru/veteran-vnesnej-razvedki-igor-prelin-otkrytoe-pismo-vladimiru-putinu/. At the time of writing, I still had not located Prelin himself.

Chapter 4: Operation Successor: 'It Was Already After Midnight'

1 Author interview with Vavilov, January 2013

2 Author interview with Pugachev, February 2016

3 Arkady Ostrovsky, 'Ailing Yeltsin will not Stand Down', *Financial Times*, October 30 1998. The Kremlin aide is deputy chief of staff, Oleg Sysuyev, who turned out to be a close Primakov ally. He told the newspaper Yeltsin was about to outline a new reduced role in a speech to parliament in the New Year and would hand over day-to-day running of the economy to Primakov.

4 Author has copy of this six-page letter to the chairman of the State Duma, Gennady Seleznyov, dated February 1 1999

5 Author interview with Pugachev, February 2016

6 Author interview with Turover, May 2013

7 Turover provided to author a series of documents which show Banco del Gottardo acting as an intermediary in the payment of Soviet-era foreign debts, mostly owed for supplies of strategic equipment, through various barter schemes. One document, signed March 9 1994 by Russia's first deputy finance minister Andrei Vavilov and foreign economic trade minister Oleg Davydov, announces the creation of the 'Joint Russian-Swiss Banking Club Gottardo'. When asked about this by the author, Vavilov said the plans for Banco del Gottardo to act as an intermediary in paying down the Soviet-era debt had never gotten off the ground. But numerous documents provided by Turover show that Banco del Gottardo continued to act in this role for at least three years. Banco del Gottardo's role in making these payments has never been disclosed by the Russian government. Indeed, at the time, officially there was an international moratorium on any payments of foreign debt by the Russian Federation. Other foreign creditors were not paid. Another

document dated March 4 1994 appoints Turover as Banco del Gottardo's adviser for 'all matters pertaining to our relationship with the government authorities and agencies of the Russian Federation and of our dealings with financial, commercial and economic entities, companies and corporations of the Russian Federation'. Another protocol dated June 2 1997 proposes that the Russian government will pay outstanding debts owed to Swiss trading firm NOGA through the sale of Russian air defence systems built by the Mari-El Engineering Works [the maker of Russia's highly strategic S-300 air defence system] through NOGA. This was another deal that has never been disclosed by the Russian government.

8 Author interview with Turover, May 2013

9 Ibid.

10 Yury Skuratov, *Kremlyevskie Podryady Mabeteksa*, pp.63–4

11 Author interview with Turover, May 2013

12 Author interview with Skuratov, October 2013; the sums Skuratov names Tatyana Dyachenko as spending in his book *Kremlyevskie Podryady*, pp.185–6, however, sound much less. He cites credit card documents sent by the Swiss prosecutors as showing Tatyana and her sister Elena spent in total 'many tens of thousands of dollars'. Tatyana, he said, on one occasion spent $13,000 in one day. He also adds he has copies of Tatyana Dyachenko's bank accounts which show she spent more than $100,000 in three years.

13 Author interview with Skuratov, October 2013; again, Skuratov's *Kremlyevskie Podryady*, p.185, makes the sum spent by Yeltsin sound far less. He

cites Turover as telling the *New York Times* that the amount spent by Yeltsin himself was 'purely symbolic'.

14 Author interview with Turover, May 2013

15 Skuratov, *Kremlyevskie Podryady*, p.76

16 Thane Gustafson, *Wheel of Fortune: The Battle for Oil and Power in Russia*, p.90, The Belknap Press of Harvard University Press, Cambridge, Massachusetts, 2012

17 Author interview with Skuratov, May 2014

18 Skuratov, *Kremlyevskie Podryady*, pp.78–9

19 Ibid.

20 Ibid., p.80

21 Ibid., p.78; Skuratov cites Swiss prosecutor Daniel Devaud as saying MES may have earned as much as $1.5 billion through the oil sales, while only $200m of this amount went towards funding the Kremlin reconstruction

22 Author interview with Pugachev; Skuratov in *Kremlyevskie Podryady*, p.95, describes the close relationship between Borodin's Kremlin Property Department and Pugachev's Mezhprombank. It says Mezhprombank was the main creditor of the Kremlin's Property Department and also says Mezhprombank serviced foreign loans under finance ministry guarantees, including for the Kremlin reconstruction.

23 Borodin had even estimated its holdings as being worth $600 billion in a press conference he gave in January 1999. This figure is almost certainly overblown, but Borodin had claimed it was based on an evaluation given to him by US experts.

24 Author interview with Pugachev, May 2014 (Yumashev said Borodin bought apartments for 'everyone' – author interview October 2017)

25 Author interview with Pugachev, June 2018

26 Author interview with Pugachev, February 2016; see also Skuratov in *Kremlyevskie Podryady*, p.95

27 One document provided by Pugachev to the author is a letter from the Patriarch Alexei II to Yeltsin dated March 21 1996. In it, Alexei II calls on Yeltsin to appoint Pugachev as his representative to the Russian president. 'During one of our most recent meetings (February 1), I raised the question of the expediency of having a person who could act as an intermediary between you and I to decide more operatively questions between the Church and the president, taking into account the complicated internal situation in the country and the fateful times in which we live. In my view, Sergei Viktorovich Pugachev, the chairman of Mezhprombank, could be such a person as I mentioned to you. I know S.V. Pugachev well as a good Christian who has done a lot to help the Church in its restoration.'

28 Mezhprombank's financial arm in San Francisco was called International Industrial Bank Corp.

29 Documents seen by author include one note of thanks from Tatyana Dyachenko to Pugachev thanking him for his help with the 1996 election campaign, as well as correspondence between Pugachev and Fred Lowell, a San Francisco lawyer with close ties to California's Republican Party. Lowell brought in George Gorton, a former aide to Pete Wilson, the Californian Governor, who worked on the campaign as a consultant together with Joseph Shumate and Richard Dresner. Officially they were hired by Oleg Soskovets, deputy prime minister in Yeltsin's government. But

Felix Braynin, one of Pugachev's employees at International Industrial Bank Corp in San Francisco, was the first and most direct connection with them. The story of the US consultants is told in this article by Michael Kramer, 'Rescuing Boris', *Time* magazine, June 24 2001. The role of the US consultants in the re-election campaign later drew controversy because of Tatyana Dyachenko's claim they had overstated their importance. However, it may well also be the case she wanted to minimise their impact because it was not good politically for it to be known US consultants had assisted Yeltsin. Their role in the campaign had been kept a secret until the 2001 *Time Magazine* article.

30 Skuratov, *Kremlyevskie Podryady*, pp.60–1

31 Ibid.

32 Author interview with Pugachev, February 2016

33 Skuratov, *Kremlyevskie Podryady*, p.62

34 Ibid.

35 Ibid., p.81; author interview with Pugachev, February 2016, during which he said he'd leaned on Vavilov to provide the finance ministry guarantees for the bonds

36 Author interview with Pugachev, February 2016

37 Paul Beckett and David S. Cloud, 'Banking Probe Reaches Yeltsin Family – Cayman Accounts Now Draw US Scrutiny', *Wall Street Journal*, September 22 1999. The *WSJ* reported the money was paid into the accounts by Belka Energy, Mr Dyachenko's oil trading company, which it said, in turn, had dealings with Runicom, Abramovich's Swiss-based oil trader. A lawyer for Belka told the *Washington Post* (Robert O'Harrow Jr 'Bank Subpoenas Trading

Firm', *Washington Post*, October 1 1999) that the funds had been paid for Dyachenko's work for the company and that there was no connection to any criminal activity.

38 'Podrobnosti Dela Mabeteksa', Vremya MN, January 28 1999; author interview with Turover, May 2013; author interview with Skuratov, October 2013

39 Author interview with Pugachev, February 2016

40 Author interview with Skuratov, October 2013

41 Skuratov, *Kremlyevskie Podryady*, p.25

42 Ibid., pp.34–44

43 Ibid., p.29

44 Ibid., pp.54–5

45 Author interview with Skuratov, October 2013

46 Author interview with Turover, May 2013

47 Author interview with Skuratov, October 2013

48 Diary entries of this period seen by author include three days of meetings with 'Tanya' and 'Valya', as Yumashev and Dyachenko were affectionately known, from January 27 1999, in the immediate aftermath of the raid on Mabetex; as well as numerous other meetings with Valya, Tanya, Bereza (as Berezovsky was known), Putin and Voloshin throughout the year.

49 Author interview with Pugachev, February 2016

50 In an October 2017 interview, Yumashev conceded that it may have been Pugachev who procured the tape, but would not elaborate further: 'I don't know who found the tape. Probably it was Pugachev, because he had good relations with Khapsirokov. And Khapsirokov was head of the property department of the prosecutor's office.' Yumashev said it was 'totally possible' that it was important for Pugachev because he was involved

somehow in the Mabetex affair through his work with Borodin. But he insisted the case did not influence the Kremlin's decision to oust Skuratov: 'I repeat for Yeltsin – and in our conversations with business, with Chubais, with Gaidar – what was important was that the prosecutor general had been turned into an instrument for business instead of dealing with real criminal cases. Skuratov, because of human weaknesses connected to the fact he thought he could do business with people who gave him bribes and prostitutes, he lost his independence. The position of the Kremlin was that a prosecutor general who could be manipulated did not have the right to occupy such a position.' In 2000 Khapsirokov went to work for Pugachev at Mezhprombank, and in 2001 he was appointed as an aide to Voloshin, who was then Kremlin chief of staff.

51 David McHugh, 'Primakov Plan Sees Sidelined President', *Moscow Times*, January 27 1999

52 Author interview with Yumashev, October 2017

53 Simon Saradzhyan, 'Primakov to Clear Jails for Corrupt', *Moscow Times*, February 2 1999

54 Author interview with Yumashev, October 2017

55 Simon Saradzhyan, 'Prosecutor Resigns as Sibneft Oil Raided', February 3 1999

56 Michael Wines, 'Yeltsin Son-in-law at Center of Rich Network of Influence', *New York Times*, October 7 1999

57 Author interview with Berezovsky associate, June 2018

58 Yumashev made way for Nikolai Bordyuzha, also a representative of the security services, who enjoyed much closer relations with Primakov.

59 Author interview with Yumashev, October 2017

60 Author interview with Pugachev, January 2015

61 Sarah Karush, 'Kremlin Rulers Set Up at Elite Hospital', *Moscow Times*, March 17 1999

62 Natalya Shulyakovskaya, 'Prosecutor Skuratov Slips Back to Work', *Moscow Times*, March 10 1999

63 The Swiss prosecutor Carla del Ponte had telephoned Skuratov with the news that the raids on Mabetex had, as they'd hoped, unearthed copies of the Yeltsin Family credit cards paid down and guaranteed by Pacolli. Though the direct evidence linking the probe with the Family was not made public then, the pieces were in place for a revolt.

64 David McHugh, 'Upper House Reinstates Prosecutor', *Moscow Times*, March 18 1999

65 Author interview with Pugachev, February 2016

66 Ibid.

67 Author interview with Pugachev, June 2018

68 Sarah Karush, 'Prosecutor Steps Up Pressure on Yeltsin', *Moscow Times*, March 24 1999

69 'Ilyukhin Nashel Scheta Yeltsina', *Kommersant*, March 24 1999

70 Author interview with Pugachev, February 2016

71 Author interview with Yumashev, October 2017

72 Author interview with Pugachev, January 2015

73 Author interview with Russian tycoon close to Luzhkov, April 2018

74 Author interview with Pugachev, January 2015

75 Later it turned out that Borodin was among them.

76 Author interview with Pugachev, February 2016

77 Ibid.

78 In *Kremlyevskie Podryady*, pp.354–6, Skuratov gives a slightly different version of events that night. He says he later found out (through a deputy who spoke to Rosinsky) that Rosinsky had indeed been brought into the Kremlin by the FSB at 2 a.m., but that he'd been taken in to see Voloshin, who showed him the tape and then a pre-prepared criminal case. Voloshin told him to go to Tatyana Dyachenko's unoccupied office to work on it, and said that if he had any difficulty there were two deputy prosecutor generals on hand. According to this account, Putin and Stepashin had been in the office with Voloshin, while Chaika and Demin's cars were seen parked at the Kremlin that night. No mention of Pugachev is made. However, it is possible that Rosinsky may not have mentioned Pugachev if he was the one who was organising the reward for him. (Skuratov also says he thinks the reason this happened is because the next day the prosecutors' office was planning to arrest Berezovsky.)

79 Valeria Korchagina, 'Yeltsin Loses Vote to Oust Skuratov', *Moscow Times*, April 22 1999

80 Author interview with Pugachev, February 2015

81 Ibid.

82 Author interview with Yumashev, October 2017

83 Yeltsin had wanted to fire Primakov months before, in the winter. But his aides, Yumashev said, held him back: 'We understood that in winter powerful forces were still behind Primakov, and the Kremlin was still weak. In winter the consequences of the default still had not passed. But by spring it was clear we were coming out of the crisis and it

was possible to take tough political moves.'

84 Author interview with Turover, May 2013

85 Author interview with Skuratov, June 2014

86 Author interview with Pugachev, February 2016. There were also worries about how Stepashin had continued to maintain relations with Primakov, with whom he'd been close since the days when he headed the FSB.

87 Stepashin later claimed it had been made clear to him from the start that he could be replaced by Aksyonenko. Stepashin interview with *Nezavisimaya Gazeta*, January 14 2000; Pugachev however claims that Aksyonenko was only ever a marginal candidate, and that Yeltsin had taken a dislike to his aggressive behaviour, which was similar to that of a Soviet factory boss.

88 Ibid.; Skuratov's *Kremlyevskie Podryady* also states Pugachev's bank was the biggest creditor to the Property Department.

89 Author interview with Pugachev, September 2014

90 Author interview with Yumashev, October 2017. Yumashev was referring then to December 1998–March 1999 just after he stepped down as chief of staff to make way for Bordyuzha and then Voloshin: 'The main task at this time was to find someone who would be president . . . and Putin at this moment – I had no idea about Putin. I had several thoughts along the way about who could be president. For example, I had the idea that it could be [Sergei] Yastrzhembsky. If there hadn't been this crisis [over Yastrzhembsky's backing for Luzhkov] then one of the strongest candidates could have been Yastrzhembsky. He spoke brilliantly. He was handsome and interesting. He was an absolute liberal . . . And honestly I looked at who was in government and in government there were candidates who could have been president. For example there was Aksyonenko [the railways minister] who was an absolute workaholic. The only sector that continued to function well despite the terrible crisis was the railways which was thanks to the organisational talents of Aksyonenko . . . In his understanding of what we needed to do with the market and ideologically, he was suitable.' In addition, Yumashev said, by the time Yeltsin appointed Stepashin prime minister that May Putin 'was a candidate. But he was not the main candidate . . . Stepashin came up at this moment because Yeltsin considered that he had political experience and Chubais was very active in support of him. The opinion of Chubais was very important for Boris Nikolaevich. Putin continued to work as secretary of the Security Council and of course did not dream of becoming president.'

91 Ibid.

92 Even darker forces led by a rogue general, Lev Rokhlin, disaffected by the futile losses and bloodshed of the war in Chechnya, had been suspected of plotting a coup against Yeltsin earlier that year – until Rokhlin was stopped in his tracks by his mysterious and brutal murder just weeks before Putin's appointment as FSB chief. In the circumstances, 'the Yeltsin Family really did need their own person in charge of the FSB', said Leonid Nevzlin, another Yeltsin-era oligarch from Khodorkovsky's Menatep.

93 Author interview with Yumashev, October 2017

94 Author interview with Sobchak's

widow, Lyudmilla Narusova, June 2014; *Delo Sobchaka*, film by Ksenia Sobchak and Vera Krichevskaya, Moscow, 2018

95 Yumashev also said that he thought Putin confided in him about helping Sobchak escape because 'We had fairly open relations. And in my view, he considered that if he didn't tell me he would undermine me. When a deputy takes such a suicidal act – and I'd recommended him to Yeltsin and he worked in my team – he thought he did not have the right to take such action without warning me.' Author interview with Yumashev, October 2017

96 Ibid.

97 Ibid.

98 Ibid.

99 Author interview with former close Putin associate

100 Author interview with senior Russian banker/foreign-intelligence operative, December 2018

101 Author interview with close Berezovsky associate, October 2019

102 Berezovsky had also initially supported Aksyonenko to take over as PM.

103 Masha Gessen, *The Man Without a Face: The Unlikely Rise of Vladimir Putin*, pp.18–19. Author interview with Leonid Nevzlin, July 2018, in which Nevzlin also said he believed Berezovsky could well have played a role in helping propel Putin to the post of FSB chief. Berezovsky knew Putin's predecessor as FSB chief, Nikolai Kovalyov, hated him. 'Kovalyov was not a bad guy,' Nevzlin said. 'But he very much hated Berezovsky. This is why they replaced him . . . He hated him so much you can't imagine. Berezovsky met a few times with Kovalyov and he always saw him as an enemy.'

104 Author interview with Berezovsky associate, July 2018

105 Author interview with Alex Goldfarb, July 2015. Berezovsky did however claim in his interviews with Gessen, *The Man Without a Face*, that in mid-July 1999 he'd gone to Putin and suggested he become president. However, he never went into any detail and Yumashev and Dyachenko however have said that at that point the decision had already been made.

106 Melissa Akin and Natalya Shulyakovskaya, 'Swiss Tie Kremlin to Money-Laundering', *Moscow Times*, July 15 1999; Andrew Higgins, 'Yeltsin Aide is Focus of Corruption Probe – Swiss Investigators Allege Money-Laundering', *Wall Street Journal*, July 16 1999

107 Author interview with Pugachev, August 2019

108 'Luzhkov Schitayet "Politicheskoi Provokatsii" Vozbuzhdeniye FSB Ugolovnovo Dela, v Kotorom Figuriruet Firma Evo Zheny', Interfax, July 17 1999

109 Author interview with Pugachev, February 2016

110 Author interview with Yumashev, October 2017. Yumashev denied that Pugachev could have played any role in Putin's rise to power. He insisted Pugachev was exaggerating it all. 'In fact he played a most minimal role in all the political stories of the time,' he said. 'We spoke with him, yes. But I also spoke with dozens of other businessmen as chief of staff – with Potanin, with Khodorkovsky and Alekperov . . . It was important for us that they were our allies.' He did concede that Pugachev had known well Khapsirokov, the official from the prosecutor general's office who'd supplied the Skuratov tape and that it may well have been Pugachev who procured the tape. He also conceded that Pugachev had

worked closely with Borodin including on the Mabetex contracts. But Yumashev claimed that the idea to forward Putin as Stepashin's replacement came initially from Voloshin, who then served as Kremlin chief of staff. 'The main initiator was Voloshin. He considered that because the situation in the Caucasus was escalating – there was a constant threat of terrorism – to go in when there was less than a year before presidential elections with a PM who was under the heel of his wife . . . and who it was dangerous to give the country to . . . it was clear that it was not possible to remove the PM three months before elections. The person who would do this would lose the election. The new PM should have at least a year for the country to get to know him. It was clear we needed to do it fairly fast and not delay till autumn. Therefore we of course took part in these discussions. It was me, Tatyana, Voloshin and Chubais. We had fairly rowdy discussions. Chubais considered it a mistake . . . He believed that to remove Stepashin now when he had worked only three months would be to demonstrate the Kremlin's total inadequacy. He believed the Duma would not approve Putin because it didn't know him.'

111   Other businesspeople had not served as adviser to a succession of Kremlin chiefs of staff, as Pugachev did (documents seen by the author show). They'd also not had the same cosy chats with Yumashev, like the one in the recording about how they'd rushed to bring Putin to power. Diary entries show Pugachev's frequent meetings at that time with Yumashev and with Dyachenko. A log of telephone calls from Pugachev's downtown Moscow office shows that

he and Yumashev spoke at least eighty-eight times in 1999 on Pugachev's office line alone, not including calls from mobile phones or from Pugachev's office in the Kremlin. The log also indicates the depth of Pugachev's other connections in the Kremlin: there are calls between him and Putin, and with Tatyana Dyachenko; there are meetings with Voloshin, calls with prosecutor general Vladimir Ustinov, and messages that 'Derevo' – a nickname for Berezovsky – had rung.

112   Author interview with Yumashev, October 2017

113   Author interview with Pugachev, March 2015. Chubais did admit he'd done everything he could to stop Putin's appointment, telling Lyudmilla Telen, *Pokolenie Putina*, p. 53 that: 'I considered that Stepashin the candidate had greater chances of being elected than did Putin the candidate. I fought for my point of view right to the end. Right up till that moment [on August 9] when Yeltsin informed Stepashin of his removal.' Yeltsin, also, in *Midnight Diaries* p.332, writes that Chubais made a last-ditch bid to stop the appointment over the weekend, but he only found out about it much later. 'Chubais could have changed everything,' Pugachev admitted. 'For Yeltsin, Yumashev was family. But he respected Chubais as a great professional. If he'd managed to tell him don't touch Stepashin, then probably [Putin's appointment] wouldn't have happened.' (Also in *Midnight Diaries*, p.329, Yeltsin writes that he first calls Stepashin and Putin (separately) to his office to inform them of his decision on August 5. But then takes the weekend to think further about it.) In his book *Vremya Berezovskovo*, Pyotr Aven, the Russian

oligarch and Alfa Bank president, has also spoken of Chubais's last-ditch efforts that Sunday to call a 'meeting of the oligarchs' to form a consolidated position of big business. 'It was clear that Stepashin would most probably be ousted on Monday morning, but it was possible to try and do something over the weekend,' said Aven. 'At this meeting Chubais spoke very clearly against Putin's candidacy.' Aven also tells of how Chubais asked him to meet with Putin and persuade him to decline the appointment. Aven says he went to Putin's dacha that Sunday evening but when they met, Putin told him he'd already agreed.

114 Author interview with Pugachev, August 2019. 'In this case, he was not acting as the president or the tsar. He was acting as a grandfather who feared for Tanya most of all, and for his grandchildren,' Pugachev said.

115 Brian Whitmore, 'Yeltsin Sacks Stepashin, Anoints Putin', *Moscow Times*, August 10 1999

116 Putin's candidacy barely got the majority needed, by only six votes.

117 Author interview with Yumashev, October 2017

118 Reports suggest that the Family had indeed been planning for a second Chechen war: Voloshin, the Kremlin chief of staff, had allegedly been detected by French intelligence meeting a Chechen rebel leader, Shamil Basayev, at a villa on July 4 on the outskirts of Nice a month before the Chechens began their armed incursion into Dagestan – John Dunlop, *The Moscow Bombings of September 1999*, pp.66–8. Later, Stepashin gave a series of interviews in which he admitted that a plan to launch a fresh military action against Chechnya – to even seize Chechen territory – had been under discussion in the

Kremlin months before, when he was still prime minister, and even suggested that the plans had been part of discussions to destabilise the situation and impose emergency rule: Dunlop cites three interviews Stepashin gave: one to *Frankfurter Rundschau* in February 2000, in which he said plans had been under way since March to close the Chechen border and create 'a sanitary cordon' around Chechnya 'like the Berlin Wall'. 'In July, we decided to seize territory [in Chechnya] north of the Terek'. He was admitting plans to invade Chechnya were authorised before the Chechens began the armed incursions into Dagestan in August. Another to Michael Gordon, 'A Look at How the Kremlin Slid into the Chechen War', *New York Times*, February 1 2000, in which Stepashin said that in March the plan had been only to secure Chechnya's borders, but by July it had expanded to seizing the top third of Chechnya, with special forces going after rebels. The third, with Russian newspaper *Moskovsky Komsomolets* in September 1999, cited him as indicating that Berezovsky had been seeking to provoke a limited conflict that would enable Yeltsin to impose emergency rule. 'As for the version of a conspiracy, [one needs to realise that] having provoked a war, it is difficult in that region to quickly gain a victory.. It is another matter [altogether] that certain agreements were possible, in order to destabilise the situation and to bring it under Emergency Rule. Now that is a version.'

119 Gleb Pavlovsky, 'Eksperimentalnaya Rodina', Moscow, July 2018

120 Author interview with two close Berezovsky associates, October 2019. Both confirmed Berezovsky knew the Chechen leader Shamil Basayev.

121 Author interview with Pugachev, February 2016

122 Carlo Bonini and Giuseppe D'Avantso, 'Svizerra, carte di credito accusano Eltsin', *Corriere della Sera*, August 25 1999

123 Author interview with Yumashev, October 2017

124 Author interview with Pugachev, February 2016

125 Andrew Higgins, 'Former Legislator Clears Yeltsin Family', *Wall Street Journal*, September 28 1999

126 Author interview with Pugachev, February 2016

127 Author interview with Yumashev, October 2017

128 Raymond Bonner and Timothy L. O'Brien, 'Activity at Bank Raises Suspicion of Russian Mob Tie', *New York Times*, August 19 1999

129 Paul Beckett and David S. Cloud, 'Banking Probe Reaches Yeltsin Family – Cayman Accounts Now Draw US Scrutiny', *Wall Street Journal*, September 22 1999. A lawyer for Mr Dyachenko has said the funds were payment for work for the oil trading firm, Belka Trading, and were not connected to any illicit activity.

130 The document from the Swiss prosecutors' office, dated July 28 2000, showed prosecutors were investigating a $235m transfer through Banco del Gottardo to an account held in East-West United Bank in Luxembourg by a company called Questor Corporation Ltd, which the prosecutors said Dyachenko was the beneficiary of. In response to written questions, Yumashev said any suggestion that Tatyana had ever received such funds was 'absolute lies. Tatyana never had any offshore companies – any companies abroad or in Russia. And if this transfer took place, then Tatyana never had any relation to this company.'

131 Author interview with Pugachev, May 2014

132 Author interview with Pugachev, September 2014

133 Primakov, 'Vosem mesiatsev plus', pp.222–3: Primakov writes that after he was fired from his post as prime minister, Putin rang him and proposed he meet with the FSB leadership. Putin brought the entire top ranks of the FSB to Primakov's dacha, where they toasted him. 'This was a serious gesture, and I don't think Putin agreed the details with anyone,' Primakov wrote. Then, when Putin in turn had been appointed PM, he accepted an invitation to attend Primakov's seventieth birthday celebrations, and again gave a speech. 'I of course had not invited one person from Yeltsin's inner circle,' Primakov wrote. Primakov says they stayed in close contact after Putin's election as president.

134 Valentin Yumashev, 'My glotnuli svobody I otravilis yeyu', interview with *Moskovsky Komsomolets*, January 31 2011

135 Gleb Pavlovsky, 'Eksperimentalnaya Rodina', Moscow, July 2018

136 Author interview with Turover, May 2013

Chapter 5: 'Children's Toys in Pools of Mud'

1 Author interview with former senior KGB officer close to Putin, August 2018

2 Ibid.

3 Author interview with Graham, June 2014

4 Pavlovsky, 'Eksperimentalnaya Rodina', July 2018. 'From 1996 to the end of Yeltsin's presidency, we spoke in the Kremlin not about a "successor" but of strengthening power,' Pavlovsky said.

5 Author interview with Illarionov, September 2015

6 Ibid.

7 Author interviews with Pugachev, September 2014, August 2018

8 Pugachev's claim that the decision had been taken earlier, almost as soon as Putin was appointed as prime minister and announced as Yeltsin's successor, fitted much better with what actually happened then. Two other Kremlin officials also indicated that the decision had been taken long before. In one interview with *Newsweek International* (January 10 2000), Anatoly Chubais, the former Kremlin chief of staff and privatisation tsar, said the idea had long been known and discussed, while Gleb Pavlovsky, the Kremlin spin doctor, said the decision had been made earlier in the year. ('Eksperimentalnaya Rodina', July 2018)

9 Author interview with close Putin ally, August 2018

10 Oksana Yablokova, Simon Saradzhyan and Valeria Korchagina, 'Apartment Block Explodes, Dozens Dead', *Moscow Times*, September 10 1999

11 Valeria Korchagina, Simon Saradzhyan, 'Tensions Grow as Toll Rises to 118', *Moscow Times*, September 15 1999

12 Sergei Yushenkov, a leading liberal MP, was shot dead outside his house in April 2003, a year after he became part of an independent public commission set up to investigate the apartment bombings. Yury Schekochikin, a well-known investigative journalist who'd also joined the commission, died three months later from a mysterious illness that bore the hallmarks of poisoning by radioactive materials. A former FSB colonel Mikhail Trepashkin who'd also joined the commission was arrested in October 2003 and jailed for four years in a military prison for alleged improper handling of classified materials shortly after he shared information with a journalist indicating an FSB agent may have been involved in the bombing of 19 Guryanova Street.

13 Said Islamyev, 'Thousands Flee Grozny as Bombs Fall', *Moscow Times*, September 25 1999

14 Brian Whitmore, 'Real Target of Airstrikes May Be PR', *Moscow Times*, September 28 1999

15 Putin in helicopter and tent – https://www.youtube.com/watch?v=8Xn7p-JQmATI ; www.ntv/ru/video/1749560

16 Brian Whitmore, 'Prime Minister's Popularity Rating Skyrockets', *Moscow Times*, November 30 1999

17 Brian Whitmore and Simon Saradzhyan, 'Moscow Awash in Explosion Theories', *Moscow Times*, September 14 1999

18 'Gennadiya Seleznyova Predupredili o vzryve v Volgodonske za tri dnya do terakta', Newsru.com, March 21 2002

19 John Dunlop, *The Moscow Bombings of September 1999: Examination of Russian Terrorist Attacks at the Onset of Vladimir Putin's Rule*, pp.170–1; 'Taimer Ostanovili za Sem Chasov do Vzryva: Terakt Predotvratil Voditel Avtobusa', *Kommersant*, September 24 1999; 'Nezavisimoye Rassledovanie: Ryazansky Sakhar', NTV, March 24 2000: before Putin's clampdown on the media NTV ran a nearly hour-long discussion programme on the events in Ryazan, where residents, including the one who reported it all, Alexei Kartofelnikov, spoke of their disbelief it had been an exercise and demanded answers from the FSB.

20 Ibid., pp.170–1; see also Pavel Voloshin, 'Chto bylo v Ryazani: sakhar ili geksogen?', *Novaya Gazeta*, February 14 2000; and 'Taimer Ostanovili za Sem Chasov do Vzryva: Terakt Predotvratil Voditel Avtobusa', *Kommersant*, September 24 1999

21 Dunlop, *The Moscow Bombings of September 1999*, pp.172–7; Simon Saradzhyan, 'Police Find Dummy Bomb in Ryazan', *Moscow Times*, September 24 1999; 'Taimer Ostanovili za Sem Chasov do Vzryva: Terakt Predotvratil Voditel Avtobusa', *Kommersant*, September 24 1999

22 'Nezavisimoye Rassledovanie: Ryazansky Sakhar', https://www.youtube.com/watch?v=K-lEi_Uyb_U

23 Ibid.: the programme shows footage of Rushailo addressing law enforcers at the interior ministry headquarters September 24 and telling them an explosion in Ryazan has been prevented. It also includes footage of Patrushev emerging to tell a TV reporter thirty minutes later that it was no more than an exercise; there was only sugar in the sacks.

24 Patrushev had started out in Leningrad KGB counter-intelligence with Putin, and then moved to head the city's contraband division. By 1994 he'd moved to Moscow, where he served as head of the FSB's all-important internal security division.

25 Alexander Litvinenko and Yury Felshtinsky, 'FSB Vzryvayet Rossiyu'. The authors cite a statement, apparently issued by the Ryazan FSB soon after Patrushev claimed the incident was no more than an exercise, as saying: 'As it became known, the device discovered 22.09.99 that was an imitation of an explosive device was part of an inter-regional exercise. The news of this was unexpected for us and came after the moment when the FSB had uncovered the place of residency in Ryazan of those who'd placed the explosive device and when it was preparing to detain them.' It also quotes the head of the investigative division of the Ryazan FSB, Yury Maksimov, as saying on March 21 2000:

'We took the events that night very seriously, as if it was a military situation. The news that this was an FSB exercise was totally unexpected for us, and came at the time when we had uncovered the places of residency of the individuals who'd placed the imitation (as it later turned out) device and were preparing to detain them.' Anatoly Medetsky, 'Sacks in the Basement Still Trouble Ryazan', *Moscow Times*, September 24 2004

26 'Nezavisimoye Rassledovanie: Ryazansky Sakhar'; Medetsky, 'Sacks in the Basement Still Trouble Ryazan'

27 'Nezavisimoye Rassledovanie: Ryazansky Sakhar'

28 Alexander Litvinenko and Yury Felshtinsky, 'FSB Vzryvayet Rossiyu'; *Blowing up Russia*, documentary film, producers Jean Charles Deniau and Charles Gazelle, 2002

29 Medetsky, 'Sacks in the Basement Still Trouble Ryazan'

30 'Nezavisimoye Rassledovanie: Ryazansky Sakhar'

31 Igor Korolkov, 'Fotorobot ne pervoi svezhosti', *Moskovskie Novosti*, November 11 2003; M.I. Trepashkin, 'Na pervom fotorobote byl agent FSB', chechenpress.com, September 18 2003; see also Scott Anderson, 'None dare call it conspiracy', *GQ*, September 2009

32 Ibid.

33 Author interview with former Kremlin official, December 2014. Kremlin spokesman Dmitry Peskov said the claims made by the former Kremlin official were 'total rubbish'. 'Don't pay any attention to this insider. He doesn't know anything,' Peskov said.

34 Ibid.

35 Author interview with Yumashev, October 2017

36 Brian Whitmore, 'Real Target of Airstrikes May be PR', *Moscow Times*,

September 28 1999; *Vremya MN* article, September 27 1999, in which Putin states: 'This time we will not put our boys under fire . . . We will use all modern forces and means to destroy the terrorists. We will destroy their infrastructure. We will use special forces only to clean up territory. We will protect our people. Of course, this demands time and patience.'

37 Pavlovsky, 'Eksperimentalnaya Rodina', July 2018

38 Author interview with person close to Yeltsin Family, July 2018. One theory could be that the Family had worked with Putin and the FSB to instigate the Chechen incursion into Dagestan, as a way of provoking a second Chechen war that would propel Putin to power, while the apartment bombings in September had been the FSB – namely Patrushev – taking matters into their own hands and going far beyond anything originally planned to propel Putin to power. One close Berezovsky associate (author interview October 2019) however also suggested the bombings could have been carried out by Chechens taking revenge for not being paid for the earlier armed incursions into Dagestan – if indeed those incursions had been planned as a way to help spur Putin's vault to power.

39 See Chapter 1

40 Author interview with former member of Red Army Faction, March 2018

41 Author interview with Russian oligarch, July 2018

42 Author interview with senior Russian banker with links to foreign intelligence, January 2019

43 Pavlovsky, 'Eksperimentalnaya Rodina'

44 Patrick E. Tyler, 'Russian Says Kremlin Faked "Terror Attacks"', *New York Times*, February 1 2002

45 Alexander Goldfarb and Marina Litvinenko, *Death of a Dissident*, pp.180-2. The book cites Berezovsky as describing his qualms when at the end of August 1999, after Putin became prime minister, he visited him in his new office and saw a statue of Felix Dzerzhinsky, the founder of the Soviet secret police, on his desk. He'd worried that Putin was still attached to the KGB, and wondered if it was not too late to find another successor. It was not until he sent Abramovich to Putin's birthday party on October 7, and Abramovich reported back that there was no sign of other spies at the party, that he took the decision to back Putin.

46 Author interview with Berezovsky associate, June 2018

47 Brian Whitmore, 'Agendas Clash on Sunday TV News', *Moscow Times*, October 12 1999

48 Andrei Zolotov Jr, 'Media Wars Turn to Blood and Guts', *Moscow Times*, October 26 1999

49 Author interview with Berezovsky associate, June 2018

50 One person close to Berezovsky said Berezovsky had earlier intercepted correspondence between Primakov and Skuratov that showed he was number one on an arrest list (author interview July 2018)

51 Michael McFaul, 'Russia's 1999 Parliamentary Elections: Party Consolidation and Fragmentation', demokratizatsiya.pub/archives/08-1_McFaul.PDF: The polling data cited by McFaul shows Fatherland-Russia's rating had dropped from 28 per cent in July.

52 Andrei Zolotov Jr, 'Shoigu's Unity Rides on Putin's Coattails', *Moscow Times*, December 4 1999

53 'Putin Soars High on War's Wings', *Moscow Times*, December 1 1999

54   Sarah Karush, 'Pro-Kremlin Parties Sweep into Duma', *Moscow Times*, December 21 1999

55   Author interview with Yumashev, October 2017

56   Boris Yeltsin, *Midnight Diaries*, p.6

57   Putin FSB meeting Dec 1999: https://www.youtube.com/watch?v=6xkLdz-rniyo

58   Vladimir Putin, 'Rossiya na Rubezhe Tysyacheletii', December 27 1999. The article is no longer available on the government portal it was published on www.government.gov.ru. But can be read here: myruwin.ru/Vladimir-putin-rossija-na-rubezhe-tysjacheletij

59   Putin, 'Rossiya na Rubezhe Tysyacheletii'

60   'Vladimir Putin Obnarodoval Svoyu Programmu', *Nezavisimaya Gazeta*, December 30 1999

61   Yeltsin, New Year's Eve speech, YouTube citation https://www.youtube.com/watch?v=qoZb8QqXooA

62   Author interview with former senior government official close to the security services, January 2014

63   Author interview with former senior Kremlin official, November 2017, in which he said that under a Luzhkov/Primakov leadership, 'What took Vladimir Vladimirovich seventeen years would have happened in four years. All this has been dragged out.' Also author interview with former presidential economic adviser Andrei Illarionov, September 2015, in which he said: 'If it had been Primakov there would not have been an initial period of economic reform as there was under Putin. But Primakov would also not have been as tough in liquidating the opposition. It would have been easier to overturn his regime in two or three or four years. There would have been a union of democrats and oligarchs against the KGB, and there would have been a chance to overturn the KGB regime. Primakov would not have been in a condition to bring in the younger generation of KGB, and he would not have been able to maintain the stability of the regime.'

64   Catherine Belton, 'Putin Campaign Cranks Through Regions', *Moscow Times*, March 22 2000

65   Putin election night, https://www.youtube.com/watch?v=DhQynqCX-WAkn

66   Catherine Belton, 'Putin Walks his Way into Women's Hearts', *Moscow Times*, March 9 2000

67   Catherine Belton, 'Luzhkov Shows Putin About Town', *Moscow Times*, March 24 2000

68   Author interview with Pugachev, September 2014

69   Anatoly Sobchak, 'Kak Rossiya Poteryala Flot na Baltike I Kto v Etom Vinovat?', *Moskovskie Novosti*, October 6 1998, retrieved from https://web.archive.org/web/20131029211741/http://datarhiv.ru/51/85

70   Elena Masyuk, 'Volodya Tolko ne Bronzovei', *Novaya Gazeta*, November 9 2012, interview with Lyudmilla Narusova

71   FBI report on the empire and associates of Semyon Mogilevich, 1995, obtained by author.

72   Author interview with Narusova, June 2014

73   'Sobchak Ostavil Dver Otkrytoi', *Kommersant*, February 22 2000

74   Ibid.; '*Kommersant* Speculates about Sobchak's Death', *Moscow Times*, February 23 2000

75   Masyuk, 'Volodya Tolko ne Bronzovei'

76   Author interview with former Traber associate, November 2015

77   Catherine Belton, 'Thousands Say

Farewell to Sobchak', *Moscow Times*, February 25 2000

78 Masyuk, 'Volodya Tolko ne Bronzovei'

79 When the author interviewed Narusova in June 2014, she declined to answer questions about her previous comments to *Novaya Gazeta*

80 Author interview with Pugachev, August 2016

81 Author interview with Pugachev, May 2015

82 Catherine Belton, 'Putin Wins, Promises no Miracles', *Moscow Times*, March 28 2000

83 Vitaly Mansky, 'Svidetely Putina', 2018

84 Author interview with Putin ally, March 2015; author interview with former senior government official, January 2013

85 Catherine Belton, 'Aluminum Sale Gets Stamp of Approval', *Moscow Times*, March 10 2000

86 Author interview with Putin ally, March 2015. He later clarified: 'One condition was clear for me, and that was for four years he wasn't to interfere in the running of the economy. That was very clear, but I can only presume.'

87 Author interview with Yumashev, October 2017

88 It seems clear that Putin and the Yeltsin Family were grafted together. One symbol of the merging of the houses of Putin's men and the Yeltsin Family appeared soon after he came to power. Just months after the election, a little-noticed oil trader was born. It was named Urals Energy and it was owned by two business partners of Gennady Timchenko and by Leonid Dyachenko. ('Sky's the Limit for reborn Urals Energy', *Platts Energy in East Europe*, March 31 2006)

89 Author interview with Pugachev, July 2015

90 Author interview with Nevzlin, July 2018

Chapter 6: 'The Inner Circle Made Him'

1 Yeltsin's speech at the 2000 presidential inauguration of Putin, www.youtube.com/watch?v=Q2AF_2gHHeQ

2 Inauguratsionnaya Rech Vladimira Putina 7 maya 2000 goda, *Moskovskie Novosti*, www.mn.ru/blogs/blog_reference/80928

3 He'd then been sent to serve briefly as security chief for the Karelian republic on Russia's strategic border with Finland.

4 Author interview with person close to Patrushev, February 2015

5 Author interview with Putin ally, August 2018

6 Author interview with person close to Patrushev, February 2015

7 Such as the works of Halford Mackinder, an English academic who at the turn of the century had written some of the founding tracts of geopolitical theory that influenced foreign policy during the Cold War

8 A former member of the Red Army Faction, however, said Ivanov had often appeared in Dresden with Putin.

9 Author interview with former FSB colleague of Ivanov, June 2014

10 Report written by Yury Shvets with input from former FSB officer Alexander Litvinenko and aired during the London High Court inquiry into Litvinenko's killing. It can be found at webarchive.nationalarchives.gov.uk/20160613091026/https://www.litvinenkoinquiry.org/files/2015/03/INQ006481.pdf

11 Author interview with person close to Ivanov, June 2018

12 webarchive.nationalarchives.gov.uk/20160613091026/https://www.litvinenkoinquiry.org/files/2015/03/INQ006481.pdf

13 Author interview with former

St Petersburg businessman, Andrei Korchagin, January 2015

14 Author interview with former close Putin ally, January 2017

15 Author interviews with two people close to Sechin: one in February 2015, the other in August 2018

16 Author interview with person close to Sechin, February 2015

17 Ibid.

18 Ibid.

19 Ibid.

20 Author interview with associate of Kharchenko, the former head of the Baltic Sea Fleet, March 2014; and author interview with former Putin ally, August 2018

21 Author interview with person close to Cherkesov, November 2015

22 Author interview with former senior US official, June 2014

23 Author interview with Pugachev, September 2014

24 Catherine Belton, 'A Russian Volley over the ABM Treaty', *Business Week*, November 9 2001

25 For a discussion of these assurances, see the analysis by Svetlana Savranskaya and Tom Blanton, of George Washington University, of recently released documents from the National Security Archive, 'NATO Expansion: What Gorbachev Heard', December 12 2017, https://nsarchive.gwu.edu/briefing-book/russia-programs/2017-12-12/nato-expansion-what-gorbachev-heard-Western-leaders-early

26 Ian Traynor, 'Putin Urged to Apply the Pinochet Stick', *Guardian*, March 31 2000

27 Hans Leyendecker and Frederik Obermaier, 'Diskrete Geschäfte am Affenfelsen', *Suddeutsche Zeitung*, April 11 2013

28 Author interview with Pugachev, September 2013

29 Author interview with Kremlin insider, December 2014

30 Author interview with Pugachev, February 2015

31 According to estimates by the International Monetary Fund; see Prakash Loungani and Paolo Mauro, 'Capital Flight from Russia', International Monetary Fund Policy Discussion Paper, June 1 2000

32 Author interview with Bogdanchikov, August 2013

33 Alexander Voloshin, then Kremlin chief of staff, said: 'The republics were not paying taxes. There was war in Chechnya. Some republics were refusing to send troops to the army. Debts for wages and pensions were mounting, and the popularity of the president was just 4 per cent. Against this background, the Communists were strong, and so were Primakov and Luzhkov. The enemies were strong and we were weak. There was a real risk the country could collapse.'

34 Author interview with Yakunin, June 2013

35 Author interview with Yakunin, November 2016

36 Alan A. Block and Constance A. Weaver, *All is Clouded by Desire*, p.125, International and Comparative Criminology, Westport, Connecticut, 2004

37 Author interview with Christian Michel, May 2005

38 Author interview with Putin associate, May 2013

39 Andrew Jack, 'Putin Appears to Distance Himself from Oligarchs', *Financial Times*, February 29 2000

40 'Oligarchs Will Become Extinct, Putin Vows', Agence France-Presse, March 18 2000

41 Author interview with person close to Putin, August 2018

42 Author interview with Berezovsky associate, June 2018

43 Nikolai Vardul, 'Kak Putin Budet Upravlyats Stranoi', *Kommersant*, May 3 2000

44 Maura Reynolds, 'Russia Raids Media Company Critical of Kremlin', *Los Angeles Times*, May 12 2000

45 David Hoffman, 'Putin Moves to Bolster Central Rule; Plan would Rein in Regional Governors', *Washington Post*, May 18 2000

46 Gregory Feifer, 'Berezovsky's Letter Dominates News', *Moscow Times*, June 1 2000

47 Author interview with Berezovsky associate, June 2018

48 Author interview with Yumashev, October 2017

49 Ibid.

50 Guy Chazan and Alan Cullison, 'Russia's Oligarchs Protest Arrest of Media Magnate', *Wall Street Journal*, June 15 2000

51 Igor Semenenko, 'Suit Filed to Undo Norilsk Auction', *Moscow Times*, June 21 2000

52 Dmitry Zaks, 'Tax Police Raid Russian Business Giants Following Putin Threat', Agence France-Presse, July 11 2000

53 Andrew Kramer, 'Tax Police Open Case against Auto Giant', Associated Press, July 12 2000

54 Dmitry Zaks, 'Putin Vows to Punish Russian Oligarchs as Tax Police Strike Again', Agence France-Presse, July 12 2000

55 Sergei Shagorodsky, 'Russian President Defends his Heavy-Handed Policies', Associated Press, July 13 2000

56 Marielle Eudes, 'Russian Business Barons Want Frank Talk with Putin', Agence France-Presse, July 14 2000

57 Nick Wadhams, 'Berezovsky's Announcement he Will Resign from Russia's Parliament Another Riddle', Associated Press, July 17 2000

58 Maura Reynolds, 'Putin Reaches Out to Oligarchs', *Los Angeles Times*, July 29 2000

59 Author interview with Pugachev, December 2013

60 Andrei Savitsky, 'Favorit', *Nezavisimaya Gazeta*, November 6 2001; see also 'Semya Kopilka', *Moskovsky Komsomolets*, June 28 2000; 'Sekretniye Druzya Putina', *Moskovsky Komsomolets*, April 4 2001; Konstantin Remchukov, 'Bodrym Shagom k BoNY-2', *Vedomosti*, November 27 2001; Andrei Savitsky, 'Syn Otvechayet za Otsa', *Nezavisimaya Gazeta*, November 30 2001; Mikhail Kozyrev, 'Tuvynets Pugachev', *Vedomosti*, December 26 2001

61 Henry Meyer, 'Russian Media Magnate Says Government Forced Sale in Prosecution Deal', Agence France-Presse, September 18 2000

62 Ibid.

63 'Berezovsky Warns About More Possible Terrorist Acts in Russia', Interfax, August 10 2000

64 Author interview with former close Putin ally, January 2015

65 Guy Chazan, 'Putin Lambasts the Media Over Coverage of Sub Disaster', *Wall Street Journal*, August 31 2000

66 Ibid.

67 Author interview with Berezovsky associate, June 2018

68 Goldfarb and Litvinenko, 'Death of a Dissident', p.210

69 Vladimir Isachenkov, 'Oligarch Says Kremlin Moves to Take His Share in Television Station', Associated Press, September 4 2000

70 'Pavlovsky Outlines Kremlin's Information Security Plans', IPR Strategic Information Database, September 26 2000

71 'Russian Tycoon Berezovsky Fears Return to Russia', Agence France-Presse, November 14 2000

72 Author interview with Nevzlin, July 2018

73 Author interview with Pugachev, March 2015

74 Andrei Zolotov Jr, 'Putin Backs Foreign Investor at NTV', *Moscow Times*, January 30 2001

75 Ibid.

76 Author interview with Pugachev, March 2015

77 'Media Most Chief Compares NTV Seizure to August 1991 Coup', BBC Monitoring Report of Ekho Moskvy interview, April 14 2001

78 'NTV Raid Shows "KGB in Power" in Russia: Ex-Dissident', Agence France-Presse, April 14 2001

7: 'Operation Energy'

1 More than 70 per cent of oil extracted and 87 per cent of gas production went to the domestic market mostly to prop up the military industry: Sergei Yermolaev, 'The Formation and Evolution of the Soviet Union's Oil and Gas Dependence', March 29 2017, Carnegie Endowment for International Peace

2 Yermolaev, 'The Formation and Evolution of the Soviet Union's Oil and Gas Dependence'

3 Thane Gustafson, *Wheel of Fortune: The Battle for Oil and Power in Russia*, p.76, The Belknap Press of Harvard University, Cambridge Massachusetts, 2012. The book describes how Yeltsin signed a decree November 1992 creating the first three vertically-integrated oil majors – Lukoil, Yukos and Surgutneftegaz, in which the state was to retain a 45 per cent stake for three years when a decision would be made about their privatisation. The rest of the industry went into a temporary state company Rosneft, which fast was cannabilised by corporate raiders who sought to take prime production units.

4 Gustafson, *Wheel of Fortune*, p.90

5 Oil revenues were 35.5 per cent of total federal revenues in 1996, and 27.4 per cent in 1997, according to Goohoon Kwon, 'The Budgetary Impact of Oil Prices in Russia', IMF Working Paper, August 1 2003, p.4 www.imf.org/external/country/rus/rr/2003/pdf/080103.pdf

6 Author interview with Pannikov, April 2008

7 Robert Cottrell, 'Russia's Richest Man Reveals Himself', *Financial Times*, June 21 2002

8 The company was financially on its knees because in the first half of the nineties it was forced to sell most of its output to the state at fixed low internal prices under the rules that governed the oil trade then, while it bartered some oil to pay for services.

9 Miller was the sea port's director for investment and development from 1996 to 1999, at the same time as the port was under the control of Ilya Traber, the Russian mobster who was a key intermediary between Putin's security men and the broader Tambov organised-crime group. Miller brought with him another official from the sea port: Alexander Dyukov, who'd worked as its general director from 1998 to 1999, and then as the head of its oil terminal, who was appointed to first serve as the head of Sibur, the petrochemicals giant, and then later in Putin's second term as head of Gazprom's newly created oil arm, Gazpromneft. Another of Traber's closest allies, a KGB man named Viktor Korytov, became deputy head of Gazprombank.

10 Author interview with senior banker

close to security services, May 2016

11 Author interview with Pugachev, December 2014

12 Author interview with Pugachev, June 2018

13 Author interview with senior banker close to security services, May 2016

14 Author interview with person close to Putin, January 2015

15 Author interview with senior banker close to security services, May 2016

16 Ibid.; author interview with oil executive close to security services, January 2014

17 Melissa Akin, 'Tax Police Target Boss of Lukoil', *Moscow Times*, July 12 2000; also see Elizabeth LeBras and Natalya Neimysheva, 'Report – Oil Evades $9 Billion in Taxes', *Moscow Times*, November 29 2000

18 Anna Raff, 'Lukoil Financial Officer Abducted', *Moscow Times*, September 13 2002

19 'Lukoil Case Closed', *Moscow Times*, February 13 2003

20 Natalya Neimysheva, 'Illuziya Lgot', *Vedomosti*, February 6 2003

21 Author interview with senior oil industry executive, March 2014

22 Author interview with Milov, September 2013

23 Author interview with Khodorkovsky, September 2015

24 Jeanne Whalen, 'Oil Tender Pricing Formula Proposed', *Moscow Times*, August 16 1997; Boris Aliabayev, 'Kremlin Pledges Fair Oil Auctions', *Moscow Times*, November 12 1997

25 Author interview with senior Western banker participating in the sale, September 2013

26 Akimov's association with Soviet foreign intelligence was noted by three sources: 'He was serving as an officer in the active reserve,' said one senior Russian banker who knows Akimov well. 'His father was a colonel in the KGB.'; 'It was not possible to have a high post in one of the foreign Soviet banks without such connections to the KGB,' said Vladimir Milov, the former deputy energy minister; Akimov could only have gained such a position through close connections with the KGB, said an executive who worked with him closely. In those days, the Soviet foreign banking network was a key channel for the financing of Soviet strategic operations. When in 1979 eight trash bags of paperwork were stolen from the Soviet foreign bank in Paris, Eurobank, a book was published a few months later based on the missing documents which detailed how the bank had financed the Communist Party in France. A position in this system was prestigious and coveted work. Akimov's first posting was in 1985 as deputy head of the Soviet external trade bank, Vneshtorgbank, in Zürich, and he rose fast through the system.

27 Vladimir Pribylovsky, Akimov biography, Anticompromat.org/akimov/akimbio.html; see also Irina Reznik and Anna Baraulina, 'Cold War Banker to Putin Billionaires Walks Sanctions Wire', Bloomberg, October 24 2014; Irina Mokrousova, 'Bankir pod Prikrytiem', Forbes Russia, April 2 2015; Alexander Birman, 'Orden Natsionalnovo Dostoyaniya', *Zhurnal Kompaniya*, May 16 2005; Akimov had created IMAG with the full sanction of the Politburo and the Supreme Soviet of the Russian Federation – and he'd used its funds to provide the first outside financing for Timchenko's Kirishineftekhimexport oil trader in St Petersburg, according to Timchenko's partner in the oil trader, Andrei Katkov.

Akimov had also kept close company with a partner of Martin Schlaff, the Stasi agent who'd worked with the Dresden foreign-intelligence chief, Herbert Kohler, to siphon funds to preserve the networks of the Stasi through fake shipments of embargoed electronic goods as the Berlin Wall collapsed. The close ties between Akimov and Schlaff were to emerge much later in Putin's presidency when they forged a central European trading hub for Gazprom gas in Austria. Serving as a deputy to him at Donau Bank and later at IMAG was a former colonel of the Austrian security services, Peter Haenseler. Haenseler took care of the housekeeping, Donau Bank's fleet of cars, the upkeep of the offices and securing passports while working on other 'special missions', according to the person who worked with Akimov.

28   Two sources: one person who worked closely with Akimov (January 2014) and senior KGB operative who worked with Putin (March 2014) also indicated Donau Bank played a role in the transfer of Communist Party funds abroad before the Soviet collapse. The person who worked closely with Akimov also said Akimov continued to work in Donau Bank after the Soviet collapse, and after he'd created IMAG in 1990, after his official departure from the bank. See also 'The History of Soviet and Russian Banks abroad', in chapter penned by the former head of OstWestHandelsbank, Sergei Bochkarev. Bochkarev reveals that when the heads of the Soviet foreign banks travelled to Frankfurt in the autumn of 1991 to urgently discuss the survival of their institutions, Akimov travelled too. The person who worked closely with Akimov said Akimov knew well

Grigory Luchansky, the head of the Vienna-based Nordex trading group, an alleged organised-crime leader at the intersection of work with the KGB moving money out of the Soviet Union on the eve of the collapse. Later Luchansky also formed a joint business with Schlaff. 'The fact that Luchansky knew Akimov well is well known. They met in Vienna,' said the person who worked closely with Akimov. The former deputy energy minister, Vladimir Milov, also alleged Akimov was close to another major organised-crime figure who worked closely with the KGB, Semyon Mogilevich (author interview, November 2013). Akimov's Gazprombank was later to set up a Vienna-based gas trader, Rosukrenergo, with Dmitry Firtash, a close associate of Mogilevich.

29   Author interview with Rair Simonyan, Medvedev's close colleague at the Institute for World Economy, September 2013; See also Birman, 'Orden Natsionalnovo Dostoyaniya', Zhurnal Kompaniya, May 16 2005; Reznik and Baraulina, 'Cold War Banker to Putin Billionaires Walks Sanctions Wire', Bloomberg, October 24 2014

30   Author interview with senior Western banker involved in Akimov's bid; see also Medvedev's official biography: https://www.gazprom-neft.ru/company/management/board-of-directors/medvedev/

31   Author interview with Charlie Ryan, November 2013

32   Ibid.; and 'Eastern Oil Bidding Has Begun', Moscow Times, October 11 1997

33   'Russia's Yukos Pays $775 million for 45 per cent stake in Eastern Oil', Dow Jones, December 8 1997; John Thornhill, 'Russian Oil Group wins Control of Rival', Financial Times, December 9 1997

34 Author interview with Ryan, November 2013

35 Author interview with person who worked closely with Akimov; see also Ilya Zhegulev, 'Nevzlin Poprosil Zaschity u Genprokurora', gazeta.ru, July 21 2004; 'Delo o dvukh pokusheniyakh na ubiistvo direktora avstriiskoi kompanii East Petroleum, Yevgeniya Rybina', *Vremya Novostei*, July 4 2003; and interview with Rybin, Oleg Lurye, Vslukh, September 10 2003

36 Author interview with person close to Rybin, January 2014

37 Ibid.

38 Ibid.

39 Author interview with senior banker close to the security services, May 2015

40 Author interview with Michel, May 2005

41 Author interview with Khodorkovsky, May 2014

42 Author interview with Khodorkovsky, September 2015

43 Catherine Belton, 'Kremlin, Big Oil on Collision Course', *Moscow Times*, January 28 2003; Jeanne Whalen, 'In Russia, Politics vs Pipelines – Kremlin Hesitates to Give Oil Firms Power to Invest in Infrastructure', *Wall Street Journal*, January 29 2003

44 Author interview with Khodorkovsky, February 2003

45 Dmitry Zhdannikov and Andrew Hurst, 'Standing at a Crossroads', Reuters, January 27 2003

46 Valeria Korchagina, 'Cabinet Agrees to Slash Tax Burden', *Moscow Times*, April 24 2003

47 Khodorkovsky's exchange with Putin at RSPP meeting, https://www.youtube.com/watch?time_continue=20&v=u6NKb79VN8U

48 Torrey Clark, 'Tycoons Talk Corruption in Kremlin', *Moscow Times*, February 20 2003

49 https://www.youtube.com/watch?time_continue=20&v=u6NKb79VN8U

50 Author interview with Kondaurov, May 2014

51 Author interview with person formerly close to Putin, June 2018

52 Author interview with Vavilov, January 2013

53 Author interview with Kondaurov, May 2014

54 Catherine Belton, '$36 Billion YukosSibneft Joins the Global Elite', *Moscow Times*, April 23 2003

55 Andrew Jack and Carola Hoyos, 'Yukos Eyes Up Western Partnership', *Financial Times*, September 24 2003

56 Author interview with former Yukos shareholder, September 2013

57 Arkady Ostrovsky, 'Yukos to Expand Beyond Russia', *Financial Times*, September 28 2003

58 Author interview with Khodorkovsky, September 2015

59 Author interview with former senior Kremlin official, November 2013

60 Gregory L. White and Jeanne Whalen, 'Why Russian Oil is a Sticky Business – Energy Barons are Wielding More Clout in Parliament at a Critical Time for Putin', *Wall Street Journal*, August 1 2003

61 Author interview with senior Western banker, November 2013

62 Moises Naim, 'Russia's Dilemma: It's Sinking While it's Swimming in Oil', *The Australian*, December 15 2003

63 Goohoon Kwon, 'The Budgetary Impact of Oil Prices in Russia', Working Paper, August 1 2003, www.imf.org/external/country/rus/rr/2003/pdf/080103.pdf

64 Victoria Lavrentieva, 'Gref Says it's Time to Squeeze Big Oil', *Moscow Times*, February 20 2003. Oil-sector net income was rising far faster than the tax take,

giving a lot of room for the government to take more. See: 'Russian Oil Companies Got Richer by $20 Billion', *Finansoviye Izvestia*, January 24 2003

65   Author interview with senior Western banker, November 2013

66   'Doklad Soveta po Natsionalnoi Strategii: "Gosudarstvo I Oligarkhiya"', https://web.archive.org/ web/20150325094708/http://www.utro. ru/articles/2003/05/26/201631.shtml; the report was published on the news website utro.ru, May 26 2003

67   Author interview with Belkovsky, May 2016

68   Author interview with one of the participants in the meeting, a former Yukos shareholder, May 2015

69   Stenogram of Putin's press conference June 23 2003, www.kremlin.ru/events/ president/transcripts/22028

70   Simon Saradzhyan and Valeria Korchagina, 'Head of Yukos's Parent Company Arrested', *Moscow Times*, July 3 2003

71   Ibid.

72   'Yukos Value Falls $2 Billion on Arrests', Combined Reports (Reuters, MT), *Moscow Times*, July 4 2003

73   Valeria Korchagina, 'Four Yukos Murder Probes Opened', *Moscow Times*, July 21 2003

74   Catherine Belton, 'The Oil Town that Won't Forget Yukos', *Moscow Times*, April 25 2006

75   Chrystia Freeland, 'A Falling Tsar', *Financial Times*, November 1 2003

76   Belton, 'The Oil Town that Won't Forget Yukos'

77   Author interview with person close to Yukos shareholders, May 2014

78   Valeria Korchagina, 'Prosecutors Summon Khodorkovsky', *Moscow Times*, July 4 2003

79   Catherine Belton, 'Stocks See Blackest Day Since 1998', *Moscow Times*, July 17 2003

80   Catherine Belton, 'Khodorkovsky Sees Totalitarian Threat', *Moscow Times*, July 22 2003

81   'Putin Says Yukos Case All About Murder', *Moscow Times*, September 22 2003

82   Author interview with former Yukos shareholder, September 2013

83   Ibid.

84   Andrew Jack and Carola Hoyos, 'ExxonMobil May Offer $25 Billion for 40 Per Cent of Yukos', *Financial Times*, October 2 2003

85   Catherine Belton, 'Yukos Targeted in Three New Raids', *Moscow Times*, October 6 2003

86   Ibid.

87   Caroline McGregor, 'President Reassures Investors', *Moscow Times*, October 6 2003

88   Catherine Belton, 'Yukos Chief – "It's Just Not Fair"', *Moscow Times*, October 7 2003

89   Author interview with Pugachev, May 2014

90   Catherine Belton, 'Khodorkovsky Arrested on Seven Charges', *Moscow Times*, October 27 2003

91   Ibid.

92   Valeria Korchagina, 'The Elite Demand Some Answers', *Moscow Times*, October 27 2003

93   Author interview with Gololobov, August 2018

94   Author interview with former senior GRU officer, April 2005

95   Author interview with oil executive linked to the FSB, January 2014

96   Valeria Korchagina and Maria Danilova, 'Putin Defends Attack on Yukos', *Moscow Times*, October 28 2003

Chapter 8: Out of Terror, an Imperial Awakening

1 Author interview with Pugachev, February 2016

2 Putin would no longer have to share the running of the economy with the Yeltsin-era holdovers. According to one close former ally, this had been part of the agreement Putin had made with the Yeltsin Family when he came to power.

3 Natalia Yefimova, Torrey Clark and Lyuba Pronina, 'Armed Chechens Seize Moscow Theater', *Moscow Times*, October 24 2002. See also description in Steven Lee Myers, *The New Tsar: The Rise and Reign of Vladimir Putin*, Simon & Schuster, London, 2015

4 Michael Wines, 'Chechens Kill Hostage in Siege at Russian Hall', *New York Times*, October 25 2002

5 'Russian NTV Shows Previously Filmed Footage with Hostage-Takers' Leader, *BBC Monitoring Former Soviet Union*, October 26 2002

6 Eric Engleman, 'Armed Chechens Hold Hundreds of People Hostage in Moscow Theater', Associated Press, October 23 2002

7 'Events, Facts, Conclusions – Nord Ost Investigation Unfinished', Regional Public Organisation for Support of Victims of Terrorist Attacks

8 Luc Perrot, 'Russia Marks Anniversary of Moscow Theater Hostage Siege', Agence France-Presse, October 23 2003

9 Michael Wines, 'Hostage Toll in Russia Over 100; Nearly All Deaths Linked to Gas', *New York Times*, October 28 2002

10 Sergei Topol, Aleksandr Zheglov, Olga Allenova, 'Antrakt posle Terakta', *Kommersant*, October 23 2003

11 Susan B. Glasser and Peter Baker, 'Gas in Raid Killed 115 Hostages; Only 2 Slain by Rebels; More than 600 Remain Hospitalised in Moscow', *Washington Post*, October 28 2002: It took at least two days before the authorities were ready to disclose the full extent of the death toll, another two before they named the gas. Doctors trying to treat the hostages had been left till then in the dark about what they were dealing with; stocks of a standard antidote were in short supply or absent.

12 Valeria Korchagina, Lyuba Pronina and Torrey Clark, 'Man, a Bottle, a Shot, Then Gas', *Moscow Times*, October 28 2002

13 Michael Wines, 'Russia Names Drug in Raid, Defending Use', *New York Times*, October 31 2002

14 Sergei Topol, Aleksandr Zheglov, Olga Allenova, 'Antrakt posle Terakta', *Kommersant*, October 23 2003

15 Author interview with former Kremlin official, March 2015

16 Ibid., March 2015 and June 2018

17 Topol, Zheglov and Allenova, 'Antrakt posle Terakta', *Kommersant*, October 23 2003

18 David McHugh, 'Doctors Say Knockout Gas Killed All But Two of the Victims of Moscow Hostage Crisis', Associated Press, October 27 2002

19 Topol, Zheglov and Allenova, 'Antrakt posle Terakta', *Kommersant*, October 23 2003

20 Irina Khakamada, then vice speaker of the Duma, 'Obraschenie Iriny

Khakamady', January 14 2004, https://graniru.org/Politics/Russia/President/m.56704.html (Khakamada made the statement as part of her failed bid for the presidency in the 2004 presidential race.) This statement is also cited by the report by relatives of dead hostages: 'Events, Facts, Conclusions – Nord Ost Investigation Unfinished', Regional Public Organisation for Support of Victims of Terrorist Attacks

21 Anne Nivat, 'Chechnya: Brutality and Indifference', *Crimes of War Project*, January 6 2003. Nivat's account is cited by John Dunlop, the senior fellow on Soviet and Russian politics at the Hoover Institution, in a report on the siege for 'RFE/RL Organised Crime and Corruption Watch', January 8 2004. Nivat says the GRU, the Russian military-intelligence service, had announced Movsar Barayev's arrest two months before the siege.

22 Yury Schekochikin, 'Nezamechenniye Novosti nedeli kotoriye menya udivili', *Novaya Gazeta*, January 20 2003: Schekochikin reported that a mother of one of the terrorists had told him her daughter, recognised by her from television footage as one of the terror-ists, had long been imprisoned in a Russian penal colony. 'She cannot understand how her daughter reached Moscow as a terrorist from a prison cell.' See Dunlop too for more on this, as well as Nivat, who reported two mothers from a Chechen village in the region where Barayev's men came from as saying their daughters had been arrested at the end of September

2002 and had later resurfaced as suicide bombers.

23 *Kommersant* buried the finding that the bombs were dummies at the bottom of the story – the first half of which was devoted to the indictment of a group of Chechens accused of being involved in preparing a string of terrorist attacks in Moscow, including the Dubrovka siege – and no one else picked it up.

24 Politicians leapt to praise a successful operation. Using the gas had been the only choice. 'We found ourselves in a situation between a horrible tragedy involving the deaths of all the hostages and an incredible disgrace had we met all the demands of the hostage-takers', the Moscow mayor, Yury Luzhkov, said.

25 Caroline Wyatt, 'Moscow Siege Leaves Dark Memories', BBC, December 16 2002. The report cites opinion polls as showing 83 per cent of Russians were satisfied with Putin's rule.

26 Valeria Korchagina, 'Duma Seeks Probe of Theater Attack', *Moscow Times*, October 30 2002

27 Timur Aliyev, 'Chechens Vanish in Veil of Darkness', *Moscow Times*, December 23 2002

28 'Moscow Gunmen Threaten to Begin Killing Hostages Sat', Dow Jones, October 25 2002. The report cites Russia's deputy interior minister Vladimir Vasiliev as saying Maskhadov was behind the attack, while Russian TV networks aired a video of Maskhadov saying the rebels had shifted from guerrilla warfare to an 'offensive' strategy, adding: 'I am

certain that in the final stage there will be a still more unique action, similar to the jihad, that will liberate our land from the Russian aggressors.' Russia's state-controlled Channel One later claimed the tape had been made five days before the hostage-taking, but it emerged that it had actually been made months earlier, during the summer. See also John B. Dunlop, 'RFE/RL Organised Crime and Corruption Watch', January 8 2004, which cites Maskhadov's spokesperson as saying Maskhadov was referring to a military operation against federal forces, not to any hostage-taking. Dunlop also cites Putin's spokesman Sergei Yastrzhembsky as saying Maskhadov could no longer be considered 'a legitimate representative of this resistance'. In NTV's interview with Barayev, the apparent leader of the hostage-takers, Barayev said they were acting on the orders of 'our supreme military emir', named as rebel leader Shamil Basayev, and that Maskhadov was the president, and 'we are very much under his command'.

29 Steven Lee Myers, 'Russia Recasts Bog in Caucasus as War on Terror', *New York Times*, October 5 2002

30 Andrew Jack, 'Moscow Siege May be Linked to Al Qaeda', *Financial Times*, October 24 2002. Russian security forces also said they'd intercepted calls made by the Chechen hostage-takers to the United Arab Emirates and Turkey.

31 Steven R. Weisman, 'US Lists 3 Chechen Groups as Terrorist and Freezes Assets', *New York Times*, March 1 2003

32 Nabi Abdullaev, 'There are No Rebels Left for Peace Talks', *Moscow Times*, November 1 2002

33 Author interview with Pugachev, February 2015

34 Author interview with Pugachev, March 2013

35 Ibid.

36 Author interview with Voloshin, November 2013

37 Catherine Belton, 'Anointed Enigma: The Quiet Rise of a Dedicated Dmitry Medvedev', *Financial Times*, February 28 2003

38 Catherine Belton, Valeria Korchagina and Alex Nicholson, 'Yukos Shares Frozen, Voloshin is Out', *Moscow Times*, October 31 2003

39 Pyotr Netreba, 'Otstavka Voloshina Sovpala s Kontsom Epokha Yeltsina', *Kommersant*, November 3 2003, interview with Kudrin

40 Belton, Korchagina and Nicholson, 'Yukos Shares Frozen, Voloshin is Out'

41 Ibid.

42 Catherine Belton and Lyuba Pronina, 'The Duma of a New Political Era', *Moscow Times*, December 9 2003

43 Catherine Belton, 'Homeland a Force to be Reckoned With?', *Moscow Times*, December 5 2003

44 Belton and Pronina, 'The Duma of a New Political Era'

45 Francesca Mereu and Oksana Yablokova, 'United Russia Set to Get 300 Seats', *Moscow Times*, December 22 2003. United Russia won 37.6 per cent of the vote, and a majority of seats after independent deputies joined its ranks.

46 Author interview with senior banker close to the security services, May 2016

47 Author interview with Kasyanov, January 2013

48 'Gazprom Off Reform Agenda', Reuters, *Moscow Times*, September 29 2003

49 'President Putin Demands Stopping of Hysterics and Speculations about Arrest of Khodorkovsky', ntv.ru, October 29 2003

50 Author interview with Kasyanov, January 2013

51 Alexander Bekker and Vladimir Fedorin, 'Interview: Mikhail Kasyanov, predsedatel pravitelstva RF: Reformy vo vsekh sferakh budut prodolzheny', *Vedomosti*, January 12 2004

52 Valeria Korchagina, 'Gazprom Cuts Supplies to Europe', *Moscow Times*, February 19 2004

53 Ibid.

54 Caroline McGregor, 'Putin Fires Kasyanov 19 Days Before Vote', *Moscow Times*, February 24 2004

55 Author interview with Kasyanov, January 2013

56 Caroline McGregor, 'Putin Picks Fradkov for Prime Minister', *Moscow Times*, March 2 2004

57 Author interview with Kasyanov, January 2014

58 Simon Saradzhyan, 'Early Returns Give Putin 70 Per Cent', *Moscow Times*, March 15 2004

59 Author interview with Pugachev, March 2015

60 Author interview with Pugachev, May 2013

61 Valeria Korchagina, 'Duma Set to Revive the Soviet Anthem', *Moscow Times*, December 6 2000

62 Natalia Gevorkyan, Natalia Timakova, Andrei Kolesnikov, *In the First Person: Conversations with Vladimir Putin*, pp.11–12, Vagrius, Moscow

63 Ana Uzelac, 'Putin, Bush Reach Across the Divide', *Moscow Times*, June 18 2001

64 Author interview with Russian tycoon, November 2013

65 Author interview with Pugachev, March 2016

66 The Russian parliament ratified a treaty calling for the creation of a single economic space between the four former Soviet republics in April 2004; earlier Putin's government had called for the rouble to be the unified currency for the union. Askold Krushelnycky, 'Parliaments Ratify Treaty on Single Economic Space', RFE/RL, April 21 2004

67 Author interview with descendant of white Russian emigré close to Putin, May 2014

68 Earlier that year, the newly-installed pro-Kremlin leader, Akhmad Kadyrov, had been killed in a huge bomb blast at a football stadium, and the vote count was barely in on the man to replace him, the former Chechen interior minister, another Kremlin loyalist. The day before the Beslan attack, it was announced Alu Alkhanov had been elected with 74 per cent of the vote. The vote – as well as a Kremlin-organised referendum the previous year for Chechnya to remain as part of the Russian Federation – had been widely denounced by human rights groups as rigged. Most of the republic's infra-structure was still in ruins following

the years of carpet-bombing in Putin's military campaign.

69 Simon Ostrovsky, 'Over 300 Killed in School Carnage', *Moscow Times*, September 6 2004

70 Ibid.

71 Simon Saradzhyan, '30 Women and Children Freed in Beslan', *Moscow Times*, September 3 2004

72 'Hostage Takers Demands in N Ossetia Not Changed', Interfax, September 1 2004; see also Peter Baker and Susan B. Glasser, 'Hundreds Held Hostage at School in Russia; Many Children Seized in Town near Chechnya', *Washington Post*, September 2 2004, and Kim Murphy, 'Critics Detail Missteps in School Crisis', *Los Angeles Times*, September 17 2004

73 Andrew Jack, 'Siege Gunmen Release 26 Mothers and Babies', *Financial Times*, September 2 2004

74 Murphy, 'Critics Detail Missteps in School Crisis'

75 'Svidetel na Protsesse po Delu Kulaeva utverzhdaet, chto Maskhadov byl gotov priekhats v Beslan dlya peregovorov c terroristami ob osvobozhdenii zalozhnikov', Interfax, December 22 2005

76 Ibid.; see also Simon Ostrovsky, 'Over 300 Killed in School Carnage', *Moscow Times*, September 6 2004

77 C.J. Chivers, 'For Russians, Wounds Linger in School Siege', *New York Times*, August 26 2005; Kim Murphy, 'Aching to Know', *Los Angeles Times*, August 27 2005. Russia initially denied it had launched the thermobaric Shmel flamethrowers at the school, but in 2005, a senior Russian prosecutor acknowledged that they had been used: see also Anatoly Medetsky and Yana Voitova, 'A Reversal Over Beslan Only Fuels Speculation', *Moscow Times*, July 21 2005. The prosecutor, Nikolai Shepel, denied that the flamethrowers could have sparked the fire that engulfed the school. He claimed the type deployed, RPO-A, did not have an incendiary effect. An independent investigation conducted by Stanislav Kesayev for the North Ossetian regional administration, however, found traces of phosphorus on bodies, a sign that the incendiary PRO-Z shells had been used.

78 Chivers, 'For Russians, Wounds Linger in School Siege'; see also 'Russia: Beslan Reports Compared', RadioFreeEurope/RadioLiberty, January 3 2007, for comments by eyewitness Kesayev on the Russians' use of tanks: 'As the head of the republican commission and as a person who was at the site of the tragedy, I continue to say that tanks began to shoot long before hostages left the building'; also the testimony given by Kesayev's aide, Izrail Totoonti, during the trial of one of the terrorists involved in the siege, in 'Zarema, a kovo nam seichas ubyvats?', *Kommersant*, December 23 2005. Totoonti said: 'I heard the shots of tank fire for the first time at about 2 p.m. It was before we began dragging the hostages out of the school.'

79 Chivers, 'For Russians, Wounds Linger in School Siege'

80 Ibid.: An independent investigation said the terrorists had forced them to wave their clothing as an indication to

federal forces they should hold their fire. But the gunfire did not stop.

81 Chivers, 'For Russians, Wounds Linger in School Siege'

82 Ibid.

83 Kim Murphy, 'Critics Detail Missteps in School Crisis', *Los Angeles Times*, September 17 2004

84 Ibid.

85 Nikolai Sergeyev and Zaur Farniev, 'Kommisiya Zavershila Terakt', *Kommersant*, December 23 2006

86 Ibid.

87 Chivers, 'For Russians, Wounds Linger in School Siege'; see Kim Murphy, 'Aching to Know', *Los Angeles Times*, August 27 2005 for a detailed account of former hostages describing how the roof began shaking while they were still held in the school. The article cites one former hostage, an army explosives expert, as saying he believed it was tank fire 'because the whole building was shaking, and these weren't grenades, it was something more serious than that . . . By that time, I was more afraid of our own people than the terrorists'; see also 'Russia: Beslan Reports Compared', and 'Zarema, a kovo nam seichas ubyvats?'

88 'Russia: Beslan Reports Compared'

89 Nikolai Sergeyev and Zaur Farniev, 'Kommisiya Zavershila Terakt', *Kommersant*, December 23 2006

90 Yury Savelyev, 'Beslan: Pravda Zalozhnikov', www.pravdabeslana.ru/doklad/oglavlenie.htm; Maria Danilova, 'Russian Lawmaker Makes Beslan Claims', Associated Press, August 30 2006

91 Andrew Osborne, 'Kremlin to Blame for Beslan Deaths, Claims Russian MP', *Independent*, August 30 2006

92 'Video Rekindles Russian Debate on Blame for Beslan Death Toll', Associated Press, July 31 2007

93 Murphy, 'Aching to Know'

94 Author interview with former Kremlin insider, August 2017

95 Catherine Belton, 'Putin is Facing his Biggest Challenge', *Moscow Times*, September 9 2004

96 Ibid.

97 'Poll: Putin's Popularity at 4-Year Low', *Moscow Times*, September 23 2004

98 Address by Vladimir Putin, September 4 2004, www.kremlin.ru/events/president/transcripts/22589

99 Belton, 'Putin is Facing his Biggest Challenge'

100 Nabi Abdullaev, 'Putin: Scrap Popular Vote for Governors', *Moscow Times*, September 14 2004

101 Nikolai Petrov, 'Putin's Reforms are Dangerous for Russia', *Moscow Times*, September 15 2004

102 Simon Saradzhyan, 'Putin Lashes Out at the US', *Moscow Times*, September 8 2004; Guy Faulconbridge, 'Putin Targets Terrorist Financing', *Moscow Times*, October 6 2004

103 Author interview with former Kremlin insider, August 2017

104 Jason Burke, 'London Mosque link to Beslan', *Observer*, October 3 2004. A Russian official, Ilya Shabalkin, federal forces spokesman for the North Caucasus, confirmed to the *Moscow Times* that the mosque attendee, Kamel Rabat Bouralha, had been arrested by Russian forces while trying

to cross the Russian-Azeri border, but declined to comment on whether he had played a role in the Beslan attack. (See: Valery Dzutsev, 'Report: 3 British Residents Assisted in Beslan Attack', *Moscow Times*, October 5 2004)

105 Valeria Korchagina, 'Putin Tells West not to Meddle in Ukraine', *Moscow Times*, July 27 2004

106 Simon Saradzhyan, 'Putin Goes on Stump in Ukraine', *Moscow Times*, October 27 2004; Francesca Mereu, 'Putin's Campaign has Kiev on Edge', *Moscow Times*, October 28 2004

107 Anatoly Medetsky, 'Outrage as Yanukovych Takes the Lead', *Moscow Times*, November 23 2004

108 Oksana Yablokova, 'Youthful Pora Charges Up the People', *Moscow Times*, December 3 2004

109 Author interviews with two people close to Putin: one in March 2014, the other November 2014

110 Simon Saradzhyan, 'President Lashes Out at the West', *Moscow Times*, December 24 2004

111 Vladimir Putin, Annual State of the Nation Address, April 25 2005, www.kremlin.ru/events/president/news/33219

112 Vladimir Putin, Annual State of the Nation Address, May 26 2004, www.kremlin.ru/events/president/news/31034

113 Vladimir Putin, Annual State of the Nation Address, April 25 2005, www.kremlin.ru/events/president/news/33219

Chapter 9: 'Appetite Comes During Eating'

1 Catherine Belton, 'Ex-Yukos Chiefs Face Trial Together', *Moscow Times*, June 17 2004

2 Peter Baker, 'Russian Oil Tycoons Lose Bid for Release', *Washington Post*, June 17 2004

3 See Leonid Ragozin, 'When Russian Officials Nightmare Your Business, You Can Lose Everything – Even Your Life', Bloomberg, January 29 2018. The situation was to escalate to such an extent that by 2015, 200,000 business-related criminal cases had been opened, of which only 46,000 had gone to trial. Yet 83 per cent of the businessmen involved in the 200,000 cases had lost their businesses. See also Kathrin Hille, 'Business Behind Bars', *Financial Times*, August 10 2018, for further figures on pre-trial detention of businesspeople, which reached a peak in 2016 at 6,856.

4 According to EBRD statistics and Vladimir Milov, former deputy energy minister and independent economist; Author interview with former government official, 2012; see also 'Russian Anti-Monopoly Watchdog Says State Grip on Economy Rises', *Vedomosti*, May 6 2019. The report cites the Federal AntiMonopoly Service as saying the state's share of Russia's GDP was more than 50 per cent by 2013

5 Author interview with Michel, January 2013

6 Interview with Vladimir Putin, *New York Times*, October 5 2003, www.nytimes.com/2003/10/05/international/06PTEXT-CND.html

7 Catherine Belton, 'NTV Speculates on Yukos, Terrorists', *Moscow Times*, September 27 2004

8 Ilya Bulavinov, 'Sergei Ivanov – Eto Ne Smena Epokh, a navedenie poryadka', *Kommersant*, November 17 2003

9 Catherine Belton, 'Kremlin Playing Oil

Game for Keeps', *Moscow Times*, December 29 2003

10 John McCain, Remarks to Senate, November 4 2003, https://www.aei.org/research-products/speech/senator-mccain-decries-new-authoritarianism-in-russia/

11 Author interview with Thomas E. Graham, September 2018

12 Graham, for one, had always been a hard-nosed sceptic who earlier than his colleagues in the nineties had pointed out the dangers of viewing Russian politics of the Yeltsin era as a black-and-white battle between Yeltsin's young reformers and the Communists. Then a diplomat in Moscow, he'd pointed out the risks the clan-driven politics of the oligarchs posed to democracy. For more on this see Hoffman, *The Oligarchs*, pp.322–3

13 Author interview with Graham, September 2018

14 Belton, 'Kremlin Playing Oil Game for Keeps'

15 Andrew Jack, 'Facing Judgment: Turmoil at Yukos Drains Investors of Their Confidence in Putin's Russia', *Financial Times*, June 16 2004

16 Catherine Belton, 'Nevzlin Offers Shares for Freedom', *Moscow Times*, February 17 2004

17 For more on the sophisticated use of judicial orders in Russia and how they became entrenched, see paper by Thomas Firestone (former resident legal adviser, US Department of Justice, US Embassy Moscow), 'Criminal Corporate Raiding in Russia', *The International Lawyer*, Vol. 42, No. 4 (Winter 2008), pp.1207–29

18 Catherine Belton, 'Banks Warn that Yukos May Default', *Moscow Times*, April 27 2004

19 Jack, 'Facing Judgment'. Despite insisting that all their actions were in line with the law, the day before the start of Khodorkovsky's trial, Yukos's management let it be known that they'd offered a deal to the government in which they could issue shares to pay off the tax bill.

20 Catherine Belton, 'Putin Tip Powers Yukos Recovery', *Moscow Times*, June 18 2004

21 Author interview with Kremlin insider, June 2017

22 Author interview with Temerko, June 2016

23 Ibid. Temerko said that when he worked with the defence ministry he was a civilian, but that three- and four-star generals worked under him.

24 Ibid.

25 Ibid.

26 Catherine Belton, 'Police Surround Yukos Headquarters', *Moscow Times*, July 5 2004

27 Peter Baker, 'Court Defeat Brings Yukos to Verge of Bankruptcy', *Washington Post*, July 4 2004

28 Catherine Belton, 'Khodorkovsky Offers Deal, Deadline Passes', *Moscow Times*, July 8 2004

29 Erin E. Arvedlund, 'Yukos Says it Offered to Pay $8 Billion in Back Taxes', *New York Times*, July 12 2004

30 Valeria Korchagina, 'Yukos Production Unit to be Sold', *Moscow Times*, July 21 2004

31 Denis Maternovsky, 'Putin Aide Named Head of Rosneft', *St Petersburg Times*, July 30 2004

32 Author interview with Temerko, June 2016

33 Guy Faulconbridge, 'Dresdner Will Set a Price for Yugansk', *Moscow Times*, August 13 2004

34 Author interview with Graham, September 2018

35 Renaissance Capital employed several senior executives from the Russian intelligence services. Igor Sagiryan served as its general director and then president from 1999 to 2009. Sagiryan graduated from Moscow's US Canada Institute, a known hub for preparing foreign-intelligence cadres, and then served for two years as a consultant to the International Department of the Central Committee, the same institution headed by Valentin Falin that was in charge of payments for strategic operations, in the two years before the Soviet Union's fall. Another was Yury Sagaidak, a former KGB spy deported from the UK in 1989, who served as deputy general director from 1999 to 2006. RenCap also employed Yury Kobaladze, a former KGB general, from 1999 to 2007.

36 Gregory L. White and Chip Cummins, 'Russia to Form Energy Giant Open to West But Led by Kremlin', *Wall Street Journal*, September 15 2004

37 Ibid.

38 Peter Baker, 'Russia State Gas, Oil Firms Merge; Aim is to Create Dominant International Supplier', *Washington Post*, September 15 2004

39 Catherine Belton, 'Gazprom to Grab Rosneft, Alter Market', *Moscow Times*, September 15 2004

40 Guy Faulconbridge, 'Second Leak Puts Fair Price on Yugansk', *Moscow Times*, October 4 2004

41 Guy Faulconbridge, 'Yugansk Goes on the Block for $8.6 Billion', *Moscow Times*, November 22 2004

42 Ibid.

43 Author interview with Temerko, June 2016

44 Faulconbridge, 'Yugansk Goes on the Block for $8.6 Billion'

45 Martin Sixsmith, *Putin's Oil: The Yukos Affair and the Struggle for Russia*, p.175 (the author also spoke with Misamore)

46 Author interview with Temerko, June 2016

47 Author interview with Charles Ryan, the US banker who then served as head of Deutsche-UFG, a Moscow brokerage in which Deutsche Bank held a 40 per cent stake, and who worked closely with Gazprom and Kudrin to bring the Western banks on board

48 Catherine Belton, 'Foreign Banks to Lend Gazprom $13.4 Billion', *Moscow Times*, December 8 2004

49 Author interviews with two people familiar with the matter: September 2018 and November 2013

50 Catherine Belton, 'Yukos Files for Bankruptcy Protection in Houston', *Moscow Times*, December 16 2004

51 Catherine Belton, 'Report: Gazprom Loan Put on Hold', *Moscow Times*, December 17 2004

52 Including a tanker of crude it sent to Houston in 2002

53 Alex Nicholson, 'Putin Defends Yukos Unit Sale', Associated Press, December 23 2004

54 Guy Faulconbridge, 'Mystery Bidder Wins Yugansk for $9.4 Billion', *Moscow Times*, December 20 2004; Catherine Belton, 'Putin Says He Knows Mystery Buyer', *Moscow Times*, December 22 2004

55 Belton, 'Putin Says He Knows Mystery Buyer'

56 Andrew Osborn, 'Rumours Abound as Mystery Buyer is Tracked Down to London Bar', *Independent*, December 21 2004

57 Belton, 'Putin Says He Knows Mystery Buyer'

58 Ekaterina Derbilova, Irina Reznik, Svetlana Petrova, 'Pobeditel, pokhozhy na 'Surgutneftegaz', *Vedomosti*,

December 21 2004. The executives were identified as Igor Minibayev and Valentina Komarova, both mid-level managers at Surgutneftegaz.

59   Author interviews with Milov, November 2013, with a former Timchenko business partner June 2014, and with senior Russian banker, May 2015; corporate records showed that Baikal Finance Group had been founded by another obscure company, OOO Makoil, which was owned by another Surgutneftegaz executive, Alexander Zhernovkov, who later served on Surgut's board. 'Baikal Finance Group was the structure of Gennady Timchenko,' said one former Timchenko business partner.

60   Anna Raff, 'State-Owned Rosneft Buys Mystery Buyer of Yukos Unit Auction', Dow Jones Newswires, December 23 2004

61   Author interview with Western banker working with Gazprom on the Yugansk bid, November 2013

62   'Kto Oplatil "Yugansk"', Vedomosti, June 3 2005; Catherine Belton, 'The Money Trail Leading to Yugansk', Moscow Times, June 6 2005. The central bank data showed that on December 30 2004, $5.3 billion was transferred from a federal treasury account with the central bank to state-owned Vneshekonombank. The same day, Vneshekonombank received the same sum in promissory notes from subsidiaries of Rosneft, and Rosneft in turn received the same sum in its account at Sberbank, another state bank. Then Baikal Finance Group, which also had an account at Sberbank, transferred the remaining $7.6 billion it owed for Yugansk to the justice ministry. Analysts said it looked as if Rosneft had transferred the funds to Baikal Finance Group.

63   Catherine Belton, 'Chinese Lend Rosneft $6 Billion for Yugansk', Moscow Times, February 2 2005

64   Catherine Belton, 'Putin Demotes Advisor Illarionov', Moscow Times, January 11 2005

65   Author interview with Illarionov, January 2005

66   Catherine Belton, 'Houston Court Rejects Yukos Appeal', Moscow Times, February 28 2005

67   Author interview with Temerko, June 2016

68   Author interview with Western intermediary involved in the process, January 2017

69   Ibid.

70   Isabel Gorst, 'Exxon and Rosneft Sign Arctic Deal', Financial Times, August 30 2011

71   These emails have been obtained by author, and are part of ongoing litigation in the Netherlands.

72   Catherine Belton, 'Half of Rosneft IPO Goes to 4 Buyers', Moscow Times, July 17 2006

73   Author interview with Temerko, June 2016

74   Catherine Belton, 'Banks Want Yukos Ruled Bankrupt', Moscow Times, March 13 2006

75   Ibid.

76   Catherine Belton, 'Creditor Banks Sell Yukos Loan to Rosneft', Moscow Times, March 16 2006

77   Catherine Belton, 'Western Banks Fund Rosneft Move on Yukos', Financial Times, March 21 2007

78   Catherine Belton, 'Analysts Skeptical as BP Quits Yukos Auction at First Stage', Financial Times, March 28 2007

79   Catherine Belton, 'Russian Bargain That Comes at a Price', Financial Times, April 5 2007

80   Ibid.

81 Catherine Belton, 'The State's Unsated Appetite', *Financial Times*, April 20 2007

82 Catherine Belton, 'Yukos Finally Expires, Victim of its Battle with the Kremlin', *Financial Times*, May 11 2007

83 Khodorkovsky's Closing Arguments, April 11 2005. Full transcript: www.freerepublic.com/focus/news/1382298/posts

84 Valeria Korchagina, 'Yukos Trial Ends with Applause', *Moscow Times*, April 12 2005

85 Eyewitness account based on documentary material. The Moscow City Court responded to a request for comment about the account by saying it was 'invention which does not require any comment. The legality and the justification of the rulings made as a result of the criminal cases have been checked by all the courts of the country, and have also been studied by the European Court of Human Rights. The rulings have been confirmed as legal.' (The ECHR ruled, however, in January 2020 that Khodorkovsky had been denied a fair trial in 2009 and 2010 when he was convicted for a second set of charges of embezzlement and money laundering. The Russian judge's refusal to 'allow the defence to examine prosecution and defence witnesses and to submit important expert or exculpatory evidence' violated Khodorkovsky's rights, the ECHR found.)

86 Ibid.

87 Ibid.

88 Valeria Korchagina, 'So Far, Verdict Appears to be Guilty', *Moscow Times*, May 17 2005

89 Catherine Belton, 'Judges Drag Out Verdict for a Second Day', *Moscow Times*, May 18 2005

90 Lyuba Pronina, 'Nine Years for Khodorkovsky and Lebedev', *Moscow Times*, June 1 2005

91 Catherine Belton, 'Shock and Then Boredom in Court', *Moscow Times*, June 1 2005

92 Ibid.

93 Eyewitness account

94 Ibid.

95 Ibid.

96 Ibid.

97 Valeria Korchagina, 'Court Rejects Khodorkovsky Appeal', *Moscow Times*, September 23 2005

98 Ibid.

99 Nabi Abdullaev, 'Khodorkovsky Jailed in Polluted Chita', *Moscow Times*, October 21 2005

100 Eyewitness account

101 Ibid.

102 Kathrin Hille, 'Business Behind Bars', *Financial Times*, August 10 2018

Chapter 10: Obschak

1 Pavel Miledin, Anna Scherbakova, Svetlana Petrova, 'Sogaz prodali v Piter. Samy pribylny v Rossii strakhovschik dostalsya banku "Rossiya"', *Vedomosti*, January 21 2005

2 Author interview with Vladimir Milov, October 2011

3 Catherine Belton, 'A Realm Fit for a Tsar', *Financial Times*, December 1 2011

4 See the excellent Neil Buckley and Arkady Ostrovsky, 'Putin's Allies are Turning Russia into a Corporate State', *Financial Times*, June 18 2006

5 Author interview with senior banker, Geneva, December 2013

6 Buckley and Ostrovsky, 'Putin's Allies are Turning Russia into a Corporate State'

7 Author interview with Kolesnikov, September 2011; Oleg Roldugin, 'Kak za Kammenym Ostrovom, Kuda Peresilsya znamenity Putinsky Dachny Kooperativ "Ozero"', *Sobesednik*, February 26 2014

8 A performer at one of these events was later to describe it all: Natalia

Vetlitskaya, 'Netsenzurnaya Skazka', LiveJournal, August 15 2011

9   Author interview with Sergei Kolesnikov, September 2011

10   Ibid.; see also Yevgenia Albats, 'Chisto Konkretny Kandidat', *New Times*, February 26 2012, for tapes on this

11   Author interview, September 2011

12   Author interview with Kolesnikov, September 2011

13   Ibid.

14   According to one former intermediary for the KGB and documents siphoned from the Soviet Union by a defecting KGB officer, Vladimir Mitrokhin

15   Author interview with Kolesnikov, September 2011

16   Author interview with former KGB officer, March 2014

17   Author interview with Kolesnikov, September 2011

18   According to documents provided by Kolesnikov to author

19   Author interview with Kolesnikov, September 2011; and documents provided to author

20   According to documents provided by Kolesnikov to author; Aktsept was owned by one of Putin's relatives, the grandson of his uncle, Mikhail Shelomov, and it owned a 4.5 per cent stake in Bank Rossiya. Abros was owned 100 per cent by Bank Rossiya.

21   Aleksei Rozhkov, Irina Reznik, Anna Baraulina and Yelena Myazina, 'Pristroili 3% Gazproma. "Sogaz" kupil Kompaniyu upravlyayushchuyu rezervami "Gazfonda"', *Vedomosti*, August 23 2006; Belton, 'A Realm Fit for a Tsar'

22   From the start, Leader Asset Management and Gazfond had been hand in glove. The two companies shared the same offices, and the walls of Gazfond's conference room bore Leader's logo. Details of how Gazfond's

$6 billion pension funds were managed were scarce. (Details of what happened to the $7.7bn Gazprom stake held on the balance sheet of Gazfond were scarcer still – by 2008, in fact, these shares had disappeared without any explanation or report.) Gazfond, however, had immediately been pulled into Bank Rossiya's orbit. Nikolai Shamalov, the business partner of Kolesnikov, the dentist turned Siemens representative turned Putin's friend, had his son Yury appointed head of Gazfond in August 2003, before the process of transfers had even begun.

23   Gazfond had accumulated a 20 per cent stake in a Moscow power-generation company called Mosenergo – and at the end of 2006 Gazprom's board of directors ruled that it would swap its controlling stake in Gazprombank (50 per cent plus one share) for Gazfond's 20 per cent stake in Mosenergo, then worth $1.8 billion. When, shortly after the deal (early 2007), a new law came into force barring pension funds from owning more than 10 per cent of non-traded stocks, Gazfond transferred the stake to Lider Asset Management, thereby giving Bank Rossiya control.

24   Belton, 'A Realm Fit for a Tsar'; see also Boris Nemtsov and Vladimir Milov, 'Putin I Gazprom', *Nezavisimy Ekspertny Doklad*, October 2 2008

25   Author interview with Milov, September 2011

26   Belton, 'A Realm Fit for a Tsar'

27   Author interview with Milov, September 2011. The estimate included the 3 per cent stake in Gazprom held by Gazfond, worth $7.7 billion; see also Nemtsov and Milov, 'Putin I Gazprom', for this estimate.

28   Author interview with Milov, September 2011

29 Ibid.

30 Author interview with Kolesnikov, September 2011

31 Ibid.

32 Ibid.

33 After Kolesnikov's allegations first appeared, Shamalov sold the stake he held in the palace to another businessman close to Putin's Kremlin, Alexander Ponomarenko. See Rinat Sagdiev and Irina Reznik, 'Troe iz Dvortsa', *Vedomosti*, April 4 2011

34 Author interview with person familiar with Shamalov and Putin

35 Author interview with Peskov, November 2011

36 Author interview with Kolesnikov, September 2011

37 The film is called *Brilliantovaya Ruka*. Sergei Pugachev also confirmed that behind the scenes Putin was nicknamed Mikhail Ivanovich after the police chief in this film.

38 Author interview with Kolesnikov, September 2011

39 Bank Rossiya had become a nest for all of Putin's closest cronies. His key business allies shifted in and out as shareholders: only Kovalchuk remained constant as its biggest shareholder, owning 37.6 per cent at the beginning of 2005 when the acquisition of the Sogaz shares was completed. Timchenko's International Petroleum Products oil trader had held 20.7 per cent between 1998 and 2002, while his other trader Kinex continued to hold this stake until 2003. It was also, for a time, a point of intersection with some of the organised-crime interests Putin had consorted with. For two years between 1998 and 1999, Gennady Petrov, a leader of the Tambov organised-crime group, held a 2.2 per cent stake in the bank, while one of his business partners, Sergei Kuzmin, held another 2.2 per cent, part of a network of close overlapping businesses that appeared at the time to hold as much as 14 per cent. It was a telltale sign of the alliance with organised crime that Putin's KGB men had forged to run the city – and then the country – in their own interests. This alliance was later to surface all too clearly when Spanish prosecutors arrested Gennady Petrov in Spain in 2009 as part of a far-reaching investigation into Russian money laundering through Spanish real estate. The case was based partly on wiretaps on which Petrov and his business partners were caught discussing connections at the highest level of Kremlin power. All the while, Petrov's wife had remained a resident of the Kamenny Ostrov compound, where Kolesnikov, Kovalchuk and other Bank Rossiya shareholders had lived.

40 Yevgenia Albats, 'Chisto Konkretny Kandidat', *New Times*, February 26 2012

41 Author interview with former KGB officer, May 2013

42 Author interview, December 2012

43 Belton and Buckley, 'On the Offensive: How Gunvor Rose to the Top of Oil Trading', *Financial Times*, May 14 2008

44 Ibid.

45 Ibid.; author interview with former Petroval trader, May 2007. (Gunvor rarely disclosed its earnings. In 2008, Tornqvist would only say annual profits were expected to be 'in the hundreds of millions' on revenues of $70 billion. But other oil traders said that sum sounded distinctly low: one estimated that Glencore – which then also did not disclose its profits – made about $6 billion on revenues of $140 billion in 2007.) The first year Gunvor began publicly disclosing its profits in 2010, it

said net profit after tax that year was $299 million on revenues of $96 billion.

46   Author interview, Geneva, February 2013

47   When I interviewed Tornqvist in 2008, he would only say the third shareholder was 'a private businessman who has nothing to do with politics'. The third shareholder was exposed by Roman Shleynov in 2012 as Pyotr Kolbin, another St Petersburg businessman who Timchenko's Geneva associates described as a 'close friend' of Putin's. See: Roman Shleynov, 'Tainstvennym tretim vladeltsem Gunvor byl Peterburgets Petr Kolbin', *Vedomosti*, October 8 2012. One of Timchenko's former closest business partners said he could only tell the story of who Kolbin was 'in ten years time'.

48   Andrei Vandenko, 'Gennady Timchenko: Za Vsyo v Zhizni Nado Platits. I za znakomstvo s rukovodstvom strany tozhe' (interview with Timchenko), ITAR-TASS, August 4 2014

49   Ibid. In the interview, Timchenko says Edward Snowden taught him 'to use this technology more carefully. We are watched.'

50   Andrew Higgins, Guy Chazan and Alan Cullison, 'The Middleman: Secretive Associate of Putin Emerges as Czar of Russian Oil Trading – In First Interview, Gennady Timchenko Denies Ties', *Wall Street Journal*, June 11 2008

51   Author interview with Pugachev, September 2014. Timchenko, through his lawyers, said any suggestion there has been some kind of 'secrecy' around his relationship with Putin is absurd.

52   Ibid.

53   Luke Harding, 'Secretive Oil Firm Denies Putin has Any Stake in its Ownership: Company Rejects Claims it Benefits from Kremlin Ties', *Guardian*, December 22 2007

54   'Russian President Says Claims That He Has Amassed a Personal Fortune Are Nonsense', Associated Press, February 14 2008

55   Author interview with Pugachev, January 2015

56   Author interview with former KGB officer and close Timchenko associate, May 2014

57   Author interview with Russian tycoon close to Putin, September 2014

58   US Department of Treasury, 'Treasury Sanctions Russian Officials, Members of the Russian Leadership's Inner Circle, and an Entity for Involvement in the Situation in Ukraine', March 20 2014, https://www.treasury.gov/press-center/press-releases/Pages/j23331.aspx. The US Treasury did not provide any details. Some signs of a close financial relationship between Timchenko and Putin's family emerged in a 2015 investigation by Reuters. In 2012, Timchenko transferred ownership of a $3.7 million mansion on the coast of southern France in Biarritz for an undisclosed price to the man who was soon to become husband to Putin's youngest daughter, Kirill Shamalov. (Stephen Grey, Andrei Kuzmin and Elizabeth Piper, 'Putin's Daughter, a Young Billionaire and the President's Friends', Reuters, November 10 2015) A year after Shamalov's 2013 wedding to Putin's youngest daughter, he also acquired a 17 per cent stake in Russia's biggest petrochemicals giant, Sibur, from Timchenko for an undisclosed price with the help of a $1 billion loan from the closely allied Gazprombank. (Jack Stubbs, Andrei Kuzmin, Stephen Grey and Roman Anin, 'The Man Who Married Putin's Daughter and then Made a Fortune', Reuters, December 17 2015) (A Timchenko spokesman said

the transfer took place at a market price.)

59 This section is based on dozens of hours of interviews the author conducted with Geneva-based associates of Timchenko between December 2012 and April 2015. Signs of Goutchkov's banking connections with Timchenko appeared in a cache of leaked bank records from HSBC shared by the International Consortium for Investigative Journalists. According to these, Timchenko and his daughter Xeniia opened accounts at HSBC's private bank in Geneva at the end of March 2007 – just six weeks after HSBC announced that Goutchkov and his team had joined it to run Russian private banking from Julius Baer, the 180-year-old private Swiss bank. Goutchkov declined to comment, saying Swiss banking secrecy law prevented him from doing so. HSBC also declined to respond to questions on Goutchkov's clients, but it indicated that it was aware his Russia connections ran deep, saying it hired him because of its desire to grow its presence in the Russian market. Two years after he joined its private bank, HSBC launched a $200 million drive to expand its presence in Russia, and Goutchkov joined HSBC Russia's board.

60 Two people who have had direct dealings with Goutchkov, December 2012 and September 2013.

61 Author interviews, Geneva, December 2012 to April 2015; see also interview Goutchkov gave to banki.ru: 'Ivan Goutchkov: 'Rossiya – odna iz takikh stran, kuda seichas vygodno investirovats', December 30 2015

62 Author interview with former HSBC colleague in Moscow, July 2013.

63 Author interview, Geneva, May 2013

64 Author interviews with two of Goutchkov's Geneva associates, April 2013, December 2013, January 2014, March 2014, January 2014, March 2015

65 Ibid. Petrotrade was the part of Rappaport's empire that made most of the billionaire's money. It owned a vast, belching oil refinery in Antwerp, Belgium, that had long been supplied with shipments of Soviet crude via the Soviet oil-trade monopoly.

66 Author interviews with one associate, September 2014, with the second in Geneva, December 2013, and a third in April 2014

67 Author interview with Geneva asssociate, Geneva, December 2013. Through his lawyers, Timchenko denied visiting the Valaam monastery with Goutchkov and Putin.

68 Author interviews with two Goutchkov associates, September 2014, and Geneva, December 2012, as well as May 2014

69 Author interview with Goutchkov associate, Geneva, December 2013

70 Author interview with former senior KGB officer and close associate of Geneva money men, June 2014

71 Author interview with Putin ally, January 2017

72 One senior US official said in an interview September 2015: 'When you've got at your disposal billions of dollars, not all of it can be personal.' It was understood that Timchenko was 'a custodian of Putin's private wealth and of strategic slush fund type accounts'. Another senior US official said in a separate interview then that in drawing up sanctions against Putin's allies in business, the US government was precisely targeting this type of wealth. 'We believe that some of the cronies' wealth, particularly Timchenko's but also . . . others, is being

enmeshed in Putin's money. One of the ways he can stash his private assets is that they can do it for him: he has to entrust this to the people he trusts, so there is no paper trail. Then the Russian oligarchs, and the cronies in particular, are ordered by Putin to spend the money on projects for the state.' Timchenko's lawyers said neither Timchenko nor any of his companies hold or manage, or have ever held or managed, any of Putin's assets. 'Our client and his companies do not have any relationship or have had any relationship with any of Mr Putin's assets.'

73 See Chapter 2

74 Author interview with Pannikov, April 2008; see also Belton and Buckley, 'On the Offensive'

75 Author interview, August 2019

76 Author interviews with three people close to de Pahlen

77 Author interview, Geneva, December 2013

78 Author interviews, Geneva, May 2014, and with Malofeyev, April 2014

79 Author interview with former senior Russian foreign-intelligence officer, May 2018. See also Roman Shleynov, 'Kak Knyazya Aleksandra Trubetskovo zaverbovali v Svyazinvest', *Vedomosti*, August 15 2011

80 Ibid., also Shleynov article; Trubetskoy was working there at the time the Soviet KGB officer Vladimir Vetrov defected to the West with a list of Soviet officers working on technology smuggling. But Trubetskoy had continued to work at Thomson, supplying Shchegolev and TASS with computers.

81 Author interview, Geneva, May 2014

82 Ibid., and author interview with senior Western banker who then served the interests of the Politburo and was friends with de Pahlen, June 2014

83 Author interviews with former KGB associates, March 2014 and March 2013

84 Author interview, Geneva, December 2013

85 Author interviews, Geneva, May 2014, and with Malofeyev, April 2014

86 Author interview, Malofeyev, April 2014

87 Author interviews with two of the Geneva money men, Geneva, May 2014

88 Author interview, Geneva, May 2013

89 Author interview, Geneva, December 2013

90 Author interview, Geneva, May 2014

91 Author interview, Geneva, March 2014

92 Ibid.

93 Author interview with Rybachuk, October 2018

94 Simon Saradzhyan, 'Russia Rethinks its CIS Policy', *Moscow Times*, August 24 2005

95 Author interview with Rybachuk, October 2018

96 Ibid.

97 Catherine Belton, 'The Mob, an Actress and a Pile of Cash', *Moscow Times*, November 27 2003

98 Ibid.

99 Author interview with Rybachuk, October 2018

100 Andrew Kramer, 'Russia Cuts Off Gas to Ukraine as Talks on Pricing and Transit Terms Break Down', *New York Times*, January 2 2006

101 Andrew Kramer, 'Russia Restores Most of Gas Cut to Ukraine Line', *New York Times*, January 3 2006

102 Catherine Belton, 'Rosukrenergo Emerges as Winner in Gas Deal', *Moscow Times*, January 10 2006

103 Steven Lee Myers, 'Ukraine's Leader Dismisses Parliament's Vote to Fire Premier', *New York Times*, January 12 2006

104 Author interview with Rybachuk, October 2018

105 According to the contract, Rosukrenergo was to buy 41 billion cubic metres of cheaper gas from Turkmenistan, and up to 15 billion cubic metres from Kazakhstan and Uzbekistan. Only 17 billion cubic metres was to be bought from Russia at the $230 per 1,000 cubic metre price, and almost all of that could be sold to Europe at $280 per 1,000 cubic metres for an immediate profit, since Ukraine only required 60 billion cubic metres of gas annually.

106 Author interview with Rybachuk, October 2018

107 Ibid.; see also Isobel Koshiw, 'Dmytro Firtash: The Oligarch who Can't Come Home', *Kyiv Post*, December 26 2016

108 Ibid.; Rybachuk suggested the deal had been done through Firtash's close relations with Yushchenko's brother Petro. (Firtash flew Petro and Yushchenko's other relatives to the United States soon after his inauguration as president, a former Western official said.) Also part of Firtash's network was a Syrian businessman with close links to Syrian and Russian security services, Hares Youssef, who Rybachuk claimed was a 'cashier' to the Yushchenko Family.

109 Catherine Belton, 'Gas Trader Keeps Orange Team Apart', *Moscow Times*, March 24 2006

110 Andrew Kramer, 'Ukraine Leader Forced to Name Ex-Rival as Prime Minister', *New York Times*, August 3 2006

111 Author interview with Rybachuk, October 2018

112 Author interview with Russian tycoon who knows Firtash and Putin, October 2018

113 Account based on author interviews with former associates of Mogilevich, and former Western officials, as well as

US Department of Justice document on Mogilevich operations, of which author has a copy

114 Author interview with former Mogilevich associate, March 2018; author interview with former Western official, September 2018

115 Author interview with two former Mogilevich associates: one in March 2018, the other July 2018

116 Author interview with former Mogilevich associates, March and April 2018

117 Author interview with Gordon, May 2007

118 Author interview with former Mogilevich associate, March 2018. Mikhailov is widely regarded as the head of the Solntsevskaya. The FBI in the nineties named Mikhailov as a leader of the Solntsevskaya organisation, which it said was the most powerful Eurasian organised-crime organisation involved in weapons trading, narcotics and money laundering. Mikhailov was arrested in Switzerland in 1996 and jailed for two years, accused of being a member of a criminal organisation. A key witness was shot dead. He was later acquitted by a jury, awarded compensation and returned to Russia.

119 Ibid.

120 Ibid.; the second former Mogilevich associate also confirmed that Mogilevich was the go-to man for these groups for organising investments, because they didn't know how to do it themselves.

121 Author interview with former Western official, September 2018

122 Author interview with former Mogilevich associate, July 2018

123 Author interview with former Western official, September 2018

124 FBI Archives: FBI Ten Most Wanted Fugitives, October 21 2009, https://archives.fbi.gov/archives/news/stories/2009/october/mogilevich_102109

125 Gregory L. White, David Crawford and Glenn R. Simpson, 'Ukrainian Investor Hid Identity to Win Business', *Wall Street Journal*, April 28 2006

126 Stefan Wagstyl and Tom Warner, 'Gazprom's Secretive Ukrainian Partner Tells of Lone Struggle to Build Business', *Financial Times*, April 28 2006

127 For more information on this, see Tom Warner, 'Disputed Links to an Alleged Crime Boss', *Financial Times*, July 14 2006; and Global Witness report, 'It's a Gas: Funny Business in the Turkmen-Ukraine Gas Trade', July 25 2006. In addition, the US Department of Justice launched an investigation into Firtash's links with Mogilevich: see Glenn R. Simpson, 'US Probes Possible Crime Links to Russian Natural Gas Deals', *Wall Street Journal*, December 22 2006

128 WikiLeaks: cable from US ambassador to Ukraine: 'Ukraine: Firtash Makes his Case to the USG', December 10 2008, https://wikileaks.org/plusd/cables/08KYIV2414_a.html. Firtash has since sought to row back on some of these comments, telling *Time* magazine in 2017 he was never Mogilevich's partner. 'He's Ukrainian . . . Half the country knows him. So what? . . . Knowing him doesn't mean answering to him.'

129 Author interview with former Mogilevich associate, March 2018

130 Author interview with Rybachuk, October 2018. Yanukovych was the gruff, tough-talking former governor from the grit and steel mills of east Ukraine, which had always maintained close links to Russia. He'd spent his teenage years in and out of prison, and then became close to the region's biggest steel tycoon, Rinat Akhmetov, whose own past was steeped in the region's mobster wars. Akhmetov had been the biggest financial backer of Yanukovych's Party of Regions. But when one of Yanukovych's closest aides introduced him to Firtash sometime in 2006, Yanukovych welcomed having an alternative. 'He was told, "You will have your own cashier. You won't depend on Akhmetov now,"' said Rybachuk, the former chief of staff to Yushchenko. 'At some point Firtash successfully represented the influence of Putin over Yanukovych. The idea was to really corrupt him.'

131 According to a lawsuit filed in the US by Yulia Tymoshenko, the former Ukrainian prime minister, in 2012. 'President Yanukovych's US Advisor to be summoned as a respondent in Tymoshenko's claim against Rosukrenergo', interview with Tymoshenko lawyer in Zerkalo Nedeli, *Gorshenin Weekly*, February 13 2012

132 Hans-Martin Tillack, 'A Tale of Gazoviki, Money and Greed', *Stern Magazine*, September 13 2007

133 Author interview with senior banker, August 2013

134 See Chapter 1; this from Bundestag investigation

135 Forster, *Auf der Spur*, p.86

136 In one deal in 2005 he'd acquired a Bulgarian mobile-phone operator from the alleged Russian mobster who owned much of Russia's aluminium industry in the nineties, Michael Cherney, reaping nearly a billion euros in profit when he flipped the mobile operator soon after to Telekom Austria.

137 Schlaff's close associate Michael Hason took a seat on its board, while Schlaff's close business partner, an oil trader named Robert Novikovsky (whose Jurimex company had sold oil to Belarus from the Russian oil major Surgutneftegaz, linked to close Putin ally Gennady Timchenko), held a

20 per cent stake in it. Another Akimov deputy from IMAG, Peter Haenseler, the former colonel from the Austrian secret services, also reportedly played a role in establishing it: Roman Kupchinsky, 'The Shadowy Side of Gazprom's Expanding Central European Gas Hub', *Eurasia Daily Monitor*, Vol 5, Issue 217, Jamestown Foundation, November 12 2008

138 Ibid. The outfit also overlapped with Rosukrenergo: a board member from Rosukrenergo, a Swiss accountant named Dr Hans Baumgartner, was president of the Centrex Vienna arm and helped set up the broader group.

139 Tillack, 'A Tale of Gazoviki, Money and Greed'; Kupchinsky, 'The Shadowy Side of Gazprom's Expanding Central European Gas Hub'

140 Roman Kupchinsky, 'Gazprom's European Web', Jamestown Foundation, February 2009

141 Gidi Weitz, 'The Schlaff Saga: Money Flows into the Sharon Family Accounts', *Haaretz*, September 7 2010. A grain-trading company owned by his close associate Robert Novikovsky had transferred $3 million into the bank accounts of Sharon's two sons in 2002, just as Schlaff was stepping up a lobbying campaign to establish a floating casino off the coast of Israel. The Israeli police investigation, however, stopped at the Austrian border. When they tried to question Schlaff and his Vienna associates, they found themselves blocked. 'Schlaff is a man of influence and standing in Austria, which, although a European country – let's say it isn't always the most properly run,' an Israeli police investigator told Israeli newspaper *Haaretz*.

142 Ibid.

143 Kupchinsky, 'Gazprom's European Web'

144 Cable from US ambassador to Italy Ronald P. Spogli, January 26 2009, disclosed as part of WikiLeaks cache: https://wikileaks.org/plusd/cables/09ROME97_a.html

145 Author interview with Michel Seppe, September 2013

146 Author interview with Rybachuk, October 2018

147 Author interview, Geneva, December 2013

Chapter 11: Londongrad

1 Andrew Higgins, 'You Don't Often Find this Kind of Mogul in the Arctic Snow – Russian Tycoon's Whim Drags Baffled Friends, Bodyguards into Aiding Blighted Region', *Wall Street Journal*, June 13 2001

2 Ibid.

3 The tycoon invested a total of $2.5bn into reconstructing the region, according to Abramovich's spokesperson.

4 Author interview with tycoon close to Abramovich, October 2017

5 See Chapter 10

6 Author interview with tycoon close to Abramovich, October 2017

7 Catherine Belton, 'Shvidler Questioned Over Taxes', *Moscow Times*, October 14 2003; 'Chelsea Boss made Millions from Tax Break; Insight', *Sunday Times*, September 14 2003. In 2003, Troika Dialog, the Moscow investment bank, estimated the tax breaks granted by the region gave the oil firm a windfall of £400m ($640m) since 2000. The tax schemes were in force until 2005.

8 In 2001 Sibneft's effective tax rate was just 9 per cent, at the same time as Yukos's was 13 per cent.

9 Igor Semenenko, 'Abramovich Questioned in Sibneft Fraud Case', *Moscow Times*, May 31 2001

10 Catherine Belton, 'Sibneft Hit with

$1 Billion Tax Claim', *Moscow Times*, March 3 2004

11 A spokesperson for Abramovich later said the tax breaks had been granted as a way of funding the Chukotka reconstruction project. He claimed the regional administration had passed a law stating that at least 50 per cent of tax breaks had to be reinvested into the region.

12 Recording of conversation between Yumashev and Pugachev. In an interview with the author in November 2017, a close Abramovich associate claimed that Abramovich really had wanted to do something good for Chukotka, and to change life there. He'd first seen the 'entire horror' of the region when he was elected to parliament as a deputy for the region in December 1999, and 'after he saw all this considered that he could do more to help as governor'. But he admitted that to some degree it became a trap, and that Putin had then asked him to go and work in Kamchatka, but he had refused. 'He was exhausted from Chukotka. It was an absolutely thankless and difficult task, and he really was tired. It was physically very difficult, because to get there you need to sit in a plane for ten hours, and then there were periods when for three or four weeks you couldn't fly out because of the weather – even though there could have been urgent business in Moscow. It was difficult work. And when his term was over, he was glad that he'd been able to do a lot with his team. They cardinally changed the social structure there. They built a lot of schools and houses and brought in cultural events and took children to the south on planes, and so on and so forth. And this took a lot of effort and money. And he worked there four or five years – I don't remember – but when the end came he said, "That's

it. I have no strength left, and I am stepping down." Vladimir Vladimirovich tried to persuade him to work further, but he said, "Vladimir Vladimirovich, I worked. Let me retire now."'

13 Author interview with Yasin, May 2013

14 Author interviews with former Western government officials, September and October 2018

15 Neil Buckley, 'Rich Rewards for Riding Rollercoaster – A New Model for Participation by Foreign Companies has Been Seen in Recent Months, Driven by Political Priorities', *Financial Times*, October 11 2005

16 Ibid.

17 Arkady Ostrovsky, 'Economy: New Found Wealth Starts to Spread', *Financial Times*, October 10 2006

18 Neil Buckley, 'Russia's Middle Class Starts Spending', *Financial Times*, October 30 2006

19 Ostrovsky, 'Economy: New Found Wealth Starts to Spread'

20 Buckley, 'Russia's Middle Class Starts Spending'

21 Masha Lipman, 'Russia's Non-Participation Pact', Project Syndicate, March 30 2011

22 Ibid.

23 Author interview, Geneva, March 2014

24 Author interviews with former Western officials, September and October 2018

25 Stefan Wagstyl, 'Challenge of Change Faces Old and New: The Citizens of All EU Member States Must Adapt to the Fulfilment of a Dream', *Financial Times*, April 27 2004

26 Arkady Ostrovsky, 'Equity Offerings Signal Maturity', *Financial Times*, October 11 2005

27 Astrid Wendlandt, 'Russian Executives Become Hooked on Lure of London', *Financial Times*, February 4 2004

28 Author interview with Nigel

Gould-Davies, October 2018. See also: Nigel Gould-Davies, 'Russia's Sovereign Globalisation – Rise, Fall and Future', Chatham House research paper, January 2016

29 Buckley, 'Rich Rewards for Riding Rollercoaster'

30 Author interview with Gould-Davies, October 2018

31 Ostrovsky, 'Equity Offerings Signal Maturity'

32 Wendlandt, 'Russian Executives Become Hooked on Lure of London'

33 Author interview with Gololobov, August 2018

34 Joanna Chung and Sarah Spikes, 'Rosneft Follows the Road to London', Financial Times, June 24 2006

35 Kate Burgess, Joanna Chung, Arkady Ostrovsky and Helen Thomas, 'Dicey Russian Flotations challenge London Investors' Appetite for Risk', Financial Times, December 6 2005

36 Author interview with former Abramovich associate, June 2017

37 Author interview with Pugachev, September 2017

38 Ibid.; Pugachev said Putin had first raised it with him a year before Abramovich bought Chelsea, suggesting that he, Pugachev, buy the club as a way of increasing Russia's influence. 'Before the deal happened, Putin told me this was the best way to infiltrate England,' he said. 'He said it's the same as buying up all the pubs. "We'll get such depth."'

39 Author interview with Russian tycoon, May 2018

40 Author interview with former Abramovich associate, June 2017

41 Author interview with Russian tycoon, May 2018

42 Author interview with person close to Abramovich, November 2019

43 See page 9

44 Author interview with Temerko, August 2018

45 Arkady Ostrovsky, 'Moscow Offers Gazprom $7 Billion for Stake', Financial Times, June 15 2005

46 Neil Buckley, 'Watchdog Alarmed at Russia's Market Growth', Financial Times, February 16 2006

47 Catherine Belton, 'Gazprom Scoops Up Sibneft for $13 Billion', Moscow Times, September 29 2005

48 Catherine Belton, 'Fortunes Go to Kremlin Favourites', Moscow Times, September 23 2005.

49 Neil Buckley and Arkady Ostrovsky, 'Rosneft Looks to US Banker to head IPO', Financial Times, March 15 2006

50 Joanna Chung, 'Bankers to Reap $120 Million on Rosneft IPO', Financial Times, June 27 2006

51 Catherine Belton, 'Yukos Asks London to Halt IPO', Moscow Times, June 26 2006

52 George Soros, 'Rosneft Flotation Would Spur Putin on', Financial Times, April 26 2006

53 Robert Amsterdam, 'Rosneft IPO Represents Nothing But the Syndication of the Gulag', Financial Times, May 1 2006

54 Gregory L. White, 'Capital Gains: Flush with Oil, Kremlin Explores Biggest Ever IPO', Wall Street Journal, April 18 2006

55 Catherine Belton, 'Half of Rosneft IPO Goes to 4 Buyers', Moscow Times, July 17 2006

56 Ibid.; and Joanna Chung, 'Yukos Challenges Rosneft $10 Billion Flotation', Financial Times, July 17 2006

57 Chung, 'Yukos Challenges Rosneft $10 Billion Flotation'

58 Belton, 'Half of Rosneft IPO Goes to 4 Buyers'

59 Ibid.

60 Catherine Belton, 'An IPO Built on Greed and Ambition', Moscow Times, July 7 2006

61 Ibid.

62 Stephen Fidler and Arkady Ostrovsky, 'Yukos Case Highlights Role of Foreign Banks', *Financial Times*, March 24 2006

63 Catherine Belton and Joanna Chung, 'Sberbank Issue to Fall Short of Russian Record', *Financial Times*, February 22 2007. Sberbank was Russia's biggest savings bank. It held 60 per cent of the country's retail deposits, and as Russia's economy boomed with the surging oil price its shares had soared more than 1,020 per cent in the past three years. There was the small issue, however, of the insider dealing in which the state-controlled bank had handed out billions of dollars in loans to a Kremlin-connected tycoon who'd used the funds to amass a large stake in it.

64 Catherine Belton and Joanna Chung, 'VTB Sets Price for $8.2 Billion Offering', *Financial Times*, May 11 2007

65 Catherine Belton, 'VTB Chief Hopes Offering will Seal Bank's Independent Future', *Financial Times*, May 2 2007. Alexander Khandruyev, the central bank's former deputy chairman, told me, 'It's a bank for government special projects. It gives credit lines and guarantees where the risks are high.'

66 Catherine Belton, 'Risks Brushed Aside in Race to Take Part', *Financial Times*, April 20 2007

67 Ibid.

68 Catherine Belton, 'The Secret Oligarch', *Financial Times*, February 11 2012

69 Another example of this new generation was Alisher Usmanov, an Uzbek-born tycoon who became one of Russia's richest men. In his case, Usmanov was able to parlay a top position at Gazprom into the transfer of metals assets from Gazprom to himself, building a metals empire and a 1.5 per cent stake in Gazprom itself. The state gas giant's surging share price had helped double his fortune between 2005 and 2006. Usmanov too was seen as a proxy for the Kremlin's interests.

70 Belton, 'The Secret Oligarch'

71 Ibid.

72 Kerimov had initially co-owned Vnukovsky Airlines with Sergei Isakov, a Russian businessman who forged ties deep in Saddam Hussein's Iraq, as did Kerimov. Towards the end of the nineties Kerimov had purchased the last remaining part of the former Soviet monopoly oil trader Nafta Moskva, by which he inherited a financial network that had once been closely connected with the KGB. The Studhalter family, who ran the Swiss holding company he took over, had been routing money for the KGB since the Soviet collapse. Then they'd managed funds for Boris Birshtein's Seabeco and the KGB colonel Leonid Veselovsky, who'd written the Communist Party memos on ways to survive the transition to a market economy. Kerimov had graduated to trading oil in Saddam Hussein's oil-for-food scheme, an operation that had been largely run out of the United Nations by Russia's foreign-intelligence service.

73 Author interview with senior Western banker, autumn 2011; see also Belton, 'The Secret Oligarch'

74 Ibid.

75 Ibid.

76 Catherine Belton, 'I Don't Need to Defend Myself: An Old Dispute Returns to Haunt Rusal's Deripaska', *Financial Times*, July 13 2007

77 Catherine Belton, 'Close to the Wind', *Financial Times*, October 25 2008

78 Ibid.; Catherine Belton, 'Court Freezes Tycoon's Stake in Vimpelcom', *Financial Times*, October 27 2008

79 Catherine Belton, 'Moscow to Lend $50

Billion to Indebted Businesses', *Financial Times*, September 30 2008; Catherine Belton and Charles Clover, 'Moscow Dictates Rescue of Oligarchs', *Financial Times*, October 14 2008; Catherine Belton, 'Too Big to Fail', *Financial Times*, July 28 2009

80 Author interview with Russian tycoon, May 2015

81 Author interview with senior Western banker, December 2011

82 Author interview, Geneva, January 2015

83 Nicholas Shaxson, 'A Tale of Two Londons', *Vanity Fair*, March 13 2013

84 Author interview with Russian tycoon, July 2015

85 Author interview with former senior Western banker, August 2015

86 Author interview with Russian tycoon, May 2018

Chapter 12: The Battle Begins

1 'Vystuplenie I diskussiya na Munchehnskoi konferentsii po Voprosam Politiki Bezopasnosti', February 10 2007, www.kremlin.ru/events/president/transcripts/24034

2 Carl Schreck, 'Putin Castigates US Foreign Policy', *Moscow Times*, February 12 2007

3 Charles Clover, Catherine Belton, Dan Dombey and Jan Cienski, 'Countdown in the Caucasus: Seven Days that Brought Russia and Georgia to War', *Financial Times*, August 26 2008; Peter Finn, 'A Two-Sided Descent into Full-Scale War', *Washington Post*, August 17 2008; see also Dan Bilefsky, C.J. Chivers, Thom Shanker and Michael Schwirtz, 'Georgia Offers Fresh Evidence on War's Start', *New York Times*, September 16 2008

4 Clover, Belton, Dombey and Cienski, 'Countdown in the Caucasus'

5 Charles Clover, 'The Message from Moscow: Resurgent Russia Bids to Establish a New Status Quo', *Financial Times*, August 12 2008

6 Stefan Wagstyl, 'Medvedev Signals He will Meet Obama Soon', *Financial Times*, November 13 2008

7 FT Reporters, 'Russia Halts Missile Plans for Eastern Europe', *Financial Times*, January 28 2009

8 Strobe Talbott, 'A Russian Reset Button Based on Inclusion', *Financial Times*, February 24 2009

9 Stefan Wagstyl, 'Obama Signals Backing for Medvedev', *Financial Times*, July 6 2009

10 Charles Clover and Daniel Dombey, 'Russia Hails New US Tone on Missiles', *Financial Times*, March 3 2009

11 Stefan Wagstyl, 'Obama and Medvedev Agree Arms Deal', *Financial Times*, July 6 2009

12 'Medvedev Hopes his Visit to Silicon Valley will Boost Russian Business', RIA Novosti, June 24 2010

13 'Obama Tries Burger Diplomacy with Medvedev', Agence France-Presse, June 24 2010

14 Author interview with Kolesnikov, September 2011

15 Catherine Belton, 'Medvedev Plan could See Putin's Return', *Financial Times*, November 5 2008

16 Charles Clover, 'Putin is Booed at Martial Arts Fight', *Financial Times*, November 20 2011

17 Charles Clover, Courtney Weaver and Catherine Belton, 'Tens of Thousands Protest Against Putin', *Financial Times*, December 10 2011

18 Catherine Belton, 'Prokhorov Pushes to Exploit Shift in Mood against Putin', *Financial Times*, February 29 2012

19 Author interview with Russian tycoon, February 2012

20 Charles Clover, 'Putin Turns up

Nationalist Rhetoric', *Financial Times*, February 23 2012; see also Charles Clover and Catherine Belton, 'I Will Transmit This to Vladimir', *Financial Times*, May 5 2012

21 Neil Buckley, Charles Clover and Catherine Belton, 'Tearful Putin Claims Election Victory', *Financial Times*, March 4 2012

22 Charles Clover, 'Protestors Defy Troops on Moscow Streets', *Financial Times*, December 6 2011

23 Catherine Belton, 'Navalny Charged with Large-Scale Embezzlement', *Financial Times*, July 31 2012

24 Author interview with former close associate of Abramovich, June 2017

25 Author interview with Russian billionaire, July 2018

26 Lucia Ziobro, Assistant Special Agent in Charge of FBI's Boston Office, 'FBI's Boston Office Warns Business of Venture Capital Scams', *Boston Business Journal*, April 4 2014; Kyle Alspach and Michael B. Farrell, 'FBI Warns of Russian Investors; Tells State Tech Firms that Venture Capitalists May Seek to Give Sensitive Data to Military', *Boston Globe*, April 8 2014

27 Peter Baker, 'Medvedev Aims to Lift Ties with US Business', *New York Times*, June 23 2010

28 By the end of Medvedev's presidency, Timchenko, for instance, had soared up the rich list compiled by *Forbes* every year with an estimated fortune of $14.1 billion. The wealth he commanded had surged partly due to his acquisition of Russia's second-biggest gas producer, Novatek, after the 2008 financial crisis.

29 Author interview with Pugachev, September 2014

30 One example was in 2004, when Pugachev claimed Putin had asked him for an emergency $100 million in financing to finance the building of apartments for the military.

31 Author interview with Pugachev, March 2015

32 Elena Mazneva, 'Nazval Khozyaina. Odin iz krupneishikh Podryadchikov Gazproma Stroigazmontazha Raskryl Vladetsa', *Vedomosti*, December 9 2009; author interview with Pugachev, March 2015

33 The pipeline was named Nord Stream. 'Stroigazmontazh Vyigral Tender na Stroitelstvo Uchastka "Gryazaovets–Vyborg (597–917km)" Severo–Yevropeiskovo Gazoprovoda', AK&M, May 26 2008

34 Author interview with Pugachev, March 2015; documentary evidence

35 Ibid. Rotenberg did not respond to a request for comment.

36 Stroigazmontazh became Gazprom's biggest contractor. In 2011 it was receiving nearly a sixth of Gazprom's total $53 billion investment programme, while critics pointed out that the state gas giant's pipeline costs were many times higher than those of any of its European contemporaries.

37 Catherine Belton, 'Businessmen are Serfs in Putin's Russia, Warns Sergei Pugachev', *Financial Times*, October 8 2014

38 Ibid.

39 Author interview with Pugachev, September 2014; court documents

40 Ibid.

41 Ibid.

42 'President Rossii Prizval Perestats "Koshmarits" Maly Biznes', RIA Novosti, July 31 2008

43 Belton, 'Businessmen are Serfs in Putin's Russia'

44 Author interview with Russian tycoon, June 2015

45 Author interview with Pugachev, September 2014

46 Author interview with Konstantin Makienko, deputy director of Tsentr AST, June 2015. See also: Yegor Popov, Ivan Safronov, Yana Tsinoeva, 'Kakov Flot, Takov I Prikhod', *Kommersant*, March 5 2015, and Yegor Popov, 'Sudostroenie ushlo v glukhuyu oboronu', *Kommersant*, March 1 2016 – for figures on overall fall in shipbuilding: The newspaper notes a 41 per cent drop in ship production in 2014, and a further 23 per cent in 2015.

47 See for example Alexander Shvarev, 'Sud Izuchit Khischeniya na Severnoi Verfi', *Rosbalt*, November 28 2014

48 See Alexander Burgansky, 'Rosneft: Paradigm Shift', Renaissance Capital, October 3 2017

49 'Support for Putin Sinks to Lowest Point in 12 Years, Poll Says', *Moscow Times*, December 4 2013. Also see: 'Pollster Says Approval for Putin at 12-Year Low', *Moscow Times*, January 25 2013

50 Author interview with senior Western banker, August 2014

51 'Russia Issues Dark Warning to Ukraine against EU Trade and Cooperation Deal', Associated Press, September 21 2013

52 'Ukraine's EU Trade Deal will be Catastrophic, says Russia', Kazakhstan Newsline, September 23 2013

53 Roman Olearchyk, 'Ukraine Students: 'Youth of the Nation . . . for Euro Integration', *Financial Times*, November 28 2013

54 Roman Olearchyk, 'Kiev Streets Erupt in Clashes with Police', *Financial Times*, January 19 2014

55 Simon Shuster, 'Exclusive: Leader of Far-Right Ukrainian Militant Group Talks with TIME', *Time Magazine*, February 4 2014; see also Neil Buckley and Roman Olearchyk, 'Fringe and Extremist Groups Carve Role in Ukraine Protests', *Financial Times*, January 30 2014

56 Neil Buckley and Roman Olearchyk, 'Ukraine Commemorates Bloody Events that Led to War', *Financial Times*, February 20 2015

57 FT Reporters, 'Ukraine Crisis: Pretext and Plotting Behind Crimea's Occupation', *Financial Times*, March 7 2014

58 Kathrin Hille and Neil Buckley, 'Vladimir Putin, Strongman of Russia Gambling on Western Weakness', *Financial Times*, March 7 2014

59 Author interview with Yakunin, March 2014; Catherine Belton, 'Putin Ally Accuses US of Trying to Destroy Russia', *Financial Times*, March 7 2014

60 Author interview with Yakunin, March 2014

61 Author interviews with senior banker close to the Kremlin, March 2014; see also Neil Buckley and Roman Olearchyk, 'Crimea Tensions Echo Georgia of 2008', *Financial Times*, March 1 2014; Roman Olearchyk, Jan Cienski and Neil Buckley, 'Russia Wages Media War on Ukraine', *Financial Times*, March 4 2014; Belton, 'Putin Ally Accuses US of Trying to Destroy Russia'

62 Belton, 'Putin Ally Accuses US of Trying to Destroy Russia'

63 Mattathias Schwartz, 'Who Killed the Kiev Protestors? A 3-D Model Holds the Clues', *New York Times Magazine*, May 30 2018

64 Buckley and Olearchyk, 'Ukraine Commemorates Bloody Events that Led to War', *Financial Times*, February 20 2015

65 Ibid.

66 Author interviews with senior banker close to the Kremlin and with former senior Kremlin official, March and April 2014

67 Author interview with former aide to Gorbachev, March 2014

68 'Obrascheniye Presidenta Rossiskoi Federatsii', March 18 2014, www.kremlin.ru/events/president/news/20603

69 In this context, Putin also said: 'In the case of Ukraine our Western partners crossed a red line. They behaved crudely, irresponsibly and unprofessionally. They knew very well that millions of Russians live in Ukraine and in Crimea . . . Russia turned out to be on a threshold from which it could not back down.'

70 'Obrascheniye Presidenta Rossiskoi Federatsii', March 18 2014, www.kremlin.ru/events/president/news/20603

71 Dana Priest, James Jacoby and Anya Bourg, 'Russian Disinformation on Facebook Targeted Ukraine Well Before the 2016 US Election', *Washington Post*, October 28 2018

72 Neil Buckley, 'Russia Relies on Destabilisation to Achieve Strategic Ends in Ukraine', *Financial Times*, July 15 2014

73 Neil Buckley, Stefan Wagstyl and Peter Spiegel, 'How the West Lost Putin', *Financial Times*, February 3 2015

74 US Department of Treasury, 'Treasury Sanctions Russian Officials, Members of the Russian Leadership's Inner Circle, and an Entity for Involvement in the Situation in Ukraine', March 20 2014, https://www.treasury.gov/press-center/press-releases/Pages/jl23331.aspx

75 Ibid.

76 Richard McGregor, Peter Spiegel and Jack Farchy, 'US Targets Vladimir Putin's Inner Circle', *Financial Times*, March 20 2014

77 Andrew Jack and Roman Olearchyk, 'Pro-Russia Separatists Strengthen Grip', *Financial Times*, April 14 2014; and Neil Buckley, Roman Olearchyk, Andrew Jack and Kathrin Hille, 'Ukraine Crisis: "Little Green Men" Carefully Mask their Identity', *Financial Times*, April 16 2014

78 Neil Buckley, 'Russia Relies on Destabilisation to Achieve Strategic Ends in Ukraine', *Financial Times*, July 15 2014

79 Geoff Dyer, Peter Spiegel and Kiran Stacey, 'US Sanctions Target Major Russian Companies', *Financial Times*, July 17 2014

80 Peter Spiegel and Geoff Dyer, 'EU and US Toughen Sanctions on Russia', *Financial Times*, July 30 2014

81 Buckley, Wagstyl and Spiegel, 'How the West Lost Putin', *Financial Times*, February 3 2015

82 Roman Olearchyk, 'Weapons Withdrawal Agreement raises Hopes of End to 18 Months of Bloodshed', *Financial Times*, October 2 2015

83 'Death Toll Up to 13,000 in Ukraine Conflict, Says UN Rights Office', *Radio Free Europe*, February 26 2019

84 Author interview with Kremlin official, November 2017

85 Author interview with Pugachev, September 2014

86 Author interview with senior banker with connections to the security services, February 2016

87 Author interview with Russian tycoon, September 2015

88 Author interview with Yakunin, March 2014

89 Author interview with former Timchenko partner, November 2014

90 Hille and Buckley, 'Vladimir Putin, Strongman of Russia Gambling on Western Weakness'

91 Ibid.

92 Kiran Stacey and Peter Spiegel, 'No 10

Denies Putting City's Interests First',
Financial Times, March 4 2014; Caroline
Binham, 'Sanctions Proposals Threaten
London's Role as Global Legal Hub',
Financial Times, April 10 2014

93 Author interview with Pugachev, April
2015

94 Ibid.

95 Alex Barker and Peter Spiegel, 'Ukraine
PM Warns EU Against Putin's Divide
and Conquer Tactics', *Financial Times*,
March 19 2015

Chapter 13: Black Cash

1   For the fullest account of how the leak
came about, see Bastian Obermayer
and Frederik Obermaier, *The Panama
Papers: Breaking the Story of how the
Rich and Powerful Hide Their Money*,
One World, 2016

2   Luke Harding, 'Mossack Fonseca:
Inside the Firm that Helps the Super-
Rich Hide Their Money', *Guardian*,
April 8 2016

3   Bank Rossiya registration documents
downloaded from egrul Russian corporate website show that Roldugin became
a Bank Rossiya shareholder in a 2005
share emission, acquiring a 3.96 per
cent stake for 375 million roubles; see
also Yelena Vinogradova, Ivan Vasilev
and Rinat Sagdiev, 'Millioner ot
Muzyki', *Vedomosti*, April 4 2016

4   For the fullest account of the ICIJ find-
ings related to Roldugin, see Luke
Harding, 'Sergei Roldugin, the Cellist
Who Holds the Key to Tracing Putin's
Hidden Fortune', *Guardian*, April 3 2016;
Roman Anin, Olesya Shmagun and
Dmitry Velikovsky, 'The Secret Caretaker',
Organised Crime and Corruption
Reporting Project, April 3 2016

5   Author interview with tycoon close to
Putin, April 2016

6   Ibid.

7   Steven Lee Myers, Jo Becker and Jim
Yardley, 'It Pays to be Putin's Friend',
New York Times, September 28 2014

8   See Yelena Vinogradova, Ivan Vasilev
and Rinat Sagdiev, 'Millioner ot
Muzyki', *Vedomosti*, April 4 2016

9   Anin, Shmagun and Velikovsky, 'The
Secret Caretaker'

10 The tycoons were Arkady Rotenberg
and Suleiman Kerimov. Ibid. The
Panama Papers showed that Roldugin
was the owner of two offshore firms:
Sonette Overseas from 2007 to 2012,
in the BVI, and International Media
Overseas (IMO), in Panama. He was
represented in both by two St
Petersburg businessmen affiliated with
Bank Rossiya's top management, Oleg
Gordin and Aleksandr Plekhov.
Plekhov and Gordin both held shares
in two other BVI companies linked to
the network, Sandalwood Continental
and Sunbarn Ltd. The Roldugin-
linked Sandalwood received the rights
to 4 billion roubles ($59 million) and
$200 million in two complex deals for
a payment of just $2 from companies
owned by tycoon Suleiman Kerimov;
the documents showed that Sunbarn
Ltd was to receive a $185 million loan
for ten years at 2 per cent interest from
close Putin ally Arkady Rotenberg.
The OCCRP story said it was not clear
whether this agreement was ever
enacted, as there were no other documents relating to it.

11 Ibid.; Harding, 'Sergei Roldugin, the
Cellist Who Holds the Key to Tracing
Putin's Hidden Fortune'

12 Anin, Shmagun and Velikovsky, 'The
Secret Caretaker'

13 The son of Putin ally and FSB director
Nikolai Patrushev, Dmitry Patrushev,
was appointed senior vice president at
VTB in 2007. He graduated from the

FSB academy the year before, according to his official biography. The son of Patrushev's successor as FSB chief Alexander Bortnikov, Denis Bortnikov, was appointed deputy chairman of VTB North West in 2007.

14 Luke Harding, 'Revealed: The $2 Billion Offshore Trail that Leads to Vladimir Putin', *Guardian*, April 4 2016

15 Harding, 'Sergei Roldugin, the Cellist Who Holds the Key to Tracing Putin's Hidden Fortune'

16 Vladimir Soldatkin, 'Putin Says Panama Papers Leaks are Attempt to Destabilise Russia', Reuters, April 7 2016

17 Harding, 'Sergei Roldugin, the Cellist Who Holds the Key to Tracing Putin's Hidden Fortune'. The $231 million in loans from Rotenberg to one of the Bank Rossiya/Roldugin-connected companies, for instance, was given shortly after Rotenberg was granted a state contract to build part of a $40 billion gas pipeline linking Russia across the Black Sea to Bulgaria, Serbia and Hungary.

18 Anin, Shmagun and Velikovsky, 'The Secret Caretaker'

19 Author call to Igora reception desk, November 2018

20 Jack Stubbs, Andrei Kuzmin, Stephen Grey and Roman Anin, 'The Man who Married Putin's Daughter and then Made a Fortune', Reuters, December 17 2015

21 Ibid. The year before the wedding, Timchenko also transferred to Kirill an ornate $3.7 million villa perched on a clifftop overlooking the beach at Biarritz for an undisclosed sum.

22 'Zemanovce sponszorovala pavucina firem napojena na Putinova pravnika', iDNES.cz, November 3 2018

23 Filip Novokomet, Thomas Piketty and Gabriel Zucman, 'From Soviets to Oligarchs: Inequality and Property in Russia, 1905–2016', National Bureau of Economic Research, August 2017, http://www.nber.org/papers/w23712. The Russian central bank recorded $534 billion in outflows after it began recording data in 1994.

24 Ibid. Inequality between Russia's rich and poor also accelerated. According to Credit Suisse, by 2014 Russia's wealth inequality was the world's highest, with the top 10 per cent holding 85 per cent of household wealth (compared to 75 per cent in the United States).

25 Tatyana Likhanova, 'Chelovek, Pokhozhy na Millera, stroit dachu, pokhozhyu na Dvorets v Petergofe', *Novaya Gazeta*, No. 39, 9–15 June 2009, http://novayagazeta.spb.ru/articles/5210/. Gazprom vociferously denied that the palace had anything to do with Miller, but in 2009 local journalists found evidence of a connection: a notice tacked to a fence surrounding the development named the palace's builder as one of Gazprom's biggest contractors, Stroigazkonsulting. The firm was one of the crony companies that received tens of billions of dollars in pipeline construction contracts from Gazprom every year. It was co-owned by the daughter of another of Putin's closest comrades, Alexander Grigoryev, the former head of the St Petersburg FSB. According to Kolesnikov (author interview), the other co-owner of Stroigazkonsulting, a Jordanian named Ziyad Manasir, was also a cashier for the Putin regime.

26 Roman Anin, ' "Dacha Yakunina" ushla v Offshory', *Novaya Gazeta*, June 17 2013. Anin, an investigative reporter at Russia's independent *Novaya Gazeta*, dug up ownership documents for the plot of land occupied by the mansion, and found that Yakunin had owned it

from 2007 to 2011. It had then been transferred to a Cyprus company, the ownership of which was difficult to trace, but which had a direct link to a company run by Yakunin's son. The mansion was estimated to be worth tens of millions of dollars, while Yakunin's official salary was estimated at $1.5 to $2.5 million per year.

27 Boris Nemtsov and Leonid Martenyuk, 'Putin. Itogi. Zimnaya Olimpiada v Subtropikakh', Moscow, 2013, https://www.putin-itogi.ru/zimnyaya-olimpiada-v-subtropikax/

28 Ibid.

29 Ibid.; Aleksandra Mertsalova, 'Maloe Koltso Postroit Kompaniya Timchenko', *Izvestia*, June 9 2012; *Novoye Vremya*, 'Sochi-2014: Doroga v Spisok', *Forbes*, February 18 2013; 'Timchenko Oprovergayet Poluchenie Podryada po Druzhbe', RIA Novosti, February 5 2014

30 Boris Nemtsov and Leonid Martenyuk, 'Putin. Itogi. Zimnaya Olimpiada v Subtropikakh', Moscow, 2013, https://www.putin-itogi.ru/zimnyaya-olimpiada-v-subtropikax/; Ilya Arkhipov and Henry Meyer, 'Putin Buddy Gets $7 Billion of Deals for Sochi Olympics', Bloomberg, March 19 2013

31 Arkhipov and Meyer, 'Putin Buddy Gets $7 Billion of Deals for Sochi Olympics'; 'Benefitsiary Olympiady. Reiting-2014', https://www.rospres.net/finance/13802/, January 30 2014

32 Author interview with senior Russian banker, January 27 2018

33 Timchenko's wife and daughter were awarded the Order of Friendship for 'strengthening friendship and cooperation with Russia'. Yakunin was weighed down with an entire armoury of awards: he'd received the Medal of Pyotr Stolypin, the tsarist-era reformer, for his work 'deciding strategic tasks for the socio-economic development of the country'; the medal for 'Irreproachable Labour and Excellence of the First Degree' for his 'contribution in developing Russia's transport system'; the Order of Alexander Nevsky, a Russian grand prince canonised for fighting off German and Swedish invaders, for helping prepare the Olympic Games; the Order of Friendship, and numerous others. For Rotenberg there was the Order of Sergei Radonezhsky, one of Russia's most venerated saints, for his assistance restoring a cathedral; the Order of Friendship; and an Honourable Gramota for his preparation of sportsmen for the London 2012 Olympic Games. Author interview with Russian tycoon who told me of Rotenberg's desire to acquire a personal coat of arms, March 2015

34 Author interview with three people familiar with the situation, May 2013, January 2018, October 2018

35 Dmitry Velikovsky, Olesya Shmagun and Roman Anin, 'Iz Strany Vyveli 700 Milliardov Rublei. "Novaya Gazeta" otvechayet na Vopros: Komu Dostalas Eta Grandioznaya Summa', *Novaya Gazeta*, March 19 2017; Luke Harding and Nick Hopkins, 'How Dirty Money from Russia Flooded into the UK – and Where it Went', *Guardian*, March 20 2017

36 Author interview with senior banker, January 2018; Yury Senatorov, 'Sledy Dvukh Milliardov Vyveli na Khishcheniya', *Kommersant*, August 15 2019; Ilya Rozhdestvennsky, 'Obysky u krupneishevo Podryadchika RZhD', *Vedomosti*, August 15 2019

37 Jack Stubbs, Andrey Kuzmin, Stephen Grey and Roman Anin, 'Russian Railways Paid Billions of Dollars to Secretive Private Companies', Reuters, May 23 2014

38 Irina Reznik, Evgeniya Pismennaya and Gregory White, 'The Russian Banker Who Knew Too Much', Bloomberg, November 20 2017

39 Ilya Rozhdestvennsky, 'Obysky u krupneishevo Podryadchika RZhD', Vedomosti, August 15 2019

40 'The Russian Laundromat', Organised Crime and Corruption Reporting Project, August 22 2014, https://www. reportingproject.net/therussianlaundromat/russian-laundromat.php

41 Harding and Hopkins, 'How Dirty Money from Russia Flooded into the UK'

42 Dmitry Velikovsky, Olesya Shmagun and Roman Anin, 'Chi 700 Milliardov rublei Vyvodili iz Rossii Cherez Moldaviyu', Novaya Gazeta, March 19 2017; Matthias Williams, 'Moldova Sees Russian Plot to Derail Money Laundering Probe', Reuters, March 15 2017

43 'Dvoyurodny Brat Premer-Ministra RF Vladimira Putina, Igor Putin, Voshel v Sovet Direktorov Russkovo Zemelnovo Banka', RIA Novosti, April 16 2012

44 'The Russian Laundromat Exposed', Organised Crime and Corruption Reporting Project, March 20 2017, https://www.occrp.org/en/laundromat/ the-russian-laundromat-exposed/

45 Author interview with senior Russian official, October 2018

46 'The Russian Laundromat Exposed'; Harding and Hopkins, 'How Dirty Money from Russia Flooded into the UK'; Velikovsky, Shmagun and Anin, 'Chi 700 Milliardov rublei Vyvodili iz Rossii Cherez Moldaviyu'

47 'Dvoyurodny Brat Premer-Ministra RF Vladimira Putina, Igor Putin, Voshel v Sovet Direktorov Russkovo Zemelnovo Banka', RIA Novosti, April 16 2012. Grigoryev and Putin had already been partners in an earlier venture, a construction company named SU-888, which received billions of roubles in state contracts in Moscow and in Russia's far east. They'd first connected when Igor Putin chaired a pipeline construction outfit that worked as a key subcontractor for companies owned by the president's closest business allies, Gennady Timchenko and Arkady Rotenberg.

48 'U Promsberbanka Smenilis Aktsionery, a v Sovet Direktorov Voshel Kuzen Putina', banki.ru, October 24 2012

49 Tatyana Aleshkina, 'Zerkalniye Sdelki Deutsche Banka Svyazali s Vyvodom Deneg Cherez Promsberbank', RBK Daily, December 16 2015; Ed Caesar, 'Deutsche Bank's $10 Billion Scandal', New Yorker, August 29 2016; Reznik, Pismennaya and White, 'The Russian Banker Who Knew Too Much'; author interviews with senior banker, January and June 2018

50 See findings by New York State Department of Financial Services, which fined Deutsche $425 million over the mirror trades for a description of the scheme: https://www.dfs.ny.gov/ docs/about/ea/ea170130.pdf

51 Reznik, Pismennaya and White, 'The Russian Banker Who Knew Too Much'

52 Author interview with Wiswell colleague, January 2017

53 Author interview with former senior Deutsche banker, September 2015

54 Reznik, Pismennaya and White, 'The Russian Banker Who Knew Too Much'

55 New York State Department of Financial Services: https://www.dfs.ny.gov/docs/ about/ea/ea170130.pdf

56 Author interviews with former trader on equities desk at Deutsche Bank Moscow, May 2017

57 Reznik, Pismennaya and White, 'The Russian Banker Who Knew Too Much'

58 Ibid.; author interview with former senior Russian banker, January 2018

59 Author interviews with Roman Borisovich, April and June 2017

60 Author interview with senior Russian banker with ties to the security services, May 2017

61 Author interview with former senior Deutsche banker, May 2017

62 The mirror trades converted rouble cash into dollars in a way that allowed it to disappear from company books, turning it into untraceable black cash, a process known in Russia as *obnalichivaniye*.

63 Author interview with former senior Deutsche banker, May 2017

64 Reznik, Pismennaya and White, 'The Russian Banker Who Knew Too Much'

65 Author interview with senior Russian banker, January 2018

66 Reznik, Pismennaya and White, 'The Russian Banker Who Knew Too Much'; author interviews with senior Russian banker, January 2018 and June 2018

67 Grant D. Ashley, Assistant Director, Criminal Investigative Division, Federal Bureau of Investigation, Senate Subcommittee on European Affairs, Washington DC, October 30 2003, https://archives.fbi.gov/archives/news/testimony/eurasian-italian-and-balkan-organized-crime

68 See Declaration of Robert A. Levinson (former FBI agent specialising in international organised crime) in United States District Court for the District Court of Delaware for further info on Ivankov case, https://www.deepcapture.com/wp-content/uploads/Ivankov-Case.pdf

69 Reznik, Pismennaya and White, 'The Russian Banker Who Knew Too Much'

70 Author interviews with senior Russian banker, January and June 2018

71 Ibid.

72 See for example Leonid Nikitinsky, 'Who is Mister Dvoskin?', *Novaya Gazeta*, July 22 2011

73 Author interview with former senior Russian banker, January 2018

74 Author interview with former interior ministry investigator, September 2012; author interviews with senior Russian banker familiar with Dvoskin, January and June 2018; Anastasia Stognei and Roman Badanin, 'Federalny Reserv: Rassledovanie o tom, kak FSB kryshuet banki', Proekt media, August 1 2019

75 Author interview with former senior Russian bankers, July 2019 and June 2018

76 Olga Plotonova, '11 Per cent Organizatsii ne Platit Nalogov'– Sergei Ignatyev, Predsedatel Banka Rossii', *Vedomosti*, February 20 2013

77 Author interview with former FSB officer, June 2014; author interview with senior Russian banker with ties to the security service, May 2016

78 Author interview with senior Russian banker with ties to the security service, May 2016

79 Catherine Belton, 'Austria Link to Moscow Bank Killing', *Financial Times*, May 27 2007

80 'Murdered Russian Central Banker's Visit to Estonia', US Embassy cable, Part of WikiLeaks datadump, https://wikileaks.org/plusd/cables/06TALLINN1009_a.html; see also: Nico Hines, 'Russian Whistleblower Assassinated After Uncovering $200 Billion Dirty Money Scandal', Daily Beast, October 10 2018

81 Natalya Morar, 'Vyshie Chinovniki Uvodyat Dengi Na Zapad', *New Times*, May 21 2007

82 Catherine Belton, 'Austria Link to Moscow Bank Killing', *Financial Times*, May 27 2007

83 The Diskont Bank scheme had involved a simpler route. Hundreds of millions of dollars were zipped offshore from a web of Russian front companies through Diskont Bank's correspondent account with Austria's Raiffeisen Bank. The Austrian interior ministry launched its own investigation, and found that more than $112 million from three offshore companies had been transferred through Diskont's account in Raiffeisen to another fifty offshore firms in the space of four days shortly before it froze the account. Alexei Frenkel, the banker serving a 19-year jail sentence for Kozlov's killing, has claimed he was set up to be the fall guy for the murder by Dvoskin and Myazin. See: Sergei Khazov-Kassia, 'Pismo iz Labytnangi. Bankir Frenkel obvinyayet General FSB', Radio Svoboda, August 7 2019

84 Luke Harding, 'Russian Millions Laundered via UK Firms, Leaked Report Says', Guardian, February 26 2018

85 Bruun and Hjejle, 'Report on the Non-Resident Portfolio at Danske Bank's Estonian Branch', September 19 2018

86 Catherine Belton, 'Tax Scam Points to Complicity of Senior Russian Officials', Financial Times, April 13 2012

87 Author interview with senior Russian banker, June 2018

88 Full text of 'Russian money laundering: hearings before the Committee on Banking and Financial Services, US House of Representatives, One Hundred Sixth Congress, first session, September 21, 22, 1999'

89 Ibid.

90 Andrew Higgins, Ann Davis and Paul Beckett, 'Money Players: The Improbable Cast of Capitalist Converts Behind BONY Scandal', Wall Street Journal, December 30 1999; Robert O'Harrow Jr, '3 Firms Links to Russia Probed', Washington Post, October 21 1999; Paul Beckett and Ann Davis, 'Fourth Firm, Sinex Bank, Called a Focus in Laundering Inquiry', Wall Street Journal, October 15 1999

91 Testimony of Jonathan M. Winer, Former Deputy Assistant US Secretary of State, US House of Representatives Committee on Banking and Financial Services, March 9 2000

92 Higgins, Davis and Beckett, 'Money Players'

93 Bonner and O'Brien, 'Activity at Bank Raises Suspicions of Russia Mob Tie'. Mogilevich's men had artificially pumped up its stock price, filing false accounts, and later Mogilevich and his closest associates were indicted for defrauding investors.

94 Timothy L. O'Brien and Raymond Bonner, 'Career Singed in Global Bank Fires', New York Times, August 23 1999; Testimony of Jonathan M. Winer, US House of Representatives Committee on Banking and Financial Services, March 9 2000

95 Testimony of Jonathan M. Winer, US House of Representatives Committee on Banking and Financial Services, March 9 2000

96 See Chapter 10

97 According to a former Western official and a former Mogilevich associate

98 Author interviews with three former Mogilevich associates, March and April 2018

99 Ibid., and FBI report on Mogilevich empire obtained by author

100 Author interview with former Mogilevich associate, April 2018

101 FBI report on Mogilevich empire. Mogilevich had always insisted he was no more than a businessman. He'd been

so sure of himself he even told associates that one day he wanted to make the *Sunday Times* rich list. 'He is just the bogeyman the West likes to connect to everything,' Mogilevich's lawyer Zeev Gordon told me.

102 Author interview with former Mogilevich associate, July 2018

103 Testimony of Jonathan M. Winer, US House of Representatives Committee on Banking and Financial Services, March 9 2000

104 Author interview with Winer, December 2018

105 Timothy L. O'Brien and Raymond Bonner, 'Banker and Husband Tell of Role in Laundering Case', *New York Times*, February 17 2000

106 Tom Hays, 'Bank of New York to Pay $38 million in Fines', *Washington Post*, November 8 2005

107 Author interview with Yury Shvets, May 2018. Mogilevich's links with the Russian foreign-intelligence service had even been mentioned in conversations between the Ukrainian president Leonid Kuchma and the head of the Ukrainian security service, which were taped and then leaked after the Ukrainian official who made them fled to the US. In one of the conversations dated February 10 2000, the head of the Ukrainian security service, Igor Smeshko, told Kuchma how Mogilevich had been a 'special agent of the KGB, from the first department, the PGU [the foreign-intelligence arm]'. He told of how 'when the Soviet Union collapsed, before the KGB had created department K [the arm of the security services that oversaw corruption and banking transactions – and in fact played a big role in facilitating black-cash transfers], when one colonel . . . tried to arrest Mogilevich, he was beaten about the head and told: "Don't go there! This is the top ranks of the PGU."'

108 Testimony of Jonathan M. Winer, US House of Representatives Committee on Banking and Financial Services, March 9 2000

109 Author interview with former Mogilevich associate, March 2018

110 Author interview with Galeotti, October 2018

111 Caroline Binham, 'Trail of Dirty Money from Danske Bank leads to London Laundromat', *Financial Times*, October 3 2018

112 Author interview with independent expert on money laundering Graham Barrow, November 2018

113 Binham, 'Trail of Dirty Money from Danske Bank Leads to London Laundromat'

114 Author interview with Graham Barrow, November 2018

115 Author interview with British MP, September 2018

116 Author interview with former senior KGB officer, August 2019

117 Roman Anin, 'The Russian Laundromat Superusers Revealed', Organised Crime and Corruption Reporting Project, March 20 2017

Chapter 14: Soft Power in an Iron Fist: 'I Call Them the Orthodox Taliban'

1 Author interview with Malofeyev, April 23 2014

2 Ibid.

3 Sevastyan Kozitsyn, 'Na Volniye Khleba. Avtor IPO "Irkuta" pokkinul MDM Bank radi svoevo biznesa', *Vedomosti*, February 15 2005; Bela Lyaub, 'Marshall Vlozhitsa v Oteli', *Vedomosti*, April 18 2006; Anastasia Golitsyna, 'Sborshchik Kontenta. Marshall Capital Partners skupaet

Provaiderov', *Vedomosti*, June 25 2007

4 Gyuzel Gubeidullina and Maria Dranishnikova, '"Aktsionernaya Stoimost Nutriteka Uletuchilas" – Konstantin Malofeyev', interview, *Vedomosti*, June 7 2010

5 See the foundation's website for board members: www.fondsvv.ru/about #about_directora

6 Oleg Salmanov and Igor Tsukanov, 'Nezavisimiye na Svyazi. Gosudarstvo menyaet chinovnikov v sovetakh goskompanii na nezavisimykh direktorov', *Vedomosti*, January 12 2009

7 Timofei Dzyadko and Igor Tsukanov, 'Direktor Gostelekoma. Rukovoditel Rostelecoma, na baze kotorovo obyedinyayutsya krupneishie gosudarstvenniye telekommunikatsionniye kompanii, budut byvshy investbankir iz Marshall Capital', *Vedomosti*, July 14 2010

8 Timofei Dzyadko, Irina Reznik and Igor Tsukanov, 'Kak Kupili Telekomy. Stats krupneishim minoritariem dochek Svyazinvesta Gazprombanku, Vozmozhno, Pomog sam Rostelecom', *Vedomosti*, September 20 2010; Vladimir Lavitsky and Inna Erokhina, 'Rostelecom zafiksiroval Novovo Aktsionera', *Kommersant*, September 7 2010

9 Author interview with Yurchenko, June 2014; see also Igor Tsukanov and Timofei Dzyadko, 'Yevgeny Yurchenko Protiv Marshalov Svyazi', *Vedomosti*, September 15 2010

10 Author interview with Yurchenko, June 2014

11 See the excellent Orysia Lutsevych, 'Agents of the Russian World: Proxy Groups in the Contested Neighbourhood', Russia and Eurasia Programme, Chatham House, April 2016, www.chathamhouse.org/sites/default/files/publications/research/2016-04-14-agents-russian-world-lutsevych.pdf

12 Author interview with Malofeyev, April 23 2014

13 Lutsevych, 'Agents of the Russian World'

14 Author interview with former senior Soviet foreign-intelligence officer, May 2018

15 Lutsevych, 'Agents of the Russian World'

16 https://www.youtube.com/watch?v=gQ-fXZbV9_4

17 Lutsevych, 'Agents of the Russian World'

18 Author interview with Batozsky, January 2015

19 Valery Litoninsky, 'Nazvali sebya Vlastyu: Noviye Nachalniki Donetska', korrespondent.net, May 19 2014

20 Boris Gont, 'Donetskaya Respublika 2005 I DNR 2014: ot fashistov k MMM-schikam', *Bukvy*, May 16 2015

21 Author interview with Batozsky, January 2015

22 V Rosii Vidayut Pasporty Gromadyan Donetskoi Respubliki, tsn.ua, March 1 2012, https://tsn.ua/politika/v-rosiyi-vidayut-pasporti-gromadyan-doneckoyi-respubliki.html

23 Author interview with Batozsky, January 2015

24 Jan Cienski, 'Oligarch Tries to Stamp Kiev Authority on Restive East', *Financial Times*, March 7 2014

25 Roman Olearchyk, 'Ukraine Tensions Rise as Two Die in Donetsk Clashes', *Financial Times*, March 14 2014; Jan Cienski, 'Russian-Speaking Activists Demand their Own Referendums', *Financial Times*, March 17 2014; Neil Buckley, 'Ukraine's Ousted President Demands Regional Referendum', *Financial Times*, March 28 2014

26 Roman Olearchyk, 'Turchynov Blames Russia for Unrest in East Ukraine', *Financial Times*, April 7 2014

27 John Reed, 'Donetsk Governor Plays Down Rebel Threat', *Financial Times*, April 25 2014; John Reed, 'Mob Storms State Security HQ in Donetsk', *Financial Times*, May 3 2014; Guy Chazan, 'Separatists Urge Russia to Annex Donetsk', *Financial Times*, May 13 2014

28 Darya Aslamova, 'Vice-Premyer Donetskoi Narodnoi Respubliki Andrei Purgin: Ukraina postavila na Donbasse Krest. Yei lyudi zdyes ne nuzhny', *Komsomolskaya Pravda*, July 8 2014

29 Courtney Weaver, 'Donetsk Chaos Leads to Split in Separatist Ranks', *Financial Times*, May 31 2014

30 Author interview with Batozsky, January 2015

31 Aleksandr Vasovic and Maria Tsvetkova, 'Elusive Muscovite with Three Names Takes Control of Ukraine Rebels', Reuters, May 15 2014

32 Arkhipov, Meyer and Reznik, 'Putin's Soros Dreams of Empire as Allies Wage Ukraine Revolt', Bloomberg, June 16 2004

33 Ibid.

34 'Marshal Malofeyev. Kak Rossiisky Raider Zakhvatil Yugo-Vostok Ukrainy', *The Insider*, May 27 2014 (citing a biography written by Strelkov taken from emails hacked by a group calling itself 'Anonimny International')

35 Vasovic and Tsvetkova, 'Elusive Muscovite with Three Names Takes Control of Ukraine Rebels'

36 Arkhipov, Meyer and Reznik, 'Putin's Soros Dreams of Empire as Allies Wage Ukraine Revolt'

37 Ibid.

38 Courtney Weaver, Kathrin Hille and Neil Buckley, 'Pretext and Plotting Behind Crimea's Occupation', *Financial Times*, March 7 2014

39 Author interview with Batozsky, January 2015

40 Dmitry Volchek, 'Operatsiya "Dary Volkhov". Kak RPTs stala otdelom administratsii Putina', Radio Svoboda, March 10 2018

41 'Marshall Malofeyev. Kak Rossiisky Raider Zakhvatil Yugo-Vostok Ukrainy', *The Insider*, May 27 2014, cites phone calls between Strelkov and Malofeyev intercepted by the Ukrainian security services.

42 Author interview with Malofeyev, April 23 2014; Arkhipov, Meyer and Reznik, 'Putin's Soros Dreams of Empire as Allies Wage Ukraine Revolt'; Courtney Weaver, 'Oligarch Emerges as Link Between Russia and Rebels', *Financial Times*, July 25 2014

43 EU sanctions issued July 30 2014, Council Implementing Regulation (EU) No. 826/2014

44 Weaver, 'Oligarch Emerges as Link Between Russia and Rebels'

45 Arkhipov, Meyer and Reznik, 'Putin's Soros Dreams of Empire as Allies Wage Ukraine Revolt'

46 Author interview, April 23 2014

47 www.fondsvv.ru/about#about_directora

48 Author interview with Geneva money man, May 5 2014

49 See Chapter 2

50 Author interview with Batozsky, January 2015

51 Author interview with Carpenter, September 2015

52 Author interview with former senior Russian foreign-intelligence officer, May 2018; see also Roman Shleynov, 'Kak Knyazya Aleksandra Trubetskovo zaverbovali v Svyazinvest', *Vedomosti*, August 15 2011; Shchegolev served undercover as a correspondent for Russian state news agency ITAR-TASS

53 Author interviews with Geneva money men, December 2012 to April 2015; see Chapter 12

54 Author interview with former senior Russian foreign-intelligence officer, May 2018; see also Shleynov, 'Kak Knyazya Aleksandra Trubetskovo zaverbovali v Svyazinvest'

55 Goutchkov sat on the board of Infra Engineering, the company that was receiving more than 80 per cent of Rostelecom's contracts. Vladislav Novy, 'Svyazisty Podklyuchili Diplomatichesky Kanal. Eks-Glava MID Igor Ivanov voshel v Sovet Direktorov "Infra Engineering"', *Kommersant*, August 7 2012

56 Shleynov, 'Kak Knyazya Aleksandra Trubetskovo zaverbovali v Svyazinvest'

57 Andrew Higgins, 'Foot Soldiers in a Shadowy Battle Between Russia and the West', *New York Times*, May 29 2017

58 See Neil MacFarquhar, 'How Russians Pay to Play in Other Countries', *New York Times*, December 30 2016; and 'Martin Nejedly: Zemanovci volici jedi gothaj, foie gras je pro jine', interview with Nejedly, denik.cz, October 4 2014

59 'Zemanovce sponszorovala pavucina firem napojena na Putinova pravnika', iDNES.cz, November 3 2018

60 Higgins, 'Foot Soldiers in a Shadowy Battle Between Russia and the West'; Ondrej Soukup, 'Hackeri odhali "otce" proruskych akci v Cesku. Na organiszaci demonstraci ve stredni Evrope dostal 100 tisic eur', *Hospodarske Noviny*, March 13 2017

61 Andrew Higgins, 'Out to Inflame EU, Russians Stir up Fringe', *New York Times*, December 25 2016; for more details read Dezso Andras, 'A Glorious Match Made in Russia', *Index*, September 28 2014, https://index.hu/

english/2014/09/28/a_glorious_match_made_in_russia/

62 Author interview with Geneva money man, May 5 2014

63 Author interviews with Geneva money man, December 19 2013, and July 21 2014, a second Geneva money man confirmed Bionda's role in setting up the deal as well as his initial role in introducing Total to Timchenko, December 20 2013, the story was confirmed by a third Geneva associate, March 2014. Total declined to comment.

64 See website for Economic Council of Franco-Russian Chamber of Commerce: https://www.ccifr.ru/ekonomicheskij-sovet/sostav/

65 See cable from US ambassador to Moscow, William Burns, discussing the Institute's creation: https://wikileaks.org/plusd/cables/08MOSCOW375_a.html

66 Author interview with former senior Russian foreign-intelligence officer, May 2018

67 Ibid.

68 https://wikileaks.org/plusd/cables/08MOSCOW375_a.html

69 Author interview with de Pahlen, May 12 2014

70 The loan was given by First Czech Russian bank, a Czech bank that at the time of the loan (2014) was majority-owned by a Russian named Roman Popov, who previously worked as the deputy head of the finance department of Stroitransgaz, a Russian pipeline-construction company acquired by Timchenko in 2007. The bank continued to be the main financial institution servicing Stroitransgaz's accounts after Timchenko acquired the company in 2007 until the end of 2014 (after the loan was extended), according to a Stroitransgaz spokesperson (Andrei

Krasavin, 'Radikalniye Svyazi', *Kompaniya*, March 28 2016). Popov retained his position as head of the bank, while Stroitransgaz's president Viktor Lorents (before and after Timchenko's acquisition of the company) owned a 25 per cent stake in the Czech bank. Timchenko's lawyers said Timchenko played no role in the bank's decision to extend the loan to Front National.

71 Karl Laske and Marine Turchi, 'The Third Russian Loan of Le Pen', Media Part, December 11 2014

72 Agathe Duparc, 'Les Casseroles de Konstantin Malofeev, oligarque Russe soutien du Front National', Media Part, February 21 2016

73 Author interview with Antonio Fallico, June 2014

74 WikiLeaks cable: https://wikileaks.org/plusd/cables/09ROME97_a.html

75 Author interview with de Pahlen, May 12 2014; Bernard Odehnal, 'Gipfeltreffen mit Putins funfter Kolonne', *TagesAnzeiger*, June 3 2014

76 Author interview with Malofeyev, June 2015

77 James Marson, 'Deepening Ties Between Greece and Russia Sow Concerns in the West', *Wall Street Journal*, February 14 2015; Sam Jones, Kerin Hope and Courtney Weaver, 'Alarm Bells Ring over Syriza's Russia Links', *Financial Times*, January 28 2015

78 Robert Coalson, 'New Greek Government has Deep, Longstanding Ties with Russian Eurasianist Dugin', Radio Free Europe, January 28 2015

79 The Malofeyev associate is Alexei Komov, Russia's representative to the US 'pro-family' conservative movement, the World Congress of Families, and Malofeyev's right-hand man in his Vasily the Great charitable foundation.

See Anton Pospelov, 'Miroviye Elity. Beseda s Poslom V semirnovo Kongressa Semei v UN Alekseem Komovym', Pravoslavie.ru, September 5 2013; Tizian di Giovanni and Stefano Vergine, '3 Million for Salvini', *L'Espresso*, February 28 2019; Alberto Nardelli and Mark di Stefano, 'The Far-Right Bromance at the Heart of Italy's Russian Oil Scandal', BuzzFeed, July 12 2019

80 Di Giovanni and Vergine, '3 Million for Salvini'; Nardelli and di Stefano, 'The Far-Right Bromance at the Heart of Italy's Russian Oil Scandal'

81 Di Giovanni and Vergine, '3 Million for Salvini'

82 The deal was first reported by the *L'Espresso* journalists. BuzzFeed's Alberto Nardelli followed, publishing a tape recording of Savoini's conversation in October 2018 discussing the deal: see 'Revealed: The Explosive Secret Recording that Shows how Russia Tried to Funnel Millions to the "European Trump"', BuzzFeed, July 10 2019

83 Author interview with former senior KGB officer, August 2019

84 Nardelli, 'Revealed: The Explosive Secret Recording that Shows how Russia Tried to Funnel Millions to the "European Trump"'

85 Sam Jones and Valerie Hopkins, 'Austrian Vice-Chancellor Filmed Seeking Covert Deals', *Financial Times*, May 18 2019

86 Author interview with Geneva associate, March 23 2014

87 The US Department of Justice was reported in November 2014 to have launched a money-laundering probe into whether Timchenko transferred funds from corrupt deals into the US financial system: Christopher M. Matthews and Andrew Grossman, 'US Money Laundering Probe Touches

Putin's Inner Circle; Federal Prosecutors Investigating Financial Transactions Involving Billionaire Gennady Timchenko', *Wall Street Journal*, November 5 2014. The probe did not appear to yield any results. In an interview with Russian state news agency ITAR-TASS, Timchenko said . he couldn't travel to Europe because he had 'serious reason to fear a provocation by the US secret services. Believe me, this is not an invention, but absolutely concrete information which I can't tell you the details of for obvious reasons': Andrei Vandenko, 'Gennady Timchenko: Za Vsyo v Zhizni Nado Platits. I za znakomstvo s rukovodtsvom strany to zhe', August 4 2014, ITAR-TASS, https://tass.ru/top-officials/1353227

88 Author interviews with Geneva associate, July 21 2014; October 1 2014; December 9 2014. Timchenko said Bionda had no connection to any of his activities in China.

89 Vandenko, 'Gennady Timchenko: Za Vsyo v Zhizni Nado Platits. I za znakomstvo s rukovodtsvom strany to zhe'

90 Author interview with Geneva associate, March 19 2014

91 Author interview with another Geneva associate, March 28 2014

92 Author interview with Geneva associate, March 16 2015

93 Author interview with another Geneva associate, March 28 2014

94 Author interview with Geneva associate, February 25 2013

95 Jesus Rodriguez, 'Gerard Lopez, manual para hacerse millionario', *El Pais*, December 27 2015

96 Through a company he owned called Sunray Energy, Bionda had long held a stake in the Lotus Formula One racing team. The smashed-up bumper he kept in his office, the other half kept thousands of miles to the east in Putin's gymnasium, was a memento from one of the races. The car was being driven by Vitaly Petrov, the son of a Russian business partner of Ilya Traber, the alleged Russian mobster who'd worked closely with Putin when he controlled the St Petersburg port and oil terminal, when it crashed into a barrier at the Monaco Grand Prix. The young Petrov was so close to the Putin regime that Putin had also taken his car for a spin when Russia first held a Formula One race, in St Petersburg in 2010. In some ways, Petrov was part of the family. The Genii group through which Bionda held his stake in the Lotus Formula One racing team was founded Lopez.

97 Catherine Belton, 'In British PM Race, a Former Russian Tycoon Quietly Wields Influence', Reuters, July 19 2019. Since the publication of this article, Temerko's lawyers have said it was 'inaccurate' and 'defamatory'. Reuters said in a statement: 'We stand by the story'. The article cites Temerko as saying his relations with people in the Russian security services were 'formal' and not 'personal'. He denied having any ongoing links with the Russian security services.

98 Banks's future wife, Ekaterina Paderina, had been saved by a local MP, Mike Hancock, who nearly ten years later became embroiled in scandal when it emerged that one of his parliamentary aides, another young Russian woman, was deported from the UK because MI5 suspected she was a Russian spy.

99 Public statement on NCA investigation into suspected EU referendum offences, September 24 2019

100 Adam Ramsay, 'National Crime Agency

Finds "No Evidence" of Crimes Committed by Arron Banks's Brexit Campaign', *OpenDemocracy*, September 25 2019. In addition, Transparency International UK tweeted in response: 'It has been clear for some time that the rules on political donations provide weak protection against funds from overseas, but the interpretation taken by law enforcement in this case makes it non-existent.'

101 Caroline Wheeler, Richard Kerbaj, Tim Shipman and Tom Harper, 'Revealed: Brexit Backer's Golden Connection', *Sunday Times*, June 10 2018

102 The fund, Charlemagne Capital, became one of a select group of foreign investors participating with the Russian Direct Investment Fund in a lucrative offering of shares in the state diamond monopoly Alrosa one month after the UK's referendum on leaving the EU. The Alrosa shares were sold at a discounted price in an offering conducted at lightning speed. Regulatory filings show Mellon owned a 19.4 per cent stake in the fund at the time of the deal (Charlemagne Capital Limited OPD – Charlemagne Capital – Replacement, *Regulatory News Service*, September 30 2016). Mellon relinquished his position as a non-executive director at the fund at the end of 2016 when the fund was merged into the Cayman Islands-registered Fiera Capital (Charlemagne Capital Limited Scheme Effective, *Regulatory News Service*, December 14 2016).

103 Author interview with Yakunin, June 2013

104 See Josh Craddock, 'Russia Positions Herself as "Light to the World" During Pro-Family Conference', Aleteia (an online Catholic news organisation), September 23 2014; Anton Shekhovtsov, 'A Rose by Any Other Name: the World Congress of Families in Moscow', http://anton-shekhovtsov. blogspot.com/2014/09/a-rose-by-any-other-name-world-congress. html?m=1. The World Congress of Families pulled its name from the event at the last minute because of the US sanctions regime, but all of its leaders still showed up. See also Casey Michel, 'How Russia Became the Leader of the Global Christian Right', *Politico*, February 9 2017

105 Craddock, 'Russia Positions Herself as "Light to the World" During Pro-Family Conference'

106 Author interview with Narusova, June 2014

107 Author interview with Yakunin, November 2016

108 Ibid.

109 Author interview with Malofeyev, April 2014

110 Author interview with Yakunin, February 2017

111 Author interview with Yakunin, November 2016

112 Author interview with Yakunin, February 2017

113 Joseph Biden, 'Brookings Hosts Vice President, Joe Biden, for Remarks on the Russia–Ukraine Conflict', Brookings Institution, May 27 2015, https://www. brookings.edu/wp-content/ uploads/2015/05/20150527_biden_tran-script.pdf

114 According to transcripts of wire-tapped calls obtained by the author that were part of the Spanish prosecutors' case. See also: Anastasia Kirilenko, 'Intercepted Calls Expose Ties between the Tambovskaya Gang, head of FSB's Economic Security Service, and the Prosecutor of St Petersburg', *The Insider*, January 8

2019. To Michael Carpenter, then Biden aide on Russia, the investigation was a real watershed for understanding how Putin's Russia worked. 'It was a key moment that underlined the fusion of Russian organised crime with structures of the state.' (Author interview, January 2018)

115   See wikileaks cable reporting on Grinda: https://wikileaks.org/plusd/cables/10MADRID154_a.html

116   Author interview with Anton Surikov, September 2009

117   Author interview, January 2018

118   Author interview with former senior Western intelligence officer, October 2016

119   Author interview with Frank Montoya Jr, July 2019

120   Author interview with Temerko, June 2016

Chapter 15: The Network and Donald Trump

1   Author interview with Tchigirinsky, May 2018

2   Ibid.

3   'In a narrow circle they were open, and they were working on ways for reform. The cracks were already visible. These were very interesting times,' said Tchigirinsky.

4   He'd met Bruce Rappaport, the Swiss banker through whom so much Soviet oil money ran, in Geneva. He met Marc Rich, the controversial metals trader with whom the Soviets also dealt in the twilight years of the Soviet Union, and was introduced to Alfred Taubman, the owner of Sotheby's auction house, with whom he became firm friends. Tchigirinsky also said he'd arranged a historic first meeting between the new Israeli ambassador to Russia, the legendary General Haim Bar-Lev, the first Soviet ambassador to

Israel, Alexander Bovin, and his mentor Mikhail Milshtein, the former Soviet military-intelligence chief, at Milshtein's Moscow dacha.

5   Author interview with Tchigirinsky, May 2018

6   Author interview with Tchigirinsky, July 2018

7   Author interview with Tchigirinsky, May 2018

8   Author interview with Shvets, August 2019

9   A cable, dated February 12 2010, from the US embassy in Moscow downloaded by WikiLeaks spoke of Luzhkov's alleged ties with the Solntsevskaya group: https://wikileaks.org/plusd/cables/10MOSCOW317_a.html

10   Author interview with Tchigirinsky, October 2019

11   Author interview with Tchigirinsky, April 2019

12   Ibid.; author interview with Martin Greenberg's wife, May 2019, who confirmed that her husband had travelled to the Soviet Union with Alfred Luciani and that both men had worked on drafting Atlantic City's casino regulations: Greenberg went on to serve as president at the Golden Nugget. Author interview with Guy Michaels, a former law-firm colleague who confirmed that Greenberg had subsequently gone on to represent bondholders in Taj Mahal restructuring. Luciani did not respond to a request for comment.

13   Author interview with Tchigirinsky, April 2019

14   Author interview with Tchigirinsky, May 2018

15   Ibid.; see also Nikolai Sergeyev, 'Umer Glava Evikhona', Kommersant, April 11 2014, for official confirmation of their partnership

16 Official registration information for the translation agency OOO Linkon shows Tchigirinsky was a partner too.

17 'Chapter 11 for Taj Mahal', Reuters, July 18 1991

18 Julie Baumgold, 'Fighting Back: Trump Scrambles off the Canvas', *New York Magazine*, November 9 1992

19 Ibid.

20 'Taj Mahal is Out of Bankruptcy', *New York Times*, October 5 1991; for further details of the restructuring see court discussion of prepackaged bankruptcy agreement before the state of New Jersey Casino Control Commission, available online: https://www.washingtonpost.com/wp-stat/graphics/politics/trump-archive/docs/trump-financial-stability-hearing-vol-iv-6-18-1991.pdf

21 Josh Kosman, 'Icahn, Ross Saved Trump Brand from Taj Mahal Casino Mess', *New York Post*, November 25 2016; see also court hearing above for Icahn role

22 For representation by Martin L. Greenberg of bondholders: see court discussion of prepackaged bankruptcy agreement before the state of New Jersey Casino Control Commission, available online: https://www.washingtonpost.com/wp-stat/graphics/politics/trump-archive/docs/trump-financial-stability-hearing-vol-iv-6-18-1991.pdf

23 Author interview with Tchigirinsky, April 2019

24 Baumgold, 'Fighting Back'

25 Robert L. Friedman, *Red Mafia*, pp.132–3, Little, Brown, 2000; see also 'The Tri-State Joint Soviet-Émigré Organized Crime Project', https://www.state.nj.us/sci/pdf/russian.pdf

26 Jose Pagliery, 'Trump's Casino was a Money Laundering Concern Shortly After it Opened', CNN, May 22 2017; see also treasury documents on settlement between US Department of Treasury's FinCEN and Trump Taj Mahal Associates, obtained by CNN: https://assets.documentcloud.org/documents/3727001/Responsive-Docs-for-17-205-F-Pagliery.pdf; also good on this is Seth Hettena, *Trump/Russia: A Definitive History*, pp.25–7, Melville House, 2018

27 FBI Report on Mogilevich empire obtained by author

28 Affidavit of Lester McNulty, special agent of the FBI, in United States District Court Southern District of New York, March 31 1995

29 See Hettena, *Trump/Russia*, p.27; and Hettena blog for fragment of FBI document on Ivankov's visits to Taj Mahal: https://trump-russia.com/2017/10/06/the-russian-gangster-who-loved-trumps-taj-mahal/

30 The film *Na Deribasovskoi khoroshaya pogoda, ili Na Braiton-Bich Opyat idut Dozhdy* can be found online on Yandex.ru

31 Author interview with Tchigirinsky, May 2018

32 In 2008 *Forbes* estimated his fortune at $2.5 billion

33 Ekaterina Drankina, 'Moskovskaya Neftyanaya Vykhodit na Rynok', *Ekspert*, April 24 2000

34 Matthew Swibel, 'The Boomerang Effect: Billionaire Tamir Sapir Earned a Bundle Exploiting Russia. Now Crony Capitalism is Getting the Better of Him', *Forbes*, April 17 2006

35 Motoko Rich and William Neuman, '$40 Million Buys Ex-Cabby His Own Corner of 5th Avenue', *New York Times*, January 10 2006; Dan Morrison, 'A Man of Many Interests', *Newsday*, December 31 2000

36 Cherney told me in a May 2007 interview that they'd always had to cooperate

with elements of the KGB – there was no other way to get ahead in business then: 'They would force you to sell through state structures. You had to pay the state racket. What was the black market then? It was just grey business. I was outside the system, but I always went along the edge of the law.'

37 In a September 2019 interview with Russian state television channel NTV, Kislin boasted of his friendship with Trump, claiming that he'd fed him borscht several times and telling of how he'd given Trump the loan for 700 TV sets in the seventies. www.ntv.ru/video/1771880

38 Author interview with Tchigirinsky, May 2018

39 Author interview with Yury Shvets, former senior KGB officer from foreign-intelligence department, May 2018. Agalarov declined to comment.

40 One of Agalarov's business partners later said that another part of his business in the nineties tied Agalarov directly to 'quasi-government agencies in Russia'. Agalarov was organising trade conferences in the former Soviet Union, which the partner said was 'a sensitive mixture of politics, negotiation and money'.

41 'Leila I Emin', *Izvestia*, February 6 2006 – in which Agalarov is named as a shareholder in the Cherkizovsky market; for an excellent description of Cherkizovsky and how it operated see Andrew E. Kramer, 'Huge Profits Spell Doom for a 400-Acre Market', *New York Times*, July 28 2009

42 One of the main Cherkizovsky owners, Telman Ismailov, was seen deep in discussion with Arif when Arif was arrested in Turkey in 2010 for hosting a yacht party with underage prostitutes: 'Telman Ismailov Popal v Skandalnuyu Istoriyu v Turtsii', *Trend*, October 4 2010. The newspaper reported Ismailov was called in by police to testify in the case. Also among those on the yacht were Arif's Kazakh business partners 'the trio' of Kazakh businessmen, led by Alexander Mashkevich, behind ENRC.

43 Author interview with Shvets, May 2018

44 Jon Swaine and Shaun Walker, 'Trump in Moscow: What Happened at Miss Universe in 2013', *Guardian*, September 18 2017

45 Author interview with Shvets, May 2018

46 See United States General Accounting Office, 'Suspicious Banking Activities: Possible Money Laundering by US Corporations Formed for Russian Entities', October 2000. A November 28 2000 letter from Citigroup's global counsel, Michael A. Ross, to the US General Accounting Office confirms that Kaveladze is the person directing these suspicious money flows. It states that Citigroup did not detect any illegal activity in the Kaveladze-related accounts, which he began to open from October 1991, but that it has since closed all of them, pointing out insufficiencies in the bank's procedures which failed to detect 'questionable activity'; see also Raymond Bonner, 'Laundering of Money Seen as "Easy"', *New York Times*, November 29 2000

47 Press release: 'Levin Releases GAO Report on Vulnerabilities to Money Laundering in US Banks', November 29 2000; for the KGB ties of the Latvian banker, see Knut Royce, "San Francisco Bank Linked to Laundering Probe at Bank of New York', Center for Public Integrity, December 9 1999

48 Letter from Citigroup's global counsel, Michael A. Ross, to the US General Accounting Office, November 28 2000

49 Ibid.

50 Author interview with former Kremlin official, June 2018; author interview with former senior Russian intelligence officer, May 2018

51 Author interview with person familiar with the matter, May 2018

52 Royce, 'San Francisco Bank Linked to Laundering Probe at Bank of New York'; Sam Zuckerman, 'Russian Money Laundering Scandal Touches S.F. Bank', *San Francisco Chronicle*, September 23 1999; Robert O'Harrow Jr, '3 Firms Links to Russia Probed', *Washington Post*, October 21 1999: Andrew Higgins, Ann Davis and Paul Beckett, 'Money Players: The Improbable Cast of Capitalist Converts Behind BONY Scandal', *Wall Street Journal*, December 30 1999: $8 million had been transferred through Benex out of accounts at the Bank of New York into accounts at the Commercial Bank of San Francisco. In addition, the Nauru-registered Sinex Bank, through which many of the payments to Benex were first transferred from Russia, had a correspondent account at the San Francisco bank.

53 Author interview with Shvets, May 2018

54 Author interview with Shvets, August 2019; author interview with former Mogilevich associate, March 2018, who said: 'After the Department of Justice closed down the Bank of New York scheme they began to send money through the Trump organisation. The Trump organisation had channels that could never be open to the Russians or Seva at that time . . . The money the Russians had access to was a lot bigger than any US investor by that time . . . The Russians didn't give a damn about whether the money was safe. Trump could give them access no one else could. For Mikhas and Seva a couple of hundred million dollars is not much money. But for Trump it's a lot of money. A hell of a lot of money.' Alan Garten, the Trump Organization's general counsel, didn't respond to a request for comment.

55 Author interview with Shvets, August 2019

56 Garten told the *FT* in relation to Bayrock: 'When you do due diligence you act in good faith and try to look at all relevant material, but there's only a certain degree that you can look at things. You can do as much as possible, but you are limited to public records.' Tom Burgis, 'Dirty Money: Trump and the Kazakh Connection', *Financial Times*, October 19 2016

57 Timothy L. O'Brien and Eric Dash, 'Is Trump Headed for a Fall?', *New York Times*, March 28 2004

58 Ibid.

59 Timothy L. O'Brien, 'Trump, Russia and a Shadowy Business Partnership', Bloomberg, June 21 2017

60 Author interview with Sater, May 2018. He was vague about when this first meeting with Trump was – first he said 2000, then 2001. In a January 23 2008 deposition for a *New York Times* legal case, he said his first meeting with members of the Trump Organization was in 2001, or 'more than likely beginning 2002'. Later lawsuits filed by Jody Kriss, the former Bayrock finance director, said Sater joined Bayrock in 2002.

61 Author interview with two former Mogilevich associates, March and July 2018

62 Author interview with Sater, May 2018

63 United States v. Felix Sater, Criminal Docket No. 98 CR 1101, letter from DoJ filed under seal to Judge I. Leo Glasser, August 27 2009

64 See also court documents related to charges against Sater: United States of

America against Felix Sater, signed by Zachary Carter, United States Attorney Eastern District of New York; transcript of sentencing against Sater (there named John Doe, and in the transcript as 'Felix Slater') before the Honorable I. Leo Glasser, United States District Senior Judge, October 23 2009; Complaint and Affidavit in Support of Arrest Warrants, Leo Taddeo Affidavit, April 1998; press release from United States Attorney, Eastern District of New York, '19 Defendants Indicted in Stock Fraud Scheme that was Protected and Promoted by Organised Crime', March 2 2000, https://www.washingtonpost.com/wp-stat/graphics/politics/trump-archive/docs/press-release-doj-howard-safir-bayrock.pdf

65 Further details of the scheme mentioning A.R. Baron involvement in United States of America against Frank Coppa et al.; for link with Bank of New York/Benex scheme, see Glenn R. Simpson and Paul Beckett, 'UK Probe Possible Link Between Russian Case, A.R. Baron', *Wall Street Journal*, September 24 1999

66 Author interview with Sater, May 2018

67 Author interview with Shvets, May 2018; author interview with former Mogilevich associate, March 2018

68 United States v. Felix Sater, Criminal Docket No. 98 CR 1101, letter from DOJ filed under seal to Judge I. Leo Glasser, August 27 2009

69 Ibid.

70 Ibid.

71 Friedman, *Red Mafia*, pp.55–7

72 United States v. Felix Sater, Criminal Docket No. 98 CR 1101

73 Author interview with Shvets, August 2019; Kalmanovich was assassinated in November 2009. Around that time, Sater ended his cooperation with the FBI.

74 Author interview with former Mogilevich associate, March 2018

75 Author interview with former Mogilevich associate, July 2018

76 Author interview with Sater, May 2018

77 Ibid.

78 See Chapter 13. In 2018 Myazin was convicted for embezzling funds from the Promsberbank connected to the Moldovan and Deutsche Bank schemes, while Dvoskin remained free. See also Leonid Nikitinsky, 'Who is Mister Dvoskin?', *Novaya Gazeta*, July 22 2011

79 Author interview with Sater, May 2018

80 Ibid.

81 Ibid.

82 Arif was also connected with Aras Agalarov, through Azeri co-owners of the Cherkizovsky market, who were associates of his.

83 Mashkevich started out in business in the late eighties as a vice president at Seabeco, the trading firm set up by Boris Birshtein, named by the FBI and Swiss intelligence as an associate of the Solntsevskaya. (A former Mogilevich associate claimed the trio continued to work with the Solntsevskaya.)

84 Author interview with Sater, May 2018

85 Ibid.

86 Andrew Rice, 'The Original Russia Connection', *New York Magazine*, August 7 2017

87 Ibid.; Felix Sater deposition, April 1 2008, in Trump v. O'Brien

88 Author interview with Sater, May 2018

89 O'Brien, 'Trump, Russia and a Shadowy Business Partnership'

90 The first story on the Trump/Bayrock interest in the project was Tom Stieghorst, 'Trump Eyes Oceanfront Land Aventura Firm to Market Project in Lauderdale', *South Florida Sun-Sentinel*, December 12 2003. Trump is described as the developer, while

Bayrock is just mentioned as partner. But later, when it all went pear-shaped, the truth emerged: Trump was only there to take a licence fee, and was not the developer: Michael Sallah and Michael Vasquez, 'Failed Donald Trump Tower Thrust into GOP Campaign for Presidency', *Miami Herald*, March 12 2016. (Bayrock purchased land for $40 million, and then received a further $139 million loan for construction.)

91 Glen Creno and Catherine Burrough, 'Trump Raises Stakes: Camelback's Glitzy Boom Continues', *Arizona Republic*, November 13 2003; Sater deposition, April 1 2008, in Trump v. O'Brien, p.60, also makes it clear that Phoenix and Fort Lauderdale were the first projects Bayrock proposed to Trump. 'Q: You said you introduced certain opportunities to Mr Flicker and Mr Reese [Trump Organization executives]. Initially what opportunities were those? A: Fort Lauderdale and Phoenix. And we discussed generally which areas countrywide and world-wide the Trump Organization was interested in expanding into and what were the opportunities for mutually working together on these various opportunities.'

92 Michael Stoler, 'Parking Lots and Garages go the Way of the Dinosaurs', *New York Sun*, February 16 2006; the Bayrock 2007 prospectus has more details on the project

93 Trump discloses the 18 per cent stake he owns in Trump SoHo in a 2007 deposition he gave in Donald J. Trump v. Timothy L. O'Brien. See: assets.documentcloud.org/documents/2430267/trumps-lawsuit-on-net-worth.pdf See also: O'Brien, 'Trump, Russia and a Shadowy Business Partnership'

94 Copy of Trump Casino Holdings LLC Petition for Chapter 11 Bankruptcy, filed November 21 2004

95 Author interview with Blum, December 2018. Alan Garten, general counsel for the Trump Organization, did not respond to a request for comment.

96 Tom Burgis, 'Tower of Secrets: The Russian Money Behind a Donald Trump Skyscraper', *Financial Times*, July 12 2018

97 Jody Kriss and Michael Ejekam v. Bayrock Group LLC et al., United States District Court, Southern District of NY. The initial version of Kriss' racketeering lawsuit is available: www.documentcloud.org/documents /3117825-Qui-Tam-Complaint-With-Exhibit-a-and-Attachments.html#document/p1. See also: Andrew Rice, 'The Original Russia Connection', *New York Magazine*, August 7 2017. The lawsuit was subsequently amended twice in which some of these specific claims were removed. Bayrock settled the lawsuit in February 2018. See: 'Trump-Linked Real Estate Firm Settles Suit by Ex-Employee', Bloomberg, February 23 2018

98 Ibid.; Marc Champion, 'How a Trump SoHo Partner Ended Up with Toxic Mining Riches from Kazakhstan', Bloomberg, January 11 2018. The claim about Bayrock accessing cash accounts from a chromium refinery in Kazakhstan was also later dropped from the lawsuit after allegations that it had been obtained improperly.

99 Craig Shaw, Zeynep Sentek and Stefan Candea, 'World Leaders, Mobsters, Smog and Mirrors', *Football Leaks, The Black Sea*, December 20 2016

100 Jody Kriss and Michael Ejekam vs Bayrock Group LLC et al., United States District Court, Southern District of NY. The initial version of Kriss's

racketeering lawsuit is available: www. documentcloud.org/documents/ 3117825-Qui-Tam-Complaint-With-Exhibit-a-and-Attachments. html#document/p1; O'Brien, 'Trump, Russia and a Shadowy Business Partnership'

101 Ibid.

102 Robyn A. Friedman, 'Trump Puts Stamp on Project; Father and Son Add Famous New Yorker as Partner to Build Sunny Isles Towers', *South Florida Sentinel*, January 30 2002

103 Nathan Layne, Ned Parker, Svetlana Reiter, Stephen Grey and Ryan McNeill, 'Russian Elite Invested Nearly $100 Million in Trump Buildings', Reuters, March 17 2017

104 Ibid.

105 For good accounts of Shnaider's career, see Tony Wong, 'Meet the Man Behind Trump Tower', *Toronto Star*, December 4 2004; Heidi Brown and Nathan Vardi, 'Man of Steel: Alex Shnaider Became a Billionaire in the Dimly Lit Steel Mills of Eastern Europe. How Will He Handle the Glare of the Western World?', *Forbes*, March 28 2005; Michael Posner, 'The Invisible Man; But for the Car, it Might Be', *Globe and Mail*, May 27 2005

106 1995 FBI report on Mogilevich empire obtained by author

107 Bayrock prospectus 2007

108 See Chapter 2

109 FBI report on Mogilevich empire

110 The Swiss intelligence report, obtained by the author and dated June 2007, notes Birshtein's 'close connections' with the Solntsevskaya organised-crime group. (A 2005 lawsuit filed in Ontario by Birshtein's son, Alon, claims that in 1995, while he was residing in Belgium, Birshtein became the subject of an international criminal investigation. 'Russian, American, Swiss and Belgian police suspected that the Defendant was a member of the Solntsevskaya Mafia . . . They believed he was an accomplice of a notorious Russian gangster named Sergei Mikhailov', a copy of the lawsuit says.

111 Charles Clover, 'Questions over Kuchma's Advisor Cast Shadows', *Financial Times*, October 29 1999

112 Mark MacKinnon, 'Searching for Boris Birshtein', *Globe and Mail*, December 29 2018. When reached by telephone, Birshtein declined any further comment to me. The Birshtein lawyer cited in the Globe report, Gavin Tighe, said he was no longer instructed by Mr Birshtein when this author contacted him for further comment.

113 Alain Lallemand, 'Coordination. Des Retards, des délais dépasses, des incohèrences', *Le Soir*, January 18 2017

114 Burgis, 'Tower of Secrets'

115 Ned Parker, Stephen Grey, Stefanie Eschenbacher, Roman Anin, Brad Brooks and Christine Murray, 'Ivanka and the Fugitive from Panama', Reuters, November 17 2017

116 Ibid.

117 Ibid. In an interview with Reuters, Nogueira said he could not recall making any of the claims on the recording, and denied laundering cash through the Trump project or handling drugs money.

118 Ibid. The criminal case against Altshoul for mortgage fraud was dropped a year later; the case against Kavalenka was also dropped in 2005 after the main witnesses, alleged prostitutes, failed to turn up in court.

119 Donald Trump, 'Mr. Trump Strongly Defends his Good Name', *Wall Street Journal*, November 28 2007

120 Bayrock prospectus 2007

121 Author interview with Tchigirinsky, July 2018

122 Jody Kriss and Michael Ejekam v. Bayrock Group LLC et al., United States District Court, Southern District of NY

123 Ibid.

124 In Iceland, FL Group went bankrupt. But in Delaware, one of its property arms, FLG Property I, continued to operate, documents obtained by the author show.

125 Sallah and Vasquez, 'Failed Donald Trump Tower Thrust into GOP Campaign for Presidency', *Miami Herald*, March 12 2016

126 According to documents obtained by author.

127 O'Brien, 'Trump, Russia and a Shadowy Business Partnership'

128 Ben Protess, Steve Eder and Eric Lipton, 'Trump Organization will Exit from Its Struggling SoHo Hotel in New York', *New York Times*, November 22 2017

129 Gary Silverman, 'Trump's Russian Riddle', *Financial Times*, August 14 2016

130 Cribb, Chown, Blackman, Varhnham O'Regan, Maidenberg and Rust, 'How Every Investor Lost his Money on Trump Tower Toronto (but Donald Trump Made Millions Anyway)', *Toronto Star*, October 21 2017

131 Author interview with Blum, December 2018

132 Felix Sater deposition, April 1 2008, in Trump v. O'Brien

133 Ibid.

134 'Ispaniya Vernet Rossii Khranitelya Kompromata', *Rosbalt*, June 10 2013

135 Author interview with Sater, May 2018

136 Nikolai Mikhailev, 'Rossiya Umenshilas v Razmerakh', *RBK Daily*, March 14 2012

137 Alan Cullison and Brett Forrest, 'Trump Tower Moscow? It was the End of Long, Failed Push to Invest in Russia', *Wall Street Journal*, November 30 2018

138 Irina Gruzinova, 'Milliarder Aras Agalarov: "Ya ne umeyu zarabatyvats na gosudarstvennikh stroikakh"', *Forbes Russia*, March 11 2015

139 Author interview with Tchigirinsky, May 2018

140 Author interview with senior Moscow banker, January 2017

141 Anthony Cornier and Jason Leopold, 'Trump Moscow: The Definitive Story of How Trump's Team Worked the Russia Deal During the Campaign', BuzzFeed, May 17 2018

142 Matt Apuzzo and Maggie Haberman, 'Trump Associate Boasted that Moscow Business Deal "Will Get Donald Elected"', *New York Times*, August 28 2017

143 'Read the Emails on Donald Trump Jnr', *New York Times*, July 11 2017

144 Jo Becker, Adam Goldman and Matt Apuzzo, 'Russian Dirt on Clinton? "I Love it," Donald Trump Jnr. Said', *New York Times*, July 11 20217

145 Ibid.

146 Philip Bump, 'A Timeline of the Roger Stone–Wikileaks Question', *Washington Post*, October 30 2018

147 Ibid.

148 David Filipov and Andrew Roth, ' "Yes We Did": Russia's Establishment Basks in Trump's Victory; Russians Couldn't Help Gloating a Bit Over Trump's Win', *Washington Post*, November 9 2016

149 Andrew Osborn, 'Donald Trump's Foreign Policy "Almost Exactly the Same as Putin", Kremlin Says', Reuters, November 10 2016

150 Author interview with Shvets, August 2019

151 Author interview with senior Russian official, February 2017

152 Author interview with Shvets, August 2019; Donald Trump, Open Letter, 'There's Nothing Wrong with America's Foreign Defense Policy that a Little Backbone Can't Cure', *Washington Post*,

September 2 1987. Accessed from: https://assets.documentcloud.org/documents/4404425/Ad-in-The-Washington-Post-from-Donald-Trump.pdf

153 Sater deposition, April 1 2008, in Trump v. O'Brien

154 Ibid. Sater said Bayrock paid $250,000 to the Trump Organization for the Trump Tower project in Phoenix 'to kick off the contract with them for services rendered' as well as an 'ongoing monthly' payment for development services – though he said he could not remember how much this payment was. Garten, the Trump Organization general counsel, did not respond to a request for comment on how much the Trump Organization received in such fees from Bayrock, or whether similar arrangements were in place for the Bayrock projects in Fort Lauderdale and Trump SoHo.

155 Transcript of full interview of Millian with ABC News, July 2016

156 Author interview with Shvets, August 2019

157 Author interview with Zatulin, October 2016

158 Author interview with Yakunin, July 2016

159 Author interview with Yakunin, November 2017

160 Ibid.

161 Shane Harris, Josh Dawsey and Ellen Nakashima, 'Trump Told Russian Officials in 2017 He Wasn't Concerned About Moscow's Interference in US Election', Washington Post, September 28 2019

162 Sharon LaFraniere, Nicholas Fandos and Andrew E. Kramer, 'Ex-Envoy to Ukraine Testifies "False Claims" Propelled Ouster', New York Times, October 12 2019

163 Author interview with Tchigirinsky, May 2018

164 Transcript of Trump–Putin press conference, Helsinki, July 16 2018, www.kremlin.ru/events/president/news/58017

165 Ibid.

166 Author interview with Galeotti, February 2018. See also Simon Shuster, 'How Putin's Oligarchs got Inside the Trump Team', Time, September 20 2018

167 Author interview with former close associate of Russian billionaire, June 2017

168 Author interview with senior Western banker, May 2013

169 Author interview with senior Russian businessman, March 2017

170 Author interview with Tchigirinsky, May 2018

171 Author interview with Graham, May 2018

172 Author interview with former close associate of Russian billionaire, June 2017

173 'Kremlin Says Mueller's Russia Investigation is Pointless', Reuters, May 29 2018

174 Author interview with Shvets, August 2019

175 Knut Royce, 'FBI Tracked Alleged Russian Mob Ties of Giuliani Campaign Supporter', The Center for Public Integrity, December 14 1999. Royce details how Kislin gave $14,250 in direct donations to Giuliani between 1994 and 1997, as well as hosting fundraising events. He also describes a 1996 Interpol report which shows that Kislin's Trans Commodities traded metals for Mikhail Chernoy, the reputed Russian mobster. Kislin boasted of his personal friendship with Trump, claiming in a September 2019 interview with Russian state TV channel NTV that he'd fed him borsch several times: https://www.ntv.ru/video/1771880

176 https://www.ntv.ru/video/1771880

177 Ibid.

178 Darren Samuelson and Ben Schreckinger, 'Indicted Giuliani Associate Attended Private '16 Election Night Party for "Friend" Trump', *Politico*, October 11 2019. The article mentions a photo Parnas posted of himself with Trump at the White House in May 2018. Trump dismissed its significance, 'because I have a picture with everyone'.

179 Aubrey Belford and Veronika Melkozerova, 'Meet the Florida Duo Helping Giuliani Investigate for Trump in Ukraine', Organised Crime and Corruption Reporting Project, July 22 2019

180 See also Rosalind S. Helderman, Tom Hamburger, Josh Dawsey and Paul Sonne, 'How Two Soviet-Born Emigres Made it Into Elite Trump Circles', *Washington Post*, October 13 2019

181 Aram Roston, Karen Freifeld and Polina Ivanova, 'Indicted Giuliani Associate Worked on Behalf of Ukrainian Oligarch Firtash', Reuters, October 11 2019. For the amounts splurged by Parnas and Fruman, see Michael Sallah and Emma Loop, 'Two Key Players Spent Lavishly as They Dug for Dirt on Biden', BuzzFeed, October 9 2019

182 Vicky Ward and Marshall Cohen, '"I'm the Best Paid Interpreter in the World": Indicted Giuliani associate Lev Parnas touted windfall from Ukrainian Oligarch', CNN, November 1 2019

183 Matt Zapotosky, Rosalind S. Helderman, Tom Hamburger, Josh Dawsey, 'Prosecutors Suspect Ties between Ukrainian Gas Tycoon, Giuliani Associates', *Washington Post*, October 23 2019

184 Opening Statement of Ambassador William B. Taylor to House Intelligence Committee, October 22 2019

185 Author interview with former senior Russian banker, September 2019

186 Author interview with senior Russian businessman, March 2017

Epilogue

1   For the best account of what happened to Shestun, see Arkady Ostrovsky, 'A Russian Tale: The Rise and Fall of Alexander Shestun', *The Economist*, December 22 2018; see also Shestun's official biography for details of his nineties-era business career: cyclowiki.org/wiki/Aleksandr_Vyacheslavovich_Shestun

2   Ostrovsky, 'A Russian Tale'

3   Author interview with senior Russian banker, June 2018

4   Anna Krasnoperova, 'Arestovanny Aleksandr Shestun Rasskazal o Korruptsii v FSB', *The Insider*, June 26 2018, https://theins.ru/news/107934

5   'Tebya pereedut katkom – general FSB ugrozhayet v Administratsii prezidenta', pasmi.ru, April 20 2018, https://pasmi.ru/archive/208765/ (with audio and video recording)

6   'FSB Schitaet Gubernatora Vorobyova Opasnee Banditov', Pasmi.ru, November 11 2018, https://pasmi.ru/archive/223752/ (also with audio recording)

7   Ibid. Lalakin was the head of the Podolsk group in the Moscow region that the former head of Promsberbank, Alexander Grigoryev, and Ivan Myazin had worked with on the Moldovan and mirror-trade schemes.

8   Author interview with Kremlin insider, February 2017

9   Author interview with Russian tycoon, February 2017

10 Aleksei Navalny, 'Kto Obyedaet Rosgvardiyu', FBK, August 23 2018

11 Author interview with Russian tycoon, September 2019

12   Author interview with Western lawyer, September 2019. Until Crimea, Putin had repeatedly pledged to make Russia the fifth-largest world economy by 2020. It seemed on track to do so. In 2011, the Centre for Economic and Business Research predicted Russia would attain the number four slot by 2020 (see Philip Inman, 'Brazil passes UK to Become World's Sixth Largest Economy', *Guardian*, December 26 2011). In 2013, Russia ranked as the world's number 8 economy, according to the IMF. In 2019, it was number 11.

13   Author interview with former senior government official, April 2019

14   'Korotko o tom, skolko milliardov I na kakie strany tratit Rossiya', Telekanal Dozhd, November 15 2018. See also: Andrei Biryukov and Evgeniya Pismennaya, 'Russia Dips into Soviet Playbook in Bid to Buy Allies Abroad', Bloomberg, October 23 2019. By 2022, Russia was expected to double annual export lending to foreign countries to $6bn, Bloomberg reported, a return to the days of Soviet practices.

15   Author interview with Milov, September 2018

16   Author interview with Khodorkovsky, July 2016

17   Author interview with senior Russian banker, June 2018

18   Author interview with Russian tycoon, January 2019

19   Author interview with senior Russian banker, January 2019

20   Author interview with Pugachev, July 2015

21   Author interview with Pugachev, September 2014

22   Author interview with Pugachev, January 2019

Index